**FRANCES WILSON** is a biographer and critic. *Burning Man* was longlisted for the Baillie Gifford Prize for Non-Fiction 2021, shortlisted for the Duff Cooper Prize 2021 and the James Tait Black Prize, and was a finalist for the 2022 Plutarch Award. Her previous book *Guilty Thing: A Life of Thomas De Quincey* was longlisted for the Baillie Gifford Prize for Non-Fiction 2016 and shortlisted for the National Book Critics Circles Award, the *LA Times* Book Awards and the BIO Plutarch Prize. It was named Book of the Year in the *Guardian*, *Times Literary Supplement*, *Spectator* and *Telegraph*, and cited by Booklist as one of the ten best-reviewed books in America during 2016. *How to Survive the Titanic: Or, the Sinking of J Bruce Ismay* won the Elizabeth Longford Prize for Historical Biography and *The Ballad of Dorothy Wordsworth* won the British Academy Rose Mary Crawshay Award. She lives in London.

*Guilty Thing: A Life of Thomas De Quincey*
*How to Survive the Titanic: Or, the Sinking of J. Bruce Ismay*
*The Ballad of Dorothy Wordsworth*
*The Courtesan's Revenge: Harriette Wilson, the Woman Who*
*Blackmailed the King*
*Literary Seductions: Compulsive Writers and Diverted Readers*

# BURNING MAN

## The Ascent of D. H. Lawrence

FRANCES WILSON

BLOOMSBURY PUBLISHING
LONDON · OXFORD · NEW YORK · NEW DELHI · SYDNEY

BLOOMSBURY PUBLISHING
Bloomsbury Publishing Plc
50 Bedford Square, London, WC1B 3DP, UK
29 Earlsfort Terrace, Dublin 2, Ireland

BLOOMSBURY, BLOOMSBURY PUBLISHING and the Diana logo
are trademarks of Bloomsbury Publishing Plc

First published in Great Britain 2021
This edition published 2022

A catalogue record for this book is available from the British Library

ISBN: HB: 978-1-4088-9362-3; PB: 978-1-4088-9365-4; EBOOK: 978-1-4088-9363-0;
EPDF: 978-1-5266-4470-1

2 4 6 8 10 9 7 5 3 1

Typeset by Newgen KnowledgeWorks Pvt. Ltd., Chennai, India
Printed and bound in Great Britain by CPI Group (UK) Ltd, Croydon CR0 4YY

MIX
Paper from
responsible sources
FSC® C171272

To find out more about our authors and books visit www.bloomsbury.com
and sign up for our newsletters

*To Ophelia Field*

I always feel as if I stood naked for the fire of Almighty God to go through me … One has to be so terribly religious to be an artist. I often think of my dear Saint Lawrence on his gridiron, when he said 'Turn me over, brothers, I am done enough on this side.'

D. H. Lawrence, *Letters*, 25 February 1913

# Contents

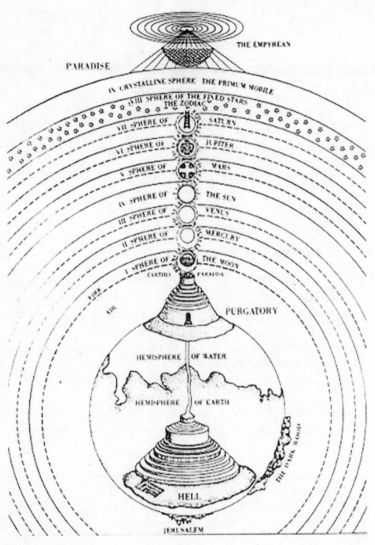

Medieval Cosmology

# Argument

Everyone who knew him told tales about D. H. Lawrence, and D. H. Lawrence told tales about everyone he knew. The tales that Lawrence told about his friends, who consequently became his enemies, can be found in his fiction, and the tales that his friends – and enemies – told about Lawrence can be found in the numerous memoirs and portraits that appeared after his death, and the spate of novels which feature a thin and bearded prophet. He also, again and again, told tales about himself: no writer before Lawrence had made so permeable the border between life and literature, or held so fast to his native right to put everything he was into a book.

*Burning Man* is a triptych of self-contained biographical tales which take as their subject three versions of Lawrence. My focus is his middle years, the decade of superhuman energy and productivity between 1915 when *The Rainbow* was prosecuted, and 1925 when he was diagnosed with tuberculosis. 'Inferno' is set largely in England, 'Purgatory' is set largely in Italy, and 'Paradise' takes place largely in the American Southwest. I say largely because after 1912 Lawrence, who was a different man in every place, was never in the same place for more than a few months; he and his wife Frieda roamed the world like gypsies and slept like foxes, in dens. Because Lawrence believed there was no progress without contraries, each of these tales sees him in battle, and because he was always in battle, I have selected those battles that have been granted the least attention. In doing so I give major roles to those figures otherwise assumed to be minor and minor roles to those figures generally considered major; episodes and experiences that earlier biographers have passed over in a paragraph are here placed centre stage. I look closely at the novels because they mattered to Lawrence and tell us who he was at the time of writing, but I do not consider them his major achievement. When F. R. Leavis placed *The Rainbow* and *Women in Love* on his Great Books List, he consigned the best of Lawrence to the periphery where it has remained ever since, so that readers today have no sense of either his range or the preternatural strangeness of his power. One aim of this book is to reveal a lesser-known Lawrence through introducing his lesser-known works.

Both censored and worshipped in his lifetime, Lawrence's afterlife has been one of peaks and troughs. 'If there was one person everybody wanted to be after the war, to the point of caricature,' said Raymond Williams, 'it was Lawrence.' In 1960, after Penguin had been tried at the Old Bailey for issuing an unexpurgated edition of *Lady Chatterley's Lover*, Lawrence was hailed as the mascot of the sexual revolution, but when, in 1969, Kate Millet skewered him in *Sexual Politics* for his submissive heroines and bullying heroes, he became one of those figures whose name triggers a psychological lockdown.

Lawrence is still on trial. When I was growing up in the 1980s my mother wouldn't have his novels in the house and my (female) tutor at university refused to teach him. Being loyal to Lawrence, especially as a woman, has always required some sort of explanation, so here is mine. Like many readers, I came to him as a teenager and knew him only as a writer of fiction. Not all of it was good and not all of it was sane, but there was still nothing to compare. He asked the same questions as I did and I liked his fierce certainties: his belief in the novel as 'the one bright book of life', his belief in himself as right and the rest of us as wrong, his insistence that the unconscious was an organ like the liver; I liked the fact that his women were physically alive and emotionally complex while his men were either megaphones or homoerotic fantasies, that he cared so much about the sickness of the world, that he saw in himself the whole of mankind; I liked his solidarity with the instincts, his willingness to cause offence, his rants, his earnestness, his identification with animals and birds, his forensic analyses of sexual jealousy, the rapidity of his thought, the heat of his sentences, and his enjoyment of brightly coloured stockings.

The Lawrence I have returned to in my own middle years, this time as a biographical subject, is composed of mysteries rather than certainties. Where I once found insight, I now find bewildering levels of naivety; for all his claims to prophetic vision, Lawrence had little idea what was going on in the room let alone in the world. His fidelity as a writer was not to the truth but to his own contradictions, and reading him today is like tuning into a radio station whose frequency keeps changing. He was a modernist with an aching nostalgia for the past, a sexually repressed Priest of Love, a passionately religious non-believer, a critic of genius who invested in his own worst writing. Of all the Lawrentian paradoxes, however, the most arresting is that he was an intellectual who devalued the intellect, placing his faith in the wisdom of the very body that throughout his life was failing him. Dismantle his contradictions, however, and you take away the structure of his being: D. H. Lawrence, the enemy of Freud, impressively defies psychoanalysis.

How can biography do justice to Lawrence's complexities? Just as writers of fiction might provide a disclaimer declaring that what follows is a work of imagination not based on real characters, and writers of non-fiction might provide a disclaimer declaring that what follows is not a work of imagination and very much based on real characters, I should similarly state that *Burning Man* is a work of non-fiction which is also a work of imagination. I should further declare that I am unable to distinguish between Lawrence's art and Lawrence's life, which was equally a work of imagination, and nor do I distinguish Lawrence's fiction from his non-fiction. I read his novels, stories, letters, essays, poems and plays as exercises in autofiction, which genre he pioneered in order to get around the restrictions of genre. 'Art for my sake,' he quipped, but he was being entirely serious. Accordingly, his letters are stories, his stories are poems, his poems are dramas, his dramas are memoirs, his memoirs are travel books, his travel books are novels, his novels are sermons, his sermons are manifestos for the novel, and his manifestos for the novel, like his writings on history, his literary criticism and the tales in this book, are accounts of what it was like to be D. H. Lawrence.

# Inferno

William Blake, *The Lovers' Whirlwind*

# Part One

*Dante belonged to the close of the great medieval period,
called the Age of Faith. His chief work, the 'Divine Comedy',
tells of his visionary visit to Hell, where the violent,
passionate men of the old world of pride and lust are kept in
torment; then on to Purgatory, where there is hope; then at
last he is conducted by Beatrice into Paradise. It is the vision
of the passing away of the old, proud, arrogant violence
of the barbaric world, into the hopeful culture such as the
Romans knew, on to the spiritual peace and equality of a
new Christian world. This new Christian world was beyond
Dante's grasp. Paradise is much less vivid to him than the
Inferno. What he knew best was the tumultuous, violent
passion of the past, that which was punished in Hell. The
spiritual happiness is not his. He belongs to the old world.*

Lawrence H. Davison, *Movements in Modern European History* (1921)

D. H. Lawrence's nightmare began in 1915, the year the old world ended,[1] sliding in horror, as he put it, down into the bottomless pit.[2] He was thirty years old – the notional middle of his life – and lost in a dark wood. The wood was on the slopes of Hampstead Heath, an ancient commons in North London which rises 499 feet above sea level and covers 790 acres, forty of them oak and beech copses. Lawrence and his wife, Frieda, were living in an enclave of the Heath called the Vale of Health; as hidden as a nest at the top of a tree, the Vale of Health is one of the weirdest parts of the city, and hardest to find.

It is reached from Highgate village by crossing through North wood and Springett's wood, and from Hampstead village by following the Georgian terraces on Well Walk to the long incline of East Heath Road, which tapers the rim of the wilderness. As the road enters woodland, a dense, narrow path – easy to miss – opens to the right. Cutting through the trees, the path is bordered by a thicket of brambles and holly, and just when it seems to be leading nowhere, it ends at a mishmash of Regency and neo-Gothic cottages which included, when Lawrence was there, a fairground tucked behind the fishing pond. North of the Vale, by the Spaniards Inn where the highwayman Dick Turpin's father had once been landlord, wounded soldiers in their hospital colours of blue and red sat in rows on benches, and lower down on Parliament Hill, recruits in khaki practised their drills. Lawrence described autumn leaves burning in heaps and 'smouldering' in a 'funeral wind': 'and the leaves are like soldiers'.[3] His image echoes Shelley's 'Ode to the West Wind':

> the leaves dead
> Are driven, like ghosts from an enchanter fleeing,
>
> Yellow, and black, and pale, and hectic red,
> Pestilence-stricken multitudes.

At night, searchlights in great straight bars fingered their way over the sky, 'feeling the clouds, feeling the body of the dark overhead',[4] and once when Lawrence and Frieda were walking home a Zeppelin hovered above them like a 'long oval world, high up'. It was as if, Lawrence told his new friend Lady Ottoline Morrell, the cosmos had 'burst at last',

> the stars and moon blown away, the envelope of the sky burst out,
> and a new cosmos appeared, with a long-ovate gleaming central
> luminary, calm and drifting in a glow of light, like a new moon,
> with its light bursting in flashes on the earth, to burst away the
> earth also.[5]

The falling flakes of flame reminded Lawrence of Milton's war in heaven, but when Frieda, who was German, looked at the Zeppelin she saw the men she had danced with as a girl now come to kill her.

The names of his many homes were often symbolic and Lawrence, who was tubercular, would spend his life in pursuit of vales of health. But there was nothing essentially healthy about this particular vale which, 200 years earlier, had been a malarial swamp known as Gangmoor. The first workman's cottage to be built when the swamp was drained in 1720 was called Hatchett's Bottom and at the turn of the nineteenth century, when there were nine more cottages and four houses, a resident was still able to describe the Vale as 'a pit in the heath'.[6] Number 1 Byron Villas, whose ground-floor rooms Lawrence rented, was a bay-windowed, red-brick Edwardian terrace backing on to a large ditch filled with nettles and berries. The topography was like that of his birthplace: the mining village of Eastwood, on the border between Nottinghamshire and Derbyshire, was also surrounded by pits, down which Lawrence's father, a collier, had been lowered every day since he was seven years old.

Lord Byron was as embedded in the Nottinghamshire landscape as the mines. Newstead Abbey, the Byron family's ancestral seat, was ten miles from Lawrence's home and the myth of the wicked milord who quarrelled with his wife and turned his back on his country was part of local heritage. After his exile, Byron evolved from a fashionable poet into an incendiary device, and it was in Byron Villas that Lawrence also became a Romantic outlaw. Byron knew the Vale of Health because, exactly 100 years before the Lawrences discovered it, his friend Leigh Hunt, released from a two-year prison sentence for libelling the Prince Regent, had moved with his growing family into a spindly white house overlooking the precise spot where Byron Villas was later built.

The inspiration for the unworldly Harold Skimpole in *Bleak House*, who reminds his friends that 'I am a child, you know!', Hunt was a poet, critic, journalist and translator of Dante. In prison, after painting the walls and ceiling of his cell with flowers and clouds, he began his long poem *The Story of Rimini*, about Paolo and Francesca, the lovers glued in an eternal embrace in the wind tunnel that is the second circle of hell. The poem was completed in the Vale of Health, where Hunt also wrote the article on 'Young Poets' which launched the careers of Shelley and Keats. His Hampstead home thus became the centre of the Romantic circle in London: Shelley, Keats, Byron and Charles and Mary Lamb all made their way up the hill for musical evenings with Hunt and his family.

The Lawrences moved to the Vale of Health on 4 August 1915, the first anniversary of the war. Two months later Lawrence's fourth novel, *The Rainbow*, was published and one month after that, on 13 November, the book was brought before the bench at Bow Street Magistrates' Court and sentenced to death, the 1,011 remaining copies burned by a hangman outside the Royal Exchange. Sir Herbert Muskett, speaking for the prosecution, concluded that it was 'a disgusting, detestable and pernicious work', a 'mass of obscenity of thought, idea, and action', and his judgement was supported by the novel's critics, whose reviews were read out as evidence.[7] 'The wind of war,' wrote one reviewer, 'is sweeping over our life. A thing like *The Rainbow* has no right to exist in the wind of war.' Another reviewer described Lawrence's characters as 'lower than the lowest animal in the zoo', and a third condemned the book as 'a monotonous wilderness of phallicism'.[8] Twenty years earlier, the same magistrates' court had charged Oscar Wilde with gross indecency; in 1907, Emmeline and Christabel Pankhurst were sent from here to serve three months in prison; and in 1910 Dr Crippen stood before the Bow Street bench charged with murdering his wife.

*The Rainbow* is a mythico-historico-biblical account of the sexual awakening of three generations of women in the Brangwen family, who live quiet lives on the Nottingham–Derbyshire borders. Beginning in 1840, a late Romantic moment where men are still in wordless communication with nature and women, the book closes in 1905 when railway lines, mineshafts and a rash of red houses have corrupted the local landscape and the lives of its inhabitants. Lawrence makes no mention of the war but his letters, in which he thundered and roared like the Old Testament God, were about little else. 'The war is just hell for me,' he repeated, 'like one of those nightmares where you can't move.' The Underground was 'a tube full of spectral, decayed people', the Battersea Recruiting Office, where he submitted the medical certificate exempting him from military service, was 'the underworld of spectral submission', and London itself 'seems to me like some hoary massive underworld, a hoary ponderous inferno. The traffic flows through the rigid grey streets like the rivers of hell through their banks of dry, rocky ash.'[9] Lawrence's rage and despair went beyond, by many miles, that felt by his anti-war friends like Bertrand Russell, who served six months in Brixton prison for his opposition to militarism, E. M. Forster, who volunteered in the Red Cross in Alexandria, and David Garnett, who avoided conscription by joining the Friend's War Victims Relief Mission.

Not that Lawrence was a pacifist. On the contrary, the suppression of his 'big and beautiful work', as he called *The Rainbow*, confirmed his conviction that 'one must retire out of the herd and then fire bombs into it'.[10] He believed deeply in conflict and thought incessantly about killing people – he would like, he said, 'to kill a million Germans – two million' – but he did not believe in crowd mentality, machinery or the wholesale destruction of civilisation.[11] Had the war been conducted by noble savages shooting tufted arrows to defend their own land rather than by mud-caked soldiers firing machine guns for reasons they did not fully understand, he would have protested less. Given his commitment to the necessity of opposition, it is odd that Lawrence's biographers take at face value his triumph at avoiding conscription, and evade the suggestion that his nervous collapse during 1915 might relate to his sense of having failed as a man. Lawrence's response to the war was further complicated by the fact that, at the same time as hating herds, he insisted that the word 'man' had 'no meaning' in the singular; it was in unison – as colliers, soldiers, brothers-in-arms – that men had 'all their significance'.[12] Lawrence had therefore, by his own lights, become a man without meaning.

Because the relevant correspondence has disappeared from the archive of his agent, J. B Pinker, it is not possible to know precisely what the prosecutors objected to in *The Rainbow*. The novel's obscenity, even they admitted, was hard to locate: 'although there might not be an obscene word to be found in the book,' Herbert Muskett declared, 'it was in fact a mass of obscenity of thought, idea, and action'.[13] The brief affair between Ursula Brangwen and her teacher, Winifred Inger, singled out for criticism, was certainly not phallic and nor was it a crime. Five years later, the Lord Chancellor would oppose a bill criminalising lesbianism on the grounds that 'of every thousand women, taken as a whole, 999 have never even heard a *whisper* of these practices'. The problem with *The Rainbow* was the author himself: a bearded upstart whose lack of patriotism was proven by his marriage to a German aristocrat who had left her husband and children to be with him, whose sister was the book's dedicatee, whose father was a Prussian officer, and whose cousin, Manfred von Richthofen, was an ace fighter pilot known as the Red Baron; Baron von Richthofen was the only German name known to every British soldier. Lawrence's so-called friend Richard Aldington said he 'knew in his bones' that the reason for the book's prosecution was not its 'filth' but the author's anti-militarism.

Lytton Strachey, who ran into Lawrence at a party during this time, reported that he had 'rarely seen anyone so pathetic, miserable, ill, and obviously devoured by internal distresses'.[14] Methuen, *The Rainbow*'s publisher, did nothing however to defend their author, his masterpiece or his reputation. Instead, as Lawrence later put it in 'The Bad Side of Books', his editor 'almost wept before the magistrate', claiming to have not read the vile book himself and to have been wrongly advised by the reader who had.[15] Nor did the Society of Authors, to whom Lawrence now turned in the hope that they would help reverse the court's decision, offer any support: there was nothing, they regretted, that they *could* do in the current circumstances.[16] Apart from his friend Catherine Carswell, who was sacked by the *Glasgow Herald* for her positive review of *The Rainbow*, not a single writer spoke up for Lawrence in the press, 'lest', as he put it, 'a bit of the tar might stick to them'. For the rest of his life he submitted to publication 'as souls are said to submit to the necessary evil of being born into the flesh'.[17]

Lawrence's immediate response to the conviction of *The Rainbow* was to consign the magistrate and the prosecutor and the reviewers and the editors to the circle of hell reserved for cowards and philistines: 'I curse them all, body and soul, root, branch and leaf, to eternal damnation.' England having become enemy territory, he arranged an immediate passage to New York, sailing on the *Adriatic* on 24 November.[18] He would transfer all his life to America, a world beyond the rainbow where, Lawrence explained, 'life comes up from the roots, crude but vital. Here the whole tree of life is dying. It is like being dead: the underworld.'[19] From New York, he and Frieda planned to continue down to Florida so that, beneath a perpetual sun, he could be reborn. 'There must be a resurrection,' Lawrence insisted, explaining his departure.[20] His doctor advised against a winter sea passage, but Lawrence never listened to doctors: he postponed his departure, he said, because he wanted to fight for his novel.

In late December he and Frieda left Byron Villas and spent Christmas with Lawrence's sister Ada in the Midlands, where he received a present from Ottoline. 'Your letter and parcel came this morning,' Lawrence told her on 27 December, 'but why did you give me the book, the Shelley, you must value it. It is gay and pretty. I shall keep it safe.' The

Shelley was a first edition of *Prometheus Unbound, with Other Poems*;
the other poems included 'Ode to the West Wind' and 'To a Skylark',
and the theme of the volume was rebirth. *Prometheus Unbound* is a verse
drama about the Titan's release from the rock to which he was chained
by the gods for giving fire to mankind, and the poem's unrepresentable
topography replicates that of Dante's *Paradise*. The imagery of *Prometheus
Unbound*, Shelley explained in his preface, was drawn from the
operations of the human mind, a procedure 'unusual in modern poetry,
although Dante and Shakespeare are full of it, and Dante more than any
other poet and with greater success'. Shelley, more than any other poet,
was filled with Dante. Lawrence's thank-you letter to Ottoline ended
with a postscript telling her that they would be leaving for Cornwall
the following Thursday, the penultimate day of the old year. This is the
nearest he could get to self-exile, and he packed Ottoline's present in his
luggage.

Ottoline knew that Lawrence liked Shelley because that April he had
enjoyed a book called *Shelley, Godwin and their Circle* by H. N. Brailsford,
which described the impact of William Godwin's anti-marriage, anti-
ownership, free-love treatise *Political Justice* on the Romantic poets. 'To
these young men,' Brailsford wrote, 'the excitement was in his picture of
a free community from which laws and coercion had been eliminated,
and in which property was in a continual flux actuated by the stream of
human benevolence.' This free community was how Lawrence wanted
to live as well. '*Very* good,' he reported to Ottoline. 'I like Brailsford. Can
I meet him?' Brailsford was a friend of Bertrand Russell, and Lawrence,
Russell told Ottoline, was 'very like' Shelley, '– just as fine, but with
a similar impatience of fact. The revolution he hopes for is just like
Shelley's prophecy of banded anarchs fleeing while the people celebrate
a feast of love.'[21] Hectic, pale, combative and combustible with a high
voice and a shrill laugh, Lawrence was compared by his circle to Shelley,
while Shelley's circle thought that Shelley – described by Hazlitt as a
fanatic who 'put his friends into hell' – was like Dante.[22]

Lawrence resembled Shelley in temperament and physique only. In
other respects they were opposites, Shelley being sexually unrestrained
and politically radical, and Lawrence being uxorious and largely
conservative. Mad Shelley, as the poet was known at school, was
expelled from Oxford for writing a pamphlet called *The Necessity of
Atheism* after which he eloped, aged seventeen, with a fifteen-year-old

girl called Harriet Westbrook. Three years later, in 1814, he abandoned Harriet – who was pregnant with their second child – and ran away with the teenage Mary Godwin, daughter of William Godwin. In late 1815 Harriet drowned herself, and Mary's half-sister, Fanny (also in love with Shelley), took an overdose of laudanum. Implicated in both suicides and considered 'an outcast', as he put it, from human society, Shelley found refuge, in the autumn of 1815, with the Hunts in Hampstead and it was here that he and Mary began their married lives in early 1816 before, later that spring, exiling themselves to Italy. It was serendipitous that Lawrence shared for a moment the same piece of earth as the man he considered 'our greatest poet', but then, as he put it in 1913, he was 'always trying to follow the starry Shelley'.[23]

Everyone who saw Lawrence in 1915 commented on how unhinged he had become, and the sightings were legion. In early January, when the war was in its infancy, he decided to form his own free community based on Godwinian lines. 'About twenty souls,' Lawrence suggested, could 'sail away from this world of war and squalor and found a little colony where there shall be no money but a sort of communism as far as necessaries of life go'.[24] He called his colony Rananim and gave it a heraldic emblem of 'a phoenix argent, rising from a flaming nest of scarlet, on a black background'. The search for recruits now on, Lawrence invited more or less everyone he met, often within moments of meeting them, to join him. In letters to friends he drew sketches of his phoenix emblem, and in *The Rainbow* Will Brangwen carves a similar phoenix into a butter stamper. The phoenix rising soon came to represent not Rananim but Lawrence himself. 'It gives me a real thrill,' he confessed to Ottoline Morrell, when he sent her his 'new badge and sign'. 'Does that seem absurd?'[25] It does seem a little absurd to give oneself a personal logo, but then Lawrence thought in symbols.

On 21 January he was introduced to E. M. Forster at a lunch party hosted by Ottoline in her Bloomsbury home, and the following day Duncan Grant invited Forster, David Garnett and the Lawrences to tea in his studio. It was not a success. Upset by the evident attraction between Grant and David Garnett (who were beginning an affair), Lawrence focused his distress on the paintings themselves. Garnett recalled that he held his head 'on one side, as though in pain' and looked more 'at the floor than at the pictures'. Embarrassed by his behaviour, Forster slunk away, muttering something about his mother and a train, while Frieda tried to save the day by exclaiming heroically, 'Ah, Lorenzo! I like this one so much better! It is beautiful!'[26] By the time the Lawrences left, Grant was rocking silently, apparently nursing a toothache. Grant's canvases, Lawrence reported to Ottoline, were 'silly experiments in the futuristic line'. Art, he believed, should aim to represent an entire cosmos. It should contain an image of the 'Absolute ... a statement of the whole scheme – the issue, the progress through Time – and the return – making unchangeable eternity'. Resurrection, the Absolute and Sodomy were Lawrence's themes of the year.[27] His crisis was religious, emotional, philosophical, sexual and ethical; it involved everything and is written into every page of *The Rainbow*, because, as he said, 'one sheds one's sicknesses in books'.[28]

Two days after Duncan Grant's tea party, Lawrence and Frieda moved into a cottage in Greatham near Pulborough in Sussex, with panoramic views of the South Downs. Lawrence thought the house, which belonged to friends, monastic and he loved the calm curvaceous landscape. From here he wrote to Forster that 'It is time for us now to look all round, round the whole ring of the horizon – not just out of a room with a view.'[29] He was speaking metaphorically (and referring to Forster's novel), but this panoramic perspective was precisely what Lawrence asked for in a view and he tested the character of his friends on their response to the one from the Downs to the sea. Forster agreed to visit Lawrence for three days and in February the two men walked to the viewing point, Lawrence pointing out the snowdrops and early signs of spring. He was finishing *The Rainbow* and Forster had just completed *Maurice*, his tale of homosexual love that would remain unpublished until 1971. They will have talked about their books and Forster very probably showed Lawrence his manuscript; the evidence that Lawrence knew *Maurice* can be found in the pages of *Lady Chatterley's Lover*, a closely observed heterosexual retelling of Forster's story, and it was after Forster's visit that Lawrence added to *The Rainbow* the affair between Ursula Brangwen and Winifred Inger.

Lawrence had admired *Howards End*, whose Anglo-German, mind–body union between the mental Margaret Schlegel and the physical Henry Wilcox recalled his own marriage, but Forster found impossible what he called the 'team spirit' of the Lawrences. The two men had been, Lawrence reported to Bertrand Russell, 'on the edge of a fierce quarrel all the time'. The quarrel concerned Forster's homosexuality – of which Lawrence only now became aware – and he veiled his abhorrence behind an attack on his guest's celibacy: why could Forster not act on his instincts and 'fight clear to his own basic, primal being?' He was all mind-consciousness and thus 'dead'. After one particularly gruelling session in which he was attacked on all fronts, Forster took himself to bed 'muttering', Lawrence reported, 'that he was not sure we – my wife and I – weren't just playing round his knees'.[30] In his thank-you letter, Forster explained to Lawrence why he wouldn't be taking up their offer to come again:

> I like the Lawrence who talks to Hilda [the maid] and sees birds
> and is physically restful and wrote *The White Peacock*, he doesn't
> know why; but I do not like the deaf impercipient fanatic who has
> nosed over his own little sexual round until he believes that there
> is no other path for others to take: he sometimes interests and
> sometimes frightens and angers me, but in the end he will bore
> [me] merely, I know.[31]

The difference between the Lawrence who was physically at peace and the 'deaf impercipient fanatic' had long been recognised by Lawrence himself. 'The trouble is, you see,' he had told his first love, Jessie Chambers, 'I'm not one man, but two.'[32] Jung, also split, called his extroverted false self No. 1 and his submerged true self No. 2; I will similarly refer to Lawrence's opposing personalities as Self One and Self Two.

He delivered *The Rainbow* to his typist on 2 March, and three days later went to stay with Bertrand Russell at Trinity College. Lawrence and Russell had been introduced by Ottoline the previous month and Russell was electrified, as everyone was, by the erudition and energy of the collier's son. When Lawrence later wrote in 'A Rise in the World' that 'I rose up in the world 'Ooray! / rose very high, for me. / An earl once asked me down to stay / and a duchess came for tea', he was referring to Russell (whose brother was an earl). 'I feel frightfully important coming to Cambridge,' he told Russell at the time, '– quite momentous the occasion is to me. I don't want to be horribly impressed and intimidated, but am afraid I may be.'[33] Having pined for a cloistered world of medieval men, Lawrence cannot have failed to be 'horribly impressed' by Cambridge, but he left no record of the impact of its monastic splendour. He sat at high table between Russell and the philosopher G. E. Moore, and over coffee the professors walked around the room with their hands behind their backs, discussing the Balkans about which, Lawrence thought, they knew nothing. He later impersonated their after-dinner strutting. Lawrence, however, went down as well as Russell hoped he would: the mathematician G. H. Hardy 'was *immensely* impressed' by the outsider and felt he had at last met 'a real man'.[34]

There is a snobbery attached to this remark because Lawrence, thin as a wire with a high-pitched voice, was nothing like a 'real man'. He was euphemistically described by his friends as ethereal, the vagueness of which elides the fact that Lawrence was not One of Us; what G. H. Hardy meant by 'real' man is that he was not a gentleman. Lawrence told Forster that he had become 'classless', but this was neither how he was seen by others nor how he really saw himself. Only David Garnett told the truth about how Lawrence was perceived among the upper-class literati: he was 'a mongrel terrier among a crowd of Pomeranians and Alsatians', he looked 'underbred', his 'nose was short and lumpy', his chin 'too large and round like a hairpin', and his 'bright mud-coloured' hair was 'incredibly plebeian'. He was 'the type of plumber's mate who goes back to fetch the tools',

> the weedy runt you find in every gang of workmen, the one who keeps the other men laughing all the time, who makes trouble with the boss and is saucy to the foreman, who gets the sack, who is 'victimised', the cause of a strike, the man for whom trades unions exist, who lives on the dole, who hangs round the pubs, whose wife supports him, who bets on football and is always cheeky, cocky and in trouble. He was the type who provokes the most violent class-hatred in this country: the impotent hatred of the upper classes for the lower.[35]

It is important to hold this description in mind as Lawrence rises in the world.

The next morning Russell took him to meet Maynard Keynes, and Lawrence made his own discovery about 'real men' in Cambridge. 'We went into his rooms at midday,' he recalled, 'and it was very sunny.'

He was not there, so Russell was writing a note. Then suddenly a
door opened and K. was there, blinking from sleep, standing in his
pyjamas. And as he stood there gradually a knowledge passed into
me, which has been like a little madness to me ever since. And it
was carried along with the most dreadful sense of repulsiveness –
something like carrion – a vulture gives me the same feeling. I begin
to feel mad as I think of it – insane.

What happened in Keynes's rooms was 'one of the crises of my life.
It made me mad with misery and hostility and rage … I could sit and
howl in the corner like a child, I feel so bad about it all.'[36] The visit had
been, Russell conceded to Ottoline, 'rather dreadful' and Lawrence left
'disgusted with Cambridge'. But because Russell was equally upset by
sodomy, he and Lawrence 'made real progress towards intimacy. His
intuitive perceptiveness is *wonderful* – it leaves me gasping in admiration.'[37]

So what did happen in Keynes's rooms? What did Lawrence actually
see when suddenly the door opened 'and K. was there'? His accounts of
his various crises – sexual or otherwise – always hold something back.
Was someone else in the bedroom? His description operates like the
memory of a primal scene: the location, the time of day, the sunlight,
the writing of the note, the opening door, the 'knowledge' passing into
him followed by the 'little madness'. Lawrence became conscious in that
moment of something which, unconsciously, he had known all along.

Back home he went straight to bed with a cold, telling Russell that
he was 'struggling in the dark – very deep in the dark'. He saw evil
everywhere, especially in himself, he wanted to love but also 'to kill
and murder'. He wrote to Russell with a special request: 'I wanted to
ask you please to be with me – in the underworld – or at any rate to
wait for me … I feel there is something to go through – something
very important. It may be that it is only in my own soul – but it seems
to grow more and more looming.'[38] Lawrence told Ottoline that what
he saw 'plainly' with Keynes in Cambridge made him 'sick' but that
Shelley 'believed in the principle of Evil, coeval with the Principle of
Good. That is right … Do not tell me there is no Devil.'[39]

His descent continued. On 17 April, David Garnett came to stay,
bringing his friend Francis Birrell. The two men were, Lawrence realised,
'like Keynes and Grant' and he began to dream of beetles; his underworld
was crawling with insects. Homosexuality, he told David Garnett, is 'so

wrong, it is unbearable. It makes a form of inward corruption which truly makes me scarce able to live.'[40] But he also acknowledged his need for male intimacy. 'All my life I have wanted friendship with a man,' he later wrote. 'What is this sense? Do I want friendliness? I should like to see anybody being "friendly" with me. Intellectual equals? Or rather equals in being non-intellectual ... Not something homosexual, surely?' This was the question.[41] What Lawrence saw in Cambridge, he told David Garnett, was 'enough to drive one frantic', so what kind of friendship had he been imagining when he included in his first novel, *The White Peacock*, the scene in which Cyril and George dry one another after a swim?

> I left myself quite limply in his hands, and, to get a better grip of me, he put his arm round me and pressed me against him, and the sweetness of the touch of our naked bodies against the other was superb. It satisfied in some measure the vague, indecipherable yearning of my soul; and it was the same with him. When he had rubbed me all warm, he let me go, and we looked at each other with eyes of still laughter, and our love was perfect for a moment, more perfect than any love I have known since, for either man or woman.[42]

This episode, said Forster, was the 'the most beautiful' in a novel which he privately thought 'the queerest product of subconsciousness that I have yet struck'.[43] John Middleton Murry described Lawrence's ideal of a *Blutsbrüderschaft* – a 'blood brotherhood' he proposed to Russell and also to Murry himself – as an 'instinctive, infra-personal sense of solidarity with men ... which he simultaneously desired and repudiated'. He desired it in his novels and repudiated it in his life, just as he admired it in Forster's novels but repudiated it in *his* life. Self One and Self Two would never resolve their quarrel about homosexuality.

On 22 April the Germans fired poison gas into the trenches at Ypres. Wilfred Owen, in 'Strange Meeting', described the sleeping soldiers groaning in the 'profound dull tunnel'; by the 'dead smile' of one, he knew 'we stood in hell'. In letters, Lawrence now described himself as 'dead', but he was also preparing to go into battle for what he knew to be one of the great English novels. 'I hope you are willing to fight for this novel,' Lawrence wrote to his agent on 23 April. 'It is nearly three years of hard work, and I am proud of it, and it must be stood up for.'

I'm afraid there are parts of it Methuen won't want to publish. He must. I will take out sentences and phrases, but I won't take out paragraphs or pages ... You see a novel, after all this period of coming into being, has a definite organic form, just as a man has when he is grown. And we don't ask a man to cut his nose off because the public won't like it: because he must have a nose, and his own nose too.

Apart from a few sentences and phrases, Methuen let *The Rainbow* through with its nose intact. The book's content was disguised behind a cover showing a girl in a barn wearing a pink dress fainting into the arms of a man in a frock coat. It looked like the illustration in a women's magazine, and Lawrence hated it.

The Bible, Lawrence said, was a 'great confused novel', and *The Rainbow* was his version of the Old Testament. Rejecting traditional Christianity, Lawrence nonetheless hung his story on the fiery furnace, Noah's Flood, God's Covenant of the rainbow and the love between Jonathan and David. His Holy Family is composed of Lydia Lensky, a Polish widow (with the same given name as his mother), Tom Brangwen, a farmer with 'inarticulate, powerful, religious impulses', and Lydia's daughter Anna, whom Tom Brangwen learns to love as his own. Tom loves easily and openly: at school, he had loved a 'warm, clever boy who was frail in body, a consumptive type. The two had had an almost classic friendship, David and Jonathan, wherein Brangwen was the Jonathan, the server.'[44] Lawrence, whose first name was also David, returned all his life to the love between the two men. Theirs was the original *Blutsbrüderschaft*: his 'love to me', says David in The First Book of Samuel after Jonathan is slain, 'was more wonderful than the love of women'.

Lydia (like Frieda) is older than her husband and her foreignness makes her unreachable, but the balance of her mysterious femininity and his mysterious masculinity makes their 'long marital embrace' a success. The Brangwen farm, The Marsh, is as eternal and unchanging as myth, and Lydia practises her own form of 'fundamental religion'. Anna, who tries to drag her parents into consciousness, marries her cousin Will Brangwen, a lace-maker in Nottingham, who shares the Brangwen soul: 'there was something subterranean about him, as if he had an underworld refuge'. Anna, with her own powerful religious impulses, dances naked in her bedroom, as David did before the Lord and as Frieda also liked to do.

Anna begets Ursula, the woman of the future. 'Whither to go' is Ursula's great question, 'how to become oneself?' She falls in love with a soldier, decides not to marry him (wherein lay the novel's anti-patriotism) and then discovers she is pregnant. In the novel's climax Ursula finds herself in a fugue state, walking and walking 'along the bottommost bed ... there was nothing deeper ... Why must one climb the hill? Why must one climb? Why not stay below? Why force one's way up the slope? Why force one's way up and up when one is at the bottom?' She goes up the slope to bed and is delirious for two weeks, during which time she loses her baby. When she recovers she sees from her window the 'insentient triumph' of life: a stream of people 'in the streets below, colliers, women, children, walking each in the husk of an old fruition ... They were all in prison, they were all going mad.' The 'stiffened bodies' of the colliers:

> seemed already enclosed in a coffin, she saw their unchanging eyes, the eyes of those who are buried alive: she saw the hard, cutting edges of the new houses, which seemed to spread over the hillside in their insentient triumph ... she saw the dun atmosphere over the blackened hills opposite, the dark blotches of houses, slate roofed and amorphous ... and she was sick with a nausea so deep that she perished as she sat.

Lawrence's novel ended with an olive branch. The rainbow that bended and strengthened itself over the blackened hills on the book's last page, like the rainbow that appeared after the flood in Genesis, symbolised fresh growth. The destroyed world would be born again. Ursula saw in the faint, vast gathering of form and colour 'the earth's new architecture', the promise that the 'old, brittle corruption of houses and factories' would be 'swept away' and a 'new clean, naked' world would be born, built on a 'living fabric of Truth'.

'Now,' Lawrence told his typist, Viola Meynell, when he posted the manuscript, 'off and away to find the pots of gold at its feet'.[45] But he had set his rainbow in the sky too soon, he later concluded, 'before, instead of after, the deluge'.[46]

Cornwall, where the Lawrences arrived on 30 December 1915, was eight hours from London by train but the journey to Penzance took them further and further out of the known world. The house, on the north coast between Newquay and Padstow, had been loaned to them by the popular horror-fiction writer J. D. Beresford, and it came with a housekeeper who provided puddings and pies. This was 'not England', Lawrence stressed. In its 'stark, bare, rocky directness of statement' Cornwall was Lyonesse, the land of King Arthur and Tristan and Iseult, now sunk beneath the waves. For the next eighteen months the 'strong and completely unsaddened' Cornwall served as pathetic fallacy; the landscapes that Lawrence inhabited always also inhabited him.

'This is the first move to Florida,' he optimistically wrote on the night they arrived. 'Here already one feels a good peace and a good silence, and a freedom to love and create a new life.'[47] But Cornwall was no replacement for the high skies of Florida, because Lawrence and Frieda had entered the wind tunnel. 'Here the winds are so black and terrible,' he told Ottoline. 'They rush with such force that the house shudders.'[48] 'I shall just go where the wind blows me,' he told his Russian friend S. S. Koteliansky, known as Kot, 'the wind of my own world'.[49] The winds were so great, Lawrence said, they make 'one laugh with astonishment'. 'I feel pushed to the brink of existence,' he told Murry, and 'might as well be blown over the cliffs here in the strong wind, into the rough white sea, as sit at this banquet of vomit, this England, this Europe'. The 'twilight of all twilights' was 'drawing on, and one could only watch it and submit'. No sooner had Lawrence arrived than he fell ill with the chest infection that nearly killed him every winter. 'I am absolutely run to earth,' he told Murry, 'like a fox they have chased till it can't go any further.'[50] He no longer spoke to Russell on the grounds that the philosopher did not share his own sense of infinity, and his only real friends, Lawrence now said, were Murry himself, Murry's girlfriend Katherine Mansfield, and the twenty-one-year-old Philip Heseltine, on the run from conscription. Heseltine was an Etonian music critic and composer with an interest in the Celtic revival; Lawrence thought him 'empty and uncreated', which qualities made him a good disciple, and Heseltine, who thought Lawrence 'perhaps the one great literary genius of his generation',[51] joined him in the cliffside house, bringing his newly pregnant girlfriend, Minnie, known as Puma. Back in London Ottoline received letters from Lawrence complaining about the behaviour of Heseltine and Puma, and letters from Heseltine stirring up trouble between Ottoline and Frieda; each man was upset to discover the other's disloyalty and Heseltine soon returned to London where he told his friends in the Café Royal that Lawrence was 'a bloody bore determined to make me wholly his and as boring as he is'.[52] Frieda, scared that Lawrence would die from misery, asked Russell to join him in the underworld but Russell refused.

Lawrence had devolved from the prophet of resurrection to a misanthrope preaching mass extermination. The Cornish men, he ranted, were 'detestably small-eyed and mean – real cunning nosed peasants' with the 'souls of insects'.[53] If 'squashed', he imagined, 'they would be a whitey mess, like when a black beetle is squashed'. Cornwall, he repeated, was cold, dark and eternal, but Lawrence was not afraid of the dark; he liked the 'terrifying rocks, like solid lumps of the original darkness, quite impregnable: and then the ponderous cold light of the sea foaming up: it is marvellous'.[54] He binged on Dostoevsky who was currently all the rage, having been translated into English by Constance Garnett, the wife of Lawrence's mentor, Edward Garnett, and the mother of David (who saw Lawrence as the plumber's mate). Lawrence had watched Constance Garnett at work in her Surrey home, The Cearne, where he said 'she would finish a page and throw it off on a pile on the floor without looking up, and start a new page. The pile would be this high – really almost to her knees, and all magical.'[55] Ottoline sent Lawrence copies of *The Possessed* and *The Idiot*; he already knew *Notes from the Underground* and had read *The Brothers Karamazov* twice, first in 1913 and again in 1915.

He was, for the moment, Dostoevsky's literary double. The two novelists arrived at the same time in the world of English letters, and Constance Garnett's translation of *Karamazov* was reviewed in the *Athenaeum* in tandem with Lawrence's second novel, *The Trespasser*. *The Trespasser*, the *Athenaeum* noted, recalled 'the best Russian school' and Lawrence's 'poetic realism' was of 'a Dostoevskian order': Dostoevsky's Russia shared with Lawrence's England the same tightness in the air; ordinary life took on the intensity of hallucination; casual conversation was fervent argument, the characters – all informing on one another – lived on the verge of brain fever and waited for a prophet to lead them. Murry had asked Lawrence to collaborate with him on a book about Dostoevsky, but Lawrence's admiration for the Russian kept turning to seething hate and so Murry was now writing the book by himself. Lawrence nonetheless shared his opinions about Dostoevsky in letters to Murry, and in his *Reminiscences of D. H. Lawrence*, Murry cited these as the cause of the breakdown in their relationship: 'It started with Dostoevsky. Lawrence was all against him for his humility and love.'

Lawrence channelled his nihilism into a theory of his philosophy called 'Goats and Compasses', written from his sickbed. The book was never published and the manuscript was lost, but Philip Heseltine's friend Cecil Gray described it as 'Lawrence at his very worst: a bombastic, pseudo-mystical, psycho-philosophical treatise dealing largely with homosexuality – a subject, by the way, in which Lawrence displayed a suspiciously lively interest at the time'.[56] Ottoline, who also read 'Goats and Compasses', thought the argument 'deplorable tosh'. Baffled by how her gentle friend could 'preach this doctrine of hate', she blamed Frieda. Fighting with Frieda, Ottoline reasoned, required Lawrence to 'suppress his human pity, his gentle and tender qualities … and this makes him raw and bitter inside'.[57] Lawrence's friends all hated his wife.

Lawrence and Frieda left the shuddering house in early spring and moved further down the coast, into a whitewashed cottage called Higher Tregerthen, five miles from St Ives and one mile from the isolated village of Zennor. They had found, Lawrence thought, for £5 a year, the best place to live in England and he straight away painted the walls pale pink, the cupboards bright blue, hung daffodil-yellow curtains and a washing line, and dug a vegetable patch for carrots, beans, potatoes, onions, cabbages. A one-up, one-down with an outside privy and no cooker or running water, the cottage stood immediately adjacent to a row of three other cottages which had been knocked together, the third of which was fashioned as a mock-castellated tower. The conversion of the buildings had been done by the previous tenant, a writer called Guy Thorne whose bestselling 1902 novel *When It Was Dark*, about an attempt to disprove the Resurrection, bringing darkness and chaos to the world, was the Edwardian equivalent to *The Da Vinci Code*.

The gales in Zennor were just as severe as those in Newquay. 'How the winds from that untamed Cornish sea rocked the solid little cottage, and howled at it,' Frieda wrote of Higher Tregerthen, 'and how the rain slashed it, sometimes forcing the door open and pouring into the room.'[58] When, in the dark, the door flew open, it seemed that 'the ancient spirits and ghosts of the place blew into my cottage. In the loneliness I seemed to hear the voices of young men crying out to me from the battlefields: "help us, help us, we are dying". Despair had blown in on the night.'[59] Higher Tregerthen lies in a lunar landscape of windswept, treeless, snake-filled fields shaped by Celtic farmers two millennia ago and strewn with Druid sun circles, granite pyramids, volcanic rock, megalithic burial chambers and the stone remains of prehistoric constructions. 'Nowhere,' Lawrence said, 'can it be so black as on the edge of a Cornish moor, above the western sea, near the rocks where the ancient worshippers used to sacrifice.' Lawrence believed that the rocks contained the souls of the dead, and when he followed the track to the cliffs he felt the presence of Phoenician traders and their donkeys. He would 'go out into the blackness of night and listen to the blackness, and call, call softly, for the spirits, the presences he felt coming downhill from the moors ... "Tuatha De Danaan! Be with me. Be with me." And it was as if he felt them come.'[60]

Behind Higher Tregerthen is a giant boulder called Eagle's Nest beneath which Lawrence liked, on calm days, to sit and write, while the front of the house looked down through fields bordered by drystone walls to a farm called Lower Tregerthen, tenanted by a family called Hocking. The Hockings, also anti-war, regarded their eccentric neighbour as a friend. Here Lawrence bought supplies of milk, cream and eggs, got the dung to fertilise his vegetables, taught French to Stanley, the youngest of the four children, and sat chatting in the kitchen while Mrs Hocking fried potatoes. There was a horse called Blossom and a dog called Nell who stole food from the Lawrences' larder. When he was an old man, Stanley Hocking recalled that once when Lawrence was helping them to cut the furze they heard 'the most horrible noises' coming from the sea, 'torpedoes, depth charges, aeroplanes overhead and airships, destroyers dropping depth charges, proper pandemonium'.[61] Fountains the size of mountains erupted from the water.

For all his descriptions of Cornwall as the second circle of hell, Lawrence found it familiar terrain and the reason he felt so at home at Higher Tregerthen was partly because of his fondness for the Hockings and partly because the landscape, mined since the early Bronze Age, was a prehistoric version of his birthplace. Fifty years earlier the Cornish tin mines had been the finest and most productive in the world, but with competition from abroad the pits were closing and the miners emigrating to Australia and North America. The engine houses that once buzzed and whirred now stood barren and silent on the clifftops, while the submarine mines which stretched beneath the Atlantic, from where, during storms, the miners could hear the rumble of boulders above them on the seabed, were as lost as Lyonesse.

Lawrence described the topography of his childhood, with its tapering chimneys, black headstocks and wheels spinning fast against the sky, as a cross between ugly industrialism and rural idyll. In an essay called 'Nottingham and the Mining Countryside', written when he was dying in France and would never see the place again, he remembered Eastwood as occupying a 'lovely position on a hilltop, with a steep slope towards Derbyshire and a long slope towards Nottingham'. Eastwood, which he pictures as though it were Dante's Florence, '*might*', Lawrence added, have been like 'one of the lovely hill towns in Italy, shapely and fascinating', had the original miners' cottages not been demolished and replaced by 'great hollow squares of dwelling planked down on the rough slope of the hill'. The front windows of these sloping blocks looked to the street and the back doors opened on to the stinking ash pits where the households' excrement was deposited.

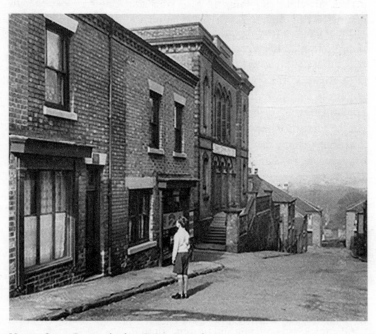

Victoria Street, Eastwood, where Lawrence was born.

Victoria Street, where Lawrence was born on 11 September 1885, ran steeply downhill to the River Erewash which divided the white limestone and ash trees of Derbyshire from the red sandstone and oak trees of Nottingham. It was from the Erewash that the colliers' wives collected the water to wash the coal dust from their husbands' backs. When he was two, the family moved further down the hill to the end house of a block called The Breach. Their new house had an outside lavatory in a row of other outside lavatories in what was known locally as the middle lane; Lawrence never forgave Barber, Walker and Co., the colliery company which employed his father and owned The Breach, for this ugliness and indignity. A hawthorn hedge 'as tall as tall trees' separated the front garden from a brook, over which a sheep bridge led into the meadows. Setting out for work at dawn, Lawrence's father Arthur would walk through these meadows looking for baby rabbits, one of which he once brought home as a pet for his children. Philip Larkin, who admired Lawrence hugely, may have had Arthur Lawrence in mind when he described in his poem 'The Explosion' the bearded, cursing colliers in their pit boots returning home after a catastrophe in the mine, one of them chasing rabbits and another 'with a nest of lark's eggs' which he showed to his family before lodging them 'in the grasses'. When Lawrence was six, the family moved to Walker Street at the top of the same hill. He called their new home Bleak House because it stood open to the west wind that swept in from Derbyshire, but the name refers also to the gloom cast by his parents' rows. In his early poem 'Discord in Childhood', Lawrence described how the wind shaking the ash tree outside his bedroom combined with the angry voices from downstairs to create the music of his childhood.

> Outside the house an ash-tree hung its terrible whips,
> And at night when the wind arose, the lash of the tree
> Shrieked and slashed the wind, as a ship's
> Weird rigging in a storm shrieks hideously.
>
> Within the house two voices arose in anger, a slender lash
> Whistling delirious rage, and the dreadful sound
> Of a thick lash booming and bruising, until it drowned
> The other voice in a silence of blood, 'neath the noise of the ash.

The house on Walker Street gave him the first view that Lawrence ever owned. In *Sons and Lovers*, the novel based on his coming of age, he described the view as 'spread out like a convex cockle-shell' on the 'brim of the wide, dark valley',[62] and in a letter to a friend written from Florence in 1926 he gave typically precise directions: 'Go to Walker St – and stand in front of the third house – and look across at Crich on the left, Underwood in front – High Park woods and Annesley on the right: I lived in that house from the age of 6 to 18, and I know that view better than any in the world.'[63] The view included the chimney pots of The Breach below, a sign that the Lawrences were rising in the world, 'Ooray. Rising was Mrs Lawrence's principal objective, and she ensured that none of her sons would go down the pit. 'We must all rise into the upper classes!' she counselled. 'Upper! Upper! Upper!'[64]

While Lawrence saw in Eastwood the England of Robin Hood, the coal-blasted earth held for him a biblical beauty. 'When I was a boy,' said Paul Morel, the Oedipal hero of *Sons and Lovers*, 'I always thought a pillar of cloud by day and a pillar of fire by night was a pit, with its steam, and its lights, and the burning bank – and I thought the Lord was always at the pit-top.'[65] In *Sons and Lovers*, The Breach became The Bottoms where the Morels lived, and The Bottoms was positioned, like limbo, above the circles of hell: 'The Bottoms succeeded to Hell Row', the novel begins.

Hell Row was a block of thatched, bulging cottages that stood by the brook-side on Greenhill Lane. There lived the colliers who worked in the little gin-pits two fields away. The brook ran under the alder trees, scarcely soiled by these small mines, whose coal was drawn to the surface by donkeys that plodded wearily in a circle round a gin. And all over the countryside were these same pits, some of which had been worked in the time of Charles II, the few colliers and the donkeys burrowing down like ants into the earth, making queer mounds and little black places among the corn-fields and the meadows.[66]

Lawrence liked to measure his terrain in prepositions: before, behind, between, above, below. Hell Row was beneath The Bottoms, the Erewash was between Nottinghamshire and Derbyshire, the brook ran under the alder trees, the coal below was brought above by donkeys treading their eternal circle.

'What was there in the mines that held the boy's feelings?' Lawrence later wondered. 'The darkness, the mystery, the otherworldliness, the peculiar camaraderie, the sort of naked intimacy: men as gods in the underworld, or as elementals.'[67] In his 1918 poem 'Miners', written after the Minnie Pit Disaster in which 156 colliers lost their lives, Wilfred Owen hears in his 'whispering hearth' the moans of 'the men / Writhing for air' and sees 'white bones in the cinder-shard', and thinks of those 'that worked dark pits / of war'. As he gazes into the burning coal, the miners and the soldiers become one. Lawrence, who searched all his life for a form of fraternity, also compared the camaraderie of the colliers with that of soldiers in the trenches. When he looked back on the 'curious, dark intimacy of the mine', it was as if, he reflected, 'there was a lustrous sort of inner darkness, like the gloss of coal, in which we moved and had our real being'.[68] He saw coal as a 'symbol of something in the soul' and never lost the sense that his real being belonged to this glossy inner darkness.

But before he romanticised his father as a collier-aesthete, Lawrence despised him as a semi-literate drunk. When Lawrence's mother, Lydia Beardsall, first met Arthur Lawrence at a dance, he was handsome and graceful and told her that he was a contractor, which was true. Arthur Lawrence was a butty, a form of subcontractor who had charge of a section of the coalface. A butty was paid by the pit owner for the quantity of coal he dug and he in turn paid the wages of the men who worked under his direction, but Lydia understood by 'contractor' that Arthur worked at a desk in a collar and shirt and brought back a fixed salary, not that he went down the pit, came home black and was paid weekly by the load. This deception was the source of her lifelong bitterness. Lydia Lawrence was a snobbish and unhappy woman who wrote verse and liked reading; Arthur was a happy traditionalist who loved the intimacy of pub and pit. Their son later learned that for his father the upperworld of women was an uglier and more dangerous place by far than the underworld of men, which had about it a sublime and primitive splendour.

George Orwell, who went down a mine in the 1930s, found that 'most of the things one imagines in hell are there: heat, noise, confusion, darkness, foul air, and, above all, unbearably cramped space'. Bent double in intense temperatures, Arthur Lawrence dug with his pick while the coal dust settled in his eyelids, throat and nostrils. Before even reaching the coalface, he had braved more dangers than most men do in a lifetime: dropped a thousand feet into the bowels of the earth, he crawled through corridors with his tools, cold tea and lunch of bread and lard; the scabs on his spine formed by banging against the roof of the mine were known by the colliers as 'buttons on the back'. Above his head, supported by wooden props, was what Orwell described as a 'tolerable-sized mountain' composed of 'hundreds of yards of solid rock, bones of extinct beasts, subsoil, flints' and 'roots of growing things'.

It was only when he saw naked miners at work that Orwell realised 'what splendid men' they were. The miner was 'a caryatid', 'superhuman', as solid and black as an 'iron statue'. It was 'impossible', said Orwell, not to feel 'a pang of envy' for his 'toughness'. These were men with 'the most noble bodies; wide shoulders tapering to slender supple waists, and small pronounced buttocks and sinewy thighs, with not an ounce of waste flesh anywhere'. Orwell spoke for Lawrence not only here, but when he described how the work of the miner had forced him to confront his own 'humiliation' as an 'intellectual'. It was only 'because miners sweat their guts out' that 'superior persons' were able to 'remain superior'. Where, Orwell asked, would we be without coal? The underworld is as essential to the overworld as the root to the flower. Everything we do involves coal, from 'crossing the Atlantic' and 'baking a loaf to writing a novel'.[69]

Little has been made of Lawrence's sense of the underworld, which formed the backdrop of his youth and worked a seam through his writing. He was always aware of what lay beneath him: in London he lived above tube trains, in Cornwall he lived above tin mines; he lived above sepulchres in Italy and Malta, and kivas in New Mexico. He described Paul Morel, his fictional alter ego in Sons and Lovers, as born into the split between dark and light: when Mrs Morel went into labour, Mr Morel was down the mine, hewing away at a piece of rock that needed to be cleared for the next day's work. In a passage he later cut from Sons and Lovers, Lawrence described his father's daily cycle in terms of the Divine Comedy. 'Mrs Morel always said the after-life would hold nothing in store for her husband. He rose from the lower world into purgatory, when he came home from the pit, and passed into heaven in the Palmerston Arms.'

A sickly child, Lawrence had not been expected to survive. He told Frieda that he had suffered from 'bronchitis' since he was two weeks old, and his childhood friend George Neville remembered that Lawrence, aged eight, 'had that little, troublesome, hacking cough that used to bring his left hand so sharply to his mouth – a cough and an action that he never lost'.[70] Lacking the energy for school sports, he read books instead and played with the girls. At home he was also to be found with the women: he liked smelling flowers, darning clothes, trimming hats and helping his sister make rag rugs. So completely did he inhabit the consciousness of the women in his world that reviewers of *The White Peacock* assumed that its author was female.

The fourth of fifth children, he was baptised David Herbert but known as Bertie or Bert because he refused to answer to his first name. 'You don't like the name of David!' his headmaster thundered across the hall. 'David is the name of a good and great man.'[71] This was the point: the sole member of his own party, Lawrence preferred not to share his identity with another chosen one. It was Bertie's elder brother Ernest who first bore the burden of their mother's savage loving. George, her eldest child, took after his father and was therefore irrelevant to Lydia; then came sensitive Ernest, followed by Emily, Bert and Ada. The girls, like George, didn't matter to Mrs Lawrence because she could not possess their souls and, when Ernest moved to London to work as a clerk, his visits home, in his frock coat and silk hat, were the high points of the month.

Lydia Lawrence was a martyr, and her children worshipped her for being so. She kept an immaculate house on the money left over from her husband's pay after he had been to the pub, and she gave her children everything they needed to rise upwards. The English class system consisted of the subtlest gradations and Lawrence described his mother, whose own father was an engineer in the Sheerness dockyard with less money than Arthur Lawrence, as middle class. The Beardsalls, Lydia believed, were greatly superior to her husband's people, and the central myth of Lawrence's childhood was that his mother not only came from a different world but belonged to a different species; his parents even spoke different languages, his father employing the local dialect and Lydia speaking the King's English. In his late poem 'Red Herring', Lawrence boiled his background down to a playground chant:

The Lawrence family: back row: Emily, George, Ernest; front row: Ada, Lydia, DH Lawrence, Arthur

My father was a working man
　　　　and a collier was he,
at six in the morning they turned him down
　　　　and they turned him up for tea

My mother was a superior soul
　　　　a superior soul was she,
cut out to play a superior role
　　　　in the god-damn bourgeoisie.

We children were the in-betweens
　　　　little nondescripts were we,
indoors we called each other *you*
　　　　outside, it was *tha* and *thee*.

But time has fled, our parents are dead
　　　　we've risen in the world all three;
but still we are in-betweens, we tread
　　　　between the devil and the deep sad sea.

In legend, the in-betweens – spawn of miscegenation – are always extraordinary and Lawrence was fascinated by hybrid forms: centaurs, satyrs, fauns, plumed serpents and men like King David who were both human and divine. Zeus and Leda created Helen, the most beautiful woman on earth; the father of Jesus was God, and the great god Pan, in whom Lawrence saw an image of himself, was the son of Hermes and a wood nymph.

His parents' conflict was the story of Lawrence's life; he internalised it, contained it and examined it from every perspective. His mother was all mind, his father all body; his mother was pure will, his father pure instinct. Having identified entirely with his mother, he then identified entirely with his father; he mined down into the experience of both and explored as no novelist had done before 'the woe that is in marriage'. 'Marriage is the great puzzle of our day,' Lawrence wrote in 'On Being a Man'. 'It is our sphinx-riddle. Solve it, or be torn to bits, is the decree.'[72] He had no interest in solving it through an understanding of his parents' personalities. Their battle was not personal but elemental: Arthur Lawrence was Man, Lydia Lawrence was Woman. He did not 'so much care about,' Lawrence explained to Edward Garnett, 'what the woman *feels* – in the ordinary usage of the word'. He cared only about 'what the woman *is* ... inhumanly, physiologically, materially ... what she is as a phenomenon (or as representing some greater, inhuman will)'.[73] Accordingly, there was only one marriage for D. H. Lawrence, and that was between heaven and hell. His mother moved upwards while his father went down, and she took her children with her. 'O I was born low and inferior', Lawrence wrote in 'The Saddest Day',

> but shining up beyond
> I saw the whole superior
> world shine like the promised land.

> So up I started climbing
> to join the folks on high,
> but when at last I got there
> I had to sit down and cry.

While Lawrence lived inside his parents' conflict, it would be, wrote Jessie Chambers, 'a great error to suppose that his early life was unhappy'.[74] His childhood was happy, but with a worm at its heart. May, Jessie's sister, who sometimes ate her tea with the Lawrences, described the happiness and unhappiness as coexisting. The Walker Street parlour would be filled with 'banter and laughter', she recalled, until Arthur Lawrence arrived. She then 'felt Bert draw himself together',

> humping himself up and bending his head over his plate. When the father talked to me, the son twitched my dress or nudged me. He hardly answered when his father spoke to him. His mother kept her eyes down and spoke only in monosyllables. But the father talked, and ate and handled the food as the man who paid for it all. He chatted amiably with me, and his young daughter told of some prank that made us laugh. But his son nudged me so hard I felt I was misbehaving. There was such a hateful feeling coming from Bert that I was almost frightened. It was as if Prince Charming had turned into a toad.

The tension climaxed when Arthur Lawrence poured his tea into his saucer to cool it down before slurping it up, at which point the children stifled their giggles. When Arthur left the room, the 'gaiety returned'.

'He hates his father,' Mrs Lawrence would announce, with such pride and regularity that her son's hatred became his badge of honour. 'I tried to find a word to fit Bert's attitude,' May Chambers continued, 'and discovered it was *vengeful*.' Arthur Lawrence ignored the 'jagged waves of hate and loathing' emanating from his son but, said May Chambers, 'the queer behaviour of mother and son made me tremble internally till I couldn't swallow my food'.[75]

Raised in a violent family, Lawrence became a violent husband. His father beat his mother and when Lawrence was fifteen his father's brother, who lived a mile away, killed his son with a kitchen pot and was found guilty of manslaughter. There was no evidence during these hellish meals in Walker Street that Bert revered his father's glossy underworld or believed that the mines were where he had his real being, and Paul Morel prays every night to the Lord to 'let my father die'. Years later, when he regretted his treatment of his father, Lawrence described the control his mother had wielded over the home, suggesting that it was Lydia rather than Arthur who had inflicted the worst damage. The nights when her husband was in the pub, Lydia Lawrence 'would gather the children in a row' where they sat 'quaking' in anticipation of his return. While they waited, she 'would picture his shortcomings blacker and blacker to their childish horror'.

At last the father would come in softly, taking off his shoes, hoping to escape unnoticed to bed, but that was never allowed him. She would burst out upon him, reviling him for a drunken sot, a good-for-nothing father. She would turn to the whimpering children and ask them if they were not disgusted with such a father. He would look at the row of frightened children, and say: 'Never mind, my duckies, you needna be afraid of me. I'll do ye no harm.'[76]

Jessie Chambers said that Walker Street had a tension unlike anything she had known before. It was as though 'something unusual might happen at any minute. It was somehow exciting, yet it made me feel a little sick … happenings there had sharp edges and a dramatic quality that made them stand out in one's memory.' This 'strangely vibrating atmosphere' was the result of 'the strong emotional tension between mother and son, and in a directly contrary sense, between husband and wife, and father and son'.[77]

In Lawrence's fiction, which is filled with the packing of bags and the slamming of doors, the waves of wrath tend to overwhelm those of love. Leaving home became his great subject, in some ways his only subject. After Lawrence left his father's house, he made it a policy never to have a home of his own; he perched instead on the highest possible branch of the highest possible tree. Then, having recreated on his perch the strangely vibrating atmosphere of Walker Street, he flew to another branch as soon as he possibly could.

The Walker Street parlour was furnished with books, pictures and a piano, making it an unusual room for a collier's family. Included among the books were the twenty-two green-bound volumes of the *International Library of Famous Literature* edited by Richard Garnett, father of Edward Garnett. The volumes were a gift from Ernest and thus regarded in the family 'with reverence amounting to awe'.[78] Here Lawrence discovered American literature in the form of Edgar Allan Poe's *Tales of Mystery and Imagination*, extracts from the *Autobiography* of Benjamin Franklin, Louisa May Alcott's *Little Women* ('Little Woman' was the name Lawrence gave his mother) and Nathaniel Hawthorne's *The Scarlet Letter*. If the mining town was composed of young enthusiasts singing Mendelssohn duets and reading the *Divine Comedy*, this was partly thanks to Lydia Lawrence's model of plain living and high thinking. Without her backing, Lawrence would not have won the scholarship to Nottingham High School which ensured that, between the ages of twelve and fifteen, his education was as good as that of any middle-class boy.

He was always aware of the dramatic potential of his childhood, and he captured the tension in his early plays, *A Collier's Friday Night* and *The Daughter-in-Law*, which anticipated the kitchen-sink dramas of the 1950s. *A Collier's Friday Night* opens with chatter between a Mother and her daughter which ends abruptly when the Father returns home black from the pit: 'A man comes home after a hard day's work to folks as 'as never a word to say to 'im, 'as shuts up the minute 'e enters the house, as 'ates the sight of 'im as soon as 'e comes in th' room—!' The son, Ernest (the Lawrence figure), then comes home from college and announces, 'Fancy! Swinburne's dead.' When Ernest's friend Maggie arrives for her Friday-night literature lesson, they discuss Francis Thompson's new essay on Shelley, in which Thompson describes the poet's childlike love of sailing paper boats. Maggie compares Ernest to Shelley:

ERNEST (*flattered at the comparison*): But I don't make paper boats. I tell you, you think too much about me.[79]

Later, the Mother expresses her loathing of Maggie and Ernest comforts her: 'I don't care for her – really – not half as I care for you. Only, just now – well, I can't help it, I can't help it. But I care just the same – for you – I do.' ('I wish I could write such dialogue,' said George Bernard Shaw of Lawrence's plays. 'With mine I always hear the sound of the typewriter.') But as good as Lawrence's dialogue are his stage directions, and the Mother and son's exchange about Maggie is preceded by this:

*There is in their tones a dangerous gentleness – so much gentleness that the safe reserve of their souls is broken.*

Maggie is a portrait of Jessie Chambers, the girl described by Lawrence as 'the anvil on which I have hammered myself out'.[80] Jessie is also the model for Muriel in *The White Peacock* and for Miriam Leivers in *Sons and Lovers*, and she gave her own version of her relationship with Lawrence in *D. H. Lawrence: A Personal Record*, published under the pseudonym 'E.T.' When Jessie met Lawrence in the spring of 1901, he was fifteen and in his last year at Nottingham High School, and she was fourteen with a 'dark rosy face, a bunch of short, black curls, very fine and free, and dark eyes'.[81] He compared her to Emily Brontë, because Jessie was also, Lawrence explained to her, 'intense and introspective' and 'governed entirely by your feelings'.[82]

Having already left school in order to take on her role as the family drudge, Jessie was yearning to complete her education and Lawrence offered to teach her French and Arithmetic. Her parents were tenant farmers with a tribe of children and a love of literature: Mr Chambers read *Tess of the D'Urbervilles* aloud to Mrs Chambers when it was serialised in the local paper, Jessie went about reciting Wordsworth's 'Lucy Gray', and the family fought over copies of the *English Review*. Their farm, on the edge of a wood three miles from Eastwood, was called The Haggs and this was Lawrence's ideal home. He later said that he was happiest when he was either there or on his way there, cutting through the alley in the woods, and circling the pond with the overhanging oaks. 'Whatever I forget,' Lawrence wrote to Jessie Chambers's brother in 1928, 'I shall never forget The Haggs – I loved it so':

Jessie Chambers

I loved to come to you all, it really was a new life began in me there. The water-pippin by the door – those maiden-blush roses that Flower [the horse] would lean over and eat – and Trip [the bull-terrier] floundering round – And stewed figs for tea in winter, and

38

in August green stewed apples. Do you still have them? Tell your
mother I never forget, no matter where life carries us. – And does
she still blush if somebody comes and finds her in a dirty white
apron? or doesn't she wear work-aprons any more? Oh I'd love to be
nineteen again, and coming up through the Warren and catching
the first glimpse of the buildings. Then I'd sit on the sofa under the
window, and we'd crowd round the little table to tea, in that tiny
little kitchen I was so at home in.[83]

This was the rural idyll that Lawrence tried to recreate in Rananim,
and that he rediscovered at Lower Tregerthen farm. The Hockings'
horse was called Blossom and their dog Nell, and Mrs Hocking made
fried potatoes rather than stewed apples, but Lawrence similarly loved
to walk down to the farm and join the family around the fire.

Three traumatic events marked the start of his sixteenth year. The
first was in September 1901 when, having now left school, Lawrence
took a job as a clerk in a prosthetics factory in Nottingham where the
women 'were filthier than anybody he had ever conceived'. The new
boy's prudishness only encouraged them and one day, according to
George Neville, a 'number of girls rushed upon him, seized him, threw
him down, and attempted upon him the Great Indignity'. Lawrence
lashed out at them 'with teeth, hoof and claw,'; he tore their dresses,
bit their fingers and arms, scratched their faces, kicked them and
eventually drove them off; his ferocity would always startle people.[84]
The impact of the assault, Neville wrote, cannot be underestimated
and this may have been the reason for Lawrence's lifelong horror of
being unexpectedly touched. The second event took place two months
later when, after one of his weekend visits home, Ernest, aged twenty-
two, picked up an infection on his return journey and died two days
later. Lawrence now became his mother's favourite and no sooner had
he been promoted than he too – in the third traumatic event of the
autumn – fell dangerously ill: 'The doctor says there is a spot about the
size of a crown on his lungs that is clear. If that can be kept clear, he
may live.'[85]

In the synopsis of *Sons and Lovers* that he later sent to Edward
Garnett, Lawrence described how Mrs Morel 'selects' her sons 'as
lovers – first the eldest, then the second. These sons are *urged* into life
by their reciprocal love of their mother – urged on and on.'[86] This is

what happened now: Lawrence pulled through his illness because of his mother's determination, and was effectively raised from the dead. When he regained consciousness he found that his voice had broken (insofar as it would ever break), which meant that he had become a man. Told by the doctor to give up his job at the factory, he convalesced for a year and then accepted a post as a pupil-teacher at the British School in Eastwood, where he undertook 'three years' savage teaching of collier lads'.[87]

These separate experiences formed one rolling catastrophe. Lawrence's illness, which coincided with the death of Ernest, was brought on – George Neville firmly believed – by the sexual assault at work; the death of Ernest led to Lawrence's elevation as his mother's lover; and his illness was clearly the start of his tuberculosis. Tuberculosis, which Lawrence believed to be caused by an excess of love, might therefore be seen, in his reasoning, as a sexually transmitted disease. 'I don't think,' said Aldous Huxley, 'one can exaggerate the importance of the disease in Lawrence,' but Lawrence always denied that he had TB: 'I am not really afraid of consumption,' he casually informed a friend in 1913. 'I don't know why – I don't think I shall ever die of *that*.'[88] His denial was part of the culture: despite being responsible for one death in eight, TB was not talked about, even by doctors to their patients. Kafka, writing from the sanatorium where he would die in April 1924, noted that 'in discussing tuberculosis ... everybody drops into a shy, evasive, glassy-eyed manner of speech'.[89] Lawrence's disease made itself apparent, so Huxley observed, in 'dips and rises and dips and rises' throughout the year.[90] Critically ill every winter, he was stronger by Easter and consequently, Lawrence said, 'those three days in the tomb' took on 'a terrible significance and reality to me'.[91] Accordingly, the most important events in his life tended to take place during Holy Week.

Until the tubercle bacillus was discovered in 1882, proving that consumption was the result of an airborne infection rather than an inner disposition, it hid its horrors behind a mask of sensibility. The image of tuberculosis as an internal flame that consumed the body was born of Romanticism ('youth grows pale, and spectre-thin, and dies', wrote Keats – himself consumptive – in 'Ode to a Nightingale'), and a version of the internal combustion theory is what Lawrence preferred to believe, arguing that 'Any excess in the sympathetic mode from the upper centres tends to burn the lungs with oxygen, weaken them with stress, and cause consumption. So it is just criminal to make a child too loving … It means derangement and death at last.'[92] His excess-of-love diagnosis was later displaced by an excess-of-rage diagnosis. Lawrence's lungs were 'crocky', he explained, because he shut his 'rages of trouble well within my belly'.[93] This was repeated on his deathbed, where Lawrence blamed Europe for his condition: 'The root of all my sickness is a sort of rage. I realise now, Europe gets me into an inward rage, that keeps my bronchials hellish inflamed.'[94] There is no medical link between rage and consumption, but those who live with consumptives often describe their emotional combustibility, and Lawrence's furies became legendary.

His temper was never apparent at The Haggs, however, where he now resumed his visits, spending so much time on the farm that his mother said he might as well pack his things and move in. Her son's love of 'the Haggites' was, for Lydia, the deepest possible betrayal and it is striking,

Lawrence in 1908

41

when we consider how close she and Lawrence had become during his illness and how jealous she was of his preferred family, that he persisted in returning there. 'Nothing will stop me,' Lawrence told Jessie, 'unless your mother and father say I can't come.'[95] The farm was the refuge for Lawrence that the pub had been for his own father, and he received the same silent treatment when he sloped guiltily home to Bleak House. Frieda would be similarly jealous when Lawrence disappeared for long periods to Lower Tregerthen farm, where she was also convinced he was conducting an affair.

'In our home,' Jessie recalled, Lawrence 'was a synonym for joy – radiant joy in simply being alive'. The Lawrence who cast a spell over his friends was born at The Haggs, where he realised himself completely. 'Ah, you Haggites see the best of me,' he liked to say.[96] His magic lay in the nakedness of his presence and the quality of his concentration: there was nothing that Lawrence did not take in. He brought a 'holiday atmosphere'[97] and controlled the family temperature; the Chambers children were nicer to one another when Lawrence was around. There was 'a quality of lightness about him,' said Jessie, 'something that seemed to shine from within'.[98] Lawrence liked to invent games and play charades, but he also enjoyed the creativity of chores and, without waiting to be asked, he would peel onions, fetch water, brush the hearth and help with the harvest. 'Work goes like fun when Bert's there,' Mr Chambers remarked.[99] Lawrence even taught the Chambers children how to waltz, having been taught himself by his father. 'Father says one ought to be able to dance on a three penny bit,' he explained.[100] This was the only occasion, May Chambers recalled, that Bert had 'allowed his father to have any good points. He talked a lot about Mr Lawrence's knowledge of dancing. It was easy to see how proud he was of him as an authority.'

Most of his time with Jessie was spent in the woods, where Lawrence had also been taught by his father the name of every bird, tree and flower. He moved through the natural world with the grace of a faun and in years to come the ranting, monological side of Lawrence's character would always be tempered by the child of Pan. It was in the woods, Jessie recalled, that he told her about William Blake, whose 'wife was a poor girl whom he taught to read, and also to print and engrave, and what a marvellous helpmate she was to him'. Jessie was Lawrence's helpmate too, and 'for a little time we lived with Blake and his wife'.[101] Blake was another respectable working-class prophet with a distrust of science and a vision of a new Jerusalem, and Lawrence's entire philosophy – 'Without Contraries is no progression' – was lifted from 'The Argument' in Blake's *Marriage of Heaven and Hell*, which 'Infernal' book tells of the poet's visit to the underworld. Robert Burns, the Ploughman Poet, was also 'a sort of brother' to Lawrence, who at one point began to write 'a sort of life' of Burns which was really, like everything he wrote, a sort of autobiography: 'I'm not Scotch. So I shall just transplant him to home – or on the hills of Derbyshire.'[102] Lawrence was saturated in Romantic poetry: 'over and over again', Jessie said, he read aloud his favourite Shelley, 'Ode to the West Wind', from her edition of *Palgrave's Golden Treasury* which he carried in his pocket.[103] Whitman's *Leaves of Grass* 'was one of his great books',[104] and among the other poems which had 'meant the most' to him were Keats's Odes and Wordsworth's Immortality Ode ('The Rainbow comes and goes'). These, Lawrence said, were 'woven deep' into his consciousness and gave the 'ultimate shape' to his life.[105] One Christmas he gave Jessie a selection of Shelley, while she gave him Blake's *Songs of Innocence* and *Songs of Experience*. Reading together Francis Thompson's essay on Shelley, published in the *Dublin Review* in 1908, they learned that 'the aboundingly spontaneous Shelley' – a 'poet of ascendency' forever 'struggling towards higher things' – was unappreciated in his own age.[106] The rise of Shelley was noted by Lawrence.

A modernist only by mistiming, there was little to interest him in the aesthetics of his own age. The Romantic period was as close to Lawrence as the modernist revolution is to us now: he could feel its roots and he grew from its soil. When Lawrence's father was born in 1846, Wordsworth was poet laureate and when Lawrence himself was born, Wordsworth had been dead for only thirty-five years. Wordsworth was a hallowed paternal presence in late Victorian England whose influence can be felt in Lawrence's reverence for nature, blanket hatred of industrialism and overriding sense of wonder. 'Wonder' was a favourite word of both Wordsworth and Lawrence: 'Oh, for the wonder that bubbles into my soul,' Lawrence wrote in 'Song of a Man Who Has Come Through'. The problem with modernity, Lawrence believed, was that the wonder had gone.

When she was sixteen and he was seventeen, Jessie and Lawrence went every Thursday evening to the library to choose their books. It was, she said, 'the outstanding event of the week' and she describes this period of their lives as 'a kind of orgy of reading. I think we were hardly aware of the outside world.'[107] Jessie and Lawrence worked their way through the canon of English literature and a great deal more besides: Fenimore Cooper's *The Last of the Mohicans*, Pierre Loti's *Pêcheur d'Islande*, Virgil's *Georgics*, Schopenhauer's *Essays*, William James's *Varieties of Religious Experience*. Jessie's account of their reading suggests that they consumed more literature in five years than most educated people do in a lifetime. This was the apprenticeship which enabled Lawrence to hold his own at high table in Trinity College, Cambridge.

It was when he was 'nineteen or so,' Jessie recalled, that his 'fatal division began to manifest itself'.[108] What happened was this: Lawrence now understood himself to be a great man in need of a guiding woman. 'Every great man – every man who achieves anything, I mean – is founded in some woman,' he explained to Jessie. 'Why shouldn't you be the woman I am founded in?' Forced to confront the nature of their relationship, they 'became self-conscious', said Jessie, 'and aware of a barrier'.[109] That barrier was Lydia Lawrence. His relationship with Jessie, Lydia explained to her son, was becoming a problem and people would talk: they should either get engaged or break it off. The ultimatum forced Lawrence to examine his feelings for Jessie and he duly discovered that he loved her, but as a woman in whom to 'found' himself and not 'as a husband should love his wife'.[110] On Easter Monday 1906 – when Lawrence was twenty – he mournfully suggested to Jessie that they could get married, so long as she understood his position; this way, he reasoned, they could at least continue their conversations about literature. Jessie now realised that Lawrence moved and breathed under the 'incapacitating' pressure of his mother: 'I was conscious of a fierce pain, of the body as well as the spirit ... I saw the golden apple of life that had been lying at my fingertips recede irretrievably.'[111]

The magical Bert who brought joy to the Haggites still existed after what was now referred to as 'the Easter Monday episode', but he was ghosted by a 'dehumanised' other self who 'utterly negated life'. Lawrence at first understood his division in terms of the difference between love and desire: he could not love the object of his desire and he could not desire the object of his love. Self One loved Jessie but, to Self Two, Jessie 'had no significance at all'. There was a similar split in

Lawrence between the self who lived and the self who wrote: 'I have a second consciousness somewhere actively alive,' he would tell a later muse, Helen Corke. 'I keep on writing, almost mechanically.'[112] This second, writerly consciousness is what led Forster to conclude, when he read *The White Peacock*, that Lawrence had 'not a glimmering from first to last of what he's up to'.[113]

The accounts of young Lawrence in the memoirs of Jessie Chambers and George Neville tell us something about the complexity of his attitude to sex and sexuality, and something about the difference between his male and female friendships. Neville, who married the girl he made pregnant while 'spooning' in an alley, describes Lawrence as his naive sexual inferior – which is how Lawrence would be seen by men for the rest of his life – while Jessie, like all of Lawrence's women, realised that 'the whole question of sex had for him the fascination of horror'.[114] Neville's *Memoir of D. H. Lawrence* was subtitled *The Betrayal*, a term associated with Lawrence except that in this instance it is Neville who sees himself as betrayer because he revealed those facts that would embarrass his friend the most. Neville suggests that because he did not play football or cricket, Lawrence was never part of male changing-room culture, and he was thus able to maintain his innocence until his late teens. He illustrates this level of innocence with an anecdote.

One afternoon, Neville arrived at Bleak House to find Lawrence copying his favourite painting, Maurice Greiffenhagen's *An Idyll*, which shows a semi-naked shepherd grabbing hold of a semi-naked girl. Neville laughed at Lawrence's penmanship, saying that his shepherd looked more like a scarecrow; he then, to demonstrate what a naked man in his full vigour really looked like, took off his clothes and flexed his muscles. Lawrence was transfixed. He leaned forward in his chair, 'his elbows resting on the table, the cup of his hands supporting his face, upon which was an expression of perfectly rapt adoration. That is a very strong expression to use, but it is the only one that will express … what I wish to convey. Lawrence adored strength and beauty with a kind of envious adoration.' 'I had no idea,' he said to Neville. 'Good gracious! You're positively a pocket Hercules.'[115] From now on, under the guise of drawing him, Lawrence apparently gazed at Neville's naked body at every opportunity and Neville, enjoying the attention, took Lawrence swimming in the local lake; the homoerotic bathing scene in *The White Peacock*, Neville said, was taken from life.

Maurice Greiffenhagen, *An Idyll*

But this was by no means the first time Lawrence had seen a well-built naked man: his father was naked a good deal of the time. After his daily bath, when the family took turns to wash his back, Arthur Lawrence would wear only his towel. Lawrence describes Mr Morel's body in *Sons and Lovers* as 'wonderfully young', 'muscular, without any fat. His skin was smooth and clear. It might have been the body of a man of twenty-eight, except that there were, perhaps, too many blue scars, like tattoo-marks, where the coal-dust remained under the skin.' Lawrence gazed at male bodies as though they belonged to a different species. 'It seemed strange', Paul Morel thought of his own naked father, that they were of 'the same flesh'.[116]

The early twentieth century was an age which idealised robust masculinity, and Lawrence was unsexed by his sensibility and physical fragility. Even the name 'Bertie', Jessie told him, sounded feminine which is why she always called him Lawrence, and yet she noted how unhappy he was to discover hairs on his chin.[117] Neville, meanwhile, observed that he gave the women in his drawings 'incipient moustaches', and that the only time Lawrence had ever physically attacked him was when Neville explained, again in relation to the unreality of his drawings, that women's bodies were not smooth like dolls, but had pubic hair. Lawrence's concern about his own sexuality might explain his assessment of the sexuality of Shelley, the man to whom he was regularly compared. To most readers, Byron and Wordsworth represent Romantic manliness while Shelley, like an angel, is genderless. But, to Lawrence, Shelley was the most male figure *in the world*. 'I can think of no being in the world so transcendently male as Shelley', Lawrence wrote in his 'Study of Thomas Hardy'. 'He is phenomenal. The rest of us have bodies which contain the male and the female,' but not Shelley. Drawing up a list of 'maleness' in high art, Lawrence ranked Shelley above 'Plato and Raphael and Wordsworth, then Goethe and Milton and Dante, then Michelangelo, then Shakespeare, then Tolstoi, then St Paul'.[118]

When Lawrence told Neville that he wanted a woman, Neville replied that:

If you wanted a woman, because, being a healthy, red-blooded sort of a chap, you had begun to feel a real urge towards women, I would say nothing at all about it … It would be natural … But what you told me was that you wanted a woman merely as an experience; so

47

that you might be able to write better from your chosen point of view. That wouldn't assist you to write; you would be relating an experience from an imitation instead of the real thing.[119]

The importance of Neville's point cannot be overstated. Lawrence wanted a woman behind him not because he desired her sexually but in order to explore her point of view; this is what every woman who ever stood behind Lawrence while he wrote a book would realise, once she had been drained and discarded. And there is no clearer example of his need to inhabit female experience than the long gestation of *Sons and Lovers*, which began as a novel called *Paul Morel* and was filtered through the mediums of Lydia, Jessie and finally Frieda.

In September 1906, when Lawrence was twenty-one and had spent three years teaching, he went to Nottingham University College to study for a Teacher's Certificate. His 'favourite Prof.', he told Jessie, was the French lecturer, Ernest Weekley: 'He really *is* a gentleman. He's quite elegant. He leans back in his chair and points to the blackboard, too elegant to get on his feet.'[120] At the same time as praising the louche elegance of Professor Weekley, Lawrence told Jessie that he had 'never really had a father' and she understood this to mean that he was asking the university, 'perhaps unconsciously', to 'make up for his lack'.[121] Ernest Weekley, meanwhile, told his wife, Frieda, that he had 'a genius' in his evening class, but Mrs Weekley, currently enjoying an affair with a genius of her own, who in turn believed that she too was a genius, took the information in her stride.[122]

Two years later, Lawrence moved to South London to take up a job at Davidson Road Boys' School in Croydon, and in June 1909 Jessie copied out four of his poems and sent them to Ford Madox Hueffer at the *English Review* (after the war, Hueffer changed his Germanic name to Ford Madox Ford). The launch of the *English Review* in December 1908 had been a cause of great excitement at The Haggs: the first number opened with new tales by Thomas Hardy ('A Sunday Morning Tragedy') and Henry James ('The Jolly Corner'), and serialisations of *Some Reminiscences* by Joseph Conrad, H. G. Wells's *Tono-Bungay* and Tolstoy's 'The Raid: A Volunteer's Story', translated by Constance Garnett. The second issue, which appeared the following month, was devoted to Dante Gabriel Rossetti, and the third, in February 1909, ran three poems by Yeats. Hueffer, who received twenty manuscripts a day, recalled the arrival of Jessie's envelope: it was 'the year when my eyes first fell on words written by Norman Douglas, G. H. Tomlinson, Wyndham Lewis, Ezra Pound, and others ... My secretary looked up and said: "You've got another genius?" I answered: "It's a big one this time." '[123] Lawrence understood the term 'genius' to mean that he was less advantaged than his social superiors. 'They never called Lawrence a professional writer,' Frieda later wrote, '– always a genius. That made him angry. "That's my label," he later said, "– a genius – and with that I am dismissed." '[124]

When Hueffer replied to Jessie expressing interest in the poet, Lawrence was on holiday with his mother and sister Ada on the Isle of Wight, where they rented a house in Shanklin. In a small act of control, Jessie decided that rather than tell him now that he had been plucked from obscurity and placed among the galaxy of literary stars, she would wait until mid-August when Lawrence returned to Eastwood. So in September 1909, when he had just turned twenty-four, Lawrence went to London to meet the great Hueffer. What would he do, Hueffer wondered, if this son of a coalminer called him 'Sir'? Would it cause the boy 'pain and confusion' were Hueffer – a socialist – to deter him from doing so? But when Lawrence appeared at the office of the *English Review*, 'leaning against the wall beside the doorway', Hueffer saw not a forelock-tugging ingénu but 'bewilderingly ... a fox. A fox going to make a raid on the hen-roost before him.'[125] The effeminate adolescent patronised by George Neville had evolved into a young man whose poise was cool, hypnotic and threatening. The transformation in Lawrence was down to one thing: he had turned from a human being into a writer.

Talking with the fox, Hueffer realised the extent of his reading: 'I have never met any young man of his age who was so well read in all the dullnesses that spread between Milton and George Eliot. He moved amongst the high things of culture with a tranquil assurance.'[126] Hueffer offered to look at anything that Lawrence cared to send him, and so Lawrence showed him the manuscript of *The White Peacock*. It was, Hueffer thought, disappointingly middle-class; Lawrence should be marketing his class authenticity and achieving for prose what Wordsworth achieved for poetry, 'to show', as Wordsworth put it in the preface to *Lyrical Ballads*, 'that men who did not wear fine clothes can feel deeply'. So that autumn Lawrence wrote his short story 'Odour of

Chrysanthemums', in which a collier's wife learns her husband has been killed in an accident. The story draws heavily on the atmosphere of Lawrence's childhood: the dark red coals of the fire, the saucepan on the hob, his mother straining the potatoes and mashing the tea, the tension of waiting for the latch to lift on the door. Hueffer would publish 'Odour of Chrysanthemums' in the *English Review* in 1911, but it was as a lyric poet and not as a fiction writer that Lawrence first became known. The November 1909 issue of the *English Review* opened with three poems by D. H. Lawrence: 'Dreams Old and Nascent', 'Discipline' and 'Baby Movements'. Lawrence's poems contain none of the vast ambition that would weigh down his novels; his writing was always at its best when it happened glancingly, and his most successful poetry catches him off-guard in a moment of absorption. In 'Baby Movements' the poet watches his landlady's toddler run across the grass.

> When the bare feet of the baby beat across the grass
> The little white feet nod like white flowers in the wind,
> They poise and run like ripples lapping across the water;
> And the sight of their white play among the grass
> Is like a little robin's song, winsome,
> Or as two white butterflies settle in the cup of one flower
> For a moment, then away with a flutter of wings.

In 'Dreams Old and Nascent', Lawrence is already positioned at a window – where his most important scenes would take place – and in pursuit of the sun:

> I have opened the window to warm my hands on the sill
> Where the sunlight soaks in the stone ...

While the poet's hands are warming on the sill, 'The clink of the shunting engines is sharp and fine, / Like savage music striking far off'. His poems always reappeared in his prose – like Shelley, Lawrence did not believe in the difference as anything more than an operating distinction – and we hear the soundtrack again in the opening lines of 'Odour of Chrysanthemums':

The small locomotive engine, Number 4, came clanking, stumbling down from Selston with seven full wagons. It appeared round the corner with loud threats of speed but the colt that it startled from among the gorse which still flickered indistinctly in the raw afternoon, outdistanced it in a canter.

His ascent was rapid. A story, 'Goose Fair', appeared in the *English Review* of February 1910, and *The White Peacock* was bought by Heinemann and published the following January. Lawrence's mother lived long enough to hold a copy in her hands: 'And though she loved me so much, I think she doubted whether it could be much of a book, since no one more important than I had written it … This David would never get a stone across at Goliath. And why try? Let Goliath alone.'[127] Whenever he was asked if it was hard, as the son of a collier, to find literary success, Lawrence replied that no, 'I *did not* find it hard.'

I never starved in a garret, nor waited in anguish for the post to bring me an answer from editor or publisher, nor did I struggle in sweat and blood to bring forth mighty works, nor did I ever wake up and find myself famous … It all happened by itself, without any groans from me.[128]

But it did not happen by itself; it was Jessie who launched him and Lawrence, who loathed patronage, never forgave her.

Being launched as a writer was easier than being launched as a lover, and Lawrence was trying out various women. The autumn of his debut in the *English Review* he announced his engagement to a fellow teacher called Agnes Holt. 'It doesn't matter *who* one marries,' he repeatedly explained to Jessie.[129] Offering what he called 'the dirty coin of marriage' improved his chances of getting beyond the kissing stage, but Agnes Holt was like all the others in that she 'refused to see that a man is male'. She wanted 'sentimentality', Lawrence wanted 'naked life'. Meanwhile his 'old fire' for Jessie 'burned up afresh' and he also discovered another girl who ' "interests" me', a twenty-seven-year-old teacher called Helen Corke. What happened between Lawrence and Helen Corke shows us the fox inside the hen-roost.[130]

By coincidence Helen Corke had also been on the Isle of Wight in early August 1909. She had taken rooms in Freshwater, on the opposite coast to Shanklin, with her married lover, Herbert Macartney. When they returned to the mainland on 5 August, Helen continued down to Cornwall with two friends and Macartney went home to his wife and children in Wimbledon where, two days later, he killed himself. Helen heard of Macartney's death through a report of his funeral in the local paper. Electrified by the tragedy and by his proximity to the lovers, Lawrence used it as the plot for his second novel, *The Trespasser*. He called Macartney 'Siegmund' and Helen 'Helena' while Siegmund's wife was named Beatrice – but his Beatrice, Siegmund explained to Helena, 'is as dead – ay, far more dead – than Dante's'. Dante's Beatrice had always irritated Lawrence, who preferred real to idealised women. 'Why do we slur over the actual fact', he wrote in his 'Study of Thomas Hardy', 'that Dante had a cosy bifurcated wife in his bed, and a family of lusty little Dantinos?' He must mean by 'bifurcated' that her legs were forked, and Dante's refusal to mention his sensual wife, Lawrence believed, made the *Divine Comedy* 'slightly dishonourable'.[131] As for his own bifurcation, Lawrence explained that there was a 'second me, a hard, cruel if need be, me that is the writer which troubles the pleasanter me, the human who belongs to you'. This 'second me,' he explained, 'belongs to nobody, not even to myself'.[132]

The relationship between Siegmund and Helena is charged by sexual frustration. Their long kisses leave Siegmund unsatisfied and Helena contented; she was one of those women for whom 'passion exhausts itself at the mouth'. While Lawrence's 'second me' wrote about Siegmund's frustrated desire for Helena, Lawrence found his 'first me' longing for Helen Corke. This, Helen understood, was the result of 'putting himself, imaginatively', in the place of Siegmund and 'I must not,' she told herself, 'confuse the man with the artist: when this work is finished he will see me from another angle.'[133] Once Siegmund and Helena return to England, their lives close in. 'Now,' says Siegmund as he opens the gate of his Wimbledon villa, 'for the beginning of Hell!' For the domestic Inferno Lawrence drew on childhood memories. When Siegmund enters the living room, 'the clock, with its deprecating, suave chime, was striking ten'.

> Beatrice was sewing, and did not raise her head. Frank, a tall, thin lad of eighteen, was bent over a book. He did not look up. Vera

had her fingers thrust in among her hair, and continued to read the magazine that lay on the table before her. Siegmund looked at them all. They gave no sign to show they were aware of his entry; there was only that unnatural tenseness of people who cover their agitation. He glanced round to see where he should go. His wicker arm-chair remained by the fireplace; his slippers were standing under the sideboard, as he had left them. Siegmund sat down in the creaking chair; he began to feel sick and tired.[134]

On his second day home, Siegmund locks his bedroom and attaches the suitcase belt to a hook on the back of the door: 'he performed his purpose methodically and exactly. In every particular he was thorough, as if he were the servant of some stern will.' Beatrice, unable to open the door, asks the window cleaner to raise his ladder to the casement and there he sees Siegmund's body swinging, 'his face hardly recognisable'. The suicide of her lover hits Helena 'like a brick … She felt as if something had crashed into her brain, stunning and maiming her',[135] but 'Beatrice was careful not to let the blow of Siegmund's death fall with full impact upon her.'

As it were, she dodged it. She was afraid to meet the accusation of the dead Siegmund, with the sacred jury of memories. When the event summoned her to stand before the bench of her own soul's understanding, she fled, leaving the verdict upon herself eternally suspended.[136]

Lawrence described the book as 'a work of fiction upon a frame of actual experience' – which might describe all his prose – but it is more curious than this.[137] The fascination of *The Trespasser* lies in the force of sympathy felt by the twenty-four-year-old bachelor for the sexually frustrated middle-aged husband. Lawrence realised as he wrote that he had vitally misread the drama of his own family. 'I have always believed,' he told Jessie, 'it was the woman who pays the price in life. But I've made a discovery. It's the man who pays, not the woman.'[138] The book's genius, however, lies in the title. Lawrence had raided Helen Corke's grief but all novels, as he now understood them, were acts of trespass and all novelists were trespassers. 'Trespassing', he explained, is a 'word invented in Hell'.[139]

As Lydia lay dying of cancer in December 1910, to ease their mother's pain, Lawrence and his sister Ada gave her a lethal dose of morphine. In *Sons and Lovers* he describes Paul crushing the morphia pills into powder to put in Mrs Morel's milk and placing the feeding cup between her lips. Writing this section of the novel made Lawrence so tense that he became ill. It was a mercy killing, but a killing nonetheless, and a continuation of their strange form of incest: Lydia had brought Lawrence into the world and Lawrence led Lydia out of it. Right until the end they were one another's axis and orbit. After the funeral, Lawrence told Jessie 'in a strangled voice', 'You know – I've always loved mother.' 'I know you have,' Jessie replied. ' "I don't mean that," he returned quickly. "I've *loved* her, like a lover. That's why I could never love you." '[140] He then handed Jessie a draft of his poem 'The Bride', in which he described his mother's corpse.

> Nay, but she sleeps like a bride, and dreams her dreams
> > Of perfect things.
> She lies at last, the darling, in the shape of her dream;
> > And her dead mouth sings
> By its shape, like the thrushes in clear evenings.

But there was another bride in Lawrence's life as well, because six days before his mother's death he became engaged again, this time to a teacher called Louie Burrows. He needed Louie to advise him on the women in *Paul Morel*; could she explain, for example, how Miriam would respond to Mrs Morel's jealousy and how Mrs Morel would feel about Miriam's love for her son? When his new fiancée proved unable to help, Lawrence made the audacious decision to pass the manuscript on to Jessie herself for comment. Jessie, reading with her usual care, thought it 'tired', 'second hand' and 'story-bookish' and told Lawrence to 'write the whole story again, and keep it true to the life',[141] which meant including an account of his brother's death. So Lawrence rewrote *Paul Morel*, this time in virtual collaboration with Jessie Chambers.

In February 1912, after another critical bout of pneumonia, he resigned from his teaching post (the last salaried job he would ever have), broke off his engagement to Louie Burrows and sent his rewritten novel to Jessie. 'As the sheets of manuscript came rapidly to me,' Jessie recalled,

'I was bewildered and dismayed … I began to perceive that I had set Lawrence a task far beyond his strength.' She had hoped her suggestions would allow him to exorcise his mother but he had exorcised Jessie instead. 'His mother had to be supreme,' Jessie at last understood, 'and for the sake of that supremacy every disloyalty was permissible.'[142] Jessie called *Paul Morel* a lie and Lawrence called it a novel. 'Of course it isn't the truth,' he explained. 'It isn't meant for the truth. It's an adaptation from life, as all art must be.'[143] Jessie was the first of Lawrence's friends to be consigned to the circle of the hell reserved for those who showed what she called 'devotion to his genius'.[144]

There are many accounts of the cost of stirring Lawrence's daemon into action, but none so raw as the tale told by Jessie Chambers in *A Personal Record*. Their differing viewpoints are caught in the textual annotations to *Paul Morel*, where Jessie corrects his memory. Lawrence described the struggle between Mrs Morel and Miriam for the possession of Paul's soul as taking place when he was seventeen rather than twenty, thus robbing Jessie of three precious years. 'Not yet, please!' she exclaimed in the margin; it was of vital importance that Lawrence's division did not appear until his twentieth year. He also attributed thoughts to Miriam that Jessie did not consider her younger self ready to have: 'She knew she and Paul were woven together unconsciously', Lawrence wrote of Miriam aged sixteen, to which Jessie responded: 'Miriam never knew this until Paul insisted on it' during the Easter Monday episode. Lawrence's account of that episode was so wrong that Jessie sent him a revised version 'nearer to the actual spirit of the time', which he ignored.[145]

Jessie, who knew Lawrence in his pupal stage and watched his transformation, made an observation in *A Personal Record* which takes us to the core of his biographical mystery. 'What was it that Keats said,' she asked, 'about a great man's life being an allegory and his works a comment on it? Something of that belongs to DHL.'[146] What Keats said was this: 'A Man's life of any worth is a continual allegory – and very few eyes can see the Mystery of his life – a life like the scriptures, figurative – which such people can no more make out than they can the hebrew Bible. Lord Byron cuts a figure – but he is not figurative – Shakespeare led a life of Allegory; his works are the comments on it.'[147]

Jessie alone saw that Lawrence, too, lived a life of allegory.

# Part Two

The *Divine Comedy*, whose events begin on the Good Friday of 1300 and continue through Holy Week, opens with the most famous landscape, or rather dreamscape, in Western literature. Midway through the journey of his life, Dante discovers himself in a dark wood. His exact phrase is 'midway through the journey of *our* life' (*nostra vita*), meaning that this is a collective as well as a personal journey, and that the reader is equally lost. Is he asleep or awake, and does he even know?

> I cannot clearly say how I had entered
> the wood; I was so full of sleep just at
> the point where I abandoned the true path.
>
> (*Inferno*, Canto 1, 10–12)

He emerges from the wood to find himself at the foot of a hill which we assume to be Purgatory because at the summit, bathed in divine light, is Paradise. Dante starts to climb, but his path is barred by wild animals. Afraid, he turns back and meets the shade of Virgil, who has been summoned here by Beatrice, who was herself sent by St Lucia and the Virgin Mary. On behalf of 'the three such blessed women', Beatrice instructs Virgil to guide Dante to Paradise via a different route; he will be able to ascend the mountain of Purgatory only after descending the pit of the Inferno.

> Therefore, I think and judge it best for you
> to follow me, and I shall guide you, taking
> you from this place through an eternal place,
> where you shall hear the howls of desperation

and see the ancient spirits in their pain,
as each of them laments his second death ...

*(Inferno*, Canto I, 112–17)

Virgil is not a randomly chosen guide; he is Dante's favourite poet and the man who knows his way around hell – in Book 6 of *The Aeneid*, Aeneas, led by the Cumaean Sibyl, goes down to the underworld where he is ferried by Charon across the River Acheron. Dante has in fact been following Virgil for years, studying his wisdom and imitating his style.

'O light and honour of all other poets,
may my long study and the intense love
that made me search your volume serve me now.
You are my master and my author, you –
the only one from whom my writing drew
the noble style for which I have been honoured.'

*(Inferno*, Canto I, 82–7)

So the Christian and the Pagan begin their journey down through the nine circles of the Inferno and up the seven terraces of Purgatory, at the top of which Virgil leaves Dante in the care of Beatrice, who takes him into Paradise where he sees the face of God. Dante crosses banks and bridges, ramparts and rivers, waterfalls and ravines, ditches and deserts; he climbs up and he climbs down; he is rained upon by fire; he moves into and out of consciousness; he is carried in the arms Virgil and on the back of Geryon, lowered by giants to the lowest circle of hell and lifted by Beatrice through the nine spheres of Paradise. His topography, like that of Lawrence, is nothing if not precise.

The *Inferno* is the part of the *Comedy* that Dante's readers have most enjoyed, not least because of his hierarchical ordering of punishment and the combination of people – historical, biblical, mythical and those known to him personally – that he consigns to hell. The first circle is reserved for pre-Christians like Virgil who were not baptised and must therefore live in limbo; the second circle is a wind tunnel in which lustful and adulterous lovers are blown about on the storms of their own passion; in the third gluttons mired in sludge are rained upon by ice; in the fourth, hoarders and squanderers push boulders with their chests; the wrathful and sullen in the fifth circle choke in the River Styx; the heretics in the sixth circle are consigned to flaming tombs; the seventh circle is a vast Piranesi-style penitentiary in which murderers are sunk in boiling blood and fire, suicides are turned into trees, profligates are savaged by hounds, and sodomites run on burning sand beneath a rain of fire. In the eighth circle fraudulent counsellors are held in tongue-shaped flames, falsifiers are plagued with scabs, flatterers are buried in excrement, Simoniacs are turned upside down in baptismal fonts while fire burns their feet, false prophets walk with their heads facing backwards, hypocrites wear robes lined with lead, and thieves and falsifiers are turned into snakes. In the ninth circle, presided over by a silent, three-headed Lucifer, the treacherous, including Cain and Judas Iscariot, are frozen in an icy lake.

Dante Alighieri, the son of a burgher, was born in Florence in 1265 and educated by monks. He married, had three children, became a member of the Guild of Doctors and wrote an emotional autobiography called *La Vita Nuova* in which, through a sequence of lyric poems with prose commentaries, he described his love for Beatrice and his grief following her early death. The Florentines were a combative people and, caught in the feud between two houses, the Guelphs and the Ghibellines, Dante was exiled from the city on pain of death. Aged thirty-five – midway through the journey of his life – he became a wanderer, crossing the Apennines by night and pacing the forests of Ravenna. He no longer had a home, wrote Lawrence H. Davison in *Movements in European History*, a school textbook published in 1921, but Dante was 'never homeless. He was a learned, cultured man, and such a man was at home everywhere in Europe.' He was sheltered in the homes of nobles who 'gave him simple little rooms within the thick walls of their great castles', and in these rooms, looking from his 'loop-hole window at the wild hills or at the river', he plotted his revenge on his enemies. Dante's *Comedy* is the great epic of *Schadenfreude*, and the writing of it was an act of therapeutic vengence.

Lawrence H. Davison imagined the poet's exile as a form of freedom:

From his writing in his lonely rooms he would go down the cold, massive stone stairway to the hall where the family dined, and there he would sit in conversation with the lords and the clergy, an honoured if penniless guest. He knew the bitterness of dependence, but still we must believe he was happy, composing his work and having converse with generous men.

According to Davison, the *Divine Comedy* is an allegory of history. In the medieval world, however, where visions were taken seriously, Dante's experience was read as both allegorical *and* autobiographical: he saw what he said he saw, and it was his audacity that gave the *Comedy* its supreme strength. Dante alone, the poet told his readers, had been singled out to make this pilgrimage through the levels of the afterlife; his fortitude in exile had been rewarded with the highest possible honour. Written not in Latin but in a Tuscan dialect, the poem was composed in *terza rima*, a three-line rhyme scheme Dante invented himself and called *concatenatio*, or 'beautiful linkage', because the second line of each stanza rhymes with the first and last lines of the next, thus joining the verses together like a chain. The effect of *terza rima* is propulsive: we are driven onwards, downwards, upwards, through forests, up cliff faces, over rivers, lakes, ledges and ravines.

There are two Dantes in the poem: Dante-the-poet and Dante-the-pilgrim, and it is important to distinguish between them. Lawrence would share the poet's temerity and dual vision: he too would be the author and the hero of his works, he too considered himself human and divine, his Inferno was also both symbolic and horribly real, and he too wrote his friends and enemies into his books. He would also share the pilgrim's social discomfort. 'One has to be a blind mole', wrote Osip Mandelstam in his sublime essay *Conversation about Dante*,

> not to notice that throughout the *Commedia* Dante does not
> know how to behave, does not know how to act, what to say,
> how to make a bow … The inner anxiety and the heavy, troubled
> awkwardness which attend every step of the unselfconfident mind,
> the man whose upbringing is inadequate, who does not know what
> application to make of his inner experience or how to objectify it in
> etiquette, the tortured and outcast man – it is these qualities which
> give the poem all its charm … and they create its background, its
> psychological drama.[1]

Lawrence structured his life – 'that piece of supreme art', as he called it – around Dante's great poem in the way that James Joyce shaped

*Ulysses* around *The Odyssey*.[2] This was his primal plan, the complex figure in the Persian carpet that Lawrence's biographers – because they have been looking from a flat perspective – have failed to see. Followed horizontally on a map, Lawrence's movements look like a mad flight: the journey that began with a detour when he went to Cornwall rather than Florida in the winter of 1915 goes haywire as he then ricochets around the globe, but if we unfold his journey in terms of descent and ascent, then the apparent chaos reshapes itself. Follow his footsteps and you see that every house Lawrence lived in, from birth to burial, was positioned at a higher spot than the last; he rose from underworld to empyrean.

It was not an especially erudite or eccentric move on Lawrence's part, to use Dante as his guiding principle; he was always led by poets rather than by novelists and saw himself as a figure of allegory. Knowledge of Dante was not then confined to the few and Lawrence knew the *Divine Comedy* as well as he knew Shakespeare, Homer and the Bible, which he described as 'the supreme old novels'.[3] He discussed the *Divine Comedy* as though it too were a novel, this being his term of praise for a book that contained everything, and it was as a creative artist that he approached the allegory whose movements he probably internalised aged seventeen, when he and Jessie hurled themselves upon the corpus of literature available in the Eastwood local library. Sections of *Inferno*, translated into blank verse by H. F. Cary, could be found in the twenty-two volumes of the *International Library of Famous Literature* on the Lawrence family shelves, but Dante was everywhere in Lawrence's world. Blake, Gustave Doré and the Pre-Raphaelites all illustrated scenes from Dante's life and poetry that sold as popular prints, and Rodin's *The Kiss* was modelled on Paolo and Francesca. Dante dominated the imaginations of Lawrence's contemporaries T. S. Eliot, Ezra Pound, Joyce and Yeats. 'I love Dante almost as much as the Bible,' said Joyce; 'he is my spiritual food, the rest is ballast.'[4] His own aim, said Pound, was to write 'an epic poem which begins "In the Dark Forest", crosses the Purgatory of human error, and ends in the light'.[5] By 1921, the 600th anniversary of his death, Dante was hard to avoid, especially in Italy where Lawrence was then living and the national poet was commemorated in parades, readings, festivals and screenings. In 1922, when Nancy Mitford visited Florence she saw the film of *L'Inferno* which was, she said, 'most bloodthirsty and exciting. Eleven murders close to with details, a man's hands chopped off *very* close to and full of detail, a man dying of starvation and eating another man *very very* close to.'[6]

'Dante and Shakespeare divide the modern world between them,' wrote T. S. Eliot in his essay 'Dante'. 'There is no third.'[7] If Shakespeare measured our moral girth, Dante scaled our heights and depths. References to the *Divine Comedy* are embedded in Eliot's poetry, most famously in the Italian epigraph to 'The Love Song of J. Alfred Prufrock' and in *The Waste Land*, where a line from Canto 3 of *Inferno* is used to describe the London rush hour:

A crowd flowed over London Bridge, so many,
I had not thought death had undone so many.

The purpose of this passage, Eliot explained in another essay, 'What Dante Means to Me', was to 'establish a relationship between the medieval inferno and modern life';[8] seven years earlier Lawrence had established the same relationship when he described the London traffic to Ottoline Morrell, as 'flow[ing] through the rigid grey streets like the rivers of Hell through their banks of dry, rocky ash'.[9] But his own debt to Dante, Eliot concluded, lay not in the number of allusions to his work but in the understanding that the poet was servant rather than master of his language. Lawrence, whose debt to Dante has barely been recognised, saw Dante not as a poet at all but as a cartographer who plotted the route to Paradise, and he chose Shelley as his guide through hell because Shelley had been there before. 'Hell', as Shelley put it in 'Peter Bell the Third', 'is a city much like London,' where 'all sorts of people' are 'undone'.

The Romantics, who invented Dante in English, found in him a spokesman for their own turbulent times. Dante, said Byron, was 'the poet of liberty', and none of the events in Dante's life – 'Persecution, exile, the dread of a foreign grave' – could shake his principles.[10] For Leigh Hunt, Dante's 'discordant' sort of 'greatness' lay in 'his being the offspring of two persons of diametrically opposed natures, – a fierce, saturnine father' and 'a gentle mother'.[11] Eliot expanded on Dante's bifurcation: if you were to combine, he said, 'the massive quality of Milton, the sense that every word is being held in place by a gigantic pressure', with the 'air and fire of Shelley ... then you will know what

Dante is like'.[12] And it was Shelley on whom the *Divine Comedy* made the deepest impression; no body of poetry contains more adaptations from, allusions to and imitations of Dante than that of Percy Bysshe Shelley. Shelley, said Eliot, was 'the one English poet of the nineteenth century who could even have begun to follow those footsteps'.[13]

Shelley's years in Italy were dominated by Dante, whom he now read in Italian. His 'Ode to the West Wind', which meant so much to Lawrence, was written in *terza rima*, and his translation of the opening section of *Purgatory*, Canto 28, posthumously published as 'Matilda gathering flowers', was the first attempt at rhymed *terza rima* in English. For Byron, Hunt and Keats, *Inferno* was the *Comedy*'s central book and the adulterers, Paolo and Francesca, the book's central figures. In Canto 5, Dante enters the storm in the second circle of hell where he finds, blowing about like autumn leaves, 'now here, now there, now down, now up', Paolo and his sister-in-law Francesca di Rimini, who were known to Dante personally before they were murdered by her jealous husband (Paolo's brother). The wind blows the couple towards the pilgrim, and Francesca explains that their lips first met when she and Paolo read 'Launcelot du Lac' together and learned of the love between the knight and the queen that destroyed King Arthur's kingdom. Here lies the difference between Dante-the-pilgrim and Dante-the-poet: the pilgrim is so moved by Francesca's tale that he falls into a faint, while the poet punishes her actions by hurling her into hell.

*The Story of Rimini* is Hunt's defence of liberty: his own Paolo and Francesca are guilty of nothing more than acting on what he calls 'one genuine impulse of the affections'.[14] A pro-love, anti-marriage treatise, *The Story of Rimini* was dedicated to Byron at the time that Byron's marriage collapsed amid rumours of his relations with his half-sister, Augusta Leigh. Writing to Augusta from Venice in 1819, Byron compared their punishment to that of Paolo and Francesca, whose 'case fell a good deal short of *ours* – though sufficiently naughty'. Dante, he said, at least allowed his lovers to suffer together.[15] Byron, who made his own translation titled 'Fanny of Rimini', used Francesca's speech as epigraphs to the cantos of *The Corsair*, and Keats dreamed that he too found himself 'whirling' in the second circle of hell, his lips joined to those of a beautiful woman. It was one of 'the most delightful enjoyments I ever had in my life',[16] and Keats's sonnet to 'Paolo and Francesca' was duly composed on the pages of his copy of Cary's translation of *Inferno*.

that second circle of sad Hell,
Where in the gust, the whirlwind, and the flaw
Of rain and hail-stones, lovers need not tell
Their sorrows. Pale were the sweet lips I saw,
Pale were the lips I kissed, and fair the form
I floated with, about that melancholy storm.

The Romantics turned the second circle of sad hell into a desirable address, and this was where Lawrence now lived too. Paolo and Francesca symbolised his union with Frieda, but then he had always seen storms as a symbol of marriage.

Back in Cornwall, in the spring of 1916, Lawrence and Frieda pressed Murry and Katherine Mansfield to take over the empty cottages; Katherine could use the tower as her study, and Philip Heseltine, Lawrence suggested, could rent a room from them. This was the perfect place to set up Rananim: they could pool their resources, live off the land, share books and ideas and eat together in the evenings. But the Murrys did not much want to be with Lawrence in the darkness: they disliked Philip Heseltine, an eccentric who rode his motorbike naked, and were anyway going through an unusual period of happiness together in the South of France. When Heseltine also turned down the invitation, the Murrys were inundated with so many appeals from Lawrence that they reluctantly broke their resolve, arriving in Cornwall on 4 April 1916. 'We'll all be happy together,' Lawrence ordered.[17] Murry agreed, telling the ever curious Ottoline that they felt serene about the future. Katherine Mansfield, meanwhile, provided a weather report:

Today I can't see a yard, thick mist and rain and a tearing wind with it. Everything is faintly damp. The floor of the tower is studded with Cornish pitchers catching the drops ... It's very quiet in the house except for the wind and the rain & the fire that roars very hoarse and fierce.[18]

Lawrence thought Mansfield as a writer 'false' because she was, like Turgenev, too critical and detached. It was Murry, his most important – and most treacherous – friend, who absorbed Lawrence's attention, and Murry's blend of mediocrity and ambition (he was Salieri to Lawrence's

Mozart) earned him the title of best-hated man of letters. Leonard Woolf called him 'Pecksniffian' and Virginia Woolf claimed he was 'the one vile man I have ever known'.[19] Born to play a supporting role, Murry, the son of a South London civil servant, described his young self as 'a bundle of antennae, feeling out for a new social persona' which never came fully into focus.[20] He won a scholarship to Christ's Hospital in Horsham, the alma mater of Coleridge, Leigh Hunt and Charles Lamb, where he shed his lower-middle-class roots, nurtured a Romantic sensibility and refashioned himself as a gentleman. His critical style was confessional, and Lawrence described *Still Life*, the first of Murry's Russian-inspired novels, as 'the kind of wriggling self-abuse I can't make head or tail of'.[21] After studying Classics at Oxford, Murry founded, aged twenty-one, an avant-garde quarterly of the arts called *Rhythm* and he and Lawrence would later start a short-lived magazine called *The Signature*. It was his making and his misfortune that Murry spent his formative years with D. H. Lawrence and Katherine Mansfield, and he carved a career from his intimacy with both. Among his sixty publications are three sour books about Lawrence; the first, *D. H. Lawrence: Two Essays* appeared months after his friend's death, the second, *Son of Woman: The Story of D. H. Lawrence*, was published a year later, and two years after that, in 1933, he produced his *Reminiscences of D. H. Lawrence* and also his biography of Katherine Mansfield. Further reminiscences of both were shared in 1935 in Murry's autobiography *Between Two Worlds*.

Murry was an innocent when he met Katherine Mansfield, but the wily Mansfield, born into a prominent family in New Zealand, had already accumulated a complicated back story. Two affairs with women; a pregnancy which was covered up by marrying a man called George Bowden whom she left two hours later; a miscarriage. She settled in London in 1910 and was introduced to Murry when she submitted a story to *Rhythm*; her first collection, *In a German Pension*, appeared in 1911. The relationship between Mansfield and Murry was largely unhappy; they infantilised one another and spoke in baby talk. Mansfield complained that Murry was 'not warm, ardent, eager, full of quick response, careless, spendthrift of himself, vividly alive' or '*high* spirited', and soon after befriending Lawrence and Frieda she began a relationship with the writer Francis Carco, who was all of those things. She then returned to Murry again and then left him again, and so the wheel turned.[22]

Katherine Mansfield

We know what happened in Higher Tregerthen because Mansfield and Murry wrote regular letters, and Lawrence devoted a chapter (called 'The Nightmare') of *Kangaroo* to his recollections. Mansfield's accounts of Lawrence describe Self One quietly enjoying his painting and sewing while Self Two 'simply *raves*, roars, beats the table, abuses everybody'.[23] In 'The Nightmare' Lawrence described his mouthpiece, Richard Lovell Somers, as having lived in Cornwall in 'semi-fear' during the war. Everything he and his German wife did was watched by the coastguards, the police or the locals. Because their letters were opened and read, the couple censored what they wrote. It was a cack-handed form of surveillance and the more sinister for being so.

A chimney of his house was tarred to keep out the damp, that was a signal to the Germans. He and his wife carried food to supply German submarines. They had secret stores of petrol in the cliff. They were watched and listened to, spied on, by men lying behind the low stone fences. It is a job the Cornish loved. They didn't even mind being caught at it: lying behind a fence with field-glasses, watching through a hole in the drystone wall a man with a lass, on the edge of the moors ... A whole intense life of spying going on all the time.[24]

The Lawrences were being spied on by the Murrys as well, on orders from Ottoline, spymaster general. Otherwise known as Lady Utterly Immoral or Lady Omega Muddle, Ottoline Morrell was a six-feet-tall redhead with the face of a handsome horse. The daughter of Lieutenant-General Arthur Cavendish-Bentinck, sister of the 5th Duke of Portland and great-great-niece of the Duke of Wellington, her husband Philip Morrell was a Liberal politician and her current lover was Bertrand Russell. Lawrence, who thought the upper classes superior to the common folk, especially liked titled women, but what mattered most to him about Ottoline Morrell – apart from the fact that, phonetically, she shared the same name as Paul Morel – is that she had been raised in Welbeck Abbey, twenty miles from Eastwood, and her family owned parts of the coalfields his father had worked. Beneath the Abbey was a network of underground tunnels built by Ottoline's dotty uncle so that he might visit the gardens and stables without having to encounter another human being. As a child Lawrence had known servants who worked in this eccentric house and now he knew Ottoline herself: he was rising in the world, 'Ooray. Lawrence had what Ottoline called a 'romantic feeling' for her grand family and Ottoline had a romantic feeling for Lawrence's miners: 'how I wished I could talk to those men,' she recalled, 'or share their good solid tea, and so bridge the gulf that lay between us'.[25]

During the brief period of their friendship, Ottoline got the very best of Lawrence. She was his 'Sybil' and he was her trophy. Katherine Mansfield described him as 'perceptibly over-eager in aristocratic company',[26] and Lawrence's letters to Ottoline are certainly keen to please; Frieda, who was jealous, destroyed at least one of them before he had a chance to send it. But equally eager were the letters that Ottoline received from Mansfield (whom she had yet to meet) and Murry: her daily postbag was bursting with missives from mortals currying favour. The chief subject of the Murrys' letters was Frieda, who had been battling with Ottoline for months and now accused her, in a letter of her own, of wanting 'some sort of unwholesome relationship' with Lawrence – which was probably true.[27] The two women were rivals for his attention, but Ottoline had the upper hand because she owned a grand house in the country, Garsington Manor, and a grand house in Bloomsbury, and could afford to be generous, while Frieda, also well born, had nothing to offer but the genius of which no one but herself was convinced. Frieda's principal complaint was that Ottoline did not treat her as Lawrence's equal.

Amused by Frieda's accusation, Ottoline forwarded her letter to the Murrys who shared the same address as the Lawrences. Frieda, assuming that an envelope addressed to her home in Ottoline's hand was surely meant for herself, duly unsealed it and out fell the contents. All hell was let loose, and Murry, Ottoline's loyal informant, sent his mistress a report of the damage:

> Lawrence is at present completely on F's side in the quarrel (which isn't a quarrel but an indecent attack), and he spent a long while trying to convince us that for us to remain friendly with you was black treachery to him ... I don't quite know how to diagnose the condition of them both for you. In many ways L seems to me to be so much happier, much younger than I have known him for the last two years. On the other hand he has bought this at a price. I feel he has quite definitely lost something ... I feel he will not create anything very much in the future.
>
> F is *monstrum, horrendum, informe, ingens*. Really, we are frightened of her ... We have tried to like her for three years now and we haven't got any further towards the end. There is in her an ultimate vulgarity which does appal us both. And that is the reason why she turned so against you, I think.

His letter ended by reminding Ottoline 'how much we both love you'. By the autumn, he had dropped the plural.[28]

Ottoline Morrell

Murry had been introduced to Lady Utterly Immoral in 1915, during a February weekend spent with Lawrence in Greatham. Lawrence had forewarned her that Murry, whom he had met two years earlier, was 'one of the men of the future', and 'my partner – the only man who quite simply is with me', but his partner was unable to live up to the praise. When Lawrence tested their characters with the view from the top of the Downs, Murry sloped behind in a sulk. In his diary, he admitted that he had been 'jealous and sad', 'painfully aware that L was the centre of attraction'. Unable to compete with L as a writer or a personality, Murry felt left out when he and Ottoline talked about Forster and Russell (whom he did not yet know), and to gain their attention he told 'strangely exaggerated stories' about his own past and then 'resented L's laughter'.[29]

Frieda had no idea that their friends found her *monstrum* and *horrendum*. She thought Katherine 'exquisite' and enjoyed the way she gave 'small events a funny twist'. The two women made potpourri together and painted wooden boxes and had what Frieda called 'those delicious female walks and talks'. Katherine, tired of being told how exquisite she was, described Frieda as 'evil hearted' and sex-obsessed. The Lawrences saw everything as a sexual symbol: the babbling brook, the granite boulders, the grass and leaves and trees. Higher Tregerthen might better be called The Phallus, Katherine suggested, and Frieda enthusiastically agreed.[30]

By the middle of May, relations between the two couples had irretrievably broken down. 'The heights,' Murry told Ottoline, 'were always wuthering,' and Lawrence had become Heathcliff, 'a man possessed, now by an angel, now by a devil … it was painful to see him so transformed and transfigured by the paroxysms of murderous hatred, of his wife, of us, of all mankind, that swept over him'. He seemed 'dangerously ill' and 'expects something of Katherine and me which we can't give – a certain intimacy … which being *demanded* is utterly impossible to give'. The letter ends with Murry's refrain: 'I hope for our sakes that you love us as much as we do you.'[31] The intimacy Lawrence demanded was the *Blutsbrüderschaft* which he saw as the male equivalent to marriage; worried that this might involve a pagan bloodletting ceremony, Murry played his hand in his usual fashion, both encouraging and resisting his friend's demands.

It is little wonder, given the failure rate of his friendships, that Lawrence required commitment. Nor is it surprising, when we compare the seediness of his current social circle to the wholesomeness of the Haggites, that he began to suffer from what he called 'androphobia'. He wanted to shoot everyone he saw 'with invisible arrows of death' and shake insect powder over all fat men in white flannel trousers.[32] In his own letters to Ottoline, Lawrence ranted about humanity's 'insect-like stupidity',[33] which included the leech-like Allies hanging on to England's rotten body. Insects were everywhere; both Murry and Frieda became 'bugs who have fed on my life'. When Lawrence lost his temper, which happened every time he was contradicted, he got into a 'frenzy' so exhausting that he then had to go to bed, from where he would cry into the night that 'Jack is killing me.' Murry ('Jack') believed, however, that Lawrence was killing *him*, and everyone thought that Frieda was killing Lawrence. The man they had once loved, Mansfield told Ottoline, 'is completely lost, like a little gold ring in that immense German Christmas pudding'.[34]

Lawrence was in a frenzy because he evidently suffered from claustrophobia, which is unsurprising given his father's job. It is striking that he was only ever angry inside a house; outside, Lawrence became a different person, and he spent as much time outside as he could. He rarely wrote, for example, in a closed room, preferring to sit beneath an open sky with his pad of paper on his knees. He described himself between 1916 and 1918 as 'trapped' inside 'the black walls of the war', and compared his trap to the one in Edgar Alan Poe's story 'The Pit and the Pendulum', 'where the walls come in, in, in, till the prisoner is almost squeezed'.[35] The very idea of houses now horrified him. 'A real panic comes over me,' he said, 'when I feel I am on the brink of taking another house. I truly wish I were a fox or a bird – but my ideal now is to have a caravan and a horse, and move on for ever.'[36] The only time during his eighteen months in Higher Tregerthen that Lawrence left the area of St Ives was when he was escorted sixty miles to the barracks at Bodmin for a medical examination, and had his naked body prodded by doctors.

*Women in Love* was begun on 24 April 1916, the onset of the Easter Rising in Ireland. Lawrence went at the novel with breakneck speed, which was the speed he always employed for writing. Murry claimed not to know that his friend had begun a new book, which rings true; he had thought him incapable of creating 'anything very much in the future', and Lawrence never made a fuss about writing. Producing a book or a story or an essay or a poem was simply another act of living which demanded to be done well, and he considered his production of sentences to be no more important than those other daily tasks of cleaning, cooking, hemming curtains and painting furniture. We have an idea of Lawrence's writing routine from the advice he gave to a fellow novelist, which was to sit down with a pen for an hour a day – 'the same hour – that's very important' – and 'write bit by bit of the scenes you have witnessed, the people you know, describing their reactions as you know they react, not as you imagine they should'. Then, 'when you've done 80,000 words, throw down your pen'.[37] So bit by bit Lawrence's impressions of Cornwall and his companions found their way into his neatly written pages. He never suffered from writer's block; his novels might grind to a halt while he worked out what a protagonist would do next (which depended on what Lawrence himself did next), but he was rarely stuck for words. Words came out of him like a running flame; *Women in Love*, he said, wrote itself.

Those who noticed that Lawrence was 'dangerously ill' did nothing to alert any medical authorities; instead, they filed their reports on the lunatic from the safety of their tower. 'Frieda and I do not even speak to each other at present,' Mansfield informed Kot, who was also a loyal friend of Lawrence's.

Lawrence is about one million miles away, although he lives next door. He and I still speak but his voice is very faint like a voice coming over a telephone wire. It is all because I cannot stand the situation between those two, for one thing. It is degrading – it offends ones soul beyond words. I don't know which disgusts one worse – when they are very loving and playing with each other or when they are roaring at each other and he is pulling out Frieda's hair and saying 'I'll cut your throat, you bitch' and Frieda is running up and down the road screaming for 'Jack' to save her!![38]

Lawrence has been judged for his treatment of women, and Frieda's brand of womanhood has been judged as harshly. Constance Garnett found her slow-witted and excessively sexual, Ottoline thought her egotistical, Huxley considered her 'incurably and incredibly stupid – the most maddening woman I think I ever came across',[39] and Diana Trilling describes her as 'a swamp'.[40] Lawrence's friends, with the exception of H.D., all loathed her but none more than Kot, whom Frieda at least knew to be her enemy. 'It hurts me very much when you think I do not count as a human being,' she told him, '– but then you do not think much of women, they are not human beings in your eyes.'[41] While the case for Frieda's defence notes that she was a liberated woman *avant la lettre*, the prosecution adduce the facts that she left three children to run off with a man she barely knew, that she was tasteless and irresponsible, that she had no evident talents apart from sex, that she sat with her legs apart, that she smoked in the face of her tubercular husband while he scrubbed the floors and cooked her breakfasts, that she got fatter while he got thinner, got stronger while he got weaker and slept with anyone she felt like sleeping with. In their summing up, they argue that Frieda ruined Lawrence's writing and shortened his life.

He may well have lived longer under the care of another woman; Huxley, who was with Lawrence in his last months, told Frieda to her face that she was 'a fool and a criminal'.[42] And had he married Jessie Chambers a different writer would certainly have emerged. 'You can put anything you like in a novel,' Lawrence wrote. 'So why do people *always* go on putting the same thing? Why is the *vol au vent* always chicken!'[43] His pre-Frieda novels, *The White Peacock* and *The Trespasser*, are chicken *vol au vent*: conventional in form, lyrical in style, Hardyesque in plot. With Frieda by his side, the *vol au vent* was loaded with everything he could find in the cupboard. As his novels evolved into the quarrelsome and self-sabotaging creatures we now recognise as Lawrentian, Lawrence restyled himself as the prophet that Frieda wanted him to be. Without Frieda there would be no *Rainbow* or *Women in Love*, and *Sons and Lovers* would not be the merciless killing machine that it became.

Frieda, who had reason enough to lose her mind during the war, stayed sane, says Trilling, because she didn't have a mind to lose: 'In her mindlessness she held Lawrence together.'[44] Mindlessness, for Lawrence, was a term of high praise. Barred from seeing her family in Germany as well her children in London (when she tried to intercept her daughters on their way to school, their nanny screamed at them to run away), Frieda was regarded by the English, including her former and current husbands, with suspicion and hatred. It was Lawrence, however, who had the nervous collapse because this was how their marriage worked. He occupied centre stage at all times but she, broad, brazen, beaming and fresh as the morning air, is there in every scene, following him around the world with her aimless bonhomie, commenting on his novels, adding silly postscripts to his letters. The immense, immovable fact of Frieda is as inconvenient to Lawrence's biographers as it was to his friends but, as Huxley explained, 'Frieda wasn't a person' for Lawrence, she was his 'food ... a vital organ of his own body'. Frieda was the axis to his orbit and Lawrence, said Huxley, was 'in some strange way, dependent on her presence, physically dependent ... I have seen him on two occasions rise from what I thought was his deathbed, when Frieda, who had been away, came back after a short absence.'[45]

While Lawrence cast versions of himself as the hero of his own story, Frieda's problem as a heroine – and she wanted very much to be seen as such – is that, beyond the satisfaction of her immediate carnal desires, she didn't much believe in anything. In Lawrence's novels, the Frieda-figures like Ursula Brangwen are the voice of common sense: soft, ironic, pliable and amused. But in life Frieda was an essentially comic figure, the kind of bawdy, red-cheeked matron found in the art of Otto Dix and in German expressionist theatre. 'It was evident', Lawrence said of Frieda's representative in *Mr Noon*, his unfinished comic novel about their 'true and terrible marriage', 'that she was all distraught, bewildered, roused, and yet not having any direction.'[46] Without goal or ambition, Frieda's one achievement (not inconsiderable) was in putting up with Lawrence. Sturdiness under pressure was in the blood: 'It took a German like Frieda,' said Trilling, 'to stay entirely sane and make a successful career of the lunacy of her marriage.' Lawrence's opposite, Frieda understood his need for opposition. She also, vitally, understood the essential Lawrentian conundrum: that on the one hand sex should be stripped of the burden of love and all other mental trappings, but on the other hand sex without love is pure filth. 'It's odd,' continues Trilling,

> the way biographers always take what Lawrence says at face value when they come to dealing with the depression he ascribes to his hatred of the war and skip the looming fact that the outbreak of the war and the outbreak of Lawrence's first period of acute emotional disturbance coincided almost exactly with the legitimization of his union with Frieda.[47]

She is surely right. Lawrence and Frieda married on 13 July 1914, one month after her divorce came through and fifteen days after the assassination of the Archduke Ferdinand at Sarajevo. But Trilling is wrong to think that it was 'disastrous' for Lawrence to have married Frieda. Their marriage was seen by others as a catastrophe, but this is not how Lawrence saw it. Marriage was his plot and his message to the world. 'Your most vital necessity in this life,' he preached, 'is that you shall love your wife completely and implicitly and in entire nakedness of body and spirit.'[48] He believed in marriage not because it simplified sexual relationships but because it made sexual relationships more complex: marriage mattered because it was so damned hard. 'I'm not coming to you *now* for rest', he told Frieda when they ran away together in 1912, 'but to start living. It's a marriage, not a meeting ... One is afraid to be born, I'm sure.'[49] *The Rainbow*, the product of their honeymoon days, was a celebration of their perfect balance. 'You will find her and me in the novel,' Lawrence told Garnett, referring to Frieda's input. 'The work is of me and her, and it is beautiful, I think.'[50] Lawrence's original title was 'The Wedding Ring' and it was Frieda who called it *The Rainbow* because rainbows, composed from fire and water, symbolised their union: she was a full-flowing stream and he was a burning flame. The magistrate's pronouncement on the novel was thus a pronouncement on Lawrence's marriage. *Women in Love* – which he called *The Rainbow*'s 'sister novel' – would therefore be Lawrence's infernal book.

The day that Lawrence met Frieda Weekley, 17 March 1912, the *Titanic* was poised in Southampton docks to make her maiden voyage and, in the Arctic wastes, Captain Oates left his tent in a blizzard telling Captain Scott that he might be some time. Ice was in the news that year, and Frieda's sister-in-law would accuse her of being as blind as the 'Titanic iceberg' to the 'mischief' she was causing.[51]

Following the death of his mother, Lawrence described himself, in one of his favourite images, as 'a leaf blown in the wind'.[52] He decided to drift towards Germany, and so asked Professor Weekley for a letter of recommendation to a university where he might teach, and Weekley invited him to Sunday lunch at his home in Private Road, Mapperley, a residential area in the Nottingham suburbs. The professor's wife was an impossibly exotic creature to wash up in a red-brick villa in the English Midlands – a Teutonic blonde with a large bosom, green eyes, straight white teeth and a distinguished profile; Lawrence compared her to 'a cat that looks round in the sunshine and finds it good'.[53] Weekley was in his study when their guest arrived, and so Frieda entertained him for the

Lawrence in 1913

half-hour before lunch, 'French windows open, curtains fluttering in the spring wind, my children playing on the lawn'.[54] What happened in those crucial thirty minutes? By the time they sat down to eat, Lawrence had decided that Frieda was his destiny.

Frieda tells us what they talked about in her memoir, *'Not I, But the Wind ... '*, and Lawrence confirms her account in *Mr Noon*. Both were at turning points in their lives, and Frieda's description of herself is as follows:

> I had just met a remarkable disciple of Freud and was full of
> undigested theories. This friend did a lot for me. I was living like
> a somnambulist in a conventional set life and he awakened the
> consciousness of my own proper self ... Fanatically I believed
> that if only sex were 'free' the world would straightaway turn into

a paradise. I suffered and struggled at outs with society, and felt absolutely isolated. The process left me unbalanced. I felt alone … I could not accept society. And then Lawrence came.

She described, of course, his Shelleyan demeanour:

I see him before me as he entered the house. A long thin figure, quick straight legs, light, sure movements. He seemed so obviously simple … He said he had finished with his attempts at knowing women. I was amazed at the way he fiercely denounced them. I had never before heard anything like it. I laughed, yet I could tell he had tried very hard, and had cared. We talked about Oedipus and understanding leapt through our words.[55]

She *laughed* at Lawrence's sexual misadventures, and it was her laughter that seduced him. Sex was Frieda's favourite subject. Mabel Luhan later described it as her only subject: 'So long as one talked of people and their possibilities from the point of view of sex, she was grand.'[56] She was therefore at her shining best with their lunch guest. Lawrence, like his mother, was brittle and judgemental, but Frieda was like his father, 'soft, non-intellectual, warm' with 'that rare thing: a rich and ringing laugh'.[57] Lawrence needed teasing, and his relationship with Frieda began as it would go on: he expounded and despaired and denounced the world and she laughed at him. In whatever form she later figured in his novels, Frieda was always mocking; her opposition was essential to Lawrence because, as he put it, 'In the tension of opposites all things have their being.'[58]

A production of *Oedipus Rex* was running in Nottingham, but for Frieda Oedipus was not a Greek king but a complex. In the discarded and posthumously published *Mr Noon*, written in 1920 and 1921, Gilbert Noon (the Lawrence surrogate) and Johanna (the Frieda surrogate) also talk about Oedipus when they first meet. Gilbert tells Johanna that his mother is no longer alive and Johanna replies,

Well I think you're lucky. Mothers are awful things nowadays, don't you think? … they all want to swallow their children again, like the Greek myth … There isn't a man worth having, nowadays, who can get away from his mother. Their mothers are all in love with them,

77

and they're all in love with their mothers, and what are we poor
women to do? ... They're all Hamlets, obsessed by their mothers,
and we're supposed to be all Ophelias, and go and drown ourselves
... Ha—mother-love. It is the most awful self-swallowing thing.

Gilbert was 'struck all of a heap' by Johanna's talk; he 'watched and
listened' while she glowed with 'zest and animation'.[59]

If Frieda's world was sex, Ernest Weekley's world was words. Like
Lawrence, Weekley was to become a prolific writer and his first book,
*The Romance of Words* – an exploration of semantic wanderings, phonetic
accidents, folk etymologies, homonyms and family names – was due to
appear later that month. The lunch conversation doubtless turned to
this imminent publication and Lawrence noted Frieda's lack of interest
in Weekley's conversation. 'You are quite unaware of your husband,' he
later told her. 'You take no notice of him.'[60] He lingered at the house all
afternoon and then walked back to Eastwood – five hours through the
darkness – absorbing what had taken place. Relationships for Lawrence
always began and ended suddenly; a single meeting was usually enough
for him to suggest that he and his new friend pool their resources and set
up an alternative community. But the force of his thesis that the blood
was wiser than the intellect rests on this first meeting with Frieda, and
he insisted for the rest of his life that his instincts about her had been
correct. The next day he wrote to say that 'You are the most wonderful
woman in all England', which Frieda already knew.[61]

Frieda's lack of moorings was essential to Lawrence, as was her class.
'She is ripping,' he told Edward Garnett,

she's the finest woman I've ever met ... she is the daughter of Baron
von Richthofen, of the ancient and famous house of Richthofen –
but she's splendid, she is really ... Mrs Weekley is perfectly
unconventional, but really good – in the best sense. I'll bet you've
never met anybody like her, by a long chalk ... oh, but she is the
woman of a lifetime.[62]

Casting Frieda as a Prussian Molly Bloom, Diana Trilling misses an
important point. The problem with Frieda for literary historians is not
that she was a fool but that she could not write – at least, she could not
write in English – and therefore left no record of her voice. Having no

style of her own, she tried to impersonate Lawrence but her sentences lack narrative energy; they move without traction and are dull to read. Having learned from her husband that writing should be spontaneous, Frieda threw down words which say nothing at all. An example of what Trilling calls 'the catastrophic naivety'[63] of Frieda's style is the following paragraph, where she discusses her husband's consumption, and the constant proximity of death:

> I hated that death and I fought against it like a demon, unconsciously on my own. I did not know he was consumptive till years later when the doctor in Mexico told me. All my life with him there was this secret fear that I could not share with him. I had to bear it alone. Then in the end I knew, and it was an awful knowledge, that I could do no more. Death was stronger than I.[64]

Why was Frieda's battle 'unconscious', and if she did not know that Lawrence was consumptive until the doctor in Mexico told her, then how could she have borne this 'secret fear' throughout her 'life with him'? Frieda presents herself as a martyr, but the person who carried the secret, fought a demonic and unconscious battle against it and bore it alone was Lawrence. 'Not I, But the Wind ...' is vague, lazy and dishonest – which does not mean its author was a fool.

It was important to Lawrence that Frieda, like his mother, was already married, but it was particularly important that she was married to a man of parts he considered a father-figure and happened to be called Ernest. It cannot have been irrelevant that Frieda's husband shared the name of the brother whose death had allowed Lawrence his pre-eminent position in his mother's love. Nor irrelevant that Frieda had married down, as his mother liked to pretend she had, or that Ernest Weekley was from a lower-class home and was determined, like Lawrence, to rise in the world.

History is never on the side of the cuckold and it does not help Weekley's cause that he, like his former wife, was a dreary writer, but he was in other respects – as Lawrence clearly saw – a worthy rival. The second of nine children, Weekley grew up in Hampstead, in a house on Well Walk formally occupied by John Constable: in 1923, the Weekley house would be endowed with a blue plaque. The Weekleys were hardworking and pious, and at the age of seventeen Ernest was already a schoolteacher. By studying at night he earned an external degree from the University of London, after which he won a scholarship to read Medieval and Modern Languages at Trinity College, Cambridge for which he was awarded a first-class degree with distinctions in German and French. He then spent a year at the Sorbonne, and taught English at Freiburg University before being offered a job at University College Nottingham. It was on a walking holiday in the Black Forest – the kind of holiday that Lawrence would choose – that he met and fell in love with the twenty-year-old Frieda von Richthofen. Their marriage took place in Freiburg on 29 August 1899, and when they returned from their honeymoon, Weekley informed his parents-in-law: 'I am married to an earthquake.'[65]

'I thought Ernest was Lancelot,' Frieda later explained, which suggests that, unlike Francesca, she had misread 'Launcelot du Lac'. Ernest, like King Arthur, possessed what Frieda called moral 'absoluteness' while Frieda, like Guinevere, understood all too easily, as she put it, how a woman could 'love another man when she was married'.[66] It was Lawrence who was Lancelot.

Both the professor and the servants were away when the trespasser visited Private Road for the second time, on Easter Sunday. While her three children hunted for eggs in the garden, Frieda tried to boil the kettle for tea but did not know how to light the gas. Lawrence scolded her lack of practicality, which he also found attractive. The day sounds happy enough but it would be wrong to assume that his discovery of Frieda left Lawrence careless with joy: he felt the weight of destiny. On Easter Monday – the sixth anniversary of their fatal Easter Monday episode – Jessie ran into Lawrence at the railway station. 'The misery I saw depicted on his face was beyond anything I had ever imagined. Utterly lonely, he looked as if his life had turned to complete negation.'[67] Three weeks later, Lawrence took Frieda and the children to the Derbyshire farm where Jessie's sister, May, now lived with her husband, William Holbrook. The party walked to the farm through the spring woods and Lawrence floated paper boats on the stream, as Shelley liked to do. It was now that Frieda 'suddenly' knew that she loved him.[68]

Shortly afterwards Jessie saw Lawrence for the last time, again at her sister's farm. His misery had lifted, but he was 'tongue-tied' around her. He said nothing about the existence of Frieda but revealed, 'with forced brightness', that he was shortly going to Germany. When she rode away she turned back to look at Lawrence who waved as he always did, raising his hat. She later received a letter from him with a German postmark, containing 'a hysterical announcement of a new attachment he had formed'. Lawrence and Frieda had run off together, and Jessie's 'deepest' response was relief: 'At last I was really free.'[69]

Lawrence too was free: Jessie was the last of his female friends to come from the lower orders. From now on he devoted himself either to ladies of rank like Lady Ottoline and Lady Cynthia Asquith, daughter-in-law of the Prime Minister, or to the well-connected upper-middle classes, like the psychoanalyst Barbara Low and the Scottish writer Catherine Carswell, former mistress of Maurice Greiffenhagen – whose painting, *The Idyll*, Lawrence spent so much of his youth trying to copy. Carswell, who was sacked by the *Glasgow Herald* for giving *The Rainbow* a positive review, remembered that the first letters she received from Lawrence were written on coroneted notepaper and that Lawrence, on both occasions, explained to her that 'My wife's father was a baron.' Mary Cannan, another friend, had been married to J. M. Barrie before running off with the novelist Gilbert Cannan, and the poet Dollie Radford moved in the same circles as George Bernard Shaw. These women – mother-figures for Lawrence – managed, by keeping a wary distance, not to fall out with him.

Because Frieda depicts herself as blown hither and thither on the winds of circumstance, she says nothing in *'Not I, But the Wind ...'* about flirting with Lawrence on that first meeting. She instead records that she was the surprised recipient of his immediate desire. He fell in love with her at first sight despite the fact that 'I hardly think I could have been a very lovable woman at the time. I was thirty-one and had three children. My marriage seemed a success.'[70] To whom did her marriage seem a success? Frieda had ceased to be a respectable bourgeois wife long before Lawrence came to lunch, and had he not turned up on her doorstep that day she would have run off with someone else instead. Her most recent lover was currently serving time in a Zurich jail, while a previous lover was hiding in an insane asylum to avoid arrest for assisting in a suicide.

Frieda had been leading a double life since 1904 when she had her first affair, with a forty-year-old lace-maker called Will Dowson who was married to a suffragette. Will Dowson owned a car and would drive

Frieda to Newstead Abbey and Sherwood Forest, where she ran naked through the oak trees. Apart from these afternoon trysts, Frieda posed as a Nottingham housewife: the remains of the Sunday roast were eaten cold on Mondays, the washing was done on Tuesdays, the ironing on Wednesdays, she was 'at home' to visitors on Thursdays and the house was cleaned on Fridays. She shopped in the mornings because it was not done to shop in the afternoons; she made polite calls on other wives. But every Easter she returned to Germany to see her elder sister and here she was 'reborn', as she called it, into her 'intrinsic self'.

There were three Richthofen girls, and Frieda was in the middle between Else and Johanna. Their father was a Prussian officer with a gambling problem, and they were raised in the German garrison town of Metz. In her novelised memoir, 'And the Fullness Thereof …', Frieda said that her parents hated each other with a 'hatred' that was 'murderous', which makes them sound like Arthur and Lydia Lawrence. Frieda, who felt 'instinctively sorry for all men', sided with her father; but Lawrence was fond of her mother, and his letters to Baroness von Richthofen are among his best.[71]

Her sisters were Frieda's closest friends. Else was earnest and intelligent, Johanna was beautiful and superficial, and Frieda was elemental; her father called her Fritzl, short for Huitzilopochtli, the Aztec god of war (the Baron had been reading Prescott's *History of the Conquest of Mexico*). Storing away Frieda's stories, Lawrence returned to Huitzilopochtli in *The Plumed Serpent*. The first man she kissed was her cousin, Kurt von Richthofen: it was in the garden on Easter Sunday, and she 'went off like a fire cracker' – Frieda was not one of those women for whom passion exhausts itself at the mouth. The Germany of her childhood was under the grip of Prussia, the supreme patriarchal power, and because her family moved in court circles, Frieda was able to witness first-hand the foppery of Kaiser Wilhelm. Johanna married the aide-de-camp of the Crown Prince, but Else, who resisted Prussianism, carved for herself a different path altogether and it was she whom Frieda tried to emulate. Else's career was not unlike that of Ernest Weekley: aged seventeen, she became a schoolteacher, after which she paid her way through a distinguished higher education, studying Economics at Heidelberg University under the brilliant Max Weber, philosopher, jurist, political economist and one of the founders of sociology.

Frieda von Richthofen

Following the completion of her doctoral thesis, on the attitude of German authoritarian political parties to worker-protector legislation, Else became the first female inspector of factories in the state of Baden-Württemberg. She was in love with Weber, but because he was married she chose one of his students instead, the decent and pedantic Edgar Jaffe who was a professor of Political Economy.

The Jaffes believed in free love and during Easter 1907 Else became pregnant by the psychoanalyst Otto Gross, husband of her former schoolfriend Frieda Schloffer. This other Frieda, known as Friedel, was also pregnant by Gross; Friedel and Else, who remained close, would both call their newborn sons Peter. Friedel Gross was an unusual woman; determinedly anti-bourgeois she now signed a pact of perfect freedom from her increasingly manic spouse, who had given up washing, sleeping and changing his clothes. That same Easter, Frieda Weekley came to visit Friedel Gross in Munich and heard about the exciting new marital arrangement. Frieda was eating schnitzel in the Café Stefanie, in the bohemian Schwabing district of the city, when Gross appeared, looking like an eagle dressed as a mountaineer and smoking a rolled-up cigarette in a seven-inch holder. The Café Stefanie, where the countercultural community met to exchange ideas, was his headquarters and when Gross talked to Frieda about Sigmund Freud, she suggested that 'The Lord can't have been such a bad psychologist as not to have known that Eve would want the apple the minute it was forbidden.'[72] Gross later recalled, in one of his ecstatic letters to her, how Frieda 'chose' him that day in her 'great aristocratic way';[73] Lawrence had a similar experience of being chosen by Frieda in Private Road.

Frieda did not want Gross as a lover as much she wanted, momentarily, to enjoy the marital freedom of Else Jaffe. The affair between Frieda and Gross lasted ten days in total but was followed by an intense year-long correspondence which she treasured like gold bullion for the rest of her life, carting it up mountains, down canyons and across oceans. Gross's love letters were the reference that guaranteed Frieda's quality. They also provided the script for the relationship she felt she was born to have, and she straight away showed them to Lawrence in order that he might learn both parts of the score. Gross presented their love as the stuff of which revolutions were made: it was an attack on patriarchy, religion, monogamy, marriage, authority, the family unit, sexual repression, sexual possession and sexual jealousy. He and Frieda embraced a Paradise of lawless, unrestricted behaviour, a new erotic world order:

My Beloved,

I thank you that you exist – that I may know of you – I thank you for all the courage, all the hope, all the strength that has come into me from you. Only now, little by little, am I able fully to realize how all my powers have been revitalised through you … the *woman of the future* … I *know* now what people will be like who keep themselves unpolluted by all the things that I hate and fight against – I know it through *you*, the only human being who *already*, *today*, has remained free from the code of chastity, from Christianity, from democracy and all that accumulated filth – *remained free through her own strength* – how on earth have you brought this miracle about, you golden child – how with your laughter and your loving have you kept your soul free from the curse and the dirt of two gloomy millennia?[74]

The effect of Gross's Frieda-worship on a woman whose Mondays were otherwise spent dealing with Sunday's leftovers cannot be underestimated. From now on Frieda led a bifurcated existence: invisible in Mapperley, she was a genius in Munich. 'Genius' was the word she and Gross used to describe one another: Frieda had 'a genius for living', Gross told her and Gross, said Ernest Jones that same year, was 'the nearest approach to the Romantic idea of genius I have ever met'.[75]

Ernest Weekley was easy enough prey for Lawrence, who knew all about married men who were admired at work and mocked at home. Lawrence knew it was the man who paid the price, and that Weekley's pride would be destroyed by his wife's adultery. But he also knew the consequences of being trapped in a loveless marriage, and that intellectual men like Weekley were anti-life. Otto Gross, however, was one hell of an act to follow. He was, as his name implied, vast and untamed; Gross was a deviant wrecking-ball, a cocaine-addicted sociopath whose father, like Lawrence's father, was his natural enemy. But while Lawrence's Oedipal battle was a kitchen-sink drama, Gross's was of Dostoevskian *ampleur*. Otto Gross was the son of the great criminologist Hans Gross, author of a famous book called *Criminal Investigation*, and his surrogate father was Sigmund Freud, for whom Gross and Jung were his most talented disciples. Gross saw sickness as a sign of health; it was the world and not the individual that needed to change: 'The psychology of the unconscious is the philosophy of the revolution,' he proclaimed. 'It is called upon to enable an inner freedom.'[76] Fathers, Gross argued – Freud included – were responsible not only for repressing their sons but for the repressive structure of the family, and society, as a whole. The cure Gross suggested was anarchy, for which he was duly punished: Hans Gross disinherited his son, had him arrested and incarcerated in lunatic asylums, and Freud expelled him from the psychoanalytic community. It was Frieda, said Gross, who freed him from the 'giant shadow of Freud'.[77] The very fact of her being had defeated Freud's masculine theorising: of all the laurels Gross crowned her with, this was the one Frieda treasured the most.

Otto Gross was a Nietzschean prophet, which is what Frieda needed Lawrence likewise to be. The weight of this burden is described in *Mr Noon*, where Johanna explains to an increasingly depressed Gilbert Noon that her previous lover, who had also been her sister's lover, was 'far, far more brilliant than Freud'.

> He made me believe in love—in the sacredness of love. He made me see that marriage and all those things are based on fear. How can love be wrong? It is jealousy and grudging that is wrong. Love is so much greater than the individual.[78]

Gilbert mockingly suggests to Johanna that she and another of her lovers had whooshed around 'in unison of pure love through the blue empyrean, as poor Paolo and Francesca were forced to whoosh on the black winds of hell'.[79] It was clear that Lawrence and Gross were opposites: Lawrence, for one thing, believed deeply in the marriage contract. But in other respects they were marching to the same drum. Lawrence was also a mother-worshipper who would attack Christianity and democracy and rewrite Freudian psychoanalysis in his own image, and both men saw Frieda as the ultimate prize in their Oedipal battle.

At the same time that Gross was lavishing praise on Frieda, he was continuing his affair with Else, who gave birth to her Peter in December 1907. Gross wanted both sisters by his side, but Frieda, for once, shone the brightest. Else was a figure of high seriousness while Frieda was freedom itself. Friedel, who also worshipped Frieda, said that she only had to look at Frieda's freedom for the world to seem brighter. Gross rhapsodised to Frieda about Else's lack of sexual jealousy, but Else was very jealous indeed and found his affair with her sister hard to bear. When she complained to him about it, Gross wondered what the 'cause' of her 'suffering' could be: 'I cannot understand it,' he said, and when Else then exchanged him for another lover, Gross ranted about her 'betrayal' in a thirty-five-page letter to Frieda.[80] Frieda, meanwhile, was simply happy to be back in a gang of three German sisters, and to celebrate their family unit she gave Gross a ring with an image of three female figures, representing herself, Else and Friedel. 'You won't find 3 people like the 3 of us on every street corner,' she told him.[81]

She briefly considered leaving Ernest Weekley for Otto Gross and taking her children with her, but decided she did not 'have the right to gamble with the existence of a good fellow'.[82] It was Else who begged her sister not to take the risk: could Frieda not see that Gross had 'almost destroyed' his wife, Friedel? Weekley's love, Else stressed, was 'greater' than Gross's, as though Frieda was being auctioned to the highest bidder.[83] As a lover, Else conceded, Gross was of course 'incomparable' but as a man he was 'not able to constrain himself even for a quarter of an hour'. Frieda agreed. 'He was a marvellous lover,' Johanna explains to Gilbert Noon,

> but I knew it was no good. He never let one sleep. He talked and talked. Oh he was so marvellous. I once went with him to a zoo place. And you know he could work up the animals, by merely looking at them, till they nearly went mad ... And he talked to you while he was loving you. He was wonderful, but he was awful.—He would have sent me mad ... He simply lives on drugs ... The only thing I couldn't quite stand, was that he would have two women, or more, going at the same time.[84]

Nor did Gross inhabit, as Frieda did, the material world. 'He lived for his vision, and on visions alone you cannot live.'[85] When, some years later, Kafka met Gross on a train with his new wife and child, he described the atmosphere as 'reminiscent of the mood of the followers of Christ as they stood below him who was nailed to the cross'.[86]

The correspondence between Frieda and Gross ended in 1908, at the same time as Gross became a patient of Jung's in the Burghölzli psychiatric asylum in Zurich, where Jung diagnosed him as schizophrenic and

Gross then escaped by jumping over the wall. Three years later Frieda began another affair, this time with an anarchist-artist and former railway worker called Ernst Frick. Frick was attractive for a number of reasons: he was a disciple of Gross, he was on the run for detonating a bomb outside a police barracks in Zurich (in protest against the arrest of a fellow anarchist), and he was, inevitably, the current lover of Friedel. Frick and Friedel were part of a utopian community based on Monte Verità, or Mountain of Truth, above the lakeside resort of Ascona in the foothills of the Swiss Alps. The pulse of the European protest system, Ascona was a vegetarian, sun-worshipping, Pan-worshipping, women-worshipping, peasant-worshipping, sandal-wearing, naturist Paradise of the kind that Lawrence would try to replicate. It was established in 1900 as a commune where artists, writers, theosophers and dancers could build their own cabins and till the land. Isadora Duncan came here, as did Paul Klee, Carl Jung, Rudolph Steiner and Hermann Hesse. Insofar as he lived anywhere, Otto Gross lived on Monte Verità where in 1906 – the year before he met Frieda – he assisted his first suicide by providing his patient and lover, Lotte Hattemer, with the dose of cocaine she needed to kill herself. When Frieda met Ernst Frick in 1911, Gross, now back on the mountain, was organising orgies in barns. In March that same year he assisted the suicide of another patient and lover, Sophie Benz, after which he too went on the run and hid from the police in an asylum.

Life with Frick, reported Friedel, 'was almost as difficult as with Otto – without the unheard of happiness Otto was able to live and give'.[87] She was relieved to be sharing her burden with Frieda again and hoped that Frick and Frieda might go away together. In August 1911, Else lent Friedel the money to pay for Frick to visit England, where he arrived in late September. There is no record of his address, but it was probably in London where he was visited by Frieda when she could get away. On returning to Germany in late October 1911, Frick was arrested for the Zurich bomb of four years earlier and Frieda, who was secretly sending him money, planned to attend his trial. So when Frieda left Weekley in May 1912, Friedel assumed it was for Frick.

As fortune would have it, Frieda was expected to be at a party in Metz to celebrate her father's fifty years of military service at the same time that Lawrence was planning his own trip to Germany. Telling no one that they were travelling together, they met outside the Ladies'

Room at Charing Cross station on 3 May 1912, caught the boat train from Dover and crossed the grey Channel to Ostend. Lawrence had in his luggage *Paul Morel*, which he was close to finishing, and in her own luggage Frieda had her letters from Gross.

This being the first of Lawrence's many voyages, it is worth observing him as a traveller. Because he wrote, read and thought at breakneck speeds, he tends to describe his journeys as though they too took place at high velocity. He complained bitterly about most things, but never about the tedium of being at the mercy of public transport with its breakdowns and cancellations and discomforts. The fact of forward motion was enough for Lawrence, and being rarely in a hurry (despite the rapidity with which he lived), he liked the traveller's lack of agency. The situationist Guy Debord would later philosophise the unplanned journey as 'la dérive', but Lawrence was the first modern drifter. He could write, read and think on boats, buses and trains just as well as anywhere else; he liked missed connections, altered plans, sudden and spontaneous diversions. Life, said Birkin in *Women in Love*, should be 'a series of accidents – like a picaresque novel', and it was the picaresque rather than the predictably shaped, pre-plotted life that Lawrence also wanted. What he experienced on the boat train to Dover and the passage to Ostend would become an addiction for him: the absolute necessity to move.

Having no home, mother or job to return to, Lawrence didn't much mind where he blew so long as he was with Frieda, but when Frieda dropped her children with their grandparents on Well Walk that early May morning she had every intention of coming back for them. She was simply visiting her family in Germany, as she did every year, only this time with her new lover in tow. Pressurised by Lawrence, she had now told Weekley about Gross and Frick, but said nothing about leaving him for Lawrence – because she was not leaving him for Lawrence. How could she? What could Lawrence possibly offer Frieda and her three young children? He had no job or prospects, no money or intention of getting any, and no home or interest in ever having one. As far as Frieda was concerned, she was enjoying an affair with the type of man she enjoyed having affairs with. Lawrence was, she explained to Friedel, 'like Gross and Frick'.[88]

'I could stand on my head for joy,' Lawrence exclaimed, 'to think I have found her.'[89] His great happiness over the next few months was equally to do with discovering 'the vast patchwork of Europe' with its 'multiplicity of connections ... magnetic and strange'.

> There seemed to run gleams and shadows from the vast spaces of Russia, a yellow light seemed to struggle through the great Alp-knot from Italy, magical Italy ... and from far-off Scandinavia one could feel a whiteness, a northern, sub-arctic whiteness.

From the 'massive lands of Germany' Lawrence could see England from the outside: 'tiny she seemed, and tight, and so partial'.[90] In Nottingham, Weekley received, on 10 May, a letter from Lawrence.

> You will know by now the extent of the trouble. Don't curse my impudence in writing to you. In this hour we are only simple men, and Mrs Weekley will have told you everything, but you do not suffer alone. It is really torture to me in this position. There are three of us, though I do not compare my sufferings to what yours must be, and I am here as a distant friend, and you can imagine the thousand baffling lies it all entails. Mrs Weekley hates it, but it has had to be. I love your wife and she loves me. I am not frivolous or impertinent. Mrs Weekley is afraid of being stunted and not allowed to grow, and so she must live her own life. All women in their natures are giantesses.[91]

Lawrence was addressing Weekley not as Frieda's husband but as his former professor, a man who understood nothing about women. Weekley must no longer think of Lawrence as his most promising pupil, he implies, because the power balance has shifted. Dante was shocked to discover his own former tutor, Brunetto Latini, in the seventh circle of hell, and the encounter between the two men, generally celebrated for its tenderness, is in fact a moment of astounding violence. Latini, outed by Dante as a sodomite and condemned to run for ever on burning sands, thinks only to praise the genius of his charge: 'If you pursue your star,' Latini tells Dante, 'you cannot fail to reach a splendid harbour.' Lawrence, who made Weekley's life a daily hell, now cast him into the circle of the Inferno reserved for those former friends to whom he owed a debt.

In Munich, where he was able to go to the ubiquitous Café Stephanie himself, Lawrence met Frieda's sister Else, who was now living with

Alfred Weber, brother of the more famous Max. Else and Edgar Jaffe had achieved an amicable separation which included shared custody of their three children – one of them sired by Gross – and Frieda, in her innocence, assumed that Weekley would be similarly flexible. With no money of her own or home to go back to, Frieda was now bound to Lawrence, and the 'storms of letters', as Lawrence called Weekley's correspondence, began.

Every time another letter arrived the lovers were, as Frieda put it, 'thrown out of our paradisial state'.[92] 'The children are miserable,' Lawrence told Garnett, 'missing her so much. She lies on the floor in misery – and then is fearfully angry with me because I won't say "stay for my sake". I say "decide what you want most, to live with me and share my rotten chances, or go back to security, and your children".'[93] Mothers, Lawrence argued, must relinquish their spawn, and the sooner the better. 'If my mother had lived,' he told Frieda, 'I could never have loved you, she wouldn't have let me go.'[94] In a letter to Else, of December 1912, Lawrence explained that he was preventing Frieda's children from a future debt crisis.

> Whatever the children may miss now, they will preserve their inner liberty, and their independent pride will be strong when they come of age. But if Frieda gave up all to go and live with them, that would sap their strength because they would have to support her life as they grew up. They would not be free to live of themselves – they would first have to live *for her*, to pay back. The worst of sacrifice is that we have to pay back. It is like somebody giving a present that was never asked for, and putting the recipient under the obligation of making restitution, often more than he could afford.[95]

He controlled his jealousy of Frieda's lovers but not of her children. In the poem 'She Looks Back', Lawrence described:

> The mother in you, fierce as a murderess, glaring to England,
> Yearning towards England, towards your young children,
> Insisting upon your motherhood, devastating.

Thus their long fight began. While Frieda wanted credit for Lawrence's rebirth, Lawrence worked to destroy the mother in her and reduce the self-image that had been inflated by Gross. He recorded their arguments in his play *The Fight for Barbara*, written in October 1912, which was, Lawrence said, 'word for word true'.[96] 'It's I who've given you your self-respect,' says Barbara/Frieda. 'Think of the despairing, hating figure that came into Mrs Kelly's drawing room – and now look at yourself.' 'It's time someone taught you you're not as great as you think,' responds Wesson/Lawrence. 'You're not the one and only phoenix.' Barbara's father, Sir William, then offers – as Baron von Richthofen also did – his own opinion: 'Touch a married woman, and you're a scoundrel … It destroys the whole family system, and strikes at the whole of society. A man who does it is as much a criminal as a thief, a burglar, or even a murderer.'[97] Dante, who put Paolo into hell, agreed.

*The Trespasser* – Lawrence's novel of adultery – was published on 23 May 1912, and on 9 June he posted the manuscript of *Paul Morel* to Heinemann: 'I know it's a good thing, even a bit great.'[98] But Heinemann rejected it on the grounds that he had 'no sympathy for any character in the book'. Lawrence's response was to 'curse the blasted, jelly-boned swines, the slimy, the belly-wriggling invertebrates, the miserable sodding rotters, the flaming sods, the snivelling, dribbling, dithering palsied pulse-less lot that make up England today'. Christ on the cross, he continued, must have similarly hated his countrymen: ' "Crucify me, you swine," he must have said through his teeth … "Put in your nails and spear, you bloody nasal sour-blooded swine, I laugh last." '[99]

There was now no going back for either Lawrence or Frieda, and so they went forward, walking south to Italy through the valley of the Isar, sleeping in haylofts. Following the road at the foot of the Tyrol mountains, they passed avenues of crucifixes. In his essay 'Christs in the Tyrol', included in his unguarded and loose-limbed travel book *Twilight in Italy*, Lawrence saw himself in all of them: 'So many Christs there seem to be: one in rebellion against his cross, to which he was nailed; one bitter with the agony of knowing he must die, his heart-beatings all futile; one who felt sentimental, one who gave in to his misery.'[100] Staying the night in Bad Tölz, they continued up through Lenggries and crossed the Brenner Pass.

They were joined en route by David Garnett and his handsome friend Harold Hobson, both of whom had spent their childhoods the Fabian way, swinging from trees, camping in the woods, staging theatrical productions and diving naked into ponds. There was a glamour for Garnett and Hobson in being with the lovers, and their evening entertainment involved Lawrence reading aloud Weekley's storm of letters, with their 'bowel-twisting' displays of suffering. 'I do not live any longer, except as a broken, meaningless automaton, which works for the sake of my children, whom I must save out of the inferno of their mother's infamy.'[101] How, Weekley wailed, could Frieda demean herself by absconding with 'a man who was not a gentleman?' Weekley, Frieda scoffed, was 'not so very grand himself'.[102] But there *was* a grandness to Weekley, who offered Frieda a flat in London if she would only give up Lawrence. His suggestion would have allowed his wife her independence as well as her children, but by now she could not give up Lawrence. She had become, Frieda announced, 'an anarchist', and Lawrence, like Gross and Frick before him, was 'the only revolutionary worthy of the name'.[103]

The party of walkers rose through the wet Alpine forests to the rocky plateau beyond Ginzling, into the southern Tyrol and onwards towards the sun. They reached the Dominicus Hütte at the end of August, and David and Lawrence climbed the rock to the snowline. Ahead of them lay 'a vast precipice, like a wall, and beyond that a cluster of mountain peaks, in heaven alone, snow and sky-rock. That was the end.'[104] The next day all four climbed the Pfitscher Joch – Harold Hobson a little quiet – and here they parted, the young men returning home and Lawrence and Frieda heading on to Sterzing, to take the high road on to Italy. Alone again, Frieda told Lawrence that, at the Dominicus Hütte, Harold 'had' her in a hay hut. This was the second time that summer Lawrence had been forced to recognise that Frieda must live largely and abundantly; back in May she had slept with an officer in Metz and Lawrence, taking his cue from Gross, responded with a shrug. She could do what she liked – who was he to stunt her growth? His own sex drive, meanwhile, had become 'a steady sort of force, instead of a storm'.[105]

Lawrence and Frieda crossed into Italy and took the train to Trento, a 'pure Italian ancient decrepit town'. Here, on the steps beneath the monument to Dante, Frieda sat down and wept. She had, she said, 'walked barefoot over icey stubble', suffered rain and hunger and cold, her clothes were tattered and drab, and now there was a cockroach in the bedroom of their hotel.[106] Following what she called a 'dantesque sunrise', they caught the train to Lake Garda and then the steamer to Villa di Gargnano, another decrepit town – this one stretching up against the rocks – where they rented cheap rooms for the winter.[107] Their bedroom, 'clean as a flower', faced the lake which lay 'dim and milky' every dawn, the mountains dark blue behind. Lawrence, who never moved into a new house without scrubbing the floors, taught Frieda to cook and clean and she was soon an enthusiastic washerwoman. He now, for the fourth time, rewrote *Paul Morel*, renaming it *Sons and Lovers*. The first draft had been overseen by Louie Burrows, the second and third drafts guided and corrected by Jessie Chambers, and for the final draft it was Frieda who advised Lawrence about the emotional lives of Miriam and Mrs Morel, even writing, she said, the 'female' bits because only she understood the hot love between mother and child. ' "Well, I don't love her, mother," ' Paul now says of Miriam, 'bowing his head and hiding his eyes on her shoulder in misery. His mother kissed him a long, fervent kiss. "My boy!" she said, in a voice trembling with passionate love.'[108] Frieda also understood the kind of woman that Lawrence needed, and so was able to explain Paul's problem with Miriam:

'I wish you could laugh at me just for one minute – just for one minute. I feel as if it would set something free.'

'But' – and she looked up at him with eyes frightened and struggling – 'I do laugh at you – I *do*.'

'Never! There's always a kind of intensity. When you laugh I could always cry; it seems as if it shows up your suffering. Oh, you make me knit the brows of my very soul and cogitate.'

Slowly she shook her head despairingly.

'I'm sure I don't want to,' she said.[109]

'I lived and suffered that book,' Frieda proudly recalled in *'Not I, But the Wind …'*, but she did not live it or suffer it as much as Jessie Chambers. 'It's one of the creepiest episodes in Lawrence's history,' says Diana Trilling, 'the two of them, Lawrence and Frieda, sitting there poring over Jessie's detailed revisions of Lawrence's earlier love affair while back in England, alone, Jessie dug and dug, dredging up every last memory as she cherished it, insisting that Lawrence do her the justice in fiction that she felt he had denied her in real life.'[110] The result was the first English modern novel, and the book in which Lawrence discarded his former self.

Lorenzo, as his wife now called him, loved the healthy, proud Italian peasants and the cheap red wine, but by April 1913 they were back in Edgar Jaffe's Bavarian mountain cabin in Irschenhausen, with its clear view of the Alps. 'The deer feed sometimes in the corner among the flowers,' Lorenzo wrote, and 'fly with great bounds when I go out'.[111] In contrast to Lake Garda, Germany had that same 'beastly, tight, Sunday feeling which is so blighting in England', and in June, after thirteen months away, the renegades returned to England for a six-week visit.[112] Lawrence went to his sister's wedding in the Midlands, and Frieda hung around her son's school in London in the hope of seeing him, which she did. Enraged by her underhand behaviour, Weekley began divorce proceedings. Lawrence and Frieda stayed with Edward and Constance Garnett in their Kentish home, The Cearne, where the Garnetts noted Lawrence's jealousy and Frieda's misery; David Garnett, visiting his parents, forgave Lawrence his treatment of Frieda only when he saw spots of blood on the writer's handkerchief. It was during this visit home that Lawrence and Frieda met Murry and Katherine Mansfield and discovered a rapport.

By August the Lawrences were once again in the Irschenhausen cabin, and in mid-September, when Frieda went to Baden-Baden to see her mother, Lawrence set out on a second pilgrimage, this time walking through Switzerland to Italy where he and Frieda planned to rendezvous in Milan. Wordsworth describes in *The Prelude* his own crossing of the Simplon Pass, and Shelley's Alpine experience is recorded in 'Mont Blanc'. Lawrence was completing a well-worn Romantic rite of passage.

Alpine air was considered good for consumptives and, while Lawrence walked, Thomas Mann was beginning *The Magic Mountain*, set in the fictional Berghof sanatorium in Davos. Lawrence followed the Rhine to Schaffhausen and headed south, thirty miles, to Zurich. Here he surveyed from a hilltop the expanse of Lake Zurich spreading beneath him 'like a relief map'. He was always moved by lakes and also by views, which he saw as a form of extended consciousness and a representation of something lost. But something in this view disturbed him: he 'could not bear to look' at it: 'It seemed to intervene between me and some reality.' Crossing to another hill, he looked down on the lake again: 'I hated it.' His boots rubbed and it started to rain; he followed the shore of the lake and stopped for tea in a villa where he chatted to two elderly ladies. Was he Austrian, they asked? Lawrence then said something extraordinary, which seemed to intervene between himself and reality. He replied that yes, he was Austrian; he came from Graz where his father was a doctor. 'I said this because I knew a doctor from Graz who was always wandering about, and because I did not want to be myself ... I wanted to be something else.'[113] The wandering doctor from Graz was Otto Gross, who five years earlier had been treated in the Zurich hospital by Jung. Meanwhile, Gross's disciple Ernst Frick was also in Zurich, serving his jail sentence for blowing up the town's police station, and hoping that Frieda Weekley would one day visit him.

Lawrence's decision to come alone to this loaded place was testament to the power of Frieda's past but also to his desire *to be something else*. He was rehearsing the role of Otto Gross, but mad Gross – who epitomised the Romantic idea of genius – was the mirror image of Mad Shelley. Both men were vegetarian sexual anarchists, suicide-inducing hell-raisers, lethal to women and at war with the fathers who disowned them. Shelley's notes to the utopian allegory *Queen Mab* describe the world as Gross also understood it:

Love withers under constraint: its very essence is liberty; it is compatible neither with obedience, jealousy, nor fear ... A husband and wife ought to continue so long united as they love each other; any law which should bind them to cohabitation for one moment after the decay of their affection would be a most intolerable tyranny ... Love is free: to promise for ever to love the same woman, is not less absurd than to promise to believe the same creed.[114]

Frieda, Lawrence said, was aiming 'in the Shelley direction, at the mid-heaven spiritual, which is still sexual but quite spiritually so. Sex as open and as common and as simple as any other human conversation.'[115] Lawrence was heading in the Shelley direction himself because in late September 1913, on the advice of Edgar Jaffe, he and Frieda took a house in the Gulf of Spezia, 'an hours walk', Lawrence said, from 'Shelley's place'.[116]

In the spring of 1822, when they had been married for five years, the Shelleys, with their friends Jane and Edward Williams, settled on the

Gulf of Spezia in a former boathouse called Casa Magni where the sea came up to the portico. Here Shelley fell in love with Jane Williams, and Mary nearly bled to death following a miscarriage. She had already lost two children who had been born full term. 'No words can tell you how I hated our house & the country about it,' Mary recalled, having lost count of the number of houses they had now moved into and out of. 'Shelley reproached me for this – his health was good, and the place was quite after his own heart.' The Gulf of Spezia, two miles along the shore from Lerici, on the eastern tip of Liguria, is a wide bay subdivided into smaller bays shadowed by what Mary described as 'wood covered promontories crowned with castles'. Mary hated the 'desolation' of it all; 'the beauty of the woods', she said, 'made me weep and shudder – so vehement was my feeling of dislike that I used to rejoice when the winds & waves permitted me to go out in the boat so that I was not obliged to take my usual walk among the tree shaded paths'.[117] Dante likened the landscape around Lerici to the ledges of Purgatory:

> By this time we had reached the mountain's base,
> discovering a wall of rock so sheer
> that even agile legs are useless there.
> The loneliest, most jagged promontory
> that lies between Turbia and Lerici,
> compared with it, provides stairs wide and easy.
>
> (*Purgatory*, Canto 3, 46–51)

The village of Fiascherino, where the Lawrences now settled, was above a 'little tiny bay half shut-in by rocks, and smothered by olive woods that slope down swiftly'. There were no roads to the village – not even a mule track. 'One gets by rail from Genoa or from Parma to Spezia, by steamer across the gulf to Lerici, and by rowing boat round the headlands to Fiascherino, where is the *villino* which is to be mine,' Lawrence told Edward Garnett. The *villino* was a 'flat, pink, fisherman's house' and the garden was 'all vines and fig trees, and great woods on the hills all around', beneath which levels of terraces led down to the sea.[118] Lawrence, a weak swimmer, liked to go out in his boat and look for shellfish. 'If you can't be a real poet,' Frieda warned him from the shore, 'then you'll drown like one, anyhow.' Her divorce was now finalised, with Weekley gaining custody of the children, and so Frieda was of course miserable, but Lawrence, she told Garnett, 'hated me for being miserable, not a moment of misery did he put up with ... In revenge I did not care about his writing.'[119]

Leaning on the rocks of the bay along from Casa Magni, Lawrence worked on his new novel which was originally called 'The Sisters', currently titled 'The Wedding Ring' and later split into the sister novels, *The Rainbow* and *Women in Love*. Looking on to the same sea, Shelley had written *The Triumph of Life*, his response to *Inferno*. Composed, like the *Divine Comedy*, in *terza rima*, Shelley's last major work was the unrolling of a 'waking dream' in which a 'great stream of people' were 'hurrying to and fro'. He compares 'this perpetual flow' to 'gnats upon the evening air', and the swarm is charged by a chariot driven by a blindfolded, four-faced figure leading a pageant of historical characters including Kant, Napoleon, Voltaire and Catherine the Great. The shade of Rousseau, looking like 'an old root which grew / To strange distortion out of the hill side', serves as the dreamer-poet's Virgilian guide. This parade, Rousseau explains, is 'Life's hellish triumph'. The poet asks Rousseau where he comes from and where he is going, and Rousseau tells his strange story, at the end of which Dante himself makes an appearance:

> Before the chariot had begun to climb
> The opposing steep of that mysterious dell,
> Behold a wonder worthy of the rhyme

> Of him whom from the lowest depths of Hell
> Through every Paradise & through all glory
> Love led serene, & who returned to tell

> In words of hate & awe the wondrous story
> How all things are transfigured, except Love.

With *The Triumph of Life*, Shelley's assimilation of Dante was complete. The streams of wailing people in *Inferno* ('I should never have believed / that death could have undone so many') trail behind a banner rather than a chariot, while their faces are stung by horseflies and wasps. Lawrence employed the same imagery in the closing pages of *The Rainbow*, where

Ursula watches from her window the streams of colliers, women and children all walking, like husks, in another 'insentient triumph' of life.

Two months after the Shelleys moved to the Gulf of Spezia, Leigh Hunt arrived in Italy with the aim of starting, with Byron and Shelley, a journal called *The Liberal*. On 1 July Shelley sailed around the coast from Lerici to Livorno to be reunited with his friend, bringing with him a letter from Mary begging the Hunts not to move to Lerici: 'I wish I could break my chains and leave this dungeon.'[120] Six days later, having helped them to settle into their new home on the ground floor of Byron's palazzo, Shelley set sail for home, but his boat was caught in a storm. His drowned body, identified from the copy of Keats in his pocket, washed ashore at Viareggio and was cremated on the beach where he was found. In Fournier's 1889 painting, *The Funeral of Shelley*, Hunt stands by the martyr's pyre flanked by Byron and his 'bulldog', Edward John Trelawny, who described in *Recollections of the Last Days of Shelley and Byron* how Shelley, doused in frankincense, salt and wine, 'made the yellow flames glisten and quiver'. His brains, Trelawny gleefully reported, 'literally seethed, bubbled, and boiled as in a cauldron, for a very long time' after which the 'corpse fell open and the heart … laid bare'. Shelley's ashes were put in a box and Hunt gave the burning heart to Mary, who kept it with her for the rest of her life.[121]

Lawrence realised Shelley's genius in this place. He was writing his novel but thinking about poetic metre, which for his own purposes he compared to 'a bird with broad wings flying and lapsing through the air'.[122] Consolidating his theory of lyric poetry, he told Henry Savage (a critic who briefly became a friend after writing a nice review of *The White Peacock*) that:

> It seems to me a purely lyric poet gives himself, right down to his sex, to his mood, utterly and abandonedly, whirls himself round … till he spontaneously combusts into verse. He has nothing that goes on, no passion, only a few intense moods, separate like odd stars, and when each has burned away, he must die. It is no accident that Shelley got drowned – he was always trying to drown himself – it was his last mood.[123]

And Shelley's last mood was recorded in his last lyric, 'Lines Written in the Bay of Lerici'.

At the same time as he was channelling Shelley in the Gulf of Spezia, Lawrence was also 'going for Whitman' who, he told Henry Savage in January 1914, 'is quite great'. Whitman was Shelley's opposite, and by pitching the poets against one another, Lawrence wrestled with his own oppositions. Shelley was bodiless but Whitman's body was central to his poetry: 'I am the poet of the body, / And I am the poet of the soul,' Whitman sang in 'Song of Myself'. A former printer and newspaper editor, Whitman loved bodies, especially if they were young, working-class and male, and in *Leaves of Grass*, which he called 'the new Bible', he 'resolved to sing' of 'manly attachment'. These twelve untitled poems of indeterminate length were born in what Whitman called 'the gush, the throb, the flood of the moment', an immediacy he emphasised by writing in free verse and employing ellipses rather than formal punctuation. The never-ending lines rolled onward, the body of the poet and the body of his work flowing freely as one.[124] 'I celebrate myself,' Whitman began, 'I lean and loaf at my ease.' When *Leaves of Grass* was published in 1855, it was accompanied by a lithograph of the loafing messiah himself, a wide-brimmed hat pushed to the side of his handsome head, a loose white shirt open at the neck, one strong hand on his hip, the other in his trouser pocket. In 'I Sing the Body Electric', Whitman provided his image with a commentary:

The expression of a well-made man appears not only in his face,
It is in his limbs and joints also … it is curiously in the joints of his
    hips and wrists,
It is in his walk … the carriage of his neck … the flex of his waist
    and knees … dress does not hide them.

There has never been an author-photo to compare with the power of Whitman's lithograph, which was not only a new image of a poet but a new image of a man: modern, sensual, independent, cocksure. For Lawrence, still encased inside collars as stiff as clerical dog collars, such physical flexibility was a revelation. So too was Whitman's joy in male comradery:

The wrestle of wrestlers … two apprentice-boys, quite grown, lusty,
goodnatured,

nativeborn, out on the vacant lot at sundown after work,
The coats vests and caps thrown down ... the embrace of love and
resistance,
The upperhold and underhold – the hair rumpled over and
blinding the eyes [...]

Whitman wanted to 'loosen' himself enough to 'swim with the swimmer, and wrestle with wrestlers, and march in line with the firemen'. Lawrence was also, he now confessed to Savage, 'just learning – thanks to Frieda – to let go a bit'. Whitman was synonymous with spontaneity, comradeship and the 'one identity'; democracy was his great subject and what he meant by the word 'manly friendship'. Whenever Lawrence changed his mind about democracy, he changed his mind about Whitman. 'The fault about Whitman,' Lawrence suggested to Henry Savage,

is, strictly, that he is too self-conscious to be what he says he is: he's
not Walt Whitman, I, the joyous American, he is Walt Whitman,
the Cosmos, trying to fit a cosmos inside his own skin ... Whitman
is like a human document, or a wonderful treatise in human
self revelation. It is neither art nor religion nor truth: Just a self-
revelation of a man who could not live, and so had to write himself.
But writing should come from a strong root of life: like a battle
song after a battle. – And Whitman did this, more or less. But
his battle was not a real battle ... he was like a wrestler who only
wrestles with his own shadow – he never came to grips. He chucked
his body into the fight, & stood apart saying, 'Look how I am
living.' He is really false as hell.[125]

Lawrence, that other self-wrestling human document, was – as ever – talking about Lawrence, and never more so than when he criticised Whitman's habit of turning individuals into types: 'Whitman did not take a person: he took that generalised thing, a Woman, an Athlete, a Youth. And this is wrong, wrong, wrong.'[126]

*The Wedding Ring,* meanwhile, kept on missing 'being itself' and Lawrence discarded the book eleven times. When Edward Garnett described the manuscript as 'shaky', Lawrence laid out, in a now famous letter, his project: Garnett was not to 'look in my novel for the old stable ego of the character. There is another ego, according to whose action the individual is unrecognizable, and passes through, as it were, allotropic states.' His characters, Lawrence explained, were not 'defined' in the traditional way but fell into 'some other rhythmic form, like when one draws a fiddle-bow across a fine tray delicately sanded, the sand takes lines unknown'.[127] Lawrence's thoughts on character in the novel recall Keats's suggestion that 'the poetical Character ... has no self – it is every thing and nothing – it has no character'.[128] In this same letter to Garnett – the last Lawrence sent from Fiascherino – he employed his most Shelleyan metaphor. Shelley had described, in *A Defence of Poetry*, 'the mind in creation' as 'a fading coal, which some invisible influence, like an inconstant wind, awakens to transitory brightness'.[129] Lawrence now explained that 'diamond and coal are the same single element of carbon. The ordinary novel would trace the history of the diamond – but I say, "Diamond, what! This is carbon." And my diamond might be coal or soot, and my theme is carbon.'[130]

On 8 June 1914, Lawrence and Frieda packed their bags and left their *villino*; Frieda went to visit her mother in Baden-Baden and Lawrence 'wandered' back 'over Switzerland – 'mid snow and ice like Excelsior – finishing up with Exhibitions in Bern'. He was always casual about his walking marathons, which on this occasion covered twenty-eight miles a day. From Bern he caught the train to Heidelberg where on 18 June he can be found with Alfred Weber, 'hearing the latest things in German philosophy ... all very interesting'.[131] By 24 June he and Frieda were back in England, and on 13 July they got married in South Kensington registry office, with Murry and Katherine Mansfield as witnesses. 'Heaven, how happy we all were!' recalled Murry. 'The time of being jolly together had really begun.'[132]

Two weeks later Lawrence was invited to a dinner hosted by the American poet Amy Lowell, in her suite in the Berkeley overlooking Green Park. The occasion brought together the poets described by Ezra Pound as 'Imagist': Pound himself, Amy Lowell, Richard Aldington, his wife Hilda, who wrote as H.D., and, for the moment, Lawrence. 'They discussed him before he came in,' H.D. recalled.

> Someone heard he was tubercular, was that true? He had run away with someone's wife, a baroness, was that true? His novel was

Lawrence and Frieda on their wedding day, with Murry, 13 July 1914

already being spoken of as over-sexed (sex-mania), was that true?
A damn shame if they suppress it. Then the little man came in,
looking slender and frail in evening dress that ... made him look
like a private soldier of the already pre-war days, in mufti.[133]

The meeting was of great importance to H.D., and Lawrence now
joined her cast of mythological characters.

He then honeymooned alone with three male friends on yet another
walking tour, this time in the Lake District. Coming down to Barrow-
in-Furness on 4 August, they heard that war had been declared and 'it
was the spear through the side of all sorrows and hopes'. Five days later,
the news from Methuen was that *The Wedding Ring* had been turned
down.[134]

The newlyweds had wanted to return to Spezia, but the war put
an end to their plans. So they rented an 'ugly' red-brick house in the
village of Chesham in the Chiltern Hills, where Lawrence became
ill with a 'long, slow, pernicious cold' that lingered for months.[135]
During his illness he grew a fox-red beard, and when he rose from
his deathbed, 'very sick and corpse-cold',[136] he decided not to
shave: soldiers were clean-shaven and gentlemen wore moustaches,
but Lawrence was no gentleman. His beard marked him out as a satyr,
a martyr, a prophet and an enemy of the people; Christ had a beard
and so did Walt Whitman, but Lawrence looked, so H.D. thought,
like Vincent Van Gogh.

Frieda wanted to be in London where her children now lived with
their grandparents, who had moved from Hampstead to Chiswick in
order to be near good schools, and she considered moving to the city
by herself, precisely as Weekley had suggested. Being remarried, she
hoped she might be granted formal visitation rights. Lawrence, tired of
her complaints, told her to live in London if that was what she wanted,
but Ottoline realised that this could never happen because he was 'too
timid and sensitive to face life alone'.[137] In June 1915 Frieda found, for £3
a month, 1 Byron Villas, the small unfurnished flat in the Vale of Health
where the Lawrences were living when *The Rainbow* was published.
Richard Aldington and H.D. lived further down the hill in Christchurch
Place where H.D. was mourning her stillborn daughter – the result, she
believed, of the shock she suffered when Aldington told her that the

*Lusitania* had sunk. Lawrence, who likened H.D. to Persephone, was, she thought, 'the only one who seemed remotely to understand what I felt when I was so ill'.[138] Then two weeks before *The Rainbow* was prosecuted news came to Byron Villas of another lost child: Peter Jaffe, Else's six-year-old son by Otto Gross, had died.

In Higher Tregerthen, on 6 May 1916, Lawrence and Frieda had one of their fights and Mansfield, who witnessed it, described the event in two separate letters. In the first, sent to Kot, she wrote the following, which is worth quoting in full because she was such a good storyteller.

> Let me tell you what happened on Friday, I went across to them for tea. Frieda said Shelley's Ode to a Skylark was false. Lawrence said: 'You are showing off; you don't know anything about it.' Then she began. '*Now* I have had enough. Out of my house – you little God Almighty you. I've had enough of you. Are you going to keep your mouth shut or aren't you.' Said Lawrence: 'I'll give you a dab on the cheek to quiet you, you dirty hussy.' Etc Etc. So I left the house. At dinner time Frieda appeared. 'I have finally done with him. It is all over for ever.' She then went out of the kitchen & began to walk round and round the house in the dark. Suddenly Lawrence appeared and made a kind of horrible blind rush at her and they began to scream and scuffle. He beat her – he beat her to death – her head and face and breast and pulled out her hair. All the while she screamed for Murry to help her. Finally they dashed into the kitchen and round and round the table. I shall never forget how L. looked. He was so white – almost green and he just hit – thumped the big soft woman. Then he fell into one chair and she into another. No one said a word … Suddenly, after a long time – about a quarter of an hour – L. looked up and asked Murry a question about French literature.

Frieda and Lawrence then began to reminisce about a particularly rich and delicious macaroni cheese they had enjoyed.[139]

In the second letter, sent to entertain Ottoline, Katherine described having tea with the Lawrences when 'for some unfortunate reason I mentioned Percy Shelley'. Frieda said 'his skylark is awful Footle' and Lawrence came back with 'You only say that to show off. It's the only thing of Shelley's that you know.' The fight then began, with Mansfield positioned like Alice between the Cook and the Duchess as saucepans and flatirons were 'hurtled through the air'. She and Murry felt sorry for Lawrence but had not 'one atom of sympathy for Frieda'. Murry, wrote Katherine, 'just didn't feel that a woman was being beaten', and Katherine herself 'never did imagine anyone so thrive upon a beating as Frieda'.[140]

What was increasingly apparent about the Lawrences' marriage is that it was a piece of theatre, performed before an audience. Lawrence had proved his talent for dramatising domestic life in his plays, and for these scenes with Frieda, which we might call 'The Collier's Son's Friday Night', he even slipped into dialect. While other men might beat their wives in private and perform their affection in public, Lawrence beat his wife in public and was affectionate when he thought no one was looking. Mansfield thought that Frieda provoked Lawrence, but on this occasion Frieda had every reason to believe that Lawrence would agree with her assessment of 'Ode to a Skylark' because his rage about Shelley's bodiless bird had become as much a set piece as his fights with Frieda. In *Point Counter Point*, his novel of literary London, Aldous Huxley gives Mark Rampion, the prophet based on Lawrence, the same diatribe: 'Don't talk to me of Shelley. No, no,' says Rampion during a party. 'There's something very dreadful about Shelley. Not a human, not a man. A mixture between a fairy and a white slug.' Shelley, Rampion goes on, had 'no blood, no real bones and bowels', and his treatment of women was 'shocking, really shocking'. He made them feel wonderfully 'spiritual' until he 'made them feel like committing suicide', and he went around 'persuading himself and other people that he was Dante and Beatrice rolled into one, only much more so'. Rampion then recites 'Ode to a Skylark' with the full 'elocutionist's "expression"' after which he picks up the thread of his monologue. 'The lark couldn't be allowed to be a mere bird, with blood and feathers and a nest and an appetite for caterpillars. Oh no!' Round and round Rampion goes, until he ends up where he began. 'If you are a slug, you must write about slugs, even though your subject is meant to be a skylark.'[141] In the poem 'I am in a Novel', Lawrence responded to Huxley's portrait of him: 'If this is what Archibald thinks I am / he sure thinks a lot of lies.' But Lawrence's same skylark-rant had already appeared in print in 1914, in his *Study of Thomas Hardy*.

Why should Shelley say of the skylark:

'Hail to thee, Blithe spirit! – bird thou never wert'

Why should he insist on the bodilessness of beauty, when we cannot know of any save embodied beauty? Who would wish that the skylark were not a bird, but a spirit? If the whistling skylark were a spirit, then we should all wish to be spirits. Which were impious and flippant.

Like his bodiless bird, Lawrence continued, Shelley 'never lived. He transcended life. But we do not want to transcend life, since we are of life.'[142]

Lawrence's own skylark is described in his manifesto for free verse, 'The Poetry of the Present', with its magnificent opening line: 'It seems when we hear a skylark singing as if sound were running forward into the future.'[143] In Lawrence's new interpretation of Shelley, the poet gives us the frozen past and for 'the unrestful, ungraspable poetry of the sheer present, poetry whose very permanency lies in its wind-like transit', we must, he says, turn to Whitman.

Whitman's is the best poetry of this kind. Without beginning and without end, without any base and pediment, it sweeps past forever, *like a wind that is forever in passage*, and unchainable. Whitman truly looked before and after. But he did not sigh for what is not. The clue to all his utterance lies in the sheer appreciation of the instant moment, life surging itself into utterance at its very well-head … Because Whitman put this into his poetry, we fear him and respect him so profoundly … He is so near the quick.[144]

Only in free verse can we feel that 'Now, *now*, the bird is on the wing in the winds.' In Lawrence's own poetry his birds are flashing feathered things with comic bodies, nimble feet and a taste for worms. His hummingbird 'races down the avenues' and goes 'whizzing through the slow, vast succulent stems', his Blue Jay 'runs in the snow like a bit of blue metal', his turkey cock has 'wattles the colour of steel which has been red hot and is going cold, / Cooling to a powdery pale-oxidized sky-blue'. But while his birds are marvellously 'of life', Lawrence could equally, like Shelley, transcend life. The final page of *The Rainbow* is a case in point: what, after all, is a rainbow if not bodiless beauty?

Lawrence's problem with Shelley was not only that the poet was *all* spirit and thus one-sided (only two opposites can make a whole) but that he contradicts himself. 'Shelley wishes to say, the skylark is a pure, untrammelled spirit, a pure motion. But the very "Bird thou never wert" admits that the skylark *is* in very fact a bird, a concrete, momentary thing.' So it was not only Frieda who Lawrence was wrestling on the night of Saturday 6 May 1916, but also Shelley.

The next month, when the foxgloves stood against the walls of Higher Tregerthen like, Mansfield thought, an 'encampment of Indian braves', the Murrys left Wuthering Heights for their equivalent of Thrushcross Grange, 'a soft valley', as Lawrence snidely called it, 'with leaves and the ringdove cooing'.[145] Claire Tomalin suggests that Mansfield took with her a memento of Zennor in the form of the consumption that Lawrence had passed on like a vampire's kiss; having wanted to kill Murry and Frieda, it is a fitting enough irony that he killed Mansfield instead. Two years later she was describing her own fits of tubercular temper as 'really terrifying' and like 'Lawrence and Frieda over again. I am sure I am more like L than anybody. We are *unthinkably* alike, in fact.'[146]

Lawrence, who never understood why the Murrys (or anyone else) would not want to live with him, now moved into Katherine's tower to finish *Women in Love*. The usual plan for a novel, he believed, was to take two couples and develop their relationships.[147] His two couples were Ursula Brangwen and Rupert Birkin, and Ursula's artistic sister Gudrun (based on Mansfield) and Birkin's friend Gerald Crich. But Birkin and Gerald are also a couple and in the chapter called 'Gladiatorial', Lawrence pitched them against one another, like Whitman and Shelley, when they take off their clothes for a wrestling match.

> So the two men entwined and wrestled with each other, working nearer and nearer. Both were white and clear, but Gerald flushed smart red where he was touched, and Birkin remained white and tense. He seemed to penetrate into Gerald's more solid, more diffuse bulk, to interfuse his body through the body of the other, as if to bring it subtly into subjection, always seizing with some rapid necromantic foreknowledge every motion of the other flesh, converting and counteracting it, playing upon the limbs and trunk of Gerald like some hard wind.[148]

The interfused bodies are lifted from *Leaves of Grass*, but the image of Birkin playing 'like some hard wind' upon Gerald's tree-like trunk is from 'Ode to the West Wind': 'Make me thy lyre,' wrote Shelley, 'even as the forest is.' A self-playing instrument, the lyre (whence 'lyric') is the quintessential metaphor for Romantic inspiration, and 'for the poet to yield himself to and be borrowed by the wind is', as the critic Merle Rubin puts it, 'almost *the* Shelleyan stance'.[149] Lawrence had used the trope of a tree as a lyre in *Sons and Lovers*, where Paul Morel lies in bed listening to his father banging his fist on the table below while the wind comes 'through the tree fiercer and fiercer' and 'all the cords of the great harp hummed, whistled, and shrieked'.[150] Shelley expands on the image in *A Defence of Poetry*:

> Man is an instrument over which a series of external and internal impressions are driven, like the alternations of an ever-changing wind over an Æolian lyre; which move it by their motion to ever-changing melody.[151]

By depicting Gerald as both a wrestler and a tree bending to Birkin's inspiration, Lawrence's contraries found their balance.

*Women in Love* is as different from her sister novel as Frieda from Else Jaffe. *The Rainbow* looked back to the organic past but *Women in Love*, whose subject is movement, runs into the future. 'Let's wander off,' says Birkin to Ursula. 'My God,' thinks Ursula at the book's exhausting close, 'how far was she projected from her childhood, how far was she still to go! In one life-time one travelled through aeons.'[152] Will Brangwen was a man of the land with no language for desire, but his granddaughters are nomads in brightly coloured stockings who articulate complex sexual needs. *The Rainbow* had been about family and roots but *Women in Love* is about breaking free. 'What had she to do with parents and antecedents?' Ursula thinks as she sheds her connections. 'She knew herself new and unbegotten.'[153] Birkin, too, is uninterested in what came before him; unlike Paul Morel, the new Lawrentian hero has no class, no history, no parents to contend with; he comes from nowhere.

Those characters guided by mind rather than blood exist in a state of frenzy: the sculptor Loerke speaks in a 'satirical demoniac frenzy' and his factory frieze contains a 'frenzy of chaotic motion'; Gerald, whose father dies in a 'frenzy of inhuman struggling', then half-strangles the continually frenzied Gudrun in a 'frenzy of delight'. *Women in Love* was a novel of revenge whose subject was not love but hate, or rather the ways in which love and murderous hate form two halves of the same emotion. 'Murder,' Lawrence believed, 'is a lust utterly to possess the soul of the murdered', and the desire to kill the loved object is as basic as any other instinct.[154] As a child, Gerald Crich accidentally kills his brother when they are playing a game, and Ursula and Gudrun wonder whether it was an accident at all. 'Perhaps there *was* an unconscious will behind it,' says Ursula. 'This playing at killing has some primitive desire for killing in it, don't you think?'[155] When Gerald's sister Diana then drowns at the water party, she is found with her arms 'tight round the neck' of her fiancé. 'She killed him,' says Gerald.[156] Before he meets Ursula, Birkin is involved with Hermione Roddice, a society hostess with a country estate and a 'long, grave, downward-looking face' which had in it 'something of the stupidity and unenlightened self-esteem of a horse'.[157] A woman of iron will who controls her guests like marionettes, Hermione tries to kill Birkin with a paperweight of lapis lazuli. He is quietly reading Thucydides when, on the other side of the room, Hermione puts down her pen.

> She could not go on with her writing. Her whole mind was a chaos, darkness breaking in upon it, and herself struggling to gain control with her will, as a swimmer struggles with the swirling water. But in spite of her efforts she was borne down, darkness seemed to break over her, she felt as if her heart was bursting. The terrible tension grew stronger and stronger, it was most fearful agony, *like being walled up.*

A 'voluptuous thrill' like 'shocks of electricity' runs down her arms as she picks up the weight and brings it down on Birkin's head. The sensation is 'pure bliss' but the act is incomplete, and so Hermione takes up the stone again. 'She lifted her arm high to aim once more, straight down on the head that lay dazed on the table. She must smash it, it must be smashed before her ecstasy was consummated, fulfilled for ever.' Birkin, quick as a flash, shields himself beneath the volume of Thucydides and the blow comes down on the book instead, 'almost breaking his neck'. Rising, he confronts his killer. 'No you don't, Hermione ... I don't let you ... It isn't I who will die. You hear?'[158]

The scene is emblematic of the rage felt by generations of Lawrence's women readers, and it is curious that Hermione Roddice did not become iconic in the days when Lawrence was being bashed over the head by exasperated English Departments the world over. When the novel appeared, however, Ottoline noted that she had given Lawrence a present of a similar lump of lapis lazuli, Frieda recalled that she had recently broken an earthenware plate over his head when he was peacefully doing the washing-up, and Murry himself will have seen that the entire passage mirrored the murder of the father in *The Brothers Karamazov*. 'I snatched up that iron paperweight from his table,' says Smerdyakov, 'do you remember, weighing about three pounds? I swung it and hit him on the top of the skull with the corner of it. He didn't even cry out. He only sank down suddenly, and I hit him again and a third time. And the third time I knew I'd broken his skull.'[159]

Birkin and Ursula begin their infernal journey in Beldover, a mining town of 'powerful, underworld men who spent most of their time in the darkness',[160] and when they leave for the Alps – taking the same Dover-to-Ostend passage as Lawrence and Frieda in May 1912 – they descend further into the darkness. In the chapter called 'Continental', 'darkness' is used a dozen times in two pages: the 'darkness' on the boat is 'palpable', the boat's crew are 'dark as the darkness', Ursula and Birkin 'fall away into the profound darkness ... dark fathomless space ... surpassing darkness ... profound darkness ... honey of darkness'; Birkin finds himself 'falling through a gulf of infinite darkness, like a meteorite plunging across the chasm between the worlds'. Disembarking from the ship is like 'disembarking from the Styx into the desolated underworld'; around them 'spectral people' are 'hurrying with a blind, insect-like intentness through the grey air'. They journey by train 'out of the darkness', through further 'wet flat dreary darkness' and into 'level darkness'.[161] In the mountains beyond Zurich they find themselves in deep snow, and at a hotel in Innsbruck they rendezvous with Gudrun and Gerald. Their downward journey now becomes a more spatially complex one, best described as *upward descent*, when the party move to a mountain hostel. Ursula understands that she has arrived at her destination, 'the navel of the world',[162] a great cul-de-sac where the valley is shut in beneath the roof of the sky and the perpendicular walls of snow and black rock. The higher they climb, the lower they sink and Ursula and Birkin flee this upside-down topography in horror.

Gerald, losing his mind over Gudrun's affair with the 'insect' artist Loerke, tries to strangle her. The desire comes over him as suddenly as Hermione's desire to kill Birkin: both sensations are 'voluptuous' and both executions are 'bliss'. Gudrun's throat was 'beautifully, so beautifully soft, save that, within, he could feel the slippery chords of her life. And this he crushed, this he could crush. What bliss! Oh what bliss, at last, what satisfaction, at last!' He then, like Captain Oates and Dr Frankenstein, heads off into the snow, struggling through 'a wind that almost overpowered him with sleep-heavy iciness'. He is found frozen in 'a pit' among the rocks and precipices. To retrieve his body the mountain guides drive stakes into the wall and attach a rope to 'haul themselves up the massive snow-front, out on to the jagged summit of the pass, naked to heaven'.[163]

The lowest circle of hell, referred to as 'Caina' by Francesca di Rimini because it is where brother-killers like her husband are destined to go, is at the frozen centre of the world. Dante departed from the traditional image of the burning pit when he turned the base of his Inferno into a deep-freeze whose temperature is controlled by Lucifer's vast bat-wings fanning their glacial winds of hate. The damned are submerged in the solid ice of Cocytus, in the middle of which is Lucifer himself, a three-faced colossus, his three mouths gnawing on the three betrayers: Judas, Brutus and Cassius.

Dante and Virgil are lifted down to this ice-bound impasse on the back of the giant Antaeus whom Dante mistakes, from the distance, for a tower, and they escape by climbing up Lucifer's legs, using his hairs as a ladder. What happens on Lucifer's legs is of immense spatial complexity. When they reach thigh-level, Virgil turns himself and Dante around so they appear to be descending again; he explains that Lucifer's thigh is the globe's circle of gravity, and so what had been upside-down is now the right way up. Lucifer is in fact standing on his head with the stars above his feet – the position in which he landed when he was thrown from Paradise.

There are wonderful things in *Women in Love*, but it is not the flawless masterpiece that Lawrence believed he had written. It is an experiment in the art of fiction produced at a time of unendurable stress. The ambition to replace character with 'rhythms' is laudable, but we only have to compare the result with Virginia Woolf's *The Waves* to see that Lawrence has failed. *Women in Love* lacks the immersive environment of *Sons and Lovers*, the atmospheric grandeur of *The Rainbow* and the hypnotic pull of *The Trespasser*. The book's tension comes not from whether or not the characters will destroy one another but from the pressure that Lawrence exerts on his reader. Are we prepared, like Ursula, to follow Birkin come what may, or will we remain in our towers and observe his proceedings from a distance? Only if we agree with Birkin on all counts does the novel become the prophetic event that Lawrence wanted it to be, and the only people who agree with Birkin are teenagers. .

But while Lawrence allows Birkin appalling indulgences, such as driving his motorcar like 'an Egyptian Pharaoh', he also sees how maddening his spokesman can be and therefore gives us Ursula, whose role it is to save the tale from the teller. When Birkin tells Ursula that he wants their relationship to be 'a pure balance of two single beings; – as the stars balance each other', she reflects that while she likes him very much, 'why drag in the stars?'[164] When Birkin tells her that he wants 'a woman I don't see', Ursula asks, 'What did you ask me to tea for, then?'[165] When Birkin describes his vision 'of a world empty of people, just uninterrupted grass and a hare sitting up', Ursula asks if this is all he believes in, 'the end of the world, and grass?'[166] But the blithe spirit is soon knocked out of her. When Birkin explains, at the end of the novel, that she is not enough for him and he also needs intimacy with a man, Ursula does not come back with a quip. She simply accepts that some things are past all understanding.

It is not only Ursula who does not understand Birkin; the reader is also confused. This is not because Birkin is passing through, as Lawrence explained to Garnett, 'allotropic states', but because *Women in Love* is incomplete. In its original conception the novel began not with the chapter called 'Sisters' where Ursula and Gudrun, at home in Beldover, discuss their views of marriage, but in the snowy upperworld of the Tyrol, where Birkin and Gerald – brothers – are on a climbing holiday in the mountains: 'The acquaintance between the two men was slight and insignificant. Yet there was a subtle bond that connected them.' The original opening, now known as the 'Prologue' and published among Lawrence's miscellanea, makes sense of *Women in Love* by providing a context for Birkin's antagonism to Hermione and his belief that he can never be completed by Ursula. Birkin, although intimate with women, does not desire them. Instead he feels a 'passion of desire' for Gerald

Crich, and for the type of Cornish man who has 'the eyes of a rat', 'dark, fine, rather stiff hair and full, heavy, softly-strong limbs'. He is also 'roused' by the 'manly, vigorous movement' of those men he sees in the streets.[167] This was an astonishingly brave piece of writing which would, had Lawrence not discarded it – through fear of censorship, no doubt – have led to a different novel entirely. Removing the opening was like taking a nose from a face, but Lawrence also destroyed his novel's most dazzling effect: *Women in Love* began and ended with Birkin and Gerald in the same Alpine landscape; he framed the novel inside a great wall of rock and snow from which no one can escape.

It took Lawrence seven months and three separate drafts to complete *Women in Love*, which was delivered to Pinker, his British agent, in November 1916. In his haste, an error slipped in. After Ursula and Birkin flee the mountain, Gudrun and Loerke discuss their pleasure in 'the achieved perfections of the past. Particularly they liked the late eighteenth century, the period of Goethe and of Shelley, and Mozart.'[168] The point Lawrence wants to make is that Gudrun and Loerke have a taste for the artificial and overwrought, and he clearly means Schiller not Shelley; he knows very well that Shelley's period was not the late eighteenth but the nineteenth century. This is the only mention of Shelley in *Women in Love,* and each time he rewrote the novel Lawrence repeated the mistake, thus digging the Romantic deeper and deeper into the perfections of the past while Whitman, as Lawrence put it in his essay on the great American poet, went 'forward in life knowledge'.[169]

In a statement intended to accompany the American edition of the novel, Lawrence explained that *Women in Love* – whose gestation was coterminous with the Battle of the Somme, the beginning of modern, mass-industrial warfare – was produced during 'a great hail storm' of 'abuse and persecution' (his own). Although the book 'did not concern the war itself', Lawrence wrote, the 'bitterness of the war may be taken for granted in the characters'.[170] What the reader hears in its pages, however, is an echo of Byron's poem 'Darkness', written at another apocalyptic moment, on a black day in July 1816 when 'the fowls went to roost at noon'.

The first year of Byron's exile was known as 'the year without a summer'. In Indonesia, Mount Tambora erupted, hurling twenty-five miles of gas and ash into the stratosphere, burying villages beneath boiling lava and extinguishing the sun. Ten thousand people died instantly, their cultures and language wiped out. Two years of climatic chaos followed: a 300-mile-wide mushroom cloud circled the earth, floods in China washed away harvests, summer crops in Massachusetts froze at the roots, brown snow fell in Hungary, red snow fell in Italy, harvests failed across Europe, thousands starved and, to replace the horses that died of hunger, the bicycle was invented. 'The world was void,' wrote Byron in 'Darkness'; 'Seasonless, herbless, treeless, manless, lifeless'. Byron wrote 'Darkness' by the shores of Lake Geneva where he was idling with Shelley, and *Frankenstein*, which Mary Shelley began at the same time, was born from the same climatic disaster. The intensity of the atmosphere was exacerbated because Byron, being famous, was spied on by tourists with telescopes on the opposite side of the lake, who elaborated on their findings in gossipy letters home. 'There was no story so absurd that they did not invent at my cost,' he complained. 'I believed they looked on me as a man-monster.'[171] He was also spied on by his doctor, Polidori, who was being paid by Byron's publisher to report back on the poet's activities.

After John Middleton Murry had abandoned him in Zennor, in June 1916, Lawrence began a Whitmanesque romance with William Henry, the dark-haired eldest of the Hocking sons. It was Frieda who was now abandoned as her husband spent more and more time at the farm, bringing in the harvest, riding the horse, sitting up late with his new friend. Lawrence had turned against her, she said – without a trace of irony – because of 'the bit of German in me'. Lawrence must have been aware, at least on some level, that he was putting his wife in the position occupied by his mother when he transferred his affection to the Haggites. In *Kangaroo*, where William Henry Hocking is renamed – also without a trace of irony – John Thomas, Lawrence described the pleasure of 'drifting back to the common people'. Biographers have suggested that the two men made love among the haystacks, for which there is no evidence. We know nothing about William Henry's sexuality other than that he was currently courting the woman he married in 1919, but we do know that Lawrence, for all his investment in the life of the instincts, repressed his desire for male intimacy. It was Frieda who started the rumour about their affair because, whenever she and Lawrence had a fight, he would make his way down to the farm and talk to William Henry 'about the sun, and the moon, the mysterious powers of the moon at night, and the mysterious change in man with the change of season, and the mysterious effects of sex on a man'.[172] The Cornish farmers, Lawrence told Murry, talked 'freely of the end of the world', and he was thus able to play the part of the man who would lead them out of the darkness.[173] 'One stormy night,' Stanley Hocking recalled, when the 'wind was blowing' around the black rocks of Zennor and Lawrence and William Henry were sitting by the fire, Frieda, terrified by a 'band of thunder', ran down the field and hammered on the door to be let in.[174] Whenever Lawrence's grand German wife arrived at the farm, the talk and laughter always stopped.

The winter of 1916–17 was severe and Lawrence began to complain that he could no longer breathe in this country, which we can take as both literal and metaphorical. He and Frieda were joined for Christmas by an American couple they had met in Hampstead during *The Rainbow* debacle. Robert Mountsier was writing articles about the war for the American press and Esther Andrews was a former actress who now worked on *Women's Wear Daily*. While Mountsier, who would play an important role in Lawrence's life, is one of those figures who appears, as it were, in parenthesis, all we know about Esther is that Frieda was convinced that she seduced Lawrence.

In London, Ottoline heard that she had been cast as the 'villainess' in *Women in Love* and demanded to see the manuscript, a copy of which Lawrence duly delivered. 'Lawrence has sent me his *awful* book,' she reported to Russell in January 1917. 'It is so loathsome one cannot get clean after it – and a most insulting chapter with a *minute* photograph of Garsington and a horrible disgusting portrait of me making me out as if filled with cruel devilish *lust*.'[175] Even Virginia Woolf, always willing to cock a snook at Ottoline, thought the parody tasteless. 'My word,' Woolf said of Lawrence, 'what a cheap little bounder he was, taking her money, books, food, lodging and then writing that book.'[176] Ottoline threatened to sue the publisher for libel, but *Women in Love* did not yet have a publisher and was unlikely to get one while she was ostentatiously waiting, rock in hand. So, with his novel effectively suppressed in England, Lawrence decided to pitch it to America instead: 'And poor vindictive old Ottoline can be left to her vanity of identifying herself with Hermione.'[177]

Lawrence, his relationship with Frieda at its lowest ebb, now collected together his poems about her – most dating from their happy days in Lake Garda – and turned them into a poetic novel with the explanatory title *Look! We Have Come Through!* His foreword explained that the poems were to be seen not as 'so many single pieces' but as 'an essential story, or history or confession ... revealing the intrinsic experience of a man during the crisis of manhood, when he marries and comes into himself'.[178] The foreword is followed by an 'Argument' in which Lawrence proposes his subject:

> After much struggling and loss in love, and in the world of man, the protagonist throws in his lot with a woman who is already married. Together they go into another country, she perforce leaving her children behind. The conflict of love and hate goes on between the man and the woman and between these two and the world around them, till it reaches some sort of conclusion, they transcend into some condition of blessedness.[179]

The idea of the poetic 'Argument' was lifted from Milton's *Paradise Lost* and Blake's *Marriage of Heaven and Hell* (a prose prophecy with an Argument in verse). Lawrence's journey, similarly epic, is represented as undertaken alone; the struggle and the loss have been on his side only; it is not 'we' but *he* who has come through; it is Lawrence we are asked to look at.

Despite its textual armour, *Look! We Have Come Through!* is a remarkably naked collection. Not all the poems are good – there are too many for that – and Lawrence is right that they cannot stand alone. But as a cycle exploring the poet's experience of love, they belong to the tradition of Dante's *Vita Nuova*, Shelley's *Epipsychidion*, Meredith's *Modern Love* and, later, Ted Hughes's *Birthday Letters*. Lawrence's dead mother is commemorated in a ghoulish lyric called 'Hymn to Priapus':

> My love lies underground
> With her face upturned to mine,
> And her mouth unclosed in a last long kiss
> That ended her life and mine.

Frieda makes her appearance, in the allegorical 'Ballad of a Wilful Woman', as the Madonna on a 'plodding palfrey'. Leaving her suckling child with Joseph, the wilful woman goes off with 'a dark-faced stranger' down to the 'flashing shore'.

She follows his restless wanderings
Till night when, by the fire's red stain,
Her face is bent in the bitter stream
That comes from the flowers of pain.

Lawrence records, in 'First Morning', the first time that he and Frieda made love – 'The night was a failure / but why not –?' – and in 'She Looks Back', a play on the Orpheus myth, he describes Frieda 'straining with a wild heart, back, back again, / Back to those children you had left behind'. In 'Frohnleichnam' Lawrence makes a claim which would have surprised both Frieda and Jessie Chambers:

You have come your way, I have come my way;
You have stepped across your people, carelessly, hurting them all;
I have stepped across my people, and hurt them in spite of my care.

The centrepiece, 'Song of a Man Who Has Come Through', is Lawrence's revision of 'Ode to the West Wind'. 'Not I, not I, but the wind that blows through me', the poet begins, having given us now two senses of 'through', currently his favourite preposition. The man has come through the storm, but the wind is also coming through the man as though, like Gerald Crich, he were a lyre.

Not I, not I, but the wind that blows through me!
A fine wind is blowing the new direction of Time.
If only I let it bear me, carry me, if only it carry me!
If only I am sensitive, subtle, oh, delicate, a winged gift!
If only, most lovely of all, I yield myself and am borrowed
By the fine, fine wind that takes its course
through the chaos of the world …

Shelley's west wind is the prophetic force of change, and his 'Ode' closes on a note of hope:

O Wind,
If Winter comes, can Spring be far behind?

In 'Craving for Spring', the final poem in *Look! We Have Come Through!*, Lawrence echoes, in his own penultimate line, Shelley's optimism. 'Ah, do not let me die on the brink of such anticipation!'

The spring of 1917 brought a lethal virus to France. Soldiers in the trenches found themselves with headaches, fever and loss of appetite; this developed into bronchial pneumonia or septicaemic blood poisoning. In the final stages of the illness, which became known as the Spanish flu, the worst afflicted would succumb to cyanosis, when their lips and faces turned purple as their lungs filled with choking fluid.

Spring in Cornwall brought the composer Philip Heseltine, on the run from conscription. He and his pregnant girlfriend Puma, who had lived with the Lawrences in their first Cornish home, had found their way into *Women in Love* as the combative bohemian Halliday and his pregnant, and faithless, girlfriend Possum. When he discovered the libel, Heseltine sued Lawrence's publisher. Since last seeing Lawrence, Heseltine had adopted, for his compositions, the nom de plume of Peter Warlock, and his current reading included Eliphas Levi's *History of Transcendental Magic*, from which he was learning how to conjure demons. The occultist Aleister Crowley, when he too came to Zennor, raised the devil on a path after performing a black mass in the church. There were other occultists here as well; Meredith Starr and his aristocratic, biracial wife Lady Mary used the mine shafts for naked meditation, filling the air with omens and what Lawrence described as 'destructive electricity'. One night the Starrs performed a lengthy concert of their own composition called 'East and West' in which Starr, dressed in 'a long nightgown', played his violin and 'intoned' spectrally from behind a curtain. It was, said Lawrence, 'the greatest event in Zennor for some time'.[180] Philip Heseltine rented a house on top of the moors with views of the sea to both the east and west, allowing him to follow the sun over the course of the day, but when his military exemption came under review, he fled to Ireland where he met W. B. Yeats and became interested, as everyone then was, in theosophy.

Heseltine would doubtless have left his own memoir of Lawrence had he lived long enough to do so, but he died of coal-gas poisoning – probably by his own hand – in December 1930. Hailed at the time of his funeral as the greatest of English songwriters, his name came up again when the art critic Brian Sewell, born seven months after Heseltine's death, claimed to be his natural son. The importance of Philip Heseltine to Lawrence is that he brought to Cornwall his twenty-one-year-old friend Cecil Gray. Another musician on the run from conscription, Gray rented an old house grandly called Bosigran Castle, which stood on the cliffs near Pendeen, four miles from Higher Tregerthen. Here, describing himself as an anchorite monk, he worked on setting Flaubert's *La Tentation de Saint Antoine* to music. Plump, fair and bespectacled with a taste for cocaine, Cecil Gray fits into Lawrence's Cornish life like the second generation of children in *Wuthering Heights*, whose narrative begins when the turbulence caused by Cathy and Heathcliff is over. And just as the second half of *Wuthering Heights* is erased by the power of the first half, Gray's role in Lawrence's Inferno tends to be overlooked. But it was he who would bring the story of Lawrence's time in the underworld to its grand finale.

Lawrence threw himself into the task of cheering up Bosigran Castle, scrubbing the floors and painting the furniture, which tasks revealed, Gray thought, a 'Dostoevskyan' abjection. In his memoir *Musical Chairs*, Gray says that he saw the Lawrences every day and they become a single household. But, according to Lawrence, Gray came over only 'fairly often'. During one of Gray's visits it seems likely that he and Frieda went to bed together; Lawrence was always down at Lower Tregerthen farm and Frieda wanted to avenge herself on his supposed affairs. The wives of admired men are catnip to their acolytes and Gray, like all those who spent time with Frieda, became an authority on Lawrence's sexual appeal, potency and performance. Lawrence, explained Gray, 'was definitely not attractive to women in himself, as apart from the seductive magic of his pen. His physical personality was puny and insignificant, his vitality low, and his sexual potentialities exclusively cerebral.'[181]

It was in wartime Cornwall, when he and Frieda were living like pioneers, that Lawrence became interested in nineteenth-century American literature. Earlier in the year he had read Herman Melville's *Moby Dick*, and he followed this up with *Typee* and *Omoo*, which described island societies peopled by unspoiled savages. He then read James Fenimore Cooper's *The Pioneers*, *The Prairie*, *The Deerslayer* and *The Pathfinder*, Hector St John de Crèvecoeur's *Letters from an American Farmer* and Hawthorne's *The Blithedale Romance*. 'It surprises me,'

Lawrence told Amy Lowell, now acting as his American patron, 'how much older, over-ripe and withering into abstraction, this American classic literature is, than English literature of the same time ... But how good these books are!' Like Columbus, Lawrence had discovered a long-inhabited land.[182]

Robert Mountsier had suggested that he act as Lawrence's American agent, thus igniting Lawrence's desire to 'transfer' all his life, as he put it, to America, but the war made this transfer impossible and so he turned himself into a critic of American literature instead. *Studies in Classic American Literature*, the greatest work of literary criticism of the age, began life as a series of proposed lectures to be delivered in New York called 'The Transcendent Element in American (Classic) Literature' before swiftly evolving into a 'ten-barrelled pistol' of eight essays, a 'thrilling blood-and-thunder, your money-or-your-life kind of thing: hands-up America!'[183] No one before Lawrence had suggested that American literature was anything other than a roughly textured collection of adventure stories, let alone that these tales might contain their own classics, and Lawrence – with the supreme confidence later shown by F. R. Leavis and Harold Bloom – drew up his own canon. Passing over Emerson, Thoreau, Emily Dickinson and Mark Twain, he selected Benjamin Franklin's *Autobiography*, Crèvecoeur's *Letters from an American Farmer* and all of Hawthorne, Fenimore Cooper, Edgar Allan Poe, Melville and Whitman. What these writers revealed, he argued in the first of his essays, 'The Spirit of Place', is that America was not the fresh-faced child of Europe but its untranslatable 'other'. Lawrence was the first to employ the word 'other' in the sense of radical alterity, but then otherness – sexual otherness, the otherness of plants, birds and animals – was his subject as much as 'oneness' was Whitman's. We tend to think, Lawrence wrote, in terms of 'likeness and oneness' but 'must learn to think in terms of difference and otherness'.

> There is a stranger on the face of the earth, and it is no use our trying any further to gull ourselves that he is one of us, and just as we are. There is an unthinkable gulf between us and America, and across the space we see, not our own folk signalling to us, but strangers, incomprehensible beings, simulacra perhaps of ourselves, but *other*, creatures of an other-world.[184]

121

Lawrence discovered in American 'classics' a version of his own duality: what distinguishes these texts, he argued, is their *unconscious duplicity*: in each case a simple tale disguises a complex symbolic meaning. Lawrence's essays on American literature similarly operate on two levels: to reach the lower level, we have to work through what he called his 'personal philosophy' which he now described, in a metaphor he returned to, as having 'got off my chest'.

Those areas of Lawrence's thinking which are most derided, from his dismissal of evolution to his faith in the ganglia at the pit of the stomach, come from theosophy and because his personal philosophy was deeply rooted in this pseudo-religion, it is necessary to introduce the theory and its founder, Madame Helena Blavatsky. For all his sense of himself as an outsider, Lawrence often swam with rather than against the tide; everyone he knew believed in the importance of free sexual expression, for example, and everyone he knew was interested in theosophy. A medley of Freudian and Jungian psychoanalysis, Mesmerism, Zoroastrianism, Buddhism, Hinduism, Neoplatonism, Occultism, Darwinism, Orientalism, Egyptian mythology, Paracelsus, anthropology and cosmology, theosophy sounds to us like mumbo-jumbo, but it served an important purpose to the late Victorians by suggesting a belief system with more wonder than Christianity and a theory of progress less depressing than Darwin's. 'All the best part of knowledge,' Lawrence said in *Psychoanalysis and the Unconscious*, 'is inconceivable',[185] and by returning the inconceivable to an over-explained world, theosophy laid the groundwork for the alternative lifestyles and therapies of the later part of the century. Blavatsky's aim was to condense the Victorian smorgasbord of spiritual and scientific movements to a single source that could serve as the ultimate authority, and this she found in an ancient Tibetan 'Master' called Morya whose teachings she disseminated through two divinely dictated theosophical bibles, *Isis Unveiled* (1877) and *The Secret Doctrine* (1888).

Lawrence thought *The Secret Doctrine*, which he read in Zennor, 'in many ways a bore, and not quite real. Yet one can glean a marvellous lot from it, enlarge the understanding immensely.'[186] One of the things he now better understood was the earth's 'circuit of vital magnetism', and he discovered in classic American literature a power-plant of untapped energy of precisely the kind Blavatsky had described. Europe and America, he explained in 'The Spirit of Place', represent the poles of positive and negative vitalism, which is why European men were compelled to sail in the direction of the New World. Like migrating birds, 'without knowing or willing', these mariners were borne 'down the great magnetic wind'.[187] Everything and everyone in the universe was connected to a vast electrical grid and to understand this connectivity, Lawrence wrote in his essay on Hawthorne, 'it is necessary again to consider the bases of the human consciousness'.[188]

The reason why Lawrence's understanding of human anatomy bears no relation to that of his doctors is again down to Madame Blavatsky, although his theories recall those of the popular scientists of the Enlightenment who argued that bodies contained waves of invisible fluid known as humours. According to theosophy, consciousness itself is housed in the body, and the body is a magnet whose front is the 'live end' and whose back 'the closed opposition'. The unconscious mind is located in the great nerve centres of the solar and cardiac plexus and composed of 'seven planes', each one charged with positive or negative energy. This body-electric plugs into a universal transmission network of high-voltage power lines; the current of physical attraction is the same as the circuit that sets Marconi wires vibrating, and the bond between mother and child is also the product of animal magnetism: the newly born baby moves, Lawrence would argue, with 'magnetic propulsion' to the breast; the 'first consciousness' of the child is a 'great magnetic or dynamic centre' which pushes 'in its circuits between two beings: love and wrath, cleaving and repulsion', the child's screams send out 'violent waves' as though 'the air were surcharged with electricity' and the mother's subsequent anger, like 'an outburst of lightning', allows the 'storm' to subside.[189]

This was the body-electric that Lawrence described in *Women in Love*, where Hermione feels 'shocks of electricity' running up and down her arm when she attacks Birkin, and Gerald – who electrifies, and thus destroys, the mines – gives off 'a sort of electric power' which Gudrun finds 'turgid and voluptuously rich … He would be able to destroy her utterly in the strength of his discharge.'[190] This same body dominated Lawrence's reading of classic American literature; electricity was everywhere but especially in Whitman. 'I sing the body electric,' Whitman sang in 'Song of Myself'.

> The armies of those I love engirth me and I engirth them,
> They will not let me off till I go with them, respond to them,
> And discorrupt them, and charge them full with the charge of
> the soul.

Whitman's body is the surging afflatus through which the 'threads ... connect the stars'.

> Mine is no callous shell,
> I have instant conductors all over me whether I pass or stop,
> They seize every object and lead it harmlessly through me.

Edgar Allan Poe was similarly, Lawrence wrote, 'a lodestone' and his women 'the soft metal', while love, in Poe's *Tales of Mystery and Imagination*, 'acts as an electric attraction rather than a communion between self and self'.[191] Lawrence's American was 'a virtuous Frankenstein monster' animated by lightning bolts; this was the term he used to describe Benjamin Franklin, that other experimenter with lightning. Franklin, Lawrence argued, 'autonomised himself' when he took the goal of moral perfection to its extreme.[192] The startling connection between Benjamin Franklin and Victor Frankenstein was, as Lawrence saw it, entirely logical: Franklin and Mary Shelley were simply tuning into the same electrical waves.

The abstractions of Shelley feature heavily in Lawrence's American essays. If Shelley and Franklin, he argued, who 'conceive of themselves in terms of pure abstraction, pure spirit, pure mathematical reality', compose one half of an American, then Rousseau and Crèvecoeur, who 'exist in terms of emotion and sensation', compose the other half.[193] Lawrence prefers Crèvecoeur's child of nature to Franklin's virtuous monster because Crèvecoeur, like Lawrence, sees the 'wild otherness' of animals, 'the pride, the recoil, the jewel-like isolation of the vivid self'. Crèvecoeur's birds are not like Shelley's 'little singing angel' but creatures possessed of 'dark, primitive, weapon-like souls'.[194] They are creatures like Melville, whom Lawrence sees as less sailor than seabird. Melville 'does not pit himself against the sea, he is of it. And he has that inscrutable magic and mystery of pure sea-creatures.' Lawrence's encounter with Melville, 'The greatest seer and poet of the sea, perhaps in all the world', is the most exciting moment in modern criticism. *Moby Dick*, derided and forgotten, was for him one of the world's 'strangest, and most wonderful books'. Beneath the tale of the whale hunt lay the 'tormented symbolism': the sea was a symbol, whiteness was a symbol, the *Pequod* was a symbol.[195]

Lawrence's ten-barrelled pistol of essays was loaded by Madame Blavatsky and pointed firmly at Murry, whose *Fyodor Dostoevsky: A Critical Study* was published in August 1916. 'The Russians', Murry announced, were a new 'phenomenon which has lately burst upon our astonished minds'. Lawrence responded by saying that Dostoevsky could 'stick his head between the feet of Christ, and waggle his behind in the air'.[196] In his foreword to *Studies in Classic American Literature*, Lawrence was in better temper: 'Two bodies of modern literature,' he argued, 'seem to me to have come to a real verge, the Russian and the American.' Murry represented the Russian body, and Lawrence represented the American. Dostoevsky, explained Lawrence, 'burrowed underground, into the decomposing psyche', while 'Whitman has gone further, in actual living expression, than any man.'[197] Whitman's verse is 'like the song of a bird. For a bird doesn't rhyme and scan.' He loosened the poetic line and his 'whole soul' thus 'speaks at once, in a naked spontaneity … unutterably lovely'.[198] So while Constance Garnett translated Dostoevsky's words for an English readership and Murry translated Dostoevsky's thought for the same public, Lawrence proposed himself as the interpreter of America's 'untranslatable otherness'.[199]

Up in Bosigran Castle in the summer of 1917, Cecil Gray, working on his opera, was discovering that Cornwall was a 'magical country' where the magic was 'black'. He loved the wild flowers and the evening frogs and the swallows dipping and skimming through the towers of the derelict engine houses next to his house, but when autumn came the beauty gave way to what he could only describe as 'a growing *malaise*'. What distinguished the Cornish spirit of place, Gray recalled in *Musical Chairs*, was the way in which 'the boundary line between the subjective and the objective' became 'vague and indecisive', so that you began to distrust the evidence of your senses.[200] Lawrence agreed, describing Cornwall in *Kangaroo* as 'a country that makes a man psychic'.[201] Gray was troubled by noise from the tin mines which were haunted by malevolent sprites known as 'knockers', and the constant hammering – like the knocking at the gate in *Macbeth* or the 'tapping at my chamber door' in Edgar Allan Poe's 'The Raven' – found its way into Lawrence's wind-poems. 'Song of a Man Who Has Come Through' ends with the dreaded sound:

What is the knocking?
What is the knocking at the door in the night?
It is somebody wants to do us harm.

'Knock, knock, 'tis no more than a red rose rapping,' wrote Lawrence in 'Love Storm', it is the 'west wind rapping'. He returns to the image in 'The Wind, the Rascal':

The wind, the rascal, knocked at my door, and I said:
My love is come!

The wind that autumn lifted the sea on to the land, wrecking the Hockings' turnip fields and smashing Lawrence's pea-rows. In early October Lawrence and Frieda went to Bosigran Castle for supper. They were singing German folk songs around the piano when there came a knocking at the door. Six armed officers burst in to inform them that a candle flickering through an upstairs window was, they believed, signalling to a German submarine. There were strict rules about blackout times in coastal regions and Gray was fined £20, but the episode had more severe repercussions for the Lawrences. On 12 October Lawrence returned with William Henry from Penzance to find Frieda in distress: their cottage had been searched; his papers were disturbed, letters from Baroness von Richthofen had been removed and Frieda's sewing was all over the floor. Later that afternoon four officers appeared with a formal expulsion order: the Lawrences, supposed leaders of an espionage circle, had three days in which to leave the county.

'I cannot even conceive how I have incurred suspicion,' Lawrence blustered to Lady Cynthia Asquith, 'have not the faintest notion,'[202] but he had been as contentious as it was possible to be since his arrival eighteen months ago, raging against the war, the Resurrection, the Government, the English and the world in general to anyone who was prepared to listen and to many who were not. So with no money and nowhere to go the couple were chased out of Cornwall by a pitchfork-wielding mob. Taking only their essentials – including Ottoline's lump of lapis lazuli – they caught the night train to Paddington where Lawrence sat among the soldiers 'perfectly still, and pale, in a kind of after death'.[203] Once they arrived in London, Lawrence told Cecil Gray that 'the people are not people any more. They are factors, really ghastly, like lemures, evil spirits of the dead. What shall we do, how shall we get out of this Inferno?'[204]

As they approached the City of Dis, Dante and Virgil discovered that the devils in the watchtowers had been alerted to their presence through a complex signalling system:

> I say, continuing, that long before
> we two had reached the foot of that tall tower,
> our eyes had risen upward, toward its summit,
>
> because of two small flames that flickered there,
> while still another flame returned their signal,
> so far off it was scarcely visible.

(Inferno, Canto 8, 1–6)

'Now you are caught, foul soul!' shouted the boatman who rowed them across the River Styx.

# Part Three

Exiled from his country of exile, Lawrence returned to the exact spot in which he had made the decision, in November 1915, to go to Cornwall in the first place. In October 1917, the Lawrences found themselves back on Well Walk, the road linking Hampstead Underground to the Vale of Health, as the guests of Dollie Radford, who lived four doors down from the house in which Ernest Weekley had been raised and where Frieda had left her children with their grandparents on the morning of 3 May 1912. Frieda's response to the proximity of her new life to her old life has not been recorded, but when Lawrence walked on the Heath, he recalled not the Zeppelin nights of 1915, but Lower Tregerthen. 'In his eyes he saw the farm below,' he said of Somers in *Kangaroo*, '– grey, naked, stony, with the big, pale-roofed new barn – and the network of dark green fields with the pale-grey walls – and the gorse and the sea. Torture of nostalgia. He craved to be back, his soul was there.'[1] They lasted in Hampstead a week and then accepted an invitation to stay with Hilda Aldington, who was now living in Mecklenburgh Square, a handsome block of Georgian houses on the edge of Bloomsbury between Coram's Fields and Gray's Inn Road. Lawrence got out of the Inferno by trading it for the underworld of Hades and Persephone.

Since last seeing one another in 1915, Lawrence and H.D. had exchanged letters and manuscripts. She sent him poems which he commented upon, and he sent her drafts of *Women in Love* and *Look! We Have Come Through!*, both of which 'revulsed' her: she thought the former too 'frenzied' while the latter contained 'too much body and emotions'.[2] She and Lawrence were crucially divided on the subject of bodies. Why, H.D. wondered, 'in your interminable novels, do you not write – to someone, anyone – as you write me in your letters?'[3] Lawrence's 'flaming letters', as H.D. called them, which she kept in

Hilda Doolittle

a special box together with the miniature of her mother, were later destroyed by Aldington which is why they are not included in his *Collected Letters*, but H.D. knew them by heart and described their content in her *roman-à-clef*, *Bid Me to Live*:

> He had written about love, about her frozen altars; 'Kick over your tiresome house of life,' he had said, he had jeered, 'frozen lily of virtue,' he had said, 'our languid lily of virtue nods perilously near the pit,' he had written, 'come away where the angels come down to earth.'[4]

The suggestion that she 'come away' with him was seen by H.D. as a 'flare' in the darkness. Lawrence had written this particular letter in the summer of 1916, after the Murrys had fled Higher Tregerthen and at a time when Aldington was having one of his affairs. H.D. returned to it repeatedly, obsessively; it was a turning point in her life. 'You said I was a living spirit,' she explains in *Bid Me to Live*, 'but I wasn't living until you wrote to me, "We will go away together."'[5] In reply to his suggestion, H.D. sent Lawrence what she called her 'Orpheus sequence' in which she explored the afterlife of her marriage. When Eurydice dies from a snake bite, Orpheus descends to the underworld to retrieve her and charms Hades with the music of his lyre. He can have his wife back, Hades says, on condition that she walk behind him through the caves into the upperworld; should he turn round to look at her she will be lost to him for ever. Unable to hear her footsteps, Orpheus turns round to look, and consigns Eurydice to perpetual night.

The sequence was originally written as a dialogue between husband and wife, but Lawrence told H.D. to stay with the 'woman vibration' and so it became Eurydice's own lament.

So you have swept me back,
I who could have walked with the live souls
above the earth,
I who could have slept among the live flowers
at last;

so for your arrogance
and your ruthlessness
I am swept back
where dead lichens drip
dead cinders upon moss of ash;

so for your arrogance
I am broken at last,
I who had lived unconscious,
who was almost forgot;

if you had let me wait
I had grown from listlessness
into peace,
if you had let me rest with the dead,
I had forgot you
and the past.

H.D. was a poet Lawrence 'feared and wondered over', and she offered him and Frieda her rooms, he said, 'with a wild free hand'.[6] The rooms consisted of a large first-floor bedsit with three French windows opening on to a balcony overlooking the square, and the temporary use of a top-floor bedroom with a dormer window which belonged to her friend John Cournos, a Ukrainian Jew known for his grey fedora hat, polka-dot ties, spats, gloves and walking stick. While Cournos was in Petrograd decoding Marconigrams for the British, he lent his bed to an American beauty called Dorothy Yorke with whom he had been in love for the last six years. His relationship with Dorothy, Cournos believed, was on the verge of becoming something, and he asked H.D. to look after her until his return. But when Aldington, away at Officers' Training Camp, came home for leave, he too fell for Dorothy Yorke, and so he and she now slept together on the top floor while H.D. slept alone downstairs. H.D. saw shapes and patterns everywhere, and this current rearrangement she compared to the 'concentric, geometric, exactly patterned circles of hell'.[7]

Cournos's rage at losing Dorothy Yorke was levelled not at Aldington but at H.D. herself who, he believed, had encouraged the situation because she thrived on *situations*. She later conceded his point. Terrified of again becoming pregnant, H.D. had stopped sleeping with her 'great, over-sexed officer' of a husband who in turn complained that his wife had, as he put it, 'no body'.[8] H.D.'s bodilessness, however, was part of her art. When Amy Lowell published, without permission, H.D.'s photograph in *Tendencies in Modern American Poetry*, H.D. was furious: 'It's not that picture, but any picture! The initials, "H.D.", had no identity attached; they could have been pure spirit. *But with this I'm embodied.*'[9]

Richard Aldington was back at camp when the Lawrences, Cornish mud still caked on their boots, arrived at Mecklenburgh Square. Lawrence now slept on the top floor, Dorothy Yorke shared the couch with Frieda, and H.D. had the campbed behind the Chinese screen. 'One seems to be, in some queer way, vitally active here,' Lawrence told Gray. 'And then, people, one or two, seem to give a strange new response.'[10] This new response came in the realisation that he, Frieda and H.D. could form what H.D. described as 'a perfect triangle'.[11] No sooner had Lawrence arrived than he announced that 'Frieda was there forever on his right hand, I was *there* for ever – on his left.' He duly passed on to H.D. the lapis lazuli paperweight given to him by Ottoline: 'I'm sick of the Ott,' he explained. 'She bores me.' Lawrence and Ottoline would not speak to one another again.[12]

The Lawrences brought their own situation to bear on H.D.'s situation. 'Frieda and I were alone together in the big room,' H.D. recalled of their first night together, when Frieda said 'that she had a friend, an older man who had told her that "if love is free, everything is free"'. Frieda went on to confide that 'Lawrence does not really care for women. He only cares for men. Hilda, *you have no idea what he is like.*'[13] It is all so believable: Frieda quoting Otto Gross, clearly still her guide and master, Lawrence's fantasy of having both women bathe his feet, Frieda's warning Hilda off with her *sotto voce* 'confidence' about her husband's sexuality. But H.D., her self-absorption having long perverted her judgement, understood Frieda to be encouraging rather than discouraging an affair between herself and Lawrence, on the grounds that Frieda herself would then, as she apparently explained, be 'free' for Cecil Gray: the Lawrences, H.D. insisted, had it 'all fixed up between them'. In which case the concentric circles which had become a triangle would turn into a square.[14]

This was a radical misreading of the Lawrences' game. Frieda, who considered herself free for Cecil Gray anyway, would never allow her husband to be similarly free and would certainly not pave the way for his relationship with a woman he had compared to Isis. But H.D. assumed that Lawrence was in love with her – why else would he tell her to 'kick over' her 'tiresome house of life' and accompany him to 'where the angels come down to earth'? The woman who interpreted her world through symbols was blind to Lawrence's own runes: he was suggesting by his imagery not that she leave the tiresome house of Aldington but that she reinvigorate her Shelleyan verse; her figures were as lifeless as the bird that never wert. When Lawrence talked about her 'frozen lily of virtue', it was not a reference to her marriage bed but a criticism of her symbolism: no living thing, least of all a lily, should be frozen. 'A waterlily', as Lawrence put it in 'The Poetry of the Present', 'heaves herself from the flood, looks around, gleams, and is gone.'[15]

H.D. later said that she envied the women who wrote memoirs of Lawrence as though they had found him 'some sort of guide or master', but this is what she did too.[16] *Bid Me to Live*, which she began in 1921 and worked over for the next forty years before it was published in

1960, is precisely about how Lawrence became her own 'guide'. She described *Bid Me to Live* as 'word for word' true, and when we consider her version of the truth we should remember that the novel was written on the advice of Freud, with whom H.D. had a three-month analysis in 1932. In order to 'break the clutch' on her memory, Freud suggested that she tell the tale of Lawrence 'straight, as history, no frills'.[17] Her story therefore reads like a session of psychoanalysis: the significance of gestures and phrases are returned to, anatomised, held up to the light; incidental events are considered in relation to the grand and eternal narratives, pattern is given precedence, the surface gives way to the symbols beneath. But, despite the Freudian overdetermination, Frieda and Lawrence sound exactly like Frieda and Lawrence ('shut-up, shut-up, shut-up, you damn Prussian, I don't want to hear anything you can tell me'), and H.D. herself blows around in the wind, her refusal of agency, like that of Frieda, creating the chaos in which she thrives – which is what John Cournos held against her. 'Homeless, they had found each other,' H.D. says of Lawrence's arrival at Mecklenburgh Square, and his 'cerebral contact' now 'renewed her'. She elevates and mystifies her relationship with Lawrence not, as one of H.D.'s biographers has suggested, because she was veiling the truth of their affair, but because she elevated and mystified people.

The central scene of *Bid Me to Live* positions all the players on the stage. It is the day after Lawrence's announcement that Frieda and H.D. will be for all eternity on his right and left sides; Frieda has gone shopping for 'old-time fags' with Dorothy Yorke, leaving Lawrence, unwell with a cold, alone with H.D. The writers start to write, Lawrence in the armchair with a notebook and pencil and H.D. on the other side of the room. She soon becomes aware of his gaze, and a magnetic track forms across the dim afternoon light. When she replayed the sequence of events, which she did for the rest of her life, she believed that she had been looking through the window at the branches of the plane tree, thinking about a poem, when he 'turned to look at her'. As though responding to 'a certain signal', H.D. rose and:

> moved toward him; she edged the small chair toward his chair.
> She sat at his elbow, a child waiting for instruction. Now was the
> moment to answer his amazing proposal of last night, his 'for all
> eternity'. She put out her hand. Her hand touched his sleeve. He

shivered, he seemed to move back, move away, like a hurt animal, there was something untamed, even the slight touch of her hand on his sleeve seemed to have annoyed him.

Last night he had 'blazed at her', but today 'only a touch on his arm made him shiver away, hurt, like a hurt jaguar'. Lawrence hated to be touched. Seconds later there were voices at the door as Frieda and Dorothy returned; H.D., her offending hand back on her lap, attended to their arrival and Lawrence, without looking up, continued to push his pencil along the pages of his notebook. 'She did not know, would she ever know, whether his gesture had been personal repugnance, some sort of *noli me tangere* (his own expression) or whether his over-subtle awareness had sensed this interruption.' Frieda came in laughing and now that she was back in the room, talking about 'this damn war' and puffing away on her smokes, Lawrence was once again moored. H.D. suddenly saw – 'she was astonished by the clarity of her perception' – a mask where his face had been: 'the eyes were wrinkled with his laughter, the eyes were drawn slant-wise up toward the ears'. Lawrence had turned from a pale man in an armchair to a satyr, and it was Frieda, H.D. understood, with her 'pre-war German distinction', who made the 'aura' around him.[18]

Having thought that he would save her from the death of her marriage, H.D. had been returned to Hades when Lawrence turned to look at her. She was back in her role of Eurydice, but she had also reconstructed the scene in *Women in Love* where Hermione and Birkin are similarly alone in a room and Hermione, pulled by some magnetic force, puts down her pen, picks up the lapis lazuli and makes her way over to Birkin.

Hilda Doolittle was born in 1886 in the Pennsylvanian town of Bethlehem; the name of her birthplace was one of the reasons why Lawrence was drawn to her. Her father was an astronomer, and she was fifteen when she met the sixteen-year-old Ezra Pound at a Halloween party. Pound was what William Carlos Williams described as a 'physical phenomenon' while Hilda, Williams said, had the impatience of 'a wild animal'.[19] She was a strikingly beautiful creature, six feet tall and slender as a reed with a high forehead and cheekbones. When she was nineteen, Hilda and Pound became engaged; three years later he went to England and by the time she joined him in 1911, he had fallen in love with

Dorothy Shakespear. Losing her men to women called Dorothy became one of Hilda's patterns. In 1912 she and Pound were having tea in the British Museum when she showed him three of her poems, 'Epigram', 'Hermes of the Ways' and 'Priapus'. 'But', he told her, 'this is poetry,' and he wrote 'H.D. Imagiste' at the bottom of the page. Thus was born her nom de plume. H.D.'s voice, Pound told Harriet Monroe at *Poetry* magazine (for which he was the British agent), had 'the laconic speech of the Imagistes ... Objective – no slither; direct – no excessive use of adjectives, no metaphors that won't permit examination. It's straight talk, straight as the Greek!'[20]

Pound was a troubadour in a purple hat, green shirt and black velvet jacket but Aldington, whom H.D. married in 1913, was as conventionally English, she said, as a side of roast beef. Their union mirrored that of Katherine Mansfield and Murry. In each case a brilliant and bisexual expatriate woman attached herself to a handsome and priapic intellectual opportunist who would make a career out of knowing Lawrence. Murry and Lawrence had at least been friends, but Aldington, who met Lawrence on no more than a handful of occasions and never liked him, became the self-appointed guide to his life and work. While Lawrence had nothing much to say about Aldington, Aldington was incontinent on the subject of Lawrence. In addition to his two memoirs, *D. H. Lawrence: An Indiscretion* and *D. H. Lawrence: An Appreciation*, he produced an off-hand biography subtitled *Portrait of a Genius, But...* edited his personal selections of Lawrence's poetry and essays, compiled an edition of Lawrence's letters, an anthology of his travel writing and a bibliography of his works, wrote essays on Lawrence in journals and provided opinionated introductions to fourteen of his paperback editions. He also destroyed Lawrence's letters to his wife, H.D., and says nothing, in *Portrait of a Genius, But...*, about the subject's six-week stay in his own home, a stay that would alter the direction of H.D.'s life. It is in the biographer's remit to edit those facts that don't fit, but what are we to make of this sudden silence in the unstoppable flow of Aldington's authority? He clearly agreed with H.D. that Lawrence was in love with her. After all, why would Lawrence want a fat German Christmas pudding who was always mocking him when he could have a thin American goddess who took him entirely seriously?

H.D. and Lawrence were, as Katherine Mansfield might have said, '*unthinkably* alike' and he was right to fear her poetry. H.D. was a great poet with a strong and spectral voice, *but* ... the self-fascination of her prose suggests something of what it was like to know her. Her determination to turn everyone into a classical type was irritating, and Lawrence found it excessively so. She wrote not to explore herself but to come into that self through symbols and situations, every situation symbolic of another, so while there was no other woman like H.D., H.D. was also every woman who had ever been wounded. Aldington, with his 'Roman head', was sometimes the Marble Faun and sometimes Dionysus, and Lawrence had 'an Orpheus head, severed from its body'. 'You jeered at my making abstractions of people,' she says to Lawrence in *Bid Me to Live*, '– graven images, you called them. You are right. [Aldington] is not the Marble Faun, not even a second-rate Dionysus ... you are right. He is not Dionysus, you are not Orpheus. You are human people, Englishmen, madmen.'[21]

Obsessed with connections and coincidences, H.D. found in Lawrence plenty to keep her occupied: the mirroring of their initials, for one thing, and for another the accident of their birthdays – he was born on 11 September 1885 and she was born on 10 September 1886, which meant that for one day of the year they were 'twinned'. She later accidentally 'substituted' her father's birthday for the day on which Lawrence died, and when she first met Freud, his smile and his beard reminded her of Lawrence. Because her mother was Moravian, Aldington thought that H.D. and Lawrence recognised in one another their Puritan stock. 'Of course, behind both is the ancient Norse-Teuton-Saxon strain, hating big cities, and crazy about ideal little "communities".'[22] One of their schemes was to form a community in the Andes together with the unlikely combination of Cecil Gray, William Henry Hocking and Dorothy Yorke.

But Cecil Gray, who hated the idea of being stuck on a snowy mountain with Lawrence and Frieda, had now read *Look! We Have Come Through!* – which was published in November 1917 – and accused Lawrence of lying about the state of his marriage. 'Look,' Lawrence defensively replied, 'we have come through – whether you can see it or not.'[23] Warming to his subject, Gray, having also heard from Frieda about H.D.'s hero-worship, reprimanded Lawrence for surrounding himself with 'unproud, subservient, cringing' women, to which Lawrence responded that such women represent 'a new world, or underworld, of knowledge and being'. This 'ecstatic subtly-intellectual underworld', which was 'like the Greeks – Orphicism – like Magdalene at her feet-washing', stood in contrast to what Lawrence now described as the 'emotional sensuous underworld' of Frieda and Gray, which was 'an underworld which is forever an underworld, never to be made whole or open'.[24]

The suspicion with which Lawrence and Frieda were treated by the authorities continued in London, where they were required to report to the local constabulary and bothered by policemen lurking in the stairwell and outside the building. Much of Lawrence's time in Mecklenburgh Square was spent on a scheme to get *Women in Love* published in a private edition, but he also began here another novel with the symbolic title of *Aaron's Rod*. He had no grand vision for this book – all grand visions had been wasted on *The Rainbow* and *Women in Love* – and so what he wrote was simply a summing-up of present circumstances. The hero, Aaron Sissons, works at a Midlands colliery but is also a musician (his flute is his 'rod'). He sees the world in terms of music: the sloping street, with its pattern of lighted windows and dark outhouses, looks like a piano keyboard, or a 'succession of musical notes'.[25] When he sits in the pub he reflects on his 'secret malady', which is a 'strained, unacknowledged opposition to his surroundings, a hard core of irrational, exhausting withholding of himself'.[26] Aldington, H.D. and Dorothy Yorke appear in the form of a party of upper-class revellers in the local big house: Aldington is Robert Cunningham, 'a fresh, stoutish young Englishman in khaki', H.D. is his wife Julia, 'a tall stag of a thing … hunched up like a witch', and Dorothy is 'a cameo-like girl' who is called Josephine Hay on page 37 and Josephine Ford on page 38. Cecil Gray – who visited Mecklenburgh Square that autumn – is cast as Cyril Scott, 'a fair, pale, fattish young fellow in pince-nez and dark clothes'.[27] Cunningham drinks red wine by the throatful, Cyril Scott silently absorbs gin and water, and Julia, sucking on cigarettes, monitors the sexual tension between her husband and Josephine while keeping Cyril Scott in tow.

Lawrence's celebration of marriage being over, Aaron's adventure begins when he leaves his wife and children and takes his flute to London. Here he meets a man called Lilly who comes from the same district and the same class: 'Each might have been born into the other's circumstance.' Like the biblical Jonathan and David, Aaron and Lilly have 'an almost uncanny understanding of one another'[28] and form a bifurcated version of Lawrence himself, the kind of fractured self who appears in a dream. When Lawrence reached this point, the novel ground to a halt. He said it was because he found people boring and you can't have fiction without people, but it was also because he found plot boring and he couldn't have fiction without forward movement. Having no idea what Aaron would do next, he left him with Lilly in London and put the novel aside.

Aldington was coming home for Christmas and so on 30 November, the Lawrences moved again, this time perching for two weeks in 'a bourgeois little flat' in Earl's Court owned by Cecil Gray's mother. They returned to Mecklenburgh Square for a party where Lawrence now cast them all in a reconstruction of The Fall. Aldington and Dorothy were Adam and Eve, H.D. was the dancing Tree of Life, Gray was the Angel at the Gate, Frieda, slithering along the carpet, was the serpent, and Lawrence, leaning against the fireplace, was 'Gawd Almighty'. She and Gray, Lawrence now told H.D., were 'made for one another', which H.D. of course took as divine intervention, and so she created another pattern.

She later understood what Lawrence had meant by throwing her into Gray's arms: Gray 'was conditioned, like herself, to some special way of feeling. He felt as she did, more like a bird or a fish.'[29] H.D. and Gray now slept on the downstairs couch while Aldington and Dorothy slept together upstairs, and when Gray returned to Cornwall in the new year, he invited H.D. to visit him. Lawrence, hearing the news, came back to Mecklenburgh Square in February 1918 to explain that he was 'not happy' about this development. Rather than staying in Bosigran Castle, he suggested that H.D. use Higher Tregerthen instead, from where she and Gray might visit one another. Assuming that he was jealous, H.D. saw Lawrence as 'Dis of the under-world, the husband of Persephone. Yes, he was her husband.'[30] But Lawrence was continually pressing Higher Tregerthen on people, including Virginia and Leonard Woolf, in order to cover the rent which had been paid for a year in advance.

As for Cecil Gray, he had become another bug sucking at Lawrence's life. 'I don't know why you and I don't get on very well when we are together,' Lawrence now told him.

> But it seems we don't. It seems we are best apart. You seem to go winding on in some kind sort of process which just winds me in the

other direction. You might just tell me when you think your process is ended, and we'll look at each other again. Meanwhile you dance on in some sort of sensuous dervish dance that winds my brain up like a ticking bomb. God save us, what a business it is even to be acquainted with another creature.[31]

The Lawrences were again wanderers, taking refuge where it was offered, and for the first six months of 1918 they stayed in Dollie Radford's cottage in the village of Hermitage, near Newbury in Berkshire. Here, between a wood and a railway, they reached the fag-end of their poverty. Lawrence, in shoes without socks, was down to one set of clothes – a green- and red-striped blazer and a pair of grey flannel trousers. Because he washed them every night, the sleeves of his blazer and the hems of his trousers had shrunk so that his wrists and ankles protruded.

On the Western Front, 70,000 American troops had now been hospitalised with the Spanish flu, a third of whom lost their lives. The virus had spread to Germany, killing 400,000 civilians, and then to Britain where it would eventually kill 228,000. The British Prime Minister, David Lloyd George, was infected; so too were the American President, the German Kaiser, Kemal Atatürk, the King of Spain and Mahatma Gandhi. The worst epidemic since the outbreak of cholera in 1849, people were dropping in the streets gasping for air, cities were sprayed with chemicals, and the white anti-germ mouth mask became as familiar a garment as a hat or coat. Because porridge was thought to protect you, Lawrence and Frieda lived on porridge; because cigarette fumes were thought to kill the virus, Frieda increased her smoking.

Meanwhile, in March, H.D. arrived in Cornwall, where she had followed Lawrence. The final section of *Bid Me to Live*, written in the pages of a notebook bought from the Zennor post office, is addressed to Lawrence directly as though he had cast a spell on her. 'This notebook is a replica of the one you were writing in that day' – that day being the one when he turned to look at her in Mecklenburgh Square.[32] Cornwall was just as he had said: 'It was not England', it was 'out of the world, a country of rock and steep cliff and sea-gulls'.[33] She walked the path that he had walked, which had also been walked by Phoenician traders, and she wondered if the Druid sun circle that she had admired was the same Druid sun circle Lawrence had told her about. To the right of Bosigran Castle, down the 'crest of the stony hill', was Higher Tregerthen. H.D. went there too but the door was locked; she saw through the windows Lawrence's bookshelves and blue and orange cushions: 'Perhaps you would say I was trespassing,' she wrote.[34] She discovered on the moor a leaf that looked like parsley and decided to send it to Lawrence to identify, because Cecil didn't know his plants. The room in which she now sat with her notebook had been painted by Lawrence, who had also chosen the lamp and the chairs. He had once told her that Bosigran Castle was haunted, but the knockers 'were not', she said, 'ghostly presences' because 'they knocked forcibly, almost violently, and often'.[35] Once the wind flicked aside the curtain so that the candle flashed a code to the ships; Gray fixed the curtain in place with a pile of books. 'We don't want to be kicked out,' he said. So H.D. and Lawrence had after all 'gone away together. I realise your genius, in this place.' Possessed as she was by Lawrence, it is small wonder that Gray felt unappreciated: 'You do not pretend to love me any more than you do,' he wrote to H.D. that March. '… Why are you so elusive, so unapproachable?'[36]

'Somewhere, somehow,' H.D. insisted, 'a pattern repeated itself … All this was meant to happen.'[37] Lawrence, the medium between herself and Gray, had sent her 'a flare'; 'they cannot stop you signalling', she wrote.[38] He had drawn her to this country where everything had a meaning: the path was 'a hieroglyph. It spelt something,' the damp sleeve of her coat 'was another story of a fleece'; Lawrence had called her Isis and there, on the mantelpiece, were statues of Osiris, the murdered Egyptian king, and Isis, his sister-bride; Freud would have similar statues in his study in Vienna. Whenever the self-absorption of H.D.'s pattern-finding threatens to suck the life from her prose, the sharpness of an image – such as the wind lifting 'a very visible dark wing from the sea' – slaps the sentence awake.[39]

'I have not seen Hilda for some time,' Lawrence shrugged in June, 'but believe she is happy in Cornwall – as far as it is possible to be happy, with the world as it is.'[40] The Lawrences had now moved to Mountain Cottage, near Wirksworth in Derbyshire. He was back home in the navel of England, the land of iron and coal, and feeling 'very lost … and exiled'. The house, paid for by Lawrence's sister Ada, stood on 'the rim of a steep deep valley, looking over darkish, folded hills', and he felt as though he were 'on a sort of ledge half-way down a precipice, and didn't know how to get up or down'.[41] He accepted an offer of £50 from Oxford University Press to write a history textbook because so long as his novels were untouchable, textbooks would have to do. The original title was *Landmarks in European History* but he changed *Landmarks* to *Movements* because movement, at this moment in European history, was impossible. And because of the scandal still attached to his name, he agreed with his editor that he should publish the book – not least because it was for children – under a pseudonym, and he chose Lawrence H. Davison. The voice, however, is unmistakably D. H. Lawrence. *Movements in European History* bears scant relation to the usual dry feed supplied to classrooms. It might be said to bear scant relation to European history in general, resembling more a covert autobiography or a collection of vivid short stories called 'Rome', 'Christianity', 'The Germans' and so forth. The past, Lawrence told the schoolchildren, was the warring of opposites: 'the passion of fighting and violence, and the passion for blissful holiness'.[42] Looking down from his own window on to the wild hills, he now gave, for the first and final time, his interpretation of the *Divine Comedy*: the poem was Dante's version of the passing of the old, familiar, cruel world into an abstract future in which he had no place. In the book's epilogue Lawrence universalised his own psychology:

> Every man has two selves, among his manifold Self. He has a herd-self, which is vulgar, common, ugly, like the voice of the man in the crowd. And he has a better self, which is quiet and slow, and which is most of the time puzzled. From his better self, he is almost dumb. From his herd-self, he shouts and yells and rants.[43]

The final horror of Lawrence's war occurred on his thirty-third birthday, the 'sacred' age when Christ had died. He was told to attend another medical examination, this time in a schoolhouse in Derby where, with 'an indescribable tone of jeering, gibing shamelessness', he and the other men, including a large, shy collier, were told to strip naked and wait on benches until it came their turn to be weighed and measured. While the officials traded jokes across the room, a young medic put his hand between Lawrence's legs to cup his genitals, and Lawrence felt his 'eyes going black'. He bent over while the medic inspected his anus, jesting all the while. Lawrence vowed that day that he would never be touched again, and never again be at 'the disposal of society'.[44]

An armistice was declared on 11 November, and Lawrence – briefly in London – spent the night singing German songs. David Garnett described him as 'ill and unhappy, with no trace of that gay sparkling love of life in his eyes which had been his most attractive feature six years before'. There was nothing to celebrate, Lawrence prophesied, because 'the war was not over, since hate and evil had become stronger than ever; so it would soon break out once more'.[45] Eight million soldiers had died in combat; six million civilians had died through war-related privations. That same month the *English Review* ran the first of five of his essays on classic American literature, and Lawrence saw Aldington, who was 'very fit'. He also saw Hilda who was, Lawrence now learned, six months pregnant. The father of the child was not Aldington but Cecil Gray, who had since abandoned her, as Lawrence now did too. 'I hope never to see you again,' he wrote in the last of the burning letters that H.D. would ever receive from him.[46]

It is tempting to apply her own levels of scrutiny to Lawrence's final words. Had he indeed been in love with H.D., and *was* he jealous of Gray? Did he still expect her to be there on his left-hand side and Frieda on his right? 'Poor Hilda,' he said in December. 'Feeling sorry for her, one almost melts. But I *don't* trust her.'[47] If Lawrence felt betrayed, was that betrayal spiritual, sexual, emotional or artistic? Biographers have found various hidden meanings to this tale; Janice Robinson boldly suggests that the child was Lawrence's and that H.D. and Aldington covered the tracks. But this is wide of the mark, not least because H.D. became pregnant in Cornwall when Lawrence was hundreds of miles away and forbidden from entering the county, but also because Lawrence, if not completely impotent, was almost certainly infertile, which realisation must have added to his sexual anxieties. His violent reaction to H.D.'s pregnancy was entirely in keeping with his character. Lawrence was jealous not of Gray but of the baby: nothing was guaranteed more to inspire his jealousy than the love between mother and child. His reaction was also in keeping with his naivety: Cecil Gray was supposed to be an anchorite monk and H.D. a blithe spirit. Despite Lawrence's marriage, the whole question of sex still had for him 'the fascination of horror', and the only conception allowed for a woman from Bethlehem was the immaculate sort. Lawrence had believed in the bodilessness of Hilda Aldington, but she was now all too evidently embodied.

By the end of November he was safely back in his fortress on the ledge, but this time alone because Frieda had gone to Hermitage after one of their fights. 'The wind is getting-up,' Lawrence wrote to Katherine Mansfield, who was in bed with TB. 'This place is a wind-centre, I warn you.'[48] He offered to send her his latest story, 'The Fox', set in post-war, influenza-ravaged Cornwall. A fox has been raiding the hen-roost of an isolated farm run by two women called Banford and March. One day March sees him and he sees her. 'He knew her. She was spellbound.' Soon afterwards a young man with blue eyes called Henry also appears at the farm and March is again spellbound: Henry *was* the fox 'and she could not see him otherwise'.

Between Christmas 1918 and April 1919, Lawrence was ill with the flu. 'A putrid disease,' he told his Scottish friend Catherine Carswell on the last day of February; 'I have never been so down in the mud in all my life.'[49] He was bed-bound for much of the time, occasionally taking walks which only weakened him more. Between fifty and a hundred million people died of the same virus, and so Lawrence's survival – which Frieda put down to sheer willpower – is something of a miracle. H.D.'s daughter was born on the last day of March. She called the baby Perdita – the lost one – after the child in *The Winter's Tale* who is born in prison because her father, King Leontes, wrongly believed that the queen had betrayed him. When, in late April, Lawrence was well enough to move, he and Frieda left Mountain Cottage. Black clouds sank over the Derbyshire hills, blotting out the dawn; he watched from the window as the thunderstorm broke and 'hail lashed down with a noise like insanity ... "Come hail, come rain"'. He would leave this country, he decided, 'forever'.[50]

Six months later we find him alone in London, Frieda having gone to Germany to visit her mother and sisters. Aldington, who saw him in Kot's flat, thought he seemed 'not to care' if he never saw Frieda again. Hunched up in a chair by the gas fire, a convenience he particularly despised, Lawrence 'was in a peculiar mood', Aldington recalled, 'which I thought at first was due to the indecency of a gas fire. But no, it went much deeper than that ... He was literally "satirical", like a wild half-trapped creature, a satyr desperately fighting to get free.' The two men walked together through the West End as the theatres were emptying,

Lawrence's red beard creating a 'sudden little whirlpool of mob hostility'. Aldington thought he cut a pitiful figure: 'There was no place for him in that rather sinister, post-war world. Either he must escape from it or it would crush him. He had to go into the wilderness or perish, cease to be the unique thing he was.'[51]

Lawrence finally left England on 13 November 1919, the fourth anniversary of the destruction of *The Rainbow* and the year that saw the births of the German Nazi Party, the Italian Fascist Party and the Irish Free State. The air was bitterly cold when he said goodbye to his country, and Catherine Carswell, who saw him off at Charing Cross, gave him a present of a camel-hair coat-lining. Through the window of the train the snow on the Downs hung like a shroud, and from the stern of the boat from Folkestone to Boulogne, England looked like 'a grey, dreary grey coffin sinking in the sea behind, with her dead grey cliffs, and the white, worn-out cloth of snow above'.[52]

He was flying south for winter. Like Aristotle, Lawrence believed that moving south was moving up, nearer to the sun.

# Purgatory

*The Divine Comedy*, fresco by Domenico di Michelino

# Part One

*On a dark, wet, wintry evening in November 1919 I arrived in Florence, having just got back to Italy for the first time since 1914.*

D. H. Lawrence, *Memoir of Maurice Magnus*

His boat docked in Boulogne on the evening of 13 November and Lawrence crawled by train across France, arriving in Italy two days later. Before the war, border crossings had been liberating but since 1915, when the passport photo became a fixture on the travel scene, the innocence of movement was lost. Passport photos, in which everyone looks like a criminal, turned frontiers into places of ritual trepidation and Lawrence's newly endorsed mugshot was a reminder that he was a creature of the state.

The station forecourt at Turin was filled with soldiers and a familiar, pre-war swagger. Lawrence took a cab and headed towards Val Salice, ten minutes outside the city, where he had arranged to stay with a philanthropical shipbuilder called Sir Walter Becker, a friend of a friend, who owned a villa inside a gated park. Knighted only three weeks earlier, Sir Walter, Lawrence told Cynthia Asquith, was a 'C.B – O.B.M or O.B something – *parvenu*, etc'. Dinner having begun, he waited in the well-appointed hall. 'It was spacious, comfortable and warm; but somewhat pretentious; rather like the imposing hall into which the heroine suddenly enters on the film.'[1] Lawrence would often compare his experience of Italy to scenes in a film, a medium he was fascinated by but claimed to dislike because, he felt, the camera turned bodies into an abstraction. An extra place was laid at the table for the guest – the only man not in a dinner jacket – who then goaded his host in 'a sincere half-mocking argument' where Sir Walter stood up 'for security and bank-balance and power, I for naked liberty. In the end, he rested safe on his bank balance, I in my nakedness. We hated each other – but with respect.'[2]

After two nights he left Turin, and to thank the Beckers he sent them a gift of *Twilight in Italy*, the product of his pre-war Italian excursion, which Sir Walter thought 'a very good book, although I do not see why he named it thus', and *Sons and Lovers*, 'which', Sir Walter confessed, 'left as it were a bad taste in my mouth'.[3] Lawrence then returned to Lerici, but it was no longer the same so he kept going south. 'The South! The South, The South! Let me go south – I must go south,' he wrote to Cynthia Asquith.[4] In the south, he reasoned, 'the past is so much stronger than the present, that one seems remote like the immortals, looking back at the world from their otherworld'.[5]

Florence was 'strange to me', Lawrence recalled, 'seemed grim and dark and rather awful on the cold November evening'.[6] He arrived on Wednesday 19 November, and headed from the station to the heart of the city. The Arno was rushing like 'a mass of *café au lait*'[7] and hooded carriages clattered over the bridges, the drivers crouching on their box seats beneath shiny umbrellas. It was a city of umbrellas. A pair of bullocks beneath a green umbrella shambled into a trot as the whip-thong flickered between their shanks and, further on, two men, arm in arm beneath another umbrella, made their nimble way. Even the bats, he wrote in his poem 'Bat', had wings 'like bits of umbrella'.

Lawrence had written in advance to Norman Douglas to find him a cheap room, and sure enough there was a note from Douglas waiting at Thomas Cook's in the Via Tornabuoni, giving the name of a *pensione*. Douglas 'has never', said Lawrence, 'left me in the lurch'.[8] They knew one another from the *English Review* where Douglas had been assistant editor and he had invited the Lawrences to a luncheon to celebrate their marriage. Frieda liked Douglas because he spoke to her in German, but the two men were natural enemies, which pleased them both. Douglas, according to Lawrence, was a sybarite with a 'wicked red face and tufted eyebrows',[9] and Lawrence, according to Douglas, was 'peevish and frothy',[10] an 'inspired provincial' with a 'shuddering horror' of nakedness. 'I don't like it! I don't like it! I don't like it!' he recalled Lawrence squealing when he saw Florentine boys in shorts. 'Why can't they wear trousers?'[11] Lawrence and Douglas also had a good deal in common: each was in search of a lost civilisation, each at his best around birds, beasts and flowers, and each a capricious and dangerous friend.

Norman Douglas

Maurice Magnus

Muffled in his coat, the beard now bushier and even more ragged, Lawrence made his way down the Lungarno, Douglas's note in his pocket. It was the hour when, under the arches of the Ponte Vecchio, the swallows and bats change guard. He had passed the bridge and was watching the night fall on the swollen river when he saw two men approaching, one tall and portly, the other short and strutting, with 'a touch of down-on-his-luck' about them both.[12] They might have been Mephistopheles and Faust or Laurel and Hardy: both were 'buttoned up in their overcoats', Lawrence noted, and wearing 'curly little hats'. For every one of the tall man's strides, the short man took five little struts. 'Isn't that Lawrence?' boomed Douglas – for it was he – the voice florid and grandiose. 'Why of course it is, of course it is, beard and all! Well how are you, eh? You got my note? Well now, my dear boy, you just go to the [Balestri] – straight ahead, straight ahead – you've got the number. There's a room there for you. We shall be there in half an hour. Oh, let me introduce you to Magnus –'[13]

So it was at the spot where Dante first spoke to Beatrice that Lawrence first spoke to Maurice Magnus, and the irony was not lost on him. Dante had loved Beatrice from afar for nine years when, walking with her companions on a May morning in 1283, she greeted him by the Ponte Vecchio. Nor would the other legends of the Ponte Vecchio have escaped Lawrence's notice. A stone inscription at the entrance to the bridge, one of thirty plaques in Florence quoting lines from the *Divine Comedy*, records the spot where on Easter morning 1216, Buondelmonte de' Buondelmonti was murdered on his way to his wedding, thus initiating the feud between the Guelphs and the Ghibellines which led to Dante's exile. Florence was the cradle of European banking, and it was on the Ponte Vecchio that the concept of bankruptcy was said to have originated, after soldiers broke ('rotto') the benches ('banco)' of those merchants unable to pay their debts.

'First let me give an exact account of my experience with Magnus.' The opening line of his *Memoir of Maurice Magnus* had the terse efficiency of an affidavit, so Lawrence cancelled it and began again. 'One dark, wet, wintry evening in November 1919 I arrived in Florence, coming from Spezia.' Nor would this do. He crossed through the first word and the last three: 'On a dark, wet, wintry evening in November, 1919,' he now wrote, 'I arrived in Florence, having just got back to Italy for the first time since 1914.' Lawrence's final draft catches him on the wing, landing in Dante's birthplace as if from nowhere. It has been five years since he was last in this country: now it is a dark, wet, wintry evening; then it was twilight in Italy.

When he reworked the beginning of the *Memoir of Maurice Magnus*, it became a piece of writing, and the 'best single piece of writing, *as writing*', he believed, that he had ever done.[14] But it is still an 'exact account' of the facts. The *Memoir* contained, Lawrence explained to his American agent, Robert Mountsier, 'just literal truth, so when you've read it you'll know all there is to know'.[15] At the same time, however, as providing an exact account of his encounter with Magnus – in the form of a breakdown of meals consumed, monies exchanged and islands visited – the *Memoir* reveals almost nothing about the peculiar nature of their relationship or why, as Frieda put it, Maurice Magnus left Lawrence feeling so 'deeply disturbed'.[16] The only truths we learn are these: that Lawrence and Magnus spent, altogether, no more than two weeks in one another's company, that Magnus had a habit of turning up unexpectedly and bleeding money out of Lawrence, and that Lawrence felt he owed Magnus a debt. The question raised by the *Memoir of Maurice Magnus* is the complex nature of that debt.

The *Memoir* was begun in the Sicilian hilltop town of Taormina in November 1921 and completed in January 1922, the year of *Ulysses*, *The Waste Land*, *Jacob's Room* and C. K. Scott Moncrieff's translation of the first volume of *À la recherche du temps perdu*. It was, 'after all', wrote Ezra Pound to T. S. Eliot, 'a grrrreat litttttterary period'.[17] Willa Cather called it the year 'the world broke in two',[18] and Lawrence's ambivalence about that break is the defining feature of the *Memoir of Maurice Magnus*. The events he describes had taken place two years before but Lawrence's recall needed no correction: apart from revising his opening line and rethinking some later sentences, his sixty handwritten pages are as neat and unblotted as the work of a medieval scribe.

It is not an easy text to categorise. Mark Kinkead-Weekes describes the *Memoir* as 'Lawrence's one attempt at biography', but it is a good deal more complex than this.[19] It was written as an introduction to a memoir by Maurice Magnus himself, initially called *Dregs: Experiences of an American in the French Foreign Legion*, but to preserve his subject's anonymity Lawrence referred to Magnus throughout as 'M—', while Douglas is referred to as 'D—'. When Magnus's book was published in 1924, Lawrence's carefully chosen title was replaced, with bland imprecision, by the heading 'Introduction', while *Dregs*, the title carefully chosen by Magnus, was replaced with the less flavoursome *Memoirs of the Foreign Legion*. It was Lawrence's name alone that appeared on the cover, which read: *Memoirs of the Foreign Legion by M.M., with an Introduction by D. H. Lawrence*. Lawrence's introduction to Magnus's strange story was, his critics agree, the best single piece of writing *as writing* that he had ever done – which means that D. H. Lawrence's best single piece of writing is an unclassifiable document virtually unknown to the majority of his readers. This is because until recently the *Memoir of Maurice Magnus* has been hard to find. Having nothing to add to the cult of the priest of love, it soon went out of print, and by the time the priest himself became unfashionable, Lawrence's *Memoir* had fallen into the oubliette of extinct books. And because no one has reprinted Magnus's *Memoirs of the Foreign Legion*, Lawrence's introduction is in the curious position of having survived, or rather of having destroyed, the book whose purpose it was to promote.

His subject in the *Memoir* is, among other things, conflict, and Lawrence's response to Magnus was, as ever, conflicted. He liked Magnus, he hated Magnus, he was attracted to Magnus, he was repelled by Magnus, he pursued Magnus and was pursued by Magnus, he was kind to Magnus, he was cruel to Magnus, Magnus was a hero, Magnus was a villain, Magnus was a clown. While Magnus took on a great many meanings for Lawrence, Lawrence meant nothing at all to Magnus, which reversed the usual pattern for both men.

Between 1920 and 1923, Magnus turned up in Lawrence's writing much as he turned up in his life: suddenly, and in the unlikeliest of places. Cast as a minor character – that most offensive of roles – Magnus is affable Mr May in *The Lost Girl*, Lawrence's least angry and most amused novel, bumbling Mr Mee in the women-fearing *Aaron's Rod*, the mosquito in *Birds, Beasts and Flowers* ('Queer, what a big stain my sucked blood makes / Beside the infinitesimal faint smear of you!'), and Bibbles the 'snub-nosed bitch' who appropriated Lawrence in Taos, 'As Benjamin Franklin appropriated Providence to his purposes'. In his poetry, Lawrence depicted Magnus as a parasitical beast, and in his prose, he compared him to a round-bellied bird whose jaunty tail sticks out, just a little, behind. In his pursuit of Paradise, however, Maurice Magnus took on a major role: replacing Shelley as Lawrence's guide, he led the pilgrim up the mountain of Purgatory.

Fresh-faced and twinkly-eyed by the Ponte Vecchio, his soft brown hair greying at the temples, Maurice Magnus was, Lawrence stressed, 'just the kind of man I had never met: little smart man of the shabby world'.[20] The name itself was arresting: 'Maurice' was the eponymous hero of Forster's unpublished novel and Magnus, Latin for 'great', was a name with freight. It was carried by Christian saints, German dukes, the medieval kings of Norway and Sweden, and Lawrence was endlessly amused by the contrast between the little man and his magnificent moniker. To preserve his subject's anonymity, Lawrence considered changing his name to Gross but Magnus, who seemed 'about forty' and was 'common' like 'an actor-manager', could not have been less like Lawrence's Austrian doppelgänger.[21] Lawrence's portrayals of Magnus recall the busy little melancholics in Edward Lear's menagerie, creatures like the Scroobius Pip who sang with a chippetty flip or the Jumblies who sailed away in a sieve. Magnus in turn assessed the stick-thin and threadbare Lawrence: he 'eyed me in that shrewd and rather impertinent way of the world of actor managers: cosmopolitan, knocking shabbily around the world'. Having weighed him up, Magnus 'greeted me in a rather fastidious voice, and a little patronisingly'.

'How much does it cost?' I asked Douglas, meaning the room.

'Oh, my dear fellow, a trifle. Ten francs a day. Third rate, tenth rate, but not bad at the price. Pension terms of course – everything included – except wine.'

'Oh no, not at all bad for the money,' said Magnus. 'Well now, shall we be moving?'[22]

Cherubic Magnus, his little legs 'perching' behind him, and demonic Douglas with his tufted eyebrows, were on their way to the post office. Magnus knew a shortcut. He 'knew', wrote Lawrence, 'all the short cuts of Florence. Afterwards I found that he knew all the short cuts in all the big towns of Europe.'[23] Lawrence, meanwhile, continued to the *pensione* on the Piazza Mentana, five minutes from the house in which Dante was born.

The *pensione* was a vast mausoleum with lonely corridors and over-large furniture, but Lawrence 'didn't care. The adventure of being back in Florence again after the years of war made one indifferent', and he preferred dark, uncosy dreariness to the film-star glitz of Sir Walter's centrally heated mansion.[24] In the *Memoir of Maurice Magnus*, Lawrence described his room on the third floor of the Balestri as 'stone-comfortless'; in his letters home he called it 'nice'. Unlike Lucy Honeychurch in Forster's *A Room with a View*, Lawrence was given a south-facing room looking over the Arno, which was like being 'in a castle with the drawbridge drawn up'.[25]

All travel, for Lawrence, was time-travel, an escape from the tawdriness of the present into what he called the 'strange, vast, terrifying reality of the past'.[26] The Florence his window looked down on was not a city divided between socialists and fascists but the late medieval Republic, crucible of the Renaissance; the present Italian conflict, Lawrence said, recalled that of the Guelphs and the Ghibellines. To see Italy as Lawrence saw it in 1919, we must return to *Movements in European History*, the proofs of which he was still waiting to receive.

His aim in the book, Lawrence H. Davison had explained in the 'Introduction to Teachers', was to give schoolchildren 'some impression of the great, surging movements which rose in the hearts of men in Europe, sweeping human beings together into one great concerted action, or sweeping them apart for ever on the tides of opposition'. One way of showing the effect of such movements was to compare them to earthquakes, or what Lawrence called 'disasters from without': earthquakes 'should be predictable. Yet no one can predict them.'[27] The most remarkable of these earthquakes was the Renaissance, which 'offered to man visions, beautiful adventures, marvellous thoughts', as if his soul were 'set free into all the air and space and splendour of free, pure thought and deep understanding'.[28] In the Middle Ages, 'man was alive, but blind and voracious. In the fourteenth and fifteenth centuries, however, he awoke. The human spirit was then like a butterfly which bursts from the chrysalis into the air. A whole new world lies about it.'[29] This world, which Dante saw in its larval form, was by the late fifteenth century presided over by Lorenzo the Magnificent, poet, despot and patron of Michelangelo. Under the Medici, Florence turned into a brothel: new money flowed in, women bared their breasts, pagan pleasures replaced Christian piety. Then into Lorenzo's court came Savonarola, the fox whose 'bright eyes burned'.

In one of the most dramatic moments of *Movements in European History*, Lawrence imagines Lorenzo on his deathbed:

> When Lorenzo was dying, in 1492, Savonarola was his confessor.
> The dark, fanatic monk bent over the dark, subtle Lorenzo, who
> was so wise in his wisdom of the world and the ages … 'Wilt thou
> restore Florence to liberty, and to the enjoyment of her popular
> government as a free commonwealth?' sternly said the fanatic friar.
> Lorenzo turned his dying face away, as if weary at this question, and
> said no more.[30]

It is a scene worthy of Baron Corvo's *Hadrian VII*. When Lorenzo was dead, the Medici fled Florence and the city fell under the Savonarola's spell. A 'strange change' then took place: 'After all the games and sports and carnivals of Medici days, men became desperately religious. The city looked suddenly grey, for none wore bright clothes any more.' The cultured Florentines 'ceased to be human men and women' and became 'like frenzied demons. Truth, beauty, happiness, wisdom, these meant nothing to such fanatics. They wanted magical violence and wonderful horrors.' A Bonfire of Vanities, sixty feet high, its tiers like the branches of a Christmas tree, was constructed in the Piazza della Signoria, in front of the Palazzo Vecchio. Here the fanatical Florentines, in white robes with olive wreaths around their heads, flung their gaming tables, books of poetry, fans and perfumes and priceless pictures. Botticelli, now old and lame, threw in his own drawings and paintings, 'and then, to loud chanting, the whole pyre of worldly treasures was burned'.[31] Six years later Savonarola himself was burned, 'like a hot coal quenched',[32] in the same piazza and his ashes scattered in the Arno. And six years after that, in September 1504, Michelangelo unveiled on the site his seventeen-foot-tall, six-ton marble nude of David the giant-killer: tense, frowning and ready for combat.

Lawrence, who refused to answer to David and was known by his friends as Lorenzo, was as severe a puritan as Savonarola. He identified with all three figures, but it was Dante whose ascent he continued to follow.

After an hour Douglas tapped on the door. 'Why here you are,' he roared, '– miles and miles from human habitation!'[33] He had told the concierge to put Lawrence on the second floor and now insisted that he complain, but Lawrence liked his far-off regions.

Douglas's room was piled with books and papers and thick with the 'queer smell' of smoke, whisky and sleep; he didn't believe in opening windows because, he explained, 'a certain amount of nitrogen' was 'beneficial'. Magnus was already there, resting neatly on the bed in a grey suit bound with grey silk braid. 'Sit down! Sit down!' Douglas ordered, 'wheeling up a chair'. They were drinking whisky, which made Magnus's pink face go 'yellowish'. Douglas said that he would need to starve himself to afford the whisky in Florence, but he was 'starved to death' anyway by 'the absolute muck they call food here', and Magnus suggested that if they each bought a bottle – 'you can get the one at twenty-two, and I'll buy the one at twenty-eight' – Douglas could eat 'just the same'. Lawrence, appalled by their expenditure, took in their covenant of friendship. 'So it always was. Magnus indulged Douglas, and spoilt him in every way,' making sure he saw the dentist, the tailor, the barber, and ate and drank his fill. 'And of course, Douglas wasn't grateful. *Au contraire* –! And Magnus's pale-blue, smallish round eyes, in his cockatoo-pink face, would harden to indignation occasionally.' Like Jonathan and David, their souls were knit together, and 'I between them,' wrote Lawrence, 'laughed and took no notice.' This wasn't the literal truth he had promised the reader so he crossed through this sentence and replaced it with, 'And I between them just wondered.'[34]

Both epicures, Magnus and Douglas discussed the menu.

'Look here,' said Douglas. 'Didn't you say there was a turkey for dinner? What? Have you been to the kitchen to see what they're doing to it?'

'Yes,' said Magnus testily. 'I forced them to prepare it to roast.'

'With chestnuts – stuffed with chestnuts?' said Douglas.

'They *said* so,' said Magnus.

'Oh but go down and see that they're doing it. – Yes, you've got to keep your eye on them, got to. The most awful howlers if you don't. – You go now and see what they're up to.' Douglas used his most irresistible grand manner.

Thus Magnus was despatched to check that the turkey was not being boiled in 'old soup-water' or 'stuffed with old boots'. His kitchen interventions were clearly part of their routine, and the bird, Magnus was able to report, would be roasted but without chestnuts. 'What did I tell you! What did I tell you!' cried Douglas. 'They are absolute—!', and off he went into his 'improprieties'. The party enjoyed a second round of whisky, and when they sat down to dinner where the waiter handed the chestnut-less turkey to Douglas who pushed it and prodded it and 'grumbled frantically, sotto voce, in Italian … getting into a nervous frenzy'. The atmosphere of Douglas and Magnus was as frenzied as that of *Women in Love*. Magnus selected the choicest bits of flesh and placed them on Douglas's plate, who demanded more bread (bread still being rationed), which got Magnus into a tizz, and so he handed over his own slice, the 'crumb part' of which Douglas threw on the floor before calling for more wine. 'We always drank heavy, dark-red wine at three francs a litre. Douglas drank two thirds, Magnus drank least. He loved his liquors, and did not care for wine.' Their talk was 'gay and noisy' and unbuttoned, with 'Douglas telling witty anecdotes and grumbling wildly and only half whimsically about the food'. They drank a litre of wine, ordered another, and after supper retired upstairs for more whisky.[35]

Lawrence woke the next morning to the whooshing of the Arno below, the ringing of bells, the banging of carts and the jingle of trams. Florence was a noisy city. After his coffee, he called in to see Magnus.

Image of the Harpie, 1497

The 'little pontiff' was in demi-toilette, mincing about in a blue silk kimono with a 'broad border of reddish purple'. Lawrence, who enjoyed brightly coloured clothes, was fascinated by Magnus's wardrobe and his soft, feminine form: he looked 'like a sparrow painted to resemble a tom-tit'.[36] Half woman, half bird, Magnus was like a Harpie, the death-spirit that haunts the wood of suicides in Dante's seventh circle of hell.

Magnus's room was fastidiously tidy and ornamented with vanities: silver-topped bottles of pomades and powders and 'heaven knows what' stood on the dressing table. Everything Magnus owned was expensive and 'finicking': a 'trouser stretcher', ivory-backed brushes, 'thick leather silver-studded suit-cases'. By his bed was an ornately bound prayer book and a life of St Benedict: a Catholic convert, Magnus aspired to join the Benedictines in the monastery at Monte Cassino, although, Lawrence noted, he had not yet begun his theological studies. 'Douglas said he only chose the Benedictines because they lived better than any of the others', but Magnus really chose the monastic life, Lawrence thought, because 'he loathed women, and wished for a world of men'.[37]

He was not at all, Lawrence realised, 'just the common person' he appeared to be, and yet Magnus '*was* common, his very accent was common, and Douglas despised him'. An American who had spent most of his life in Europe, Magnus spoke with a twang, but his voice was otherwise 'precise' with 'an odd high squeak'. Lawrence's voice, with its East Midlands accent, was also high-pitched, his laugh even more so, reaching at times the level of a scream. 'I wondered over him and his niceties and little pomposities,' Lawrence recalled. 'He was a new bird to me.'[38]

Magnus had turned forty-three on 7 November and Douglas insisted that they celebrate his birthday on Saturday night with a dinner, which gave him an excuse to feast on hare with truffles, champignons and cauliflower, followed by zabaglione. Because he was leaving for Rome the next day, this would be their last supper. 'You aren't going before you've given us that hare,' said Douglas. 'Don't you imagine it my boy. I've got the smell of that hare in my imagination, and I've damned well got to set my teeth on it.' So on Saturday morning Magnus rose with the first light to buy hare and mushrooms at the old market while, on Saturday afternoon, Douglas and Lawrence trailed over Ponte Vecchio in search of a suitable present. 'I shall have to buy him something—have to—have to—' Douglas fretted. He wanted to spend no more than five francs and all he could find for that price was a saint-medal, which was presumably ironical. Lawrence, an expert present-giver who loved precious stones, found for four francs at the Mercato Nuovo a little bowl of amber-coloured Volterra marble. Magnus was delighted: 'Thank you a thousand times Norman,' he said. 'That's charming! That's exactly what I want.' This is the first sign in his *Memoir* of Lawrence's identification with Magnus: the bowl is exactly what he would have wanted too. That night, for twelve francs a head, the three of them ate 'good, good food' until their stomachs were tight. When they left the table, Douglas instructed the waiter to deduct from the bill the half-litre of wine that remained in the flask.[39]

There is no sign in Lawrence's portrait of himself of the half-crazed satyr described by Aldington. The Lawrence of the *Memoir* is Self Two, who was quiet and slow and most of the time puzzled; he returns to the word 'puzzle' throughout. It is Douglas instead who represents the herd-self, who shouts and yells and rants. Lawrence is the voice of reason at a bacchanal, the straight man (in both senses) in a comic act, a Christ figure tempted from his fast by two devils. His mood, however, is certainly satirical. The writer H. M. Tomlinson, who was present during one of Lawrence's later drawing-room impressions of Norman Douglas, conceded that in this particular party-piece Lawrence surpassed himself, catching with lethal precision Douglas's voice and gestures. Lawrence pictured Douglas, Tomlinson said, 'as grotesquely and alarmingly as a cinema-camera in a "close-up"', and as the performance gathered in momentum Tomlinson found himself thinking, 'Yes, that was Douglas; his glance went like that sideways when he dropped a slow and artful comment, and that was the way he spoke when irritated, and those exaggerations mocked his ordinary movements.' Everyone laughed. But reflecting on the performance afterwards Tomlinson 'saw that the excellent mimicry was no truer a representation of Douglas than one of his old hats. All that was important was left out, because it was not important to Lawrence.'[40] Lawrence's 'novelist's touch in biography' would be Douglas's complaint as well.

Despite the comic set pieces in his writing, the most complex of which is the Florentine section of the *Memoir*, Lawrence is traditionally described as humourless. According to Douglas, he had 'not a trace of humour', and while 'no one', said Philip Heseltine, 'had a keener sense of the absurdities and weaknesses of others ... of true humour, the humour of God and man as opposed to angel and devil, Lawrence was fundamentally incapable'.[41] It was his sense of the absurdities of others that made him such a terrifying mimic: Lawrence was, said David Garnett, 'a natural copy-cat' and 'the only great mimic I have ever known'. His genius for mimicry, thought Garnett, was rooted in his class. Lawrence seized on 'the slightest affectation of manner or social pretence ... One realised the enormous aesthetic enjoyment which the poor are afforded by the spectacle of the imbecilities of the rich, of the endless "copy" which they provide.'[42] Brigit Patmore described Lawrence's impersonations as less '*acting*' than 'demoniacal possessions', and demoniacal possession was, accordingly, his most accomplished routine. Aware of his own frenzied and fanatical tendencies, Lawrence was drawn to frenzy and fanaticism in others. May Chambers, the sister of Jessie, remembered his performing the word 'fanatic' in a game of charades: 'He went up to the attic dressed like an old crone to fetch down her lazy son. His shrill, withering vituperation made me shiver.' 'You acted a bit too well,' they told Lawrence. 'You *became* a fanatic.'[43] Frieda similarly described his impression of the fanatical revivalist parson – the Eastwood Savonarola – who had terrified Lawrence as a child:

He would work his congregation up to a frenzy; then, licking his finger to turn the imaginary pages of the book of Judgement and suddenly darting a finger at some sinner in the congregation: 'Is *your* name written in the book?' he would shout.

A collier's wife in a little sailor hat, in a frenzy of repentance, would clatter down the aisle, throw herself on her knees in front of the altar and pray: 'O Lord, our Henry would 'ave come too, only he dursn't, O Lord, so I come as well for him, O Lord!' It was a marvellous scene! First as the parson then as the collier's wife Lawrence made me shake with laughter.[44]

Lawrence, said David Garnett, made them all laugh 'until laughing was an agony', but it was less mirth than hysteria. Douglas, however, never laughed at Lawrence's satires. Charles Duff recalled in his memoir of Norman Douglas that while Douglas 'preferred the humorously satirical to the serious ... there were some subjects about which I never heard him speak other than seriously. One was D. H. Lawrence.'[45]

PART ONE

Max Beerbohm, *'A flask of Bombarolina; and Mr. Norman Douglas bent on winning an admission that the rites of the Church are all a survival of Paganism pure and simple.'*

This was a great age of parody, and shortly before Lawrence left England in 1919, Max Beerbohm's *Seven Men* appeared. One of the most curious and perfect books ever written, *Seven Men* is a collection of biographical fantasies about figures from the 1890s who find themselves at sea in the twentieth century, and Beerbohm – a friend of Douglas and one of these figures himself – wanders among his creations. In the opening story, 'Enoch Soames', Beerbohm and the illustrator William Rothenstein are drinking vermouth in the Café Royal when they spot a man in a soft black hat and cape, with the expression of 'a donkey looking over a gate'. He is, they realise, Enoch Soames, Catholic diabolist and author of a neglected collection of poems called 'Negations'. Some time

163

later, Beerbohm and Soames are lunching together in Soho when they are joined at their table by a stranger.

> On one side sat a tall, flashy, rather Mephistophelian man whom I had seen from time to time in the domino room and elsewhere. On the other side sat Soames. They made a queer contrast in that sunlit room – Soames sitting haggard in that hat and cape which nowhere at any season had I seen him doff, and this other, this keenly vital man, at sight of whom I more than ever wondered whether he were a diamond merchant, a conjuror, or the head of a private detective agency.[46]

The flashy man turns out to be the Devil, with whom Soames makes a pact that in exchange for his soul he will be transported a hundred years into the future to discover his posthumous reputation. Landing in the reading room of the British Library in 1997, Soames searches for his name in the catalogue. When he returns to 1897 – and before being escorted to hell – he reports to Beerbohm that the only mention of Enoch Soames to be found was a satire by Beerbohm himself, in a book called *Seven Men*.

Maurice Magnus and Norman Douglas step straight from these same pages. The fate of Magnus, who also aspired to literary immortality, is precisely that of Enoch Soames: if Maurice Magnus is heard of today, it is because of the satire by D. H. Lawrence. Could Lawrence – who also wandered among his own creations and was equally at sea in the twentieth century – have read *Seven Men*? He did not mention Beerbohm but Beerbohm mentioned Lawrence: 'Poor D. H. Lawrence. He never realized, don't you know – he never suspected that to be stark, staring mad is somewhat of a handicap to a writer.'[47] The two men could not have been more different, but in the opening section of the *Memoir of Maurice Magnus*, the detached and immaculate Max Beerbohm and the stark, staring mad D. H. Lawrence meet at the same table and share the same joke.

The person whom Lawrence most constantly mocked, said David Garnett, 'was himself ... He mimicked himself ruthlessly and continuously.' He 'acted ridiculous versions of a shy and gawky Lawrence being patronised by literary lions, of a winsome Lawrence charming his landlady, or a bad-tempered whining Lawrence picking a quarrel with Frieda over nothing.' Garnett likened these self-parodies to Charlie Chaplin, but Lawrence was more bitter and 'less sentimental' than the tramp in the curly hat.[48]

The provincial persona Lawrence adopts in the *Memoir of Maurice Magnus* serves, at least in part, as a defence against the sexualities of his companions, and he insists throughout the *Memoir* on his difference from both Magnus and Douglas, a difference manifested most forcefully in their attitudes to money. Who paid what percentage of the bill for drinks and meals was always for Douglas a bone of contention, while Lawrence was intent on holding tight to what little he had. Precisely how much this is we are kept informed of at every stage. 'I landed in Italy with nine pounds in my pocket,' he tells us in the first paragraph of the *Memoir*, 'and about twelve pounds lying in the bank in London. Nothing more. We should have to go very softly, if we were to house ourselves in Italy for the winter.' Magnus, Lawrence thought, despised him for being penny-pinching.

> 'Oh,' said Magnus. 'Why, that's the very time to spend money, when you've got none. If you've got none, why try to save it? That's been my philosophy all my life: when you've got no money, you may just as well spend it. If you've got a good deal, that's the time to look after it.' Then he laughed his queer little laugh, rather squeaky. These were his exact words.
>
> 'Precisely,' said Douglas. 'Spend when you've nothing to spend, my boy. Spend *hard* then.'
>
> 'No,' said I. 'If I can help it, I will never let myself be penniless while I live. I mistrust the world too much.'
>
> 'But if you're going to live in fear of the world,' said Magnus, 'what's the point of living at all? Might as well die.'
>
> I think I give his words almost verbatim. He had a certain impatience of me and of my presence.[49]

Lawrence, who would remember Magnus's remarks about living in fear of the world, was as frugal as anyone raised in a large family on thirty-five shillings a week, and in conversations like this he became his mother taunting her husband for spending his income on drink. Lydia Lawrence's anger about money set the tone of the house, and Lawrence later, in 'An Autobiographical Fragment', described her generation of women as reacting against 'the ordinary high-handed obstinate husband who went off to the pub to enjoy himself and waste the bit of money that was so precious to his family. The woman felt herself the higher moral being: and justly, as far as economic morality goes.'[50] Lawrence also felt himself the higher moral being as far as economic morality goes, in relation to Douglas and Magnus.

But these were happy days, spent 'mostly', he recalled in the *Memoir*, 'in one or other of their bedrooms, drinking whisky and talking'. They got through a bottle a day; Lawrence even bought a bottle himself although he drank very little of it, preferring the wine at mealtimes, 'which seemed delicious after the war-famine'.[51] In the company of Douglas and Magnus, Lawrence came back to life. They too were expatriates and here, in their otherworld, they amused one another and lived well.

The *Memoir of Maurice Magnus* tells us precisely what Magnus and Douglas sounded like, while revealing very little, beyond discussions about food and money, of their conversation. This is because, according to Douglas in *Looking Back*, Lawrence did not 'understand' in writing 'how conversation works'. 'In *Women in Love*, for example,' Douglas complained, 'we find pages and pages of drivel. Those endless and pointless conversations! That dreary waste of words! ... Lawrence never divined that conversation and dialogues are precious contrivances, to be built up *con amore*; that they should suggest a clue to character and carry forward the movement instead of retarding it; that they should be sparkling oases, not deserts of tiresome small talk.'[52] Most of our conversations, however, *are* a 'dreary waste of words', and the conversation between Douglas and Magnus, as recorded by Lawrence, is indeed a desert of 'tiresome small talk'. This is quite possibly an accurate account: according to Aldous Huxley, from the 1920s onwards Douglas talked about nothing but boys, sex and drink. Did Magnus, however, not have a wider repertoire? Did he expand, for example, on his tour of pre-revolutionary Russia, his experience as a theatrical agent, his brief marriage or his daring escape from the French Foreign Legion?

We know from his many admirers that Douglas had once been a versatile companion whose interests ranged from the formation of forest loam to the best recipe for potato salad, and that he had no patience with tourist gush ('Isn't that all rather *Cinquecento*, my dear,' he said to Nancy Cunard, when she suggested seeing Renaissance art in Florence).[53] An aesthete, a pagan and a Darwinist, aged eighteen, Douglas had contributed an article to *The Zoologist* on 'Variation of Plumage in the Corvidae', and in his twenties he published such monographs as *The Herpetology of the Grand Duchy of Baden, The Pumice Stone Industry of the Lipari Islands* and *On the Darwinian Hypothesis of Sexual Selection*.

Apart from catching his likeness, Lawrence says nothing in the *Memoir* about the life and times of Norman Douglas. He would, however, have been familiar with the details. Seventeen years older than Lawrence, Douglas was born in Austria in 1868 and was aged five when his father, a Scottish laird called John Sholto Douglas, died in a fall in the Austrian Alps. Douglas's family were a cadet branch of the Queensberry Douglases: his father shared the name of the 9th Marquess of Queensberry, father of Lord Alfred Douglas and the man who destroyed Oscar Wilde. His mother, Wanda Freiin von Poellnitz, was the daughter of a Prussian baron and the granddaughter of James Ochoncar, 17th Lord Forbes. When Douglas was eight, Wanda remarried and sent her son to school in England, which he hated. He completed his education at the Karlsruhe *Gymnasium* after which, in 1893, he joined the British diplomatic service. As a schoolboy Douglas had travelled extensively across the Mediterranean where he observed the flora and fauna, and as a diplomat he visited Finland, Poland, Istanbul, Ankara and the Lipari Islands. His career terminated, however, in St Petersburg 1895 – the year of the Oscar Wilde trial – when one of his two mistresses fell pregnant. Douglas fled to Europe, bought a villa in the Bay of Naples (where Wilde also went in 1897) and became involved with the fifteen-year-old brother of his current mistress. He then married his first cousin, after which his life rapidly changed course. By 1904 he was divorced, no longer sexually interested in adults, and – to his ex-wife's distress – the sole custodian of their two young sons. Like his good friend Hilda Doolittle, Douglas was more comfortable in the ancient world and so he bought land on Capri, the former Xanadu of the Emperors Augustus and Tiberius, where he took over their imperial role. It was Douglas's siren's song that drew to the rock all those writers and exiles who washed up on Capri in the first half of the twentieth century – including D. H. Lawrence.

In 1908, when the family fortune disappeared, Douglas took a desk job at the *English Review* in London and reinvented himself, aged forty, as a classical travel writer. His essays about Ischia and Tiberius, published in the *English Review* in 1909, reappeared in *Siren Land* in 1911. The first of his celebrations of Capri and its environs, *Siren Land* is an entirely idiosyncratic creation: erudite, curmudgeonly, witty, digressive and nostalgic. *Siren Land*, said Douglas, was simply an account of 'dreaming through the summer months to the music of cicadas'. Framed around the search for what songs the Sirens sang, it is a celebration above all of Tiberius, an inhabitant of the rock islet and 'a siren-worshipper all his life'. This was followed by *Fountains in the Sand*, about a walking tour in Tunisia, and, in 1915, *Old Calabria*, which proved his most enduring work. Then, in 1916 – the year his former wife burned to death in her bed – Douglas was obliged, as he liked to say, 'to put a slice of sea' between himself and England when he was arrested for kissing a boy in South Kensington Underground station. Skipping bail, he fled London and returned to the Mediterranean where he set himself up as a pederast and a gentleman. The following year he became a celebrity when *South Wind*, his first novel, was published. Set on a Mediterranean rock called Nepenthe (after the opiate in *The Odyssey*), whose inhabitants are caricatures of those people Douglas didn't like, *South Wind* proved an opiate for the war years. Like the island itself, which was part Capri and part Never-Never Land, the book distracted its readers from current events.

Douglas's writings on southern Italy introduced Lawrence to the Mediterranean, and to the idea that travel writing was a dual narrative involving a geographical and a symbolic journey. Before he met Lawrence, Norman Douglas had been a figure to contend with: Joseph Conrad, an early friend, encouraged him; Graham Greene, a later friend, revered him, and Evelyn Waugh emulated his ironic detachment. Nabokov admired his muscular prose but not his sexuality. Douglas, Nabokov told his wife, was a 'malicious pederast', and as such is surely the model for *Lolita*'s Humbert Humbert.[54] Nabokov ensures Douglas a part in the novel: Gaston Godin, Humbert's homosexual colleague at Beardsley College, has a photograph of Norman Douglas on his studio wall and Godin is later involved, Humbert gleefully informs us, in a '*sale histoire* in Naples of all places!'

The sight of Douglas promenading down the *strade* with an urchin by his side became a feature of Florentine life. Occasionally, when the boy's parents caught up with him, he was obliged to flee. 'Florence is taboo for me … at present,' Douglas wrote to Lytton Strachey on one such occasion in 1922, when he was hiding out in Prato. He currently went out 'thickly veiled and wearing blue glasses and a carroty beard'. Looking, in other words, like D. H. Lawrence.[55]

Before he left England, Lawrence complained that he found people 'ultimately boring'.[56] In the company of Douglas and Magnus he found them interesting again. Florence, Lawrence told Katherine Mansfield, was filled with 'extremely nice people',[57] especially those the Florentines called the *stranieri inverti*, whom Douglas called the 'pederast loungers'. This group – including Reggie Turner, best friend of Beerbohm and acolyte of Oscar, C. K. Scott Moncrieff, translator of Proust, the painter and musician Collingwood Gee, and Leo Stein, brother of Gertrude – lived in what Reggie Turner's biographer describes as a 'world without time' but was, more precisely, the world of the 1890s.[58] Reggie, like Beerbohm, was too solid a construct of the *fin de siècle* to gain a foothold in the twentieth century, and his apartment on the Viale Milton, which Lawrence knew well, was decorated with drawings by Beerbohm and photos of Wilde. Here Reggie held court, said Douglas, like an old maid in Kensington. Reggie in turn described Douglas as a combination of Roman emperor and Roman cab driver.

It is worth pausing to watch Lawrence among the bohemians because he was not, as Douglas noted, bohemian himself; he mixed with the avant-garde but did not belong there. Lawrence 'belonged' nowhere, but bohemia was as close as he would get to a convivial culture. Douglas mocked his discomfort in bohemia but bohemia was equally uncomfortable around Lawrence because he was a remover of masks, and Douglas was posing as a sybarite. A Victorian scientist with a Romantic sensibility, Douglas also belonged nowhere; he teased his audience by swishing his tail and stomping his cloven hoof, but he kept his precise nature under wraps. He led a double life: he had his 'Mediterranean' circle who discussed his wickedness at catty tea parties but he was not prepared to stand in the dock and defend the love that dare not speak its name: when he had been arrested in South Kensington station, he crossed a few borders rather than face a scandal. 'Burn your boats!' he counselled in *Looking Back*. 'This has ever been my system in times of stress.'[59] Douglas lived, like Lawrence and like Magnus, on the move and on the run.

While his larger conversations with Douglas and Magnus are not recorded, Lawrence does let slip a tender moment where Magnus says,

'How lovely your hair is – such a lovely colour! What do you dye it with?' Lawrence laughed, but Magnus was perfectly serious. 'It's got no particular colour at all,' Lawrence replied, 'so I couldn't dye it that.' Magnus didn't believe him. 'It puzzled me,' Lawrence wrote, 'and it puzzles me still.'[60]

On Sunday 23 November 1919, the pomades and powders packed up in the silver-studded suitcases, Magnus caught the midnight train to Rome, snuggled up in a first-class compartment. 'Why should I go second?' he reasoned. 'It's beastly enough to travel at all.' His plan was to continue after Christmas to Monte Cassino. Lawrence, who would be spending Christmas twenty miles away from the monastery in Picinisco on the edge of the Abruzzi mountains, asked whether he might pay the place a visit. 'Certainly,' Magnus replied. 'Come when I am there. I shall be there in about a month's time. Do come! Do be sure and come. It's a wonderful place – ah, wonderful. It will make a great impression on you. Do come. Do come.'[61]

Lawrence was always relieved whenever Magnus left. 'So the little outsider was gone, and I was rather glad. I don't think he liked me.'[62] But despite repeating that Magnus despised him, was impatient with him, didn't like him, Lawrence was determined to see him again.

Frieda was not expected until 3 December, which gave Lawrence and Douglas ten days alone. They clearly got on well: Frieda was 'thrilled at the fireworks of wit that went off' between them.[63] Douglas's influence can be seen in a postcard sent by Lawrence on 24 November (showing a picture of the Piazza della Signoria) in which he described himself as 'loafing', a word he repeated in a second card sent that same day. It was not in Lawrence's nature to loaf, but Douglas, like Whitman, defined himself as a loafer. 'I lean and loaf at my ease,' sang Whitman in 'Song of Myself'. In *Alone*, where Douglas describes his southern Italian wanderings, 'loafing' is repeated like a mantra. 'What did *you* do in the Great War, grandpapa?' Douglas imagines being asked one day. 'I loafed, my boy,' is his reply. 'I have loafed into Levanto,' Douglas drawls in the chapter on Levanto; in Rome, he makes his 'plans for loafing through the day'.[64]

When Lawrence saw Keynes emerge from his bedroom in 1915 it was one of the crises of his life. So how was he feeling now about drinking whisky in the bedrooms of homosexuals? There was a difference, for Lawrence, between the intellectual inverts of Cambridge and

Bloomsbury and the robust homosexuality of the ancient world and the 1890s. 'I myself never considered Plato very wrong, or Oscar Wilde,' he explained to David Garnett.[65] What Lawrence admired was physical strength, and Douglas, unlike Keynes, was a goliath of a man.

With Magnus now gone, Douglas moved into his friend's former room in the Pensione Balestri and tried to persuade Lawrence to take over his own unaired quarters. Lawrence stayed put on the third floor. Neither says how he occupied his time until Frieda arrived, but it was during these days that Lawrence was introduced, by Douglas, to Reggie Turner. 'I have D. H. Lawrence (*The White Peacock*, *The Rainbow* etc) with me,' Douglas wrote to Reggie.

> Would you care to meet him? If so, let me know and I will arrange a quiet dinner somewhere, ONLY WE THREE.
> I am going to prevent his meeting certain other people, because he is a damned observant fellow and might be so amused at certain aspects of Florentine life as to use it as 'copy' in some book: would be annoying.
> Read his *Twilight in Italy*, if you can get a copy – that gives you a clue as to his nature which is sympathetic and yet strangely remote.[66]

It was probably now that Lawrence produced his astonishing essay on Michelangelo's *David* with its refrain 'Perpetual sound of water'. He wrote in a clipped, staccato present tense which he called 'cinematographic' because it sounds like he is directing a film: 'Morning in Florence. Dark, grey and raining, with a perpetual sound of water'. The river churns with rain, the weir is 'a fighting flurry of waters' and out of a similar wetness blossoms David, 'corpse-white and sensitive', the 'flower of adolescence' standing up for naked liberty in the Piazza della Signoria. Frozen in 'hot excitement', David – 'the Lily, the Water-born, most dazzling nearest the sun' – is the child of the wet north and the fiery south, and he strains in wait, like the lover on the Grecian urn, for the orgasm that Florentines say 'possesses him at midnight of the New Year'. This is why, Lawrence wrote, the 'lily of Florence' is 'unforgettable, now I am safe in my upper room again'.[67]

Later, in the *Memoir of Maurice Magnus*, Lawrence mocked his innocent idealisation of David's nakedness. Here he was in the lily town, home of heavy-limbed and acrid-fearless men, with Magnus fussing around in his silk kimono in demi-toilette. Magnus's servile love for Douglas is presented as grotesque, and his pudgy body as the opposite of the Renaissance ideal. Imagine Magnus's soft pink flanks, wet with rain, displayed on a plinth, or Douglas and Magnus wrestling naked like gladiators, their glossy flesh driving 'deeper and deeper', like that of Birkin and Gerald, 'as if they would break into a oneness'.

Reggie Turner said that Douglas never read 'a line of Lawrence except the thing about Magnus',[68] but Douglas had read a good deal of Lawrence and knew exactly what he was up against. He had warned Reggie, after all, about the dangers of dining with him. Douglas knew that Lawrence's recklessness made his own insurrections look like those of a music-hall villain.

When he had been working at the *English Review*, Douglas 'persuaded', as he put it, the editor to publish two of Lawrence's early stories, 'The Prussian Officer' (originally called 'Honour and Arms') and 'Vin Ordinaire' (later renamed 'The Thorn in the Flesh'). 'The Prussian Officer', Douglas regretted, had to be cut by a third or the journal would not run it, 'and I was charged with the odious task of performing the operation'. Having conceded that the task of cutting Lawrence down by 1,500 words was odious and due to the issue of page-space, Douglas then suggested that the fault lay with Lawrence himself: 'Would Lawrence never learn to be more succinct, and hold himself in hand a little? No; he never would and he never did; diffuseness is a fault of much of his work.'[69] But there was, as Douglas knew, nothing diffuse about 'The Prussian Officer', one of the finest short stories in the language – and Douglas's amputation was not an improvement. No writer likes to be cut by an editor, and what happened at the *English Review*, which left Lawrence furious, played a small part in the later Magnus business.

Written in Germany in 1913, 'The Prussian Officer' is about the attraction of an aristocratic captain to his Bavarian orderly. 'Gradually the officer had become aware of his servant's young, vigorous, unconscious presence about him. He could not get away from the sense of the youth's person, while he was in attendance. It was like a warm flame upon the older man's tense, rigid body.' The officer is all conscious will, but the orderly 'received life direct through his senses, and acted straight from instinct'.[70] When the officer discovers that the orderly has a sweetheart, he is 'mad with irritation'; he makes the young man work in the evenings to prevent him from seeing the girl, and thrashes him – first across the face with a belt, and then on his legs. During a manoeuvre in a forest, the orderly kills the officer, and then dies himself, the next day, from dehydration. In his final moments of consciousness he gazes out at the mountains 'straight in front of him, blue and cool and tender', ranging 'across the pale edge of the morning sky'.

> He wanted them – he wanted them alone – he wanted to leave
> himself and be identified with them … There they ranked, all still
> and wonderful between earth and heaven. He stared till his eyes
> went black, and the mountains, as they stood in their beauty, so
> clean and cool, seemed to have it, that which was lost in him.[71]

The orderly's last thoughts are of wanting not to be on the mountains but to *be* the mountains, to share their certainty, clarity and ancient serenity. All mountains, for Lawrence, were magic.

The prose in 'The Prussian Officer' has an airborne, suspended quality, hallucinatory at times. In one scene the orderly spills the wine and the officer, his eyes 'bluey like fire',

> held those of the confused youth for a moment. It was a shock
> for the young soldier. He felt something sink deeper, deeper into
> his soul, where nothing had ever gone before. It left him rather
> blank and wondering. Some of his natural completeness in himself
> was gone, a little uneasiness took its place. And from that time an
> undiscovered feeling had held between the two men.[72]

This is one of the passages that Douglas cut. Public-school educated, half-Austrian and attracted to younger men, Douglas belonged to the peculiar world that Lawrence – a nobody from nowhere – seemed instinctively to understand. Added to which, Douglas's father had died on a mountain, and his own love of mountains was second to none. 'The Prussian Officer' was not Lawrence's story to tell, and nor was this the last time he would trespass on Douglas's turf. Years earlier, in collaboration with his wife, Douglas had written a collection of stories called *Unprofessional Tales* which proved his lack of talent for the genre. Lawrence's tales, Douglas now conceded, had an 'enviable flair, an enviable freshness, an enviable mastery': Douglas envied Lawrence.[73] 'It has always seemed to me possible,' suggests Douglas's biographer Mark Holloway,

> even likely, that Douglas recognised in Lawrence a quality of lyricism and spontaneity – the Shelleyan, the Blakean streak – of which he himself, at one point in his life, might have been capable, might have developed, if he had not progressed in another direction, and that perhaps it filled him with a kind of nostalgia for what might have been, a kind of envy.[74]

Like Lawrence, Douglas had pursued the shade of Shelley, visiting Viareggio in the hope that he might see the poet 'flit along' the shore, searching for the spot where they burned his body.[75] If it is hard to see how a figure as terrestrial as Douglas might have developed in a Shelleyan direction, it is because by the time he knew Lawrence the mask had eaten into his face.

'Vin Ordinaire', written in the same summer as 'The Prussian Officer', depicts the relationship between another bullying officer and his noble subordinate. Bachmann is a private in the Bavarian army, stationed in the garrison town of Metz (where Frieda was raised). His officer is a thug and a drunk, and on the day in question Bachmann, who has a fear of heights, has to climb to the top of the ramparts on a ladder. The ramparts are like 'a low cliff, along whose summit the grass and the tall daisies grew'. The exercise is the 'supreme test' for the private of 'whether his will, sufficiently identifying itself with the will of the Army, could control his body'. But his body fails him: halfway up the ladder, Bachmann feels his bladder relax and water run down the leg of his uniform. The soldiers below laugh uneasily and the officer on the summit above turns 'yellow with fury'. Gathering his nerves, Bachmann completes the climb, but before reaching the top, he is hauled over the edge by the large hands of the officer who then hisses into his face. 'Bachmann started away; the vision of the sergeant's face, the open mouth, the upper lip raised from the teeth, the snarling, barking look had shocked him away on the reflex.' His heart pounding, Bachmann jerks up his arm to protect himself and in doing so hits the officer, who staggers backwards and falls down the ramparts into the moat. Bachmann runs; in an instant he has become a deserter.[76]

These two studies of crime and punishment are Lawrence's Dostoevskian masterpieces, and in his memoirs of the French Foreign Legion, Maurice Magnus would produce his own version of them both.

When he reached Rome on the morning of 24 November, Magnus booked into the Grand Hotel by the station where he drafted a document stating that in the event of his death he left his literary material and letters to Norman Douglas. He then walked into the lobby of the Excelsior Hotel on via Vittorio Veneto and asked the Deputy Director, Leone Colleoni, to cash for him two cheques worth a total of £3,800.

Meanwhile in Florence, Lawrence found himself weary of Renaissance self-consciousness; with the exception of Michelangelo's *David*, the sharpened perceptions of Florentine art sated and appalled him. In a belligerent essay called 'Looking Down on the City', he described the state of his soul. Florence, Lawrence believed, was the birthplace of personality and thus the snake in the Garden of Eden: 'At the Renaissance, mankind, and Florence perfectly, took a new apple, and opened a new field of consciousness, a new era.' The rebirth of art was accompanied, he felt, by 'a misery in the loss of spontaneity' and 'in my tissue', he conceded, 'I am weary of personality.'[77]

Happiest when he set himself in opposition to a place, the personality of Florence now became Lawrence's psychic battleground. The only sight in Florence to move him was the view of the city from the Piazzale Michelangelo, the paved hilltop across the Arno built by Giuseppe Poggi in the mid-nineteenth century. A different man in every place, Lawrence travelled to find 'unchangeable eternity', and when he looked at the prospect of the city from the Piazzale Michelangelo, he was 'moved by a strange deep feeling which I cannot fathom: a kind of far-off emotion, like the sound of surf in the distance, heavy. Who knows what it is.'

The town lies below and very near. The river winds beneath one, under four bridges, disappearing in a curve on the left. And the brown-red town spreads out so thick, so intense, so far. One could almost stroke it with the hand. The Duomo – the naked tower of Giotto – the hawk-neck of Palazzo Vecchio – a few other churches – rising above the ruffled brown roofs, all level, far-spreading, and the hills half encircling – a strange sight. One has looked down on many cities – Turin on her plain with the Alps

flashing beyond – London in her smoke – Edinburgh. But Florence
is different, quite different: not worldly.[78]

Florence lies below and spreads out, the river winds beneath and
under the bridge, the towers and churches rise above, the mountains flash
beyond; he looks down, along and across; he sees near sides, far sides, near
distance, further nearness. Florence from above is like a vision or memory,
something that has passed away. It is the 'brown-red town' that wounds
him like a punctum. It could be the view from the house in Walker Street
where Lawrence lived when he was the same age as Michelangelo's David
and which, he once said, with its 'amphitheatre of hills', now spoiled by
'new patches of reddish houses, and darkening of smoke', he knew better
than any other view in the world.[79] Just as there was only one marriage
and one conflict, there was only one view, and Lawrence, who identified
completely with whatever place he was writing in, was rarely in the place
he was writing about. He wrote about Garsington from Cornwall, Monte
Cassino from Taormina, Cornwall from Australia, Australia from New
Mexico, and Eastwood from everywhere.

Looking down on Florence awakened in him now a 'far-off sadness,
an emotion deeper than the natural planes of emotion, unrealizable,
lying in the sub-stratum of one's being'. Only once, he recalls, has he
known a sadness similarly intolerable, and that was looking at Leonardo's
*Madonna of the Rocks* in London's National Gallery. *Madonna of the
Rocks* brought out in him 'a sadness so deep that it has hardly yet begun
to be felt: root of all our modern nostalgia and neurasthenia'. No other
painting, said Lawrence, 'touches these roots'.[80]

Preferring symbolic to imitative art, Lawrence was drawn to the
unreality of Leonardo's landscape. The Madonna and child – the origin
and centre of the world – are in a rocky place; their comfortless red-
brown cave could be the stone Ezel, where David hides from Saul. There
is a womb-like quality to the image, and not a father in sight. Luminous
in a blue and gold robe, the Madonna is resting from her journey; sheer,
red-brown rocks turn in the smoky distance to the colour of precious
stones. Cool and contained, Mary has her arm around her red-headed
child, her hand supporting his chubby shoulder as he reaches towards
his cousin, John the Baptist, patron saint of Florence, who is being
tended by an angel. The baby's plump feet, like those in Lawrence's first

Leonardo da Vinci, *Madonna of the Rocks* (1483–1486)

published poem, 'Baby-Movements: Running Barefoot', are firm and silken among the clusters of aquilegia and white narcissi.

The sadness he feels, Lawrence suggests, when he looks down on the city or across at the *Madonna of the Rocks*, is comparable to 'the pain which overcomes a man when he eats of the Tree of Knowledge'. What Lawrence sees in the painting and what he sees in the view of Florence repeat for him the birth of self-consciousness, the sudden shift from instinct to knowledge. Self-consciousness brings with it the never-ending dialectic: the ecstasy of 'delirious triumph' is accompanied by the agony 'of sin and despair'.[81] All Renaissance art describes this awakening, captured by Michelangelo in David's combination of primitive spontaneity and subtle self-awareness.

Looking down on the city from the Piazzale Michelangelo, Lawrence yearned for a return to what he called man's 'first primal consciousness', figured historically as the Middle Ages. But, he concluded when he was safe in his upper room, 'one must go right through with consciousness. Forward is the only direction. Sufficient consciousness liberates us to spontaneity again ... There is faith still in Florence.'[82]

His Florentine life was astonishingly fertile. It was also now, in the company of Douglas, that Lawrence began to formulate the six essays which compose *Psychoanalysis and the Unconscious*, the first of his two books on the controversial new Viennese science. If his repressed motive for joining in the debate was to displace Otto Gross as Frieda's psychoanalytic hero, his declared aim was to challenge Freud's understanding of the incest drive. *Psychoanalysis and the Unconscious* reads like a natal autobiography in which Lawrence returns with nostalgia to his months in the womb, his first blind suck, his first angry cry, his first expulsion of wind, his violent but necessary separation from his mother's body and the kicking into action of his nervous system. Even after birth, Lawrence explains, the Madonna and child form an island: a 'lovely, suave, fluid, *creative* electricity ... flows in a circuit between the great nerve-centres in mother and child'.[83] He might be describing Leonardo's painting.

Few writers have returned with Lawrence's intensity to their time as a foetus. In *Sons and Lovers*, the pregnant Mrs Morel, her son boiling in her belly, is locked out of the house after a row with her drunk husband. In the front garden, 'the moonlight standing up from the hills in front', she becomes aware of 'something about her'.

With an effort she roused herself to see what it was that penetrated her consciousness. The tall white lilies were reeling in the moonlight, and the air was charged with their perfume, as with a presence. Mrs. Morel gasped slightly in fear. She touched the big, pallid flowers on their petals, then shivered. They seemed to be stretching in the moonlight. She put her hand into one white bin: the gold scarcely showed on her fingers by moonlight. She bent down to look at the binful of yellow pollen; but it only appeared dusky. Then she drank a deep draught of the scent. It made her almost dizzy.[84]

This, Lydia Lawrence had explained to her son's first girlfriend, Jessie Chambers, was why Lawrence hated his father: 'It happened before he was born. One night he put me out of the house ... he's bound to hate his father.' When she said this, Jessie noted, Mrs Lawrence 'bent her head with a strange smile'.[85] When Mrs Morel went into labour, her husband was down the mine 'hewing at a piece of rock that was in the way for the next day's work'. He would not leave until the job was finished, and so worked himself into a 'frenzy'. Finally, 'wet with sweat', he threw down his tool, pulled on his coat, blew out his candle and began the 'long, heavy tramp underground', beneath the plashing of 'great drops of water'. He was a great, naked man in the rain. It was raining in the upperworld as well, and he walked home with his 'old umbrella, which he loved'. At home, Mrs Morel, who had just given birth, lay in bed listening to the rain.

'What is it?' she asked, feeling sick to death.

'A boy.'

And she took consolation in that. The thought of being the mother of men was warming to her heart. She looked at the child. It had blue eyes, and a lot of fair hair, and was bonny. Her love came up hot, in spite of everything.[86]

So it was a dark, wet, wintry evening that Paul Morel was born.

Having spent his days working, Lawrence dined with Douglas either at Betti's or Paszkowski's Café or the other trattoria on the Via Tornabuoni, frequented by the expatriate colony, which is when he would have asked him about Magnus.

'Oh, you never know what he's at,' Douglas replied. 'He was manager for Isadora Duncan for a long time – knows all the capitals of Europe: St Petersburg, Moscow, Tiflis, Constantinople, Berlin, Paris – knows them as you and I know Florence. He's been mostly in that line – theatrical. Then a journalist. He edited the *Roman Review* until the war killed it. Oh, a many-sided sort of fellow.'[87] In the *Memoir*, Lawrence passes over without comment the news that Magnus had managed Isadora Duncan, high priestess of naked liberty and representative of spontaneous movement. Isadora Duncan believed, as Lawrence did, that the body was the true self, source of all knowledge. Her solo performances, in which she enacted the shaking-off of chains, were impersonated by Julia's tree-dance in *Aaron's Rod* and Gudrun's cattle-worship in *Women in Love*. Dancing in front of the herd of oxen, 'her arms, her wrists, her hands stretching and heaving and falling and reaching and reaching and falling, her breasts lifted and shaken towards the cattle', Gudrun stamped her feet 'as if she were trying to throw off some bond, flinging her hands suddenly and stamping again, then rushing with face uplifted and throat full and beautiful, and eyes half closed, sightless'.[88] The pregnant Anna Brangwen, swaying 'backwards and forwards, like a full ear of corn' when she danced like David, also captured the spirit of Isadora Duncan. 'That isn't dancing,' sneered Will Brangwen, which is what the early critics of Duncan said as well.[89]

Magnus had also managed Duncan's lover, the set designer Edward Gordon Craig, and it was Isadora Duncan, Magnus said in his 'Memoirs of Golden Russia', who encouraged Craig to consider the origins of the theatre as 'movement'. Lawrence had come across Craig before because the editor at Oxford University Press who had commissioned *Movements in European History* was married to Craig's music manager, and John Cournos, in whose bed Lawrence had slept in Mecklenburgh Square, was a friend of Craig and had written a book called *Gordon Craig and the Theatre of the Future*. But Lawrence says nothing in the *Memoir* about Magnus's connections to modern dance and theatre.

How, Lawrence asked, did Douglas come to know Magnus? 'I met him in Capri years and years ago,' Douglas explained, '– oh, sixteen years ago – and clean forgot all about him until somebody came to me one day in Rome and said: "You're Norman Douglas." – *I* didn't know who he was. But he'd never forgotten me. Seems to be smitten by me, somehow or other. All the better for me, ha-ha – if he *likes* to run round for me. My dear fellow, I wouldn't prevent him, if it amuses him. Not for worlds.'⁹⁰

In *A Plea for Better Manners*, Douglas gave a fuller version of his first acquaintance with Magnus, and he too promised an exact account of the experience. Douglas met Magnus, he said, on Sunday 22 August 1909 – 'I know it because I had fixed to leave, and did leave, that same evening for the mountains of the Abruzzi' (where Lawrence also travelled after meeting Magnus). Magnus approached him in the street – Douglas being the emperor of Capri – and asked to borrow money; Douglas replied that lending money 'makes enemies' but he was happy to give the stranger thirty-seven francs. 'I'll never forget your kindness,' said Magnus catching the ferry to Naples, and he kept his word. For the rest of his life Magnus was in Douglas's debt.⁹¹

They did not meet again until August 1917, when Magnus once more stopped Douglas in the street, this time on the Via Corso in Rome. Magnus had recently escaped from the French Foreign Legion and was enjoying a precarious freedom, while Douglas was on the run from the London police following the incident in the South Kensington Underground station. 'And now,' Magnus said, having reminded Douglas who he was, 'you must let me do something for you in return, if I can; you really must.' 'I wouldn't prevent you for worlds,' Douglas replied.⁹² So Magnus installed Douglas in his apartment at 33 Via Margutta, giving up his bed and providing his guest with a suit, a shave and round-the-clock room service. Magnus's rooms, which he borrowed from a friend called Nathan Cobb, were a stone's throw from the Egyptian needles, Roman gateways, Renaissance churches, the Spanish Steps and the house in which Keats had died from consumption in 1821.

Magnus became Douglas's orderly. After rising at 4.30 a.m., he would work until 7.30 on *Dregs* before turning his attention to his house guest. 'Here's your shirt on the window-sill,' Magnus would tut, having brought him his breakfast. 'And your trousers hanging to the top of the wardrobe. Don't you know that trousers ought to be folded up every evening? Why have you turned them inside out?'⁹³ The two fugitives lived in this manner, with Magnus quoting from *Lives of the Saints* and Douglas quoting from Nietzsche, until October when Douglas once again, as he put it, 'got into some kind of trouble' and was obliged 'to hop over the frontier' (he was charged with offences against two brothers aged ten and twelve). By the time he hopped back again, Magnus himself was in trouble, almost certainly financial, and had hopped off to Monte Cassino until things cooled down. 'Don't want anyone to know where I am,' he wrote to Douglas on 5 October, in a letter signed 'the worried one'.

Monte Cassino, Magnus wrote to Douglas, was 'Paradise'. It 'is the only place in which one lives in unchanging time', and the life of the monk is 'the only life. I only pray that I may be able to settle all my affairs soon and be permitted to stay always.' Magnus was given a large, 'beautiful' room overlooking the valley and mountains, and his days were organised around work, mass and meals ('soup, good soup, meat, vegetables, fruit and wine'). Having itemised his routine, Magnus responded to Douglas's complaints: 'Sorry – so sorry you are lonely – you know I am sorry,' and suggested that he join him in the monastery. Before signing off, Magnus told Douglas to 'look for your slippers *under* bed ... *under* table in studio where you put your shoes on, in corner next to sofa – under book cases'.[94]

When it was safe to return to Rome, Magnus threw his energies into arranging a tour for Isadora Duncan, which failed to come off and lost them £60,000. Then, together with a man called Augusto Bazinno, he formed a company dealing in the exchange of motion pictures between Italy and America, and on 18 May 1918, Magnus set sail for New York. Nothing more is known about his foray in the movie business, which clearly failed, but Lawrence made light of it in his portrait of the entrepreneurial Mr May in *The Lost Girl*.

By Easter 1919, Magnus was back in Italy with an exclusive invitation to the Holy Week services in Monte Cassino. Here he was joined by scions of the ancient royal houses such as Prince Massimo (now ninety years old), Prince Alexandr Volkonsky and Prince Ruffo-Scaletta, and various bishops, counts, cardinals and dukes from around the world. Magnus described the experience in an article, 'Holy Week in Monte Cassino', which begins:

'Cassino – Cassino – Cassino!' yells the conductor of the train, with the accent on the 'O', after four hours of purgatory in a packed train from Rome.

For Magnus, spending Holy Week 'on that lonely mountain-top gave me much to think about ... I wondered as I left whether the monasteries will not become the centres of intellectual life again, during and after the great social upheaval which seems to be shaking our Occidental life now.' The 'better elements', he grandly observed, 'will always seek refuge' in the religious houses, 'where law and order exist'.[95]

The next time Douglas saw him, Magnus was leaning over a Roman bridge gazing into the Tiber. 'He was in pensive mood,' Douglas recalled, 'his face all puckered into wrinkles as he glanced upon the tawny flood rolling beneath that old bridge.'

There he stood, leaning over the parapet, all by himself. He turned his countenance aside on seeing me, to escape detection, but I drew nigh none the less.

'Go away,' he said. 'Don't disturb me just now. I am watching the little fishes. Life is so complicated! Let us pray. I have begun a new novel and a new love affair.'

'God prosper both!' I replied, and began to move off.

'Thanks. But supposing the publisher always objects to your choicest paragraphs? ... It is with publishers as with wives: one always wants someone else's. And when you have them, where's the difference? Ah, let us pray. These little fishes have none of our troubles.'

I enquired about the new romance. At first he refused to disclose anything. Then he told me it was to be titled 'With Christ at Harvard', and that it promised some rather novel situations. I shall look forward to its appearance.

Douglas's parody was published first in the *Anglo-Italian Review* and then, in 1921, in *Alone*. 'What good things one could relate of Maurice Magnus, but for the risk of incurring his wrath!' Douglas continued.

It is a thousand pities, I often tell him, that he is still alive; I am yearning to write his biography, and cannot afford to wait for his dissolution.

'When I am dead,' he always says.

'By that time, my dear Magnus, I shall be in the same fix myself.'

'Try to survive. You may find it worth your while, when you come to look into my papers. *You don't know half.* And I may be taking that little sleeping draught of mine any one of these days …'

Magnus, Douglas said, was 'a connoisseur of earthquakes, social and financial'. His life was 'punctuated by them to such an extent that he no longer counts events from dates in the ordinary calendar, from birthdays or Christmas or Easter, but from such and such a disaster affecting himself'. The problem with earthquake connoisseurs is that they have too many illusions and not enough interest in 'things terrestrial'. In addition to which, they positively *need* to feel pursued by cataclysms. 'Far from being damaged by such convulsions,' Douglas believed, they 'distil' from them a 'subtle' value.[96]

From his Jewish-American father, Douglas explained to Lawrence, Magnus 'inherited that all too common taint of psychasthenia (miscalled neurasthenia)'. His domestic 'refinements', on the other hand, were the result of being the only son of his indulgent mother, Hedwig Rosamunde Liebetrau, whose death in April 1912 – the same month that Lawrence met Frieda – 'was the tragedy of his life'. So Magnus, like Lawrence, had a Mother with a capital M; the Madonna and child were 'sacred' to one another and it had been Hedwig who sowed 'the seeds of that habit of reckless expenditure which proved to be [her son's] undoing'. His mother's death, thought Douglas, 'must have given him a twist that never passed off: a twist reflected in his very face which, in unguarded moments, took on as sad an expression as I have seen on any human countenance'.[97]

Magnus rarely spoke about his mother, and when he did so his voice took on 'such tremulously tender accents' that Douglas was forced to change the topic of conversation.[98] But we know, Douglas revealed to Lawrence, that Hedwig believed herself the illegitimate daughter of Wilhelm I, King of Prussia and first German Kaiser. She was therefore half-sister to Frederick III, who married the eldest daughter of Queen Victoria, making Magnus first cousin to the last German Kaiser, Wilhelm II, whose support for Austro-Hungry in the crisis of July 1914 led immediately to the Great War. Illegitimate lines are hard to trace and there is no surviving evidence to show that Hedwig Liebetrau was a Hohenzollern, but Magnus had 'Filia Regis' engraved on her headstone in the Protestant cemetery in Rome. Lawrence, whose mother also felt she belonged to a superior class and whose wife had her own connections to German aristocracy, was in no doubt about Hedwig's heritage when Douglas told him. It all made sense: possessed by what Lawrence called 'the cruel illusion of importance *manqué*',[99] Magnus resembled the Kaiser himself, another earthquake connoisseur who was now exiled in Holland. Wilhelm II, Lawrence wrote in *Movements in European History*, had reduced the German aristocracy to something 'so hollow' and 'snobbish' and 'bluff' that it '*has* to be swept away'.[100] Magnus was also, Lawrence later observed, treated like royalty at Monte Cassino where the monks made it their business to know the people who mattered, and he certainly, Lawrence concluded in the *Memoir of Maurice Magnus*, had 'royal nerves'.[101]

But Magnus said nothing to Lawrence about his bloodline: illegitimacy was a matter of shame, and the honour of his mother was at stake.

Maurice Magnus was born in New York City on 7 November 1876. His father, a scientist called Charles Ferdinand Magnus, emigrated from Poland in the 1860s and married Hedwig Liebetrau in 1867, when she was twenty-two. Magnus's mother was born in Berlin and possibly raised at court, where some injustice caused her to fall from high society. Had she become an embarrassment? Was she banished by her nephew, the Kaiser?

Hedwig's father is officially recorded as Paul Liebetrau, husband of Mary Liebetrau. Was Mary pregnant with the child of Wilhelm I when she met Paul Liebetrau, or did the affair take place later? Nothing is known about the life of Mary Liebetrau, or the life of her daughter, other than the fact that Hedwig was raised to be a strict Lutheran. Wherever he was educated – and he grew up to know every bend in every road on the French Riviera – Magnus learned to speak several languages badly, to produce indifferent prose, to mismanage money, to appreciate good food and to keep up appearances. He wanted to be known as a '*littérateur*' ('littérateur!' mocked Lawrence, '– the impossible little pigeon!'),[102] and his adventures in the world of letters can be traced through the curious trail of publications he left behind. In his early twenties Magnus wrote a play called *Eldyle* about a visionary who turns his back on the world and builds a monastery to which young and beautiful men can retreat. Two of the monks, Hyantha and Clavel, fall in love, as a result of which Hyantha dies. The life Magnus sought in Monte Cassino had clearly been a long-term fantasy.

*Eldyle* was published in 1898. In the same year Magnus is credited as a 'translator and compiler' in the *American Colonial Handbook*, volumes one and two. In 1901 he worked – probably as manager – for a new literary magazine called the *Smart Set*, which would later publish a number of Lawrence's poems and stories. In 1902 he abandoned the Lutheran church and converted to Catholicism, and by 1903 he had left America for good and was to be found in Berlin, writing articles for the *Berlin Times* and *Florence Herald*. For a brief period, Maurice Magnus was Berlin correspondent for the *New York Independent*. He disliked Germany because, he felt, its history lacked culture and its people were thugs, but his antipathy was probably a response to the Kaiser's humiliation of his mother. He expressed his feelings in a manuscript called 'The Unspeakable Prussian', which he dedicated '*to all my fellow sufferers who have come into contact with Prussian officialdom and thereby suffered indignities and outrage*'.[103]

In 1904, Magnus introduced himself to Edward Gordon Craig who, fifty years later, recorded the event in his memoirs. Craig was exhibiting his stage and costume designs at a gallery on the Königgrätzer Strasse in Berlin when in walked a dapper little man who 'carefully … told me what a great artist I was'. The 'little' stranger:

> pretended to look at each drawing carefully – eagerly – his little face
> with its tight snappy mouth peering with apparent understanding
> at what he could not for the life of him comprehend. He wasn't
> an artist – nor a connoisseur – nor an art critic. Nor did he know
> anything about the workings of a theatre …[104]

Craig was the illegitimate son of Ellen Terry and the architect Edward Godwin, and his childhood was spent in the theatre where his mother was leading lady to the actor-manager Henry Irving (the model for Bram Stoker's Dracula). By the time he met Magnus, Craig had sired eight children; the following year he celebrated the appearance of a ninth, born to Isadora Duncan. Magnus appeared just as Craig was looking for someone to take care of his business arrangements, which included setting up a school, starting a magazine, building a theatre and seeing to fruition various plans for books, exhibitions and productions including designing the sets for Hugo von Hofmannsthal's *Elektra*. Magnus recommended himself as the best person. 'A concert or a lecture to arrange? Oh, yes. A book to be published? Oh, yes – he could see to that.' When Magnus reported to Craig at the end of his first day, he 'had seen a dozen people – pulled two dozen strings – drunk three Martinis'. On his second day, Magnus handed Craig a cheque for £40. He quickly made himself indispensable, writing reports, arranging introductions and providing all the flattery Craig's ego required. 'Enthusiasm,' Craig recalled, 'was his stumbling block', while the flaw in his character was 'pepperiness', particularly around women. But when his flattery was allowed 'full swing' Magnus was 'goodness itself'.

> Then the mouth would be less tight, but the head well up, and smiling in a quite nicely condescending way, he would say 'Yes, my dear Craig, I think they are quite wonderful, these drawings – more wonderful than Rembrandt' ... and the word 'Rembrandt' had a nasty snap, and Rembrandt was seen to be hastily bolting to get away from this little chap.

Guided by Magnus, who sped through the city 'in a hundred little steps', Craig discovered the best restaurants and bars in Berlin, spent twice what he could afford on cocktails he didn't want and was entertained by his manager's 'love for and ignorance of the eighteenth century'. Magnus had many talents but he was not, Craig mused, 'a business man at all. I don't know quite what he was, and never shall know, but I know what he did – and for artists he was always doing good, or trying to. His chief quality was rapidity – he attacked things – always had ideas how to begin – and then had not the faintest hesitation in calling on people and bringing them to see me.' One of Magnus's tricks was to remove the most impressive calling cards from the trays of entrance halls. 'You never know – might be useful one day,' he explained to Craig, slipping a few into his pocket. Such a day arose when Craig and Magnus were making their way to the Deutsches Theatre but found the road blocked by Prussian guards waiting for the Kaiser's arrival. Magnus flashed one of his cards and the waves parted. On another occasion Magnus offered to bring the Kaiser himself to Craig's studio. 'Believe me,' Craig recalled, 'he could have done it.'[105] Craig, like Lawrence – and probably like the Kaiser himself – knew nothing about Magnus being the latter's cousin.

Magnus was busy in Berlin. He set up his own theatrical agency and took over the bookings for Isadora Duncan; he set up a literary bureau specialising in translation, theatrical and serial rights; he translated into (bad) German Craig's treatise on *The Art of the Theatre*, then wrote an introduction to the book and found it a publisher; he drew up the budget for Craig's proposed new theatre in Dresden, which would house his life-size marionettes. The money Magnus made for Craig was always needed, he explained, for other ventures. The proceeds of Craig's first book vanished in Magnus's care, and so did those of his quarterly journal, *The Mask*, which Magnus looked after for a brief and disastrous period. 'He was not dishonest,' Craig concluded, '– he was merely very hard up ... He never deliberately cheated me, but he could not resist helping himself, any more than he could resist trying to help me.'

Magnus was hard up because Craig did not pay him. Instead, Magnus asked for 'loans' which Craig – himself supported by handouts from his mother and from Isadora Duncan – was 'only too glad' to provide. 'Thank you, thank you *so* much. My dear Craig, I can't tell you how much obliged I am to you – some publishers were to have paid me fifty pounds last week, and failed – it's been owing to me three months already.' (Like Lawrence, Craig could not write about Magnus without recalling the particular cadence of his speech.) Eventually Craig realised that it was cheaper to pay Magnus a salary than support him on loans, but soon his funds ran out altogether and Magnus was once again living on nothing. His missives to Craig became desperate: 'send as much as you can possibly spare ... it is dreadful here', 'I waited all day for money and none came – I am weak at the knees.'[106]

After parting from Craig in 1907, Magnus accompanied Isadora Duncan on a tour of 'Golden Russia', which was perhaps the best time of his life. The grandeur of St Petersburg and Moscow, the formal dinners, the immaculate servants, the endless aristocrats, the equestrian statues, the public baths, the first-class carriages, the French champagne, the hotels and bellboys and huge fur coats all made Magnus a 'lord of life'; this is what France in the eighteenth century must have been like, he imagined, 'only here everything was on a larger scale'. When Duncan danced in the Moscow Art Theatre, Magnus met Stanislavsky – 'a saint, an artist, a gentleman, all in one' – and was able to promote the theatre of Gordon Craig. The following summer, he drew up the contract between the Moscow Art Theatre and Gordon Craig for the production of *Hamlet*, which transformed Craig's career.[107]

Magnus was excellent at his job. He put himself in the path of all the important people (knowing the right people, he believed, was the source of success), he dealt with the press, and he made sure that Isadora Duncan had everything she desired. He managed her rehearsals, organised her meals and even directed, from behind the proscenium, the lights and the curtains. The profit, of course, disappeared, but being financially chaotic herself, Isadora didn't much mind that Magnus was too.

When he returned to Europe in 1908, Magnus found himself in a rapid sequence of earthquakes. We know that on 22 August 1909 he was on Capri borrowing money from Douglas, that on 26 April 1912 his mother died and that on 10 July 1913 he married a woman called Lucy Bramley-Moore, seven years his senior, at the Church of Our Lady of Victories in London. All we know about his wife is that she was a vegetarian with what Magnus described as a 'persistent, subtle jealousy'.[108] By 1914 he was in Rome, without Lucy, editing the *Roman Review*, and in 1915 he was living in Taormina, which he left in bad odour. In March 1916, he sailed – as the only first-class passenger on board – to North Africa to join the French Foreign Legion. By 1917 Magnus had deserted the Legion and was back in Rome, where he once again ran into Douglas, and having for the moment some money – heaven knows how – insisted on repaying his friend's former kindness.

'I was glad to lose sight of him,' Gordon Craig had said when he and his manager parted company in 1907, but Magnus was never far away.[109] At the same time that he ran into Douglas once more in Rome, Magnus also ran into Craig and organised for him a performance of Bach's Matthew Passion. He stayed in touch with Isadora Duncan as well, and in the summer of 1919 arranged her tour of Switzerland. When, in late November 1919, Magnus returned to Rome from Florence and defrauded Leone Colleoni of the Excelsior Hotel, he again saw Craig who thought him 'a very changed man'. Life 'seemed to have played him so many dirty tricks that he was contemplating retiring into a monastery. So many of the "names" with which he had conjured in the past were no more, or no longer meant anything. He could see no future for himself.' These remarks were scribbled by Gordon Craig in the margins of his copy of *Memoirs of the Foreign Legion by M.M., with an Introduction by D. H. Lawrence*.[110]

* * *

On 4 December 1919, Lawrence sent his sister a postcard reporting that Frieda had now joined him in Florence: the picture on the card was of Michelangelo's *David*. Frieda arrived from Germany at 4 a.m., and Lawrence met her from the train and hired an open carriage from which to view the city in the 'moonmist'. They passed 'the pale crouching Duomo', where the top of the Giotto tower had 'disappeared into the sky', and 'the Palazzo Vecchio with Michelangelo's *David* and all the statues of men. 'This is a men's town,' Lawrence told her, 'not like Paris, where all the statues are women.' Frieda liked Douglas, and talking with him in her native tongue. The full extent of his wit, she said, was only apparent in German. She was less impressed by his self-consciously wicked friends. 'Corruption is not interesting to me,' she said. 'Nor does it frighten me. I find it dull.'[III]

Four days later, the Lawrences left for Rome, after which they caught the train further south to Cassino. 'Few places in the West represent the continuity of tradition between the ancient and the modern world as well as does Monte Cassino,' wrote Herbert Bloch in *Monte Cassino in the Middle Ages*.[112] Poised on the summit of one of the Alban mountains, halfway between Rome and Naples, the abbey surveys the Liri, 1,400 feet below. A medieval panopticon, it looks in every direction and can, in turn, be seen for miles across the valley. Lawrence saw it for the first time from the town which leans against the base of the slope, where their train pulled in on the morning of 13 December. The monastery was 'crouching there above, world-famous', he wrote in the *Memoir*. It had witnessed the turbulence of the early Christian Church, the conflict between Rome and Byzantium in the eleventh century and the glorious days of the Holy Roman Empire; popes had prayed there, Charlemagne rested there, Thomas Aquinas was educated there, Dante himself visited, and St Benedict is buried there. 'But it was impossible to call then,'[113] Lawrence said. He was with Frieda, for a start.

In his account of the life and miracles of St Benedict, Pope Gregory described how, driven from his previous monastery by the envious priest Florentius, Benedict came to the mountain by Cassino, and saw that it 'riseth in height the space of three miles' and 'seemeth to touch the very heavens'. At the top was a pagan temple of Apollo, surrounded by 'woods for the service of the devils'. Setting fire to the woods and breaking the idols, Benedict began the construction of his abbey. The devil, 'with his fiery mouth and flaming eyes', railed against the holy man and did everything in his power to disrupt his progress – crouching on rocks they needed for building, setting fire to the kitchen, knocking down walls.[114] But time and again Benedict's prayers defeated the serpent, and his great monastery was completed.

The only aspect of Benedict's life that interests Dante, when he meets the saint in the seventh sphere of Paradise, is the building of Monte Cassino. 'That mountain on whose flank Cassino lies', St Benedict explains,

> was once frequented on its summit by
> those who were still deluded, still awry;
>
> and I am he who was the first to carry
> up to that peak the name of Him who brought
> to earth the truth that lifts us to the heights.
>
> (*Paradise*, Canto 22, 37–42)

The two men led parallel lives: Dante in his exile built his mighty poem and founded modern poetry, and Benedict built his mighty monastery and founded modern monasticism.

From Cassino, the Lawrences travelled five miles by postbus to the town of Atina, and then continued another five miles by donkey and on foot to Picinisco, on the edge of the Abruzzi mountains. They had gone, Lawrence said, 'beyond the world into the pre-world', which is what he looked for in a journey.[115] The Abruzzi, which Lawrence had once thought a possible location for Rananim, his utopian community, is a wild and desolate terrain, as dense and silent as the Hercynian forest. They crossed the icy river on a plank, their luggage on the donkey's back, and for the last stretch of the journey, dwarfed beneath white peaks that grinned like devils and glittered hellishly, they scrambled goat-style down a barely formed track to the house they were renting for the winter. The cold was stunning, and they arrived stupefied with weariness. The house had been built thirty years before by a local man called Orazio Cervi, who had made money in London as an artist's model. One of the sculptors Cervi had sat for was Sir William Hamo Thornycroft whose daughter, Rosalind Baynes, had now separated from her husband and was looking to make a new start in Italy. The Lawrences had met Rosalind after the war, and it was she who had told them about the house; it was their task to report back on whether it would make a suitable home for her and her three young children. 'It's a bit staggeringly primitive,' Lawrence warned.[116] The nearest village was a heavy two-mile climb uphill.

Part Victorian villa and part peasant hovel, from the outside the building was – and still is – strong and square and important-looking, but the inside might have been scooped out of a quarry. The kitchen had an unswept stone floor, a vaulted ceiling and a large, dark open hearth: 'everything must be cooked gipsy-fashion', Lawrence reported to Rosalind, 'in the chimney over a wood-fire'. The few sticks of furniture were crude and rough, and the windows were hidden behind iron bars and drab shutters. Wooden stairs led to a bleak bedroom with a balcony that looked over the viewless terrain. There was no bath, so Rosalind's children would have to be washed in the 'big copper boiling pan, in which they cook the pig's food'. Chickens wandered in and out and the donkey, braying 'his head off', was tethered to the doorpost where he dropped his manure on the doorstep. The local men were 'brigands with skin sandals and white swathed wrapped legs' and the women dressed in 'Swiss bodices and white shirts with full, full sleeves'. They spoke an unintelligible dialect and no Italian. He was 'stunned with the strangeness of it all', Lawrence wrote, 'half-enraptured' and half-annihilated by the 'terrific beauty of the place'.[117]

He and Frieda built a fire in the kitchen and a fire in the bedroom, but the cold had sunk into the walls. 'It seems there are places which resist us,' Lawrence said of Picinisco, 'which have the power to overthrow our psychic being,' and he had struck one of them.[118] But Lawrence had also, he confessed in a letter home, 'turned into a wandering Jew. My feet itch, and a seat burns my posterior if I sit too long. What ails me I don't know, but it's on and on.'[119] It began to snow, which meant they would soon be trapped, so on Christmas Eve, he and Frieda fled.

Packing their bags and tying them to the donkey, they stalked and scrambled their way back to Atina, where they took another postbus and passed once more beneath the world-famous monastery, poised in the sky like a floating ark. In Cassino, they boarded a train to Naples where they caught the steamer to Siren Land and pulled into the rocky coast just as a magnificent red dawn rose over the Mediterranean.

Capri, where he and Frieda thawed out between late December 1919 and March 1920 was, Lawrence told his childhood friends Willie and Sallie

Hopkins, 'about 4 miles by 2 miles but really almost mountainous, sheer precipices above us even here'.[120] Since 1907 it had been possible to ascend by funicular from the marina to the 'tiny jungle' of Capri town, and this is what Lawrence and Frieda did. They slid up the cliff and took two large rooms at the top of a building called the Palazzo Ferrero, which stood in a cluster of other towers a few minutes' walk from the central campanile. The town itself, Lawrence noted, was the same size as Eastwood. Their apartment had three balconies and a roof terrace which he thought 'one of the most wonderful places in the world'.[121] Here they hung their washing, 'strange pieces of grey flannel underwear', recalled Compton Mackenzie, which might have belonged to either one of them.[122] Poised on 'the very neck of the little town, on the very neck of the island', their drying drawers fluttered alongside the bobbly roof of the Duomo. 'All the island life goes on beneath us,' Lawrence wrote of the view from his new home, 'and then, away to the right, the sea, Ischia in the distance, and the Bay of Naples: on the left the wide open Mediterranean.'[123] Beyond the Bay of Naples, clear as a picture, stood Vesuvius rolling 'her glittery white smoke'. Even in winter the Capri sun was 'brilliant, beautiful', and this was the first time for years that Lawrence had felt its force. From the edge of the rock he 'watched him go down red into the sea. How quickly he hurries round the edge of the horizon, as if he had an appointment below'.[124]

The island fascinated Lawrence, not least because he was fascinated by islands. The Blue Grotto, on the north-western tip of Capri, is a particularly Lawrentian piece of natural architecture: a sea cave flooded with brilliant emerald and blue light, it was the private swimming pool of Tiberius. But apart from in his letters Lawrence wrote nothing about Capri, and the reason for his silence is presumably that Norman Douglas had written so well about it already. Lawrence climbed Monte Solaro, Capri's highest peak, and took in the prospect: 'this island at one's feet, the dark sea all round: the mainland at Massa coming close, pale grey rock, very steep, and slopes of white-speckled villages'. There in the distance the other islands slept 'pale and delicate in the sea'.[125] When Lawrence looked down the Salernian Gulf on a blue day, towards 'the dim, sheer rocky coast' and 'the clean rock mountains', it was 'so beautiful', he thought, 'so like Ulysses, that one sheds one's avatars, and recovers a lost self, Mediterranean, anterior to us'.[126]

Capri had been devoted to pleasure for 2,000 years, and Lawrence initially liked the island's international scene, packed as it was with exiled Europeans, Russians and Americans including, until 1913, Maxim Gorky. Oscar Wilde and Lord Alfred Douglas had come here before moving on to Taormina, and the current 'personalities' included Compton Mackenzie. Lawrence had met Mackenzie and his wife, Faith, before the war, through the former actress Mary Cannan, who was now separated from her second husband, the novelist and playwright Gilbert Cannan. Mary Cannan was on Capri herself and there were 'lots of other people', said Lawrence, 'if we cared to know them'.[127] Having corrected the proofs for *Movements in European History*, Lawrence borrowed Compton Mackenzie's typewriter (on which Norman Douglas had written *South Wind*) to hammer out *Psychoanalysis and the Unconscious* before sending it to his agent.

Posing in a floppy velvet hat, blue-lined cape and orange tie, Compton Mackenzie was deputising for Norman Douglas as Capri's head of state. Freshly famous after the success of his novel *Sinister Street*, which defined the generation of 1910, Mackenzie was renting the Casa Solitaria, a Bond-style house protruding out of the limestone cliffs, 300 feet up from the sea on the island's south side. Five hundred feet above the Solitaria stands the Telegrafo summit, and in front of the house, rising from the depths like the spires of a drowned cathedral, are the great Faraglioni rocks.

Lawrence's arrival on Capri coincided with Mackenzie's discovery that during the war his wife had fallen in love with an Italian who had since died. His being cuckolded doubtless endeared him to Lawrence who, according to Frieda, had never responded so warmly to anyone before, although Lawrence later said that Mackenzie, from a line of travelling players, was too theatrical for him: 'one feels generations of actors behind him and can't be quite serious'.[128] Mackenzie, however, thought Lawrence extremely good company. For two months their friendship was unsoiled. Lawrence made his way to the Casa Solitaria on Mackenzie's thirty-seventh birthday, armed with a bottle of Benedictine; he took Mackenzie's advice on the publication of *Women in Love* and the projected reissue of *The Rainbow* (for which Mackenzie suggested he write a preface). On one occasion, according to Mackenzie, Lawrence confided that he and Frieda had never achieved simultaneous orgasm, which meant that their marriage was 'imperfect'. His only experience of 'perfect love', Lawrence allegedly also confided, had been for a 'young coalminer' when he was sixteen,[129] which is the kind of gossip that people liked to spread about Lawrence.

The two novelists planned to sail to the South Seas, and even advertised in *The Times* for a secretary. Mackenzie suggested filming the adventure, but Lawrence, wanting to return to the spirit of Melville, refused. Hearing that Lawrence had turned down Mackenzie's invitation, Magnus wrote to Douglas: 'Any chance for me? I'd love a trip to the South Sea Islands. Can't you recommend me as something?'[130]

Instead of sailing to the South Seas, Mackenzie leased the Channel Island of Herm, one mile long and half a mile wide. 'The Lord of the Isles', Lawrence wrote to him in September 1921. 'I shall write a skit on you one day.'[131] But Faith thought Herm was haunted by unhappy spirits and so they moved to the smaller and even more derelict rock of Jethou. Still not satisfied by island life, in 1925 Mackenzie bought the uninhabited Shiat Isles in the Outer Hebrides but lived on the nearby rock of Barra.

Lawrence and Compton Mackenzie would each write a skit on the other. After his death, Lawrence appeared as the 'innately' homosexual Daniel Rayner in Mackenzie's novel sequence *The Four Winds of Love*. In *The South Wind of Love*, which is set before the war, Rayner is introduced in his apron scrubbing the living-room floor while his fleshy German wife, Hildegarde, formally married to a Birmingham doctor, is having a nap upstairs. Rayner, whose consciousness 'of his own genius' was 'aggressive and self-assertive', speaks with a Midlands accent. In *The West Wind of Love* the war is over and Rayner, brutalised by the censorship of his novel and being hounded out of Wales, turns up in Rome: 'I believe that hate is becoming the driving force of his genius,' reports John, the protagonist, 'and that without it he would be lost.'[132] The Rayners then come to the island of Citrano (Capri) where Rayner discourses on the sickness of western man. ' "Man went off the track when he started to think here," he tapped his forehead, "instead of here," he pointed at his generative centre.' He later sends John a postcard from Monte Cassino: 'This place is rotten with the past,' it says. Rayner was not yet mad, John believed, but 'moving towards madness'.[133]

Mackenzie himself was the model for Cathcart, the islander in Lawrence's 1926 parable 'The Man Who Loved Islands'. Cathcart wants his first island to be 'Paradise regained' but finds instead that he has landed in Limbo, 'where all the souls that never die veer and swoop on their vast, strange errands'. He is living in 'the dark, wide mystery of time', where the 'moment begins to heave and expand in great circles' and 'the chariots of the so-called dead dash down the old streets of centuries, and souls crowd on the footways'. The island frightens him and so Cathcart moves to a smaller one near by, where the past is not so 'vastly alive, and the future is not separated off'.[134] He then buys a third island which should be his Elysium but even the baaing of the sheep proves a curse, and so he drives them over the cliff. Soon the birds themselves disappear, and there is nothing on the island left living. The story ends with Cathcart being buried by snow, like Gerald in *Women in Love* and the sinners in the lowest circle of hell, up to their necks in ice.

'The Man Who Loved Islands' is strong, spare and cruel, and Mackenzie threatened legal action. But Lawrence, who also loved islands, used his friend's experience to mock himself equally: Cathcart's first island – 'a quiet, busy little world' which he shared with a fisherman, a carpenter, a mason and the souls of all the dead – is a parody of Rananim, Lawrence's own 'island idea'.[135] Islands played a significant part in *Women in Love*: it is on an island that Gudrun dances before the cattle, and on another island that Birkin's true communion with Ursula takes place. And the same month that Compton Mackenzie was being driven from Herm by malevolent spirits, Lawrence would leave Magnus alone on an island to face his fate.

On New Year's Eve, Magnus paid for his six weeks at Rome's Grand Hotel with the money stolen from the Excelsior and then fled thirty miles south to the fishing port of Anzio, where he booked himself into the Hotel Vittoria. Meanwhile, the cheques cashed at the Excelsior were returned unpaid by the Banca Commerciale Italiana on the grounds that Mr Magnus did not have an account with the Metropolitan Trust Company on which they were drawn. Making enquiries at the US embassy, Colleoni heard that Maurice Magnus was – for reasons unknown – 'persona non grata to the authorities of his country' and that a passport visa would be denied him if he ever tried to re-enter the United States.

Posing at the Hotel Vittoria as a client of the Banca Sebasti, Magnus cashed two cheques for £200. Having stayed at the Vittoria before, he was trusted by the manageress, Maria Tomaselli, who instead of presenting him with a weekly bill agreed to let Magnus draw up a tab and pay it off on the day of his departure. He then, on 3 February 1920, wrote a final fraudulent cheque for £1,600: £1,400 to cover his bill for the past thirty-five days, and £200 to be given to him in cash. All three cheques were later returned unpaid to Maria Tomaselli.

Allowing the Hotel Vittoria to believe that he was returning to his apartment in Rome, Magnus instead fled to Monte Cassino, where the monks had been expecting him for the last six weeks. 'I don't know what my next step will be,' he wrote to Douglas when he reached the monastery, '– if there is going to be any step at all. I have drifted into a sort of resignation – the sort Heine wrote about in his "Reisebilder" – you can't fight God.'[136]

From Capri, Lawrence wrote a number of important letters. The first was to Katherine Mansfield, now dying in Menton. 'I loathe you,' he said. 'You revolt me stewing in your consumption.'[137] It's an astonishing remark even by Lawrence's standards, and one of the few occasions on which he called the dreaded illness by its name. His attack should be seen in the context of an earlier letter to Mansfield, written in December 1918, when one of his childhood friends was in the final stages of TB: 'Katherine – on ne meurt pas: I almost want it to be reflexive – on ne se meurt pas: Point! Be damned and be blasted everything, and let the bloody world come to its end. But one does not die. Jamais.'[138]

Lawrence then wrote to Magnus in Monte Cassino, whose reply had 'a wistful tone – and I don't know what made me think he was in trouble, in monetary difficulty. But I felt it acutely – a kind of appeal.'[139] Lawrence several times described Magnus as 'appealing' to him; the word can be read in both senses. That week, Lawrence had received a gift of twenty pounds (1,300 lire) from Amy Lowell in America, and so his own monetary difficulties were for the moment relieved. His thank-you letter to his benefactress pulled no punches: Lawrence resented his reputation in America as a martyred genius beaten down by establishment bully-boys. It 'irks me a bit', Lawrence told Amy Lowell, 'to have to accept a sort of charity ... I am a sort of charity-boy of literature, apparently.'[140] He then did something entirely characteristic, and passed his humiliation on to Magnus. 'I felt … I owed Magnus that dinner,' he wrote in the *Memoir of Maurice Magnus*, 'and I didn't want to owe him anything, since he despised me a little for being careful. So partly out of revenge, perhaps, and partly because I felt the strange wistfulness of him appealing to me, I sent him five pounds …'[141] It was a complex and loaded decision. 'I doubt if any man living hands out a pound note without a pang,' Lawrence began his poem 'Money Madness'.

While Lawrence hated owing anything, Magnus believed he was owed a good deal. 'Your cheque has saved my life,' he told Lawrence in his thank-you letter. 'Since I last saw you I have fallen down an abyss.'[142] His cheque, Lawrence admitted, was vengeful: he wanted to prove that Magnus was wrong to think him a puritan, he wanted to place Magnus on the rung beneath him, charity-boy wise, and he wanted to compete with Douglas, whose friendship with Magnus had equally begun with a gift of money. In *Triumph to Exile*, Mark Kinkead-Weekes describes Lawrence's trip to Monte Cassino as an irritating 'distraction' to his work, something he was 'pressed' by Magnus to do. But what Lawrence principally wanted when he sent Magnus that £5 cheque was to confirm his intention to visit the monastery by putting down a deposit.

Lawrence finally wrote to Frieda's mother in Bavaria, asking her to send on a manuscript he had left there seven years before. It consisted of 200 pages of an unfinished novel called 'The Insurrection of Miss Houghton' which, had it been completed in 1913 as intended, would have followed *Sons and Lovers*. On 12 February, the manuscript arrived. Lawrence left the first five chapters untouched, and discarded the rest (around 140 pages). 'The Insurrection of Miss Houghton', he told his publisher Martin Secker, is 'quite unlike my usual style', and will be 'quite *unexceptional*, as far as the censor is concerned'. It would make, Lawrence believed, a 'perfect selling novel'.[143] Loosely based on the true fortunes of an Eastwood family called the Cullens, who were known to Lawrence as a child, it is the story of Alvina Houghton, a would-be New Woman who lives 'like a mole' in Manchester House in the mining town of Woodhouse, a place of 'cabbage stumps' and 'rotten fences'. 'I can't stay here all my life,' Alvina declares. 'I can't bear it. I'm buried alive – simply buried alive.'[144] Alvina is twenty-five when the book begins, and has nothing to look forward to: her mother dies, her father's various businesses – a fashionable clothing store, a brick kiln and a coalmine – invariably fail. 'How many infernos,' she wondered, '… did she not travel?'[145] At this point in Alvina's story Lawrence put down his pencil and sailed for the mountain-isle of Purgatory, the place where sinners pay their debts.

# Part Two

'I always remember getting up in the black dark of the January morning, and making a little coffee on the spirit lamp, and watching the clock, the big-faced, blue old clock on the campanile in the piazza in Capri, to see I wasn't late.'[1] It was in fact 18 February 1920 when Lawrence set off for Monte Cassino, five days after Otto Gross, found frozen and starving on a Berlin street, died of pneumonia. At ten minutes to six, Lawrence crossed the campanile, 'slid' down the vertical rock in the funicular and took a rowing boat over the 'dark sea' to the steamer 'that lay there showing her lights and hooting'. He watched the dawn rise as the steamer, pushing against the wind from the snow-crests, made its way round Vesuvius and into the harbour at Naples.

Lawrence 'always loved hanging over the side', he wrote in the *Memoir*, 'and watching the people come out in boats from the little places of the shore, that rose steep and beautiful. I love the movement of these watery Neapolitan people.'[2] When Dante and Virgil were transported to Purgatory by the angel with the burnished wings, the sun 'with his arrows bright' was also 'shooting forth the day'. Lawrence's own boat was late and he reached the station at Naples just as the train was pulling out; running along the platform, he leapt on to the last carriage. 'Perhaps if I had missed it,' he mused, 'fate would have been different.'[3] What he means by this is unclear. In what way would fate have been different? Would Magnus's fate have been different had Lawrence missed his train? Or would Lawrence himself be a different man had he not gone to Monte Cassino on that particular day?

Hell had been described by poets before Dante but the shape and dimensions of Purgatory, where we shed our former selves, were his own invention. Earlier authors placed Purgatory underground, but for

Dante the border crossing between two worlds was a conical mountain in the southern hemisphere, made of the matter displaced when Lucifer's fall from heaven created the Inferno. A stairway of ledges, each eighteen feet wide – which Dante compared to the steps of the Church of San Miniato – is cut into the slope, which is composed of seven circles, one for each of the sins. Dante's Purgatory was a composite of Mount Sinai, Mount Zion, Mount Arafat, the Mount of Olives, Mount Tabor, Mount Carmel, Mount Parnassus, Mount Olympus and the mountain in Lactantius' late Latin poem 'The Phoenix', on whose peak can be found the mythical bird. Purification is not something we always achieve willingly, and a character in Samuel Beckett's *Rough for Radio* reflects on the fact that the men in Dante's Purgatory are nostalgic for who they once were. Instead of saying 'I shall be,' they lament, 'I was, I was.' Lawrence followed suit.

From the station at Cassino he hired a *carrozzella* – or what Magnus called 'a dirty little cart' – to take him to the monastery.[4] 'We twisted up and up the wild hillside,' Lawrence wrote, 'past the old castle of the town, past the last villa, between trees and rocks. We saw no one.' Dante's own progress up Mount Purgatory, which took three days, was halted when darkness extinguished the divine guiding light, and Lawrence similarly saw his journey as a race to reach the summit before sunset. At twilight, they turned the corner of the oak wood, and there it stood, rearing above him 'from its buttress in the rock', a 'huge square fortress-palace of the sixteenth century crowning the near distance'.[5] It had taken him nearly twelve hours, and every available means of transport, to get here.

The angel who holds the keys to the door of Purgatory warns Dante that having entered, he cannot look back and sigh, 'I was, I was': 'he who looks behind returns outside again'. Stepping through the portal into the white marble world, Dante hears the ringing of bells and the chanting of a *Te Deum*. When Lawrence arrived at Monte Cassino the monks were at Evensong and it was Magnus, still chubby-cheeked but 'greyer at the temples', who stepped over the threshold to greet him – Magnus always appeared to Lawrence from out of the darkness. There being no Douglas to fuss over, the host gave the pilgrim his full attention. Reaching for his hand as Lawrence stepped down from the cart, Magnus looked into his eyes 'rather like a woman who isn't quite sure of her lover'. He had a 'wistful and watchful tenderness' which

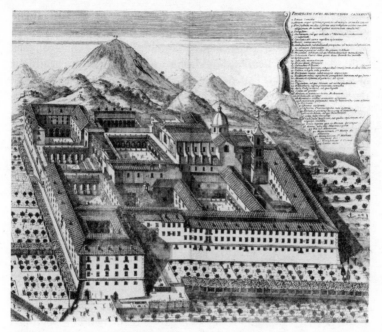

Plan of the monastery at Monte Cassino

was both 'charming' and oddly pompous in the freezing air of the vast place, with its 'ponderous stone walls' and 'masses of coldness cloaking around'.[6]

'So *very* glad to see you,' Magnus said, taking Lawrence's bag. 'I'm so *pleased* you've come.' Lawrence responded by asking Magnus for five francs to pay the driver. 'Certainly, certainly,' said Magnus, pressing the coins into the driver's palm. Lawrence, who had 125 lire (just over £1) in his pocket, could have paid the man himself, but asking Magnus to do so was a reminder that he had bought Magnus for £5. Neither had any news to share except that Magnus was 'very short of money', which, he said, 'of course is *no* news', and he 'laughed his little laugh'. 'I'm so glad to be here,' Magnus continued. 'The peace and the rhythm of life is so *beautiful*! I'm sure you'll love it.' They passed through the great door and down the covered entrance into the first courtyard. Young monks stood in clusters chatting to one another, a peasant was driving his sheep from the cloister grass and an old monk was darting into the post office. Coming towards them under the arches was a labourer with a two-handed saw, and behind him, 'hastening forward with a quick smile', was Magnus's particular friend: a handsome Maltese monk called Don Martino, fresh and bespectacled and around the same age as Lawrence. Only fifty monks now lived in the vast abbey, and 'one felt', thought Lawrence, that 'one was at college with one's college mates'.[7] It reminded him, in other words, of his traumatic visit to Cambridge.

They turned the corner into the central courtyard, attributed to Bramante, with its great well and colonnades of arches; from here a grand sweep of steps leads to the higher courtyard, at the end of which stand the doors to the Desiderian Basilica. Lawrence recorded the scene in his photographic memory, and Don Martino then led him to his rooms in the fortress walls which were down a narrow staircase and along a 'cold, naked white corridor, high and arched'. It was 'dead, silent, stone cold, everywhere'. The term 'stone cold' must, Lawrence thought, have been invented here, and he used the phrase again to describe his reaction to reading, in *Dregs*, Magnus's accounts of homosexual relationships in the French Foreign Legion. He had been given by the monks a 'charming and elegant' bedroom whose balcony looked down to the monastery garden, 'a narrow strip beneath the walls, and beyond, the clustered buildings of the farm, and the oak woods and arable fields of the hill summit: and beyond again, the gulf where the world's valley was, and all the mountains that stand in Italy on the plains as if God had just put them down ready made'.[8] Still further beyond, the sun had gone down, giving the snow a rosy glow and casting the valleys in shadow. 'One heard, far below, the trains shunting, the world clinking in the cold air.' Magnus stood there beaming, and looking wistfully at Don Martino. 'Isn't it wonderful! Ah, the most wonderful place on earth! What now could you wish better than to end your days here? The peace, the beauty, the eternity of it.' All he needed was some money, Magnus said, and he could begin his religious studies in Rome.[9]

Magnus talked about his future as a Benedictine monk, said Lawrence, 'like a boy planning a new role'. But the monastic life, in which time stood still, had long tempted Lawrence as well. He had described Higher Tregerthen as a monastery, and the ideals of Rananim were close to those of St Benedict's ethic of work, brotherhood and soil. Magnus was on the cusp of achieving for himself the life that had so far eluded Lawrence. Magnus's own 'sumptuous' bedroom was further down the corridor. He had a curtained four-poster bed, a sofa, a desk covered in papers and photographs, a table with a green-shaded electric lamp, and the usual array of powders and pomades on the dressing table. He kept the drawers of his desk locked as though they contained great secrets, and he carried, like Dante's doorkeeper, his keys on a chain. 'I always wonder what the secrets can be,' wrote Lawrence, 'that are able to be kept so tight under lock and key.' Night had now fallen, and 'from the window one saw the world far below, like a pool the flat plain, a deep pool of darkness with little twinkling lights, and rows and bunches of light that were the railway station'. Magnus, Lawrence and Don Martino sat around the table, drinking tea and talking. Lawrence had only a thin coat, so Magnus wrapped him inside a coat of his own, 'made of thick, smooth black cloth, and lined with black sealskin', with a collar also of sealskin. 'I can still remember the feel of the silky fur. It was queer to have him helping me solicitously into this coat.' Lawrence disliked being touched, but didn't flinch when Magnus tenderly buttoned his stiff, high-necked collar. He must have looked like a Prussian officer. 'So off we went, he in his grey overcoat and I in my sealskin millionaire monster, down the dim corridor to the guests' refectory.'[10]

They were waited on at supper by a lay brother 'with a bulging forehead and queer, fixed eyes' who belonged in an Italian picture, and while Magnus's Italian was as incorrect as it was possible to be, he still patronised the lay brothers. Because the food had grown cold on its journey from the kitchen, Magnus nibbled instead on a piece of bread. 'I could tell the meals were a trial for him,' wrote Lawrence, and that Magnus's 'tisickyness' was equally a trial for the lay brothers, who bore a 'grudge' against their pompous little guest.

After supper they went, 'by our two secret little selves into the tall dense nearly-darkness of the church'. Lawrence pictured them 'creeping' about like thieves, which in a sense they were, being trespassers in this hallowed place. Raised as a low Protestant, Lawrence was drawn to the headiness of high Catholicism; his pilgrimage had brought him from the parish church in Eastwood, with its fanatical pastor, to the medieval basilica where Thomas Aquinas had been educated. Magnus led Lawrence by the arm as though he were guiding him through a city, clicking on the light switches as they tiptoed from altar to altar.

> We looked at the lily marble of the great floor, at the pillars, at
> the Benvenuto Cellini casket, at the really lovely pillars and slabs
> of different coloured marbles, all coloured marbles, yellow and
> grey and rose and green and lily-white, veined and mottled and
> splashed: lovely, lovely stones – And Benvenuto had used pieces of
> lapis lazuli, blue as cornflowers.[11]

Lilies and lapis lazuli: two of Lawrence's favourite symbols. Still holding his arm, Magnus 'whispered ecstasies' in his ear, and whenever they passed an altar, 'whether the high altar or the side chapels', he performed 'a wonderful reverence, which he must have practised for hours, bowing waxily down and sinking till his one knee touched the pavement, then rising like a flower that rises and unfolds again, till he had skipped to my side and was playing cicerone once more'. Lawrence compared Magnus to Klingsor, the sorcerer in Wagner's *Parsifal*, while he was Parsifal himself, on the quest for the Holy Grail.

They crept about examining the treasures of the chancel and the roly-poly babies carved into the choir stalls and 'everything in the church – and then everything in the ancient room on the side', after which they went down to the crypt where Magnus clicked on the lights so that the 'gold mosaic of the vaulting glittered and bowed' and the 'blue mosaic glowed out'.

Lawrence was glad to get away from the glittering splendour of the church and retire to the normality of Magnus's bedroom, where he was presented with the contents of the old leather suitcase containing his host's treasures.

> He showed me a wonderful photograph of a picture of a lovely
> lady – asked me what I thought of it, and seemed to expect me
> to be struck to bits by the beauty. His almost sanctimonious
> expectation made me tell the truth, that I thought it just a bit
> cheap, trivial. And then he said, dramatic:
>     'That's my mother.'
>     It looked so unlike anybody's mother, much less Magnus's, that
> I was startled. I realised that she was his great stunt, and that I had
> put my foot in it.[12]

Of course Lawrence knew that this lovely lady was the great Hedwig herself, outcast daughter of emperors and sister of kings. It was perversity on his part to describe her image as 'a bit cheap, trivial', simply because Magnus wanted it praised. But Lawrence was the only boy ever to have had a sacred mother, or to have known the suave electricity that flows in a circuit between the great nerve-centres in mother and child. The tense silence that followed was broken by the appearance of Don Martino, who chatted happily about his former life ('I was, I was'), while all three sipped a liquor that Magnus liked and a bottle of which, Lawrence said – to compensate for his earlier cruelty – he would buy for him. They discussed politics until midnight, at which point Lawrence 'came out of the black Overcoat' and went to bed.

The following morning was bright and still and sunny. From the loophole window of his room, Lawrence 'looked down on the farm cluster and the brown fields and the sere oak-woods of the hill-crown, and the rocks and bushes savagely bordering it round'. Dante, who might have stayed in the same room when he too visited the Abbey, will have known the view. It was now that Lawrence had the first of his crises on the hill. 'He who looks behind', the doorman had warned Dante, 'returns outside again', and Lawrence's crises over the next two days were precisely to do with looking back and returning outside.

And the poignant grip of the past, the grandiose, violent past of the Middle Ages, when blood was strong and unquenched and life was flamboyant with splendours and horrible miseries, took hold of me till I could hardly bear it. It was really agony to me to be in the monastery and to see the old farm and the bullocks slowly working in the fields below, and the black pigs rooting among weeds, and to see a monk sitting on a parapet in the sun, and an old, old man in skin sandals and white-bunched, swathed legs come driving an ass slowly to the monastery gate, slowly, with all that lingering nonchalance and wildness of the Middle Ages, and yet to know that I was myself, child of the present.[13]

Farms were where Lawrence had been happiest, and his 'agony' recalls the word's single appearance in the Bible where, on the night before his betrayal and arrest, Jesus prays in the garden of Gethsemane at the foot of the Mount of Olives: 'And being in an agony he prayed more earnestly: and his sweat was as it were great drops of blood falling down to the ground.'

What agonised Lawrence in the view from his window was not the rocks or the river or the roads, but the railway. It was 'so strange', he said, to see 'the white road going straight past a mountain that stood like a loaf of sugar, the river meandering in loops, and the railway with glistening lines making a long black swoop across the flat and into the hills'. It was strange to 'see trains come steaming with white smoke flying. To see the station like a little harbour where trucks like shipping stood anchored in rows in the black bay of railway … to see all this from the monastery, where the Middle Ages live on in a sort of agony, like Tithonus, and cannot die, this was almost a violation to my soul, made almost a wound.'[14] It was not the *sight* of the trains and their tracks, as destructive to the view as windfarms today, that Lawrence could not bear: it was their sound, the savage music of his childhood.

He liked to follow an experience of height with one of depth, and when we next see Lawrence in the *Memoir*, he is safely in a crypt underground where they are attending mass. Magnus was 'scrupulous in his going up and down' while Lawrence felt like 'an outsider'. The monks 'seemed very human in their likes and jealousies', and Lawrence compared them, again, to a group of dons at Cambridge.

After mass, Magnus continued his guided tour and Lawrence's day got steadily worse. They walked in the Bramante courtyard where once there had been a Renaissance world; now it was 'dead forever' and when pilgrimages thronged in, they were 'horrible artisan excursions from the great town'. The local peasants, however, still had their white-bunched and swathed legs, but this made Lawrence equally wretched.

He and Magnus climbed the stairs of the observatory. Here, at the highest point of the monastery, they 'looked at the world below':

> Roads, railway, river, streams, a world in accurate and lively detail, with mountains sticking up abruptly and rockily, as the old painters painted it. I think there is no way of painting Italian landscape except that way – that started with Lorenzetti and ended with the sixteenth century.

The roads through the mountains from Rome, Lawrence said, came 'straight as judgment'. Today was Judgement Day.[15]

\* \* \*

When Moses was dying, God took him to the top of Mount Pisgah and showed him the Promised Land. A 'Pisgah sight' is thus a view offered and denied, and Lawrence's writing is filled with Pisgah sights. The symbolism of views he learned from the Bible, but writing about views was a skill picked up from Ruskin's art of word-painting: 'The greatest thing a human soul ever does in this world,' wrote Ruskin in *Modern Painters*, 'is to see something and tell what it saw in a plain way.' Seeing, for Ruskin, was a double act, involving both visual accuracy and historical imagination, and Lawrence, as Aldington was quick to point out, was 'strangely akin' to Ruskin, 'both in the character of his mind and in his social views'. Lawrence learned from Ruskin that mankind was 'nobly animal, nobly spiritual', and that the integrity of the Middle Ages has never been replaced. The name given to the 'Dark Ages,' writes Ruskin in *Modern Painters*, 'is, respecting art, wholly inapplicable'.

> They were, on the contrary, the bright ages; ours are the dark ones
> ... We build brown brick walls, and wear brown coats ... There
> is, however, also some cause for the change in our own tempers.
> On the whole these are much sadder ages than the early ones; not
> sadder in a noble and deep way, but in a dim wearied way, – the
> way of ennui, and jaded intellect, and uncomfortableness of soul
> and body.[16]

The *Divine Comedy* contains all this brightness, as do the illuminated manuscripts of the poem: Dante in a blue cap, red shoes and rose-pink, indigo or amber robe, beneath a cobalt vault of golden stars. Lawrence, stiff in his military coat, had come to Monte Cassino in a dim and weary age: what for Ruskin was an observation, for Lawrence was an agony.

They went from the watchtower to the bowels of the building, the 'ancient cell away under the monastery, where all the sanctity started', after which they looked round the library, with its copies of Virgil, Cicero, Ovid and Tacitus and *Divine Comedy*. Among the books and illuminations, Lawrence had his second crisis on the hill. He described himself as being overcome by tiredness and cold, but his experience sounds closer to an attack of claustrophobia: 'I could not bear it any more. I felt I must be outside, in the sun, and see the world below, and the way out.'[17] Whatever space he was in, Lawrence looked for the exit.

After supper he broached the question which had been hanging over them both. 'And what was the abyss, then?' Magnus told Lawrence about one of the cheques in Anzio – 'there should have been money to meet it, in my bank in New York' – but not about the fraudulent cheques in Rome, whose existence Lawrence never discovered. 'It is an *absolute* secret that I am here,' Magnus confided. 'As you see, I'm in a very nasty hole.' The money he had paid to Lawrence's driver was, he laughed, all he had left in the world: 'I haven't even anything to buy a cigarette or a stamp.' What happened to the £5 Lawrence had recently sent him? Of his own 125 lire, Lawrence needed a hundred to get home, so he could spare Magnus twenty-five for the bottle of liquor he had promised. Expecting more, Magnus looked 'rather crestfallen'. 'But I didn't want to give him any money this time,' Lawrence wrote, 'because he expected it.' This was also why Lawrence had called the image of Hedwig Magnus 'cheap' and 'trivial': because Magnus had expected something more. Lawrence would, however, write to various people in London recommending Magnus's articles, which he privately considered 'very self-conscious and poor'. The best of them was 'Holy Week in Monte Cassino' which Lawrence thought might sell 'because of the photographs', one of which showed the interior of the basilica while another was of the monastery from one of the terraces below.[18]

On his second night in the monastery, Magnus showed Lawrence the eighty-page manuscript of *Dregs* which he had got 'rather raggedly typed out'. Lawrence, who began reading it in bed and completed it the next morning, found himself 'moved and rather horrified' by this tale of bullying officers, proud insubordinates, shame and defiance. It was, he said, 'like a map of the lower places of mankind's activities'.[19] The story of Magnus's journey from Italy to Algeria, where he enlisted in the Legion, and then from Algeria to France when he made his escape back into Italy, is described as one of disappointing train carriages ('I was informed that a private soldier cannot travel first class', 'the second class of the Sidi Brahim did not sport any luxuries whatever'), disappointing meals ('watery soup', 'a sardine and an olive', 'a vegetable done up beyond recognition', 'a very meagre meat course', 'a second helping was charged extra', 'an orange') and disappointing hotels ('The dining-room was as ill-lighted by the weak gas as the halls'). Magnus was as disturbed by the discomfort of his bed as he was by the violence of the legionnaires, and all he learned from his trials were that 'the things one is accustomed to do become privileges after one has been deprived of them for a long time'. These 'things' include 'the cleanliness and care of a first-class hotel, the feeling of wearing clean clothes, the comfort of breakfast in bed, and lounging over the *New York Herald*'.[20]

Without Lawrence's introduction – even with Lawrence's introduction – Magnus's readers would be bewildered by the character of the author. Why would a sensitive and self-pampering man with a vocation to be a monk ever choose to join the hardest and most elite fighting force in Europe? Furthermore, why would a sensitive and self-pampering man have a vocation to be a monk? For Lawrence, Magnus's need to balance his passion for blissful holiness with his passion for violence needed no explanation: this was the eternal dialectic, the progression of history. Even so, the rigorous physical and psychological training the legionnaires underwent could never have suited a man like Magnus; their marching pace would by itself have been a problem. Rather than the usual 116-step-per-minute speed of other French units, legionnaires employ a slow 88-step-per-minute tempo known as 'the crawl'. Lawrence pictured the figure of Magnus 'in the red trousers and blue coat' of the legionnaire, 'with lappets turned up, surging like a little indignant pigeon across the drill yards'.[21]

The legionnaires were for the most part, as Magnus knew, men who needed to disappear; as such they were expected to enlist under false names. 'The idea in founding the Legion,' Magnus wrote, 'had been to give a man who had committed some error a chance to rehabilitate himself.' It was, in other words, a form of Purgatory. No questions were asked, and if they were the answers were not required to be truthful. Many a volunteer in the Legion's history had turned out to be a 'murderer, thief, cut-throat, deserter, adventurer, embezzler, forger, gaol-bird and fugitive from justice'.[22] Some, like Magnus, had even been unrecognised princes. For example, a 'simple young man' who had registered himself in the Legion as 'John Smith, or some such name' and unfortunately died shortly afterwards 'was discovered to be no other than a nephew of Emperor William II'. Magnus calculated that 'John Smith' must have been one of 'the three sons of Prince Albrecht of Prussia, Regent of Brunswick'.[23]

The composition of the Legion, Magnus discovered, was 70 per cent German. The food, manners, discipline, arrogance, insolence and 'arbitrariness' of the outfit were all German characteristics: 'it was a

German regiment of the lowest type transplanted to Africa'. Magnus found himself consorting with the dregs of German society, men who had no interest in personal redemption: 'There was nothing to redeem; a man was a living shell, with his soul dead, with no conscience or scruple, without heart or feeling, with only a belly to feed and fill with drink, and sexual organs to serve him for his depravities.'[24] The Legion licensed these men to continue as thieves and murderers: 'there was no friendship, no self-respect, no respect for others, nothing was sacred'. Those few, like Magnus, who had enrolled as innocents were 'made beasts of' so often that they became beasts themselves.

> In addition to the filth and disgusting surroundings, living among the dregs of human society, doing strenuous exercise at great expense to my purse, I was treated like a dog, a ruffian, a blackguard, an outcast. I would not stay another minute more than was absolutely necessary.[25]

After a few days a helpful German count asked Magnus how he had washed up in the Legion, having evidently 'not done anything wrong'.

> 'No one is going to believe that you have come here for idealistic purposes of doing your share to aid the Allies. They could not understand that; and any one can see that you are not a soldier born, and that you have no love for the life ... I would advise you to get out if you can – something sinister might happen to you if you don't. That is all I can say.'
>    ... I realized that what he told me was the truth. I was the butt of the officers, who were suspicious of me and partly jealous, and did everything to humiliate me, and make me feel as cheap as possible. I was the butt of the petty officers, who wished to ingratiate themselves with their superiors. I was the butt of the soldiers who thought I was not one of them, and I was the butt of others who were jealous or bore me a grudge for not lending them unlimited money.[26]

One of those who humiliated Magnus was an officer called Steinmann, 'a typical Prussian bully, mean, brutal, domineering, ignorant, sly, and cowardly, and usually in a nasty temper'.

There was a system, Magnus discovered, of *girants* (otherwise spelt *girons*, or *gironds*, meaning passive homosexual boys). Having been picked up in Marseille or Paris by soldiers on their way to the Legion, the boys then also enlisted. In exchange for sexual favours, the *girants*, who enjoyed the protection of their lovers, ran their chores and carried theirs packs on marches. The *girant* culture was embedded in legionnaire life, and rivalry over boys could lead to murder. When their protectors tired of them, the *girants* became 'public property'.

'Well, dearie, where is your protector today? Why doesn't he carry your pack?'

'Can't you walk? Did he hurt you last night?'

'I'll carry your pack if you're tired, but you must let me come and see you tonight.'

'These and other remarks,' Magnus wrote, 'were shouted across one column from another.' After the lights went out, the legionnaires would creep across the barracks to their various boys. Magnus was not, he said, 'that kind' of man – he describes himself in these pages as heterosexual – but this didn't prevent his being accosted. 'You are not bad,' said one lieutenant, pinching his cheek. 'I wouldn't mind sleeping with you.' Magnus apparently 'trembled with rage' at the suggestion. He was also accosted by an Arab in a shop, and when an Armenian in the shower put his erect member in Magnus's face, 'my disgust and indignation gave vent to a volley of contemptuous language which completely cowed him'.[27]

What would Lawrence have made of this section of *Dregs*? The answer is that it was almost certainly not included in the draft he read in Monte Cassino. Douglas, having read a still earlier draft in 1917, had advised Magnus to tone down the obscenities. The manuscript at that point contained, Douglas recalled, many unprintable 'allusions' to the 'ultra-masculine peculiarities of Legionary life'. These scenes, Douglas explained, would have to be expurgated but Magnus refused: 'I've given chapter and verse,' he proudly insisted. 'I've just tried to tell the truth.' 'You want to sell the book don't you?' argued Douglas. 'No publisher would touch it with tongs as long as it stands. Water your truth! The reader likes to think that the legionaries, for all their roughness, are brave men ready to die for their country, and not a cosmopolitan bunch of cutthroats and sharpers and sodomites.'[28]

Lawrence told Magnus that *Dregs* was 'good' and that if the last five chapters (which describe his escape) could be made 'less vague and diffuse' and given 'more detail and definite event' he would help find the book a publisher.[29] The result is that Magnus's account of his escape is the most readable part of the text. Having obtained leave to go to Paris for a night, Magnus then caught the train south to Menton on the French–Italian border. Guessing that the authorities would not look for deserters in first-class carriages, this is where he hid. From Menton he crossed into Italy on an omnibus with a Havana in his mouth, then caught the train to Naples and the boat to Spain.

Why did Magnus really join the Legion? He pictures himself as a naïf in the style of Candide and he perhaps did believe, on one level, that he was joining up to do his bit for the war. But he was also, like the other legionnaires, a man on the run, and 'near enough', Lawrence wrote, 'to being a scoundrel, thief, forger ... to appreciate their company'.[30] Nothing is said by Lawrence about the similarity between Magnus's ordeal in the Legion and his own when he was called up for the medical examination in Derby, which he counted – together with his visit to Keynes's rooms in Cambridge – as one of the crises of his life.

That afternoon, Lawrence and Magnus walked through the woods and across the moorland to a ruined convent that lies on the rocks and heath over the brow of the monastery hill. Two rooms of the convent were inhabited by a peasant farmer, and as they explored the ruins they heard a 'crying – crying, crying, crying with a strange inhuman persistence'. It might have been 'a sharp-voiced baby'. Looking for the source of the sound they came to a 'little cave-like place' and found there a 'blind black puppy crawling miserably on the floor', his mother nowhere to be seen.[31] Lawrence had recently explained, in *Psychoanalysis and the Unconscious*, his theory about the cries of blind puppies: 'there speaks the first consciousness, the audible unconscious, in the squeak of these infantile things, which is so curiously and indescribably moving, reacting direct upon the great abdominal centre, the preconscious mind in man'.[32] He had always been moved by the sudden cries of the non-human world which he saw as 'the upper mind losing itself in the inner first mind'. They passed the peasant farmer who lived in the ruin; his face was as lined as a 'gnarled bough', and he was leading an ass carrying brushwood. The 'bitch-mother', the peasant told them, had 'gone off' for the day to look after the sheep. The mind of the peasant was 'utterly blank' and he spoke 'as a tree might speak'.[33]

Lawrence was as affected by the blind pup in the cave as he was by the peasants on the slope, who were:

> crying their speech as crows cry, and living their lives as lizards among the rocks, blindly going on with the little job in hand, the present moment, cut off from all past and all future, and having no idea and no sustained emotion, only that eternal will-to-live which makes a tortoise wake up once more in spring, and makes a grasshopper whistle on in the moonlight nights even of November.

The puppy was crying, crying, crying, the peasants were crying, the crows were crying, Lawrence was crying, Magnus was crying. It was now that he and Magnus had the only conversation in the *Memoir* that Lawrence reports in full, and it ends in tears.

> 'The monks keep their peasants humble,' I said to Magnus.
>
> 'Of course!' he said. 'Don't you think they are quite right? Don't you think they *should* be humble?' And he bridled like a little turkey cock on his hind legs.
>
> 'Well,' I said, 'if there's any occasion for humility, I do.'
>
> 'Don't you think there *is* occasion?' he cried. 'If there's one thing worse than another, it's this *equality* that has come into the world. Do you believe in it yourself?'

Lawrence did not believe in equality, but nor did he know how to measure a man's superiority, and he '*could* not accept Magnus' superiority to the peasant'.

He and Magnus belonged, Lawrence explained, to the same tree as the peasant; they were the 'growing tip' of the tree, and the peasant was the 'hard, fixed tissue of the branch or trunk'. Magnus leapt on the analogy. Yes, yes, he agreed: that is what the Church believes too. 'It is terrible to be agreed with,' thought Lawrence, 'especially by a man like Magnus. All that one says, and means, turns to nothing.'[34]

Lawrence and Magnus were in danger of agreeing again, when Magnus warmed to the topic of marriage. 'They talk about love between men and women,' he said. 'Why it's all a *fraud*. The woman is just taking all and giving nothing, and feeling sanctified about it. All she tries to do is thwart a man in whatever he is doing. – No, I have found my life in my *friendships*.' Magnus and Douglas both used the terms 'friend' and 'friendship' to denote a sexual relationship. He liked the physical side of his male friendships, said Magnus, but it was the durability of his mental friendships that mattered more. Lawrence was pleased to find a point on which they could violently differ: 'With me, on the contrary, if there is no profound blood-sympathy, I know the mental friendship is trash.' Magnus looked crestfallen, as though Lawrence had been denigrating their own friendship. They walked on in silence until Lawrence suddenly said, 'I should die if I had to stay up here.' Having had no idea that he was suffering, Magnus asked why. 'Oh, I don't know. The past, the past. The beautiful, the wonderful past, it seems to prey on my heart, I can't bear it.' It was the third time on the mountain that Lawrence had looked back. 'Really?' Magnus replied, his eyes widening. 'Do you feel like that? – But don't you think it is a far preferable life up here than down there? Don't you think the past is far preferable to the future, with all this socialismo and these comunisti and so on?' Lawrence of course agreed. But he did not say so.

It was the end of a bright afternoon and they were seated on 'the wild hilltop high above the world' which had 'been one of man's intense sacred places for three thousand years'. An ancient path through the wood had once connected the pagan temples, and the great wall at the bend in the road preceded even the birth of Christ. From this 'last foothold of the old world', they looked down at 'the great white road straight as a thought, and the more flexible black railway with the railway station'. The railway workers swarmed 'like ants'. This was the new world of 'democracy, industrialism, socialism, the red flag of the communists and the red white and green tricolor of the fascisti'. And it was 'barren' down there, 'like the black cindertrack of the railway'.[35]

Both worlds, the emerging one of the present and the not-quite-dead one of the past, were an agony to Lawrence, 'but here on the mountain top was worst'. Up here he was lost; they both were. It was not only the historical past to which he could never return. It was his own past in Eastwood, and England. 'I feel one comes unstuck from England,' he wrote later that year, 'from all the past – as if one would never go back.'[36] Lawrence now confirmed the decision he had made the previous morning at the window: 'I think one's got to go through with the life down there – get somewhere beyond it. One can't go back.' He said this to Magnus, who believed with a passion that one could go back and get beyond the life down there. 'But do you call the monastery going back?' Magnus asked. 'I don't. The peace, the eternity, the concern with things that matter.'[37] This was both a Pisgah sight and a version of the angel's command to Dante at the door of Purgatory, but it also recalls Satan taking Jesus to the top of a mountain and showing him the kingdoms of the world. 'All this I will give you,' he says, 'if you will bow down and worship me.' 'Away from me, Satan,' Jesus replies.

The devil on the mountain had disrupted the progress of the monks building Monte Cassino, and Lawrence now disrupted Magnus's progress. Magnus would never be a monk, Lawrence told him; he lacked the 'vocation'. It was a cruel thing to say but Magnus, Lawrence thought, seemed relieved to be released from the weight of this intolerably vivid and exhausting place. The 'mediaeval spirit' of the wild hill summit then overcame Lawrence so powerfully that for the moment he 'was almost speechless'.

Something had happened on the mountain top: he and Magnus had formed a *Blutsbrüderschaft* of sorts. Lawrence never admits this, but it is the only explanation for what followed. Magnus put his hand on his friend's arm and, rather than freeze with horror as he usually did when he was touched, Lawrence stopped mocking him and saw who he really was:

> He seemed to understand so much, round about the questions that trouble one deepest. But the quick of the question he never felt. He had no real middle, no real centre bit to him. Yet, round and round about all the questions, he was so intelligent and sensitive.

Magnus, Lawrence's guide, had reached into the pilgrim's soul. They walked back slowly and in silence as the sun declined and the air filled with the cold of snow. Magnus kept close to Lawrence, 'very close' and reassuring, 'and I feeling as if my heart had once more broken: I don't know why. And he feeling his fear of life that haunted him, and his fear of his own self and its consequences, that never left him for long.'[38]

Returning through the great door of the monastery after the wailing and lamentations of the afternoon, the two men might have been Dante and Virgil entering, not Purgatory, but the gate to hell:

And when, with gladness in his face, he placed
his hand upon my own, to comfort me,
he drew me in among the hidden things.

Here sighs and lamentations and loud cries
were echoing across the starless air,
so that, as soon as I set out, I wept.

(*Inferno*, Canto 3, 19–24)

At the end of their visit to Purgatory, when they reach the Garden of Eden, Virgil bids farewell to Dante, and that night Lawrence announced that he would be leaving Monte Cassino. He says nothing about his third night on the mountain, but Magnus will have begged him to stay and Lawrence will have been cruel because he had shed one of his selves up here and, as he put it in his story 'A Modern Lover', 'nothing is so hateful as the self one has left'.[39]

We next see them both the following morning, 21 February, and they are two figures walking down the slope. They take not the winding carriage road but the 'wide old paved path that swoops so wonderfully from the top of the hill to the bottom. It feels like a thousand years old.'[40] Magnus is miserable, so they stop for a glass of wine, which he pays for himself. Lawrence then offers him twenty lire which Magnus refuses, not out of modesty but because it's too small an amount to do much with.

By the time Lawrence reached the station at Cassino, it had started to rain and his thin coat was soaked through. He took the train to Naples, and then the steamer to Capri: modern transport for a hurrying world. 'I let myself be carried away, away from the monastery, away from Magnus, away from everything.' For a moment on the deck of the boat the sun came out, and Lawrence 'felt that again the world had come to an end for me, and again that my heart was broken'.[41]

But what is clear is that when Lawrence dismissed Magnus's vocation as a monk, he accepted his own as a man of the future rather than the past. In the epilogue to *Movements in European History*, which he added to the proofs after his return from the monastery, Lawrence confirmed this position. When the war ended, he wrote, 'We thought the old times were coming back. They can never come. We know now that each one of us had something shot out of him. So we have to adjust ourselves to a new world.'[42]

His utopias all turned to dystopias, and the Capri he returned to at the end of February 1920 had become a 'gossipy, villa-stricken, two-humped chunk of limestone'. It was a 'cat-Cranford': Mrs Gaskell's novel of Midlands provincial life was often evoked when Lawrence wanted to describe a particular form of hell.[43] So the Lawrences sailed south to their latest Happy Isle, 'dawn-lovely Sicily', a place of rippling terraces and sudden drops, with mile upon mile of stone steps and sarcophagi cut into the rocks and mountains. Sicily had been recommended by Magnus, who had lived in Taormina in 1915 and still owed money to his landlord. 'Whatever had died for me,' Lawrence believed, 'Sicily had then not died.' Poised at the point 'where Europe ends', Sicily had, Lawrence thought, 'a good on-the-brink' feel to it.[44] The island is on the join where European and African plates collide and ten years earlier one of Sicily's many earthquakes had killed 120,000 citizens, and destroyed all but three of Messina's ninety-one churches.

Magnus had suggested that they take a house on the south-west shore, but Lawrence preferred Taormina, 'ledged so awfully above the dawn' on the eastern side of the island on the slopes of Mount Etna, whose summit was believed in medieval Italy to be the location of Mount Purgatory.[45] Today Taormina is a tourist resort but in Lawrence's time it was a refuge for expatriate artists and 'gentlemen': Wagner came here and so did Oscar Wilde; Wilhelm von Gloeden photographed his nude Sicilian boys in Taormina, and Nietzsche wrote a portion of *Thus Spake Zarathustra*. The town itself, made of narrow streets, pastel-coloured houses and old white walls, lies on ancient ground. It has its own Greek amphitheatre facing what Lawrence called the 'witch-like' Etna, her 'strange winds prowling round her like Circe's panthers'.[46]

In Canto 28 of *Purgatory*, Dante finds himself in a wood where, on the far side of a stream, he sees a garden of flowering boughs. Into this 'earthly paradise' comes a fair maiden called Matelda, his final temptation before his encounter with the jealous Beatrice. Matelda explains that the stream comes from a fountain and that drinking from one side of the stream takes away the memory of sin, and from the other side the water restores the memory of good deeds. Shelley's translation of the canto is called 'Matilda Gathering Flowers', and Lawrence, with

D. H. L.

FLORENCE, SEPTEMBER, 1921

I took this on the top of Romola's
house in the Via dei Bardi.

Catherine Carswell

the serendipity that accompanied the choice of every house he lived in, found his own earthly Paradise behind a pink and cream villa called the Fontana Vecchia or 'Old Fountain'. 'Here one feels,' he wrote, 'as if one had lived for a hundred thousand years.'[47]

Fontana Vecchia was a fortress-like house divided into two halves: the landlord and his family occupied the lower part and the Lawrences took the top floor, from which a generous terrace hung suspended over a terraced garden of magenta bougainvillea, wild cyclamen, pink gladioli, roses, snapdragons, orchids and finger-high irises that bloomed for only a day.[48] A broken Roman tomb lolled across the track and the fountain after which the house was named still spurted water, 'in a sort of little cave-place'. Marrows, beans and tomatoes grew in the sappy earth, and in the centre of the garden stood a great carob tree surrounded by an orchard of sweet-smelling citrus, olive, eucalyptus, medlar and almond trees. Fertilised by volcanic ash, Sicilian soil is endlessly bountiful: the Sikels, who first came here from Italy in the eleventh century BC, believed that their gods lived below ground, in the hot springs and boiling subterranean rivers. Legend says it was the goddesses of Sicily who first gave wheat to the world.

The sun rose every morning with 'a splendour like trumpets' and his days were filled with the clanging of goat bells.[49] Lawrence was overcome by a suave indifference and in this enchanted garden he returned to his memories of Eastwood. 'The Insurrection of Miss Houghton', which he completed in early May, contained his first, and most magnanimous, response to Magnus. He did not, Lawrence told Catherine Carswell, 'want to do a satire' because 'it all just dries up one's bowels'.[50] So he cast Magnus instead as an upmarket Charlie Chaplin.

Alvina's father, James Houghton, meets an American called Mr May who has 'been in the music-hall line as a sort of agent'. Mr May, who appears in Woodhouse as if from nowhere, was 'one of those men who carry themselves in a birdie fashion, so that their tail sticks out a little behind, jauntily'. There was a Mrs May somewhere in the background but they were no longer together; she was, Mr May explained, a vegetarian and had once ruined his buttered champignons by dousing them in old carrot water ('*Can* you imagine such a person?'). Mr May had lived in Rome and managed the career of 'Miss Maud Callum, the *danseuse*', but he was currently down on his luck, hence prospecting for show business in the collier towns of the English Midlands.[51]

With his immaculate linen, 'small felt hats' and 'face clean-shaved like a cherub', he cut quite a figure in Woodhouse, and when Mr May and James Houghton walked through the town they resembled a couple of vaudeville artists. Houghton, shabby in his overcoat and bending forward, 'nipped along hurriedly, as if pursued by fate', and Mr May, 'tight and tubby, with his chest out and his head back', recalled 'a consequential bird of the smaller species'.

The mind of Mr May was 'quick' but 'not winged', and what excites him in Woodhouse is the Cinematograph and Variety Theatre in the old cattle market, where the colliers and working girls come on a Friday night. If James Houghton could be persuaded to buy a similar 'erection', as Mr May calls it, then he, Mr May, could manage the place. So Mr Houghton invests in a frame-section building in the neighbouring town of Lumley, and Mr May works hard at the programme. Up at 5.30 a.m., he is on his way by seven, sailing through the day like a 'stiff little ship before a steady breeze'. Having done 'a fair amount of journalism', and garnered calling cards from a good number of newspapers, he takes over the publicity himself.

With 'Houghton's Picture Palace' (his 'ox-blood red erection') up and running, Mr May entertains the colliers to conjurors, contortionists, comics, performing birds, five-minute farces and popular songs. Mr May even does a turn himself as a begging dog, wearing a pug 'costoom', as he calls it. The audience love the pug: it is 'too lifelike, and too impossible'.[52] It's a surreal joke, turning Magnus, who described himself as 'treated like a dog' in the Foreign Legion, into a Chinese pug with a squashed, wrinkled face, and Lawrence repeated it two years later in 'Bibbles', his ambivalent paean to the bulldog with the 'Chinese puzzle face' and the 'wrinkling reproachful look' who appropriated him in New Mexico. Except that it was hard to tell, Lawrence said of Bibbles, who appropriated whom. Either way, he 'owned' Bibbles and 'never dreamed, till now, of the awful time the Lord must / Have, "owning" humanity'.

Lawrence loses Bibbles in Taos plaza and then finds her, 'prancing round the corner in exuberant, bubbling affection', on the trail of a 'yellow-green old Mexican woman' who tries to shoo her off, but Bibbles doesn't notice. Lawrence hates Bibbles, with 'her imbecile bit of tail in a love-flutter', but he also loves her, tearing along like a 'dust-ball' and not giving 'a rap for anybody'. 'Bibbles' is the best dog-poem in the language and while it might be an account of female promiscuity, Lawrence's fond, exasperated tone is also the one he reserved for Magnus.

Mr May, who 'must have a good hotel' (and 'if he had to clear out without paying his hotel bill – well, that was the world's fault'), is possessed of the 'private innocence' found in all Americans. He and Alvina bond immediately, but Alvina does not find him 'physically moving. Physically he was not there: he was oddly an absentee.' As for Mr May, were he to see 'the least sign of coming-on-ness' in Alvina, 'he would have fluttered off in a great dither'.[53] Lawrence's parody of Magnus contains none of his future venom, but nor does it hint at the sensitive, intelligent man he had glimpsed in Monte Cassino, who understood 'so much, round about the questions that trouble one deepest'. Mr May in his 'pug-costoom' is a violent reaction to the Mr Magnus who, on his last afternoon on the mountain, returned with Lawrence to the monastery as the air filled with snow. It is as though Lawrence were repulsed by his own affection.

When he renamed his novel *The Lost Girl*, he surely had H.D.'s baby daughter Perdita in mind, and H.D. will have seen his title as another flare sent from a window. She will have hated the novel because *The Lost Girl* is both a mad and a bad book (so 'bad', thought Katherine Mansfield, it 'ought not to be allowed'), but the madness and the badness are not necessarily related. Its badness is because Lawrence had lost interest in human psychology – 'his hero and heroine', Mansfield rightly said, 'are animals on the prowl'.[54] And its madness is the result of his tearing along like a dustball without having the faintest idea of what's coming next. 'Begun a novel – don't know if it will ever end,' Lawrence wrote on 15 March 1920. 'I may come to a full stop any moment – you never know,' he wrote on 22 March. By 31 March, when he had completed 50,000 words, he described the book as running 'out of control' and jumping 'through the port-hole into the unknown ocean', and leaving him 'on deck painfully imploring it to come home'. The first five chapters, those which Lawrence revised before leaving for Monte Cassino, do nothing to prepare us for the sudden appearance of Mr May, and the four chapters devoted to mocking Mr May do nothing to prepare us for what follows, including the anal rape of Alvina in the bedroom of her deceased mother (which page had to be spliced out of the printed book in order for the libraries to take it). There is also a problem of genre: *The Lost Girl* begins in the vein of

Arnold Bennett and then turns round to eat its own tail. The satire that dried Lawrence's bowels appears from left field, in the form of a bizarre spin on Jane Austen's *Emma*: Alvina Houghton, handsome, clever and no longer rich, lives in Woodhouse with her elderly, widowed father. There is even a minor character called Frank Churchill.

Lawrence described *The Lost Girl* as 'comic' but the only genuinely funny aspect is the arrival in the town of the faux Native American tribe, the Natcha-Kee-Tawaras, whose souls belong to the primitive world and must therefore be as respected by the reader as they are by Lawrence. The Natcha-Kee-Tawaras consist of four strapping young men: Louis and Geoffrey, who are French, Max, who is Swiss, and a feral 'yellow-eyed' Italian called Ciccio to whom Alvina, when she has given up being a New Woman, will submit: 'He gave the slight, almost imperceptible jerk of the head, backwards and sideways, as if summoning her towards him. His face too was closed and expressionless. But in his eyes, which kept hers, there was a dark flicker of ascendency. He was going to triumph over her.'[55] Led by a plump, middle-aged actor-manager-mother-squaw known as Kishwégin, the Natcha-Kee-Tawaras ride on horseback through Woodhouse dressed as braves in deerskin trousers and war paint. It is often the case in Lawrence that the passages he considered his finest are those most vulnerable to mockery.

The Natcha-Kee-Tarawa show contains a number of different acts, including yodelling, but their great turn is 'The White Prisoner', which Lawrence describes in reverential detail. Kishwégin, alone at the door of her wigwam, rocks a hanging cradle and the brave Louis brings home a white prisoner. The brave Ciccio then brings home a dead bear and tortures the white prisoner while Kishwégin continues to rock the cradle. The bear, not dead at all, then sits up and strikes Louis down.

On one occasion, when Kishwégin has a cold, Mr May takes over her role, wearing a long black plait, a short chamois dress, gaiters and moccasins. 'Can you *believe* that that's Mr. May,' Alvina laughs, 'he's exactly like a girl.'[56] The greatest of all insults for Lawrence – as for Douglas – was to describe a man as girlish. We are asked to laugh at Mr May but not at the Natcha-Kee-Tawaras themselves, who are the moral and spiritual core of the book.

While Lawrence marries his heroine to Ciccio, he does not allow her to love and be loved. After leaving the Midlands for Italy – as Frieda had also done – Alvina goes not to Lake Garda or the Gulf of Spezia, where Lawrence and Frieda had been happy, but to the very house in Picinisco in which their bones had turned cold.

The interiority denied to Alvina and Ciccio is accorded instead to the Midland and Abruzzi landscapes, and this is where the strength of *The Lost Girl* lies. Lawrence's sense of place is, as ever, preternatural: the bleak beauty of Woodhouse, the bleak beauty of Picinisco; the hellishness of Manchester House, the hellishness of the Italian villa; the never-ending depths of the mines beneath Woodhouse and the never-ending heights of the devilish Abruzzi mountains. The bride and groom travel by train across France to Italy, and from Turin to Genoa and Rome, after which the hills approach and they are among the Alban hills: Alvina is penetrating the terrain looked down on by Lawrence from Monte Cassino.

Up and up they clamber until they reach the station from where the couple go by omnibus towards the core of the mountains. Lawrence was always impressed by the Italian roads; 'splendid gestures', he called them in *Sea and Sardinia*, swinging from impossible crags, scooped 'with complete sang-froid' from the sides of hills, piercing mountain forests.[57] He loved their carelessness and disrepair and the relaxed expectation that they will be ruts and ruins in ten years' time. The final stage of Alvina's journey to her new home is a paean to the art of the Roman road, both ancient and modern. Moth-white oxen wave past the bus, followed by peasant men in black cloaks. The mountains are closing in, the rocks rise up straight into the thick darkness. Every time they turn a corner, Alvina thinks that they are 'coming out on the top of this hollow between the heights' but the road continues to coil. They reach Atina, a market town on the summit, and continue by foot through the wilderness towards Ciccio's home. When the cart can go no further, they pile their luggage on to the back of a donkey, and navigate the icy river and rocky path until they reach a Victorian villa on a bit of 'half-savage, ancient earth'. It had been built by Ciccio's uncle, Pancrazio, who was an artist's model in London in the 1890s. Suburban from the outside, it is cave-like within: the frozen kitchen is empty save for piles of straw and beans. In the bedroom on the first night, 'a real terror took hold of her ... Everything seemed electric with horror ... What would she do, where should she flee? She was lost – lost – lost utterly.'[58]

All Lawrence's novels are about the hellishness of home, but Alvina's claustrophobia in houses outstrips even that of Siegmund in *The Trespasser*, or that of Paul Morel. The only happy interior in *The Lost Girl* is the stage wigwam in Houghton's Picture Palace. If she has to 'live in this part of the world at all', Alvina says of the Abruzzi region, 'she must avoid the *inside* of it … If she was to save her sanity she must keep to the open air, and avoid any contact with human interiors.' Ciccio joins the Italian army and Alvina, in the open air, sheds her former self. The sound of men chopping wood and calling to the oxen makes her happy; hearing 'the constant speech of the passing river, and the real breathing presence of the upper snows … a wild, terrible happiness would take hold of her, beyond despair, but very like despair. No one would ever find her.'⁵⁹

Katherine Mansfield was wrong when she said there was 'not one memorable *word*' in *The Lost Girl*, and that 'the nature study' of the final chapters was 'no more than the grazing-place for Alvina and her sire'.⁶⁰ The novel has flashes of intense beauty and its compulsive appeal is precisely the result of Lawrence's having not a glimmer of what he's up to. In our final glimpse of Alvina she is, as H.D. was when Lawrence last saw her, pregnant and alone, a white prisoner wondering if her sire will ever return. She has known agony and her heart is broken. The old world is not for her: it is the New World across the Atlantic that Alvina is left gazing towards.

In late April 1920, a warrant was issued for the arrest of Maurice Magnus. After three weeks of floundering, the police received a tip-off that he was hiding in Monte Cassino (Magnus was 'denounced' by a friend, probably Nathan Cobb who had loaned him the apartment in Rome). On the morning of 24 April, with only two more pages of *Dregs* to revise – he was concluding the climax of his flight from the Legion – Magnus was warned by Don Martino that the carabinieri were currently making their way up the mountain. It was time for his second great escape. Taking 150 lire from the monastery funds and throwing a change of linen and a toothbrush into his satchel, Magnus slipped through the back of the fortress and slithered down the other side of the pathless slope, over rocks and stones and thorns, before taking the backroads to the station at Cassino.

The walk to Cassino took seven hours. From here he caught the slow train (second class) to Rome, where he changed for Naples, hiding most of the way in the lavatory. He then caught the *diretto* to Sicily, and thirty hours later knocked on Lawrence's door having had, during this time, nothing but a glass of wine and a little bread and cheese from a station café. But Lawrence was not there: he had gone down to Syracuse to see the spring flowers. So Magnus booked himself into the San Domenico, a former monastery and now the most expensive hotel in Taormina, and waited for his friend.

When Lawrence returned to his garden at the end of April, Magnus emerged through the orange trees like Dante's Matelda. 'A terrible thing has happened,' he wailed, 'and I came straight to you.' He told Lawrence about his narrow escape, adding that it would be awful were the monks to discover 'everything', and 'he laughed a little, comical laugh over *everything*, as if he was just a little bit naughtily proud of it'. Why, Lawrence asked Magnus, did he stay in the San Domenico at fifty lire at day if he had no money? The cost 'of course' was '*ruinous*', Magnus heartily agreed, but the food was better at the San Domenico than at Fichera's, a hotel which was half the price. Who, asked Lawrence, is going to cover the bill? 'Well, I thought,' said Magnus. 'You know all those manuscripts of mine? Well, you think they're some good, don't you? Well, I thought if I made them over to you, and you did what you could with them, and just kept me going till I can get a new start – or till I can get away –'. His plan was to go to Egypt (then a British colony) where he had a friend in newspapers who might get him an editorship or some such. Until then, Magnus hoped that he might stay 'very quietly' with Lawrence and Frieda and do a little writing. 'He looked up into my face, as if he were trying all he could on me. First thing I knew was that I could not have him in the house with me: and even if *I* could have borne it, my wife never could.' Frieda then came down to meet Magnus who was charming and kissed her hand in the German fashion. 'Such a beautiful place you have here,' he said wistfully. Lawrence had a lunch appointment, so he gave Magnus the 100-lire note he had in his pocket and arranged to see him again the next morning. 'You're so awfully kind,' said Magnus, but Lawrence wasn't 'feeling kind'.[61]

'Whatever do you pick up such dreadful people for?' asked Frieda when Magnus had gone. 'He's the first,' replied Lawrence. 'And even he isn't dreadful.'[62] This is how Lawrence remembered their exchange. In her own version, Frieda recalled her husband's rage, asking, 'Is it my duty to look after this man?' Magnus, said Frieda, was 'taking for granted that we would be responsible for him'.[63]

The next morning a letter addressed to Magnus arrived at the Fontana Vecchia. So he was already using Lawrence's address. Then Magnus himself reappeared in the garden and repeated how beautiful it was. 'Yes,' I said. 'But Magnus, there isn't a room for you in the house. There isn't a spare room, anyway. You'd better get something cheaper in the village.' They agreed that Magnus would find a room with an old friend of his, a waiter called Melenda, after which Lawrence would settle his hotel bill: 'But I can't do any more. I simply can't.' Magnus's eyes filled with tears, and Lawrence 'looked away at the Ionian sea, feeling my blood turn to ice and the sea go black. I loathed scenes like this.'[64]

Magnus turned up in the garden again that afternoon, and Lawrence being out, he pleaded instead with Frieda, kissing her hand, wiping away his tears and 'trembling in distress'. Her 'spine', Frieda reported to Lawrence, 'crept up and down with distaste and discomfort'. According to Frieda, Magnus was without 'meaning, or purpose' and 'made a fool of Lawrence'.[65] In Magnus's version of his encounter with Frieda, reported to Douglas, 'She, the bitch, met me and asked some supercilious questions and passed some pleasant words.'[66] Another visitor to the Fontana Vecchia that spring was a local mule-driver called Peppino d'Allura, who recalled that Frieda, once again alone, emerged naked in the garden and offered him her body, which he willingly enjoyed.

Magnus reluctantly agreed to move into Melenda's house for ten francs a day. But before doing so he had *one* last request of Lawrence: would he mind nipping up to Monte Cassino to collect his things, including his papers and trinkets and clothes? Of course, the papers were highly confidential and mustn't be shown to anyone. If Don Martino saw them, 'there's an end to me at the monastery. I can *never* go back there.' Lawrence considered the sixty-hour round-trip, the heavy leather suitcases, the interruption to his novel and the embarrassment of seeing Don Martino again under these circumstances. 'I don't want to do that,' he said, and the Ionian sea again went black. 'Why not?' Magnus asked, turning green. He could not take it in: 'You *will* go, won't you?' Magnus insisted. 'You *will* go to the monastery for my things?' Lawrence did not reply, and Magnus left the garden with the 'terrible insolence of the humble', and a small glimmer of hope.[67]

What Magnus told Douglas about their encounter is this: 'Lawrence heard my tale, was most sympathetic and ready to help me in the way I asked … I offered [him] half of the proceeds of that book, and all my other stuff, if he would help me now and go to that place on the hill and get my things and the other manuscripts. He seemed willing and was most nice.'[68] It was now that Lawrence wrote the final chapter of *The Lost Girl*, in which he left Alvina abandoned and alone in Picinisco.

As Lawrence was walking into town the next day, Magnus again appeared on his path. Taking Lawrence's hand, he looked up at him imploringly but Lawrence would not, he confirmed, be returning to the monastery. 'It was final,' he said, and Magnus 'knew it'. They walked together 'in silence', as they had done that late winter afternoon at Monte Cassino, but now it was a 'lovely, lovely morning of hot sun' with butterflies 'flapping over the rosemary hedges and over a few little red poppies'. As on the mountain top, when Lawrence had told him that he lacked the monastic vocation, Magnus seemed relieved to be denied by Lawrence, and 'seemed almost to love me for having refused him'. They reached the garden gate and Magnus asked if he might come in. Lawrence, who now cast Frieda as the jealous Beatrice, said no, because 'My wife doesn't want it.' But even that Magnus 'accepted without offence, and seemed only to like me better for it. That was a puzzle to me.'[69]

Later the same day Lawrence sent Magnus a cheque covering his hotel bill, adding 200 lire to keep him going ('What good to me,' Magnus complained to Douglas, 'were these few pounds?'). Lawrence also wrote Magnus a letter saying that he 'could *not* do any more, and didn't want to see him any more'. This, Magnus told Douglas, was 'because his wife was angry!!!!! Finis.' Playing on Magnus's horror of women, Lawrence now turned Frieda into the villain of the story. When Magnus received this news, he returned, his 'mouth dry', to the Fontana Vecchia but '– he was out – she was in – I asked her if she knew what he had written me – she said "more or less" – of course I knew it was her doing. I spoke as nicely as I could, and pleaded without losing all my dignity … she looked like nails …'[70]

If, wrote Lawrence in his *Memoir*, he had had the money to send Magnus off to Egypt to sponge off someone else, he would willingly have done so. But Lawrence *did* then have the money. He was, for the moment, relatively flush: in the first six months of 1920 he received Amy Lowell's gift, plus a second surprise cheque of £75 from Mary Cannan's husband, Gilbert, who had organised a collection in America for the charity-boy of literature, plus American royalties worth £145, plus two

$50 payments from Seltzer, plus £19 from *Land and Water* for his story 'You Touched Me', $40 from *The Dial* for his story 'Adolf' and an offer from them of $50 for the companion story 'Rex', plus a whopping $250 from *Metropolitan Magazine* for 'Wintry Peacock'. Added to which he was expecting £100 in advances for *The Lost Girl* and *Women in Love*, which was to be published in a limited American edition by Thomas Seltzer. Lawrence currently had so much money that when, in May, Catherine Carswell sent him £50, he *burned the cheque*. He then burned a second cheque for £5, sent from Kot for the royalties for the preface he had written to Kot's translation of Shestov's *All Things are Possible*.

Meanwhile, Magnus told Douglas that 'my hotel bill ate up every cent I got – Lawrence never asked me for a meal or offered a room in his most commodious house.' Magnus now sent *Dregs* to the first of several publishers in London, and wrote to an English friend asking for a thousand lire. 'If I get it,' he told Douglas, 'I shall go to Malta and from there to Egypt ... If anything happens in the meantime, look for my grave in the foreigner's cemetery and <u>I leave all my manuscripts and papers to you – and their proceeds. They are all on the hilltop.</u>'[71]

For the next ten days Lawrence heard nothing from Magnus, and when he reappeared in the garden of the Fontana Vecchia it was in the form of a note handed to Lawrence by Melenda, Magnus's landlord, who had asked him to leave. He had been paid, wrote Magnus, seven guineas by *Land and Water* for his article on 'Holy Week at Monte Cassino' (published on Lawrence's recommendation), but the post office would not give him the letter because it had been wrongly addressed. Would Lawrence kindly advance him the seven guineas, after which he would leave Sicily at once. According to Melenda, Magnus was a *mezzo signore*, a half-gentleman: he had slept beneath his roof for ten nights, made daily orders of delicious, specially cooked food, drunk as much as he could stomach and so far not paid a penny. The money, Melenda complained, was always coming tomorrow.

Lawrence's proceedings with Magnus were observed by the South African artist Jan Juta, who had come to the Fontana Vecchia in the spring of 1920 to paint the novelist's portrait. Magnus, Juta thought, was persecuting Lawrence but Lawrence was colluding in the game. On the day they were to begin their sessions, Lawrence was too angry to sit. 'If I tried,' he explained to Juta, 'I know you would paint me scarlet all over.' So they went for a walk along the mountain path that climbed behind the town. Magnus, said Lawrence, was begging for money which he then spent on luxuries, 'and now he throws his "memoirs" at me and, believe me, I am to write a foreword to them AND get them published for him … Oh, I could kill him.' So it was during Magnus's lifetime that Lawrence committed himself to writing an introduction to *Dregs*: it was a favour to his friend.

The next Lawrence heard of Magnus, he was safely in Catania, fifty miles away. 'Ah, I breathed free now he had gone,'[72] wrote Lawrence, and for a brief moment Maurice Magnus dwindled into the past.

Mary Cannan, now also living in Sicily, suggested they all take a two-day trip to Malta, paid for by her. So on 17 May, Lawrence, Frieda and Mary caught the train to the port at Syracuse, only to hear that the steamers were on strike and the next sailing would not be until the following day. They spent the evening wandering along the harbour, watching the sun dissolve behind the skyline of flat-topped hills, and the Arabs and Turks saunter beneath the pomegranate and hibiscus trees. They booked themselves into the dilapidated Grand Hotel for the night where the porter gave Lawrence an envelope addressed in the all-too-familiar hand. 'Dear Lawrence,' wrote Magnus. 'I saw you this morning, all three of you walking down the Via Nazionale, but you would not look at me … The strike of the steamboats has delayed me here. I am sweating blood. I have a last request of you. Can you let me have ninety Lire, to make up what I need for my hotel bill. If I cannot have this I am lost.'[73] Magnus, like Christ on his last night, was sweating blood to the ground. Who was Lawrence to deny him his last request?

'Well, here was a blow!' thought Lawrence: Magnus was also bound for Malta. He had no choice but to meet up with the fugitive in the hotel lounge, where Magnus explained that he had been driven to sell his precious trinkets, including his opal cufflinks. His eyes 'were swimming with tears' and Lawrence gave him a 100-lire note. The steamer to Malta was leaving that night and so Magnus paid his hotel bill and booked himself – with what remained of Lawrence's lire – a second-class ticket. At least, reasoned Lawrence, he was not travelling first class, but 'I should have gone third myself, out of shame of spending somebody else's money.'[74] It was now, inspired by the insect-smeared walls of his hotel bedroom and the blood which Magnus was both sweating and sucking, that Lawrence wrote 'The Mosquito', a summing-up of his relations with Magnus to date and a parody of his belief in a blood brotherhood.

The poet begins with respect for the insolence of the vampire: 'When did you start your tricks / Monsieur?' (Lawrence would refer, in his *Memoir*, to 'Monsieur Magnus'). Monsieur Mosquito stalks the air 'in circles and evasions, enveloping me', and the poet becomes increasingly angry as he fails to swat him:

> I hate the way you lurch off sideways into air
> Having read my thoughts against you.
>
> Come then, let us play at unawares,
> And see who wins in this sly game of bluff.

By the end of the poem Lawrence's combination of cold contempt and boiling rage, so out of proportion to its object, is presented in a language arcane enough to be comic:

> I behold you stand
> For a second enspasmed in oblivion,
> Obscenely ecstasied
> Sucking live blood
> My blood.
>
> Such silence, such suspended transport,
> Such gorging,
> Such obscenity of trespass.

Lawrence succeeds in killing the mosquito – 'the infinitesimal faint smear of you' – but what has his victory achieved? The pest was a 'nothingness' to begin with.

The 'sly game of bluff' had only just begun. After he, Frieda and Mary Cannan had boarded the steamer, Lawrence leaned on the rail of the deck and watched the passengers course up the gangplank: Arabs, Maltese, Greek and at the last minute, 'like the grandest gentleman on earth', came Magnus, 'very smart in his little grey overcoat and grey curly hat, walking very smart and erect and genteel, and followed by a porter with a barrow of luggage' (so he had managed to retrieve his belongings from Monte Cassino). The carabinieri were lounging around on the harbour front and Lawrence felt his heart quicken; but Magnus sailed past, 'his nose in the air'. Hooting and twinkling, the ship heaved into the night and Lawrence, still leaning on the rail, was watching the lights of Syracuse 'sinking already forlorn and little on the low darkness' when 'suddenly, like a *revenant*', appeared Magnus at his side. 'Oh my word,' Magnus said, 'I begin to breathe free for the first time since I left the monastery! How awful it's been! But of course, in Malta, I shall be all right.'[75] Then lurching off sideways into the air, Monsieur Mosquito reappeared, just as suddenly, on the first-class deck, smoking a cigar and comporting himself in conversation with an officer in a thoroughly first-class manner: 'Such obscenity of trespass'.

The following dawn Lawrence saw for the first time the 'heaped glitter' of Valetta, and he thought of St Paul who was shipwrecked here and 'must have struck the island from this side'. When Coleridge landed in the same harbour 115 years earlier, to take up his position of Secretary to the British Governor, he had felt like Aeneas arriving at Carthage. Lawrence watched Magnus disembark and present his passport to the Maltese official. This was the egregious little modern moment to which all pilgrims were now subjected: would he pass the examination? 'Yes, he passed all right. Once more he was free.'[76] And so off Magnus went through the tilting streets and stairways of the town.

The Knights of Malta, who came to the island in 1530 after being expelled from Rhodes, are a religious and military brotherhood whose mission, dating back to the time of the Crusades, is to defend the poor and sick. Malta's reputation as a sanctuary was confirmed in the Great War, when 20,000 hospital beds were made available for the wounded. The monks of Monte Cassino had connections on Malta, and so Magnus was in good hands: he would be safe here, looked after by two Maltese friends of Don Martino, called Mazzaiba and Salonia.*

Malta shows every sign of being a colonial outpost. The butter-yellow rocks of the port have been, Lawrence noted, 'cut straight by man', and the Maltese speak fluent broken-English. It is a place of barking dogs, military bands and bacon-and-egg breakfasts. It was also, when Lawrence was there, staggeringly hot: 'so hot', he wrote, that 'I feel quite stunned.' No sooner had Lawrence booked into the Great Britain Hotel in the Strada Reale than he ran into Magnus whose (superior) hotel was

---

*Mazzaiba and Salonia are the names given to the two Maltese in the *Memoir of Maurice Magnus*. Their real names, by which they were referred to in Lawrence's letters, were James Borg and Walter Salomone. For consistency, I have referred to the two men by their pseudonyms.

on the same street, and he now did nothing to resist him. They lunched together and went back to Magnus's bedroom for whisky: such had become their routine. Magnus was sporting a 'smart white duck suit' and Lawrence – astonishingly – paid a tailor £6 to make him a similar white suit of Indian silk. He doubtless needed cooler clothes, but this sartorial extravagance is evidence of the degree to which Lawrence resigned himself to the appeal of Magnus. The two men, it will have been noted, explored the island in identical outfits.

The steamer strike turned their two-day jolly into an eight-day sentence, and so, with nothing else to do, Lawrence joined Magnus, Mazzaiba and Salonia in the car for sightseeing excursions to St Paul's Bay and the fortress-city of Medina, the stately and impregnable former capital of the island. On the other side of Medina's walls lies the overflow town of Rabat (meaning suburb), and beneath Rabat (because the dead could not be buried beneath Medina) are the Phoenician catacombs of St Agatha and St Paul, a vast subterranean country covering more than 20,000 square feet. The underworld is entered through a shaft in the stone which opens into a cave where tables and couches hewn from the rocks impersonate the furniture of Roman villas. This is where the mourners once feasted in celebration of the life to come. Narrow corridors like the passages in a mine lead to further chambers, and gangplanks lead on to the sarcophagi where a thousand corpses once waited for the Day of Judgement. We do not know if Lawrence toured the catacombs – he says next to nothing in his letters about what happened on Malta – but it is hard to believe that he would have overlooked the opportunity.

What Lawrence did say is that he loathed Malta, a land without rivers or streams or even snakes because St Paul, surviving a snakebite, drove them all away. Lawrence described it as a 'bone-dry', 'bath-brick', 'hideous island', 'stark as a corpse, no trees, no bushes even: a fearful landscape, cultivated, and weary with ages of weariness, and weary old houses here and there'.[77] Eight days was a long time for Lawrence to remain in the same spot without writing, and the blistering heat would have made his need for constant movement difficult. The dryness of Malta gets under your skin, and Coleridge felt much as Lawrence did. Or rather, Lawrence's 'glittering' Malta sounds very like that of Coleridge, who in one of his notebook entries pictured himself after three months on the island as gasping like a fish 'on the glittering mud, the mud of his once full stream'. In a letter to his wife in the Lake District, Coleridge described Malta as 'a barren Rock ... no rivers, no brooks, no hedges, no green fields, almost no trees, & the few that are unlovely'.[78]

For Magnus, Malta was – literally – a last resort. When Lawrence said goodbye to him at the end of May, the fugitive was settling into a tiny house (rent: £6 a year, paid in advance) in a 'quiet forlorn little yellow street' in Rabat, directly above the underworld.

According to the *Memoir*, during their days on Malta Lawrence and Magnus discussed nothing but the publication of *Dregs* and various of Magnus's drama translations, and we know that Lawrence wrote to publishers on Magnus's behalf. Douglas had separately tried to place *Dregs* but, as he had predicted, no one would touch it with tongs. Magnus was determined, however, to live from his writing, and his letters from Rabat are evidence of his campaign to survive. To one editor who had turned the book down on the grounds of obscenity, Magnus grandly replied:

I believe I should deserve the reproach that 'there are some things that cannot be published' if 'Dregs' were vulgar. Only vulgarity without wit is unpublishable, or rather not permissible ... I think I have mentioned the eulogistic verdicts of Norman Douglas, D. H. Lawrence, and Douglas Goldring ...[79]

Undeterred, Magnus began a second set of memoirs, settling down in the burning heat to recall his winter tour of 'Golden Russia'.

He was making plans. In the long term, Magnus wanted to clear his name and return to what he called the 'place on the hill', but he also wrote to the Queen of Spain ('There are so few queens left now!') to enquire about 'a room in one of her country houses, or a cell in one of the monasteries she is protecting. No answer – not that I expected it.' Another plan was to go to Morocco. 'What the hell will you do in Morocco', asked Douglas, 'besides —?' There were, Magnus conceded, 'a few desirable Arabs – though I only fly to the physical when I can't have the other'. Douglas was planning a trip to Morocco himself, 'to indulge in the carnal delights'. Magnus and Douglas used code-words when what they discussed was illegal: 'Most interesting,' Magnus told Douglas, 'what you say about the Maltese and the *tobacco*. Of course you are a connoisseur of young tobacco ...'[80]

Lawrence returned from Malta at the end of May, relieved that his friend was 'shut up in that beastly island'. He hoped that Magnus had now exited the stage but had 'that fatal lurking feeling that he *hadn't*',[81] and one morning in July he came down to find once again a serpent in his garden. This one was gold and soft-bellied rather than pink and soft-bellied, and drinking not from a whisky glass but from Lawrence's water-trough. Magnus's latest incarnation as a snake recalls the circle of hell where the thieves are turned into serpents who slither into and out of one another's bodies.

A snake came to my water-trough
On a hot, hot day, and I in pyjamas for the heat,
To drink there.

In the deep, strange-scented shade of the great dark carob tree
I came down the steps with my pitcher
And must wait, must stand and wait, for there he was at the trough
before me.

Lawrence felt 'honoured' to have such a guest.

He drank enough
And lifted his head, dreamily, as one who has drunken,
And flickered his tongue like a forked night on the air, so black,
Seeming to lick his lips,
And looked around like a god, unseeing, into the air,
And slowly turned his head,
And slowly, very slowly, as if thrice adream,
Proceeded to draw his slow length curving round
And climb again the broken bank of my wall-face.

Lawrence then threw a 'clumsy log' in his direction which missed the snake but hit the water-trough with a clatter. The god 'writhed like lightning' and 'immediately I regretted it'.

And I thought of the albatross,
And I wished he would come back, my snake.

For he seemed to me again like a king
A king in exile.

That July he returned to the manuscript of *Aaron's Rod*, discarded in 1918. Breathing life back into *The Lost Girl* had been easy – the novel had effectively written itself – and Lawrence assumed that *Aaron* would be just as quickly off his hands.

In August and September of 1920 Lawrence did two remarkable things, both in response to Magnus. The first was to go back, this time with Frieda, to Monte Cassino – the place in which he had understood, with such devastating impact, the full meaning of not going back. And the second was to have an affair.

He says nothing in the *Memoir*, or anywhere else, about his second visit to the monastery, where he and Frieda stayed between 2 and 5 August as guests of Don Martino, but in the last letter Lawrence ever sent to Magnus, in July, he tells him that he is returning to the place on the hill. The subject of Magnus's plight will have arisen during Lawrence's stay: did he denounce his friend or remain loyal? Either way, he had displaced him. Lawrence was now the guide who pointed out to Frieda the Bramante courtyard, the Cellini casket, the exquisite mosaics and agonising views. In a repetition of the time they had toured Florence by moonmist, Lawrence showed his wife a town of men.

From Monte Cassino, Frieda went on to Germany to see her mother and sisters and Lawrence, once again, waited in Florence for her return. In September 1920 the lily town was in a state of civil war, as it had been under the rule of the Guelphs: fascist banners, processions, sudden shots, the shops barred and closed. Lawrence stayed not in the old *pensione* but five miles north-east in the Villa Canovaia, a thirteenth-century house in San Gervasio on a narrow lane leading up the hill to Fiesole, where tourists go to look down on the city. The house dated back to the time when the families of Dante and Beatrice had neighbouring summer villas on this same slope. Dante remembers Fiesole in *Inferno*, Canto 15, where he meets Brunetto Latini, his former tutor, on the burning sands of the seventh circle of hell and Latini, praising his pupil's fame and prophesying his fate, calls the conquerors of Florence the 'beasts of Fiesole':

But that malicious, that ungrateful people
come down, in ancient times, from Fiesole –
still keeping something of the rock and mountain –

for your good deeds, will be your enemy:
and there is cause – among the sour sorbs,
the sweet fig is not meant to bear its fruit.

*(Inferno*, Canto 15, 61–6)

Over the next few weeks, in poems born directly from Dante's lines and published in *Birds, Beasts and Flowers*, Lawrence allowed the sour sorbs and the sweet figs and all the beasts of Fiesole to fructify.

The Villa Canovaia was being rented by Rosalind Baynes (on whose behalf Lawrence had inspected the house in Picinisco), but after an explosion at a nearby munitions factory had blown out the windows, Rosalind and her three daughters decamped to a villa on the top of the hill. Lawrence, who preferred fresh air, lived in the bombed-out building like a happy hermit. He had his bedding, his portable gas stove for coffee and eleven rooms to himself. There was a large walled garden with persimmon trees and vines, a courtyard, a stone bench, a fountain, a resident nightingale, a family of tortoises and, to greet the evening, a host of fireflies. But there was no escaping the political turmoil. On one of these late-summer nights, Lawrence recalled, the fascists banged at the door of the mayor of Fiesole, getting him out of bed. They then 'seized him, stood him against the wall of his house, and shot him ... in front of his wife and children, who were in their night-dresses. Why? Because he was a socialist.'[82]

Willowy with porcelain skin and soft chestnut hair, Rosalind Baynes was lovely to look at. Her mother, Agatha Thornycroft – considered by Thomas Hardy to be 'the most beautiful woman in England' – was the model for Tess D'Urberville, and her first cousin was Siegfried Sassoon. Now aged twenty-eight Rosalind had separated from her husband, Godwin, a psychoanalyst who would later work closely with Jung. The marriage had always been sexually relaxed but, having had two daughters by Godwin, Rosalind then, during the war, produced a third by a different man, hence the divorce. On the day she first met Lawrence and Frieda, Rosalind picnicked with them in the woods where the Lawrences sang German folk songs in their 'shrill, penetrating, unforgettable voices'.[83] She then invited Lawrence to her cottage when her husband was coming to discuss the separation: Rosalind needed Lawrence to lessen her load, and he had been protective of her ever since. He saved her from the freezing house in Picinisco and then, when she stayed at Pensione Balestri in Florence, he saved her from the offensive conversation of Norman Douglas. Rosalind was Lawrence's type: he liked mothers, especially if they were from elevated backgrounds, and – having his own theories of the unconscious – he liked to pitch himself against psychoanalysts like Otto Gross and Godwin Baynes.

Rosalind did not add her memories of Lawrence to the rash of those that appeared in the 1930s. She recalled him instead in a private account, *Time Which Spaces Us Apart*, which remained unpublished until 1954. Here she described how he would climb the lane to Fiesole, bearing gifts for her girls – a salamander, a baby duck – and walk with her in the cypress woods after supper. On one of these occasions he asked about sex. Did she miss it? She did, Rosalind replied, but was 'damned fastidious' about partners: 'It's no good just making love; there must be more to it than a few pretty words and then off to bed.' Lawrence wholeheartedly agreed, adding, 'God save us from the so-called Love – that most indecent kind of egoism and self-spreading.' They were not, in other words, allowed to fall in love, but why not have 'a sex-time' together? The idea was presented in an 'off-hand' way and Rosalind was 'astounded' with happiness: 'Firenze and her lights twirled round and I felt off the world.' Nothing, however, was to happen that night. She asked Lawrence to stay but he preferred to wait. The prophet of blood-consciousness and spontaneous instinct displayed a triumph of mind over matter that must have surprised Rosalind Baynes. They kissed their troth, after which Lawrence went back down the lane.

The next night he came again for supper and Rosalind 'sweetened' her room for his visit, but still Lawrence would not stay. His returns home are recalled in 'Medlars and Sorb Apples', written in September, where he compared himself to Orpheus descending into the underworld to retrieve Eurydice.

Going down the strange lanes of hell, more and more
    intensely alone,
The fibres of the heart parting one after the other
And yet the soul continuing, naked-footed, ever more vividly
    embodied
Like a flame blown whiter and whiter
In a deeper and deeper darkness
Ever more exquisite, distilled in separation.

On the third night, Lawrence and Rosalind walked again in the cypress woods where they saw a grand turkey cock and sucked sorb apples. 'How good it is here,' said Lawrence. 'It is something quite special and lovely, the time, the place, the beloved,' and Rosalind's heart jumped 'with joy'. They sat there until it grew dark, his hand in her hand: 'And so to bed'.[84] It was 11 September, Lawrence's thirty-fifth birthday. In 'Medlars and Sorb Apples' he wrote:

A kiss, and a vivid spasm of farewell, a moment's orgasm of rupture
Then along the damp road alone.

Not only was his affair an act of will, a conscious decision to confirm his freedom from Frieda, but it leaves us with the impression of a man held at gunpoint like the Mayor of Fiesole. 'Wonderful', Lawrence reflected in 'Medlars and Sorb Apples', 'are the hellish experiences'. What followed, however, was a stream of poetry, the best he had written. Turkey cocks, sorb apples, tortoises, figs ('put your mouth to the crack, and take out the flesh in one bite') – it was now that Lawrence produced the bulk of *Birds, Beasts and Flowers*. His September 1920 was akin to Wordsworth's June 1802, and in the Romantic tradition Lawrence staged encounters between the human and non-human. In Monte Cassino he had felt the agony of being 'a child of the present'; he now celebrated what he called the 'poetry of the present', with its 'spinning of sky winds'.[85] Because the present is unfinished, the poetry of the present can have 'no rhythm which returns upon itself ... no static perfection, none of that finality which we find so satisfying because we are so frightened'.[86] The form the poetry of the present takes must be free verse, and the model was Whitman: 'There was never any more inception than there is now,' Whitman wrote in 'Song of Myself'. 'And will never be any more perfection than there is now.' For Lawrence, only in the present can we be 'in ourselves spontaneous and flexible as flame'.[87]

The language of *Birds, Beasts and Flowers*, said W. H. Auden, is so transparent that we forget the poet is there: we simply see what Lawrence sees. But *Birds, Beasts and Flowers* also reminds us of what Lawrence was like when he *was* there, in the form of his better self, walking through the woods and meadows, noting that wet almond trees look like iron sticking out of the earth and that young cyclamens prick up their ears when they wake, 'like delicate very-young greyhound bitches'. Whitman had displaced Shelley as his mentor, but the voice of these poems is Lawrence's own; so too is the quality of his noticing, the comedy of bodies and the immediacy of the encounters. His animal encounters are like quick little jokes.

Lawrence had the gifts of a botanist and the eye of a naturalist, but he refused to see the world as Darwinian. In his view, the survival of the fittest was a mock-heroic battle between man and beast: 'But I am greater than he …' Lawrence concludes in 'Man and Bat', where he describes a bat trapped in his bedroom: 'I escaped him.' He had a similar joust with the mosquito in Syracuse, and the snake in his Sicilian garden. In his encounters with the natural world he usually comes off worst, and when he reflects on his own affairs, through the agency of flowers, birds and beasts, it is in the spirit of self-parody; satirising his own limitations, Lawrence catches the inscape of 'divine otherness'. He and Frieda, carting their homes around on their backs, are a naked pair of tortoises; in relation to the regal snake in the garden, Lawrence is prosaic and petty. Reflecting on fish reveals nothing of himself.

They are beyond me, are fishes.
I stand at the pale of my being
And look beyond, and see
Fish, in the outerwards,
As one stands on a bank and looks in.

The heroine of 'She-Goat' might trip along the rocks like a woman going to mass, but suddenly she reappears,

standing like some huge, ghoulish grey bird in the air, on the

bough of the leaning almond tree,
Straight as a board on the bough, looking down like some hairy horrid God the Father in a

William Blake imagination.

Lawrence stands back in these poems and lets his daemon take front stage: this is why his amusement always ends in terror. As for the baby tortoise,

It is no use my saying to him in an emotional voice:
'This is your Mother, she laid you when you were an egg.'

He does not even trouble to answer: 'Woman, what have I to do
    with thee?'
He wearily looks the other way,
And she even more wearily looks another way still,
Each with the utmost apathy,
Incognizant,
Unaware,
Nothing.

There is no precursor for his Tortoise poems. No one but Lawrence
could have written in this way about tortoise recognition – 'Not
knowing each other from bits of earth or old tins' – or tortoise life
prospects: 'What a huge, vast inanimate it is, that you must row
against, / What an incalculable inertia'. Perhaps no one else would have
wanted to. And no one else could have engaged so thoroughly with
the martyrdom of tortoise sex, the female being so much larger than
the male.

Crucifixion.
Male tortoise, cleaving behind the hovel-wall of that dense female,
Mounted and tense, spread-eagle, out-reaching out of the shell
In tortoise-nakedness,
Long neck, and long vulnerable limbs extruded, spread-eagle over
    her house-roof,
And the deep, secret, all-penetrating tail curved beneath her walls,
Reaching and gripping tense, more reaching anguish in uttermost
    tension
Till suddenly, in the spasm of coition, tupping like a jerking leap,
    and oh!

He had plenty of time in San Gervasio to complete *Aaron's Rod* but,
like a motorcar with a faulty engine, the book wouldn't move. 'My novel
jerks one chapter forward now and then,' he told Compton Mackenzie
on 12 September. 'It is half done. But where the other half is coming
from, ask Divine Providence.' On 26 September, Lawrence complained

that 'My novel – the new one – has stuck half way.' On 7 October: 'I am stuck in the middle of *Aaron's Rod*.'

The rain in November 1920 fell straight and silent and Lawrence, who never entered a room without flinging open a window, raised his hands to the weather as though warming them before a fire. It was so wet, he said, that it was like living inside an aquarium. On the fifth day of the month, *Women in Love* was published in America and on the twenty-sixth, *The Lost Girl* was published in England: Lawrence was once again a novelist. In between these two momentous events, the postman made his way through the now bowed and sodden garden with a letter from Don Bernardo at the Abbey: did Lawrence know that Maurice Magnus had killed himself on Malta? 'The world', Lawrence wrote,' 'seemed to stand still for me.'[88]

A 'scrubby' notice in the *Daily Malta Chronicle*, sent later by Magnus's Maltese friend Salonia, contained more information: Magnus, 'a well-built man in the prime of life', had swallowed prussic acid in his bedroom as a result of financial difficulties. Mazzaiba then wrote to Lawrence to say that Magnus had owed him £55 which he needed to recover – could Lawrence help? Lawrence himself was owed £23. He also received a letter from Salonia who described Magnus's time on the island as a 'painful' and 'unsolicited' experience for himself and Mazzaiba, 'a huge farce wrapped up in mystery'.[89]

Last July, Salonia continued, Magnus had been told by the Maltese police to deposit a sum of money or, when his three months on the island had expired, he would be required to leave. Not having any money to deposit, Magnus asked Mazzaiba to stand as surety. But Mazzaiba, who had lent Magnus that £55 and was also standing surety for some cousins, passed the responsibility on to Salonia himself, who noted that Magnus, having signed a declaration stating that he would 'not be a burden to the inhabitants of these islands', also owed the local shopkeepers over £10. When Salonia refused to guarantee the visitor's debts, Magnus wrote to the police explaining that he would be leaving for Morocco in three weeks' time and asking for a period of grace. When he did not receive an acknowledgement of his letter, he began to grow anxious.

Then, on the morning of 4 November – the day before the publication of *Women in Love* – Magnus was stopped in the street by two detectives and arrested for the fraudulent cheques in Rome. He explained that he needed to change his clothes before accompanying them to the police station, and the detectives agreed to wait outside his house while he did so. Locking the door behind him, Magnus went up to his bedroom and wrote to Don Bernardo: 'I leave it to you and Gabriel Mazzaiba to arrange my affairs. I cannot live any longer. Pray for me.' Dropping the letter from the window, he asked a passing boy to post it for him but it was picked up by the police. He then wrote a second, more general message which he left on his writing table: 'In case of my expected death inform American consul. I want to be buried first class, my wife will pay.'[90] His literary executor was to be Norman Douglas, who would receive half the profits from sales of his work. The other half were to pay off Magnus's debts. Changing into his duck-white suit Magnus lay down on his bed, drank the phial of acid he carried in case of emergency and damned himself in the eyes of his God.

The detectives meanwhile were getting uneasy and tried to force open the door. When it would not give way, they got hold of a ladder and climbed through the window into Magnus's bedroom, where they found him in the last moments of consciousness. A priest was called to administer Extreme Unction and Magnus died at 11.45 that morning. He was buried on 7 November 1920, his forty-fourth birthday, in a suicide's grave. His wife refused to fund his first-class funeral and so the costs were met by Mazzaiba, Salonia, the Consul, the Vice-Consul and a mysterious American referred to in the papers stored in the Malta archive as Mr M. Out of respect for their shared faith, Mazzaiba later had Magnus's remains removed and placed in his own family plot.

'I heard ... the other day that Magnus had committed suicide,' Lawrence wrote to Douglas. 'He was found in a white suit dead on his bed in his room at Notabile, having taken poison. En voilà fini.'[91] His sangfroid disguised the Gordian knot of responses that would appear in his writing over the next two years. Lawrence had long stopped replying to Magnus's letters but Douglas and Magnus were often in touch, with regular instalments of the 'Memoirs of Golden Russia' making their way from Malta to Menton, where Douglas was currently based. Douglas sent Magnus ideas for improvements, and Magnus offered literary advice of his own: Douglas should write a history of the Protestant Cemetery in Rome – Magnus's mother was buried there, and so too was Shelley. It was a good suggestion and Douglas would have done the job well. Magnus himself was winding down: 'I haven't any energy left,' he wrote on 2 October, 'to get up and go chasing madly through the world doing odds and ends as I have been doing for the last few ages. I am tired. I want to be quiet and sit still and just go on writing in my own little way.'[92]

On 28 October he wrote what would be his last letter to Douglas, received by him on the day that Magnus died. His subject was Lawrence. 'Don't worry about Lawrence writing nasty,' Magnus reassured Douglas.

> He opened his 'heart' (!) to me here accidentally. He is looking for bisexual types for *himself*. Spoke of his innocence when he wrote 'Twilight' and 'Il Duro'. Evidently innocent no longer. Didn't like Malta because he thought the religion or something prevented their sexual expression! I didn't elucidate [sic] as I could have done even after a few days stay! He revels in all that is not just within his reach. He wants it to be within his reach. Arrives too late – regrets it – never speaks of it unless bored to death by women as here by Mrs Gilbert Cannan and his wife.[93]

There is a wealth of information in this passage. First, Douglas was increasingly anxious about being turned by Lawrence into copy. Secondly, Lawrence's conversations with Magnus on Malta extended further than helping him find publishers for his various writings. Lawrence confided in Magnus, as he did in a number of his male friends, about his homosexual curiosity; he admired Magnus for leading a bisexual life, something he too would like to do. What did Lawrence mean, that he had arrived 'too late'?

'Il Duro' ('The Hard One') is a chapter in *Twilight in Italy*. It is also the name of a peasant Lawrence had known at Lake Garda in 1914, who worked for seven years in a flag factory in America and returned with a little money. Il Duro was 'very handsome, beautiful rather, a man of thirty-two or -three, with a clear golden skin, and perfectly turned face'. He had the 'slightly malignant, suffering look of a satyr' and Lawrence compared him to Pan. He had 'seen too much' for marriage, but Lawrence knew that Il Duro 'liked me very much, almost loved me, which again was strange and puzzling. It was as if he were a fairy, a faun, and had no soul.' His presence 'gave me a feeling of vivid sadness, a sadness that gleamed like phosphorescence', and watching Il

Duro crouch on the earth 'like some strange animal god, doubled on his haunches' filled Lawrence 'with a sort of panic'. But, he concluded, 'there was nothing between us except our complete difference. It was like night and day flowing together.'[94]

Like Magnus, Il Duro left Lawrence both puzzled and panicked. Had Lawrence told Magnus about the Italian peasant when they had been talking about peasants on that freezing afternoon in Monte Cassino? Did Lawrence regret that there had been nothing between himself and this 'strange animal god'? Did he stop replying to Magnus's letters precisely because he had 'opened his "heart"' on the island to this man who seemed to understand so much, round about the questions that trouble one deepest? To prove Lawrence's point, what Magnus said now to Douglas simply dazzles: *Lawrence revels in all that is not just within his reach.* That is exactly right.

*Aaron's Rod* was still mired and so, on 28 November, Lawrence began instead a comic novel about his marriage which he called *Mr Noon*, where he returned to his courting days with Frieda and his anxiety about Otto Gross. It was an act of release, abandon even, and there is magic in *Mr Noon*; had he finished the novel it would have presented an entirely different Lawrence to the world. But by 9 December, the book came to 'a sudden stop', and in early January 1921 he and Frieda went on a nine-day visit to Sardinia, his fourth island in a year.

'Comes over one an absolute necessity to move': *Sea and Sardinia* has the finest opening line of any travel book.[95] Presented in a clipped, cinematic shot-by-shot present tense similar to that of 'David' (the other titles Lawrence considered for the book were 'Sardinian Films' and 'Films of Sicily and Sardinia'), *Sea and Sardinia* is self-parody in technicolour. The mood, like that of *Mr Noon*, is joyful and unbuttoned, but also edgy and ominous. Lawrence's best self is at the wheel in these pages and beside him, her hair blowing back, sits the 'Queen Bee', as he refers to Frieda. Husband and wife are his new comic couple, with Lawrence playing the surly worker-bee for all he's worth, while Frieda has replaced Magnus as the self-pampering Frau.

He and the 'q-b' leave Fontana Vecchia at dawn, as the sea and the sky are parting 'like an oyster shell, with a low red gape'. Closing the gate on the sloping garden where Magnus once appeared like a revenant, they slink between the rosemary hedges and make their way beneath the eucalyptus trees to the station. On the train to Palermo a child vomits twice on the floor and no one bothers to clean it up, while on the stomach-churning passage to Sardinia, the q-b remains horizontal. Lawrence now has his first sight of Mount Eryx on Sicily's western coast, and his 'darkness' quivers. 'But why in the name of heaven should my heart stand still as I watch that hill which rises above the sea … To men it must have had a magic even greater than Etna's.' All high lands, he concludes, are 'magic' when 'seen from the sea'.[96]

Then 'suddenly' there is Cagliari, 'a naked town rising steep, steep, golden-looking, piled naked to the sky … like a town in a monkish illuminated missal'. It rises before them like 'some vision, some memory, something that has passed away'. It is fiesta-time: the men are dressed as women and the women are in masques; one couple is dressed as Dante and Beatrice, 'in Paradise apparently, all in white sheet-robes, and with silver wreaths on their heads, arm in arm, and prancing very slowly and majestically, yet with the long lilt as if hitched along by wires from above'. Dante, with his long nose, high cheekbones and 'stupid wooden look,' has 'come to life', offering 'a modern criticism on the Inferno'.[97] The whole town is a marionette show.

Lawrence has brought along their 'kitchenino', containing a thermos of tea, bacon and egg sandwiches, apples, butter, sugar, salt, two spoons, two forks, two aluminium plates, a small saucepan, some methylated spirits and a knife. Food features heavily in *Sea and Sardinia*, as do the thinginess of things. At sea, Lawrence and Frieda are given thick, oily cabbage soup, leathery omelettes, slabs of meat tasting of 'dead nothingness', greenish cauliflower, leather-fleshed pears, macaroni in tomato sauce and multiple cups of coffee. In Sardinia they eat roast kid and fatty pork and turn their noses up at indifferent red wine. The food they are served is disgusting, but the food they see is delicious and the q-b would buy everything. She would live in Sardinia, Lawrence complains, simply for the eggs. In the meat and poultry and bread market they gaze at cakes, olives, sausages and dozens of different cheeses. In a fabric shop the q-b buys a roll of blue and red striped material from which to make a dress, and they rummage through 'combs and collar-studs, cheap mirrors, handkerchiefs, shoddy Manchester goods, bed-ticking, boot-paste, poor crockery, and so on'. So much for shopping: 'The question is, shall we go on? Shall we go forward?' They have to keep moving, but upwards not forwards. 'Always upwards', Lawrence says of the flights of steps in Cagliari. 'We were always climbing', he says of the roads outside the town. 'Up and up the roads go.' They rush and wind up a hill to Nuoro; the 'little engine whisks up and up' the massif of Gennargentu. In Sardinia, even the level ground is high: 'Here, in the heart of Sardinia, the life-level is high on the golden-lit plateau, and the sea-level is somewhere far away ... the life-level is high up, high, and sun-sweetened and among rocks.'[98]

Everything here rises: the myrtle scrub, the hazels, the gorges, the forests: there is no 'single peak' like Etna on Sicily. Lawrence's ascent is so rapid and continuous that you wonder how he could not by now have reached the empyrean. He too wonders this: 'On we rush', he later says; they must reach a new 'highest point of the journey'. 'I would like to go to Fonni', he writes when they can go no higher. 'They say it is the highest village in Sardinia.'[99]

It is on Mount Ortobene in Nuoro that Lawrence has his next epiphany: 'Life was not', he now understands, 'only a process of rediscovering backwards,' although 'it is that, also: and it is that intensely'.

But this morning in the omnibus I realize that, apart from the great rediscovery backwards, which one *must* make before one can be whole at all, there is a move forwards. There are unknown, unworked lands where the salt has not lost its savour. But one must have perfected oneself in the great past first.[100]

It is the revelation he had on Monte Cassino, that there is no looking back in Purgatory. But he now understood what he had to do.

Lawrence's concern in Sardinia is with the lost savour of masculinity: the local men are dressed as women, he himself is buzzing around after the queen. 'One realises, with horror, that the race of men is almost extinct in Europe', that their 'fierce singleness is quenched'.[101] Like looking down on a city, or across a landscape, or at Leonardo's *Madonna of the Rocks*, the native Sardinian men are a vision of something passed away.

After nine days, Frieda and Lawrence return to Sicily via the mainland, where they once again take the train from Rome to Cassino. 'Why, there is the monastery on its high hill! In a wild moment I suggest we shall get down and spend a night up there at Monte Cassino ... but the q-b shudders, thinking of the awful winter coldness of that massive stone monastery.'[102] It was a year ago that Lawrence first suffered the coldness of the place. He lets his plan subside, and they brew coffee instead on the station platform. Their train to Naples is filled with legionnaires from Fiume, where Gabriele D'Annunzio's fifteen-month rule over the Croatian town has ended.

Lawrence later said that he disliked Sardinia. The yellow island 'belonging to nowhere' reminded him of Malta, and *Sea and Sardinia* is in many ways a thank-you-and-goodbye letter to all of Italy: 'Italy has given me back I know not what of myself, but a very, very great deal. She has found for me so much that was lost: like a restored Osiris.' Having perfected himself in the country's great past, the lost boy was ready to move forward.[103]

When *Sea and Sardinia* was published in England in April 1923, the reviewer for the *New Statesman* compared it to the sort of 'individual' travel book written by Norman Douglas. 'Superficially there is something alike in them. The sort of people and scenes they delight in … both have the novelist's gift of introducing little dramatic incidents, depending almost entirely on the close observation of one or two sharply cut figures …'[104] Had he seen the review, Douglas would have felt his blood turn to ice and the sea go black.

*Aaron's Rod* still wouldn't move and Lawrence couldn't stay still. Leaving Sicily again in April 1921, he returned briefly to Capri where he discussed his novel with two new friends, American Buddhists called Earl and Achsah Brewster. He had not yet got Aaron out of England, and Earl Brewster recalled how, 'in his low sonorous voice with the quiet gesture of his hands', Lawrence told the story of his hero and his flute and his friendship with Lilly. It was a beautiful account, 'more beautiful than it ever could be written in a book'. And then 'suddenly', he stopped. What should Aaron do now, Lawrence asked, having left his wife and broken with the past?

> We ventured that only two possible courses were left to a man in his straits – either to go to Monte Cassino and repent, or else to go through the whole cycle of experience. He gave a quiet chuckle of surprise and added that those were the very possibilities he had seen, that first he had intended sending him to Monte Cassino, but found instead that Aaron had to go to destruction to find his way through from the lowest depths.[105]

In other words, Aaron had to visit hell before reaching Purgatory. Following this revelation, the novel now kicked into gear. Lilly left London for Malta, from where he crossed over to Syracuse and journeyed through Sicily to the mainland and up to Turin: Lawrence's journey in reverse. 'A new place brings out a new thing in man,' Lilly tells Aaron.[106] 'Come if you want to. Bring your flute.' So in Chapter 12, Aaron finally leaves England and follows the same route through France taken by Lawrence in November 1919, arriving at Turin, renamed Novara, 'on a wet, dark evening'. Sir Walter Becker is refashioned as Sir William Franks, an affable old bore whose wife, small and portly like Queen Victoria, has him parade his order medals after dinner.

Aaron 'had fallen into country house parties before, but never into quite such a plushy sense of riches', and he and Sir William argue about how to live. 'I always advise Providence plus a banking account,' says the businessman. 'I believe in chance,' says Aaron. That night the softness of his mattress robs Aaron of sleep; he 'preferred to be more uncomfortable and more aware of the flight of the dark hours'. Breakfast in bed – coffee and eggs in a silver egg cup with a frill around it – brings out Aaron's conflicted nature: the part that liked 'fine, delicate things' appreciated the luxury, while the part that preferred naked liberty wanted to 'throw the dainty little table with all its niceties out of the window'.[107]

Sir Walter Becker later told Norman Douglas of his 'astonishment' on finding, when he read *Aaron's Rod*, a detailed account of Lawrence's stay in Turin, including 'faithfully reproduced' descriptions of 'the conversations at the dinner table and afterwards, all of which, according to him, were on a despicably low level', of the 'blue silk hangings of his bedroom', the exact dimensions of the 'entrance gate, lodge and grounds' and the 'unpardonable' offence of being served breakfast in bed. Sir Walter's understanding was that he and Lawrence had formed a sympathetic friendship; he had no idea that his guest thought him a 'physically decrepit and vulgarly ostentatious plutocrat'. If Lawrence had 'at least made me out an amusing jackanapes,' he told Douglas, 'I would not have minded it, but, that I should have been the source of inspiration of such shockingly wearisome tirades, somewhat humiliates me.' Douglas explained that Lawrence 'disliked accepting help, financial or otherwise, however willingly bestowed'. While most people, however, were polite enough to 'mask their feeling of resentment' and display due gratitude, Lawrence was compelled to curse the people whose patronage he accepted. He was simply, said Douglas, 'one of the most envy-bitten mortals I have known. He was envious of other men's social rank, of their reputations and natural gifts, and chiefly of their bank-balances; even the relative affluence of his own family was a grievance to him'.[108]

As Aaron penetrates Italy, he finds himself beneath scenery that threatens to possess and obliterate him. His bedroom window at Sir William's mansion looks across a clear Alpine sky and Aaron sees the mountains 'hovering round, circling, waiting. They reminded him of marvellous striped sky-panthers circling round a great camp.' From the garden, Aaron follows the path 'upwards' to the 'steep last bit' of land where 'massive in the further nearness' stand 'the tiger-like Alps. Tigers prowling between the north and the south.' The view makes him feel as though he were asleep and being prodded awake by a long finger into a new consciousness. Dante emerged from his own sleep in the dark wood to find his ascent up the mountain of Purgatory blocked by three wild beasts; Aaron finds 'striped sky-panthers' and prowling snow tigers in the 'white-fanged' mountains and is driven back down the path. But that afternoon he starts his climb again and this time he reaches the top and sees 'over into vineyards, and a new strange valley with a winding river, and jumbled, entangled hills'[109]

Aaron arrives in Florence on a dark, wet evening in November 1919, and on his first morning goes to the Piazza della Signoria where he catches sight of 'the long slim neck of the Palazzo Vecchio up above, in the air'.

There he stood still and looked round him in real surprise, and real joy. The flat empty square with its stone paving was all wet. The great buildings rose dark. The dark, sheer front of the Palazzo Vecchio went up like a cliff, to the battlements, and the slim tower soared dark and hawk-like, crested, high above. And at the foot of the cliff stood the great naked David, white and stripped in the wet, white against the dark, warm-dark cliff of the building – and near, the heavy naked men of Bandinelli.[110]

There are three naked men in the Piazza della Signoria. David, a sack over his shoulder holding the stone he will lodge in Goliath's head, is on one side of the Palazzo door and on the other side, crowded together on one plinth, are Bandinelli's Hercules and Cacus. Hercules the demi-god stands triumphant, and crouching at his feet is the cave-dwelling, cattle-thieving cannibal. Aaron 'looked and looked at the three great naked men'; he looked at 'the great, naked men in the rain, under the dark-grey November sky, in the dark, strong inviolable square! The wonderful hawk-head of the old palace! The physical, self-conscious adolescent, Michelangelo's David, shrinking and exposing himself, with his white, slack limbs! Florence, passionate, fearless Florence had spoken herself out.'[111]

Aaron never went into town without finding an excuse to pass through the Piazza della Signoria. 'And he never passed through it without satisfaction. Here men had been at their intensest, most naked pitch, here, at the end of the old world and the beginning of the new. Since then, always rather puling and apologetic.' The statues awaken Aaron's Whitmanesque consciousness: he feels 'a new self, a new life-urge rising inside himself. Florence seemed to start a new man in him.'[112] England, since the war, had become a country of women – in terms of population, women now exceeded men by two million – but here in the piazza there was not a woman to be found.

Lawrence's recent experience with Rosalind Baynes is explored in Aaron's affair with an American marchesa in Florence. The Marchesa is musical and married; her bond with Aaron is formed when he plays his flute and 'a gleam almost of happiness seemed to light her up'. By way of symbolising that she has stolen a part of him, when Aaron leaves her palazzo that night, he is robbed by a gang of soldiers and his letter-case taken. 'Yes – and if I hadn't rushed along so full of feeling: if I hadn't exposed myself: if I hadn't got worked up with the Marchesa, and then rushed all kindled through the streets, without reserve, it would never have happened. I gave myself away.' The following night, looking across the Arno from her magnificent terrace, Aaron asks if they will be lovers. 'You don't want emotions?' he adds. 'You don't want me to say things, do you?' The Marchesa wants 'none of that', but when the deed is done Aaron knows she is 'not his woman'. He now hates her and wants to bolt. That night he goes to bed alone, for which he is 'unspeakably thankful'.[113]

Lawrence called *Aaron's Rod* 'the last of my serious English novels, the end of *The Rainbow, Women in Love* line',[114] and it is a novel about leaving the love of women altogether. In *The Rainbow* Lawrence celebrated marriage as a joining of opposites to achieve integration, in

*Women in Love* marriage is a way of preventing Birkin from growing too intimate with Gerald, but in *Aaron's Rod* marriage is the destroyer of men, and thus of civilisation itself. 'The man's spirit has gone out of the world,' explains Lilly. 'Men can't move an inch unless they can grovel humbly at the end of the journey ... That's why marriage wants readjusting.'[115]

The *stranieri inverti* appear in *Aaron's Rod* as a sort of mad-hatter's tea party. Reggie Turner is the owl-like and blinking Algy Constable (recalling Algy Moncrieff in *The Importance of Being Earnest*), and Douglas is the louche writer James Argyle, whose 'wicked whimsicality' was 'very attractive, when levelled against someone else, and not against oneself'. Argyle, thought Aaron, 'must have been very handsome in his day, with his natural dignity, and his clean-shaven strong square face. But now his face was all red and softened and inflamed, his eyes had gone small and wicked under his bushy grey brows. Still he had a presence.'[116] Argyle and his friends pose as Faustian but their atmosphere is closer to that of *Cranford*.

Argyle sees life as 'the search for a friend', by which he means lover ('same thing, same thing'). In his previous life he had been married and is thus an authority on the subject of wives. 'They've got the start of us the women: and we've got to canter when they say gee-up ... Oh, they are the very hottest hell once they get the start of you.'[117] His apartment, known by the porter as 'Paradise', is high up under the eaves in the cathedral square, level with the roof of the Baptistery of St John where Dante was baptised and whose south doors, designed by Andrea Pisano, were likened by Michelangelo to the doors to Paradise. The sunlight 'caught the façade of the cathedral sideways, like the tips of a flower, and sideways lit up the stem of Giotto's tower, like a lily stem'. ' "I love it," ' said Lilly. ' "I love this place ... the dark stripes are as they should be, like the tiger marks on a pink lily." '[118]

Where was the recently deceased Magnus in all of this? He appears as 'Little Mee', one of the more striking names in a novel filled with striking names. Little Mee, who sits through raucous luncheons 'with a little delighted disapproval on his tiny, bird-like face', might look like 'an innocent little boy', explains Argyle, who is – as ever – 'in his cups', but 'he's over seventy if he's a day. Well over seventy. Well, you don't believe me. Ask his mother – ask his mother. She's ninety-five.'[119] Little Mee soon flutters away, never to be heard of again.

If Magnus was both bird and beast, Lawrence in Florence was a flower. 'Consider the lilies,' said Christ in his Sermon on the Mount, 'how they grow. They toil not, they spin not.' Living like a lily, Lawrence explained in *Aaron's Rod*, is 'being by oneself, life-living. One toils, one spins, one strives, just as the lily does.' Lilly lives like a lily, and Aaron wants to do so too: 'The lily is life-rooted, life-central. She *cannot* worry. She is life itself.'[120] In Florence, Lilly believes, 'men for a moment were themselves, as a plant in flower is for the moment completely itself.' Lilies are everywhere in Lawrence's Florence and *Aaron's Rod* is his lily book. The symbol of the city is a red lily on a white background; Aaron's flute is 'a black rod of power, blossoming again with red Florentine lilies and fierce thorns',[121] Giotto's tower is a 'lily stem' while the Duomo is the lily's pistil. Michelangelo's *David* is 'the lily of Florence', and the Florentines are 'flower-souled' people: 'Flowers with good roots in the mud and muck, as should be: and fearless blossoms in air, like the cathedral and the tower and the David'.[122]

Paul Morel was also flower-souled: while he boiled away in his mother's belly, she fainted from the scent of lily pollen in the garden. And Lawrence himself had been flower-souled until the war was announced. He was walking that day in the Lake District with 'water-lilies twisted round my hat – big, heavy, white and gold water-lilies that we had found in a pool high up'.[123]

From Capri, where he had confided in the Brewsters about his stagnant novel, Lawrence returned to Florence in the spring of 1921, where Rebecca West and Norman Douglas called on him one day after lunching with Reggie Turner. West's account of their meeting is worth quoting in full:

> He was staying in a poorish hotel overlooking what seems to me
> … to be a trench of drab and turbid water wholly undeserving of
> the romantic prestige we have given the Arno. Make no mistake, it
> was the hotel that overlooked the Arno, not Lawrence. His room
> was one of the cheaper ones at the back. His sense of guilt which
> scourged him perpetually, which was the motive-power of his
> genius, since it made him enquire what sin it was which he and all
> mankind have on their conscience, forbade him either enjoying
> comfort or having money to pay for it, lest he should weaken.
> So it was a small, mean room in which he sat tapping away at a

typewriter. Norman Douglas burst out in a great laugh as he went in, and asked him if he were already writing an article about the present state of Florence; and Lawrence answered seriously that he was. This was faintly embarrassing, because on the doorstep Douglas had described how, on arriving in a town, Lawrence used to go straight from the railway station to his hotel and immediately sit down and hammer out articles about the place, vehemently and exhaustively describing the temperament of the people. This seemed obviously a silly thing to do, and here he was doing it. Douglas' laughter rang out louder than ever, and malicious as a satyr's.

He was probably hammering out the Florentine chapters of *Aaron's Rod*, in which case the joke was on Douglas. But Rebecca West later realised that he was writing not about Florence at all but about 'the state of his own soul at that moment', which 'he could only render in symbolic terms; and the city of Florence was as good a symbol as any other'. If Lawrence was 'foolish' to 'make allegations' about the state of the world which were 'only true of the state of his soul', then, West reasoned, 'so too was Dante, who made a new Heaven and Hell and Purgatory as a symbol for the geography within his own breast'. More than any of his other readers, Rebecca West understood what Lawrence was up to.

Lawrence was, she thought, 'one of the most polite people I have ever met, in both naïve and subtle ways'. He described to her, in a 'curious hollow voice, like the soft hoot of an owl', the journey he had made, 'up from Sicily to Capri, from Capri to Rome, from Rome to Florence', and West compared his wanderings to those of the mystic or Russian saint, who 'says goodbye and takes his stick and walks out with no objective but the truth'. Lawrence, she instantly saw, 'travelled, it seemed, to get a certain Apocalyptic vision of mankind that he registered again and again and again, always rising to a pitch of ecstatic agony'.

The following day she, Douglas and Lawrence walked together in the *campagna*. Lawrence was so thin that 'it seemed as if a groove ran down the centre of his chest and his spine, so that his shoulder-blades stood out in a pair of almost wing-like projections' (Aretaeus, a doctor in second-century Rome, described one of his tubercular patients as also having shoulder blades 'like the wings of birds'). He moved, however, 'quickly and joyously. One could imagine him as a forerunner, speeding faster than spring can go from bud to bud on the bushes, to tell the world of the season that was coming to save it from winter. Beside him Norman Douglas lumbered along stockily.' They looked, West thought, like Ormuzd, the Zoroastrian creative deity, and Ahriman the evil spirit. Bending over a flower, Lawrence's face 'grew nearly as tender as a mother bending over her child'.

During lunch, Rebecca West listened while Lawrence and Douglas 'talked for long of a poor waif, a bastard sprig of royalty, that had recently killed himself after a life divided between conflicted passions for monastic life, unlawful pleasures, and financial fraud'. He and Douglas spoke of their friend, Rebecca West thought, 'with that grave and brotherly pitifulness that men who have found it difficult to accommodate themselves to their fellow men feel for those who have found it impossible'.[124]

*Women in Love* was eventually published in England in June 1921, and was described by John Middleton Murry in *Nation and Athenaeum* as:

> five hundred pages of passionate vehemence, wave after wave of turgid, exasperated writing impelled towards some distant and invisible end; the persistent underground beating of some dark and inaccessible sea in an underworld whose inhabitants are known by this alone, that they writhe continually, like the damned, in a frenzy of sexual awareness of each other.[125]

One month earlier, Lawrence had completed *Aaron's Rod*, writing the last pages in a dark wood in Baden-Baden. It is not a mad book in the sense of engagingly bonkers like *The Lost Girl*: *Aaron's Rod* is barely sane, and its madness is bound up with its badness. Lawrence allowed his anger to spoil his beautiful story. Everyone he met during its five-year gestation appeared in parody, but playing along in the background was his row with E. M. Forster: *Aaron's Rod* is an inversion of *A Room with a View*. Forster's novel begins in Florence and continues in England, and Lawrence's novel begins in England and continues in Florence. Lawrence gives us a city of men while Forster's Florence is a city of women: Lucy Honeychurch and Charlotte Bartlett share the Pensione Bertolini with the two Miss Allens and the observant Eleanor Lavish, whose own novel, *Under a Loggia*, uses as copy the kiss in Fiesole between Lucy and George (where Lawrence had also kissed Rosalind Baynes). Lawrence's men have endless theories about women, but Forster's women find nothing in men to wonder about. 'Why will men have theories about women?' muses Lucy. 'I haven't any about men.'[126] Lawrence inverts Forster in another sense too: Forster uses Florence as the stage for a heterosexual romance, while for Lawrence Florence is a city of homosexuals.

The novel ends with Lilly in full D'Annunzio mode, shouting and yelling and ranting about love and power and how women must submit to men and how Aaron, too, must submit to Lilly. Meanwhile, Lawrence's Self One puzzled away about Magnus, and it is with these thoughts that the novel ends.

After a bomb has exploded in the café where he is sitting with Lilly and Argyle, Aaron dreams that he is in a strange country with nowhere to sleep. Passing through the mouth of a cave 'his second self' appears in what seems to be a house where tin miners are coming home from work: 'a sort of underworld country spreading away beyond him'. He wanders from 'vast apartment to apartment, down narrow corridors like the roads in a mine', until he comes to a room in which the miners are preparing to eat. 'And it seemed to him that what they were going to eat was a man, a naked man.' They are like the Morlocks of H. G. Wells's *The Time Machine*, feasting on the Eloi. Aaron's first, non-dreaming self knows that it is not in fact a man but a 'skin stuffed with meat', but he then sees the naked figure who is to be eaten walking 'slowly and stiffly across the gangway and down the corridor'. He is a man 'in the prime of life'.[127]

The queerest product of subconsciousness, Aaron's dream hangs suspended in the book's final chapter, playing no role in the plot. It is a record, surely, of a dream of Lawrence's, still fresh in his mind when he sat down that day to write. And in his dream Lawrence returned to the catacombs of Rabat, where he left Magnus to die before feasting on his body, and to the dawn boat from Capri where he sailed to the mountain isle of Purgatory.

# Part Three

Comedy begins badly and ends well, tragedy begins well and ends badly. Or, as Dante put it, tragedy is 'admirable and tranquil in its beginning, in the end fetid and horrible'.[1] The *Memoir of Maurice Magnus*, which started out as pantomime, ended in fury and despair. Magnus's suicide, Lawrence repeated in the *Memoir*'s final section, made his world stand still. He was stunned by the news; maimed. But, like Beatrice in *The Trespasser*, who was afraid to meet the accusations of her dead husband, Lawrence put Magnus on trial instead, leaving the verdict on himself suspended.

Magnus's death inspired in Lawrence a contradictory set of responses. 'I could,' he conceded, 'by giving half my money, have saved his life', but 'I had chosen not to save his life.' It was only now that Lawrence 'realized' how 'the hunted, desperate man' must have felt, what his inner life must have been, what suicide 'must have meant' to him. Even now, however, a year later, Lawrence stands by his choice: 'I still would not save his life,' he 'shall and should die, and so should all his sort'. But he also, Lawrence said in the same paragraph, respected Magnus 'for dying when he was cornered. And for this reason I still feel connected with him: still have this to discharge, to get his book published, and to give him his place, to present him just as he was as far as I knew him myself.'[2]

Six months after Magnus's death, Douglas, as his literary executor, sent to Mazzaiba for *Dregs*, declaring himself the book's 'co-writer'. There was a publisher, he explained, who was prepared to take the project on and the profit would all go to Mazzaiba. Hearing nothing back, Douglas then applied for the manuscript via Carl Loop, the US Consul in Valetta, again to no avail. Loop explained that he had 'no

*Memoir of Maurice Magnus*

authority' to dispose of any of Magnus's property 'except to satisfy local debts'.[3] The dead man's chattels now belonged to Mazzaiba who, assuming that Douglas was cut from the same cloth as Magnus, rejected his appeals and promised the manuscript to Lawrence instead: this way he could be certain of being repaid his £55. Added to which, Mazzaiba held Lawrence to blame for his loss: had he been forewarned about Magnus's leech-like tendencies, he would not now be out of pocket.

While he was hiding from the police in Taormina, Magnus, as we know, had asked Lawrence to write a foreword to *Dregs*. He considered himself a Lawrentian outlaw: *The Rainbow* had been banned for indecency, and some of this glamour might rub off on Magnus. So the introduction Lawrence now wrote served a dual purpose: to repay the money owed by Magnus to Mazzaiba, for which Mazzaiba held Lawrence responsible, and to honour his own commitment to Magnus, who similarly held Lawrence responsible for his welfare. If he could sell *Dregs* to an American publisher for $400, Lawrence reasoned, he would be able to pay his debt to Magnus, pay Magnus's debt to Mazzaiba, reimburse himself for the £23 Magnus owed to him and pass on to Douglas what was left. With Douglas, Lawrence was at least in part settling a separate score: ten years earlier, as his editor at the *English Review*, Douglas had cut 'The Prussian Officer' down to size, and Lawrence would now do the same to him.

Lawrence was in Florence for the Dante Festival on 15 September 1921, and the next month he was sued by Philip Heseltine for the libellous portrayal of himself and the Puma as Halliday and the Possum in *Women in Love*. Lawrence duly altered the appearance of Halliday and the Pussum before going ahead, in November, with his portraits of Magnus and Douglas in the *Memoir*.

Lawrence fell out with places in the same way that he fell out with people, and Europe was now 'like a bad meal' in which he had 'got indigestion from every course', 'a dead dog that died of a love disease, like syphilis'.[4] He was once again ready to shed his European skin and become an American writer. When he returned from Malta that June, Lawrence had reworked his essays on classic American literature (five of which had been published in the *English Review*) with the plan of turning them into a book.

In December 1920, the *New Republic* published Lawrence's pulpit piece, 'America: Listen to Your Own', written as the foreword to his proposed *Studies in Classic American Literature*. His thoughts about American literature had evolved since Cornwall, and he now counselled American writers to turn away from the 'lovely monuments of our European past' with their 'almost fatal, narcotic, dream-luxurious effect upon the soul', and towards the 'spirit' of their own 'dark, aboriginal continent'. The real America belonged not to the dollar princesses of Edith Wharton but to 'the Red Man'. 'America: Listen to Your Own' is Lawrence at his most daring and original: 'Now is the day when Americans must become fully self-reliantly conscious of their own inner responsibility. They must be ready for a new act, a new extension of life.'[5] He was referring to men like Henry James, Eliot and Pound, who turned to Europe because America was where art withered on the vine; the 'lovely monuments' of the European past were necessary in order for art to flourish. For writers like James, as Van Wyck Brooks put it, America 'signified failure and destruction': it 'was the dark country, the sinister country, where the earth was a quicksand ... where men were turned into machines, where genius was subject to all sorts of inscrutable catastrophe'.[6] In his life of Hawthorne, James lamented the fact that 'the flower of art blooms only where the soil is deep, that it takes a great deal of history to produce a little literature'. Hawthorne's entire genius, James continued, expressed itself in 'four novels and the fragment of another, five volumes of short tales, a collection of sketches, and a couple of story-books for children'.[7] Only James could have seen this as a paltry offering. While James created his myth of Europe, Lawrence – for whom England's 'whole tree of life' was 'dying' – nurtured his myth of America as a place where 'life comes up from the roots'.[8]

Lawrence then launched himself in *The Dial*. America's leading journal of the vanguard, *The Dial*'s remit was to 'display the role of the imagination in an age of science' and publish the best that was available in American fiction, art, anthropology, history, sculpture, philosophy, criticism and poetry.[9] He had been recommended to the journal's editor, Schofield Thayer, by Pound – 'two stories (or somethings) by D. H. Lawrence have been accepted [by Schofield] through no particular fault of my own', wrote Pound.[10] The first something, published in September 1920, was 'Adolf', Lawrence's charming account of the wild rabbit he kept as a child, and the second was 'Rex', which appeared in *The Dial*'s February 1921 issue. In March, April and July 1921 *The Dial* published Lawrence's poems 'Pomegranate', 'Apostolic Beasts' and 'Snake', and in October and November, they printed extracts from *Sea and Sardinia*, which appeared in America two years before it appeared in England.

In eleven months, *The Dial* had published Lawrence in seven issues and three different genres: his appearance in the journal consolidated his place at the very top of the American literary league. It was *The*

*Dial* that would establish the fame of e. e. cummings, Marianne Moore (who became, in 1925, the editor) and Hart Crane; Pound's *Cantos* were first published in its pages, together with Eliot's *The Waste Land*. During the 1920s, Lawrence's work would appear in thirty issues of *The Dial*, and he was reviewed in eighteen further numbers. Those issues in which he was neither published nor reviewed usually mentioned D. H. Lawrence in passing. *The Dial* did for Lawrence in America what the *English Review* had done for him in England.

In May 1921, *Psychoanalysis and the Unconscious* was published in New York. This was followed in June 1922 by a sequel, *Fantasia of the Unconscious*, which was composed in the autumn of 1921 and contained Lawrence's current thoughts on child consciousness, cosmology and dreams ('The generality of readers', he warned, will find it 'bosh and abracadabra'). Lawrence told Kot in November 1921 that 'Nowadays I depend almost entirely on America for my living',[11] and *Fantasia*, he said in the epilogue, was his 'real American book. If there had been no America I would never have written it.'[12] The *Memoir of Maurice Magnus* was thus composed in the spirit of departure: Lawrence was clearing his desk, paying his debts and burning his bridges. But he was also returning to a story he already knew. The image of the suicidal man on the burning island, his dead body discovered by a man on a ladder, had been with Lawrence since 1909 when he wrote *The Trespasser*, and his experiments in the art of fictional biography began.

When *Dregs* arrived from Malta in December 1921, Lawrence had more or less finished his *Memoir*. 'It is exactly two years since I read it first in the monastery,' he said of the manuscript now sitting on his desk.[13] He had then advised Magnus to rewrite the last five chapters, but Magnus had instead rewritten 'the whole thing' and Lawrence's reaction to the *girants* sections of the book suggests that this was the first time he had seen it. As for Magnus's pretence of horror, Lawrence was left 'stone-cold to this pink-faced, self-indulgent, morally indignant pigeon', and the *Memoir*'s final pages, coming out of sheer rage, are the work of his Self Two.

Magnus, Lawrence said, was 'a liar' and a 'hypocrite': this was his 'first grudge' against him. 'The "vice" which he holds his hands up so horrified at, in the "girants", he had it himself.' But the difference between Magnus's attitude to sodomy and that of the legionaries – as Magnus himself had carefully explained to Lawrence – was that he, like a 'gentleman', paid for his men of the 'lower classes'. But, said Lawrence, all Magnus's friendships were based on money: he seduced people in order to bleed money out of them.[14]

His reason for introducing the dead man's memoir in this unorthodox fashion, Lawrence explained, was to warn us not to take M.M. at 'face value'; this was no 'spiritual dove' cooing among the 'vultures of lust'. Magnus, who had objected to being treated like 'a dog' in the Legion and had been parodied as a pug in *The Lost Girl*, was now described by Lawrence as 'a mongrel' and 'a cur': tail-wagging and tongue-hanging, he would give anyone affection in exchange for twenty francs. 'And he to sit in judgment on the Legionaries!' Magnus was 'worse' than the legionaries themselves; they might be a tribe of cutthroats, but they at least carried their blood-passions 'defiantly, flagrantly, to depravity', while Magnus pussied around with his 'conceit of spiritual uplift'. Magnus's version of sensuality was 'the modern form of vampirism', so 'Let him die and be thrice dead.'[15]

As for the delusion that Magnus was a 'littérateur', 'I hope,' Lawrence mocked, 'this book will establish his fame as such. I hope the editor, if it gets one, won't alter any more of the marvellously staggering sentences and the joyful French mistakes.'[16] The only publisher brave enough to touch the book was Martin Secker, who cut Magnus's descriptions of the *girant* culture, including the sexual assault he suffered in the shower, plus those pages in Lawrence's introduction (quoted above) where Lawrence – as Secker put it – 'let [him]self go, on Magnus's attitude towards certain things'. The first edition of *Memoirs of the Foreign Legion by M.M.* was thus an amputated affair. Lawrence had told Secker that he didn't care what he cut; Douglas, however, who had been cautious from the start about the 'obnoxious material', did care. Magnus's manuscript had been 'expurgated thoroughly … too thoroughly for my taste', he said.[17] He also disliked the pointless and confusing change of title: *Dregs*, Douglas thought, hit just the right note.

Having argued for the prosecution, Lawrence lent himself, in the final pages of the *Memoir*, to the work of the defence. Crossing to the other side of the courtroom, he confessed that he preferred Magnus, 'scamp' as he was, 'to the ordinary respectable person' because Magnus took risks and chose death over a stint in an Italian prison. 'I like him for that. And I like him for the sharp and quick way he made use of every one of his opportunities to get out of that beastly army.' Magnus had the courage of a 'persistent louse'; he was a rat 'determined not to be trapped'; he braved 'vile experiences' and 'kept his manhood in spite of them. For manhood is a strange quality, to be found in human rats as well as hot-blooded men.' Magnus 'carried the human consciousness through circumstances which would have been too much for me' and Lawrence 'would rather have died than be so humiliated'. But Lawrence had been equally humiliated, having his genitals groped and his anus inspected by a laughing doctor in Derby. Magnus was a victim of a foul and shameful war whose ghastliness 'we haven't the soul-strength to contemplate'. It was because he did what few men have done, and fought 'open-eyed' with 'lovely, terrified courage' for his 'spirit and liberty', that Lawrence was giving him 'his place in the world's consciousness'.[18]

Only when he was finishing the *Memoir* did Lawrence write to Douglas, on 21 December 1921. 'Apparently the shades of Magnus are going to give us no peace,' he began, before explaining that he had been asked by Mazzaiba to get the 'Legion' book published. 'I don't know who really is responsible for the MS,' Lawrence said, knowing full well that Douglas owned the rights. He would take on the burden of publication in America, Lawrence continued, and was ready to 'write an introduction giving all I knew about M – not unkindly I hope' (the words 'not unkindly' were underlined by Douglas in a green pen, and an exclamation mark added in the margin). Lawrence wished 'you would do it really' – he underlined the word 'you' three times himself – 'and let me stand clear. If you will do it, I will write to an American publisher for you. – If you don't want, then I'll go ahead, rather unwillingly.' Could Douglas, Lawrence added, refresh his memory of the 'Hohenzollern myth? – who was the mother, and who the grandfather?' And might he provide some photographs of Magnus and his mother? Lawrence repeated that he would 'like best to be out of it altogether' and that if Douglas instead were to take on the burden of introducing *Dregs*, 'why, you might effect a sale'.

He then added a postscript in which he changed from future to present tense. The introduction he was ready to write was in fact, Lawrence let slip, already being written.

In my introduction I give a sketch of Magnus as I knew him in Florence, Montecassino, here, & Malta. In the first of course you figure, under a disguised name: along with me. The only vice I give you is that of drinking the best part of the bottle of whisky, instead of the worst part, like me. Do you mind at all?[19]

It was the dishonesty of a man who has packed his bags in preparation for crossing the border. Lawrence, like Magnus, was a confidence trickster and this letter to Douglas was his version of a bad cheque.

Douglas, always worried by Lawrence 'writing nasty', cannot have been reassured. What was Lawrence's game? He knew that Douglas was Magnus's literary executor, that Douglas should have been consulted on the publication at an earlier stage, that Magnus had gifted to Douglas the copyright of *Dregs*, had asked Douglas to write his biography and had left him a suitcase of papers in order to do so. Nonetheless, Douglas replied with cavalier good humour, not thinking that Lawrence – usually so careless with correspondence – would store away the letter. 'Damn the Foreign Legion,' he bellowed. 'Whoever wants it may ram it up his exhaust pipe. I have done my best.' Had Mazzaiba initially sent the manuscript to Douglas, 'the book would be published by this time', but then 'some folks are 'ard to please'.

> By all means, do what you like with the MS. As to M. himself,
> I may do some kind of memoir of him later on – independent,
> I mean, of Foreign Legions. Put me in your introduction – drunk
> and stark naked, if you like. I am long past caring about such things
> … Pocket all the cash yourself. Mazzaiba seems to be such a fool
> that he doesn't deserve any … I'm out of it and, for once in my life,
> with a clean conscience.[20]

One month later, on 26 January 1922, Lawrence posted both *Dregs* and his completed introduction, which he called *Memoir of Maurice Magnus*, to his American agent. Three weeks after that, on 19 February, he and Frieda left the Fontana Vecchia altogether.

Douglas meanwhile wrote to Grant Richards, the publisher of George Bernard Shaw and A. E. Housman, proposing that he, Douglas, produce his own 'Memoir' of Magnus to go in front of an English edition of the 'Legion' book.

> Lawrence's memoir … is sure to be full of bias. He hardly knew the
> fellow – only for 2–3 months, and moreover, Magnus owed him

money, which he never got back! My memoir would be the other way round. I knew him for 15 years or so, and moreover, he lent me money which, needless to say, he never got back. Judge if I should not be fair to his memory.

The problem for Douglas was that he would have to remain anonymous. 'If the name of the author became known,' he explained, 'I should not be able to write anything.' Did Douglas mean that he would be besieged by Magnus's creditors or that he had to protect his own sexual reputation – or both?[21] Either way, because Douglas had never been given the manuscript of *Dregs*, it was impossible for him to produce an edition, so it was Lawrence who eventually secured publication rights on both sides of the Atlantic. And by the time the renamed *Memoirs of the Foreign Legion by M.M., with an Introduction by D. H. Lawrence* appeared in England on 1 October 1924, and in America in January 1925, where it was published by Knopf, Douglas had already seen himself, drunk and stark naked, in the pages of *Aaron's Rod*. Bound in black with gold lettering down the spine, the English edition of the *Memoirs of the Foreign Legion by M.M.* looked, Lawrence noted, like a hymn book. Which is precisely what Magnus would have wanted.

While M.M.'s prose was agreed to be – as one critic put it – 'sodden, slipshod, no better than that of the average police reporter', Lawrence's introduction was applauded. 'Lawrence's introduction is one of the best things he has ever written,' said the critic for the *New Statesman*. The American reviewers concurred. Lawrence's introduction contained, said Laurence Stallings, 'one of the most extraordinary memoirs in the world'. D. H. Lawrence, concluded *The Sun*, 'has never published anything that throws so much light on his own enigmatic character'. Even those reviewers, like Ben Ray Redman in the *New York Herald Tribune*, who questioned the taste of denouncing the character of the dead man whose work is being introduced, conceded that 'it is the damnable introduction that makes this book interesting'. Frieda said that Magnus had made 'a fool' of Lawrence, Douglas said that Mazzaiba had made 'a fool' of himself, while Lawrence now made a fool of Douglas not once but twice – first in *Aaron's Rod* and then in the *Memoir of Maurice Magnus*. And by doing so he was catapulted to the first rank of writers.

\* \* \*

Douglas had suggested to Secker that he might produce his own 'introduction (little memoir): say 4000 words' to any second edition of Magnus's *Memoirs*, presumably displacing the one by Lawrence. Instead he wrote *D. H. Lawrence and Maurice Magnus: A Plea for Better Manners*, which was published privately in Florence in a print run of 500 copies, selling out in a fortnight. Two further print runs followed, after which *A Plea* was reprinted in 1925 as the centrepiece of Douglas's new collection of essays, *Experiments*. The identity of the characters referred to by Lawrence as 'D—' and 'M—' was now revealed. Douglas's 'Magnus pamphlet', as it was referred to, and Lawrence's introduction, formed what was described in *The Author* as 'a serious controversy between two literary giants'. Richard Aldington, who waded into the row with his usual glee ('It is not for me to judge my two friends in this unhappy controversy'), put it about that Douglas had been paid, by a woman with a grudge against Lawrence, £100 to write *A Plea*. Douglas denied the charge, but it rings true: in December 1924, he booked himself into the most expensive hotel in Syracuse, which implies that he was feeling flush. It was in another hotel in Syracuse that Lawrence had written 'Mosquito', and there could be no more appropriate place for Douglas to defend the honour of Maurice Magnus. His 13,000-word polemic took eight days to produce.

'All this is awkward,' Douglas coughed. 'One hates thrusting oneself forward in a matter,' and his awkwardness shows through. While trying to appear at his languorous best, he comes across as bourgeois and insecure. He writes like a man who can't get into character and so overacts instead. Of course, Douglas agrees, swirling his whisky and sinking into his wingback chair, there is no mistaking the 'wicked red face' and shabby clothes of the character called 'N— D—': 'I should recognize myself at a mile's distance, especially knowing, as I do, friend Lawrence's idiosyncrasies in the matter of portraiture: what he contrives to see and what he fails to see.' Friend Lawrence sees, for example, that Douglas asked the waiter in the *pensione* to weigh the wine they had left undrunk and deduct it from the bill, but 'fails to see' that 'the man who does not act as I did is held to be weak in the head'. Returning again and again to Lawrence's accusations of meanness, Douglas throws them back over the fence. Lawrence's entire animus against Magnus, he said, was down to a few borrowed pounds which he has 'recouped … many times over by the sale of these *Memoirs*'.

Having told Lawrence to pocket the profit himself, Douglas now told his readers that he was 'entitled to half the proceeds' of Magnus's book.[22]

Lawrence's crime as a writer, Douglas argued, was to employ 'the novelist's touch in biography'. This consists in 'a failure to realise the profundities and complexities of the ordinary human mind'. The novelist-biographer works from the 'leitmotif system' in which he 'selects for literary purposes two or three facets' and discards the rest. 'What the author says may be true,' Douglas explained, 'and yet by no means the truth.'[23] By the same token, what Douglas says of Lawrence may be true, and yet by no means the truth. The two or three facets that Lawrence selected in order to satirise 'N— D—' as a high-handed old swaggerer with a messy bedroom are the same two or three facets selected by Douglas in his own self-portraits. And the two or three facets of Magnus selected by Lawrence are brilliant enough to fully suggest the profundities and complexities of his mind. Lawrence was a catcher of quirks and the right quirks can take us straight to the mystery of character: Lawrence's Magnus is a figure of sublime ridiculousness. But while Lawrence described his introduction as the 'literal truth', he at no point described it as biographical. He had written, very specifically, a memoir, and fidelity to one's own experience is not at all the same thing as biographical truth.

According to Douglas, the occasions where Lawrence 'novelized' the biography include his claim that Magnus lived in Malta on £100 of borrowed money ('He never borrowed a hundred,' corrected Douglas. 'Apart from what he got from Lawrence ... he borrowed fifty-five: neither more nor less') and his claim that Douglas 'despised' Magnus for being 'an effeminate little bounder'. He felt towards Magnus, Douglas insisted, nothing of the sort. Magnus had been his friend, and he was not in the business of despising his friends. 'I have no fault to find with his travesty of myself, no fault whatever,' Douglas insisted. 'It is perfectly legitimate fooling and my young friend might have presented me in a far less engaging fashion, since I gave him permission to "put me in as you please".'[24] Except that, as Douglas was well aware, Lawrence's portrait wasn't fooling, and nor was it strictly legitimate. According to Aldington, 'what Lawrence wrote was a short imaginative novel about a possible (not necessarily real) Magnus', and it was 'his grave error ... to publish this as a biography'.[25]

What really nettled Douglas about Lawrence was not his novelist's touch in biography but his biographer's touch in novels. And what really provoked Douglas's anti-Lawrence pamphlet, Aldington believed, was not the satire of him in the *Memoir of Maurice Magnus* but the satire of him in *Aaron's Rod*. James Argyle was evidently homosexual, part of a tribe of other thinly disguised homosexuals. 'I can never read the book,' said Aldington of *Aaron's Rod*, 'without laughing aloud at the perfection with which Lawrence has hit off his various unconscious portrait-sitters.'[26] The problem for Douglas in being portrayed as homosexual is that this wasn't the full picture: Lawrence had selected one facet of Douglas's sexuality and discarded the rest. Douglas liked the company of boys rather than men, but he liked young girls too. He was not homosexual, he was a pederast lounger. He hated being misrepresented and he hated being parodied – not least because he hated being seen to mind ('I am long past caring about such things'). Vanity – as Lawrence well knew – did not feature in a persona built on masculinity, amorality and effortless superiority, which is why Douglas made such a good target.

What Douglas said he objected to in the character of James Argyle were the 'spiteful observations' Argyle made about his friends, which Douglas himself would 'never dream of uttering'. This was a 'damnably vulgar proceeding. There was no reason why [Lawrence] should annoy people who, while he was in the place, fed him to bursting-point and went out of their way to show him every civility in their power.' Lawrence was 'trespassing on libel'. This kind of personality-mongering 'menaces the living, wrongs the dead, and degrades a decent literary calling to the level of the chatter at an old maid's tea party' (an old maid's tea party was also how Lawrence had described the chatter of the Florentine homosexuals). Are modern writers 'too lazy or stupid', asked Douglas, to make up their own characters instead of feeding on the people they know?[27] This was thin ice because the cast list of *South Wind* – in which novel Douglas admitted that 'men cannot live, it seems, save by feeding on their neighbours' life-blood'[28] – was also composed of the people Douglas knew. But the difference between himself and Lawrence, Douglas explained in *A Plea for Better Manners*, was that 'I like to taste my friends, but not to eat them.'[29]

To get the full measure of the offence to his ego caused by the figure of James Argyle, we need look no further than Douglas's account of the Emperor Tiberius, published first in the *English Review* in 1909 and then in *Siren Land*, both of which Lawrence read. 'Let us examine this Siren-loving monster,' Douglas began. The young Tiberius was 'broad-shouldered … and tall above the common measure'. The possessor of a 'large and powerful intellect', he was 'courteous and formal, a strenuous cultivator of the "grand manner"'. Detesting all 'slipshod expressions', he was 'economical, conscientious, methodical' and 'a scorner of luxury and dissipation'. His 'frugality', of course, 'was interpreted as avarice, while an invincible shyness, peculiar to many great men, was put down to pride'. After Tiberius divorced his loathed wife and moved, as an old man, to the isle of Capri these admirable qualities were replaced by cruelty and lust: 'We have all heard of the reformed rake; Tiberius was the reverse.'[30] Bryher (the lover of H.D.) recalled the reception Douglas had received on the island in 1921, when he returned after several years away:

> The news of his arrival spread from mouth to mouth. I have never
> seen a political leader enjoy so great a triumph. Men offered him
> wine, women with babies in their arms rushed up so he might
> touch them … The *signore* had deigned to return to his kingdom
> and I am sure that they believed that the crops would be abundant
> and the cisterns full of water as a result.[31]

Douglas played the part of Tiberius right to the end. In 1952, when he returned to Capri to die, he was given a ceremonial funeral. But then 'no man was written down', as he liked to say, 'except by himself'.

Today it is hard to see how *A Plea for Better Manners* might once have trounced Lawrence's *Memoir*, but at the time of publication Douglas won the moral high ground. It was, however, a writing and not a morality contest and Lawrence outwrote Douglas on the subject of Magnus. What is lacking in *A Plea* is precisely what Douglas complained of in Lawrence: the novelist's touch in biography. Thinking it 'vulgar' to show curiosity, Douglas knew, as he conceded, 'practically nothing' about Magnus, but he was incapable of describing the man that he did know. In his account of their conversations, there are no clues to character, and Magnus's speech, astonishingly alive in Lawrence's hands, falls dead on the page when Douglas records it. 'Rather a mess in here,' Magnus says of Douglas's bedroom, in what is presented as a moment of high comedy in *Plea*. 'I'd like to tidy the room a bit, if you don't mind.'[32] Having recalled how they had met in Capri and again in Rome, Douglas summed Magnus up as 'charming' and 'a far more civilized and multi-faceted person than the reader of Lawrence's Introduction might be led to expect'. He illustrates this with examples of Magnus's generosity when he had money to spare. Lawrence's assumption that Magnus's 'off-hand manner' revealed an essential 'commonness' showed evidence, said Douglas, of a crucial failure of insight. Magnus's brusqueness was the 'mask' of a 'sensitive man', it was 'his armour, his defence against the world'. Nothing is said about the nature of this mask or what lay behind it; instead Douglas puts his energies into polishing his own persona as a bluff old railer of the old school. The difference between them is that when Douglas wrote about Magnus, he served himself, but when Lawrence wrote about Magnus, or Douglas, or anyone else who crossed his path, he served his art.

The problem for Douglas in writing about Magnus is that he had wet his powder three years earlier when he described him as an 'earthquake connoisseur'. The phrase was perfect, and there was nothing more to add. Every time he now tried to nail Magnus down, Douglas found himself quoting from Lawrence. Lawrence's description of Magnus in his kimono as 'a little pontiff' is, Douglas admits, 'admirable', 'a perfect etching – not a stroke too much or too little', and he 'commends' the phrase 'to those simpletons who say that friend Lawrence cannot write'.[33] He again turns to Lawrence to describe how Magnus looked when he was tired: '"rather yellowish under the eyes", as Lawrence picturesquely puts it'. As for Magnus's mother, she was 'his great stunt', as 'Lawrence calls her'.

Having lost the writing contest, Douglas rounds on his opponent's 'bad breeding'. He tried to generalise his argument by describing Lawrence as part of a literary vogue trading in 'low-class allusions to living people', but his hatred is aimed at Lawrence alone; no other writer is named and, in a buffoonish parody of good manners, Douglas suggests that only duelling 'would put an end to these caddish arts'. Literary codes of etiquette, he implies, are unintelligible to the sons of coalminers. He then moves on to friend Lawrence's masculinity. Lawrence was 'sexless', he belonged to 'the school of cerebral hermaphrodites', his caricatures were 'derided not with frank wit or invective or mockery or Rabelaisian laughter, but with that squeaky suburban chuckle which is characteristic in an age of eunuchs'.[34]

Lawrence, said Douglas, was one of those men who had 'never got beyond the shock of puberty'. His friend H. M. Tomlinson slavishly agreed, writing to Douglas that Lawrence's 'transition state is that of a girl'.[35] This sentence in Tomlinson's letter was marked up by Douglas with a blue crayon, as though he were putting together a file of evidence. Douglas similarly told a correspondent that 'Lawrence is all wrong about my room; table obviously untidy: as to keeping my windows shut, I can afford to do so; I haven't got a syphilitico-tuberculous throat like he has.'[36] The vileness of his remark recalls the vileness of Lawrence's letter to Mansfield: 'I loathe you ... stewing in your consumption.'

If the *Memoir of Maurice Magnus* was, as Douglas said, 'a masterpiece of unconscious misrepresentation',[37] then *A Plea for Better Manners* is a masterpiece of unconscious misreading. By fixating on Lawrence's lack of class, lack of masculinity and lack of literary etiquette, Douglas elides his descriptions of Florence, Monte Cassino, Capri, Sicily and Malta, his journeys across land and sea, his ascents and descents, his agonies and his ecstasies, the dilemma that the dead man had posed for Lawrence about whether to look backwards or move forwards, and the devastating views that Magnus had afforded him. 'Every place has its genius,' Douglas wrote in *Old Calabria*, 'if one could but seize upon it',[38] and Lawrence had seized with both hands upon the genius of Monte Cassino, one of the few places in Italy that Douglas had never been. By fixating on the *Memoir* as failed biography, Douglas avoided mention of the area in which Lawrence had excelled. The 'reader of a good travel-book', Douglas wrote in a review of Charles Montagu Doughty's *Travels in Arabia Deserta*, 'is entitled not only to an exterior voyage, to a description of scenery and so forth, but to an interior, a sentimental or temperamental voyage, which takes place side by side with the outer one'.[39] The travel writer, he suggested, travels into himself and should therefore have a self worth exploring. The *Divine Comedy* is in this sense a first-rate travel book.

Lawrence has never found a home in the canon of twentieth-century travel writers, but this is one of the places where he belongs. He perfected the art of interior and exterior movement; he discovered in geographical extremes a way to symbolise his own poles of being. Thus, without a glimmering of what he was up to, Lawrence turned his journey with Maurice Magnus into the finest piece of travel writing of the age.

\* \* \*

Lawrence at Villa Mirenda

Douglas included *A Plea for Better Manners* in the collection of essays, *Experiments*, which appeared in 1925, and in February 1926 the reviewer for the *New Statesman* praised the author for defending Maurice Magnus from Lawrence's 'brilliant but unfair portrait'. Lawrence, who had been unaware of the pamphlet, now read what Douglas had to say. His reply was in the form of a letter to the *New Statesman*: 'It is time that I said a word,' Lawrence began. 'One becomes weary of being slandered', and he quoted the letter in which Douglas gave him permission to 'do what you like with the MS ... *Pocket all the cash yourself* ... I'm out of it and, *for once in my life*, with a clean conscience.' Having now repaid Magnus's debts to Mazzaiba, Lawrence also, for once in his life, had a clean conscience. 'As for Mr Douglas,' he concluded, 'he must gather himself haloes where he may.'[40]

Three months after his *New Statesman* letter, Lawrence returned to Florence where, on the upper floor of a house called the Villa Mirenda in the hills outside the city, he wrote *Lady Chatterley's Lover*. And it was once again on the Lugarno that he and Douglas were reunited, this time in the bookshop of Pino Orioli, who would publish the first edition of *Lady Chatterley*. Lawrence and Frieda were talking when Douglas stepped through the door. 'Have a pinch of snuff, dearie,' Douglas boomed, breaking the embarrassed silence. Lawrence accepted. 'After that meeting,' Douglas recalled, 'I induced Lawrence to buy several whiskies-and-sodas for Orioli and myself; the surest way to win his regard was to make him suffer small losses of this kind.' But Lawrence played the last card. When he and Frieda were leaving Florence for Germany, they invited Douglas and Pino for a farewell lunch where Lawrence ordered a sole costing sixty lire. Having licked the plate clean he looked at his watch. 'Good God!' he announced to Frieda. 'We're just in the nick of time. Hurry up! I can't pay now, because I've only got a few coppers and a five-hundred-franc note which they'll never be able to change.' Off they rushed for a cab (paid for by Douglas), leaving their guests the bill. And as Lawrence sailed away, Douglas 'thought to detect – it may have been imagination on my part – the phantom of a smile creeping over his wan face'.[41]

David had slayed his Goliath with a single stone.

# Paradise

Dante and Beatrice ascending to heaven

# Part One

*November of the year 1916. A woman travelling from
New York to the South west, by one of the tourist trains. On
the third day the train lost time more and more. She raged
with painful impatience. No good, at every station the train
sat longer. They had passed the prairie lands and entered
the mountain and desert region. They ought soon to arrive,
soon. This was already the desert of grey-white sage and blue
mountains. She ought to be there, soon, soon she ought to
be there. The journey alone should be over. But the train
comfortably stretched its length in the stations, and would
never arrive. There was no end. It could not arrive. She
could not bear it.*

D. H. Lawrence, fragment of a novel, 1922[1]

Lawrence's Great American Novel was a tale of slow time. The train,
like the snake who came to his water-trough on that hot day in Sicily,
moved 'slowly, very slowly, as if thrice adream', drawing his slow length,
snake-easing his shoulders over the burned earth. The woman from
New York was in a hurry: she 'ought to be there, soon, soon she ought
to be there', but while she was hurtling forwards, the clock was ticking
backwards and the train, in his slackness, was resting in the sun.

All we have of this untitled fragment, started in Taos, New Mexico
on 19 September 1922, are seven handwritten pages. But the prose is as
compact and charged as a battery, and battery charge was Lawrence's
theme: the woman from New York, he continued, was a highly explosive
figure, heavy with energy like a small bison, and capable of a soft, heavy,

grateful magnetism. Her impatience was volcanic. She was approaching forty but had the round face of an obstinate girl of fourteen; her dark brows were curved horns, her forearms were muscular, her eyes had devilish grey and yellow bits like the headlights of a great machine coming full at you in the night. She was a bull in a ring but she was also, Lawrence said, a seductive serpent lying on the Western trail. Hercules had better think twice, he joked, before picking up this particular hydra. 'He had picked up a snake long ago, without hurting himself. But that was before Columbus discovered America.'[2]

This bull-like, serpent-like, much married woman who was called Sybil Mond but started out as Sybil Hamnett and then became Sybil Thomas before becoming Sybil Danks had left New York in a frenzy, and as she crossed Kansas and Oklahoma, her head was 'a mass of thoughts and frenzied ideas, almost to madness' and she was 'curiously heart-broken at being alone'. They were now only hours from Lamy where her third husband, a Russian artist whom she had 'torn to atoms and thrown to the four corners of the universe' and then put back together like Isis, was to meet her at the station. But the train 'would not arrive, *could* not arrive. Could not arrive. That was it.' Perhaps, she reasoned as they dozed on the track, 'some power of her will would at last neutralise altogether the power of the engines, and there would come an end to motion, so there they would sit, forever, the train and she, at a deadlock on the Santa Fe line'. Lawrence's America, with its theological faith in technology and Whitmanesque worship of the self, is condensed in this image of the high-voltage woman whose telekinetic power can, she believes, bring an end to motion.

His repetitions, meanwhile – 'more and more; soon, soon, soon; would never arrive, would not arrive; *could* not arrive, could not arrive' – catch Sybil Mond's sense of being trapped in the wrong speed. Twelve years earlier, in 1910, D. W. Griffiths had made Hollywood's first film, a drama called *In Old California* about the Mexican era before it became a Western state, and Lawrence, miserably aware of the impact of cinema on human consciousness, describes Sybil Mond's impatience with the train as though she were watching a silent movie, with her perception running ahead of the action. One of the disorientating effects of moving pictures for early audiences was that screen time felt out of sync with real time and this was also, for Lawrence, the effect of the Southwest. 'The time,' Lawrence said of New Mexico, 'is different there.'[3]

In her next whirl, Lawrence continued, Sybil 'sprang' from her Pullman and found 'a worn-out old Dodge' and a sixteen-year-old boy to drive it. She was in the hands of destiny: destiny had brought her to the Southwest, destiny had made her abandon the train in Trinidad. They would get to Lamy ahead of that hateful Pullman, 'she *must* get to her journey's end, she *must* arrive'. Having never been out west before, Sybil had no idea of her route through the desert but at least – at last – they were moving. Instead of a road, however, there was only a trail of sorts: the motorcar squirmed up sandbanks, rattled along riverbeds, scrambled at an angle of forty-five degrees over landslides and precipices. Banging against boulders, they lurched and jerked and shuddered through lost villages of windowless mud boxes where the Brotherhood of Penitentes scourged their backs in perpetual Purgatory. Night fell and the car had no headlights so they sniffed their way ahead, tracing the scent of the pinion and cedar. They had reached a table land guarded by mountains. Sybil's sturdy body was now so battered that she felt like a penitente herself: 'Here was a country that hit her with hard knuckles, right through to the bone.' It was impossible, she realised: they would never arrive.

So at eight o'clock that night, the Dodge dropped Sybil Mond at Wagon Mound station where she waited three hours for the slow train to Lamy which had followed the train she abandoned. She reached her destination at three o'clock the next morning.

This is as far as Lawrence got with the tale of Sybil Mond before Frieda, disliking his heroine, put an end to the writing. 'I had always regarded Lawrence's genius as given to me,' she explained in *'Not I, But the Wind...'*[4] But a different account of what happened might be that Lawrence put an end to a novel that had already stalled. We know how Sybil's story would have continued, however, because it was to be based on the society sorceress Mabel Dodge Sterne, later called Mabel Dodge Luhan and called here for convenience Mabel Dodge, who published four volumes of memoir called, collectively, *Intimate Memories*, and a separate memoir of Lawrence called *Lorenzo in Taos*.[5] Mabel, as famous when she knew him as Lawrence was himself, explained in *Lorenzo in Taos* that he 'wanted to write an American novel that would express the life, the spirit, of America and he wanted to write it around me – my life from the time I left New York to come out to New Mexico; my life, from civilization to the bright, strange world of Taos; my renunciation of the sick old world of art and artists, for the pristine valley and the upland Indian lakes. I was thrilled at the thought of this.'[6]

Mabel Dodge, the embodiment of the American will-to-power, dominates Lawrence's writing between 1922 and 1925, and she figures in his bestiary as 'a big, white crow, a cooing raven of ill-omen' and 'a little buffalo'.[7] He reflected on her life in *St Mawr* and *The Plumed Serpent*, and on her death in 'The Woman Who Rode Away' and 'None of That'. But versions of Mabel had appeared in Lawrence's writing long before they met. Mabel's type of dynamo had always been employed by Lawrence for fictional purposes; her English prototype was Ottoline Morrell, but her most recent blueprint was Alvina Houghton, who ran away from home to join the Natcha-Kee-Tawaras.

Mabel's worst quality, according to her close friend Carl Van Vechten, was also the one that made her great: 'she adored to change people',[8] and New Mexico, Lawrence conceded, 'changed me forever'.[9] *Lorenzo in Taos*, Mabel's account of 'what I went through in my friendship (if that's what it was)' with Lawrence, is the story of that change, of 'the painful days that brought about changes in us all,' and of 'the process of change, of the permutations of the spirit worked upon by spirit. It does not,' she warns, 'end happily.'[10]

Lawrence's journey to the Southwest, like that of Sybil Mond, was composed of detours and delays. On 5 November 1921, a letter arrived at Fontana Vecchia from Mabel Dodge inviting Lawrence and Frieda to live in an adobe house in New Mexico, built on Native American soil. Mabel, who had admired *Psychoanalysis and the Unconscious*, wrote to Lawrence after reading the excerpts from *Sea and Sardinia* in *The Dial*. He was to come to Taos, she suggested, to save 'the Indians' and reignite the American literary tradition. Her letter has not survived, but she recalled in *Lorenzo in Taos* that it was so long that she rolled it up 'like a papyrus'. She 'tried to tell him every single thing I could think of that I felt would draw him – simple things as well as strange ones'. She told him that Taos was 7,000 feet up in the Sangre de Cristo (Blood of Christ) mountains, so named because the highest peak reflected the scarlet colours of the setting sun; that the sun was born here; that in Taos there wasn't enough night for the sky or blue for the day; that the mountains had waterfalls which turned, in the winter, into ice sculptures and that behind the waterfalls were caves; she told him that there was a Sacred Mountain, 12,000 feet high, on whose uppermost flank was the Blue Lake from which the Taos people, who had been here since the flood, were first created. She told him that the Taos Pueblo were a tribe of 600 'sun-worshipping', rain-making 'free Indians', one of whom was her lover; that Taos was a place where 'one did not go *out* to things' but was already 'part of them. The mountain, if anything, came to one, came into the house.' She told him that his house here would be on 'a lofty, pastoral land far from railroads, full of time and ease' where the high, clear air was filled with 'an almost heard but not quite heard music'.[11] The Taos hum, also called the singing waters and the mountain music, likened by some to the seven ascending notes of a musical scale and by others to the rumbling of an engine, is believed to come from electromagnetic vibrations emanating from the Sacred Mountain. Like Prospero's Island, the air was filled with a thousand twanging instruments humming about the ears, and Lawrence absorbed the idea of Taos as a field of invisible forces.

On 8 November, Lawrence had told Earl Brewster that he wanted 'to get a little farm somewhere by myself – in Mexico, New Mexico, Rocky Mountains or British Columbia'.[12] The synchronicity of Mabel's letter was therefore remarkable. Should her description fail to draw him, Mabel enclosed in her package some herbs, 'a few leaves of *desachey*, the perfume the Indians say makes the heart light, along with a little *osha*, the root that is a strong medicine'.[13] In separate packages, Mabel sent Frieda a Native American necklace 'that I thought carried some Indian magic', and for Lawrence – with an irony she must have registered – she sent a book by Charles Fletcher Lummis called *The Land of Poco Tiempo*. Mabel translated 'poco tiempo' as 'not yet', and Charles Lummis translated it as 'pretty soon'. 'Why hurry with the hurrying world?' *The Land of Poco Tiempo* begins. 'The "Pretty Soon" of New Spain is better than the "Now! Now!" of the haggard States ... Let us not hasten – *mañana* will do.'[14] Both packages got lost in the post: *The Land of Poco Tiempo* arrived, accordingly, in its own time, but the magic necklace simply vanished into the air.

While Mabel felt the weight of her responsibility to save Native American culture, she took for granted her role as Lawrence's divine guide. In *Lorenzo in Taos*, she explained that she had 'sensed' from the start 'Lawrence's plight' and 'willed him to come', which is what Beatrice also tells Virgil in *Inferno*.

my friend, who has not been the friend of fortune,
is hindered in his path along that lonely
hillside; he has been turned aside by terror.

From all that I have heard of him in Heaven,
he is, I fear, already so astray
that I have come to help him much too late.

(Inferno, Canto 2, 61–6)

Lawrence responded to Mabel's letter as though its appearance at this juncture in his life were part of the general plan, which of course it was. This was the invitation to cross into another world that he had been waiting for. 'And so I cross into another world', he wrote in 'New Heaven and New Earth' in 1917:

shyly and in homage linger for an invitation
from this unknown that I would trespass on.

His reply to Mabel was both immediate – that same afternoon – and resigned. He 'smelt the Indian scent and nibbled the medicine' and believed, he said, that he had heard of Taos through Leo Stein, 'and even seen pictures of it' in Stein's house in Settignano. Yes, they would like to come; they could leave in January or February. He was ready 'to take the next step', in addition to which he liked 'the word' itself, which was 'a bit like Taormina'. He told Mabel that he had written a sequel to *Psychoanalysis and the Unconscious* called *Fantasia of the Unconscious* but could not write 'the third book ... till I have crossed another border'. How much, he asked, would it cost them 'per month' to keep house, taking into account that they did their own washing, cooking and cleaning? Did Taos, like Florence, harbour a 'colony' of 'dreadful sub-arty people'? Were 'the Indians dying out'? Were there any trees? How far was her home from Santa Fe? (He couldn't find Taos on the map.) Did Mabel know anything about ships from Italy to New Orleans or Galveston or Los Angeles, so that they could avoid docking in New York? He had an aversion to entering America from the east coast.[15]

When Beatrice led Dante by the hand through the vast bright air of Paradise, he too was overwhelmed with questions. What was this strange light world, with its unidentifiable sounds?

The newness of the sound and the great light
incited me to learn their cause – I was
more keen than I had ever been before.

(Paradise, Canto 1, 81–4)

Dante's mind was in a sort of frenzy. How could he be flying above
the earth, into these realms of eternal sun? His head was such a mass
of thoughts and ideas that he couldn't find the words to ask Beatrice
'how my body rises past these lighter bodies'. Understanding Dante's
confused state, Beatrice answered his questions without his needing to
voice them aloud:

And she who read me as I read myself,
to quiet the commotion in my mind,
opened her lips before I opened mine

to ask, and she began: 'You make yourself
obtuse with false imagining ...'

(Paradise, Canto 1, 85–9)

Dante's ignorance about eternity drew from Beatrice a 'sigh of pity',
and as she patiently explained the order of the universe she 'settled her
eyes' upon him 'with the same look a mother casts upon her raving child'.

Mabel Dodge is a much mocked figure. Parodied in the press as a
millionaire Pocahontas, even her biographers do not take her seriously;
in *Mabel: A Biography of Mabel Dodge Luhan*, Emily Hahn adopts a
tone of irony throughout. But what is striking about Mabel – and
Lawrence was very struck indeed – is not only how well she interpreted
her role as Beatrice, but how right she was about Lawrence. Mabel
*knew* Lawrence: she knew from within her solar plexus that the man
she was inviting to her sky-home was a borderer ready to make the
next crossing, just as she knew before he even opened his lips that his
body was failing him, and that he needed the unbreathed air of a higher
altitude in order to survive another winter.

Mabel also knew that he believed in the power of what he had called
in *Sea and Sardinia*, the 'strange, sinister spirit' of a place to 'smash our
mechanical oneness into smithereens'.[16] Here was the man, she recalled,

who could 'understand things for me' and 'describe' her home 'so that it is as much alive between the covers of a book as it is in reality'. Lawrence was 'the only person living' who could 'penetrate and define' the 'laughing, aloof, genius of Taos'.[17]

It was *Psychoanalysis and the Unconscious* that confirmed Mabel's belief in the electricity that flowed between herself and Lawrence. If Beatrice represented theology, Mabel represented theosophy, in whose esoteric Esperanto both she and Lawrence were fluent. She, like Lawrence, adopted those aspects of theosophy that best suited her; she spoke of poles and souls, sources and circuits, and the womb as a centre of consciousness: 'The womb in me roused to reach out to him,' she said of Lawrence's plight. She had, in addition, a second womb – a 'womb behind the womb' – and was able to bend the universe to do her bidding. Lawrence, Mabel believed, may well be 'the key' to 'the source'.[18]

Having received his letter, Mabel set about preparing Lawrence's headquarters. The house she had earmarked for them, 200 yards behind her own, was on Native American land that she was allowed to enter because of her relationship with a Taos Indian called Tony Lujan. Shaded by cottonwood trees, with the Sacred Mountain looming above, it was modest and low with five sun-filled rooms and a roof supported by twisted columns of pine, painted in her favourite sky-blue. 'I foresaw', said Mabel, quite rightly, that Lawrence 'would love the isolation of it out there'.[19] Leo Stein, in a letter warning Mabel about her guest, had a difference premonition: 'I wonder which will give out first: his lungs or his wits.'[20]

Lawrence wrote to Mabel again on 21 November 1921 to say that he was looking for a cargo boat from Naples to San Francisco, as it was imperative that he approach America from the Pacific. The Atlantic was a thoroughfare, but the Pacific was, Lawrence thought, Tir-na-Og. On 28 December he told Mabel that there was a boat from Bordeaux to New Orleans on 15 January 1922. If they missed this sailing, they would get the next one and be in Taos, at the latest, by March: 'I want very much to come, and wish I could start tomorrow.' He 'believed' in Taos, he added. 'I also believe in Indians. But they must do *half* the believing: in me as well as in the sun.' Mabel did not at first, she said, 'understand' what Lawrence meant 'about the Indians believing in him … but I learned later!'[21]

He did not mention that his American friends Earl and Achsah Brewster, also theosophists, were expecting the Lawrences to join them in Ceylon (now Sri Lanka), where Earl was studying Buddhism. Earl Brewster's own interest in theosophy had begun in 1890 when Annie Besant, one of the leading figures in the theosophical movement, lectured in his native Cleveland. From now on Besant – whom Brewster had never met personally – became his own telepathic guide. Having initially told Brewster that he would 'rather go to Mars or to the Moon' than to Ceylon, Lawrence as good as confirmed that they would be arriving in February. Then on 2 January 1922, he told Brewster that they would no longer be coming to Ceylon because 'the east is not my destiny'. By mid-January he had changed his mind: 'I would rather go to Ceylon, and come to America later, from the east.' Theosophists locate the centre of spiritual gravity in the East, which made the East, as Lawrence put it, 'the *source*' and America 'the extreme periphery'. Frieda, tossed about on the winds of Lawrence's indecision, explained to Mabel that 'We were coming *straight* to you at Taos but now we are not. Lawrence says he can't face America *yet* – he doesn't feel strong enough! So we are first going to the East to Ceylon.' The house that Mabel had prepared, meanwhile, had fires laid and plants at the window.[22]

The problem, said Lawrence, was his 'compass'; the 'shifty devil' swerved one way and then the other. 'I couldn't simply face America,' he told Norman Douglas, '– the magnetism shoved me away.'[23] On 20 January, Lawrence asked Kot to send him that month's issue of the *Occult Review*, which contained a description of 'The Higher Science of Rhabdomancy', the divination technique whereby a staff placed on its end and then dropped to the ground determines the direction in which we should travel.

Mabel, Frieda now suggested, should join *them* in Ceylon, and then 'we will go with *you* to Taos from the other side'. But in Taos, as Mabel had made clear, one did not come to the mountain and she would certainly not be coming to this one. 'I'd had the idea of having *him* come to *Taos*,' she wrote in *Lorenzo in Taos*, 'and I'd sit there and draw him until he came. I'd go down inside myself and call that man until he would have to come.'[24]

Only after Frieda had broken the news of their delay did Lawrence send Mabel a letter of his own. 'It is vile of us to put off Taos for the moment,' he said by way of apology. 'But I have a Balaam's Ass in my belly which won't budge, when I turn my face west. I can't help it. It just suddenly swerves away in me. I *will* come. But a detour.'[25] The Old

Testament tale of the ass who was prevented from transporting Balaam in the direction he wanted to go was a favourite of Lawrence: barred by the angel, whom Balaam could not see, the ass swerved as though magnetically into a field, banged into a wall and collapsed to the ground. On each occasion, the beast was beaten by her master for thwarting his progress.

Having explained to Mabel that he was propelled by forces against his control and that this 'detour' ('silly detour' as Mabel called it) was part of his 'destiny', Lawrence then launched an attack on everything she held sacred, beginning with psychoanalysis. 'You want to send [A. A.] Brill to hell,' he said of her New York psychoanalyst, 'and all the analytic therapeutic lot.' 'And I don't like Stein,' he said of her good friend Leo, 'a nasty, nosy, corrupt Jew.' As for 'all that "arty" and "literairy" crew' – Mabel's friends in Santa Fe – 'I know them, they are smoking, steaming shits.' This is why, he explained, he was going first 'to the old, old, east': to sweeten his blood before the 'Onslaught on to that Land of Promise of yours.'[26] Mabel now grasped that the man she had invited to live with her was built on a contradiction: 'He whom I was trying to draw to Taos because he seemed to me to have more consciousness than anyone alive was inimical to conscious activity!' She too had lived by 'hunches' and 'intuitions' until the Freudians had set her right. Lawrence, however, still let 'It' decide.[27] 'It' was Lawrence's word for the terrific, unavoidable, malevolent power to which we all at times have to answer.

But Mabel – and she must have realised this – had inadvertently given Lawrence his Get Out of Jail Free card. Because Taos was the land of Poco Tiempo, there was no hurry in arriving. 'I shall have to go to America at length,' he explained as she exploded with rage. 'But not yet.'[28] What had happened to Lawrence, that his compass swerved so violently? 'Quite why Lawrence suddenly changed his mind once again,' writes David Ellis in *Dying Game*, 'is the kind of hermeneutic puzzle of which biography is full but which no amount of biographical enquiry is ever likely to solve.'[29]

Lawrence's solar plexus was guided by a number of factors, some of which can be traced in his current writing. In January 1922, *The Dial* published, on Lawrence's recommendation, Ivan Bunin's '"The Gentleman from San Francisco", translated from the Russian by D. H. Lawrence and S. S. Koteliansky'. Lawrence's own role, he said, had been to 'rub up' Kot's translation, but as far as the editor, Schofield Thayer, was concerned the work belonged to Lawrence. 'Lawrence rewrote Koteliansky's translation,' said Thayer, 'and that accounts for its value.'[30] 'The Gentleman from San Francisco' has, accordingly, all the beauty, spareness and allegorical simplicity of one of Lawrence's own short stories.

The gentleman and his family sail from San Francisco to Capri on board the *Atlantis*, which, like all ships, has two levels. There is the upper level, where the first-class passengers are treated like royalty, and the 'gloomy and sultry depths of the inferno' where the colliers work. 'The submerged womb of the steamer' is the 'ninth circle' of hell. Down here the 'gigantic furnaces' devoured 'with their red-hot maws mountains of coal cast hoarsely in by men naked to the waist'. Once he has settled into his hotel in Capri, the gentleman has the bad taste to die. What is the hotel manager to do with his corpse? It has, straight away, to be removed from the sight of the other guests. So the gentleman from San Francisco is 'subjected to many humiliations, much human neglect', shunted from warehouse to warehouse and then back to Naples where he is 'carried at last on to the same renowned vessel which so short a time ago, and with such honour, had borne him living to the Old World'. On his return to San Francisco, the gentleman, now 'closed in a tar-coated coffin' and 'hidden far from the knowledge of the voyagers', is 'lowered deep into the vessel's dark hold'.[31]

The gentleman's humiliating passage from Naples to San Francisco is the same one that Lawrence, wretchedly ill, had until recently been planning on making himself.

'What is it?' Virgil asks Dante, when the pilgrim has been prevented by a lion, a leopard and a wolf from climbing the mountain of Purgatory. 'Why does your heart host so much cowardice?' Mabel also knew that Lawrence was 'scared', as she put it, but assumed that he was scared of her. The reason that he and Frieda wanted to meet her first in Ceylon, she believed, was to 'take a look, take even a bite and be able to spit it out if they didn't like it!'[32] Lawrence *was* scared of Mabel – which is why he asked Frieda to break the news of their delay – but he was scared of other things too. Catherine Carswell, who missed Lawrence's complexity, thought he was 'most reasonably afraid of disobeying doctor's orders by going to America in midwinter', but Lawrence was never afraid of disobeying orders, particularly those of doctors.[33] He was, however, afraid of dying and he had just spent the winter, as usual, shivering in bed and struggling to breathe. 'I do not feel quite myself even now,' he said in a letter on 15 February 1922. 'It is a misery.' Taormina, Lawrence wrote to Douglas in early March, 'would have been the death of me after a little while longer',[34] and because he underplayed the state of his health, we have to take Lawrence at his word.

The thought of 'AMERICA', Lawrence told Schofield Thayer in August 1921, made his 'knees lose their brassy strength, and feel like chocolate fondants'.[35] America represented the end of his journey; this was the subject of 'The Evening Land', written in Germany during the summer of 1921.

Oh America
The sun sets in you!
Are you the grave of our day?

Anticipating the terms of his current conflict with Mabel, Lawrence suggested that rather than coming to America, America should come to him.

I would come, if I felt my hour had struck;/I would rather you came to me.

For that matter,
Mahomet never went to any mountain
Save it first approached him and cajoled his soul.

Because America made him panic – 'I confess I am afraid of you' – Lawrence changed the location of his Paradise. It was now, he now decided, in the '*innerliche* East', where the sun rises, rather than the '*ausserliche* West', where the sun sets. On 2 February, he sent two letters confirming this Columbus-like discovery; in the first, to Kot, he wrote that 'there was once paradise down there, in Ceylon … I'm also looking for a bit of this paradise.' In the second, to Jean Starr Untermeyer, he wrote: 'They say Paradise was once in Ceylon. Was it ever in America. Or will it be? Or is America where Paradise is perfectly lost?'

His last two weeks in Sicily were taken up with Magnus. He asked Mountsier to send a copy of the *Memoir* to Monte Cassino, thus ensuring that Magnus's name was defiled in the place he loved best, and wrote to Mazzaiba to say that Magnus was an even worse rat than he had described: 'Poor Magnus. I heard of another nasty bit of swindling which he did a few days before he left for Malta.'[36] By 12 February, Lawrence was smirking like a schoolboy who had put a frog in his teacher's desk. 'I did such a "Memoir" of Maurice Magnus,' he told Mary Cannan, 'to go in front of his horrid *Legion* book.'[37]

Lawrence and Frieda left Fontana Vecchia on 19 February, taking four trunks, two suitcases, a hatbox and a piece of Sicilian memorabilia in the form of the side of a cart, five foot by two foot, with a joust painted on one panel and St Genevieve on the other. 'Oh painted carts of Sicily', Lawrence wrote in *Sea and Sardinia*, 'with all history on your panels!'[38] From Sicily they sailed to Naples where they had booked second-class berths on the RMS *Osterley*, a large passenger vessel that ran between Europe and Australia. Having imagined himself as a pilgrim on a cargo boat, Lawrence ended up in what he described as a luxurious hotel, equipped with a smoking lounge, library, lift, Marconi room and laundry.

Waving goodbye to Etna, they headed towards Crete and then Egypt, crossing to the Red Sea through the Suez Canal, an eighteen-hour journey whose proximity to the desert Lawrence found thrilling. 'Slowly came the evening,' he wrote to his mother-in-law, 'and we so still, one would have thought we no longer moved. A thousand gulls flew about, like a snowstorm, and a great black bird of prey, alone and cruel, so large, among thousands of white, screaming, fast-moving sea-birds.' The sun was sinking when they came to the Great Bitter Lake, and there was '*such* a sky, like a sword burning green and blue'. The beauty was 'superhuman. One felt oneself near the gates of old Paradise … Yes, it is a borderland.' And there, on the other side, was Mount Sinai, the mountain of Moses, 'red as old dried blood, naked as a knife', poised like a poniard 'between man and his lost Paradise'.[39]

The ship was '*so* comfortable', he complained, 'nothing but comfort',[40] but his two weeks on board were happy. He spent the days on deck translating Giovanni Verga's magnificent novel *Mastro-Don Gesualdo*, thus absorbing himself in the country he had just abandoned. After their winter of rain they sailed into 'lovely lovely weather', with the sea 'steady as a road'. Lawrence enjoyed the suspended unreality of marine life: 'I feel,' he told Rosalind Baynes, 'like a sea-bird must feel.'[41] 'Time passes like a sleep,' he told Kot, '– nothing exists except just this ship.'[42] He liked watching the passengers idle away the days and the workers getting on with their work. He felt the relief that we do when a decision is made and we are back in the hands of fate.

He was always inspired by the manliness of ships and their paraphernalia – ropes, tugboats, ladders, funnels. And he loved the movement of vessels through water; what he described, in *Sea and Sardinia*, as 'the motion of freedom ... the long, slow lift of the ship, and her long, slow slide forwards'.[43] Because Conrad was the English literary sea-captain, Lawrence's seas have never been granted the status they deserve. But he gravitated all his life towards sea-power and sea-crossings, and Melville was much on Lawrence's mind as they headed into the Indian Ocean. The final letter he sent from Fontana Vecchia had been to ask Curtis Brown, his new English agent, to send Robert Mountsier, his American agent, the essay on *Moby Dick* he had written in Cornwall, thus ensuring that Mountsier was able to present the American publishers with a complete manuscript for *Studies in Classic American Literature*.

Conrad's sea was a merciless void, James Joyce's sea was a 'great sweet mother', but Lawrence's sea was a man much like Lawrence himself, 'solitary and single', as he wrote in his poem 'The Sea', 'fruitless, phosphorescent, cold and callous', playing his 'great game around the world'. Lawrence always preferred the journey to the destination. 'I wished in my soul the voyage might last forever,' he said of the passage from Sicily to Sardinia, 'that the sea had no end, that one might float in this wavering, tremulous, yet long and surging pulsation while ever time lasted: space never exhausted, and no turning back, no looking back, even.'[44] He wished in his soul the same thing now. 'I do wonder how we shall feel when we get off and are in Ceylon,' he confided to Kot.[45]

When they reached Ceylon the horror set in. Kandy, 100 miles from the port at Colombo, would be Lawrence's Heart of Darkness. The Brewsters lived in a large old bungalow on a hill surrounded by jungle; from the verandahs he watched chameleons, lizards and tropical birds go about their business. Earl Brewster was studying at the sacred Temple of the Tooth, named for its possession of the left eye-tooth of the Buddha, and Lawrence, before he got to Ceylon, had played with the idea of also studying at the 'molar monastery'. But within a week he had decided not to enter into the Eastern experience, but to continue his absorption in Sicilian peasant life by translating the twelve stories of Giovanni Verga's *Little Novels of Sicily*.

'I love trying things and discovering how I hate them,' Lawrence later told Earl Brewster. 'How I *hated* a great deal of my time in Ceylon.'[46] He hated the four ayahs who were (he thought) planning to murder him, he hated the swamp-like humidity, the family of rats who nested in his hat, the wounded snake who dragged his length across the floor leaving a trail of blood, and the wildcats who fought on the skylight of his room at night. He hated, so he told Mabel Dodge, the hellish quality of the jungle, 'the thick, choky feel of tropical forest, and the metallic sense of palms and the horrid noises of the birds and creatures, who hammer and clang and rattle and cackle and explode all the livelong day, and run little machines all the livelong night'.[47] He remembered these noises for the rest of his life. Richard Aldington recalled that Lawrence 'once asked me if I had heard the night noises of the tropical jungle, and then instantly emitted a frightening series of yells, squawks, trills, howls and animal "help murder" shrieks'.[48]

He hated Buddhism and it's 'rat-hole temples' which looked like 'decked up pigsties'.[49] Lawrence, who also hated the cinema, hated Ceylon more: he would prefer, so he told Mary Cannan, to see Ceylon 'on the cinema: you get there the whole effect, without the effort and the sense of nausea'.[50] When Frieda and the Brewsters removed their shoes and sun-hats to pay homage to the Buddhas in the old rock caves, Lawrence, Achsah Brewster recalled, remained outside in the swamp heat, boiling in hatred, 'hat tight on his head, declaring that there was no use, he did not belong there and could not join in'.[51]

But he liked the elephants and the midnight 'devil dancing' at the torchlit festival of Pera-hera, held to celebrate the visit of the young Prince of Wales. And Lawrence liked the Prince of Wales, whose shade-like presence he described in every letter home. The 'pale, shattered' Prince, he felt, was being mocked: 'They secretly hate him for being a Prince, and make a Princely butt of him – and he knows it.' Lawrence too felt mocked: 'I find all dark people have a fixed idea to jeer at us … They jeer behind your back.'[52] But it was Lawrence who jeered: most recently he had jeered at Freud. *Fantasia of the Unconscious* opens with 'a little apology to Psychoanalysis: it wasn't fair to jeer at the psychoanalytic unconscious'.[53]

The only writing, apart from his Verga translations and letters home, that came out of Lawrence's time in Ceylon was his superb poem 'Elephant', in which he contrasts the frenzied 'fire-laughing' motion of the dancers at the Pera-hera with the 'pale and dejected' Prince 'up aloft', 'his chin on his hands', looking down on the 'huge homage of shadowy beasts'. Lawrence's spatial sense comes into full play here, with the drama of the 'nervous pale lad / up there' in the Temple of the Tooth, and the stepping homage 'down below'.

More elephants, tong, tong-tong, loom up,
Huge, more tassels swinging, more dripping fire of new
    cocoa-nut cressets
High, high flambeaux, smoking of the east;
And scarlet hot embers of torches knocked out of the sockets
    among bare feet of elephants and men on the path in
    the dark.
And devil dancers luminous with sweat, dancing on to the
    shudder of drums.
Tom-toms, weird music of the devil, voices of men from the
    jungle singing;
Endless, under the Prince.

Possessing no natural majesty, the Prince was weary and diffident, doing the rounds of his tiresome duty. He was, Lawrence thought, less a person than a fragment.

'I still am not quite sure where I am,' Lawrence said when he had been two weeks in Ceylon: 'sort of look round for myself among all this different world.'[54] Knowing where he was and knowing who he was were bound up for Lawrence, and his crisis in Ceylon – as opposed to his crisis in Monte Cassino or his crisis in Cornwall – was to do with doubting his calling. Was he really the master that Mabel believed him to be? Was he really a prince among men? When he looked around for himself in this different world, Lawrence was also in fragments. Part of him was in the frenzied devil-dancers, whose vitality he internalised. Rolf Gardiner, the English rural revivalist, described Lawrence's 'terrifying' impersonations of the dancers at the Pera-hera, 'his piercing blue eyes popping right out of his pale face as he twisted like a cobra, shuffling in his carpet slippers like one possessed by demons'.[55]

On 10 April 1922 Lawrence wrote to Mabel to say that he would come to Taos, but only after going to Australia. The problem, he told Mabel, was that 'the East doesn't get me at all'. The East no more believed in Lawrence than it believed in the wretched Prince of Wales. Lawrence hated, he said, the 'boneless suavity' of the place, 'the sort of tropical sweetness' which suggests 'an undertang of blood'. He would 'still of course distrust Taos very much, chiefly on account of the artists', but he was prepared to trust 'the Indians, yes: if one is sure that they are not jeering at one'. He would prefer, in all honesty, to come to America without having to encounter at all 'the awful "cultured" Americans' – the 'steaming shits' referred to in his earlier letter to Mabel – 'with their limited self-righteous ideals and their mechanical love-motion and their bullying, detestable negative creed of liberty and democracy'. He believed in neither liberty nor democracy, Lawrence revealed. Obliged to be at war with every country he was in, Lawrence now pitched himself in advance against the ideals on which America was built. What he believed in, Lawrence told Mabel, was the emergence of an unelected natural leader, the 'divine right of natural Kings'. In this sense he found himself 'in diametric opposition to every American – and everybody else, besides Americans – whom I come across' – which is the position that Lawrence liked best.[56] Meanwhile the primitive authenticity he had come to Ceylon in order to find was what now appalled him the most: by the time Lawrence left, his letters had degenerated into rants about being 'in the heat among the black people'.[57]

Ceylon brought out the worst in Lawrence and it is hard, on the surface of things, to understand why he hated it so much. The problem, as he saw it, was one of magnetism: 'The magnetism is all negative,' he explained, 'everything seems magnetically to be repelling one.'[58] The magnetism that had shoved him away from the West, now shoved him away from the East. But he was with people he liked – Lawrence would always like the Brewsters, and they him – and on a beautiful island filled with new and astonishing birds, beasts and flowers. Imaginatively, Ceylon was well within his reach but it was not his imagination that failed him. What is underestimated in accounts of his time in Ceylon, mainly because Lawrence himself refused to discuss it, is the dire state of his body. His health, having improved on the sea passage, worsened again in Kandy. As ever, he gave no details of his symptoms but he reported afterwards that 'I had never felt so sick in my life.'[59] Biographers have put his accounts of night sweats ('Even at night you sweat if you walk a few yards'),[60] weight loss ('One sweats and sweats, and gets thinner and thinner'),[61] inability to breathe ('the feeling that there is a lid down on everything', that the sun makes 'a bell-jar of heat, like a prison over you'),[62] enervation ('the east seems to bleed one's energy and make one indifferent to everything') and decomposition ('It isn't so much the heat as the chemical decomposition of one's blood by the ultra violet rays of the sun')[63] down to the weather. But as the father of the playwright John Mortimer put it, 'I'm always angry when I'm dying.' We cannot know how ill Lawrence became during these weeks, but we can at least imagine how it felt to be in a country the effect of whose climate so perfectly impersonated the symptoms of the illness from which he was trying to escape, making it impossible for him to tell if he was dying of consumption or dying of Ceylon.

Illness prevented Lawrence from moving, and lack of movement led to claustrophobia and paranoia. He recalled Ceylon in 'The Man Who Loved Islands': Cathcart's first island was not 'Paradise regained', as he had hoped, but Limbo, where the 'moment begins to heave and expand in great circles'.[64] In a frenzy of panic and fear, Cathcart fled to another island and, on 26 April 1922, armed with their trunks and hatbox and painted Sicilian panel, Frieda and Lawrence set sail for the great penitentiary which is located at the same point of the southern hemisphere where Dante placed Purgatory. By astonishing coincidence, also on board, heading to a theosophical convention in Sydney, was Brewer's telepathic guide Annie Besant, who was now looking out for Lawrence.

From the deck, where he finished his translation of *The Little Novels of Sicily*, Lawrence watched flying fish sprint through the waves like 'winged drops', while an albatross, with its 'long, long wings', followed the ship. The southern waters, Lawrence wrote, make 'one feel that our day is only a day. That in the dark of the night ahead other days stir fecund, when we have lapsed from existence.'[65] At sea, his balance was restored. 'No more of my tirades,' he told Cynthia Asquith, 'the sea seems so big.'[66] His Purgatory would be three months, he continued. 'Three months' penalty for having forsworn Europe'.[67] He was perfectly aware of the symbolism of his pilgrimage: 'It is strange and fascinating', Lawrence reflected as his ship smashed through the Timor Sea, 'to wander like Virgil in the Shades.'[68]

It was midwinter when the Lawrences docked in Perth, and the sky was 'high and blue and new, as if no one had ever taken a breath from it', which suggests that Lawrence could breathe again.[69] His panic now subsided. In Ceylon he had felt as though he were dying, but in Australia he felt 'unborn'. Because he liked Australia, he also resented it. It was, he complained, 'the most democratic place I have *ever* been in. And the more I see of democracy the more I dislike it. It just brings everything down to the mere vulgar level of wages and prices, electric light and water closets, and nothing else.'[70]

Between 6 and 18 May, Frieda and Lawrence stayed in a guest house in Darlington, near Perth, co-run by a woman called Molly Skinner who described Lawrence as a 'little man' with 'strange scarlet lips' and a 'fragile body'.[71] He was shrinking: Lawrence, at 5 foot 9 inches, had once been seen as a tallish man with a stoop, but since his last winter illness even he had begun to describe himself, and his fictional representatives, as little. From Perth, the Lawrences sailed to New South Wales where they rented a three-bedroomed bungalow in a mining township called Thirroul – an Aboriginal word meaning 'in a basin' – forty miles south of Sydney. The men here were mostly coalminers, Lawrence wrote, 'so I feel quite at home'.[72] Thirroul was 'haphazard and new' with unpaved streets, a wooden church and myriads of bungalows with roofs of corrugated iron. As with any colony, Englishness was everywhere, but 'crumbled out into formlessness and chaos'. The great 'loose vacancy' of Australia was, Lawrence found, 'almost terrifying' while the sense of 'do-as-you-please' liberty felt 'utterly uninteresting'.[73]

Their house, called Wyewurk ('an Australian humorism', Lawrence explained'),[74] was – of course – 'on the brink'. The garden stopped short at a twenty-foot cliff which dropped down to miles of coastline; the Lawrences felt like they were living in the sea, with foam lapping their ankles. Bread and meat were delivered to the door and so there was no need to engage with the outside world; they made no friends at all in Thirroul where, for the last time in their married life, they lived alone.

The improvement in the air was reflected in Lawrence's productivity. On 25 May, he reported to Mountsier that 'one could never make a novel out of these people, they haven't got any insides to them, to write about'. A week later – after he and Frieda had finished scrubbing the floors and killing the mice – he had immersed himself in *Kangaroo*. He began writing on 1 June and sent Mountsier the finished book on 17

July, which means that Lawrence's dreamtime in Australia was spent writing a novel about his dreamtime in Australia.

'The business of the novel', Lawrence wrote in 'Morality and the Novel', 'is to reveal the relation between man and his circumambient universe, at the living moment', and *Kangaroo* reveals Lawrence's relation to the universe at the 'living moment' of June 1922.[75] As ever, he ran at it like a man possessed and produced roughly 3,500 words a day. He wrote and wrote and wrote, except that he did not write for the whole day because he also did the housework, cooked the meals, swam at lunchtime, collected shells from the beach, supervised Frieda over the laundry requirements (reminding her to rinse in cold water with bluing in it, to bring out the whiteness), read the newspaper cover to cover, rode into the bush in a pony cart, walked in woods of golden mimosa, sent dozens and dozens of letters and consumed a book on the sympathetic power of the glands that Mabel had sent to Ceylon. So Lawrence produced his 3,500 immaculately handwritten words in the few hours of the morning he put aside to sit on the ground beneath a tree, resting his notebook on his drawn-up knees.

Variously described by him as 'a thought adventure',[76] a 'gramophone of a novel' a 'mad novel of Australia' and a 'funny sort of novel where nothing happens'[77] – all of which are true – *Kangaroo* is the story of Richard Lovatt Somers. A 'strange little bloke', Somers is a working-class Englishman and the author (like Lawrence) of a recent essay on 'Democracy', who arrives in Western Australia with his German wife, Harriett. They live alone in a bungalow by the Pacific where Somers is wooed by the supreme leader of the Diggers Clubs (organised along the same secretive and ritualistic lines as the Freemasons), known by his followers as Kangaroo, and by a communist called Willie Struthers, who asks Somers to edit a newspaper. Oscillating between these two poles allows Lawrence to reflect on his connections to other working men, his leadership potential and his current line on democracy.

But *Kangaroo* is not really a novel about leadership; it is Lawrence's 'Song of Myself'. The subject, like *Leaves of Grass*, is the author's own energy: he wrote about anything, he wrote about everything, he wrote about nothing. 'Chapter follows chapter', begins Chapter 15, 'and nothing doing.' He wrote, so Lawrence explained to one of his reviewers, 'only just what I felt',[78] and he thus proceeded by instinct. As Whitman became one with his *Leaves of Grass*, Lawrence and

*Kangaroo* shared the same being. There is no attempt to distinguish the writer from his protagonist: Richard Lovatt Somers pursues his path through *Kangaroo* in much the same vein as Lawrence had pursued his path through the pages of *Twilight in Italy* and *Sea and Sardinia*. Somers is Lawrence's most self-aware likeness, not least because of the inconsistency of his character – he is right-wing, left-wing, passionately political and not political at all – which is caught in the instability of his name. We are first introduced to Somers as R. L. Somers, a reminder that he shares his initials with R. L. Stevenson, who visited this same coast in 1890. Richard Lovatt Somers is sometimes called Lovatt (which, in the Penguin edition is spelled 'Lovat'), sometimes called Richard, sometimes called Somers, sometimes called Richard L., sometimes called Lovatt (or Lovat) Somers and usually referred to by all these appellations in the same chapter.

Nor is there any attempt to distinguish Frieda from Somers's cake-baking, home-making, inexhaustibly cheerful wife (called Harriett in Lawrence's manuscript but Harriet in the Penguin edition); *Kangaroo* allows us to see Frieda once again in full focus, and witness the Lawrence marriage at its crucial turning point. The chapter called 'Harriett and Lovatt at Sea in Marriage' begins with the suggestion that, their sexual passion for one another being over, it was time for Harriett now to 'honour and obey'. The conversations between Harriett and Lovatt have the authenticity of gramophone recordings: 'Him! A lord and master!' jeers Harriett. 'Why, he was not really lord of his own bread and butter.' And as for all this phoenix nonsense, Somers, said Harriett, was less like a phoenix rising from the ashes than like an emu standing in a railway carriage.[79] 'Of course,' she continues,

> 'you lonely phoenix, you are the bird and the ashes and the flames all by yourself! You would be. Nobody else enters in at all. I – I am just nowhere – I don't exist.'
>
> 'Yes,' he said, 'you are the nest.'[80]

*Kangaroo*, Lawrence's most modernist novel, in many ways recalls *Ulysses*, which was published the month the Lawrences sailed for Ceylon. Lawrence had not yet read Joyce's book but the synchronicity between the two is remarkable: episode 7 of *Ulysses*, 'Aeolus', is interspersed with newspaper headlines, and chapter 8 of *Kangaroo*, 'Volcanic Evidence', does something similar. Turning the pages of the Sydney *Daily Telegraph* and reflecting on his own anger – 'Well, all right then, if I *am* finally a sort of human bomb, black inside, and primed' – Somers comes across an article which he transcribes for the reader:

Earthquakes.
Is Australia Safe?
Sleeping Volcanoes.

The fact that Australia so far has had no trouble with volcanoes or earthquakes, and appears to be the most immune country in the world, accounts for our entire indifference to the whole subject.

Tracing Australia's own faultlines, and reflecting on the earthquakes in Krakatoa, Peking, Naples, Martinique and San Francisco, the article suggests that 'We know nothing whatever of the awful forces at work beneath the crust of the earth, and nothing of the internal fires.' If the earth is so unstable, Somers concludes from this 'thrilling bit of journalism', then what does it matter if a man also has 'a devil in his belly!'[81]

Lawrence, like Magnus, was an earthquake connoisseur: he was never far from earthquake territory and nor were earthquakes, human or otherwise, ever far from his thinking. He returned to them in the chapter called 'The Nightmare' in which he went back to the granite boulders of Higher Tregerthen and recalled 'detail by detail' his experiences in Cornwall, from having his naked body inspected by a team of medical men to being hounded out of the county by the police. Having held the humiliation at bay, Somers's rage now boiled up like a 'white hot lava' which breeds 'more lava fire, and more, and more – till there is an eruption ... and then the lid is blown off, as the top is blown off a hill to make a new volcano'.[82] 'The Nightmare' has a similarly combustive effect in *Kangaroo* as a whole, leaving volcanic evidence on every page.

Robert Mountsier – who had been in Cornwall with Lawrence – complained that 'The Nightmare' was a diversion too far, that this wholesale eruption had been inserted into the wrong book and should be reprinted separately alongside Lawrence's essay on 'Democracy'. But Lawrence stood his ground, and rightly so. 'The Nightmare' digs down into his present fears. 'He had known such different deep fears,' the chapter begins, and 'one could feel such fear, in Australia'. The bush in the moonlight was 'so phantom-like, so ghostly, with its tall pale trees and many dead trees, like corpses, partly charred by bush fires'. Somers's fear of this deathlike landscape made the hair on his scalp stir and go cold. Only now did Lawrence connect his fear of Australia's spirit of place with the fear he had felt in Sicily and the fear he had felt in wartime England – 'a fear of the criminal *living* spirit which arose in all the stay-at-home bullies who governed the country' – which was similar in type to the fear he had felt in Ceylon, where he had gone to escape his fear of America.[83]

When *Kangaroo* was published in 1923, Lawrence's Australian critics noted the absence of characterisation but none could fault his description of the continent itself: its 'fern-dark indifference', its 'strange, as it were, *invisible* beauty', the way 'the bush seems to recede from you as you advance, and then it is behind you if you look round'.[84] For the Brisbane *Daily Standard*, the 'Australianism in this book is racy of the soil and belongs to the soul of the land. It leaps at you, almost clutching your throat at times.'[85]

That June, Lawrence sent Mabel copies of the newly published *Aaron's Rod* and *Fantasia of the Unconscious*, but she had been able to read him all year in *The Dial*. January's edition had run Lawrence's translation of 'The Gentleman from San Francisco', in February they printed an excerpt from *Aaron's Rod* ('An Episode') describing a fascist march through Milan, and in May they began a four-part serialisation of 'The Fox'. Mabel, meanwhile, 'willed him to come'.

> Before I went to sleep at night, I drew myself all in to the core of
> my being where there is a live, plangent force lying passive – waiting
> for direction. Becoming entirely that, moving with it, speaking
> with it, I leaped through space, joining myself to the central core of
> Lawrence …[86]

Her lover, Tony Lujan, also used 'his magic to call him' and so 'together we called Lawrence'. Finally, on 9 July, they made contact: *The Land of Poco Tiempo*, which Mabel had sent the previous November, now arrived. 'Lawrence!' her handwritten inscription read, '– this is the best that has been done yet – And yet if you knew what lies untouched behind these externals, unreached by the illuminating vision of a simple soul yet! Oh come!'[87] The book had pursued Lawrence around the circumambient universe, from Taos to Taormina, from Sicily to Ceylon and from Kandy to New South Wales.

Charles F. Lummis had discovered New Mexico in 1888, and he wrote *The Land of Poco Tiempo* in 1893. Reading his account of the place, Lawrence's fear can only have intensified. New Mexico, wrote Lummis, is 'the Great American Mystery – the National Rip Van Winkle – the United States which is *not* United States'. Life here moves at its own vague pace. There are 9,000 Pueblo Indians along the Rio Grande, 'peaceful, fixed, house-dwelling and home-loving tillers of the soil' spread between nineteen compact little 'cities'. Pagan Catholics, they worship both the Virgin and the 'opiate sun' and live in box-shaped houses built of clay and pinewood.[88] To protect themselves from being raided by the Navajos, there are no front doors in the pueblo, so you enter your house by climbing a ladder which leads to an opening in the roof.

Taos pueblo, 'in its lovely, lonely valley' far to the north of New Mexico, 'is two great pyramid-tenements of six stories' divided by a stream which flows down from Blue Lake. Those on the north side of the stream are the Winter People and those on the south side are the Summer People, and the pueblo is looked down on by 'skyward miles of savage rock' with forests far between. Every rock is 'a sphinx' and 'every peak a pyramid': Taos is 'an Egypt' with a 'mythology' more complex and comprehensive than those of Greece and Rome.[89] According to legend, when the Sun and the Moon mated above the Blue Lake, their progeny slid down into the water and lived beneath the earth until they emerged through the lake's navel to build their mud homes on land. The exact travels of the sun, moon and stars are recorded by the Indians on the walls of subterranean ceremonial chambers known as kivas.

The mountainous region of north-central New Mexico is also home to the Brotherhood of the Penitentes, a secret society that combines Catholicism with magic and witchcraft. The Penitentes, wrote Lummis, have worshipped here for the last two centuries and their Holy Week procession is 'a sight that might grace a niche in Dante's ghastly gallery'. The self-flagellating men, whose swishing and thudding can be heard from 200 yards away, are followed by another man, also half-naked, dragging behind him the timber cross on which he is to be crucified. During the crucifixion, which Lummis was privileged to witness, the honoured man sobs with shame as the ropes are tightened around his wrists and ankles: '*Ay! Como estoy deshonrado!* Not with a rope! Not with rope! Nail me! Nail me!' But the practice of nailing men to the cross during Holy Week had been abolished the previous year, due to the rising death toll. As the first man ever to photograph a Penitente crucifixion, Lummis reproduced the image in the book. 'There we stood,' he recalled of the camera and the cross, 'facing each other, the crucified and I – the one playing with the most wonderful toy of modern progress, the other racked by the most barbarous device of nineteen hundred years ago.'[90]

Penitente Crucifixion Ritual, 1888

'Very interesting,' wrote Lawrence in his next letter to Mabel.[91]

On 10 August he and Frieda boarded the *Tahiti*, bound for San Francisco. They had been in Australia for exactly 100 days. Almost 9,000 miles away, Mabel was triumphant: 'I became', she believed, 'that action that brought him across the sea. Come, Lawrence! Come to Taos!... This is not prayer, but command.'[92]

The *Tahiti* stopped for a day in Wellington, New Zealand – which Lawrence thought a 'cold, snobbish, lower-middle-class colony of pretentious nobodies'[93] – and he sent Katherine Mansfield, whose birthplace this was, a postcard containing one word: 'Ricordi' (Memories). It would be the last contact they had.[94]

The ship then turned her nose towards the South Seas and Lawrence at last saw Tahiti, where Captain Cook had observed the transit of Venus, the crew of the *Bounty* had mutinied, Darwin's *Beagle* had moored and Melville had wandered like a native in one of Lawrence's favourite novels, *Omoo*. During his two days on the island, Lawrence sent a card to Compton Mackenzie: 'If you are thinking of coming here, don't. The people are brown and soft.'[95] These were the same people that Lawrence had admired in Gauguin's paintings. Lawrence, as Mabel said, always 'lived afterwards', but his response to Tahiti was particularly tiresome. Once again the reactionary hysteria at the core of Self Two smashed the genius of Self One to smithereens.

The temptation is to ignore Lawrence at moments like this, but these tensions, or rather lesions, in his character are precisely what Lawrence's biographer must seize in order to see not only the stuff of which he was composed, but the world as he saw it. Where was his xenophobia coming from? Was it the racism of the age, or did it have a deeper source? Lawrence's description of the Tahitians contains none of the panic contained in his description of the Cambridge homosexuals, but once again, faced with 'the glamour of strangeness',[96] a limit had been reached and he emerged from the encounter a littler man than we had initially thought.

His reaction was part of the nameless dread he carted from island to island. Translucently white himself, Lawrence had told Jessie Chambers many years before that 'to me a brown skin is the only beautiful one', in which case we must assume that he was less afraid of brownness than of what he called 'softness'.[97] What Lawrence saw as Tahitian 'softness' had to do with a violation of his vision of a singular, primitive masculinity. But he was not really talking about Tahitians: Lawrence was talking about Lawrence. No matter how much he insists on male superiority – and this, from now on, will be the preoccupation of his fiction and of his battles with Frieda – Lawrence is unable to convince us, just as he was unable to convince his wife, that his was not the frailer sex.

Equally tiresome, and it must have been extremely so to Frieda, is the predictability of his disappointment. Having schlepped many thousands of miles around the globe in order to delay going to America, he now dismissed not only Ceylon and Tahiti but the South Sea islands as a whole: 'These are supposed to be the earthly paradises,' he wrote to Mary Cannan. 'You can have 'em ... Travel seems to me a splendid lesson in disillusion.'[98]

Finally, to make his temper worse, at Tahiti the already crowded ship took on a further 'Crowd of cinema people', who had been making an island film directed by Raoul Walsh. The women, Lawrence thought, were like 'successful shop-girls' and the men 'like any sort of men at the sea-side'.[99] So Melville's sweet, serene Pacific was filled for Lawrence with inanity, drunkenness and flirtation. Instead of mast-head romanticism in an empty world of water, he was trapped for 5,000 miles with a swarm of Hollywood actors. As the ship staggered over the sea, Lawrence observed this new species in close-up, and he mutinied. Losing his temper, he challenged them over their coarseness. The response of the actors, so Frieda told Mabel, was to 'jeer at him'.[100]

Brimful of prophecy, Lawrence motored into Taos on 11 September 1922, his thirty-seventh birthday. At the wheel of the Ford Model T was Tony Lujan and in the back sat Mabel and Frieda. It was the time of year when the desert blooms into 'soft puffy yellow fire'.[101] In 'Autumn in Taos', Lawrence described how the aspens 'laid on one another like feathers',

And then to look back to the rounded sides of the squatting
    Rockies,
Tigress brindled with aspen
Jaguar-splashed, puma-yellow, leopard-livid slopes of America.

They drove past Los Alamos where, twenty-two years later, the atomic bomb would be born, and down through the canyon. On one side of the road the Rio Grande makes its way to the Gulf of Mexico and on the other is a perpendicular wall of red rock; the gorge then opens on to a high stretch fringed with volcanoes, as vast and endless as an African plain. This is Taos valley, the land of the sky, and above them the air crackled with electricity. A 'long, slow flash of lightning' zigzagged from above the mountain, Mabel recalled, and then the lightning crashed down on all sides. Rain fell in steel sheets and turned to bullets of hail: this year's harvest was ruined.[102]

Once the storm had passed and they could see the eagles breasting the desert, Lawrence caught his breath. 'Something stood still in my soul,' he remembered, 'and I started to attend.'[103] Here, in this absolute silence, lay America. Taos is at the same degree of latitude as Tibet – to many of the mystics who come here, Taos is the link between East and West – and the Tibetans call the light at this altitude the Ultimate Reality. 'Never', said Lawrence of this magnificent clarity, 'is light more pure and overweening than there, arching with a royalty almost cruel over the hollow, uptilted world.' It was curious, he reflected, 'that the land that has produced modern political democracy at its highest pitch should give one the greatest sense of overweening, terrible proudness and mercilessness: but so beautiful, God! So beautiful!'[104] America, like Lawrence, was built on contradictions.

Eight days earlier, on 3 September 1922, they had docked in San Francisco, which Lawrence thought 'a sort of never-stop Hades' made up of 'black, glossy streets with steel rails in ribbons like the path of death itself'.[105] A letter from Mabel enclosing two train tickets to Lamy Junction had been waiting at their hotel, and she had also sent the news that the New York Society for the Suppression of Vice was trying to ban *Women in Love* (which attempt would increase sales exponentially). While they waited for Mountsier to wire them money, Lawrence and Frieda went to the cinema. We do not know what they saw, but it could have been a Buster Keaton short, or any number of films starring Rudolph Valentino, Mary Pickford, Douglas Fairbanks or Charlie Chaplin: hundreds and hundreds of movies – Westerns, romances, comedies, epics, realist and experimental – were being churned out of the five principal studios. The Hollywood industry was running at full throttle: earlier that year, also in San Francisco, Fatty Arbuckle had been tried for the rape and killing of a young actress called Virginia Rappe, and the following year the 'Hollywood' sign was erected in the hills overlooking Los Angeles.

In the poem 'When I Went to the Film', Lawrence described film culture as a form of pornography. Cinema, he believed, detaches us from our own souls by replacing vitality with abstraction: film actors – false gods – are shadows who 'live in the rapid and kaleidoscopic realm of the abstract'.[106]

When I went to the film and saw all the black and white feelings
    that nobody felt,

And heard the audience sighing and sobbing with all the emotions
    that none of them felt,
And saw them cuddling with rising passions they none of them for
    a moment felt,
And caught them moaning from close-up kisses, black and white
    kisses that could not be felt
It was like being in heaven ...

Yet when, in January 1923, Lawrence's American publisher Thomas
Seltzer tried to sell Warner Brothers the film rights for *Women in Love*,
Lawrence and Frieda were excited by the possibility – 'it would mean
dollars!' – and disappointed when it didn't happen.[107]

Mabel saw the arrival of Lawrence at Lamy Junction as confirmation
of her power, but what Lawrence saw on the station platform was a
piece of theatre. First, regal as a pharaoh, was the expressionless Native
American Tony Lujan, with his two long braids, and then there was
Mabel herself, dressed like a fortune teller with her own hair cut into
a Betty Boop bob. At forty-three, Mabel was the same age as Frieda,
and she had the same full figure. There, however, the likeness ends.
Frieda was physical and Mabel spiritual; the two women recalled
Ursula Brangwen and Hermione Roddice: 'And was not Ursula's way of
emotional intimacy', Lawrence wrote in *Women in Love*, 'emotional and
physical, was it not just as dangerous as Hermione's abstract spiritual
"intimacy?" ... Hermione saw herself as the perfect Idea, to which all
men must come: And Ursula was the perfect Womb.'[108]

Mabel was disappointed by her first impression of Lawrence, whose
nose she thought vulgar. They came towards her down the platform
with their trunks and boxes and painted Sicilian cart panel, Frieda
fleshy and expansive, with a 'forced, false bonhomie' and her 'lower jaw
pulled a little sideways'; she had a mouth, Mabel said, like 'a gunman'.
Running along with 'short quick steps' by her side, 'agitated, fussy' and
'distraught', was the master himself.[109] The couple appeared to Mabel
exactly as Magnus and Douglas had appeared to Lawrence three years
earlier, on that wet November evening by the Ponte Vecchio, which
shows how marked was the change in his health since his illness the
previous winter. Until recently, Lawrence had moved like a forerunner,
and it was Frieda who scuttled behind.

Tony Lujan by Ansel Adams

Mabel Dodge Luhan

It was a seventy-mile drive to Taos so they ate supper in the station café, sitting in a row of four high seats at the polished wooden counter. Lawrence in his dark suit and tie and Tony in his Native American blanket sat at the far ends, shielded from one another by their women. The meal was 'an agony', wrote Mabel, who felt the air around them 'splitting and crackling ... from the singular crash of our meeting'. There was 'a vibratory disturbance around our neighborhood like an upheaval in nature. I did not imagine this,' she stressed. 'It was so.' While Tony ate with his usual calm aloofness and Frieda talked incessantly with interjections of laughter, Mabel, whose rule it was to say as little as she could, read the runes. She sensed that Frieda was 'visualising' Tony in bed and that Lawrence, being 'keyed' into Frieda, therefore 'felt things through her'. As such, he did not like Frieda thinking about Tony in bed, but Frieda, Mabel understood, 'had to see life from the sex-centre'; she was 'the mother of orgasm'. Lawrence, she believed, was tied to Frieda as a lamb to a stake: 'he frisked and pulled in an agony, not Promethean so much as Panic'. Mabel denigrates her skills as a writer but *Lorenzo in Taos* is packed with good phrases, and Panic is precisely the right word for Lawrence at this point. While her memory cannot always be trusted, her insights often have the ring of truth. She describes Frieda, for example, as 'complete, but limited' and Lawrence as 'incomplete and limited'. It is beautifully precise, and one of the wisest summations we have of the Lawrence union.[110]

Supper finished, the party went out to the motorcar where Lawrence joined Tony in the front seat. This was the first time that Lawrence had met a Native American, and he had not expected him to be at the wheel of a Ford Model T. Indians, he believed, should pass through the land like fish through water or birds through air, without making a sound or leaving a trace. Frieda, confronted with Tony's broad back, exclaimed to Mabel that this wonderful expanse of body must be a 'rock to lean on', and Lawrence, hearing a criticism of himself, apparently twitched. At this point the car broke down and they sat in silence under the vast southern sky while Tony fiddled with the engine. Frieda suggested that Lawrence, who knew nothing about mechanics, lend Tony a hand and Lawrence snapped back that he hated cars. ' "Oh, you and your hates," she returned, contemptuously.'[111]

It was now too late to drive through the canyon to Taos and so they stopped in Santa Fe, where Mabel arranged for the Lawrences to stay the night with her friend Witter Bynner, who lived in an adobe house with his former student (and current lover) Willard 'Spud' Johnson. Witter Bynner and Spud Johnson were part of the 'literaiy crew' that Lawrence had specifically not wanted to meet. Bynner was a poet whose most recent collection was *A Canticle of Pan and Other Poems*, while Spud had founded a journal called *Laughing Horse*, whose editors described themselves as a 'wrecking gang, hurlers of brickbats, shooters of barbs, tossers of custard pie'.[112] Lawrence would become their prized contributor, but the wreckage began on the driveway of Bynner's house when Tony unwittingly reversed the Ford over the Sicilian panel. The first words that Bynner thus heard from Lawrence were said in a 'fierce falsetto': 'It's your fault, Frieda! You've made me carry that vile thing round the world, but I'm done with it. Take it, Mr Bynner, keep it, it's yours! Put it out of my sight! Tony, you're a fool!'[113] Bynner kept the panel, buckled and split, for the rest of his life.

In *Journey with Genius*, his memoir of D. H. Lawrence, Bynner noted that the Lawrences were both on the run but at different stages of their escape. Lawrence would continue to 'flee each harbor', but Frieda, who had made the 'important break' (from Weekley, in May 1912), 'did not need all the subsequent little escapes from escape' that her life with Lawrence had become.[114] Frieda needed to build her nest.

When he had recovered his temper, Lawrence entertained his hosts and their guests – who included Mabel's friend Alice Henderson, co-editor with Harriet Monroe of *Poetry* – to an impersonation of Norman Douglas, whom Bynner knew. The next morning, Bynner rose early to find the Lawrences already up. Having made the bed and washed the dishes, they were now cooking breakfast. 'The night had been the Lawrences' first in an American house,' Bynner reflected. It would prove 'a mixed omen'.[115]

The relationship between Lawrence and Mabel was a battle of wills, or rather a battle in which Lawrence resisted what they both described as Mabel's 'magnetism'. The battle took the form of a bullfight, where Lawrence shook his red cape and Mabel, horns lowered and eyes narrowed, came charging forward. Their dynamic might equally be seen as a snake dance, with Mabel manipulating the serpentine Lawrence, whom she held, for the moment, in captivity.

Mabel's adobe mansion was her great accomplishment: part Spanish revival, part English country house, part Florentine palazzo, this was her magnet and soul-centre, built with the intention of changing human consciousness. Her house would be a 'headquarters for the future', she believed.[116] Here twentieth-century radicalism would find the soil in which to flourish: Mabel, who envied Tony's tribal life, created a tribe of her own along the same lines as her salon in Greenwich Village. She drew into her orbit Willa Cather, Georgia O'Keeffe and Martha Graham (who choreographed *El Penitente* during her time here), John Collier, the future Commissioner of Indian Affairs, came first in 1920 and then made Taos the base for his life's work, Ansel Adams photographed both Tony Lujan and the pueblo, Greta Garbo visited with the costume designer Gilbert Adrian, the conductor Leopold Stokowski came for the Indian songs, which contained, he said, sounds that are 'not supposed to exist' in European music,[117] and when Carl Jung made the pilgrimage to Taos described in *Memories, Dreams and Reflections*, he was granted a rare interview with an elder in the pueblo called Mountain Lake who explained that white men 'think with their heads' while Indians think with the heart. Mountain Lake, wrote Jung, had 'unveiled a truth to which we are blind'.[118]

The Big House by Ansel Adams

The Big House, as it was known, eventually had seventeen rooms, in addition to which Mabeltown consisted of five guest houses (two of them photographed for *House Beautiful* in 1922), a large gatehouse for the staff, barns, corrals and stables for the horses and a busy Mexican village on stilts for the pigeons. Mabel bought the twelve acres in 1918 and Tony designed the main building, drawing each room in the earth with a piece of whittled stick, while the men from the pueblo did the work. 'The house grew slowly,' Mabel wrote, 'and it stretches on and on.' It grew room by room, step by step, alcove by alcove, porch by porch, wing by wing. She installed central heating, soundproofing and plumbing; she designed private quarters for herself and public areas for her guests; Tony cut down trees for the support columns which were carved into rope-like twists, and Mabel invented a concoction of wood-ashes and kerosene oil to rub into the corbels that held the roof beams. A second storey appeared, and then a third, in the form of a glass lookout positioned like a bell tower which gave Mabel eyes to the pueblo three miles away. She decorated the doors with ornamental fittings from Florence; the ceiling saplings for the dining room were painted – after those in Mexico's Laguna chapel – in shades of rust and frost and charcoal; and the glossy brown floor tiles were cast in a clay oven beneath the cottonwood trees. The house was janus-faced: while it looked as primitive as the pueblo, it had every modern convenience including electricity, running water and soundproofed rooms. The front of the building was protected by bushes and trees, but the back was strung with telephone wires, radio wires and electric and power wires, all 'swinging carelessly'.[119] It took four years to build – this being the land of Poco Tiempo – and the front door commemorates the date of completion: 1922. But Lawrence took one look at Mabel's creation and giggled. It was, he said, like 'one of those nasty little temples in India'.[120]

The next day Tony drove the party down to the pueblo at the foot of the Sacred Mountain. Taos, the Indians believe, is 'the King' pueblo, crowned by the Aztec King Montezuma himself who came here before Coronado's conquest of New Mexico in 1540. Frieda exclaimed with delight at the two piles of box-tenements, cosmologically arranged on either side of the river and rising like primitive skyscrapers, and at the four kivas, layered beneath the ground into underworlds, and at the dusty plaza, with its full-skirted women in white deerskin boots and men invisible in their sheets and dogs sniffing around. But Lawrence,

The Taos pueblo

said Mabel, was 'silent and seemingly unaware'.[121] He was, however, intensely aware: why, he wondered in his writings on Taos, when the marble statues of classical antiquity stand limbless in the desert like Ozymandias, didn't these thousand-year-old clay-heaps crumble back to the earth from whence they came? He was equally struck by the adobe Catholic church, as neat and crisp as a gingerbread house. The Indians, who adopted the Madonna from the Spanish invaders, rejected the other Catholic paraphernalia like confession and Extreme Unction. They worshipped the Virgin as a goddess: every Christmas Eve, Lawrence learned, her image was removed from the altar and paraded in a starlit procession by the village elders, who warded away bad spirits by firing guns and banging drums.

Mabel compared Taos to a landscape by Leonardo, and Lawrence, for whom Leonardo's landscapes were the architecture of his own imagination, doubtless agreed. The terrain was both strange and familiar; he had been here before, and not only when he looked at the *Madonna of the Rocks*. Taos pueblo, Lawrence wrote to Brewster, was 'like looking from the top of a hill way back down to a village one has left and forgotten: a bit *écoeurant*'.[122] In his essay on 'Taos', written that October, Lawrence compared the pueblo to 'one of the monasteries of Europe', a place in which the 'spirit dwells'.[123] Taos pueblo reminded him of Monte Cassino but it also, with its flat roofs and ladder entrances, recalled the house in Rabat where Magnus had ended his life.

'The Red Wolf', written in October 1922, describes the poet standing in the pueblo at dusk, 'on the shadow's dark red rim', having 'followed the sun from the dawn through the east / trotting east and east and east till the sun himself went home'. In a Wordsworthian encounter, the poet meets 'a dark old demon' in a white sheet who says 'thin red wolf, go home'. But, the poet replies, the red wolf 'has no home, old father, / That's why I come'.

The red dawn wolf sitting 'dark at the door', lifting up his voice and howling 'to the walls of the pueblo / Announcing he's here', is an appropriate image for Lawrence's arrival on the scene as an American writer.

Things were not going according to plan, and so Mabel rearranged the players. On Lawrence's third day in Taos, she ordered Tony to take him, together with her old friend Bessie Freeman – who was visiting from Buffalo, New York – to the Apache harvest festival celebrations in the Jicarilla reservation 100 miles north-west. This required the hypersensitive Englishman, the middle-aged American woman and two Native Americans (Tony was with a companion) to sleep for four nights in tepees. 'Tony didn't want to take Lawrence,' Mabel recalled, 'but I made him!' And Lawrence didn't want to go with Tony, but Mabel made him too. Her 'need to bring Lawrence and the Indians together,' Mabel explained, 'was like an impulse of the evolutionary will ... using me for its own purposes'.[124] But the impulse was equally to bring herself together with Frieda because the best way of controlling the Lawrences, Mabel had decided, was divide and rule.

With Lawrence and Tony away, Mabel and Frieda became, for a moment, friends. 'She was good company when Lawrence was not there,' said Mabel, 'as is the case with nearly all wives.' Frieda, Mabel found, was 'hedged in by her happy flesh'. Simple and boisterous, 'any reference to the spirit ... was antagonistic to her'; the only unhappiness that Frieda would allow were those 'caused by some mishap of the bed', and one such mishap, Frieda told Mabel, had been Lawrence's affair with a young Cornish farmer during the war. Frieda had similarly warned off H.D. by telling her that Lawrence was homosexual. Her husband, Frieda suggested to Mabel, was attracted to non-intellectual men of the land, rather like the ones with whom he was currently camping. Mabel, who did not rise to the bait, had her own agenda. 'Frieda,' she announced, 'it seems to me that Lawrence lives through you. That you have to feel a thing before he can feel it. That you are, somehow, the source of his feeling about things.' Everyone in Mabel's world was a medium for someone else. 'You don't know how right you are,' Frieda cried. 'He has to get it all from me. Unless I am there, he feels nothing. Nothing. And he gets his books from me. Nobody knows that. Why, I have done pages of his books for him. In *Sons and Lovers* I actually wrote pages into it.' Mabel had unearthed, in a matter of moments, Frieda's 'great grievance'. 'Everyone thinks Lawrence is so wonderful. Well, I am something in myself, too.'[125]

The Apache party, meanwhile, went banging and lurching across the Rio Grande and over the San Juan mountains, between the dusty divides and through a desert as mottled and cracked, Lawrence thought, as the bottom of the sea once the water has been drained. An emptied basin is effectively what the New Mexico desert is: on three occasions in its volcanic past the land has been flooded by ocean.

The drive to the Jicarilla reservation, where Tony was participating in the festival, took two days, but Lawrence says nothing in any of his writing about his impressions of Mabel's lover, who remains the most enigmatic figure in Mabeltown. In Willa Cather's 1927 novel *Death Comes for the Archbishop*, the bishop of Santa Fe crosses New Mexico with a guide called Eusabio, who may have been modelled on Tony Lujan. Travelling with Eusabio, says Cather, 'was like travelling with the landscape made human',[126] but this is not how Lawrence saw Tony, whom he had called a 'fool' on their first meeting. Tony, he will have seen, was part warlock, part Buddha, part tour-guide and part playboy, and Lawrence's silence conceals a complex response. On the one hand, Tony represented the Lawrentian ideal of manhood: he was the real thing, the noble savage under whose tutelage the middle-class woman gives up her controlling will and overcooked mind. But rather than dragging Mabel by the hair to live in his pueblo, as Lawrence would have preferred him to do, Tony had left the pueblo in order to be pampered as a fetish by Mabel. It was Tony, and not Mabel, who appeared to be the captive: he had given up his wife and importance in the tribe to be bossed about by a New York socialite who wanted to save the very people he had abandoned. Tony Lujan was thus in a similar position to Frieda, who had traded her home and her children to serve the cause of Lawrence.

On the other hand, Tony was nobody's poodle. That Mabel needed Lawrence to interpret the riddles of the pueblo is because Tony himself refused to do so. The 'secretive Indian silence', as she called it, was 'torment' to a woman as inquisitive as Mabel. Her simplest questions, such as why Manuel changed his hair today from braids to a knot, would be met by Tony with the same response: 'Secret.'[127] Some nights she would wake to find Tony pulling on his clothes. 'What are you doing?' Mabel would ask. 'Dressin. Goin,' Tony would answer. 'Going *where*?' Mabel would wail. 'To the mountain,' Tony would reply. 'Oh Tony, *why*?' 'Secret.' In the early days of their relationship, before he lost his place in the pueblo, Tony disappeared into the kiva for six weeks in order to be trained as the headman of his clan. This period was 'like a death' for Mabel, whose need to unlock secrets was, she realised, her undoing. 'I wanted to know the secret of the Sacred Mountain,' she confessed, and 'the secret of the Indian's sufficiency', but while Tony taught her to hear the difference in the sound of the stream after midnight, he never explained 'why he could walk straight up a hillside with no more effort than when he went down it'.[128]

When Jung visited Taos pueblo, he too described the air as 'filled with a secret known to all the communicants, but to which the whites could gain no access'.[129] Only the pueblo, Chief Mountain Lake explained to Jung, whose rituals caused the sun to rise and set, could know the secrets of the universe. As far as Tony was concerned, the emotional demands of Mabel Dodge were a speck of dust compared to ensuring that the sun went round the earth: he had relinquished his part in the ceremonial life of the pueblo, but there was no question about where his loyalty lay. Mabel saw Tony as her conduit to ancient wisdom, but Tony saw himself as a floodwall holding back the twentieth century. His role was to monitor modern America's fascination with his people: it was Tony who arranged for Ansel Adams to photograph the pueblo, Tony who arranged for Carl Jung to speak to Chief Mountain Lake, Tony who advised John Collier on how to communicate with the Indians.

Wrapped in his blanket, he kept his hawk-eyes on the future in order to preserve the sanctity of the past.

'Indians and an Englishman', the first of Lawrence's five essays on New Mexico, was written on 18 September 1922, the day he returned from the Apache festival. It is important to remember when we read this essay that it was produced to order because Mabel considered Lawrence her writer-in-residence. She wanted Lawrence to 'take *my* experience, *my* material, *my* Taos, and to formulate it into a magnificent creation. That was what I wanted him for.'[130] More immediately, however, she wanted Lawrence to protest against the bill which had been introduced into Congress by Senator H. O. Bursum. By allotting native American land to individual Indians who could then sell it to whomever they wished – ranchers, developers, the government – Bursum's aim was to regain their territories and force the Indians into mainstream American life. Mabel rounded up her writer and artist friends to protest, but her greatest contribution was to involve John Collier, who had come to Taos in 1920 as a radical poet but now became a lobbyist for the Native Americans.

Lawrence wrote nothing about the presence of John Collier in Mabeltown, despite the fact that the Colliers and their two children lived in the house next to him. Mabel described Collier as 'a small, blond Southerner, intense, preoccupied, and always looking windblown on the quietest day. Because he could not seem to love his own kind of people ... he turned to other races and worked for them.'[131] Lawrence said something similar about Mabel: she loved the Indian world out of hatred for the white world. Once Collier had discovered Taos, he devoted his life to the fight to protect the land rights and traditions of the Native Americans in the pueblos. From 1922 he worked as a research agent for the Indian Welfare Committee, resisting the repressions instituted by the missionaries and the federal government. This involved a state campaign to uproot Native American children from their families and cultural lives by putting them in boarding schools where overcrowding, illness and corporal punishment prevailed, and the decision, in 1913, to declare all Native Americans wards of the government, which meant that they no longer owned the land on which they lived.

John Collier and Tony Lujan became a team. Because Tony trusted Collier, so too did other Indians. In a letter he later wrote to Collier, Tony described him as 'a real friend' and explained how he – Tony – spread the word throughout the pueblos that John Collier 'really likes Indians. In past time, we had Commissioners against us who tried to stop our ceremony dances and our dances-religious. They nearly destroy us; call our ways bad or immoral or something ... But John Collier fight for us ... and he save us. Now, he look far ahead and it is like he is putting a wall all around us to protect us.' Lawrence, observing all this, thought Collier a 'salvationist' who, together with Mabel and her 'poisonous white consciousness', was destroying what they wanted to preserve.[132]

The campaign against the Bursum Bill was the first time in American history that the protection of indigenous lands and culture would become a national movement, and Mabel's connectivity put her at the helm of the protest. The campaign, which became a cause célèbre, was launched by an article by Collier called 'The Red Atlantis' in which he argued that the life of the 'Pueblo Indian' was a model for all Americans and he outlined his reform ideals: 'recognition of Indian civil rights, conservation of their lands through cooperative enterprise, preservation of their communal societies, and agricultural and industrial assistance programs sponsored by the federal government'.[133] Tony Lujan and John Collier then visited the twenty-two New Mexican pueblos, from Taos to Hopi, explaining what was at stake and organising a defence in the form of an All-Pueblo Council. Lawrence put his name to Mabel's petition against the bill, but otherwise refused to be her scrivener. 'I arrive in New Mexico at a moment of crisis,' he wrote in an article published in the *New York Times Magazine* called 'Certain Americans and an Englishmen'. 'The crisis is a thing called the Bursum Bill, and it affects the Pueblo Indians. I wouldn't know a thing about it, if I needn't. But it's Bursum Bursum Bursum!! the Bill! the Bill! the Bill!'[134] Mabel, reading what Lawrence had produced on her behalf, was duly disappointed: 'it does not seem to me very good', she said.[135] Lawrence, who 'believed', so he had said in his letter from Ceylon, in the Native American and wanted them to 'believe' in him, had fallen at the first hurdle.

The Native Americans believed instead in John Collier and so did Mabel, who wrote him a letter in late November offering all she had in terms of 'energy, time, and money' to further his campaign. Her home, she said, was to be 'a base of operations *really* for a new world plan' which would save 'the whole *culture* and *agriculture* of the pueblos', while also guiding white America into a whole new way of living. She would even, she told Collier, marry Tony if that made their work 'more convenient from the worldly standpoint'.[136] In a letter to a friend, Mabel expanded on her vision:

> We want *interest* and *appreciation* of the Indian life and culture
> to become part of our *conscious* racial mind. We want *as a nation*
> to value the Indian as we value ourselves. We want to *consciously*
> love the wholeness and harmony of Indian life, and to *consciously*
> protect it.[137]

He understood nothing, Lawrence stressed in his New Mexican essays, about Native American consciousness and culture, the aim of his insistence that 'there is no bridge' between the two worlds, 'no canal of connection', being to cause maximum offence to Mabel and those other 'highbrows' who fooled themselves 'into believing that the befeathered and bedaubed darling is nearer to the true ideal gods, than we are'.[138]

Readers of the *Divine Comedy* generally prefer *Inferno* to *Paradise*. Dante's Paradise, wrote Lawrence in *Movements in European History*, 'was much less vivid to him than the Inferno' because what Dante knew best 'was the tumultuous, violent passion of the past, that which was punished in Hell. The spiritual happiness is not his. He belongs to the old world.'[139] There was also the issue – which Dante returns to – of describing that which exceeds representation. The problem with representing Paradise is that nobody understands you, and Dante therefore explains that, having now reached the uncharted terrain of eternity, his poem will have to switch, or 'leap', into a different mode:

> And thus, in representing Paradise,
> the sacred poem has to leap across,
> as does a man who finds his path.
>
> (*Paradise*, Canto 23, 61–3)

Lawrence describes a similar jolt in 'Indians and an Englishman', also published in the *New York Times Magazine*, which begins: 'Supposing one fell on to the moon, and found them talking English, it would be something the same as falling out of the open world plump down here in the middle of America.'[140] There are no perspectives on the moon, and what is most striking in Lawrence's early accounts of the landscape in New Mexico is the absence of deep, technicolour, consciousness-expanding views.

'Indians and an Englishman' continues with an appeal to the 'dear reader' to have towards Lawrence an attitude of 'amused pity', recalling the appeal to the reader of *Paradise*, Canto 2, where we are pictured in a small bark tailing behind Dante's splendid ship. Now, Dante tells us, we must 'turn back' to our 'shores again' because at this point the waters become deeper and harder to navigate.

> do not
> attempt to sail the seas I sail; you may,
> by losing sight of me, be left astray.
>
> (*Paradise*, Canto 2, 4–6)

An author's admonishment to his reader to stop reading is rare indeed, and Dante's purpose is to prevent us from being led astray. Now that the physical side of his climb has ended, we enter the metaphysical with Beatrice explaining the workings of the universe: why, for example, there are spots on the moon. We are also introduced to the cosmological complexity of Paradise, with its higher and lower heavens, and faster and slower heavens. Those heavens that are nearer to God and the empyrean, we are told, move with more speed than those which are closest to Purgatory.

In the four volumes of Mabel Dodge's *Intimate Memories*, the waters become equally hard to navigate as she too tries to explain the workings of the heavens ('What holds the stars firm in their constellations, able to withstand the awful magnetism that must attract them to one another?')[141] and to warn her readers off asking too many questions about her relationship with Tony Lujan. 'This narrative about Tony and me becomes more and more difficult to tell,' she warns, 'for I feel increasingly obliged to leave most of it unwritten, not only the secret aspects of his religious life and experience, but the secret intimacies of our own personal life together.'[142]

It was dusk when they arrived at the reservation and Tony parked the Ford at the top of a crest. Lawrence looked down from the 'high shallows' while the other two men sat beneath a pine tree to braid their hair and dress in their best blankets and turquoise jewellery. They were above a hollow basin with a lake in the distance, and what Lawrence saw on the crest below was as though projected in black and white: 'the points of Indian tents, the tepees, and smoke, and silhouettes of tethered horses and blanketed figures moving'.[143] In his later essay 'New Mexico', he described the reservation as composed of 'old Spanish, Red Indian, desert mesas, pueblos, cow-boys, penitents, all that film stuff'.[144] This was Cinema Paradiso.

The Native Americans of New Mexico were among cinema's earliest subjects. In 1912 D. W. Griffiths had shot a film in the Isleta pueblo, twenty miles south of Taos, called *A Pueblo Legend*, which starred Mary Pickford as 'the Indian girl'. *A Pueblo Legend* opens on a feast-day in the time before Columbus, with the sun priest telling the legend of the turquoise stone that fell from the sky. Mary Pickford recalled how the actors' costumes, loaned by the Museum of Indian Antiques in Albuquerque, were worn incorrectly, and so the chief ordered the crew out of the village. Three years later, when D. W. Griffiths made another New Mexican film called *The Penitentes*, he brought in Charles Lummis, author of *The Land of Poco Tiempo*, as a cultural and historical adviser.

Back at the Apache reservation, Lawrence heard rather than saw the dance. As the sun went down, he wrote in 'Indians and an Englishman', the drums started 'their strong-weak, strong-weak pulse that beat on the plasm of one's tissue'. Two elderly men then began moving, 'pat-pat, pat-pat', their feet flat on the earth 'like birds that move from the feet only', and while they danced they sang 'with wide mouths', sightless, without words or vision and in perfect hypnotic unison: 'Hie! Hie! Hie! Hy-a! Hy-a! Hie! Hie! Hie! Ay-away-away –!' A second set of drums then began thud-thudding, as though in response, and 'from the gathering darkness' other men drifted slowly in,

> each carrying an aspen-twig, each joining to cluster close in two rows upon the drum, holding each his aspen twig inwards, their faces all together, mouths all open in the song-shout, and all of them all the time going on the two feet, pat-pat, pat-pat, pat-pat, to the thud-thud of the drum.

As he listened, Lawrence was overcome by 'an acute sadness, and a nostalgia, unbearably yearning for something, and a sickness of soul came over me'. His contact with 'Red Men' was not, he confessed, 'what I thought it would be. It was something of a shock. Again something in my soul broke down, letting in a bitterer dark, a pungent awakening to the lost past, old darkness, new terror, new root-richnesses.' This visceral response to the lost past, by now so familiar to Lawrence's readers, always comes as a shock to Lawrence himself; each time his soul breaks down feels like the first time his soul has broken down, and on each occasion, with the predictability of a cuckoo clock, he knows that he cannot go back. 'There is no going back,' he now once again concludes. 'Always onward, still further.' Except that having reached his destination – Taos, Lawrence wrote, 'feels final' – there is no further that he *can* go.[145]

They ate supper at their camp, and when Tony Lujan went off to visit the tepees of his friends, Lawrence wrapped himself 'up to the nose' and wandered invisible among the Apaches in their blankets and the cowboys in their big hats and leather chaps. The 'dark air' was 'thick with enemies: that was my feeling'. He describes the world as a stage and himself as Hamlet: Lawrence cast 'a lone lorn' figure that night, while the Taos Indians in their white cotton sheets were 'like Hamlet's father's ghost'. It is striking how powerful Lawrence's father-fantasy is in this essay about dancing, underground men: 'these old men telling the tribal tale were my fathers'; he too had 'a dark-faced, bronze-voiced father far back in the resinous ages' and his mother 'lay in her hour with this dusky-lipped tribe father' who, 'like many an old father with a changeling son … would like to deny me'. Lawrence passed a group of young men playing softly on a drum and a group of old men sitting in the firelight, listening to an even older man reciting like a 'somnambulist', in a 'distant, plangent, recitative voice', the history of his tribe. This 'piece of living red earth' talked for hours and hours; some of the men who 'listened without listening' were chewing gum and others smoked cigarettes; they drifted out and filtered in and Lawrence stood wrapped in his blanket 'in the cold night, at some little distance from the entrance, looking on'. The old man's voice from its 'far-off time' was 'not for my ears. Its language was unknown to me. And I did not wish to know.' As the night thickened, the cowboys rode home and there was 'a new savagery in the air'. So Lawrence went slowly away, back over the rim and across the darkness to his own lonely camp.[146]

The Indians, said Lawrence, were 'flat shapes, exactly like men, but without any substance of reality … No deeper consciousness at all.'[147] It was a strange criticism from a man who claimed to distrust mental consciousness, but the whole business of having an inside or an outside and of being an insider or an outsider becomes paramount in Taos, where Lawrence was an outsider with an inside while Tony was an insider with, Lawrence thought, only an outside. Lawrence's letters home describe a world which is all show: 'Internally, there is nothing,' he wrote.[148]

No sooner had Lawrence and Tony Lujan returned from the Apache festival than the group dynamic changed. Mabel put it like this: Lawrence 'was annoyed that Frieda and I had become friends, and not only jealous of me, but jealous of her as well. The flow immediately ceased between Frieda and me and started between Lawrence and me. He somehow switched it.' Lawrence was jealous of Mabel and Frieda, Mabel was jealous of Frieda and Lawrence, and Frieda was jealous of Mabel and Lawrence. So the night after writing the first draft of 'Indians and an Englishman', Lawrence suggested that he and Mabel should work on a book together. Having been in America for a little over two weeks, 'he said he wanted to write an American novel,' Mabel recalled, and that 'he wanted to write it around me'. She was delighted: 'It was for this I had called him from across the world.'[149]

On the morning of 19 September, Lawrence went across to the Big House to begin work. He found Mabel sunbathing on the flat roof outside her bedroom, naked beneath a dressing gown that was like a burnous. She says that she didn't think to dress for him, but this is disingenuous. Passing by Mabel's unmade bed, Lawrence 'averted his eyes, as though it were a revolting sight'. Mabel's room was, she said, clean and light but Lawrence, just by 'passing through it, turned it into a brothel. Yes he did. That's how powerful he was.' Mabel, who felt so connected to Lawrence, had misread him: Lawrence hated slovenliness, sartorial and domestic.

Squatting on the roof, while the pigeons in their coops below paced 'amorously up and down', Lawrence fell into a 'gloomy silence'. 'I don't know how Frieda's going to feel about this,' he said, and he threw an angry look in the direction of their house below. 'Well, surely she will understand,' Mabel reassured him, at which point Lawrence launched into a tirade against Frieda who, being German, understood nothing about the 'Latin spirit' shared by himself and Mabel. Were they discussing co-writing a novel or having an affair? Mabel elides the difference, and Lawrence did too. Mabel then, having waited almost a year to do so, told Lawrence the story of her journey 'from civilisation to the bright, strange world of Taos': how she had exchanged her New York salon – 'the sick old world of art and artists' – for the 'pristine valley and upland lakes'. And 'in that hour', she wrote in *Lorenzo in Taos*, she and Lawrence 'became more intimate, psychically, than I have ever been with anyone else before'.[150] Which makes it sound less like an affair than a psychoanalytic session.

Mabel, who started out as Mabel Ganson, and then became Mabel Evans before becoming Mabel Dodge, and after that Mabel Dodge Sterne, was born in Buffalo, on the eastern shores of Lake Erie, at what she called 'zero hour'. The Native Americans had been driven away and the white Americans who now possessed the land 'were sinking down into a diseased and melancholy inanition'.[151] The only child of wealthy parents who hated one another, Mabel's childhood was gilded, and silent. Because she wrote so garrulously about herself, it is easy to overlook the significance of silence to Mabel. Her father, Charles Ganson, was treated by her mother, Sara, with a silent contempt which provoked him to despair. He would, Mabel recalled, 'shout and fling his arms about and his face would seem to break up into fragments from the running passion in him', but still Sara Ganson refused to respond.

Mabel, who imitated her mother in all things, practised this same pose, and she found in Tony Lujan someone equally taciturn: both Tony Lujan and Sara Ganson had what Mabel called 'a secret life'.[152] To her friends, Mabel spoke only in monosyllables (her voice was described as mellow, with confidential overtones), and to her servants she said nothing at all, responding to their queries with brief nods or shakes of her head. Her battle from birth was to get what she wanted: Mabel was always clear about this, objectivity being one of her finest features. She made no attempt to pretend that she was anything other than a manipulator, an exhibitionist and a bully, or to disguise the fact that jealousy was her guiding star and love an obstacle rather than a goal.

What Mabel had was energy – she saw herself as 'a Leyden jar charged to the brim' – and she employed this to create the maximum emotional flurry.[153] As a child she sexually experimented with her girlfriends, and her mother removed her from school when she became involved with a girl called Beatrice. Her first marriage, aged twenty-one, to Karl Evans, took place suddenly, and in secret. It served a dual purpose: to challenge the authority of Charles Ganson, and to prevent Karl Evans from marrying the woman to whom he was currently engaged. '*I* want you,' Mabel told him, explaining in her memoir that she wanted him not out of love but in order to prove her power. Three months after the wedding, Mabel was having an affair with her doctor, a middle-aged, married man called John Parmenter whom she first encountered after a suicide attempt. When Mabel became pregnant, she told both Karl Evans and John Parmenter that the child was theirs but, she later wrote, 'I hardly knew whose baby I was going to have.'[154]

She called the boy after John, but thought Karl was the father. There would be no electricity flowing between this mother and child: when she was handed the newly born baby, Mabel refused to look at him, deciding that she didn't 'like it', by which she meant both the infant and motherhood. This never changed. When John Evans had children of his own and Mabel offered him parenting advice, he replied by telling his mother, 'YOU, lecturing ME on children and child-love! YOU, the perfect Mother … MY GOD … There is more love in the little finger of my hand for each of my children than you ever had for me.'[155]

Two months after John's birth, Mabel was passing by her parents' house when she saw Dr Parmenter's car driving away. Her father was dying and so a visit by the doctor would not be unusual. But Mabel, being naturally suspicious, went inside and found her mother lying in a state of dishabille on the couch at the end of her bed. The air in the room throbbed and Sara Ganson lay there 'flushed and warmed, her hair, burning brightly in the light, a little loosened', while her eyes, usually cold, were 'heated and accentuated by her quickened, strong blood'. Seeing her in a state of post-coital bliss, Mabel realised that her mother was no longer a stranger but another version of Mabel herself, filled with 'the life that was my life, with the fires that I considered I alone held the key to loosen'. 'How is my father?' she asked. Dr Parmenter, Sara Ganson languidly replied, was keeping him quiet with a dose of morphine. Mabel then returned home, haunted by the picture of Parmenter 'driving his awkward body against my mother's cold sensuality'.[156]

Charles Ganson died in the autumn of 1902, and six months later Karl Evans also died, having been accidentally shot in the back while shooting ducks. Mother and daughter were now widows competing over Dr Parmenter. 'It was,' Mabel said, 'as though I had never known Karl', and to separate her rival from Parmenter, Sara Ganson arranged for Mabel and her tiny son to visit Europe.[157]

It was on the ship to France that Mabel met Edwin Dodge. He was a recently qualified architect and Mabel had an interest in interior decoration: they married straight away. She claims she was not in love with him, but the purpose of Mabel's official story was to show that her life had no meaning until she met Tony Lujan. Between 1904 and 1912, the Dodges lived in Florence: 'I will make you mine,' Mabel said when she first saw the lily town. They bought the fourteenth-century Villa Curonia at Arcetri, and while Edwin focused on the renovations, Mabel filled the rooms with the expat community, including Gordon Craig and Norman Douglas: she made a point of including theatre people and homosexuals in her circle. She also befriended Gertrude Stein, who furthered the advancement of Mabel Dodge by writing an impenetrable 'Portrait' of her which Mabel had printed and distributed around her circle. Alice B. Toklas, who kept her distance, recalled Mabel once encouraging John, then aged five, to jump from the balcony. 'Fly, my dear, fly,' she coaxed. 'There's nothing like a spartan mother,' muttered Edwin Dodge.[158]

In 1912 – the year that Lawrence met Frieda – the Dodges returned to New York, where they set up home in Greenwich Village, in an apartment Mabel decorated entirely in white. This was the bohemian quarter, the city's Left Bank. From now on things moved fast: Mabel discovered herself as a 'mover and shaker' and saw a psychoanalyst who advised her to separate from her husband. She divorced Dodge in 1913, in which year she also donated $500 to the International Show of Modern Art, held at the Sixty-Ninth Regiment Armory and known for posterity as the Armory Show. The show became what Mabel saw as her own 'little Revolution'. Here the Steins displayed, for the first time, their magnificent collection of modern art, and Mabel was asked to write a profile of Gertrude Stein for *Arts and Decoration* magazine.

When the Armory show was over, Mabel redirected the centre of Manhattan's energy to her house in the Village whose notorious Wednesday Evenings became the Jazz Age equivalent of Studio 54. Her white rooms were filled with the men and women who were shaping the future: trade unionists like one-eyed Bill Haywood, anarchists like Emma Goldman, black musicians from Harlem, suffragettes, psychoanalysts, artists and poets. Mabel supported workers' rights, women's rights, the rights of African Americans and the unemployed, and as such the press presented her – correctly – as an heiress who entertained the radicals while the workers starved. But her salon was a great success. Mabel described how, wearing a white shift dress and a vivid scarf, she would greet her guests with a limp hand and a brief, abstract smile, inwardly bubbling with pleasure.

She behaved in her love affairs like a woman deranged; being loved by Mabel was compared to a jail sentence. Her romances, she stressed, were spiritual rather than sexual, except for the one with the journalist and war correspondent John Reed. Between 1913 and 1915, John Reed was Mabel's great passion. They both believed in the immortal quality of their love: Reed was a god and Mabel the muse from whom, as she put it, he 'drew electricity'. In 1913, when Reed was writing *Insurgent Mexico*, the book about the revolution that would make him famous, Mabel pursued him into Texas and one of her Evenings went ahead without her. This occasioned the cubist artist Andrew Dasburg (also in love with her) to paint a picture commemorating 'The Absence of Mabel Dodge' which, together with Gertrude Stein's 'Portrait of Mabel Dodge', consolidated Mabel's status as the doyenne of modernism.

Mabel also now befriended Isadora Duncan who, having parted ways with Maurice Magnus, was setting up a dance school in New York. Isadora's sister, Elizabeth, became Mabel's great ally, and it was Elizabeth Duncan's dance school, in a farmhouse in Croton-on-Hudson, that Mabel helped to establish. Buying for herself the house next door, Mabel became the Croton Queen and she enrolled her son, John, now aged fifteen, in the Elizabeth Duncan school. It was here, at a dance recital, that Mabel – no longer in love with John Reed – met husband number three, the Jewish-Russian post-impressionist painter Maurice Sterne.

In his own reminiscences Sterne wondered how their marriage ever came about, given that Mabel was not his type and that he was not in her 'astral sphere'. She disliked his art, but Mabel also believed that if she had a physical relationship with a talented man, she would absorb his powers. What he was drawn to in Mabel, Sterne later realised, was her control. 'For the first time in my life I could relax, rest my will, and do what someone else decided was best.' When Mabel went into analysis with A. A. Brill, Freud's disciple and first English translator, he recommended a marital separation. And so in 1917 Sterne joined the artists' colony in Santa Fe from where, in November, he sent his wife a letter: 'Do you want an object in life? Save the Indians, their art-culture – reveal it to the world!'[159] That same month the face of a Native American man appeared to Mabel in a dream.

Mabel Dodge, whose life reads like a Freudian case-study, was a psychoanalytic lab-rat. Analysed first as a teenager, she maintained a close relationship with A. A. Brill until his death in 1944. Brill, who in 1909 had accompanied Freud to Clark University in Worcester, Massachusetts where he gave his famous Clark Lectures, was afterwards asked by Freud to set up and run a branch of the International Psychoanalytic Association in New York. Jung was Freud's man in Switzerland, and Brill was Freud's man in America: 'You are indeed the only one who can always be relied on,' Freud told him in 1932, 'who never lets a person down.'[160] Brill could equally rely on Mabel, who between August 1917 and February 1918, wrote a bi-weekly column for the *New York Journal* in which she too disseminated psychoanalytic ideas: 'Mabel Dodge Writes about the Unconscious' was the title of one of her articles. It was when Mabel invited Brill to talk at one of her Evenings that the idea of unconscious behaviour was introduced to New Yorkers for the first time. Several of her horrified guests walked out.

In December 1917, Mabel Dodge entered into 'the second half' of her life when she headed south-west from New York to 'save the Indians'. 'My heart was pounding with impatience, for in spirit I had already arrived and only my body was left behind on that smelly train.'[161] After three days of crawling across the desert, she jumped out of the Pullman several stops before Santa Fe and summoned a boy to drive her to the station. But the car had no headlights so she ended up at Wagon Mound, waiting for the train that followed the train she had abandoned.

She and Sterne, for the moment reunited, moved north to Taos, whose landscape Mabel had fallen in love with. Here, in January 1918, she first saw Tony Lujan who was 'squatting' – just as Lawrence was doing now – on the floor of his house in the Taos pueblo, beating softly on a drum and singing a wordless song. When he looked up, Mabel realised that his was the face she had seen in her dream. Tony had similarly dreamed about Mabel: 'I seen you before, already,' he said, and Mabel gave him an orange. By the summer both Tony's wife, Candelaria, and Maurice Sterne had been despatched by Mabel, and her journey of 'awakening at the different great centres' was over. Buffalo, she explained to Lawrence, had been 'the lower sex center', Florence the 'emotional, nervous, aesthetic center at the solar plexus', and New York 'the exciting frontal brain center where ideas stimulate and whirl about'.[162]

Back on the sun-roof in Mabeltown, Mabel finished telling Lawrence her story. By the time their hour was up, they had achieved what she called 'a complete, stark approximation of a spiritual union'. Lawrence then went downstairs while Mabel dressed, and they strolled over to his house. 'We were happy together,' she recalled. 'We reinforced each other.' But there ahead of them was Frieda in a pink cotton frock, hanging out the washing. Her rage was apparent from a distance of a hundred yards and Lawrence started to 'chuckle'.[163]

That night, when the Lawrences came over for supper, Mabel noted a tired serenity about them which suggested they were worn out by fighting. In 'Not I, But the Wind ... ', Frieda covers in one brief sentence her fight with Lawrence over the Mabel-novel: 'I did not want this.' So Lawrence, taking Mabel aside, now explained that 'Frieda thinks we ought to continue the work at our house.' 'With her *there*?' replied Mabel, astounded. 'Well, not in the room,' Lawrence mumbled, at least not 'all the time. She has her work to do.' Mabel then understood that she would never, as long as the Lawrences were together, have 'the chance to unload my accumulation of power'.[164]

Frieda had reason to feel threatened: Mabel wanted, she admitted, to 'seduce' Lawrence's 'spirit so that I could make him carry out certain things'. She did not find Lawrence physically attractive but she nonetheless 'persuaded' herself that she 'wanted him' because she could then imbibe some of his genius.[165] Lawrence, meanwhile, knew full well that writing a novelised biography of Mabel and Tony would be an erotic challenge, just as it had been when he wrote *The Trespasser*, his novelised biography about Helen Corke and her suicidal lover. So the following morning Mabel grudgingly turned up at the Lawrence house and shivered in a room with wide-open windows while Frieda 'stamped around, sweeping noisily, and singing in loud defiance'. Under these conditions, nothing 'vital' could 'pass' between writer and subject, and so they shut up shop for the day. Thus began the struggle between Frieda and Mabel, the body and the spirit, for control of Lorenzo's soul. 'Frieda's opposition to me,' wrote Mabel, 'released all my desire for domination.' She put it to Lawrence slightly differently: 'Frieda,' Mabel announced, 'has mothered your books long enough. You need a new mother.'[166]

Sitting beneath a cottonwood tree, Lawrence began writing immediately. He called his combustible heroine Sybil Mond, Mond meaning world and Sybil combining the name of the Greek oracle with that of Cybele, the plump mother-goddess. With her fierce brows and headlight eyes, Sybil was Isis, a sun disk between her two cow-horns. But Mabel was also, as the mother of a fatherless son, the Virgin of the Pueblo. Thus Sybil Mond was a blend of Madame Blavatsky and Madonna of the Rocks. The Pullman which brought her from New York, meanwhile, was a Balaam's ass who refused to do her bidding: Sybil willed it to go forward, but instead it rested on the track.

'I have done your "train" episode,' Lawrence told Mabel in an undated note, 'and brought you to Lamy at 3 in the morning.' Because Frieda had banned Lawrence from being alone with Mabel and Mabel refused to talk to Lawrence with Frieda in the room, he asked her to now flesh out for him, in writing, the following details:

1. The meeting with Maurice
2. John, M and You in Santa Fe
3. How you felt as you drove to Taos
4. What you *wanted* here before you came
5. First days at Taos
6. First sight of Pueblo
7. First words with Tony
8. Steps in developing intimacy with Tony
9. Expulsion of M
10. Fight with Tony's wife
11. Moving into your house.[167]

Mabel would cover most of these points in her memoirs but questions 7, 8 and 10 – the story that became 'more and more difficult' for Mabel to tell – still need answering.

Did Mabel really meet Tony Lujan in the mystical conditions she described? Maurice Sterne rubbished her official account: the drum performance in his house, he said, was 'put on to impress tourists'.

Tony was a 'show-Indian' who knew exactly how to play spiritually hungry women like Mabel because he had once toured Coney Island with a Wild West troupe. He had, in addition, been 'spying around' the Sterne house for a good while before Mabel appeared that day at the pueblo; Maurice recognised him as one of a group of Indians who turned up in their kitchen at mealtimes. He was handsome and arrogant and stood out from the others 'like a proud cock amongst a flock of meek chickens'. Mabel was 'hypnotised' by the Indians, said Sterne, particularly by their silence. What you have to understand about Mabel, he stressed, is that she was a 'dead battery' who needed constant recharging and Tony Lujan, Sterne conceded, was probably the right man for the job.[168]

We know that Tony's wife was paid by Mabel $35 a month in exchange for not naming her as co-respondent in the divorce (Mabel similarly paid Maurice Sterne $100 a month), and we know that the pueblo strongly disapproved of the union between Mabel and Tony. But who had the power in the relationship: Mabel, who was rich, or Tony, who represented everything that Mabel most valued? Lawrence wanted Mabel to dig deep. 'You've got to remember', he added at the bottom of his note, sounding like A. A. Brill, 'also the things you don't want to remember.' But without Lawrence there to 'make the dynamos inside begin to hum and discharge sparks', Mabel's battery had once again gone flat and she could not, she said, even begin to put pen to paper.[169]

She must, however, have written something for him because in a letter to Mountsier on 6 October Lawrence said: 'Am doing a M. Sterne novel of *here*, with her Indian: she makes me notes. Wonder how we shall get on with it. I don't let her see my stuff.' Frieda added to the letter a postscript: 'I *love* the land and like Mabel D … Lawr has actually begun a novel about here and Mabel D – It's *very* clever the beginning, it will be rather sardonic!'[170] So to begin with, Frieda had liked the Mabel book and mothered it herself. 'There is a kind of vitality and eternal youth in it,' she said (according to Mabel) of these opening pages, 'like nothing he had done before'.[171] It was only later, recalled Mabel, that Frieda's resistance took hold, when the relationship between Lawrence and his Beatrice had broken down.

The book that began at full throttle now lay sleeping. 'America,' Lawrence wrote home, 'makes me feel I haven't a word to say about anything.'[172]

# Part Two

Mabeltown was built on secrets and lies. Some of its residents were close to the truth, and what concerned Mabel is whether Lawrence was too.

The story of her life that she told Lawrence was a fiction, and we can read it again in the four volumes of *Intimate Memories* that Mabel began writing in the winter of 1924: *Background*, which describes her childhood in Buffalo and first marriage to Karl Evans; *European Experiences*, where she covers the years in Florence with Edwin Dodge; *Movers and Shakers*, about her Greenwich Village salon and relationship with Maurice Sterne; and *Edge of Taos Desert*, which includes her journey from New York to Santa Fe on trains so slow that she 'could hardly endure it'. The quartet concludes in 1918 with Tony and Mabel preparing to consummate their love: 'He bent a firm, gentle look down upon me and held out his hand, and I took it. "I comin' here to this tepee tonight," he said, "when darkness here. That be right?"' It was then that Mabel took the 'irrevocable step' across cultures, and left her old identity behind. '"This will be mine," I thought when I crossed the barrier between Tony and myself, and I sought in every way to become like one of them as I turned away from my own kind.' And they all lived happily ever after.[1]

*Intimate Memoirs* was intended, however, to include five further volumes which Mabel then withheld from publication, presumably on legal advice, and which are now stored among the papers she deposited in 1952 at the Beinecke Library at Yale. These suppressed volumes were then further suppressed in 1973, when her son, John Evans – only now made aware of their contents – embargoed their release until the year 2000. One of the volumes, 'Notes Upon Awareness', tells the story of Mabel's battle with manic-depression, while another, 'The Statue of

Liberty', written in 1947 when Mabel believed that Tony was having an affair with the glamorous socialite and art collector Millicent Rogers, gives the unvarnished account of her relationship with Tony Lujan: what really happened after she took the 'irrevocable step' into the tepee. 'The Statue of Liberty', whose title comes from Mabel's identification with the 'great hollow stone image' at the 'entrance to this great deluded country', is the most explosive volume of them all, and the one most relevant to Lawrence's time in Taos. Here, after being married to Tony for thirty years, Mabel revealed that their union amounted to a 'tragedy', an 'everlasting loneliness'.[2]

But what also becomes clear in 'The Statue of Liberty' is that Mabel's earlier moratorium on the subject of herself and Tony was a smokescreen: it was her relationship with her other husbands that she was unable to discuss. The set of apparently straightforward questions that Lawrence had asked in his note – about Mabel's life with Maurice in Santa Fe, her feelings as she drove into Taos, what she wanted when she first came here, her response when she first saw the pueblo – were like loaded guns.

In addition to the crisis generated by the Bursum Bill, which was all anyone spoke about, there was another crisis brewing in the pueblo where a friend of John Collier's called Eshref Shevky was conducting a survey into syphilis ('People here called the Shevkys,' Lawrence wrote on 14 November. 'Nice'). Mabel had 'protested strongly' against Shevky's belief that there was syphilis in Taos, 'for the Indians,' she said, 'are disinfectant. Nothing foul or morbid taints their neighbourhood', but she nonetheless gave him $1,000 to pay for Wassermann tests for the whole pueblo.[3] Shevky and his wife lived with Mabel while he completed the testing and Tony, as ever, acted as medium, encouraging the Indians to give their blood to this stranger and setting an example by being the first to have his own tested. The blood samples were then sent to Albuquerque for analysis and 12 per cent came back positive. Tony Lujan's blood, however, was negative.

Soon afterwards when Tony, having been out late, was undressing for bed, Mabel saw on the white sheet wrapped around his loins 'a dampened border' with 'tiny veins of blood streaking through it'. Lifting the material to her nose she was overcome by 'a wave of sickness'. It smelled of semen, and Tony then confessed that he had slept with a woman in the pueblo called Christine, who was the wife of his good friend Tony Romero. With the smell, 'a memory rushed back' to Mabel.

There was a dream I had had years ago … a dream [that] was overwhelming, yet it was only about an odour, a strange unknown effluvia that assaulted me with menace and threat and it was accompanied by a voice I had never heard before that uttered meaningfully: 'That is the odour of evil' … even to recount it now revives the terror and despair it gave me.

Her memory is presented as a dream about an odour, but dreams themselves are memories, or reworkings of an experience. What Mabel remembered may have been her first smell of semen which occurred when she was a child. The night Tony's infidelity was revealed she lay 'in the darkness beneath the pillow' and 'lived again':

the same terror and despair of the first dream experience. For I recognised then for the first time what the nature of that odour was, a recognition I had never known, an association I had never made before in waking life. For me now the primitive, physiological smell of the seminal fluid was evil, really, and destructive.[4]

Other women discovering semen on their partner's underclothes would feel jealousy and rage, but Mabel felt terror and despair. Her first response was not that Tony been unfaithful to her, but that the smell of semen *in general* was evil and destructive. Over the next few weeks she kept up appearances while living with what she called a 'nameless fear'. Her fear was confirmed when she experienced pain passing urine: Mabel had syphilis. She had been, she believed, infected by Tony who had himself been infected by Christine Romero: she knew as much by the streaks of blood in his semen. Blood in the semen, however, is not a symptom of syphilis and, given that Tony had recently tested negative, it might just as easily have been Mabel who infected Tony.

Syphilis, a bacterial infection later treated with penicillin, has four episodic stages. The first symptoms, which appear a week to three months after infection, are genital sores. When these disappear, the patient enters the secondary stage whose symptoms include a pustular rash on the palms or soles of the feet, fever, headaches, muscle pain, fatigue and swollen glands. If these are left untreated, the patient will then either develop latent syphilis, in which the disease simply hides itself away for anything up to twenty years, or progress directly to the tertiary stage, which can last up to thirty years after the initial infection. Tertiary syphilis can result in blindness, deafness, bone erosion and brain damage before causing death. In 1910, an effective treatment for syphilis was discovered in the form of an arsenic-based drug called Salvarsan and known as the 'magic bullet', in which a yellow powder dissolved in sterile water was injected into the buttocks. Mabel and Tony were treated with Salvarsan shots administered by a doctor in Santa Fe. The injection was painful, and the pain would last for around six weeks; the side effects of Salvarsan shots included rashes and liver damage.

'For the first time', Mabel said of her diagnosis, she now 'hated' her body, and for rest of her life she was 'dead' to Tony, who went on to have other affairs.[5] Her 'death' was enacted in ways apart from keeping separate bedrooms: one morning during the early stages of her Salvarsan treatment, Mabel passed out while doing up her shoe and did not regain consciousness for seventy hours (in other versions of this story, she says it was twenty-four hours). 'You been dead for three days,' said Tony, who had been praying by her bed until she eventually came round.

'I, who had never believed in "secrets!",' wrote Mabel in 'The Statue of Liberty', 'had this shameful one that hurt me with every breath I drew.' Except that she had long believed in secrets because John Parmenter, as she revealed in the final volume of her suppressed memoirs, 'Doctors: Fifty Years of Experience' (written in 1954), had contracted gonorrhoea. 'That damn bitch of Dr Sherman's has given me the clap,' Parmenter told Mabel, presumably referring to the wife or secretary of a fellow doctor. Mabel, then aged twenty-two, replied, 'Give it to me and I will take it for you', at which point, 'throwing himself passionately upon me, he did so'.[6] When Mabel met Edwin Dodge on the boat to Europe, he told her that he was syphilitic, having caught the illness from a French prostitute. Mabel was horrified but married him all the same. He was apparently past the infection stage, but 'I could never overcome my revulsion to Edwin's body, no matter how I tried.' And when she married Maurice Sterne he was in the secondary stage of syphilis, which he contracted on Bali where he was painting the natives. On learning this, Mabel 'shrank' from him 'and our intimacy lapsed away'.[7]

She came to Taos to escape from what Joyce in *Ulysses* called 'syphilisation'. Lawrence felt the same: Europe, he said, was 'a dead dog, that died of a love disease, like syphilis'. Mabel wanted 'some strong solution that would wipe out forever the world I had known' and discovered in Taos pueblo an Eden replete with an 'untarnished' Adam in the form of Tony Lujan.[8] Because the local physician, Dr Martin, was indiscreet, Maurice Sterne was treated in Santa Fe, and Mabel's growing disgust at his illness and the secrecy it entailed led her to build her pristine new house. Mabeltown was to be a refuge from 'the dismal atmosphere at home'. Here, lying next to Tony's 'wholesome' body – wholesome was a word Mabel returned to in her descriptions of Tony and the pueblo – she would start again, a virgin on virgin land.

But Mabel's homes all shared the same dismal atmosphere; each was contaminated with the same 'ghastly secret things'.[9] Her earliest memory was of visiting her father in a sanatorium where he was being treated for insanity, the result, apparently, of masturbation. But there are many indications that Charles Ganson was himself syphilitic: after Mabel's birth, for example, he was banned from entering his wife's bedroom, and he died believing himself possessed by devils. As a child, Mabel harmed herself in order to get the sympathy of doctors, and as an adult she became a pioneer of psychoanalysis. She tried, at various points of her life, to commit suicide and regarded sex as a form of murder in which she was both victim and perpetrator. She knowingly infected herself with gonorrhoea from a lover who was *in loco parentis*, and she married, in succession, three syphilitic men (Mabel married Tony in the spring of 1923). After which she lived in a state of terror lest she go mad like her father.

Mabel Dodge Luhan was a magnet for syphilis; she formed a syphilitic circuit, and at the root of her pathological behaviour was the need to confirm the filthiness of her body. She described Frieda as 'hedged in by her happy flesh' precisely because Mabel herself had what she described as 'frightened flesh'. Bodily connections being poisonous, she spent her life exploring the alternative realms of spiritual connectivity.

But venereal disease was the symptom and not the cause of her self-revulsion. Mabel's real secret, I suggest – triggered by the smell of Tony's semen – is her abuse by the syphilitic Charles Ganson. It was the odour of her father's sperm that Mabel had repressed until the night of Tony's infidelity, and the sight of her own virginal blood on the white sheet that she recalled with such 'terror and despair' when she imagined that she saw Tony's 'infected' semen.

Of all the devasting things revealed by Mabel in 'The Statue of Liberty', the most moving is the confession that she 'often wished one of those old men in the Pueblo had been my father instead of the frustrated, tortured man I had known and turned away from in my childhood!'[10] Like Lawrence, she would have preferred for herself a 'dark-faced, bronze-voiced' father. Throughout 'The Statue of Liberty' Mabel repeats the biblical lines by which she had been haunted all her life: 'the sins of the father' and 'the wages of sin are death'. Her sense of sex as a sin – her father's sin – and the horror of sexuality she rehearsed in all her marriages dates from childhood, as did her experience of her mother as a sexual rival ('I have a very bad Oedipus complex,' Mabel told Dr Brill).[11] There was also what she enigmatically referred to as a 'family secret: which I don't know'.[12] But she did know, at some level, what the family secret was, and comes perilously close at times to spelling it out: 'My father,' Mabel told Una Jeffers in 1930, 'turned me into what is euphemistically called a frigid woman at an early age.'[13] She 'had to have' Dr Parmenter, Mabel explained in 'The Statue of Liberty', 'to get the taste of my father out of my mouth and his odour out of my nostrils'.[14] Before Parmenter, the only men Mabel had known, she said, were 'boys' or 'old pigs'. If her first husband, Karl Evans, was the boy, the assumption must be that her father was the old pig, and from the sins of her father Mabel learned to be sexually inappropriate towards her own son, whose 'mother complex' she admittedly encouraged. Unable to give him maternal love, Mabel instead made sexual advances to John Evans who, in 1936, published a novel called *Shadows Flying* in which the central character tells his mother that 'If you ever so much as touch me again, so help me God, I'll murder you.' John Evans, in turn, had incestuous feelings towards his daughter, whose breasts he liked to fondle.[15]

Having come to Taos in search of Paradise, Mabel found only Purgatory. From 1923, she lived like a penitente, chained to Tony for perpetuity. 'We have injured one another,' as she put it in one of her many self-lacerating passages, '– torn each other apart.' Their punishment was to 'be together in our strange, bleak separation'.[16] Tony felt the same: the gods, he believed, had wanted their union and so he and Mabel – like Paolo and Francesca and Lawrence and Frieda – could never separate. Even when Mabel left this earth, Tony said, he was condemned to follow her.

How much of all this did Lawrence know? John Collier knew that Mabel and Tony were being treated for syphilis; the Shevkys also knew, and so too did Alice Henderson, whose daughter married Mabel's son in December 1922. Did Lawrence detect the symptoms – a pustular rash on the palms, fatigue, fever? Was he aware of their unexplained absences? Mabel and Tony went regularly to Santa Fe for their Salvarsan shots, and they disappeared into California over long periods for mercury treatments. There must have been whispered conversations, tense silences and a dismal atmosphere of 'ghastly secret things' in Mabeltown.

Lawrence's illness was also too awful to be named. He too was a pariah. He had dragged his contagious body from island to island, continent to continent, across oceans and through jungles and up mountains, telling the world that he suffered from 'the bronchials' while dreading the show of blood on the white sheet.

His journey upwards was allegorical, but also practical. Lawrence needed to breathe and so there had been reasons apart from Mabel's magic to bring him to Taos. He was looking, like all consumptives, for altitude, Between 1882, when Robert Koch discovered the bacterium that causes TB, and the late 1940s, when streptomycin was made available, tubercular patients fled to New Mexico in their thousands. The treatment for TB was rest, sunshine, mountain air, good food and a positive attitude, all of which 'the nation's sanatorium', as New Mexico was called, could provide and which were used, at the turn of the century, to alter her demographic: if a stock of white people could be drawn here and persuaded to settle, the federal government might consider the territory eligible for statehood (in January 1912, New Mexico was duly admitted as the forty-seventh state of the Union). Doctors across America therefore received promotional material claiming that Native Americans and Hispanics couldn't contract TB because Mycobacterium tuberculosis was unable to survive at this altitude: 'The lowest death rate from Tubercular Disease in America is in New Mexico,' read one leaflet. Santa Fe was advertised as the 'Land of Sunshine', Albuquerque as the 'Heart of the Well County' and Silver City as the 'City with the Golden Climate'. An article in the *Silver City Enterprise* in 1900 explained that by living in a ranch in the Rocky Mountains the consumptive 'will be outdoors in the life-giving sunshine all day long, and that is what his condition demands'. So desperate for sunshine were the 'lungers', as they were known, that in a process called heliotherapy sunlight was directed down their throats with the use of mirrors.

Consumption shaped New Mexico. When Lawrence arrived here, the lungers made up 10 per cent of the population and there were forty sanatoriums. By 1930, there were sixty sanatoriums. The disease was rampant, and the state's healthy inhabitants lived in terror of infection: the death rate of Native Americans was 800 a year and rising.[17]

Mabel was alert, as everyone was, to consumption. When John Parmenter left Buffalo in 1908 he set up a TB clinic in Geneva, and Alice Henderson had originally come to Santa Fe for the cure. Say what you like about Mabel, remembered Alice's daughter (who was also Mabel's daughter-in-law), when it looked as though her mother was dying, 'Mabel marched in and packed her up and took her out to California, to a specialist she knew out there, and made her take things easy. Mother never looked back: she lived for years afterward. Mabel did more good in five minutes than the Santa Fe doctor had done in years.'[18] The Lawrences knew they could rely on Mabel: at one point Lawrence asked her if the son of his English agent, Curtis Brown, who had 'lung trouble', could rent a house on her land, as though Mabeltown were itself a sanatorium. And Frieda asked Mabel, in confidence, to send a cable to Nottingham to find out if her daughter Elsa was consumptive and needed to be brought out here.[19] One reason why Mabel did not march in and pack Lawrence off to California, as she did Alice Henderson, is that she was ill herself. Instead she accused Frieda of effectively killing Lawrence by taking him 'to the very worst climates and the most depressing surroundings'.[20] But she also claimed, in *Lorenzo in Taos*, that Lawrence died because he was a neurotic – which is what Lawrence thought too. The reason he died however is because no one, including Lawrence himself, was able to name his illness.

Lawrence and Mabel were carriers of the plagues: together their infections could have wiped out half the population of New Mexico. And the only way of ridding the world of corruption, Lawrence believed, was by destroying it in a flood, which is what he now described as he sat down in late September 1922 to write the concluding chapter to *Kangaroo*. In their last week in Australia, Richard and Harriett are confined to the house by a storm of biblical proportions: the sea reaches the doors and the rain comes in room after room. 'It was like the end of the world.'[21]

'I don't think I can bear to be here very long,' Lawrence told Mountsier on 28 October. 'Too much on Mabel Sterne's ground … I don't choose to be anybody's protégé.' He now read *Ulysses* and a newly published novel by Carl Van Vechten called *Peter Whiffle* in which Mabel appeared in the person of the New York society hostess Edith Dale, 'a dynamo' of 'electric energy' who 'invented her own kind of wireless long before Marconi came along with his'.[22]

As ever, Lawrence worked in the mornings, keeping abreast of the industry that was his writing life. His increasingly complex publication arrangements included completing *Kangaroo*, waiting for the proofs of *England, My England* (a collection of ten short stories), *The Ladybird* (a triptych of longer stories containing 'The Ladybird', 'The Fox' and 'The Captain's Doll') and *Fantasia of the Unconscious*; placing his article about the Bursum Bill, 'Certain Americans and an Englishman' going through the manuscript of his Verga translations, putting together *Birds, Beasts and Flowers*, whose last additions were his first American poems – 'Spirits Summoned West', 'Eagle in New Mexico', 'Bibbles', 'The Red Wolf', 'Men in New Mexico', 'Autumn in Taos' – writing a book review for *Laughing Horse* and dashing off his daily letters. Perhaps the most remarkable aspect of Lawrence's writing life is his dependency on and trust in the postal service. Manuscripts, made without copies, were regularly despatched from one-horse towns; proofs from London and New York similarly journeyed across oceans to catch up with Lawrence in whatever hut he had laid his hat. He knew at any moment which of his writings were in the press, which were out to publishers, which were on hold, which proofs were expected, which needed completing and which needed rewriting. Only occasionally, as with the essays that would comprise *Studies in Classic American Literature*, did he get confused over those pages that were with his English agent and those with his American agent.

In the afternoons he and Frieda picked apples with Mabel in the orchard, bathed in the hot springs on the Rio Grande and learned to ride. Tony laughed when Lawrence's pony went cantering off down the field with its rider clinging on, he thought, like a monkey and so that was the end of any sympathy between the two men: Lawrence was increasingly unable to cope with being challenged or mocked. But he was a fast, free and fearless rider who never fell, and every day Lawrence and Frieda, initially in the company of a guide, galloped to the pueblo or down to one of the canyons or round the desert, returning at sunset. In the evenings they played charades in Mabel's house, and sometimes Mabel invited the men from the pueblo to come and play their drums and dance, which Lawrence always enjoyed. He repeats in his early letters how 'generous' and 'nice' Mabel was, but also how wilful he found Americans.

Lawrence, in turn, encouraged Mabel to do her own baking and housework: one morning she made an inedible loaf of bread, and on another she tried to wash a floor ('You don't *know* your floor,' Lawrence explained, 'until you have scrubbed it on your hands and knees!').[23] Her maids, meanwhile, stood by 'half-distressed and half-amused'.[24] Mabel's account, in *Lorenzo in Taos*, of her inability to do basic tasks is comic and self-aware: she knew what she looked like from the outside, and she knew that she and Lawrence were flirting. Once, when they were washing up together on the porch of his house, 'our fingers touched in the soap-suds and he exclaimed, with a blue and gold look through the clamour of magnetic bells: "There is something more important than love!"' 'What?' asked Mabel. 'Fidelity!' replied Lawrence, his tone 'grim'.[25] He now encouraged her not to hide her shape – which Mabel compared to a Christmas tree – inside flowing robes, but to dress as his mother had done: 'A woman is a woman. A waist-line is a waist-line.' Frieda accordingly went about in white stockings, starched petticoats, long skirts, neat aprons and peasant bodices to emphasise her magnificent bosom, and Lawrence suggested Mabel do the same. It was curious, Mabel reflected as she bought herself 'yards and yards of gingham, calico and dimity', to find herself in this sacred place, dressing up to look like Lawrence's mother.[26]

On 22 September, Lawrence wrote to his American publisher, Thomas Seltzer, asking him to send a new biography called *Herman Melville: Mariner and Mystic* by Raymond M. Weaver, and the 'MS copy of *Studies in Classic American Literature*' which he had delivered in the summer of 1921 and heard nothing of since. He wanted to take another look at the dozen essays and add to them 'the first reaction on me of America itself'.[27] This would therefore be his third version of *Studies*: the first being written in the Inferno years, and the second when he had climbed the purgatorial hill in Italy. He had 'nightmares', Mountsier despaired, 'of you spending the rest of your life rewriting it!'[28] But what Lawrence wrote in New Mexico became the definitive edition of *Studies*. He revised his opinions of some of the 'classic' writers but he did not alter the line-up: Franklin, whom Lawrence now disliked ('I can't stand Benjamin'), remained at the helm, but without the brilliant comparison with *Frankenstein* because Lawrence was no longer interested in the Shelleys. 'The Perfectibility Of Man!' he now said of Franklin's clockwork version of selfhood. 'Ah heaven, what a dreary theme!'[29]

What would dramatically change in the newly revised *Studies* was the style: Lawrence described the 'voice' of American literature as 'a new bird', and so too was the voice of his American criticism. He was 'Americanising' the essays, Lawrence explained to Mountsier and Seltzer, by making them 'much shorter',[30] 'sharper, quicker'.[31] Having never before made anything 'shorter', 'sharper' or 'quicker' during revision he slashed away at his lovely sentences so they became like irate telegrams. 'I AM HE THAT ACHES WITH AMOROUS LOVE,' Lawrence yelled in the Whitman essay that closed the collection:

CHUFF! CHUFF! CHUFF!
CHU-CHU-CHU-CHU-CHUFFFF![32]

The cinematographic style pioneered in his essay on 'David' was pushed to breaking point: 'You may think them too violent now, to print,' Lawrence warned Mountsier.[33] This final version of *Studies* will here be referred to as the 'Mabel' edition, not least because we have Mabel Dodge to thank for the book that is itself a classic of American literature.

The difference between the transcendental reflections of Zennor 1917, the enthusiastic revisions of summer 1920 and the combative, virtuoso 'Mabel' edition of *Studies* is that of hope defeated by experience. Lawrence in Taos was, once again, a disappointed man and terrible in his wrath. He was also a famous man, with James Joyce to contend with. He and Joyce, Lawrence said, usually mentioned together and doomed to be yoked through eternity, were like 'Paolo and Francesca floating down the winds of hell'.[34] The challenge he set himself was to write with authority about literature while hating the literary scene: no one disliked the pedantry of scholarship more than Lawrence, and he was going bare-knuckled into the ring. If the first and second versions of *Studies* were critical prose, the 'Mabel' edition was free verse: Lawrence measured and indented his sentences; he paid attention to his line endings; his words had rhythm. What he emphasised was his lone maleness: this is Lawrence the cowboy riding into town and slinging his pistol. The quick fire of the 'Mabel' edition of *Studies* is thus a parody of the critical discipline practised by T. S. Eliot, but it also follows, to the letter, Pound's instruction to the young American critic to 'put down exactly what you feel and mean! Say it as briefly as possible and avoid all sham of ornament.'[35] Having said exactly what he felt and meant, Lawrence blew all the other American critics out of the water.

The argument of *Studies in Classic American Literature* is that both America and its literature have a pathological attachment to 'a sort of double meaning'. These double meanings start with the tale Americans tell about themselves: the Pilgrim Fathers, Lawrence argued, say that they came here for freedom of worship but this is a lie because 'England had more freedom of worship in the year 1700 than America had.' The real reason they came here was 'to get *away*' – from home, from mother, from themselves. The Pilgrim Fathers 'were driven by IT' – by which he meant their inner magnet – and they came on the same invisible winds that also carried 'swarms of locusts'. As for 'the land of freedom' – where is the freedom in slavery and mammon and the drive for domination?[36] What we find in American literature, Lawrence suggested, are two tales sandwiched together. There is the surface tale which comes from the artist's upper-consciousness, a children's story in which everything is 'nice as pie, goody-goody and lovey-dovey', and humming away beneath is the real, demonic tale: '*Destroy! destroy! destroy!* hums the under-consciousness. *Love and produce! Love and produce!* cackles the upper-consciousness. And the world only hears the Love-and-produce cackle.'[37] To deal with this doubling, Lawrence gives his readers clear instructions: 'Never trust the artist. Trust the tale. The proper function of a critic is to save the tale from the artist who created it.'[38]

This was a reformulation of Lawrence's sense that the part of him that was a writer (his under-consciousness) knew things instinctively and should therefore be allowed to get on with the job, while the part of him that was not a writer (his over-consciousness), by trying to master and control the writing, robbed it of its magic. But Lawrence's observation also refers directly to Mabel, who was similarly putting up a double meaning. The goody-goody all-American story of her life which she had told Lawrence on the sun-roof, disguised the destructive hum in the airwaves which he had tuned into. What Lawrence now needed to do was to save Mabel's tale from the artist who created it.

The 'Mabel' edition of *Studies* is packed with references to Mabel. At times Lawrence just played with her name. 'The world,' he added to the opening chapter 'The Spirit of Place', 'is a great dodger, and the Americans the greatest.' More generally, the descriptions of America and Americans tend to be descriptions of Mabel herself: 'White Americans', he said in the closing lines of 'Henry St John de Crèvecoeur', 'do try hard to intellectualise themselves. Especially white women Americans. And this latest stunt is the "savage" stunt again.' As for Tony, Lawrence reflected in 'Fenimore Cooper's White Novels' on the 'pride' felt by an Indian man who lives with a white woman: 'he will be a big man amongst his own people, especially if the white mistress has money', but he will also 'jeer' at his mistress and 'try to destroy her white pride'.

In 'Edgar Allan Poe', Lawrence was forced to deal with the subject of tuberculosis, from which Poe had died aged forty. The cause of TB, Lawrence explained, in a repetition of his self-diagnosis, is love: 'It is love that causes the neuroticism of the day. It is love that is the prime cause of tuberculosis.' Love/neurosis messes with the wiring of the body by causing the 'sympathetic ganglia' of the breast to vibrate 'over-intensely', thus weakening the lungs and giving 'the tubercles a ripe field'.[39] Lawrence and Mabel were here in agreement. But, by the close of the essay, Poe's illness, which was also Lawrence's illness, has become a description of Mabel's illness because syphilis is also caused by excessive love. So Poe was 'doomed', Lawrence concluded.

> He died wanting more love, and love killed him. A ghastly disease, love. Poe tells us of his disease: trying even to make his disease fair and attractive. Even succeeding. Which is the inevitable falseness, duplicity of art, American art in particular.[40]

At the end of November, having revised his essays on Franklin, Crèvecoeur, Hawthorne, Fenimore Cooper, Poe and Dana, with the essays on Melville and Whitman still to do, Lawrence and Mabel had a fight. It was ostensibly caused by Mabel's living too much 'from her head': even the vast, multicoloured scarf she had knitted to keep him warm throughout the winter had been 'knitted with her head' and 'willed' on to Lawrence.[41] But the final straw seems to have been when Mabel told Frieda that Lawrence was 'not physically attractive to women' and that women didn't 'want to touch him'. Frieda apparently agreed with Mabel, describing her husband as sexually 'dry', at which point in their conversation they became aware of Lawrence standing in the doorway. The next day Lawrence told Mabel that there was 'a witch's brew on this hill' and that they had been offered a ranch in the mountains, where they would decamp with two Danish artists called Knud Merrild and Kai Gøtzsche. In Mabel's version of their departure, she begged Lawrence and Frieda to stay and Frieda promised that they would pay regular visits to Taos. 'But,' Mabel decided, 'I wanted *none of that*. I did not care for what I knew would be broken, breathless visits full of errands and practical needs. No. I wanted the flow and rhythm of daily living.' She would not remain polite friends with the Lawrences: 'Unless I could have what I wanted, I wouldn't have anything. *My* will be done!' This is the only occasion in *Lorenzo in Taos* that she uses the phrase 'none of that', which Lawrence would associate with Mabel and employ in his darkest Mabel story. The last words Lawrence said to her were: 'You are like a great cat – with your green eyes. Well, I snap my fingers at you – like that!' Lawrence, the nifty mouse caught in her paws, was making his escape.[42] The day the Lawrences left, Mabel and Tony vanished off into Santa Fe. She says it was because she couldn't bear to see them go but it was presumably also to get their Salvarsan shots.

Knud Merrild and Kai Gøtzsche, touring America in their own Ford Model T, had been passing through Taos when they met Lawrence and Frieda at a dinner party in early November. Lawrence took a shine to them both, and in an attempt to persuade them to stay longer, he passed on the copy of *The Land of Poco Tiempo* that Mabel had given him. He no longer wanted it, Lawrence explained, because he hated Mabel. Mabel in turn hated the Danes, as they were generally called, and Merrild, who also hated Mabel, taunted her by parading around in the scarf she had knitted Lawrence 'with her mind'. Lawrence and Frieda suggested to the Danes that they pool their resources and winter together in Mabel's ranch on Lobo Mountain, but Mabel vetoed the idea by saying that she wanted it for her son. Lawrence, in a fury, found two cabins to rent on a ranch lower down the mountain called Del Monte, which belonged to a man called Hawk who had moved there because of his lungs.

In *A Poet and Two Painters*, his memoir of the savagely cold winter they spent on the last foothills of the Rocky Mountains, Merrild explains that he had been reluctant to throw in his lot with the Lawrences because they hardly knew one another, but that Lawrence had bullied him into it. This is almost certainly the case: as far as Lawrence was concerned, there were practical benefits to sticking with the Danes. Not only would their friendship torture Mabel, but the two men were strong and healthy and had a car. It would be impossible to survive in the Rockies without their help.

So Lawrence's ascent continued: Del Monte Ranch, sixteen miles north of Taos, was a further 2,000 feet above sea level. He had moved from a soft, brown adobe house on a desert plateau to a dilapidated shack in a Hercynian forest. The ranch was, as ever, magnificently placed, with forests and mountains behind, desert below and further mountains to the west, but Lawrence refused to admire the view because, as he repeated, America 'was hopelessly empty in its vastness of death'.[43] Before they could settle in, there was work to be done: the cabins needed fumigating, the roofs and windows needed mending, and the walls had to be plastered and painted. In order to survive, wood had to be chopped which meant felling trees, and water had to be brought from further up the mountain. When the ice became too hard to break, they made water by melting snow in a pan. To wash, they either rode seventeen miles to the hot springs in the Rio Grande, or scrubbed themselves down with snow. Lawrence, having bolted from the Abruzzi during a winter milder than this, and then having barely survived the winter rains in Sicily, was pushing on like Scott of the Antarctic. 'We have to go on, on, on,' he now wrote in his essay on *Moby Dick*, 'even if we must smash a way ahead.'[44]

We can measure the difference between the man Lawrence was in the winter of 1922 and the man he had been five years earlier by comparing the earliest version of the Melville essay, written in Zennor 1917, with the version he wrote in the Rocky Mountains. The 1917 essay, 'Herman Melville' (which had never been published), began like this:

The greatest seer, and poet of the sea, perhaps in all the modern world, is Herman Melville. His vision is wider than that of Swinburne, and more profound than that of Conrad. Melville belongs to the sea, like one of its own birds. Like a sea-bird, he seems merely to perch on the shore, he does not belong to this land.[45]

In his revision, Lawrence divided the essay itself into two, called 'Herman Melville's *Typee* and *Omoo*' and 'Herman Melville's *Moby Dick*'. 'Herman Melville's *Typee* and *Omoo*' now began like this:

The greatest seer and poet of the sea for me is Melville. His vision is more real than Swinburne's, because he doesn't personify the sea, and far sounder than Joseph Conrad's, because Melville doesn't sentimentalise the ocean and the sea's unfortunates. Snivel in a wet hanky like Lord Jim.[46]

'The greatest seer and poet of the sea *for me* is Melville': the inclusion of 'for me', removal of 'perhaps in all the world', and replacement of sea-birds by snivelling turns the passage from critical reflection to a playground brawl. The 'Mabel' version of *Studies* is a fist-fight: Lawrence against everyone else. His schoolboy taunt about sentimentalising the sea suggests that Melville is more of a man than Lord Jim, which matters because literature – like life – is about sexual strength. But Lawrence was more of a man than Melville, because the cannibalism which so 'horrified' Melville did not horrify Lawrence at all. Eating the body of another human, he said, is much the same as – indeed, 'more valid than' – taking the sacrament. 'This is thy body, which I take from thee and eat. This is thy blood, which I sip in annihilation of thee.'[47]

'At first you are put off by the style,' Lawrence continued in the essay he now began on 'Herman Melville's *Moby Dick*'. 'It reads like journalese. It seems spurious. You feel Melville is trying to put something over you', which is exactly what the critics of *Studies* said about Lawrence.[48] The power of *Moby Dick*, Lawrence noted, lies in the way in which actuality becomes symbolic, which is equally true of the power of Lawrence's life and fiction. The *Pequod*, Lawrence wrote, with its crew of Africans and Malays and Native Americans under the deranged command of a Quaker, was the symbol of America, while the whale, 'hunted, hunted, hunted by the maniacal fanaticism of our white mental consciousness', was the 'last phallic being of the white man'.[49] If Lawrence was the great white sperm whale (Mabel described his body as 'white as lard' but 'indomitable, with a will to endure as

348

ivory endures, sinewy and resilient'),[50] and Tony Lujan was Queequeg the noble savage, then the mad captain Ahab himself was none other than Mabel Dodge.

Lawrence did not reread Melville's novels before his revision: the changes he made were the result of reading Raymond Weaver's *Herman Melville: Mariner and Mystic*, published in 1921. Weaver's biography, the first on Melville to appear, instigated the resurrection of his reputation that took place in the 1920s: had Lawrence's first reflections on 'Herman Melville' been published with his other essays on classic American literature in the *English Review* of 1918, the honour of saving Melville from oblivion would have gone to him. As it is, Lawrence's defence of Melville helped to awaken America to the presence of their sleeping giant. Before Raymond Weaver all that Lawrence, or anyone else, had previously known about Melville came from the semi-autobiographical *Typee*, in which the son of a gentleman goes to sea on a whaler, is marooned on the island of Nantucket and lives for four months among cannibals, and the semi-autobiographical *Omoo* (meaning 'rover'), in which, having mutinied with his crew off the coast of Tahiti, Melville roves the island in a state of bliss. What Lawrence learned from Raymond Weaver is that, when Melville returned to Home and Mother aged twenty-five and wrote his first three books, he was a disappointed man. He had 'found Paradise', wrote Weaver, but 'even in Paradise' he felt himself 'an exile'.[51]

After the baffled reception of *Moby Dick*, published when he was thirty-two, Melville withdrew from literature and spent his last forty years in misanthropic despair. He described himself as a seed that had flowered late, rapidly reached 'the inmost leaf of the bulb' and then fallen 'to the mould'. He became what Weaver wonderfully called 'a crabbed and darkly shadowed hieroglyph' whose life amounted to 'a quenchless and essentially tragic odyssey away from home ... in search of "the unpeopled world behind the sun"'.[52] Melville's books, said Weaver, more 'volcanic in energy' than those of any other American writer, 'are a long effort towards the creation of one of the most complex, and massive, and original characters in literature: the character known in life as Herman Melville'.[53]

The artist in Melville, Lawrence now understood, 'was so *much* greater than the man', but Lawrence was equally struck by his own similarity to the man, especially now that he too had sailed the Pacific and visited Tahiti and was also living among primitive people.[54] Lawrence's new essays on Melville, which incorporate his excitement at reading the Weaver biography, therefore put up a sort of double meaning: his reflections on Melville's life serve as the latest instalment of Lawrence's own spiritual autobiography. Melville, wrote Lawrence, 'hated the world: was born hating it' and he 'hated it to the pitch of madness'. Melville went as far as he could go from the shores of civilisation, but he could not 'escape his European self'. He was 'looking for Paradise ... Paradise. He insists on it. Paradise.'

> Then why wasn't he happy along with the savages?
> Because he wasn't.
> He grizzled in secret, and wanted to escape.
> He even pined for Home and Mother, the two things he had
> run away from as fast as ships would carry him. HOME and
> MOTHER. The two things that were his damnation.[55]

'But I should not have been happy either,' Lawrence sighed. 'One's soul seems under a vacuum, in the South Seas.'[56] When Melville returned to Home and Mother, he 'found it Purgatory':

> No more Typees. No more paradises ... A mother: a gorgon.
> A home: a torture box. A wife: a thing with clay feet. Life: a sort
> of disgrace. Fame: another disgrace, being patronised by common
> snobs who just know how to read.[57]

Melville says nothing about Purgatory in either *Typee* or *Omoo*, and Lawrence said nothing about Purgatory in his 1917 essay on Melville. But the permanence of Purgatory now became his theme: 'Poor Melville! He was determined Paradise existed. So he was always in Purgatory ... Some souls are purgatorial by destiny.'[58] Why, Lawrence asked as he wrote in the freezing conditions of his snowbound mountain cabin, 'pin ourselves down on a paradisal ideal? It is only ourselves we torture.'

'There is no Paradise,' he concluded. 'Fight, fight. That is life.'[59]

Lawrence had himself been thinking of Home and Mother. In 'Spirits Summoned West', his first American poem, he called his mother's spirit to join him 'on this high American desert / With dark-wrapped Rocky Mountains motionless squatting around in a ring'.

For virgins are not exclusive of virgins
As wives are of wives;
And motherhood is jealous,
But in virginity jealousy does not enter.

Thus Lydia Lawrence became the Virgin of the Rockies.

Once the Lawrences had left Mabeltown, the fight began in earnest. Mabel's son told everyone in Taos that Lawrence and Frieda were spongers and so his mother had to turn them out, and Tony told everyone that Lawrence was 'a snake and poison and a sick man'. The reference to Lawrence's health, Mabel triumphantly recorded, 'is almost the worst he could say!'[60] Lawrence, meanwhile, spread it around that Mabel had tried to seduce him on the sun-roof of her bedroom on the day that he had begun working on the novel about her life, which *was* the worst he could say. After hearing what Lawrence was saying about her, everything became 'too much' for Mabel and she lost consciousness while putting on her shoe. When she describes this same loss of consciousness in 'The Statue of Liberty', it was after being diagnosed with venereal disease; Lawrence's own diagnosis was that, for the first time in her life, Mabel's 'will had been defeated'.[61]

He had defeated Mabel's will in a strikingly Melvillian manner. His refusal to be her scrivener while squatting in her property recalls Bartleby, that other great creation of Melville's, who lives in the scrivener's office while repeating, when asked to do any writing, that 'I would prefer not to.' 'She wants to bully me into writing a book on her,' Lawrence now told Knud Merrild. 'Never, never, in my life shall I write that book.'[62]

*A Poet and Two Painters* is not among the best of the Lawrence memoirs. The main fault is that Merrild lifts great wads of Lawrence's prose from his novels and essays, and places them in quotation marks as examples of his current 'conversation' ('To quote Lawrence,' he explains, 'is to quote his books').[63] He thus gives us the public Lawrence whose voice we know already instead of the private Lawrence whom Merrild alone knew on the foothills of the Rocky Mountains in the winter of 1922–3. There are, however, some striking moments. One is Merrild's account of how Lawrence would insist on joining the Danes for day-long excursions through deep snow to reach Lobo peak. Because he lacked their stamina, Lawrence tended to lag further and further behind and eventually sit himself down somewhere, claiming that he was not resting but watching the birds and animals. On one occasion when the Danes were bounding ahead, 'enjoying the deep forceful breathing, bringing the cold pure air into the innermost corners of our lungs', they realised that they had lost Lawrence altogether: looking back they saw him on a tree trunk, 'a mere speck in an immense sheet of white, and so alone in the vast wilderness of rugged mountains and endless sky'.[64] Frieda warned Merrild that Lawrence was not well enough for hiking on this scale but the hikes continued nonetheless. 'When I think of it now, knowing he had a weak chest, our behaviour does seem a bit cruel,' Merrild concedes, 'but we didn't know it then.' Except that they did know it then: 'We had heard somebody say that Lawrence was a sick man, but people say so many things and we merely let it pass over our heads.'[65] They preferred, in other words, to ignore what was in front of them.

Merrild describes their winter together as a happy time but what emerges is a theatre of mutual cruelty; Lawrence even described himself at one point as 'going off the stage' when he slipped into the forest at the sound of Mabel's car.[66] On another occasion, when Frieda lit her after-supper cigarette, Lawrence, hating the way she dangled her smokes from her corner of her mouth, tried to punch her in the face. But Frieda smoked in this way precisely to provoke Lawrence. Lawrence lost his mind completely when his mongrel, Bibbles (a present from Mabel), came on heat and disappeared for the night. In his memoir's central scene, Merrild describes how Lawrence burst into their cabin and found Bibbles, freshly impregnated, sitting on Gøtzsche's lap. 'So there you are you dirty, false little bitch,'[67] Lawrence roared, striking her so hard that she fell and rolled under the table. He then slithered around on his stomach in pursuit of the dog, knocking over the furniture as he did so. Because the door was open, Bibbles bolted into the snow where Lawrence first kicked her and then, picking her up, hurled her though the air. This, presumably, is how he felt when he similarly heard that H.D. was pregnant.

Those who witnessed his rages commented on how surprising it was to see a man as fragile as Lawrence combust with such berserk energy, and the scene with Bibbles is a particularly painful example of this. Lawrence's current murderous mood was the same as his murderous mood in Higher Tregerthen. He told Merrild that he would enjoy committing a murder and that his first victim would be Mabel, whose throat he would cut. But a second victim might have been Merrild himself, whose insufferable behaviour is overlooked by all readers of his memoir, including Aldous Huxley (who describes *A Poet and Two Painters* as 'the most disinterested' of all the portraits of Lawrence).[68] Lawrence, said Merrild, was itching for a fight and we can see why he might have wanted to punch this muscle-flexing, chest-thumping Prince of Denmark, who packed the corners of his voluminous lungs with mountain air while Lawrence sat depleted on a tree stump.

Merrild, with no sense of his own aggression, spends a good deal of *A Poet and Two Painters* comparing his healthy body to Lawrence's unhealthy one. Lawrence might have been the taller man but he was otherwise, gloats Merrild, 'underdeveloped, athletically speaking', with 'thin legs like the Archbishop of Canterbury'. When Lawrence (a poor swimmer) and the Danes bathe in the hot Manby springs, Merrild – who lists in a footnote to this passage that he won the Nordic championship in backstroke in 1919 and qualified for the Danish Olympic swimming team in 1920 – gives a three-page comparison of their naked bodies. Being the first to undress, he was stepping around 'shadow-boxing' while the other two struggled out of their trousers when 'a feeling of superiority, of bodily superiority, came over me'. Merrild noticed that, while he still had his summer tan, Lawrence and Gøtzsche were white as a 'sprout of a potato in a darkroom or a tapeworm'.[69] As they swam, Merrild recalled the wrestling scene between Gerald and Birkin and wondered whether the rumours about Lawrence's sexuality were true: but 'happily', he realised, Lawrence was neither a 'hermaphrodite' nor 'the pervert he was accused of being'.[70] Few writers have been paraded naked oftener than Lawrence, who revealed no homoerotic feelings for either of the Danes, on whom he depended to buy the provisions, drive the car, chop the wood, break the ice, carry the water and mend the leaks in the roof.

The year 1923 saw the publication in America of four books by Lawrence in four different genres – *The Ladybird, Studies in Classic American Literature, Birds, Beasts and Flowers* and *Kangaroo*. The year also began with two major losses. The first was Katherine Mansfield, who died of tuberculosis in the Gurdjieff Institute in Fontainebleau. Lawrence described the Institute as 'a rotten, false, self-conscious place of people playing a sickly stunt', but he would not admit the cause of her death.[71]

The second loss was Mountsier, also associated with Higher Tregerthen and whom, Lawrence decided, he no longer liked. 'I wish now to break the connection between you and me,' he told his friend and agent.[72] And just like that, Mountsier – Lawrence's champion through the darkest of days, who paved the way for him to come to America – was directed off the stage. 'Mountsier didn't believe in me,' Lawrence told Seltzer, his American publisher, 'he was against me inwardly ... It has been ugly. First Mabel Sterne, then him.'[73] To Murry, Lawrence sent his condolences on the death of his wife. 'Feel as if old moorings were breaking all. It has been a savage enough pilgrimage these last four years.'[74]

Their six-month visas were due to expire in March, so the Lawrences planned, in time-honoured fashion, to slip over the border to Mexico. Mabel had initially suggested that she come with them, but Lawrence ruled it out: 'I don't feel angry,' he wrote in the briefest of possible letters. 'I just want to be alone.'[75] But he didn't want to be alone, as Mabel well knew, because he invited her friends Witter Bynner and Spud Johnson to join them, and Mabel would later punish Bynner for his disloyalty by appropriating Spud for herself. Lawrence and Frieda were now never able to be alone: he needed an audience for their fights and she needed witnesses. 'Lawrence was theatre,' said Bynner, 'and Frieda was life.'[76]

The Bynners, as the Lawrences called them, were a striking pair, and it is equally striking that Lawrence was now, after his days in Florence, comfortable around homosexual men. Witter Bynner, aged forty-one, had met Spud, now twenty-seven, when he taught him in a poetry course at UCLA. With three other students, Spud then founded the countercultural journal *Laughing Horse*, which he ran from Bynner's house in Santa Fe, where he lived as his 'secretary'. In addition to being one of the 'steaming shits' of the literary scene, Bynner was a six-foot-tall Harvard graduate, and his memoir of Lawrence in Mexico, *Journey with Genius*, written twenty-eight years after the journey itself, is a well-marinated character-assassination by a writer denied the status of genius himself. Like everyone else, Witter Bynner avenged himself on Lawrence by jeering at his body: 'bony, pinched, pigeon-breasted, clay-white'. Lawrence, said Bynner, 'could seldom have seen a body weaker than his own', which is why the writer shadow-boxed with 'the muscles of his mind'.[77]

They crossed into the Mexican desert at the El Paso border, and travelled the 1,200 miles to Mexico City by Pullman. Lawrence loathed the intimacy of passengers lying in their berths behind heavy green curtains, but he loved raising the blind when the lights went out and feeling the train chuffing and shunting down the wild slopes. Arriving in the capital on 23 March, they booked into a small Italian hotel by the public square on the Avenida Uruguay, where they ate minestrone soup and drank Chianti. Mexico, Lawrence thought, was more like southern Italy than America; it was another noisy, colourful, careless country with collapsing buildings and soldiers everywhere. The two places had long been linked in his imagination: it was in Italy that 'a lake-city, like Mexico',[78] had come to Aaron in the dream described at the end of *Aaron's Rod*, where he found himself hanging over the side of a boat in an underground expanse of dark blue water.

Mexico City, no longer on a lake, was on the edge of exploding. The thirty years of revolution which began in 1910 would kill 2 million citizens, and when Lawrence arrived there were soldiers riding on the roofs of cars, random shootings and the possibility of strikes at any moment. Lawrence's mood, said Bynner, was equally incendiary. Once he began ranting about the failings of Mexico he would continue for hours; the country's insurrections were, for Lawrence, a personal attack. But the immediate difference between America and Mexico, Lawrence wrote in 'Au Revoir, USA', was that the former put a 'strain on the nerves' and the latter put 'a strain on the temper'.[79]

Having done an immense amount of preparatory reading (Mexico, Mabel noted sourly, had 'some written "history"', while 'New Mexico had none'),[80] Lawrence was alive to the current political scene. The revolutionary fervour he had imagined in *Kangaroo* was all too real here. In 1911, after thirty-five years of dictatorship, Porfirio Díaz was overthrown in a coup and fled to France. One of his atrocities, Lawrence reported to Bynner, was to summon the strikers to a meeting to address their grievances, then lock them inside the building and set it on fire. The history of Mexico was one of endless, wholesale cruelty: the Mesoamericans, the Spanish, the Aztecs, Porfirio Díaz, all ruled by fear. It was an unbreakable cycle: Mexico was the land of death. Díaz was replaced by Francisco Madero who, unable to resolve the conflict between the Bolshevists, the nationalists and the conservatives, was murdered in 1913 by his trusted general, Victoriano Huerta. Huerta's own reign of terror lasted until 1914 when another coup forced him too into exile. Mexico was then controlled by warring factions until the Constitution of 1917, which expressed the ideals of the Revolution: land reform, ownership of the means of production, the banishment of foreign priests. The election of the revolutionary Venustiano Carranza in March 1917 then resulted in open war, and Carranza was murdered in 1920 when he was on the run with the state treasure. For the remainder of Carranza's four-year term, the presidency was held by Adolfo de la Huerta who was replaced, in the September 1920 elections, by Álvaro Obregón. When Lawrence arrived in Mexico, Obregón was nearing the end of his term and the question of who was to succeed him was causing further disturbance, with a rebellion led by de la Huerta gathering headway. So Lawrence's stay coincided with the first serious attempts to return the land to the people, get rid of the Catholic Church (the process described by Graham Greene as 'the fiercest persecution of religion anywhere since the reign of Elizabeth') and involve Mexican Indians in national life.

During Holy Week, when the Catholics 'grovelled' into the churches on their knees, their arms outstretched like penitents, the Lawrences and the Bynners saw the 44-minute feature film *La Vie et la Passion du Christ*, and Lawrence left the cinema feeling depressed by the grip of the Church.[81] The following day they went to a bullfight and saw a great white bull, taunted to the edge of his nerves, disembowel the matador's horse, and Lawrence left the ring before the fight was over. They then went to the National Museum where Lawrence found the Aztec carvings 'gruesome', 'ghastly' and 'sub-cruel'.[82] His letters uniformly announce that he will now be returning to England.

Two days later they visited the Mesoamerican city of Teotihuacan (the Aztec word for 'Place where the gods dwell'), thirty miles north of Mexico City. Once covering an area of thirty-two square miles, Teotihuacan was the world's largest theocracy: the building of the great pyramids of the Sun and the Moon began centuries before the birth of Christ, and 200,000 people were settled here before the city was destroyed by fire around AD 800. When the Aztecs discovered, and named, Teotihuacan it was a ruin and when Lawrence came here it was an archaeological site. Four years earlier, the snarling heads of feathered serpents had been uncovered on the outer walls of the Temple

D. H. Lawrence, Witter Bynner and Frieda Lawrence at the Pyramid of the Sun, Teotihuacan

of Quetzalcoatl, a six-layered pyramid which stands at the far end of the Avenue of the Dead. 'Quetzal' means bird and 'coatl' means snake: the god Quetzalcoatl was a plumed serpent. The walls of the pyramid had once been blue and the serpent's eyes had been black obsidian glass which glimmered in the candlelight. Beneath the great plumed heads were carvings of enormous snakes and delicate fish and shells: Quetzalcoatl belongs to the earth but comes from the water. His presence on the temple wall is as threatening as that of Cerberus at the gates of Hades, and Lawrence, whose pantheon of symbols also included birds and snakes, found in Quetzalcoatl the god he had been looking for. At least in Mexico, he said, the gods still 'bit' and their 'fangs are still obvious': America might flow with the 'same old dragon's blood', but the gods there 'have had their teeth pulled'. Mexican civilisation, Lawrence decided, 'never got any higher than Quetzalcoatl'.[83]

*Terry's Guide to Mexico*, on which Lawrence depended, gave a brief account of the history of Quetzalcoatl. God of the air and the earth, Quetzalcoatl – whose name Lawrence loved – means 'twin'. His complex mythological life included a period where he took the form of a bearded white man who ruled over a prosperous and happy country,

357

but then he angered a god and was exiled, sailing away on a skiff made of serpent skins. It was the Aztec conviction that he would one day return which ensured the success of the Spanish invasion in 1519: believing that Hernán Cortés was the incarnation of Quetzalcoatl, Montezuma handed the conquistador his empire and its gold. In the Zennor version of *Studies in Classic American Literature*, Lawrence considered the fatal Aztec prophecy about the return of Quetzalcoatl: they knew, he then wrote, through 'vibrations in the ether', that the legend describing the coming of bearded white strangers was 'a fact'.[84] It was now Lawrence who wanted Quetzalcoatl to return; the plumed serpent would preoccupy him for the next two years.

The word from Taos that April was that Mabel and Tony had got married. 'I hear Mabel married Tony,' Lawrence wrote to Mabel's friend Nina Witt. 'Why?'[85] The reasons were sound enough: the scandal of their relationship was damaging John Collier's campaign for Indian land rights, and inspectors from the Department of Interior regarded Mabeltown as 'the centre of disturbance'. Officially, Mabel was marrying Tony to help Collier with his work; unofficially, she wanted as little gossip as possible about her private life given her current health problems. Lawrence was disturbed by Mabel's news and told her so; later, by way of apology, he said that 'I would never venture *seriously* to judge', and he battled with the honesty of this self-assessment.[86] Frieda voiced their joint opinion when she wrote to Mabel's friend Bessie Freeman, 'Your world must have come tumbling about your ears, your whole world, when you heard that Mabel had married Tony', which recalls Mr May's reaction, in *The Lost Girl*, on hearing that Alvina Houghton was running away with the Natcha-Kee-Tawaras ('"Really!" Mr. May seemed smitten quite dumb. "I feel as if the world had suddenly come to an end"').[87] 'In my *head*,' Frieda continued to Bessie Freeman, 'I say: why not, but somewhere else it's *so* impossible.'[88]

The only guests at Mabel's wedding were the artist Andrew Dasburg and the actress Ida Rauh, but the story nonetheless made the news: 'Why Bohemia's Queen Married an Indian Chief' ran the headline in the *Ogden Standard-Examiner*. A Pittsburgh newspaper told its readers that Mabel Dodge Luhan (she changed the spelling of Lujan when she adopted her husband's name) was tired of the 'sophistications of New York and the European capitals' and 'soothed' by the 'primitive simplicity in which the Red Man lived'. Miscegenation between white

Americans and black Americans was a felony in some states, but by marrying Native Americans, white Americans believed they could absorb, and thus erase, the indigenous population: 'let our settlements and theirs meet and blend together,' proclaimed Thomas Jefferson, 'to intermix, and become one people'. Mabel turned the equation around: by intermixing and becoming one people, the Native American could absorb and erase the savage white man. 'The Indians will save our race,' she said in an interview with the *Denver Post*. 'A wealth of artistic sentiment will be blended in the new blood infusion with the white race.'[89] Mabel was breaking through to the America of the future.

Lawrence, meanwhile, was thinking about the future of the novel. Before leaving Del Monte Ranch, having consolidated in *Studies* his thoughts on the double consciousness of classic American literature, he dashed off an article called 'Surgery for the Novel – or a Bomb'. The modern novel, he now argued, had to grow up: '"Did I feel a twinge in my little toe, or didn't I?" asks every character in Mr Joyce or Miss Richardson or M. Proust.' The serious novel has to be convulsed out of these 'purely emotional and self-analytical stunts'. Time was, philosophy and fiction had been inseparable: 'they used to be one, right from the days of myth. Then they went and parted, like a nagging married couple', at which point 'the novel went sloppy, and philosophy went abstract dry'. The future of the novel lay in resurrecting this mixed marriage: only then could the one bright book of life 'present us with new, really new feelings'. The 'poor old novel', Lawrence diagnosed, has 'either got to get over the wall, or knock a hole through it'.[90]

Now that he was freed from Mabel, Lawrence was able to write the novel of the future about the future of America, but Mexico proved as uncongenial as Taos. 'I should never be able to write on this continent,' he complained, 'something in the spirit opposes one's going forth.'[91] So at the end of April he left Frieda with the Bynners in Mexico City and took an overnight train to Lake Chapala, 300 miles north-west in the state of Jalisco, arriving at a desert-like station in Ocotlán in the 'full dazzling gold of a Mexican morning'. The town was noiseless and the streets empty, with broken cobbles and smashed pavements: 'the stones seemed dead, the town seemed made of dead stone. The human life came with a slow, sterile unwillingness, in spite of the low-hung power of the sun.' To reach his lakeside hotel he went by boat, down the 'pale buff river' into the vast open lake, the largest in Mexico. It was heavenly on the water, where the 'aboriginal, empty silence' was like 'life *withheld*'.[92]

In the days before the Revolution, Lake Chapala – an onomatopoeic translation of the sound made by waves lapping on the shore – had been the Mexican Riviera. The haciendas were now, like everything else in Mexico, broken, but the warm climate brought songbirds, hummingbirds, snow geese, sandpipers, coots, scores of pelicans, pintails, widgeons, wildfowl, ravens and cockatoos to the water. In the village of Chapala itself, Lawrence found a cool dark house by the lake on the Calle Zaragoza whose rooms opened on to a shady verandah. This was a place where he could write, so he sent a telegram to Frieda: 'Chapala paradise. Take evening train.'[93]

Back in Mexico City, Frieda confided in the Bynners about the state of her marriage and explained why she stayed with Lawrence. The Bynners had of course witnessed the fights: there was one in particular that Bynner described in *Journey with Genius*. Enjoying her after-dinner smoke, Frieda's cigarette 'began to slant downward in the left corner of her mouth'. Lawrence's eyes lit up, he 'jerked' to his feet and 'blared' at her to 'Take that thing out … Take it out, I say, you sniffing bitch. There you sit, with that thing in your mouth and your legs open to every man in the room! And you wonder why no decent woman in England will have anything to do with you.'[94] Throwing his wine in her face, he left the room. Bynner thought he saw a tear in Frieda's eye, but it was only cigarette fume. Their smoking number was the best-rehearsed act of the Lawrence roadshow.

Because he was ill, Frieda explained to the Bynners, it angered Lawrence that she was well. She was unable to leave him because she had nowhere to go, but she wouldn't leave Lawrence anyway. And he would be happy as soon as he was writing again. Bynner wrote in his notebook that Lawrence was a man with nothing at his core but hatred. 'With the tongue of a singing serpent, he searches for Edens. And in all the lost gardens he finds on the way, he adds to the damage already done.'[95]

It had become Lawrence's habit to produce a novel in the summer months. The previous June he had written *Kangaroo* by the Pacific Ocean, the summer before he had finished *Aaron's Rod* in the forest of Baden-Baden, and the summer before that he had written *The Lost Girl* in the garden of the Fontana Vecchia. 'Quetzalcoatl', as Lawrence called his new book, was penned beneath a pepper tree on the shores of Lake Chapala. Frieda swam while he wrote, the women washed their clothes, the pelicans glided in their single stately body and the fishermen in their dugouts floated silently by.

'Quetzalcoatl', like *Kangaroo*, is a leadership novel but it is closer to the consciousness of *The Lost Girl* because Lawrence returns here to the idea of marriage as female sacrifice. He also, for the first time, confronts what it means to 'go back' into the not-quite-dead past. In 'America, Listen to Your Own', Lawrence had called on America's writers to 'catch the spirit of your own dark, aboriginal continent' and embrace the 'black Demon' at the heart of the country.[96] The black Demon of Mexico was now Lawrence's new subject: 'Quetzalcoatl', he told Seltzer, was his 'real novel of America'.[97]

The novel opens in Holy Week, with a young widow called Kate Burns walking out of a bullfight in Mexico City because a magnificent bull has disembowelled a horse. She meets a soldier called Cipriano, who looks Italian but is in fact 'pure Indian' and speaks 'English English' because he was educated at Oxford. Cipriano introduces Kate to his handsome friend, Ramón Carrasco, who is Spanish and studied Philosophy at Harvard. Ramón is the leader, and Cipriano the follower; their bond is compared to Jonathan and David.

Kate then reads in the newspaper about a strange event on Lake Chapala: women drying their washing on the shore reported seeing a naked man wade out of the water towards them. The man explained that he has come from talking to Quetzalcoatl, who lives beneath the lake and is preparing his return. Leaving Mexico City, Kate goes to Chapala herself where she remeets Ramón, who has a house by the water and starts a religious revolution by posing as the returned Quetzalcoatl with Cipriano, his deputy, as the reincarnation of Huitzilopochtli, Aztec god of war. At Cipriano's investiture as Huitzilopochtli, one man is decapitated in his honour, and five others are shot: the bodies of all six sacrifices are placed before Cipriano/Quetzalcoatl, seated on his throne.

Kate is appalled by the violence of Ramón's revolution but she understands the need to reclaim the ancient soul of the people. The Mexicans need a leader, and no man has yet proved strong enough. Ramón's vision is neither communist nor fascist but patriarchal; he wants to 'establish a system something like the old Indian village system, with a war chief, and a cacique, and a peace chief'.[98] Because the gods demand that Huitzilopochtli take a wife, Cipriano asks Kate to marry him. It is not love, he insists, but destiny. 'I am the living Huitzilopochtli,' he explains. 'It's a hard name to remember,' she replies. Rejecting Cipriano's proposal she decides to go home to her mother. The lake now becomes a kind of pasture: she sees a black and white cow being shoved into the dark belly of a boat and a bull stepping delicately up the same gangplank, a roan horse prancing along the shore and four mules looking like dark sea-horses. Yellow and white calves are 'skipping, butting their rear ends, lifting their tails, and tripping side by side to the water to drink', and a mother ass tethered to a tree tends to her newborn foal. Kate laughs with delight as the foal takes his first tentative steps, rocking on 'four loose legs' thin as hairpins. The world is being reborn. The novel ends with Kate returning to her bedroom where she tries to get on with her packing.[99]

'No,' Lawrence snapped at Mountsier, 'my new novel has nothing whatever to do with Mabel, nor with Taos, nor with the United States at all.'[100] In one sense this is true. Kate Burns is Lawrence's fantasy of Frieda after his death: brave, grief-stricken and utterly loyal to his memory when a more masculine man comes along. Frieda's future as a widow would become a preoccupation of Lawrence's writing. But Kate's complexities *as a character* have everything to do with Mabel and with Taos. Kate Burns, like Mabel, is a dynamo from whom revolutionary men draw their energy. She is fierce and opinionated with an ambivalence about her independence that reflects Mabel's own. Chapala under the rule of Ramón and Cipriano, where it is all Quetzalcoatl Quetzalcoatl Quetzalcoatl!! the Gods! the Gods! the Gods!, is a satire of Mabeltown, where it had been all Bursum Bursum Bursum!! the Bill! the Bill! the Bill! 'Quetzalcoatl' is in many ways a continuation of the novel that Mabel had wanted Lawrence to write using '*my* experience, *my* material', but it wasn't the tale she wanted him to tell. The bull-like, goddess-like Sybil Mond is now the bull-like, goddess-like Kate Burns, who finds herself involved with a 'pure-blooded' Indian who might be Tony Lujan, and a white political activist who might be John Collier. Kate's marriage to the Indian is essential to their cause, which is to return the land and customs to the native people. But in Lawrence's version of the story, the white woman refuses to be a pawn in a political deal. It is remarkable, considering how badly he was getting on with Frieda, how angry he was with Mabel and how tediously monological he would become about the need for women to submit to the natural leadership of those few remaining men who were male enough to be natural leaders, that Lawrence now wrote a novel in which the heroine is a noble and sympathetic feminist who turns down the offer of marriage to a god.

Lawrence said that he liked this new novel 'best of all', but despite giving the manuscript to Thomas Seltzer to be typed up, he did not, he repeated, consider 'Quetzalcoatl' finished. It reads however like a finished work: it has a solid base, a strong forward movement and a pleasing symmetry: beginning with an angry bull disembowelling a horse in a filthy arena, it ends with a roan horse prancing along the shore and a happy bull sailing away on mystical blue waters. With its image of the Ark, the final page recalls that of *The Rainbow*. 'Quezalcoatl' is also an inversion of *The Lost Girl*: while *The Lost Girl* closes with Alvina wondering if her Italian husband, who masquerades as a Native American, will ever return from the war and take her to America, 'Quetzalcoatl' ends with Kate Burns refusing marriage to a Mexican Indian who looks Italian but masquerades as the Aztec god of war. Lawrence's novels tend to close on a journey about to commence, but when Kate tries to get on with her packing, the reader feels that there is nothing more to say: she came in search of Paradise and found a garden on the lake. It is evidently a completed work, so why did Lawrence delay publication?

His problem with 'Quetzalcoatl' lay in the marriage plot. Should Kate have crossed the barrier between Cipriano and herself? It is this, rather than Cipriano's impersonation of Huitzilopochtli, that causes her sleepless nights. On one occasion, as she watches Cipriano swimming in the lake, Kate sees that his skin is not black but 'red', and 'would it be true for her to marry that red man there out in the water?'

> There was a gulf between him and her, the gulf of race, of colour,
> of different aeons of time. He wanted to force a way across the gulf.
> But that would only mean a mutual destruction.[101]

Should she turn away from her own kind? Herein lay the chaos of Lawrence's personal philosophy. For Mabel, miscegenation was the future but for Lawrence it was another kind of 'going back', and however much we yearn to return to the past we 'can't go back'. But

Lawrence also believed in the vitality of difference, and marriage as the home of opposition. So what prevented him from marrying Kate to her 'pure-blooded Indian'?

After he had written the last words of 'Quetzalcoatl', Lawrence and Frieda finished their packing and caught the train back to America. Crossing into Texas at the Laredo frontier, they continued to New York where he deposited the manuscript with Thomas Seltzer and booked a passage to England for 18 August. Frieda was also returning to Home and Mother; she wanted first to see her children in London and then to go on to Baden-Baden. But, at the last minute, Lawrence changed his mind about joining her. His readiness, over recent months, to return to England had depended to a large degree on his health: 'When I feel sick I want to go back,' he told the Danes. 'When I feel well I want to stay.'[102] He was currently feeling well but he also, he explained to his mother-in-law, had another Balaam's ass in his belly. The Balaam's ass that preventing him from coming to America now prevented him from leaving.

When they parted on the pier in Manhattan, Lawrence and Frieda had a fight which was so severe that Frieda assumed, as her ship sailed away, that their marriage was finished. And in a sense it was: 'He can go to blazes,' she wrote in a letter from her cabin, 'I've had enough.'[103] Neither says what the fight was about, but Lawrence presumably behaved outrageously and something broke in Frieda. Meanwhile, Lawrence wrote blithely to Murry, now a widower, asking him to look after his wife. Murry performed his duty with such assiduity that Frieda suggested they go to bed together, the thought of which, Murry wrote in his journal, 'was heaven on earth', but out of consideration for Lawrence he turned her down. 'It drove me crazy – really crazy, I think,' Murry later told Frieda, '– wanting you so badly.'[104]

His desire for Frieda coincided for Murry with his renewed regard for Lawrence. Having panned *Women in Love* in his review of the novel, Murry liked where Lawrence was going in *Aaron's Rod* and *Fantasia of the Unconscious*. '*Fantasia* was more than a book,' he wrote in *Reminiscences of D. H. Lawrence*, 'it was a message to me.' Murry was now, as he put it, 'Lawrence's man: he should lead and I would follow'. Reading *Fantasia* had been a mystical experience: it 'explained' Murry's own 'strange life' and it 'explained' Lawrence himself.[105] It also explained why Murry now wanted, and resisted, Lawrence's wife: Frieda was the conduit between the two men.

To serve Lawrence's cause, Murry had recently established a new journal called the *Adelphi* whose purpose was to spread 'the faith' that Lawrence proclaimed: 'life is important'. What Murry understood by 'life' was the reintegration of mind and body: this is what the *Adelphi* would preach in order to regenerate post-war England. 'I would prepare the place for him,' Murry said of Lawrence. 'I waited eagerly for his coming.'[106] The first issue of the *Adelphi*, in June 1923, contained a central chapter from *Fantasia*; two further excerpts from the book appeared in the July and September issues. If Lawrence was serious about saving mankind, Murry would argue, his work lay not in chopping wood in the Rocky Mountains but in editing the *Adelphi*. He was luring Lawrence back from Paradise so that the crops might once more grow and the birds sing.

Lawrence's own plan was to return to Mexico. Before crossing the border, however, he did something which seems on the surface to be utterly bizarre but on closer inspection to make perfect sense: he went to Mabel's home and met her white-haired mother.

Immediately after the fight on the pier, Lawrence received a letter from Mabel's friend Bessie Freeman – whom he had met in Taos – inviting him to Buffalo. As with all things relating to Mabel, the timing could not have been more serendipitous. 'I should like to stay a night in your Buffalo,' Lawrence replied, adding that it was 'the Buffalo also of Mabel'. He ended up spending four nights.[107]

Mabel's Buffalo was known as the Electric City of the Future because it was illuminated by hydroelectricity generated by the Niagara Falls. Lawrence liked this bourgeois, industrial town: Buffalo, he said, was like Manchester or Nottingham 'sixty years ago' and he found here 'a genuine nice feeling'.[108] Mabel's mother, Sara Ganson, had moved out of town to a place called Lewiston on the Niagara River, where Lawrence was invited for lunch. If Sara was cold and evil, Lawrence didn't notice; what he saw was a blue-blooded hostess, tolerant and sensible in her old age, enjoying devilled kidneys for breakfast. This was the real old America.

Back in Taos, Mabel knew that Lawrence and Frieda were on different sides of the Atlantic: she knew it because of the gossip, and she 'knew it out of the air'. She also knew that Lawrence had gone to the trouble of meeting her mother. No sooner was he free of Frieda, Mabel wrote triumphantly in *Lorenzo in Taos*, than 'Lawrence turned and went to

Buffalo!' She saw it as a victory, and rightly so: Lawrence later told Mabel that having stepped into her past he now knew who she really was: 'Life made you what you are: I understood so much when I was in Buffalo and saw your mother.'[109]

When *Studies in Classic American Literature* was published on 27 August 1923, Lawrence was back in Los Angeles with the Danes. He then returned to Mexico with Kai Gøtzsche: Merrild, sated by Lawrence, stayed behind. Lawrence retraced his former journey, taking Gøtzsche back to Guadalajara, Lake Chapala and Mexico City. In Taos, Mabel – rumoured to be divorcing Tony – was now spreading it about that Lawrence had a vendetta against her. As for the 'vendetta', Lawrence wrote to Bessie Freeman on 16 September, 'I'm ready.' But then Mabel herself wrote to Lawrence, begging his forgiveness. He called it her 'Peccavi, peccavi, c'est ma faute letter'[110] and replied that he hoped the gossip about her divorce was unfounded. Her marriage to Tony, he now believed, 'may even yet be the rounding of a great curve', which shows how his thoughts had progressed since 'Quetzalcoatl'.[111] Mabel then, in an act of penitential abjection, offered Lawrence her soul if he would only return to Taos. 'I submitted my will to him,' she wrote, recalling the time she asked John Parmenter to give her his gonorrhoea. 'I luxuriated in submission, for a change.'[112] And Lawrence, accepting without question their new dynamic, replied that he would 'take your submission: when you are ready'.[113]

Lawrence's letters to Mabel in the autumn of 1923 are power-crazed and sexually suggestive. He asks her to give up the messianic mission she shares with John Collier in order to join his own messianic mission. 'Don't trouble about the Indians,' he wrote from Guadalajara on 8 November.

> You can't 'save' them: and politics, no matter *what* politics, will only destroy them. I have said many times that you would destroy the Indians. In your lust even for a Saviour's power, you would just destroy them. The same with Collier. He will destroy them. It is his saviour's will to set the claws of his own White egoistic *benevolent* volition into them. Somewhere, the Indians know that you and Collier would, with your salvationist but poisonous white consciousness, destroy them.[114]

Without Frieda to keep him in check, Lawrence's megalomania and paranoia took hold. Later that month, Frieda – instructed by Murry – sent a telegram instructing her husband to 'come', and Lawrence informed Mabel on 20 November that he was sailing to England in the morning. Whatever happened between himself and Frieda – and neither yet knew if they had any kind of future – he and Mabel, Lawrence said, were 'to keep an invisible thread' between them. She was to be his handmaiden as he went forth, the 'serpent of the sun'.[115]

He boarded a ship at Veracruz which drew into the Plymouth Sound on 11 December: thus began what Murry called 'the whole strange episode of Lawrence's return to England in 1923–1924'.[116] It had been four years since he had left Dover on that bleak November morning, and watched from the deck 'the death-grey coast of Kent go out'. His first impression on returning to his native land, Lawrence wrote in an incendiary little essay called 'On Coming Home', was of 'a dead muffled sense of stillness' as though everything were 'sand-bagged'. He was once again locked inside English tightness: tight manners, tight snobbery, tight wet sunshine, tight fields inside tight hedges, tight train carriages, tight faces too tightly close to his own: 'one would like to smash something'. England was a civilisation of small things: kippers, bacon, porridge, spoonfuls of sugar; the self-deprecating manners of the dining car where each man pretends to be 'grander' than he is. There was 'not a man left in all the millions of pairs of trousers. Not a man left.'[117]

His reception party at Waterloo consisted of Murry, Kot and Frieda. Murry said that Lawrence looked 'greenish', but this will be because Lawrence suspected, from the 'chumminess' between them, that his friend was now sleeping with his wife.[118] Plus he knew that he had made a mistake in coming back for Frieda: the mountain should have come to Mohammed. 'I can't bear it,' Lawrence said five minutes after seeing her again.

Frieda had taken rooms in Hampstead, and in the cab across London Lawrence explained his vision of the *Adelphi*, which Murry wanted him to edit. The point of the journal, he insisted, was not to regenerate the country but to 'attack everything, everything; and explode in one blaze of denunciation'.[119] Accordingly, Lawrence submitted 'On Coming Home' which Murry refused to publish because it would 'only make enemies'. 'As if that weren't what I want,' Lawrence replied.[120] The visionary voice of *Fantasia* had vanished: Lawrence had returned to England as the God of War.

He and Frieda stayed in a flat in 110 Heath Street, a vertical climb further up the hill from Well Walk and upstairs from Catherine and Donald Carswell. Hampstead was preparing for Christmas; holly wreaths hung on door knockers and pyramids of oranges glimmered in greengrocers' windows. The days, so bright in New Mexico, were now reduced to the 'dull, heavy, mortified half-light' of an English winter.[121] Down the hill, on Pond Street, Murry was living in a flat above the Russian mosaicist Boris Anrep, with his friend Dorothy Brett in the little Queen Anne house next door. Although Brett barely knew Lawrence – they had met briefly during the war – she was excited by his return. And because she now attached her life to his, we need to see Brett as Lawrence saw her.

Brett, Lawrence told Mabel, is 'deaf, forty, very nice, and daughter of Viscount Esher'.[122] As with Frieda, he never tired of rehearsing Brett's family connections, but equally important to Lawrence was her virginity, and Dorothy Brett was to D. H. Lawrence as Dorothy Wordsworth was to her brother, William. On the one hand, she can be seen as a female sacrifice, part of the worshipful company of women who now made his writing possible, and the other hand, Brett was liberated by Lawrence, who airlifted her out of a dead-end existence. A shy spinster with rabbity teeth, eyes round as marbles, a shocked expression and a weak chin, Brett had, in Lawrence's imagination, no notion of sexual pleasure. Her glamorous and powerful father had been in Queen Victoria's inner circle, and Brett was raised in a newly built mock-Tudor mansion near Windsor Castle where she and her sister Sylvia had shared dancing classes with Princess Beatrice's children, watched over by the Queen. Brett later attended the funeral of Victoria and the coronation of Edward VII, but her formative experience of the mystique of power was when she was taken, aged four, to see Buffalo Bill's Wild West Show at Earl's Court and felt a connection between herself and Chief Sitting Bull. She was later allowed to learn the drums, which suggests a degree of unconventionality on her parents' part. With their brothers away at Eton, Brett and Sylvia shared a lonely childhood in the nurseries of several enormous houses where they were beaten by their drunken nanny, kept in ignorance of the wider world and paraded on the marriage market without yet knowing why their pet rats had babies.

As a debutante Brett went to the state balls where it was assumed, being the daughter of the intelligent, witty and brilliant Viscount Esher, that she too would be 'intelligent, witty and brilliant', but 'I was shy, dumb and shrinking'.[123] Aged eighteen she nearly died after her appendix burst and during a long convalescence fell in love with her kind young doctor. She later wondered if her increasing deafness was a way of not hearing the cruel jibes of her father and brothers, but if she willed it on as a means of escape, Brett's silent world soon became what she called her prison sentence. As well as her ear-trumpet she had a Marconi listening machine that she carried in a suitcase, for which she wore headphones like a radio operator. This cumbersome equipment, plus the need for snippets of conversation to be repeatedly yelled back to her, made Brett an object of condescension and comedy. In whatever circle she moved – Windsor or Garsington – she was considered the bore. Because deafness is regarded as a social inconvenience to those who have full hearing, no one among Brett's family or friends, apart from Ottoline Morrell, is known to have shown anything other than irritation with her disability. 'If it were not for my painting,' Brett wrote to Bertrand Russell in 1918, 'I would end it all … I am just the shadow of a human being.'[124] According to her mother, Brett failed on the marriage market, but Brett's version would be that she managed to get out in one piece. She responded with ferocity to any man who came near her, and found a retreat from small talk, we can imagine, in fiddling with the dials of her Marconi.

'On or about December 1910,' Virginia Woolf calculated, 'human character changed.'[125] This was the year that Roger Fry introduced the English to Van Gogh, Gauguin and Cézanne in his 'Manet and the Post-Impressionists' exhibition at the Grafton Galleries, and also the year that Brett, aged twenty-seven, left home to study at London's Slade School of Art. She now met Augustus John and Mark Gertler, renamed herself Brett (her friend Dora Carrington was similarly known as Carrington), cut her hair, embarked on her lifelong habit of wearing corduroy breeches and began a chaste romance with her professor. The following year her brother Maurice married the musical comedy actress Zena Dare, and her sister, Sylvia, married Sir Charles Vyner de Windt Brooke, the last of the White Rajahs who had ruled the Kingdom of

Sarawak, in north-western Borneo, since 1846. Sarawak, the size of England, had its own currency, flag and postage stamps and from now on 'Ranee' Sylvia wore a sarong. Because she revelled in the savagery and romance of her subjects, which included the head-hunting Dayak people, Sylvia was known as 'Queen of the Head-hunters'.

This much Lawrence knew. What he will have discovered later, when Brett became his disciple, are those things she confided to her unpublished memoirs, *My Long and Beautiful Journey*. As a sheltered fourteen-year-old, still playing with dolls and making up imaginary worlds, a friend of her father's called Lord Harcourt placed her hand on his 'burning' penis; she tried to run but 'was not quick enough. He was on me, he caught hold of me from behind and held me in a grip of iron, and began kissing the back of my neck.'[126] The experience left Brett terrified of men: aged twenty-eight, she repeatedly kicked a man who tried to kiss her under the mistletoe. Her sister Sylvia, aged twelve, had been assaulted by their father's secretary, which experience made her horrified of the male sex too. Viscount Esher, meanwhile, was attractive to women but attracted to men: Brett described her father as 'ambidextrous'. He filled his household staff with boys and explained to his daughters that 'the only thing in life is not to be found out'.[127] Brett was similarly ambidextrous: following the crush on her doctor, she fell in love with Sylvia's mother-in-law and then transferred her swain-like devotion to Ottoline Morrell, to whom she wrote daily letters: 'I love you so much that I turn to stone or else babble weakly.'[128] Ottoline described Brett as squirrel-like and highly nervous, with, she believed, that peculiar capacity that deaf people have for knowing exactly what you are thinking.

A father with an unspeakable secret, a distant mother, a mystical experience with a Native American, a childhood trauma leading to a horror of sex, an infatuation with her doctor, an early desire for women, a tendency to love obsessively, suicidal depressions, the need to inhabit a radically different world from that of her family – it is striking how similar Brett's formative experiences were to those of Mabel, as if there were only one story available for upper-class Edwardian girls.

It was winter and so Lawrence's lungs were suffering: Catherine Carswell accepted his self-diagnosis as 'a mild attack of malaria'.[129] His London life, he told the Danes, was 'gloom – yellow air – bad cold – bed – old house – Morris wall-paper – visitors – English voices – tea in old cups – poor D.H.L., perfectly miserable, as if he was in his tomb'.[130] Writing to Mabel he said that 'I don't belong over here any more. It's like being among the dead of one's previous existence',[131] which description recalls the short story by Henry James, 'The Jolly Corner', in which Spencer Brydon returns to New York after thirty years in London and confronts the ghost of the man he would have been had he not left.

The Café Royal on Regent Street was the headquarters of 'literairy' London, and in this sense a surprising location for Lawrence to host his first and only party, a post-war reunion in a plush, private room with a round table and a crew of silent, jeering waiters. But the Café Royal is also where history happens. It was where Frank Harris advised Oscar Wilde to drop his libel charge against the Marquess of Queensberry and where Max Beerbohm encountered Enoch Soames. The following reconstruction of Lawrence's party is taken from the conflicting accounts in the memoirs of Dorothy Brett, Catherine Carswell and John Middleton Murry. The host arrived late and looking 'like a God', recalled Brett, 'the light streaming down on your dark, gold hair' (Brett addresses her memoir directly to Lawrence).[132] Catherine Carswell thought Lawrence arrived looking out of his depth and 'schoolboyish: "You'll see I'm quite up to this," he seemed to be saying.'[133] Brett sat on Lawrence's right-hand side, her Marconi on the table between them. 'I am not a man,' Lawrence told her, 'I am MAN.'[134] On his left sat Mary Cannan. The order of seating then went: Kot, Donald Carswell, Mark Gertler, Catherine Carswell, Frieda and Murry. Murry was still sexually obsessed with Frieda, and Brett had been in love with Murry for the last three years. Kot, who loathed Frieda, also had a 'murderous dislike' for Donald Carswell and was on the cusp of falling out for ever with Brett over her love for Murry.[135] Gertler, whom Lawrence cast as the 'insect' artist Loerke in *Women in Love*, had recently been diagnosed with TB; Catherine Carswell hadn't wanted to come at all, and Frieda, looking on in disdain, reminded Catherine Carswell of King David's wife.

Port followed claret and the guests, most of them not used to alcohol, became unbuttoned. The purpose of the party, Lawrence announced, was to plan his return to Taos – a form of Second Coming – and he called on his followers to join him and form a new society. In other words, the Apocalypse was nigh and so the chosen few should build their ark. The gist of his speech, Carswell recalled, was 'Did the search, the adventure, the pilgrimage for which he stood mean enough to us for us to give up our own way of life and our own separate struggle with the world?'[136] Nobody much wanted to give anything up for Lawrence or New Mexico, but Mary Cannan, who had already been with him in Capri, Sicily and Malta, was the only one to turn him down directly. 'I like you, Lawrence,' she apparently said, 'but not so much as all that, and I think you are asking what no human being has a right to ask of another.'[137]

Kot, when his turn came to heave his heart into his mouth, gave a Russian-style speech in which, Carswell recorded, he smashed a wine glass after every statement:

'Lawrence is a great man.' (Bang! Down came Kot's fist enclosing the stem of a glass so that its bottom came in shivering contact with the table.) 'Nobody here realises how great he is.' (Crash! Another good wine-glass gone.) 'Especially no woman here or anywhere can possibly realise the greatness of Lawrence.' (Smash and tinkle!)[138]

Then, remembered Murry, also speaking directly to Lawrence in *Son of Woman*, 'suddenly you put your arm around my neck for the first and the last time, and said: "Do not betray me!" '[139] According to Catherine Carswell, Murry promised that he would indeed never betray Lawrence, but according to Murry himself he said, very specifically, 'I love you Lorenzo, but I won't promise not to betray you.'[140] Either way, Murry then kissed Lawrence 'fervently' according to Brett and 'effusively' according to Carswell. 'I *have* betrayed you, old chap, I confess it,' Murry – according to Carswell – told Lawrence. 'But never again. I call you all to witness, never again.'[141]

His kiss, Murry explained, was 'an affair between men' that no woman could ever understand. Catherine Carswell replied that Judas had been a man. Lawrence then leaned forward, laid his head on the table and vomited. Because Frieda remained 'stonily detached',[142] it was Brett who held Lawrence's hand and stroked his hair until he had finished. Mary Cannan and Gertler then made a swift exit, Kot and Murry put Lawrence, now unconscious, into a cab, and Donald Carswell paid for the damages. In addition to the broken glass, there was a pool of vomit to be cleaned up by the waiters. The sight of Lawrence, limp and lifeless, being supported by Kot and Murry looked for all the world, said Catherine Carswell, like Christ being carried by St Peter and St John. The following morning, sitting up in bed, Lawrence told Catherine that 'I made a fool of myself last night.'[143]

It was during this Last Supper that Murry understood for the first time how much Lawrence had suffered. 'Suddenly, in a moment of vision, I saw it – an utterly impersonal thing: suffering, of a kind and magnitude and beauty, completely beyond my experience and until that moment beyond my extremest imagination.' Human contact, Murry understood, was no longer possible for Lawrence: he was divided not only in himself but from his own species; he was utterly adrift and alone and he always would be.[144]

Catherine Carswell said in *The Savage Pilgrimage* that she regretted not joining Lawrence on the Taos ark but her obligations at home made such a move impossible. It was clear, however, that no one – especially his wife – could cope with Lawrence for long. His single recruit from that night was Brett, who agreed to join them, mainly because Murry said he was coming too which meant either that she could marry Murry or that Murry would marry Frieda, leaving Lawrence free to marry Brett. But, having promised not to betray his leader, Murry vacillated, letting them all believe until well into the following spring that he would be joining them just as soon as he had sorted out his affairs. It wasn't until May 1924, when Murry announced that he had recently married a 23-year-old contributor to his journal, that Lawrence ceased to anticipate his arrival.

Soon afterwards Kot, Gertler, Murry, Brett and Frieda were sitting around the fire in Lawrence's flat, drinking tea. Lawrence, Murry and Brett were making plasticine models of Adam and Eve, Frieda was knitting, and Brett was listening to Lawrence on her Marconi device, when Frieda, according to Brett, 'started attacking you, contradicting you, then denouncing you: finally accusing you of wanting to make a God of yourself'. Lawrence retaliated in a 'midland vernacular' that the others had not heard him speak before. He then grabbed the poker and started smashing the crockery.

It became terrible to watch and to hear – the slow, deadly words
and the steady smash of the poker, until, looking at Frieda, you say,
slowly, menacingly:

'Beware, Frieda! If you ever talk to me like that again, it will not be the tea things I smash, but your head. Oh, yes, I'll kill you. So beware!' And down comes the poker on the teapot.

Lawrence then held out his hand to Brett, who silently took it in her own. Thus her place in the Lawrence ménage was assured.[145]

Mabel could feel it in the air when things were going badly between Lawrence and Frieda, and the letters between Hampstead and Taos were currently 'an outpouring stream of power'.[146] While Frieda laughed at Lawrence, Mabel took seriously his claim to be an instrument of 'the great dark gods'. And herein lies the latest Lawrencian paradox: the more seriously he demanded to be taken, the more he denounced seriousness and insisted on the power of laughter. His letters to Mabel now describe seriousness as the 'disease' of the day, and 'an awful disease in Murry'. If only they had laughed more in Taos, 'then the vileness of 1923 need not have been'. Laughter is the true badge of courage: 'One's got to put a new ripple on the ether.'[147]

Lawrence had once more changed his shape: no longer a marauding fox or a red wolf or a plumed serpent, he now saw himself as Pan, sex-god of the mountain wilds. Pan's death, according to Plutarch, was announced by a ship's pilot on the Mediterranean and lamented by all the spirits in the air: 'The great god Pan is dead! The great god Pan is dead!'[148] But Pan had now returned and was stirring up trouble in wintry Hampstead. Lawrence's new incarnation was announced in a letter to Mabel: the fact that everyone in London hated him only 'makes me laugh. My gods, like the Great God Pan, have a bit of a natural grin on their face.' When he returned to Taos, Lawrence warned, there must be 'no seriousness' – if Pan 'gets driven too hard', he 'goes fierce'. 'The old communion,' he continued, 'was in seriousness and earnestness. The new is in fierceness, daring, knife-like trust, and laughter.'[149] And if Mabel could only leave the Indians alone, Lawrence said, 'We'll laugh last: and really laugh, not jeer.'[150]

Lawrence had long been likened to Pan: he looked and acted like a satyr, he panicked and created pandemonium, he was sex-obsessed, he lived in woodland when possible, he had an instinctive understanding of the animal world and a deep distrust of humankind. His high, reedy laugh was described by Brett as 'the ever-ready amused jeer',[151] and Aldington spoke of his 'pleasant devil's voice, with its shrill little titters and sharp mockeries'.[152] From the winter of 1923, these 'shrill little titters' enter Lawrence's writing: we hear them in his stories, his essays, his letters and *The Plumed Serpent*. But it is in an incendiary tale called 'The Last Laugh', written in January 1924, that we first hear the new ripple on the ether. Here Lawrence, having brought Pan with him from America, avenges himself on the friend who put the cuckold's horns on his head.

'The Last Laugh' opens on a winter's night in Hampstead, with a deaf woman called James and a small, balding man called Marchbank leaving the home of Lorenzo, a 'thin man with a red beard' who is 'grinning like a satyr and waving goodbye'. It has snowed and the couple are making their way home by lamplight when Marchbank hears laughter. James, putting on the headphones of her listening machine, finds that the laugh, which sounds like 'neighing', is in fact 'bursting out' of Marchbank himself. She then sees something dim in the darkness of a front garden, after which Marchbank disappears into the adjoining house for a sexual assignation with a mysterious dark-eyed woman. There are 'strange unheard voices' swirling in the air and James finds that she can, for the first time, hear them. Thunder and lightning strike the church and a gust of wind blows out the church windows; the 'chuckling, naked laughter' now comes from inside the building. Escorted by a policeman, James continues home in a state of elation. 'He's come back! Aha! He's come back!' The terrified policeman sleeps on her sofa, while upstairs James thinks about Marchbank, with whom she has been in love for two years. 'Her love for him now seems so funny!' She has 'never really wanted a man, *any* man'.

In the morning Marchbank calls in to see James, and the policeman wakes up to find he has grown a cloven hoof. Marchbank then gives a 'strange, yelping cry, like a shot animal', and 'in the rolling agony of his eyes was the horrible grin of a man who realises that he has made a final, and this time fatal, fool of himself'. Like 'a man struck by lightning', he falls down dead.[153] In his later essay 'Pan in America', Lawrence explained the cause of James's euphoria and Marchbank's fate: 'a man who sees Pan by daylight' will die 'as if by lightning'.[154]

'The Last Laugh' is a piece of mischief in which Lawrence, who made a fatal fool of himself in the Café Royal and had been made a fool of by Murry as well, now has Murry die of his own foolishness. Added to which, he has Brett cured of her love for Murry, virginity intact. But

Lawrence, as usual, was unaware of the full story: Brett had already lost her virginity to Murry; it had happened the previous April and she had been his mistress ever since. In her secret diary, written as a series of letters to the ghost of Katherine Mansfield ('Dearest Tig'), Brett told the whole story, 'For the first time in my life I slept with a man and that man was yours.'

The autumn that Murry was driven 'crazy – really crazy' with wanting Frieda, Brett told Dearest Tig that 'The return of Lawrence is great news – only it is overshadowed for me with the fear that I have a baby coming.' In which case, 'it will be difficult to keep the secret of our relationship'. Brett's pregnancy scare was a false alarm, but Murry had both Frieda and Brett eating out of his hand: 'I never refuse him,' Brett confided to Kot on Boxing Day.[155] Which means that it was Murry and not Lawrence who had the last laugh.

For readers of poetry and popular fiction, the Great God Pan did not return in the form of D. H. Lawrence because Pan had never really gone away. Lawrence would hate to be seen as moving with the zeitgeist, but Pan was, in accordance with his name, everywhere in Edwardian literature. In *Cakes and Ale* (1930) Somerset Maugham described the cult to which Lawrence subscribed. 'Thirty years ago in literary circles God was all the fashion ... then God went out ... and Pan came in. In a hundred novels his cloven hoof left its imprint on the sward; poets saw him lurking in the twilight on London commons, and literary ladies in Surrey and New England, nymphs of an industrial age, mysteriously surrendered their virginity to his rough embrace.'[156] He featured most famously in J. M. Barrie's *Peter Pan in Kensington Gardens* (1906), but Witter Bynner had himself, in 1920, published 'A Canticle of Pan', in which the Great God Pan does not, as Plutarch reported, die on the birth of Christ but visits the baby in his manger.

The spirit of Pan was behind *Laughing Horse*, and it was Spud Johnson who later typed out 'The Last Laugh'. So if Lawrence brought Pan back to London, he took him from the Bynners, who were putting together the latest edition of *Laughing Horse* in Chapala at the same time as Lawrence was writing 'Quetzalcoatl'. The pandemonium of *Laughing Horse* was more suited to Lawrence's current mood than Murry's earnest *Adelphi*, and so this is where Lawrence sent, in January 1924, his 'London Letter', a revised version of 'On Coming Home', written as a paean to Pan. 'Dear Old Horse,' Lawrence wrote, 'I've been here exactly a month, in London, and day has never broken all the time.' The neighing of the Horse was most welcome: 'Good old Horse, be patted, and be persuaded to grin and be a Centaur … let me get on your back and ride away again to New Mexico.' When Jesus was born, Lawrence continued, 'the spirits wailed round the Mediterranean: Pan is dead. Great Pan is dead.' He might be dead as a doornail in Europe but he is alive and 'making a few sparks fly, across the tops of the Rockies'.[157]

# Part Three

The idea of return had dominated Lawrence's last nine months: the return of Quetzalcoatl, the return of Pan, the return to Mexico, the return to London, the return to Hampstead. They approached America from the east, leaving Southampton on the *Aquitania* on 6 March 1924 and docking at New York six days later. In Brett's account of the voyage, Frieda doesn't exist: it is Brett and Lawrence making their lonely way across the Atlantic. As they passed Ellis Island, Lawrence hurried Brett on deck to see the Statue of Liberty, but Mabel's 'great hollow stone image' was lost in mist and cloud. New York is bitter in March, with sudden snow showers, instant ice and wind whooshing round corners. Lawrence hated it. They had tea with Willa Cather, a friend of the Brewsters and the only American novelist that Lawrence would ever meet; in what Brett described as 'his mischievous naughty-boy mood', Lawrence 'teased Willa Cather about women writers, belittling them, mocking them'.[1] Pan and his party then travelled by train to Santa Fe: three days of playing cards and seeing America pass by the window like a film. The Bynners, 'hugging and shouting', met them at the station and the next day they continued on to Mabeltown by stagecoach, Brett squeezed between Lawrence and Frieda. The snow made for a perilous journey, during which Brett held on to Lawrence's knee.

Having wintered in California (where they were getting their treatment), Mabel and Tony were not due for another few days and so the travellers had the Big House to themselves. In his Stetson hat and Western boots – he now dressed as a cowboy – Lawrence taught Brett how to ride although having been raised on a stud farm, she hardly needed his help. 'You ahead, I behind,' Brett lovingly recalled. 'You, turning your head at intervals to make sure I am all right, which

Lawrence and Frieda in Santa Fe

gives me a feeling of security I have rarely felt since.'² When Mabel's Ford rolled through the gate to the estate, with Tony tooting the horn, Lawrence, 'breathless and shaking', ran down the steps to greet them. Frieda followed, giving out her usual 'hearty sounds'. Mabel braced herself to plant a kiss on Frieda's 'hard, pink cheek', but Frieda recoiled and Lawrence 'giggled the same faint, small giggle I had heard so often before'.[3]

Up at the house Mabel was introduced to the latest member of the community. Brett, she thought, was a 'grotesque' whose 'long, thin shanks ended in large feet that turned out abruptly like the kind that children draw'. Her ear-trumpet – known as Toby – which seemed to 'suck into itself all it could from the air', was 'almost always ... pointing at Lorenzo'. Mabel saw Toby as an 'eavesdropper', a 'spy', and Brett wielded him like a truncheon, keeping him 'forever between Lawrence and the world'. She took on a similar role herself. Brett was, Lawrence explained to Mabel, 'a kind of buffer between him and Frieda', but she was also a buffer between Mabel and Lawrence.[4] Brett's first impression of Mabel was equally Hogarthian: her hostess was a woman of 'square, sturdy build', with hair 'bobbed like a Florentine boy' and a 'curved fringe' pointing down in the middle of the forehead 'like a Mephistophelian cap'.[5] While Frieda airily dismissed the relevance of Brett ('she doesn't count'), it took Mabel to see the new girl's power. Brett's presence around Lawrence, wrote Mabel – who similarly used silence to impose her authority – was as 'pervasive' as the 'air'.[6]

Lawrence and Frieda

The Lawrences moved into a two-storey house, known as the pink house, that was across the garden from the Big House, with Brett in the adjacent studio. The plan was to rendezvous for lunch and supper, and thus began, wrote Mabel, 'our second effort to live a kind of group life'.⁷ It was no easier now for Mabel to get Lawrence on his own than it had been in the autumn of 1922. She managed to detach him from his entourage only when they went riding, on which occasions, by feigning a newly discovered timidity which allowed Lawrence to protect her, she tried to prove herself as submissive a horsewoman as Brett. 'I am not the same as I was!' Mabel admitted as she 'trembled' by the side of her mare. Lawrence 'grinned' and helped her to mount. They then 'rode decorously away across the desert; no more wild riding with me in the lead and he tearing after me!'⁸

It was Mabel who recognised that Brett also hid her aggression beneath a mask of femininity. 'I cannot describe to you my increasing irritation at Brett's ridiculous ways,' she complained. One of these mannerisms was to describe everything as '*little*' as in '*Oh!* a li-ittle flower-pot!' Mabel's impersonations of Brett's whimsy made Frieda laugh and Lawrence 'sore', and Brett got her revenge when, trimming Mabel's bob, she nipped the lobe of her ear. 'I looked at Brett in amazement and, I must admit, in some admiration!' It could not be more symbolic, thought Mabel: the deaf woman had tried to 'mutilate' the ear of her rival.⁹

Lawrence now started to paint. He painted the windows of Mabel's bathroom in Aztec patterns of yellow and blue and green and red, and he painted a lovely chrysanthemum and a nimble phoenix on a cupboard door in the pink house. He painted an enormous serpent coiled around the stem of a sunflower on the walls of the outside privy, and on the upper half of a Gothic door he painted a medallion of a golden phoenix rising from a nest of flames, while Brett decorated the lower half with a carving of Adam and Eve and the tree of knowledge. ' "Here's Eve – the bitch," Brett said, viciously, "*cause* of all the trouble. Here, let's give her a good fat tummy!" ' The reason Lawrence and Brett hated Eve so much, Mabel believed, is because 'I was Eve.'¹⁰

He was woken at night by the whipping and wailing of the Penitentes, who dragged their crosses past Mabeltown on the way to Calvary. Revolted by the thought of them, Lawrence slept with his windows shut, but during the day he would walk up and down the

Calvary Road. The presence of the Penitentes was a drawback, and Lawrence was restless. Because Mabel didn't want to lose him again, she came up with a solution: she would give Lawrence her ranch on Lobo Mountain, the same one she had prevented him from living in with the Danes on the grounds that it belonged to her son, John. Two miles further up than Del Monte, the ranch consisted of 160 acres, a barn, two reasonably sized cabins and a third cabin measuring nine feet by eleven, the size of what the English call a Wendy-house. Mabel, in her capacity as Beatrice, had excelled herself: the ranch she gave Lawrence is 8,600 feet above sea level. He had reached the empyrean, where all becomes one.

Lobo, Spanish for wolf, was a mountain of wild animals and on its 'Jaguar-splashed, puma-yellow, leopard-livid slopes', Lawrence once saw two hunters carrying the corpse of a lion they had shot. 'So, she will never leap up that way again,' he wrote in 'Mountain Lion', 'with the yellow flash of a mountain lion's long shoot!'

And her bright striped frost-face will never watch any more, out of
the shadow of the cave in the blood-orange rock,
Above the trees of the Lobo dark valley-mouth!

Kiowa, as Lawrence called his ranch – after the Indian tribe who had once lived on the land – is the only home he would ever own, except that Lawrence didn't strictly own it. To prevent him from turning her gift down, Mabel put the ranch in Frieda's name. Lawrence insisted, however, on giving Mabel something in return and that something was the manuscript of *Sons and Lovers*, currently in Germany in the care of Frieda's sister, Else. The quid pro quo was, Mabel believed, a 'cold and distrustful' gesture that 'spoiled the whole exchange',[11] yet the manuscript was apparently valued at $4,000 and Mabel had originally paid $1,200 for the ranch. Having given the place to her son as a shooting lodge, she bought it back from him with a buffalo-hide coat and a small sum of money so that Lawrence could take up residence.

By April the ice had thawed and new life was stirring: the Indians were ploughing their furrows, baby burros were taking their first steps, and the wild-plum hedges were coming into flower. Mexican workers were preparing Lawrence's ranch for habitation, and over Easter he went to the pueblo at Santo Domingo to see the Dance of the Sprouting

Brett

Corn. He had compared his experience at the Jicarilla reservation to a 'stage', and while his responses to the ceremonials would evolve, Lawrence's sense of New Mexico as a theatre remained the same. This is clear in the two essays he wrote during Holy Week 1924, 'Indians and Entertainment' and 'The Dance of the Sprouting Corn'.

'Indians and Entertainment' was a response to the latest disturbance
in Taos pueblo: on Good Friday, Charles Burke, Commissioner of
Indian Affairs, arrived from Washington to advise the Indians against
keeping their boys from school in order to instruct them in religion in
the kivas. This was a further attempt, in the aftermath of the Bursum
Bill, to integrate the indigenous people into mainstream American life
by depriving them of their customs and beliefs. Eighteen months earlier
Lawrence would have complained that all anyone in Mabeltown talked
about was Burke! Burke! Burke! School! School! School!, but he now
accepted the atrocity of Burke's intervention and wrote an account of
Indian 'otherness' in which he broke through his earlier blockage.

The essay begins with an attack on the 'shadow-pictures' of films which
offer the audience 'an orgy of abstraction'. While white Americans
canoodle in the back row of the movie house, Native Americans,
Lawrence argued, have no notion of 'entertainment', and this is what
makes their dances so hard for liberals like Mabel or John Collier to
understand: 'sentimentality' always 'creeps in'. What follows is a reading
of Indian ceremonials as a form of theatre of the absurd: performances
of 'no words' meaning 'nothing at all', involving 'no spectacle, no
spectator', 'no beginning and no end', in which we cannot judge what
we see 'because there is nothing outside it, to judge'. Only when we
stop trying to root out the meaning of the dance can we appreciate its
beauty. Lawrence was adamant about this: the ceremonial dances were
a mystery to him and would remain so.[12]

So how to describe such a ceremony? This is what Lawrence set
out to achieve in his account of the Dance of the Sprouting Corn.
His solution was to imitate the dancers themselves. 'The Dance of the
Sprouting Corn' is subtle, soft re-enactment recalled with astonishing
precision. The opening lines are stage directions:

Pale, dry, baked earth, that blows into dust of fine sand. Low hills
of baked pale earth, sinking heavily, and speckled sparsely with dark
dots of cedar bushes.

The action then begins: 'Thud – thud – thud – thud – thud! goes the
drum, heavily the men hop and hop and hop, sway, sway, sway, sway go
the little branches of green pine.' The dance 'tosses like a little forest',
the bells on the knee-garters pulse and ripple, the gourd-rattles shudder, the

barefoot women, motionless as 'solid shadows', tread their steps behind the men. These lines, 'straight as rain', break into four rings and then form a star, before falling back into lines – every pattern folding into place without apparent direction, like the shifting shapes in a kaleidoscope. Meanwhile the clowns or Koshares, daubed in black and white earth, weave 'like queer spotted dogs' through the dancers, calling something up from the earth or down from the sky, catching a word from the singers, fluttering their hands in slow motion, up and down, up and down. 'They are anything but natural,' wrote Lawrence; they are like the 'blackened ghosts of a dead corn cob'. The drum then stops, breaking the trance, and the dancers silently file into line and thread their way back to the kiva, where the thud thud thud begins again, and the men hop and hop and hop, and the little forest starts once more to sway.[13]

There is no howl of misery, in either essay, about the impossibility of going back, no acute sadness or nostalgia or unbearable yearning, no insistence on the need to push onwards, no suggestion that the Native Americans lack any 'inside' or anger about being an outsider; no sense of looking through a screen or despair at the unbridgeable difference between Lawrence's own wretched world and the better one of the Indians. He just runs forward with the wonder like a half-empty ship heading into warm waters, feeling the long, slow, waveringly rhythmic rise and fall, lilting in the slow flight of the elements, winging outwards.

What is most extraordinary about 'Indians and Entertainment' and 'The Dance of the Sprouting Corn' is how little their vanishing, egoless author resembles the impossibly self-aggrandising, semi-sane bore whose fantasies of divine leadership were currently being suffered by Frieda and nurtured by Mabel and Brett.

Memoirs of Lawrence are driven by either love or hate, depending on whether they are written by women or by men. Good haters are better company than blind lovers, and Brett's adulation of Lawrence takes its toll on the reader. Brett, unlike Mabel, has no interest in Lawrence's complexity or awareness of her own. Mabel is the better writer by far, not least because – taking seriously Lawrence's moratorium on seriousness – she casts herself as a comic character in her own drama and is ready to laugh at the things that matter to her most. Take her account of greeting her guests one morning with the news that she feels 'marvellous'. 'Hah!' snorts Frieda and 'Humph' mutters Lawrence, who then blames Mabel's irritating sense of well-being on 'sheer unrestrained ego'. Strolling over to see Brett, who is of course eavesdropping from her doorway, Mabel 'screams' into Toby, 'Isn't it a wonderful day?' 'What?' Brett screams back. 'Hay? Is José cutting hay?'[14]

Mabeltown was enhanced by the presence of Ida Rauh, the former actress whom Mabel knew from her Greenwich Village days and who was now living in Santa Fe with Andrew Dasburg. Despite (or because of) her feminism, Lawrence liked Ida and with their combined talents, the evening charades were fuelled by an excess of fierceness, daring and laughter. No subject was considered off-limits: Mabel described one charade 'that represented me taking Tony to Buffalo to visit my mother!' Lawrence, 'dressed in a shawl and a big hat, flourishing a horrified lorgnette', played Sara Ganson, Ida played Mabel, and Tony, 'wrapped in his blanket', played himself, 'very seriously, making deep bows to Lorenzo'. It was 'so funny', said Mabel, that 'we couldn't finish the act!'[15] The laughter Lawrence generated always had an edge of panic. Only Brett picked up on Tony's hatred of these theatricals: 'We have a hilarious evening of charades,' she recalls in the present tense of *Lawrence and Brett*. 'You are eager, alive, and full of fun. Even Tony is roped in: solemn, bewildered, he re-enacts with Mabel their marriage. "I have married an Indian Chief," announces Mabel. "No," says Tony, with offended dignity, "not a chief." And he turns and walks solemnly out of the room, which brings the charade to an abrupt finish.'[16]

On Lobo Mountain Lawrence and Frieda moved into one of the larger cabins, the second cabin was reserved for Mabel and Tony, and Brett took the Wendy-house, which just about contained a single bed and the desk on which she typed Lawrence's manuscripts on a typewriter borrowed from Mabel. 'It's quite big enough, really,' Brett said brightly.[17] It was smaller than the larder of one of her childhood homes. That summer, Mabel and Tony were picnicking at the ranch when Lawrence began a diatribe against the decadence and corruption of society. Lowering his voice and glaring around the table, he reached his crescendo: 'only the doctors know the truth about all these "best people"! *They* know that the ratio of *syphilis* among them is enormous. They are rotten with it. The men have lost their manhood from it, the women their fertility. Our own best friends are filthy with it for all we know!' Tony, in his ancient wisdom, looked Pan in the eye and asked, 'What that syphilis? Something like TB?'[18]

In early July when the Lawrence party came down to Mabeltown for supper, Frieda and Mabel's latest protégé, a young man called Clarence, disappeared after drinking moonshine and dancing together. Lawrence went to bed in a rage and Mabel, wildly excited by Frieda's transgression, stayed awake until she heard the couple return. Creeping through the dark to Clarence's house, she asked him what they had been doing. 'I have been learning the Truth!' he replied.[19] The Truth, revealed to Clarence by Frieda, was that Lawrence was trying to murder Mabel, who would be getting weaker and sicker after each of his visits. Yes, thought Mabel, that made sense: Lawrence always talked about people 'destroying' one another, and when she had recently said to him 'you want to *kill* me, that's what you want!', he had replied, in a 'hesitating voice', 'No–o. Not exactly.'[20]

The next morning Lawrence handed Mabel his latest story. While Mabel sat on the couch reading 'The Woman Who Rode Away', as it was called, Tony and Clarence had words with Lawrence outside, and Frieda and Brett began to pack their bags.

'The Woman Who Rode Away' is a dream-like parable about a bored American wife who rides off to discover the secrets of the Chilchui people. Meeting three Indians in the desert, she goes with them over the mountains, climbing up and up through the night until they reach 'the roof of the world' where the snow 'slashes' against the heavens. When the horses can go no further, the woman crawls on her hands and knees up 'mile-long sheets of rock'. Three thousand feet below lies a lush green valley where houses glisten like little white cubes; the party descend, and the woman is taken to the earthen sun-roof of a temple in which an 'old, old man' is lying on a bed. The woman tells him that she wants to bring her heart to the god of the Chilchui, and the other men in the room, dressed in white sheets gathered into loincloths, cut her riding boots and clothes away from her with knives. The old, old man touches her naked breasts and runs his moistened fingertips down her body. It is, Lawrence says, a curiously sexless experience for the woman because she already 'feels dead'. She is then clothed by the men in a white cotton shift and imprisoned in a small house where she can hear 'the long, heavy sound of a drum'. A magical drink makes her vomit and then hallucinate: she can hear 'the vast sound of the earth going round, like some immense arrow-string booming'. Every time she is given the drink she gets a little weaker and more sick, but she now understands the oneness of the universe.

The highbrow white woman, the Indians explain to her, has 'stayed too long on the earth, the moon and the sun are waiting for her to go'. The woman's death will be an offering to the gods; she will save the tribe. On her last day she is taken on a long climb to a mountain chamber which can only be entered by a ladder descending from the roof, and then to an amphitheatre fanged with icicles, and finally to a cave over which a waterfall has frozen and behind which tunnels lead to other, smaller caves. Here she is 'fumigated' before being laid naked on a large flat stone. 'She knew she was going to die, among the glisten of this snow', but as 'she stared at the blaze of blue sky above the slashed and ponderous mountain, she thought "I am dead already."' The old, old man approaches her with his blade and she knew that when the sun had reached its reddest point, it would hit the column of ice, and 'the old man would strike … and accomplish the sacrifice and achieve the power'.[21] It is at this point that the story ends, with the figures at the sacrifice as frozen as the 'men or gods' and 'maidens loth' in Keats's 'Ode on a Grecian Urn'.

'Do you like it?' asked Lawrence when Mabel had finished reading. 'Oh, it's splendid!' Mabel replied, annoyed that the story was set in Mexico when it was clearly about New Mexico.[22] Lawrence had captured, as Mabel wanted him to, the strange, sinister spirit of the place and then called it by another name. 'The Woman Who Rode Away' was filled with messages to Mabel, who had announced herself 'dead' to Tony when she contracted syphilis, who had once been given by Tony a 'magical drink' made from cacti (called peyote) which, she said, 'revealed the irresistible delight of spiritual composition: the regulated relationship of one to all and all to one'.[23] The cave itself was inspired by a visit that she and Lawrence had made to Lucero Peak, a 10,800-foot rock above the town of Arroyo Seco; the ancient ceremonial chamber, considered by the Taos Indians to be a sacred place, can be found behind a heavy waterfall that freezes in the winter.

Lawrence described 'The Woman Who Rode Away' as 'Mabel's story to me', and Mabel called it the story 'where Lorenzo thought he finished me up',[24] but it was Lawrence and not Mabel who was 'finished up' by the tale. When *Sexual Politics*, Kate Millett's study of literary misogyny, appeared in 1969, her analysis of 'The Woman Who Rode Away' dealt the final blow to Lawrence's flagging reputation. The story, said Millett, was 'monstrous', 'demented', 'sadistic pornography', a snuff-movie 'reeking of Hollywood'. The scene, she argued, in which the woman, preparing for her sacrifice, stands between the priests while 'the throng below gave the low, wild cry' is shot in 'MGM technicolor'.[25] After Millett's verdict, Lawrence dropped off university reading lists and was thrown into the Inferno where he has remained ever since.

If 'The Woman Who Rode Away' is read as the sacrifice of a single and specific woman, then it might certainly seem like a work of sexual sadism. The tale is sick, but then we shed our sicknesses in books. Yet it can equally be read as an allegory in which modern America sacrifices the mechanical world it now worships for the cosmic world it has lost, thus displacing the power of the dynamo with that of the virgin. Either way, 'The Woman Who Rode Away' is concerned with regeneration rather than death, because the woman's sacrifice is to ensure the movement of the planets. There is nothing surprising in the tale's savagery: Lawrence's sole mission was to uncover the demonic soul of America, the 'under-consciousness' beneath the upper layer of 'nice-as-pie'. The *destroy! destroy! destroy!* that lurked beneath the surface of American literature is given here upfront, leaving us with the problem of what exactly is being destroyed: one woman, all women or the modern American ego.

While it has proved impossible to save this particular tale from the artist who created it, what Kate Millett did was to flip the tale and the teller around. She made Lawrence himself the human sacrifice, and encouraged his 'throng' of readers to strip him naked and give the 'low, wild cry' for his destruction. What matters in the biographical context however is not how critics have responded to 'The Woman Who Rode Away', but how Mabel herself responded, and Mabel let Lawrence think that she did not mind: her acceptance of his offering was part of her new 'submission'. But she told Leo Stein that Lawrence was 'too *damn* mean', and that he had 'satisfied his sadism' in a story about 'a white woman whom he makes sacrifice herself voluntarily to the Indians who finally cut out her heart'.[26]

When she had finished reading his story and the Lawrence party were being driven back to the ranch by Clarence, Mabel promised Tony that she would never contact Lorenzo again. Then a few days later a battered package arrived for her at the local post office. It was the manuscript of *Sons and Lovers*, delivered from Germany, and no sooner had Mabel ripped open the wrapping than there was 'a clap of thunder' in the clear blue sky and the rain came down in sheets. 'Well,' she said as she looked at Lawrence's handwritten pages, 'I had the essence of him in my hands. Perhaps that should have been enough for me, you think? It wasn't.'[27]

Clarence reminded Mabel every day that Lawrence '*wants* you *dead*', but Tony, now 'tired of Lorenzo', did not, Mabel said, take 'this sensational news sensationally'. Nor, however, did Mabel, who was far from tired of Lorenzo. On the contrary, she 'missed' him 'and the fun of his company, the thrill that got into everything when he was about'. Masochists need sadists and Mabel knew from her marriages that the connection between the hunter and his prey was the most thrilling one of all. Life without Lawrence was 'too peaceful' and so she broke her promise to Tony and sent a card up to the ranch, asking how her killer was doing. Lawrence replied that all was well, and she should come and see him in the 'lion's den'.[28] He presented himself as having the power, but Mabel was guiding his every move. He was living in her ranch, he had stolen her friends, he was jealous of her husband, he had met her mother; having defiantly left her in 1923, he skulked back to her in 1924, crossing the globe in order to do so. To remind Mabel that it was she who was in debt to Lawrence, Frieda now told her that the manuscript of *Sons and Lovers* was worth a good deal more than $4,000. It had been valued, she revealed, at '$50,000, at least!'[29]

Lawrence's ranch on Lobo mountain

Lawrence's next story, the novella *St Mawr*, was about a woman who 'had had her own way so long, that by the age of twenty-five she didn't

391

know where she was'. Lou Witt, as the heroine is called, is a wilful American with a European background and a sexually available mother (modelled on Sara Ganson). St Mawr is the name of the stallion that Lou buys for her husband Rico, but Rico prefers cars to horses and is anyway scared of St Mawr who attends to his surroundings 'as if he were some lightning-conductor'. The groom is a small and wily Welshman called Lewis, who considers his beard a part of his body; a second groom called Phoenix has a Mexican father and a Navajo mother. Fragments of Lawrence can be found in every character, including St Mawr himself, who is the latest incarnation of Pan. Leaving Rico in England, Lou returns with Phoenix, her mother and her horse to the 'absolute silence' of America. New Mexico feels to her 'like a cinematograph'; it is peopled by 'flat shapes, exactly like men, but without any substance of reality'. Self-conscious cowboys herd their cattle in black Ford motorcars: 'It was all film-psychology.' To get away from the movie set, Lou buys, for $1,200, a ranch in the foothills of the Rocky Mountains identical to the one in which Lawrence was now living. Lou has reached the beyond, a place of 'pure, *absolute* beauty', where the desert spread its 'eternal circles' beneath and below, the 'long mountain-side of pure blue shadow closed in the near corner'. Here the thought of sex becomes repellent to her and she decides to give herself 'only to the unseen presences'. Another female sacrifice, Lou Witt forsook the life of her body in order to become 'one of the eternal Virgins, serving the eternal fire'.[30]

The relation between the dynamo and the virgin had been noted before, in a book so Lawrentian that Lawrence himself might have written it. Sixteen years earlier, Henry Adams – grandson of John Quincy Adams – had described, in *The Education of Henry Adams*, his own struggle with the scientific and technological revolutions of the age. In the chapter called 'The Dynamo and the Virgin', Adams visits the 1900 Paris Exposition where 'the forty-foot dynamos' represent 'a moral force, much as the early Christians felt the Cross'.[31] He now understands the 'absolute *fiat* in electricity as a faith'; the energy of the dynamo has become 'divine', the dynamo is the new 'symbol of infinity'. The Virgin – by which Adams means the eternal goddess, symbol of female fecundity – was once 'the greatest force the Western world had ever felt', but modern America has never feared her. She is admired as an image of 'reflected emotion, beauty, purity' and 'taste', but not as the power that built Chartres Cathedral. The purpose of American art, said Henry Adams, was to return to the Virgin her former stature.[32]

On 3 August, halfway through writing *St Mawr*, Lawrence spat blood into a handkerchief. When Frieda called the local doctor, Lawrence hurled an iron eggcup at her head. The doctor's diagnosis, Frieda was happy to report, was that this was not at all a death sentence: the patient's lungs were 'strong' – he had nothing but a 'touch of bronchial trouble!'[33] But from now on it was Lawrence and not Mabel who got weaker and sicker, and Mabel wondered if he was bent on 'destroying himself instead of me'.[34]

After a week in bed, Lawrence told Mabel that his throat 'hurt like billy-o' but he wanted to go to the Hopi Snake Dance in Arizona. Mabel wanted this too, because he would write about it afterwards. While Lawrence wrote about the Snake Dance itself, which took place on 17 August 1924, Mabel described, in *Lorenzo in Taos*, the 400-mile drive there, which was dominated by Lawrence's hostility towards Tony. The journey contained other dangers too: cars had been swallowed by quicksand on the roads through Navajo country, and Mabel realised, as Tony sang in the front of the Ford and Lawrence fired verbal missiles at Frieda in the back, that she was 'thrice alone' with her three companions; nothing but 'a smiling, embalmed mummy'. Mulling over Lawrence's intention of destroying her, she wondered if the Sybil Mond novel might itself have been a weapon, and was sorry that Frieda had put a stop to it, 'because it would have been an easier and a quicker end' had Lawrence 'done it with the magic pen rather than by the reiterated blows he gave me with the strange power of his presence'.[35]

The Hopi Snake Dance, a petition for lightning, is the apotheosis of snake-power. In preparation for the ceremony, twelve officiating men of the tribe catch the rattlesnakes in the rocks; they wash, soothe and 'exchange spirits with them' before keeping them in the kivas for nine days. On the day of the dance the snake priests, with the snakes in their mouths, circle around one another before letting the creatures slither back down to the underground to give the gods the prayers 'which had been breathed upon them'.[36]

Lawrence had described Sybil Mond as a 'seductive serpent', but as far as Tony Lujan was concerned Lawrence was the snake, and it is hard to tell, in their own particular snake dance, whether Lawrence is dangling Mabel from his mouth, or Mabel dangling Lawrence. Lawrence's first account of the Snake Dance, 'Just Back from the Snake Dance – Tired

Out', was written in the back of the car as Tony drove them home from the ceremony. Later published in *Laughing Horse*, the piece was a fresh attack on Mabel. 'One wonders what one went for,' Lawrence began. 'The Hopi country is hideous', with 'death grey mesas sticking up like broken pieces of ancient, dry, grey bread'. The dance itself was a 'tiny little show' laid on for white Americans, involving eight 'so-called' antelope priests and a dozen 'so-called' snake priests, while the so-called snakes themselves looked like 'wet, pale silk stockings'.[37] Reading Lawrence's description, Mabel was duly disappointed – she had not taken him to the Snake Dance to have him mock and belittle it. He then agreed to do the piece again, and this time 'not for the Horse to laugh at'.[38]

In his second account, 'The Hopi Snake Dance', we see exactly what Lawrence went for and how intensely he had absorbed the ceremony and its meanings. He begins with their arrival at the 'ragged ghost' of a mesa where they join a line of black automobiles which, having 'lurched and crawled' across the desert, now moves slowly up the slope, drawing its slow length over the burned earth. While the crowd – Lawrence thinks there are 3,000 people – have come to see men hold rattlesnakes in their mouths, his own interest is in the animism of a religion in which 'all is alive'. For the Native Americans, the sun and the moon and the wind are 'the great living source of life', to which 'you can no more pray than you can pray to Electricity'. Which brings Lawrence to his central theme: today we capture electricity in 'reservoirs and irrigation ditches and artesian wells. We make lightning conductors, and build vast electric plants', but the Native Americans approach lightning 'livingly' and 'from the mystic will within'. Herein lies the gulf between the white Americans and the Native Americans: 'We dam the Nile and take the railway across America. The Hopi smooths the rattlesnake and carries him in his mouth.' To us, 'God was the beginning and Paradise is lost', and to the Hopi, 'God is not yet' and Paradise is yet to come.[39]

The snake priests, 'heavily built, rather short', with 'bobbed hair' and an 'anarchic squareness', look like Mabel. But they also, with their faces smeared in black clay, look like miners. They are 'the hot, living men of the darkness, lords of the earth's inner vital rays'. The ceremony over, the tourists 'hurry back to the motor-cars, and soon the air buzzes with starting engines, like the biggest of rattlesnakes buzzing'. The long line of black steel uncoils itself back down the slope.[40]

In April 1923, a German art historian called Aby Warburg, founder of the Warburg Institute, gave a slide lecture at Ludwig Binswanger's Kreuzlingen sanatorium in Switzerland. Five years earlier Warburg had suffered a psychotic breakdown and his Kreuzlingen Lecture, as it became known, was the result of a deal he made with his doctors. If he proved able to deliver a rational and sustained talk for one hour, drawing on material he had cellared since his journey to the American Southwest in 1897, he would be deemed sane enough to return to Hamburg. Warburg chose as his topic the Snake Dance, and he described his own performance as 'the gruesome convulsion of a decapitated frog'. The event was extraordinary in many ways, not least because Warburg, despite his extensive knowledge of Native American life and culture, had never actually seen the Snake Dance, which puts his lecture in the same category as those essays on classic American literature that Lawrence had written in Cornwall, before he had actually seen America.

Warburg went to the Southwest in order to experience life 'in its polar tension between pagan, instinctual forces of nature and organised intelligence'. The culture and religion of the Native Americans, he believed, was built on the same 'synchrony' of higher civilisation and magical causation as the Renaissance; in addition, both cultures were orientated around the symbol and 'symbolic connection'. In the Snake Dance, said Warburg, the serpent serves as the agent of lightning but also as lightning itself: one of his slides showed an image taken from the altar floor of a kiva, in which lightning is represented by serpents rather than zigzags descending from the clouds. Now that we have scientific explanations, Warburg argued, we no longer fear the snake or feel its force.

Warburg's talk, illustrated throughout with his remarkable photographs – the lightning altar in the kiva at Sia, the antelope dance at San Ildefonso – ends with an image he had captured on the streets of San Francisco. It represents, he said, 'the conqueror of the serpent cult and of the fear of lightning, the inheritor of the indigenous peoples and of the gold seeker who ousted them'. In centre frame is 'Uncle Sam in a stovepipe hat, strolling in his pride past a neoclassical rotunda. Above his top hat runs an electric wire. In this copper serpent of Edison's, he has wrested lightning from nature.'[41]

Uncle Sam, photographed by Aby Warburg in San Francisco 1895, and used in the 1923 lecture on the Snake Dance

So eighteen months before Lawrence wrote about the Snake Dance and electricity, a German in a Swiss sanatorium also wrote about the Snake Dance and electricity. Warburg's lecture was equally concerned with synchronicity, and his thoughts synchronised entirely with those of Lawrence, as he reached the empyrean.

September was a time of frenzied composition. Lawrence finished 'The Hopi Snake Dance', revised the proofs of the *Memoir of Maurice Magnus* and wrote a story which he saw as the third part of the triptych which contained 'The Woman Who Rode Away' and *St Mawr*. 'The Princess' was Lawrence's story for Brett, in which he showed that he knew (probably through Frieda) she had lost her virginity to Murry. The daughter of a Scottish aristocrat, Dollie Urquhart – 'the princess' – comes to New Mexico and is attracted to a Mexican guide called Romero who takes her on a long ride into the mountains. In a hunting lodge where they rest for the night, Dollie gives herself to Romero. The next day she tells him that she did not enjoy the experience – 'I don't care for that kind of thing' – which provokes Romero to throw her boots and breeches into a pond. He holds her captive in the hut until he is shot dead by two men from the forest service. The princess, who tells no one what happened on her excursion, remains, for all the world, 'a virgin intact'. But now 'her bobbed hair was grey at the temples, and her eyes were a little mad'.[42]

Having vented his anger with Brett, Lawrence returned to the image of Pisgah. Looking down today from the mountain, Lawrence wrote in 'Climbing Down from Pisgah', all that can be seen is a scrawny image of the globe – 'the graveyard of humanity'.[43]

'You are so near the final blessedness,' Beatrice told Dante when they had passed through the seventh sphere of Paradise, 'that you have need / of vision clear and keen.' Now that he was ending his journey, Beatrice commanded Dante to look down, for 'much of the world is there'. This was the first time that he had taken in the view, and he smiled at the 'scrawny image' of the globe.


After her crisis on the way to the Snake Dance, the life went out of Mabel. She lost touch 'with all that is human', had 'no recognition of the interests of others', was 'outside, inhuman, unloving, insentient, an exile from the earth'.[44] She went to New York for two weeks to consult Dr Brill; his repeated advice, which she always ignored, was that the cure for her melancholia was to find herself something – anything – to do. Mabel needed a project.

Her letters to Lawrence from New York are searching and desperate. She treats him as Brill's equal, and places herself entirely in their joint hands: 'Both you and Brill feel *I* have to do all the work this winter. With guidance I have to *do* the thing, whatever it is. Can you tell me *what* this thing literally is?' Lawrence replied that Mabel should 'try, try, try to discipline and control yourself'.[45] In another letter, Mabel noted that the only times she felt alive and 'flowing' were when she was in love and when she was '*writing*'. 'If I can once get started and know I want to say something – it comes. Then I am off – in a good running pace.' But she had to write '*for* someone' and Lawrence was 'positively the only audience I care to say anything to'. Lawrence, however, had dismissed her as a writer: 'I always remember your words: "I shall never consider you a writer or even a knower." And these words paralyze me …' So Mabel tentatively asked his permission: 'Shall I start a life-history or something?'[46]

When she returned to Taos, everyone was leaving: Lawrence, Frieda and Brett were wintering in Mexico (Lawrence's chest was feeling 'raw' at this altitude), and Mabel herself was returning to New York for a longer spell of analysis. In early October – when the *Memoir of Maurice Magnus* was finally being published in England – Tony took them all for a last drive through the valley. The cottonwood trees stood yellow against the windless autumnal sky, the purple mountains hung quietly around, and the world was at peace. 'Perhaps we shall look back on this afternoon,' said Mabel, breaking the silence, 'and think how happy we were.' The Lawrences left the next day. 'We'll write,' said Lawrence, leaning from the window of the motorcar.[47]

Breaking their drive in Santa Fe, Lawrence told Mabel's friends that she was 'dangerous' and 'destructive'. When this was duly reported back, Mabel finally 'gave up Lawrence'.[48] They continued to exchange letters but she no longer asked him to be her *genius loci*. That 'frail failure of a man,' she said in *Lorenzo in Taos*, had 'overcome' her.[49] She and Lawrence would never meet again, and Mabel now began, without his help, to tell the story of her life.

After a month in Mexico City, the Lawrence party travelled south to Oaxaca, the land of the Mixtecs and Zapotecs. Lawrence and Frieda took a house at 43 Avenida Pino Suárez, and Brett, with whom relations were becoming strained, booked into a hotel. 'The little town of Oaxaca is lonely,' Lawrence told Secker, 'away in the south and miles from anywhere except the Indian villages of the hills. I like it, it gives me something.'[50] Oaxaca was a place of crumbling colonial churches, bloodied Christs, walled gardens, narrow streets, dusty plazas and processions with Virgins. Lawrence, haggard and emaciated, was of course mistaken for the resurrected Jesus. In December, at the same time that Norman Douglas, holed up in his Sicilian hotel, was penning his *Plea for Better Manners*, Lawrence returned to 'Quetzalcoatl', which had been sleeping now for over a year. Writing with his usual rapidity, he doubled its length and spoiled its beauty.

Lawrence didn't simply revise 'Quetzalcoatl'. He did as he always did and started the novel again, because what he now wanted to say was no longer what he had originally wanted to say. *The Plumed*

*Serpent*, as it was renamed (because, as Lawrence's publisher said, no one could pronounce Quetzalcoatl), has the same structure as 'Quetzalcoatl' but a sourer flavour. Lawrence changed some names – Kate Burns becomes Kate Leslie, Lake Chapala is Lake Sayula – but, most importantly, he changed the ending: Kate now marries the 'savage' rather than returning to her home and mother. Cipriano's proposal is presented as a form of therapy – she needs a project and he needs a woman: 'You marry me. You complain you have nothing to do.' Socialism in Mexico, Lawrence wrote, 'is nothing but an infectious disease, like syphilis', and the implication is that Kate's marriage is syphilitic too: 'how could she marry Cipriano, and give her body to this death?' Kate, like Alvina Houghton, is held captive by her husband: 'You won't let me go!' she says to Cipriano in the final words of the novel.[51]

When Kate sits on her throne as Cipriano's goddess, the dynamo has once again become a virgin: 'How else, she said to herself, is one to begin again, save by re-finding one's virginity?' A way of ensuring that Kate re-finds her virginity is to prevent her from reaching orgasm, and this is Cipriano's great achievement. He 'drew away from her as soon as this desire rose in her' and Kate realised, 'almost with wonder, the death in her of the Aphrodite of the foam'.[52]

*The Plumed Serpent* is alien and alienating, hard to forgive and hard to forget. It is also boring, at times brutally so. Especially tiresome are the 'Quetzalcoatl hymns', a variation on the interminable pledges of tribe loyalty made by the Natcha-Kee-Tawaras: 'Who sleeps – shall wake! Who sleeps – shall wake! Who treads down the path of the snake shall arrive at the place ...' Witter Bynner thought it was the influence of Mabel that ruined *The Plumed Serpent*, which is true although not in the sense that he meant. Bynner was referring to the novel's burden of theosophy, but Mabel alone saw that the book was about her. 'I hear that Mabel thinks she is the heroine in *The Plumed Serpent*!' Frieda wrote mockingly to Bynner.[53] Lawrence, Mabel rightly said, had 'simply transposed' New Mexico for Old Mexico. 'What I wanted him to do for Taos, he did do, but he gave it away to the mother country of Montezuma.'[54] Kate Burns had been warmly inhabited by Lawrence, but Kate Leslie is his enemy and Lawrence compares her to a 'great cat, with its spasms of voluptuousness and its life-long lustful enjoyment of its own isolated individuality'.[55]

Lawrence never knew or cared what his novels were about and this is part of what makes them interesting, even when they are bad. At the level of plot, *The Plumed Serpent* is his take on *The Taming of the Shrew* and in terms of his Dantesque journey *The Plumed Serpent* is the novel in which he reaches a greater understanding of the universe. This is symbolised by the Quetzalcoatl emblem: an eagle enclosed by a serpent with its tail in its mouth. The tail-eating serpent, also the symbol of the theosophical movement, brings, Lawrence said, 'the great opposites into contact and union again'.

When Dante reached the Eternal Light he understood how all the disparate events and all the arbitrary thoughts and all the chance occurrences of all the universe were connected. Here he saw:

> ingathered
> and bound by love into one single volume –
> what, in the universe, seems separated, scattered:
>
> substances, accidents, and dispositions
> as if conjoined.
>
> (*Paradise*, Canto 33, 89–93)

'I managed to finish my Mexican novel,' Lawrence wrote to Amy Lowell. 'And on that very same day,' he continued, 'I went down, as if shot in the intestines.'[56] His collapse coincided with an earthquake in Oaxaca which made the walls of the house rock. Lawrence blamed his condition on the tension generated by Brett (who had been banished by Frieda back to the ranch), but he also described it as the 'tail-end of influenza' getting 'tangled up with a bit of malaria',[57] which makes it sound like the serpent in the Quetzalcoatl emblem. He further explained that he had a case of malaria tangled up with the 'grippe' with 'a typhoid inside', none of which would account for the pain in his intestines.[58] He was taken by stretcher to a local hotel, and three weeks later Lawrence and Frieda were back in Mexico City. Their train journey was described as a 'crucifixion' by Frieda, who cried 'like a maniac the whole night'.[59] They had planned to return to Europe for the spring, but a doctor in Mexico City took an X-ray of Lawrence's lungs and diagnosed the advanced tuberculosis that the Taos doctor had missed. She did not know he was consumptive, Frieda insisted in *'Not I, But the Wind ...'*, until the doctor in Mexico told her.

Lawrence's Self One rejected the diagnosis, but Self Two took the doctor's advice about returning to the healthy air of the Rockies. Because legislation had recently been passed which stopped consumptives from entering the United States, Lawrence, despite wearing blusher to disguise his pallor, was detained, stripped and examined at the El Paso border before eventually being let through on a six-month visa. His rage and humiliation were intensified when the officials accused him of lying about his health. The ingenuity with which he deceived himself about his symptoms probably explains the pain in his intestines: Lawrence simply displaced the location of his sickness, moving it from the upper to the lower body.

When he and Frieda returned to the ranch on 1 April 1925, Mabel was still being analysed by Brill in New York. She was also conducting an affair with a young songwriter called Everett Marcy, about whom very little is known. Carl Van Vechten described Everett as a 'callow youth' and Mabel as currently 'at her most beguiling and dangerous'.[60] Everett was also being analysed by Brill, with Mabel paying his fees, but rather than write Brill a cheque for their sessions, Mabel gave him the manuscript of *Sons and Lovers*. In a letter dated 24 April, she explained to Brill that she was 'glad' to put to 'some creative use' what had been given to her 'by Mr & Mrs Lawrence not openly in exchange for the ranch in New Mexico'.[61] But nor was the manuscript of *Sons and Lovers* openly in exchange for Everett Marcy's analysis, its being worth a great deal more than the amount that Brill would have charged Mabel.

The exchange rate in Mabeltown was fluctuating. Mabel had bought the ranch for $1,200 and given it to her son; she then bought it back from him with a buffalo-hide jacket and a pot of cash and gave it to Lawrence, but in Frieda's name. Lawrence insisted on 'exchanging' the ranch for the manuscript of his novel about a dangerous and destructive mother which Mabel then gave to Brill in lieu of payment for his analysis of her lover who was young enough to be her son. Critics of Mabel have assumed that she failed to appreciate the value of Lawrence's manuscript because she had no interest in his novels, but the opposite is the case.[62]

At the same time that Lawrence was writing *The Plumed Serpent* in Oaxaca, Mabel embarked on the project that would absorb her for the next thirty years, and the impetus behind her memoirs, she explained, was to 'save' herself from the impact of Lawrence's 'disloyalty and treachery'. Brill had counselled her to work, and 'the only work that suggested itself' to her 'was to tell Lawrence about my whole life from the beginning so he would understand more completely, so he would stop calling me dangerous and destructive'. Mabel went one step further: she would achieve in her memoirs a 'self-destruction' more assured than 'anything' that Lawrence 'could accomplish were he to take a hammer and beat my brains upon a stone'. Her aim was 'undo' herself, to 'unravel the fabric of the artificial creation',[63] and Brett, who witnessed the unravelling, described how Mabel 'wrote incessantly, without stopping, day after day, lying on her sofa with a copybook and pencil'.[64] As she wrote, Mabel's melancholy lifted and she ceased to feel, as she put it, that there were 'serpents coiling and uncoiling in madness' in her 'vagina'.[65] She wrote with the same ease and fluency as Lawrence himself, whom she no longer needed to capture the genius of Taos because spirit of place would prove to be Mabel's own genius.

*Background*, the first volume of *Intimate Memoirs*, describes the corrosive effect of capitalism on *fin de siècle* America. In a reversal of the story in which the white woman is held captive by the Indians, Mabel is born in captivity in bourgeois Buffalo, on land stolen from the natives who will eventually free her. Buffalo is a city much like Freud's Vienna, where the inhabitants repress their own 'pain and fear' and pretend 'to ignore each other's inward lives'. The culture is at an advanced state of degeneration: a man is found hanging in his bedroom, a girl disappears, and her mother does not mention her absence. The hyacinths in the garden of the Ganson mansion come up 'in rigid rows' of 'hard and ugly colours ... pink, blue, white, deeper pink'. The tulips, every leaf 'strong, aggressive, and tailored', 'would radiate in symmetrical circles of white, red, yellow, and pink'.[66]

The silence of Mabel's home was broken only by Charles Ganson's desperate rages which, being ignored, made him rage all the more. When her husband stormed upstairs and slammed his door, Sara Ganson 'would raise her eyes from the pretence of reading and, not moving her head ... grimace a little message of very thin reassurance'.[67] Deprived of maternal love, Mabel found pleasure in other women's breasts. She stroked and fondled the breasts of every female friend she had, and in one memorable passage describes how, contriving to share a bed with a servant, she spent an 'ecstatic' night rolling the sleeping woman's bosom 'from side to side' and 'slathering' it with her 'dripping lips'.[68]

The release Mabel found in writing can be felt in the freshness of her voice, the swiftness of her gait and the ease with which she turned chaos ('serpents coiling and uncoiling' in her vagina) into a tale as tailored as her mother's flower garden. She gives the impression of confessing everything, while revealing next to nothing of the truth. Framing her narrative around the drama of a wife who hates her husband and a child with incestuous longings, *Background* is Mabel's *Sons and Lovers*. It was Lawrence who showed Mabel, when he asked her questions for his novel about Sybil Mond, what happened when she wrote things down: 'I was thrilled to find how *reasonable* and *logical* life seemed,' Mabel recalled.[69] She also learned from Lawrence how to reduce a mass of psychological detail to the stark orderings of an Oedipal triangle, and Lawrence's stylistic influence can be felt from the start: Mabel's hellish home with its rigid rows of spiked hyacinths recalls the neat little front gardens of Hell Row in Eastwood, with the 'auriculas and saxifrage in the shadow of the bottom block' and 'sweet-williams and pinks in the sunny top block'.[70] Only from the back of Hell Row is it possible to smell the excrement rising from the ash-pits. Mabel learned one other trick from Lawrence too. After *Background* had been published, she was asked by a shocked friend 'how far' she thought a person was 'justified in going in art, if it sacrifices other people'.[71]

From his bed in the ranch, where he now described his consumption as 'mountain fever' brought on by lack of rain, Lawrence spent April 1925 writing a sixteen-scene play about his old friend, David the giant-slayer. Lawrence's attitude to David always tells us how he felt about himself, and his interest was no longer in David's love for Jonathan but in his relationship with his father-in-law Saul, who anoints him heir to the throne of Israel and then suffers agonies about being supplanted. Lawrence's theme is familial jealousy, and in his new-found sympathy for the king, he atoned for supplanting his own father.

David is now a trespasser with a 'fox-red' beard who brings home the head of Goliath as 'a fox brings his prey to his own hole', who eyes Saul's daughter, Merab, as a 'fox eyes a young lamb', who is pursued by Saul 'as a fox with the dogs upon him'. The play closes with David, last seen on stage stripped down to his leather loin-strap, hiding from Saul in 'a rocky place by the stone Ezel'. Jonathan, given the closing speech, describes his friend as 'subtle,' 'shrewd' and 'prudent' and says that Saul is right to fear him. David might be a 'smiter down of giants' but he would never, like Saul, go naked into the fire. He will wait, concludes Jonathan, 'till the day of David at last shall be finished, and wisdom no more be fox-faced, and the blood gets back its flame'.[72]

Mabel returned to Taos in July 1925, and in early September, the Lawrences – their visa having expired – suspended their table and chairs from the rafters with leather straps to protect them from the rats, and departed the ranch on Lobo Mountain. They left Taos, without saying goodbye to Mabel, in the same month that, three years earlier, they had first arrived. Lawrence's fortieth birthday was spent in New York, and on 25 September, he and Frieda sailed to Southampton knowing that, given the medical examination required to renew his visa, he would not be allowed to return to America. From England they went on to Italy, and settled on the top floor of a villa outside Florence, from whose windows Lawrence could see the Duomo and the hills of Fiesole. Here, in 1926, Frieda began an affair with a married officer in the Italian army called Captain Angelino Ravagli.

Lawrence's closest friends in his last years were Aldous and Maria Huxley, whom he had met through Ottoline Morrell. A tall, near-blind Etonian from a distinguished family of scientists, Huxley felt as Lawrence did about mass culture and modernity, and he would be the first reader of Lawrence's final novel, *Lady Chatterley's Lover*. 'Let's go to New Mexico in the autumn,' Lawrence suggested to the Huxleys. 'Let's be amused.' Lawrence 'often talked of the place,' Huxley recalled, 'with a mixture of love and dislike.' He longed 'to be back in that ferociously virgin world of drought and storm' but also resented 'its alienness and lunar vacancy'.[73]

Lawrence's New Mexico, with its films, Freuds and Fords, pueblos, kivas and snake dances, found its way into Huxley's next novel *Brave New World*. Set in AF (After Ford) 632, the citizens of the World State are no longer obliged to have feelings, to look any older than thirty or to inhabit family units. Monogamy, emotions and parents belong to history, and history, according to 'Our Ford', is 'bunk'. Freud, meanwhile, has revealed the dangers and perversity of family life; those who belong to the lowest social order are conditioned by electric shocks to fear books and flowers, and happiness is ensured by a drug called soma. The theatre no longer exists and silent movies have evolved into 'feelies' – a pansensual experience where the audience can not only watch but feel the giant kisses on the screen.

The old world can still be found in the Savage Reservations of New Mexico whose pueblos – 'stepped and amputated pyramids' – are places of eagles, ladders, old people, ill people, married people and religious people. In snake dances the men swarm up from their subterranean chambers and limp round and round, the drums quickening like 'the pulsing of fever in the ears' while snakes are flung into the crowd; in one pueblo a teenage boy in a loincloth is whipped during the dance by man wearing the mask of a coyote. Huxley, who had not been to New Mexico when he wrote *Brave New World*, would, like Warburg, never see the Snake Dance he described. His impression came from Lawrence's description, and the entire novel is saturated in Lawrence.

The teenage boy, whose name is John, is white but he was born in the pueblo when Linda, his pregnant mother, was accidentally left behind after visiting the reservation on holiday. Linda now has an Indian lover with hair like 'two black ropes' whom John wants to kill. The 'brave new world' itself – which phrase he learns from *The Tempest* – is the shallow, pornographic World State where the mother and son are now taken and in which John, referred to as 'the Savage', is treated as a celebrity. When Linda dies (aged forty-four), John's grief is not understood because no one knows any more what a mother is. Increasingly depressed, he retreats to a hilltop tower where he can once again flagellate himself and experience pain: 'I don't want comfort,' John says before ending his life. 'I want God, I want poetry, I want real danger, I want freedom, I want goodness. I want sin.' His hanging body is described as a compass, dithering over which direction it should take:

> Slowly, very slowly, like two unhurried compass needles, the feet turned towards the right; north, north-east, east, south-east, south, south-south-west; then paused, and, after a few seconds, turned as hurriedly back towards the left. South-south-west, south, south-east, east ...[74]

When she had completed the first two volumes of her memoirs, *Background* and *European Experiences*, Mabel sent copies of the manuscripts to her friends. Carl Van Vechten said that 'Probably, it's going to be the best thing yet done in America', Brill said it was 'one of the best books of mental and emotional evolution that has come to my attention',[75] and then, in April 1926, came Lawrence's verdict from Florence. Mabel had written, he said, 'the most serious "confession" that ever came out of America, and perhaps the most heart-destroying revelation of the American life-process that ever has or ever will be produced. It's worse than Oedipus and Medea, and Hamlet and Lear and Macbeth are spinach and eggs in comparison.' Mabel's book was 'a sort of last word', it was 'hemlock in a cup'.[76] Mabel had written, in other words, the Great American Memoir.

Lawrence liked Mabel's memoirs because her prose had a strong pulse rate and made no attempt to be literary, and because she wrote about the body, the family and the claustrophobia of homes. Having initially dismissed her as a writer or even a 'knower', his letters to Mabel in the last years of his life amount to a masterclass in writing, editing and publication. He suggested that she send the book to Sylvia Beach, who had published *Ulysses* in Paris; Mabel should, Lawrence further counselled, bring out *Background* first, 'so that there would be nothing to startle the prudes', before hitting the public with the other volumes. He advised her to 'turn off the tap' and give herself breaks, not to write if she was 'out of mood' but 'wait for grace', to write about only those things in which she had a 'burning interest' and then to write 'without reflection,' to put her pages in a safe and 'let them lie still' before returning to them at a later date. He passed Mabel's manuscripts on to Aldington and Huxley, who was 'pining' to read them; he advised her on editors, royalties, translations, foreign rights; he told her to have her books reviewed in a few good newspapers 'and no more. As little publicity as possible, and the thing makes its own way and won't be quashed. And preserve your incognito as quickly as you can.' She should, 'for once' put her 'ego aside'.[77] Finally, he warned her to change the names: 'Remember, other people can be utterly remorseless, if they think you've given them away.'[78] Not that Lawrence followed these rules himself: none of his own manuscripts were locked in a safe. Some were currently mouldering in the ranch; could Mabel, he now asked, try to salvage them?

Lawrence's essays on 'Indian Entertainment', 'The Dance of the Sprouting Corn' and 'The Hopi Snake Dance' were published in a collection called *Mornings in Mexico*, which he dedicated to 'Mabel Dodge Luhan, who called me to Taos'. His title, as Mabel will have noted, suggests that his subject was Mexico rather than New Mexico, but the centrepiece of the volume is the essay about 'New Mexico', in which Lawrence described his time there as 'the greatest experience from the outside world that I have ever had'.[79] It was now that he finally repaid his debt to Mabel. But because he gave with one hand and took away with the other, Lawrence wrote a second essay that same week, 'Introduction to these Paintings', whose subject was ostensibly the portrayal of sex in painting but actually the scourge of syphilis, brought to England by merchants trading with America. Syphilis was a disease of the 'upper classes' and while he knew, Lawrence said, 'very little about diseases', he remained 'convinced that the secret awareness of syphilis, and the utter secret terror and horror of it, has had an enormous and incalculable effect on the English consciousness and on the American'. After tracing the syphilitic line through English literature, he confided that 'I have never had syphilis myself. Yet I know and confess how profound is my fear of the disease, and more than fear, my horror.'[80]

'I feel so strongly as if my illness weren't really me,' Lawrence told Mabel in October 1929, describing it as 'bronchitis'.[81] Now aged forty-four, he was living with Frieda in a small house in Bandol near Marseille where, that winter, he wrote *Apocalypse*. Officially his exposition of 'The Book of Revelation', *Apocalypse* was the final revelation of D. H. Lawrence, his last will and testament. When Frieda's sister Else came to stay with them in January 1930, Lawrence weighed six stone. As soon as he was well enough, he told Mabel that same month, he would return to New Mexico; in the meantime he counselled her to yield 'entirely' to the needs of her body.[82] In February Lawrence agreed to be admitted to the Ad Astra sanatorium in the medieval hill town of Vence, between Nice and Antibes, beneath the steep Baou rock. From the balcony of his room he could see the coastline, and in preparation for his return to Mabel, he began to read a life of Columbus. When he developed pleurisy, he asked to be moved. 'This place no good,' he told Maria Huxley; it was the last line of the last letter he sent.

Frieda rented a local villa where Lawrence was carried on 1 March. After breakfast the next morning he sketched, on a piece of paper on his tray, a happily shining sun, a peacock, a locomotive engine of the sort that carried the coal in Eastwood and a dead man lying on his back, his beard and feet pointing straight upwards. Which was how Lawrence also appeared when his body was laid out that night.

It was appropriate, said Mabel, that he died on the second day of March because he was 'always double – split in two'.[83] He was buried in the local cemetery, in a service without speeches or prayer. 'Like a bird,' Frieda said, 'we put him away.'[84] And like a phoenix, he rose.

Lorenzo had prepared in advance his final assassination attempt on Mabel. 'None of That', written in May 1927, is about a twice-married, super-rich American 'dynamo' called Ethel Cane whose hobby is doing up houses. Ethel Cane, who likes dangerous men, especially if they like look prophets or reformers, imagines herself to be an 'extraordinary and potent woman, who would make a stupendous change in the history of man'. She meets a Mexican matador with whom she becomes sexually obsessed, but she will have 'none of that' because Ethel Cane refuses to yield to the needs of her body. One night, however, she goes to the matador's house where he hands her over to half-a-dozen 'of his bull-ring gang, with orders not to bruise her'.[85] Three days later she swallows poison, leaving half her fortune to the matador who ordered her rape. It's a grim little tale, made more malevolent by Ethel's suicide mirroring that of Magnus. 'None of That' – a catchphrase of Mabel's – operates alongside *Lorenzo in Taos* like pistols at dawn, with both parties injured but not killed.

Mabel's memoir of Lorenzo, largely completed while he was still alive but not published until 1932, was dedicated to 'Tony and All Indians' and presented as a letter to the poet Robinson Jeffers, now being groomed as Lawrence's replacement. Lawrence, Mabel concluded, failed to capture the spirit of Taos because 'somehow he could not give himself to it'. He would have, in other words, none of that. His problem, Mabel continued, was to do with the 'rarefied air. Too much oxygen will burn out the lungs. He ran to save himself from purity and died in the old country.'[86] 'It is not a pretty book,' wrote the reviewer for the New York *Evening Post*. 'To anyone who has deep regard for *Sons and Lovers*, *Women in Love* and *Aaron's Rod*, the picture of Lawrence as a sadistic, violent, arrogant, hypersensitive man must be considerably repulsive.' Brett had not realised until *Lorenzo in Taos* 'the width, depth and height of Mabel's dislike of me', and reading it in Vienna, where she was now being analysed by Freud, H.D. said that she had never laughed so much in her life.

Aldous Huxley's edition of *The Letters of D. H. Lawrence* also appeared in 1932, but without the 100 letters that Mabel published in *Lorenzo*.

His achievement was considerable: Huxley collated, in the immediate aftermath of his subject's death, nearly 1,000 pages of correspondence: it was as though he feared that Lawrence – 'the most extraordinary and impressive being' he had ever known – would vanish completely without evidence of his reality. The preface to Huxley's *Letters* remains the best account we have of what it was like to know Lawrence. 'He was an artist first of all,' Huxley wrote, 'and that fact of his being an artist explains a life which seems, if you forget it, inexplicably strange.' Lawrence's spirit was essentially 'nocturnal'; he was at home in 'the darkness of mystery' and thus denounced science in 'the most fantastically unreasonable terms'. While he was often exasperated by him, Huxley admired beyond measure his friend's 'unshakeable' loyalty to his 'own self'. This loyalty, Huxley said, was 'fundamental' in Lawrence, and 'accounts, as nothing else can do, for all that the world found strange in his beliefs and his behaviour'.[87]

As a widow, Frieda was once again free. Within weeks of Lawrence's death she and Murry slept together, and the following year she returned to her ranch accompanied by Angelino Ravagli, who now left his wife and children. She recorded her memories in *'Not I, But the Wind ...'* which was published in October 1934, eighteen months after the appearance of Brett's *Lawrence and Brett*. Frieda's memoir, *Newsweek* calculated, was the seventeenth book on Lawrence to appear since his death. In 1935 she sent Ravagli back to Vence with instructions to bring home her husband's ashes in a bespoke urn, which would be kept in a specially made memorial chapel at the end of a steep path 8,000 feet up Lobo Mountain, making his final resting place the highest point of his journey.

Ravagli's mission involved driving 100 miles through deserts and canyons to Lamy Junction, where he took a train 2,000 miles across the continent to New York, from where he sailed 3,920 miles to Marseille. From Marseille, he travelled a further 120 miles along the coast to the cemetery in Vence to supervise the exhumation. Norman Douglas heard about the procedure from Mrs Gordon Crotch, who ran the local pottery shop and looked after the writer's grave. 'So glad to get your exciting letter about Lawrence,' Douglas replied to Mrs Crotch, his enthusiasm recalling that of Trelawny over the burning body of Shelley. 'Now do tell me more – about bones and skull etc etc. I love macabre details ... send those photos of the exhumation, and I shall be delighted to pay for them.'[88]

The 'golden hoard', as Douglas called Lawrence's remains, was then taken by hearse to Marseille to be cremated, after which Ravagli let Mrs Crotch know that 'the ashes of Lawrence is all ready [sic]. I go take the boath at Villefranche at 4 April with the Lawrence's ashes.'[89]

There are several versions of what happened next. In the first version, Ravagli took the boat and handed the urn to Frieda in Taos. In the second version, Ravagli – according to his own tearful confession, made many years later – collected Lawrence's ashes and then, overwhelmed by the task ahead, dumped them in Marseille, returning to America with an empty urn which he later filled with other ashes picked up on the way to Taos. But whatever it contained – Lawrence's ashes, cigarette ash or the cinders of a fire – the urn had a will like Balaam's ass. No sooner had he cleared customs at New York Harbor than Ravagli left the urn outside the Sheldon Hotel on 49th Street, where Alfred Stieglitz was holding an exhibition of his photographs. 'Someday I'll tell you the story,' Stieglitz reported to Brett. In her joy at being reunited with her lover, Frieda then left the urn on the station platform at Lamy Junction; they had reached Santa Fe before noticing that her husband was not with them. Like the gentleman from San Francisco, Lawrence was 'subjected to many humiliations, much human neglect' in the journey to his final resting place.

Once the ashes were safely back at the ranch, Mabel and Brett agreed that they should be scattered over the landscape rather than turned into a tourist attraction in a mock chapel which Frieda thought looked like a temple to Isis but Mabel and Brett considered more like a station lavatory. Mabel therefore decided to steal the urn, but, getting wind of what was afoot, Frieda had Ravagli stir its contents into a wheelbarrow of cement which was then used to make the altar stone. When the stone was laid men from the pueblo performed a ceremonial dance, after which a storm broke out and the horses panicked as thunder and lightning circled Lobo Mountain.

A third version of what happened to Lawrence's ashes was told to me by the sister of a friend, who heard it in the 1980s when she and her husband were travelling in Taos. Lawrence was not stirred into the cement of the altar stone because Frieda, Mabel and Brett sat down together and ate him. The power of this version rests, of course, on the assumption that it was indeed the body of Lawrence that they ate.

When Dante left the dark wood to climb to Paradise up the mountain of Purgatory, his way was barred by a lion, a leopard and a wolf. Turning back he met Virgil, who had been sent by Beatrice, who had been sent by St Lucia, who had herself been sent by the Virgin Mary; and so, said Virgil, with 'three such blessed women, / concerned for you within the court of heaven', there was no need to fear the steep and savage path.

The three blessed women of Lobo mountain: Mabel, Frieda and Brett

Dorothy Brett, *Three Fates*

# Notes

Quotations from *The Divine Comedy* are from the translation by Allen Mandelbaum (Everyman, 1995).

## INFERNO: PART ONE

1  in 1915, the year the old world ended: D. H. Lawrence, *Kangaroo*, ed. Bruce Steele (Cambridge University Press, 1994), p. 216 ('It was in 1915 the old world ended')

2  'down into the bottomless pit': *The Letters of D. H. Lawrence*, ed. James Boulton et al. (8 vols, Cambridge University Press, 1979–93), 7 February 1916

3  'and the leaves are like soldiers': *Letters*, 28 November 1915

4  'feeling the clouds, feeling the body of the dark overhead': *Kangaroo*, p. 215

5  'the stars and moon blown away': *Letters*, 11 September 1915

6  'a pit in the heath': J. T. Smith, *Nollekens and his Times* (Richard Bentley & Son, 1895), p. 52

7  'a disgusting, detestable and pernicious work': Adam Parks, *Modernism and the Theatre of Censorship* (Oxford University Press, 1996), p. 21

8  'The wind of war … monotonous wilderness of phallicism': Richard Aldington, introduction to D. H. Lawrence, *The Rainbow* (William Heinemann, 1958), p. ix

9  'The war is just hell … banks of dry, rocky ash': *Letters*, 25 August 1914, 11 November 1915, 4 December 1915, 14 May 1915

10  'one must retire': *Letters*, 19 February 1916

11  'to kill a million Germans': *Letters*, 14 May 1915

12  'no meaning … all their significance': D. H. Lawrence, *Mr Noon*, ed. Lindeth Vasey (Cambridge University Press, 1987), p. 228

13 'although there might not ... obscenity of thought, idea, and action': *Modernism and the Theatre of Censorship*, p. 21

14 'rarely seen anyone so ... devoured by internal distresses': Michael Holroyd, *Lytton Strachey: A Critical Biography*, vol. 2 (Holt, Rinehart & Winston, 1968), pp. 161–2

15 'almost wept before the magistrate': D. H. Lawrence, 'The Bad Side of Books', in *The Bad Side of Books: Selected Essays of D. H. Lawrence*, ed. Geoff Dyer (New York Review Books Classic, 2019), p. 210

16 nothing ... that they *could* do: John Carter, '*The Rainbow* Prosecution', *Times Literary Supplement*, 26 February 1969, p. 216

17 'lest ... born into the flesh': 'The Bad Side of Books', p. 211

18 'I curse them all': *Letters*, 22 April 1914

19 'life comes up from the roots': *Letters*, 26 October 1915

20 'There must be a resurrection': *Letters*, 28 November 1915

21 'very like' Shelley: *The Selected Letters of Bertrand Russell: The Public Years, 1914–1970*, ed. Nicholas Griffin (Routledge, 2001), p. 240

22 'put his friends into hell': Richard Holmes, *Shelley: The Pursuit* (HarperCollins, 1974), pp. 360–2

23 'always trying to follow the starry Shelley': *Letters*, 14 October 1913

24 'sail away from this world of war and squalor': *Letters*, 18 January 1915

25 'Does that seem absurd?': *Letters*, 3 February 1915

26 'on one side ... it is beautiful!': Mark Kinkead-Weekes, *D. H. Lawrence : Triumph to Exile, 1912–1922*, vol. 2 of *The Cambridge Biography of D. H. Lawrence* (Cambridge University Press, 1996), p. 184

27 'silly experiments ... unchangeable eternity': *Letters*, 27 January 1915

28 'one sheds one's sicknesses': *Letters*, 26 October 1913

29 'It is time for us now': *Letters*, 28 January 1915

30 'on the edge ... playing round his knees': *Letters*, 12 February 1915

31 'I like the Lawrence who talks to Hilda': *Selected Letters of E. M. Forster*, vol. 1: *1879–1920*, ed. Mary Lago and P. N. Furbank (Collins, 1983), p. 222

32 'The trouble is, you see': Jessie Chambers [E.T.], *D. H. Lawrence: A Personal Record* (Frank Cass, 1935), p. 136

33 'I feel frightfully important': *Letters*, 2 March 1915

34 'was *immensely* impressed': Ray Monk, *Bertrand Russell: The Spirit of Solitude, 1872–1921* (The Free Press, 1996), p. 407

35 'a mongrel terrier': David Garnett, *The Golden Echo* (Chatto & Windus, 1954), p. 241

36 'He was not there': *Letters*, 19 April 1915

37 'rather dreadful': *The Spirit of Solitude*, p. 409

38 'struggling in the dark': *Letters*, 15 March 1915

39 'believed in the principle of Evil': *Letters*, 8 April 1915

40 'so wrong, it is unbearable': *Letters*, 19 April 1915

41 'All my life I have wanted friendship with a man': Jeffrey Meyers, *Homosexuality and Literature, 1890–1930* (Athlone Press, 1977), p. 134

42 'I left myself quite limply in his hands': D. H. Lawrence, *The White Peacock* (Penguin, 1981), p. 166

43 'the most beautiful': David Ellis, *Love and Sex in D. H. Lawrence* (Clemson University Press, 2015), p. 8

44 'inarticulate, powerful, religious … David and Jonathan': *The Rainbow*, pp. 26–8

45 'Now … off and away to find the pots of gold at its feet': *Letters*, 2 March 1915

46 'before, instead of after, the deluge': 'The Bad Side of Books', p. 210

47 'This is the first move to Florida': *Letters*, 30 December 1915

48 'Here the winds are so black and terrible': *Letters*, 16 February 1916

49 'I shall just go where the wind': *Letters*, 7 January 1916

50 'I feel pushed to the brink of existence': *Letters*, 9 January 1916

51 'perhaps the one great literary genius of his generation': letter to Delius in *Frederick Delius and Peter Warlock: A Friendship Revealed*, ed. Barry Smith (Oxford University Press, 2000), p. 187

52 'a bloody bore': Barry Smith, *Peter Warlock: The Life of Philip Heseltine* (Oxford University Press, 1994), p. 92

53 'detestably small-eyed and mean': *Letters*, 5 January 1916

54 'terrifying rocks': *Letters*, 1 February 1916

55 'she would finish a page': Carolyn Heilbrun, *The Garnett Family* (Macmillan, 1961), p. 164

56 'Lawrence at his very worst': Paul Delany, *D. H. Lawrence's Nightmare: The Writer and his Circle in the Years of the Great War* (Basic Books, 1978), p. 198

57 'preach this doctrine of hate': *D. H. Lawrence's Nightmare*, p. 198

58 'How the winds': Frieda Lawrence, *'Not I, But the Wind …'* (Viking, 1934), p. 84

59 'the ancient spirits': *'Not I, But the Wind …'*, p. 88

60 'Nowhere … can it be so black … he felt them come': *Kangaroo*, p. 226

61 'the most horrible noises': *A Mere Interlude: Some Literary Visitors in Lyonnesse*, ed. with an introduction by Melissa Hardie (The Patten Press, 1992)

62 'spread out like a convex': D. H. Lawrence, *Sons and Lovers* (Duckworth, 1913), p. 60

63 'Go to Walker St': *Letters*, 3 December 1926

64 'We must all rise': D. H. Lawrence, 'Return to Bestwood', in *The Bad Side of Books*, p. 294

65 'When I was a boy': *Sons and Lovers*, p. 321

66 'The Bottoms succeeded to Hell Row': *Sons and Lovers*, p. 1

67 'What was there in the mines': *Letters*, 31 August 1925

68 'curious, dark intimacy of the mine': D. H. Lawrence, 'Nottingham and the Mining Countryside', in *Phoenix: The Posthumous Papers of D. H. Lawrence*, ed. Edward McDonald (*hereafter Phoenix I*) (Viking, 1964), pp. 135–6

69 'what splendid men': George Orwell, *The Road to Wigan Pier* (Penguin, 2001), p. 21

70 'had that little, troublesome …': G. H. Neville, *A Memoir of D. H. Lawrence: The Betrayal*, ed. Carl Baron (Cambridge University Press, 1981), p. 40

71 'David is the name of a great man': Helen Corke, *D. H. Lawrence: The Croydon Years* (University of Texas Press, 1965), p. 119

72 'Marriage is the great puzzle': D. H. Lawrence, 'On Being a Man', in *Reflections on the Death of a Porcupine and Other Essays,* ed. Michael Herbert (Cambridge University Press, 1988), p. 216

73 'what the woman *feels*': *Letters*, 5 June 1914

74 'a great error': 'The Collected Letters of Jessie Chambers', ed. George J. Zytark, *The D. H. Lawrence Review*, vol. 12, no. 1/2 (Spring and Summer 1979), p. 59

75 'banter and laughter … swallow my food': May Holbrook, 'Some Memories of D. H. Lawrence', in *A Personal Record*, pp. 234–5

76 'would gather the children in a row': *D. H. Lawrence: A Composite Biography*, ed. Edward H. Nehls (3 vols, University of Wisconsin Press, 1959), vol. 2, p. 126

77 'something unusual might happen': *A Personal Record*, pp. 35-6

78 'reverence': *A Personal Record*, p. 92

79 'A man comes home … about me': D. H. Lawrence, *A Collier's Friday Night*, in *The Complete Plays of D. H. Lawrence* (William Heinemann, 1965), pp. 482–500

80 'anvil on which': *A Personal Record*, p. 152

81 'dark rosy face': *A Personal Record*, p. xxvii

82 'intense and introspective': *A Personal Record*, p. 130

83 'Whatever I forget': *Letters*, 14 November 1928

84 'were filthier than anybody': *The Betrayal*, p. 90

85 'The doctor says': *A Composite Biography*, vol. 3, p. 574

86 'selects' her sons 'as lovers': *Letters*, 14 November 1912

NOTES

87 'three years' savage teaching': D. H. Lawrence, 'Myself Revealed', in *Late Essays and Articles*, ed. James T. Boulton (Cambridge University Press, 2004), p. 178

88 'I am not really afraid': *Letters*, 15 September 1913

89 'in discussing tuberculosis': Franz Kafka, *Letters to Friends, Family and Editors* (Shocken Books, 1977), 7 April 1924

90 'dips and rises': Aldous Huxley et al., *A Conversation on D. H. Lawrence* (UCLA Library, 1974), p. 39

91 'those three days in the tomb': Mabel Dodge Luhan, *Lorenzo in Taos* (Alfred A. Knopf, 1935), p. 326

92 'Any excess in the sympathetic mode': D. H. Lawrence, *Psychoanalysis of the Unconscious and Fantasia of the Unconscious* (Dover Publications, 2005), p. 97

93 'rages of trouble': *Letters*, 15 September 1913

94 'The root of all my sickness': *Letters*, 26 November 1929

95 'Nothing will stop me': John Worthen, *D. H. Lawrence: The Early Years: 1885–1912*, vol. 1 of *The Cambridge Biography of D. H. Lawrence* (Cambridge University Press, 1992), p. 109

96 'Ah, you Haggites see the best of me': *A Personal Record*, p. 134

97 'holiday atmosphere': *A Personal Record*, p. 29

98 'a quality of lightness': *A Personal Record*, p. 47

99 'Work goes like fun': *A Personal Record*, p. 31

100 'Father says one ought': *A Personal Record*, p. 30

101 'wife was a poor girl': *A Personal Record*, p. 63

102 'a sort of brother': *Letters*, 17 December 1912

103 'over and over again': *A Personal Record*, p. 99

104 'was one of his great books': *A Personal Record*, p. 122

105 'woven deep': D. H. Lawrence, 'Hymns in a Man's Life', in *Late Essays and Articles*

106 'the aboundingly spontaneous Shelley': Francis Thompson, *Shelley* (Burns & Oates, 1914), p. 23

107 'the outstanding event of the week': *A Personal Record*, pp. 93–4

108 'nineteen or so': 'The Collected Letters of Jessie Chambers', p. 59

109 'became self-conscious': *A Personal Record*, p. 125

110 'as a husband should love his wife': *A Personal Record*, p. 66

111 'I was conscious of a fierce pain': *A Personal Record*, pp. 66–7

112 'I have a second consciousness': *Letters*, 11 May 1910

113 'not a glimmering': *Selected Letters of E. M. Forster*, p. 222

114 'the whole question': *A Personal Record*, p. 153

115 'his elbows resting on the table': *The Betrayal*, p. 82

116 'wonderfully young': *Sons and Lovers*, p. 198

117 'Bertie': *A Personal Record*, p. 56

118 'I can think of no being in the world': D. H. Lawrence, 'Study of Thomas Hardy', in *Study of Thomas Hardy and Other Essays*, ed. Bruce Steele (Cambridge University Press, 1985), p. 71

119 'If you wanted a woman': *The Betrayal*, p. 84

120 'favourite Prof.': *A Personal Record*, p. 76

121 'never really had a father': *A Personal Record*, p. 88

122 'a genius': *A Composite Biography*, vol. 1, p. 162

123 'the year when my eyes': Ford Madox Ford, *Mightier than the Sword: Memories and Criticisms* (Allen & Unwin, 1938), p. 98

124 'That's my label': Frieda Lawrence, foreword to D. H. Lawrence, *The First Lady Chatterley* (Penguin, 1994), p. 14

125 'leaning against the wall': *Mightier than the Sword*, p. 106

126 'I have never met any young man of his age': *Mightier than the Sword*, p. 113

127 'And though she loved me so much': 'The Bad Side of Books', pp. 207–8

128 'I *did not* find it hard': D. H. Lawrence, 'Myself Revealed', in *The Bad Side of Books*, p. 387

129 'It doesn't matter *who*': *A Personal Record*, p. 177

130 'refused to see that a man is male': *Letters*, 28 January 1910

131 'Why do we slur': 'Study of Thomas Hardy', p. 185

132 'second me': *Letters*, 27 December 1910

133 'I must not confuse': Corke, *The Croydon Years*, p. 10

134 'Now for the beginning of Hell!': D. H. Lawrence, *The Trespasser* (Duckworth, 1912), p. 196

135 'he performed his purpose … maiming her': *The Trespasser*, pp. 250–66

136 'eternally suspended': *The Trespasser*, p. 271

137 'a work of fiction': *Letters*, 1 February 1912

138 'I have always believed': *Letters*, March 1910

139 'Trespassing': *Letters*, 15 April 1908

140 'in a strangled voice': *A Personal Record*, p. 184

141 'tired', 'second hand': *A Personal Record*, p. 190

142 'As the sheets of manuscript': *A Personal Record*, p. 201

143 'Of course it isn't the truth': *A Personal Record*, p. 204

144 'devotion to his genius': *A Personal Record*, p. 201

145 'Not yet, please! … actual spirit of the time': D. H. Lawrence, *Paul Morel*, ed. Helen Baron (Cambridge University Press, 2003), p. xlvii

146 'What was it that Keats said': 'The Collected Letters of Jessie Chambers', p. 59

147 'A Man's life': *The Letters of John Keats*, vol. 2: *1819–1821*, ed. Hyder Edward Rollins (Cambridge University Press, 1958), p. 67

### INFERNO: PART TWO

1 'One has to be a blind mole': Osip Mandelstam, *Conversation about Dante*, trans. Clarence Brown and Robert Hughes (Notting Hill Editions, 2011), p. 114

2 'that piece of supreme art': *Letters*, 2 March 1915

3 'the supreme old novels': D. H. Lawrence, 'Why the Novel Matters', in *The Bad Side of Books*, p. 256

4 'I love Dante': Richard Ellmann, *James Joyce* (Oxford University Press, 1959), p. 226

5 'an epic poem': Ezra Pound, *Money Pamphlets by £* (Peter Russell, 1950), p. 5

6 'most bloodthirsty and exciting': Harold Acton, *Nancy Mitford: A Memoir* (Gibson Square Books/Hamish Hamilton, 1975), p. 45

7 'Dante and Shakespeare': T. S. Eliot, 'Dante', in *The Complete Prose of T. S. Eliot: The Critical Edition: Literature, Politics, Belief, 1927–1929*, ed. Frances Dickey, Jennifer Formichelli and Ronald Schuchard (Johns Hopkins University Press, 2009), p. 700

8 'establish a relationship': T. S. Eliot, 'What Dante Means to Me', in T. S. Eliot, *To Criticize the Critic and Other Writings* (Farrar, Straus & Giroux, 1965), p. 128

9 'flow[ing] through the rigid grey streets': *Letters*, 14 May 1915

10 'the poet of liberty': Thomas Medwin, *Conversations of Lord Byron* (Princeton University Press, 1966), p. 160

11 'discordant': Leigh Hunt, 'Mr Carlyle's Lectures', *The Examiner*, 20 May 1838, p. 310

12 'the massive quality of Milton': C. S. Lewis, 'Shelley, Dryden and Mr Eliot', *Selected Literary Essays* (Cambridge University Press, 1969), p. 204

13 'who could even': Eliot, 'Dante', p. 723

14 'one genuine impulse of the affections': Leigh Hunt, preface to *The Story of Rimini: A Poem* (John Murray, 1816), p. viii

15 'case fell a good deal short of *ours*': Lord Byron, *Selected Letters and Journals*, ed. Leslie Marchand (Belknap Press, 1982), p. 198

16 'the most delightful enjoyments': *The Letters of John Keats*, vol. 2, p. 91

17 'We'll all be happy together': *Letters*, 7 January 1916

18 'Today I can't see a yard': *The Letters of Katherine Mansfield*, ed. Vincent O'Sullivan and Margaret Scott (2 vols, Clarendon Press, 1984–7), vol. 1, p. 261

19 'Pecksniffian ... one vile man': Sydney Janet Kaplan, *Circulating Genius: John Middleton Murry, Katherine Mansfield and D. H. Lawrence* (Edinburgh University Press, 2010), p. 1

20 'a bundle of antennae': *London Magazine*, vol. 3 (1956), p. 32

21 'the kind of wriggling self-abuse': *Circulating Genius*, p. 13

22 'not warm, ardent, eager': *D. H. Lawrence's Nightmare*, p. 241

23 'simply *raves*, roars': *Letters of Katherine Mansfield*, vol. 1, p. 261

24 'A chimney of his house': *Kangaroo*, p. 227

25 'how I wished': *D. H. Lawrence's Nightmare*, p. 38

26 'perceptibly over-eager': introduction to *Letters*, vol. 2, p. 4

27 'some sort of unwholesome relationship': *Triumph to Exile*, p. 320

28 'Lawrence is at present': *Triumph to Exile*, p. 321

29 'jealous and sad': *Circulating Genius*, p. 65

30 'exquisite': *D. H. Lawrence's Nightmare*, p. 223

31 'The heights were always wuthering': *Circulating Genius*, p. 69

32 'with invisible arrows of death': *D. H. Lawrence's Nightmare*, p. 248

33 'insect-like stupidity': *Letters*, 5 May 1916

34 'immense German Christmas pudding': *Triumph to Exile*, p. 323

35 'the black walls of the war': *Kangaroo*, p. 257

36 'A real panic comes over me': Cecil Gray, *Musical Chairs; Or, Between Two Stools* (The Hogarth Press, 1948), p. 300

37 'the same hour': M. L. Skinner, *The Fifth Sparrow: An Autobiography* (Sydney University Press, 1972), pp. 115–16

38 'Frieda and I do not even speak': *Letters of Katherine Mansfield*, vol. 1, p. 263

39 'incurably and incredibly stupid': *Aldous Huxley: Bloom's Modern Critical Views*, ed. Harold Bloom (Infobase, 2010), p. 117

40 'a swamp': *The Selected Letters of D. H. Lawrence,* ed. Diana Trilling (Farrar, Straus & Cudahy, 1958), p. xxi

41 'It hurts me very much': *Letters*, 22 February 1915

42 'a fool and a criminal': *The Letters of Aldous Huxley*, ed. Grover Cleveland Smith (Chatto & Windus, 1969), p. 314

43 'You can put anything you like': D. H. Lawrence, 'The Novel', in *The Bad Side of Books*, p. 237

44 'In her mindlessness': introduction to *The Selected Letters of D. H. Lawrence*, p. xxii

45 'Frieda wasn't a person': Rosie Jackson, *Frieda Lawrence,* (HarperCollins, 1994), p. 33

46 'It was evident': *Mr Noon*, p. 128

47 'It took a German like Frieda': introduction to *The Selected Letters of D. H. Lawrence*, p. xxiv

48 'Your most vital necessity in this life': *Letters*, 7 July 1914

49 'I'm not coming to you *now* for rest': *Letters*, 16 May 1912

50 'You will find her and me': *Letters*, 3 April 1914

51 'Titanic iceberg': *Frieda Lawrence: The Memoirs and Correspondence*, ed. E. W. Tedlock (Alfred A. Knopf, 1964), p. 166

52 'a leaf blown in the wind': *A Personal Record*, p. 184

53 'a cat that looks round': *Mr Noon*, p. 123

54 'French windows open': *'Not I, But the Wind ... '*, p. 4

55 'I had just met': *'Not I, But the Wind ... '*, pp. 3–4

56 'So long as one talked': *Lorenzo in Taos*, p. 49

57 'soft, non-intellectual': *Sons and Lovers*, p. 9

58 'In the tension of opposites': D. H. Lawrence, *Birds, Beasts and Flowers* (Cresset Press, 1930), p. 105

59 'Well, I think you're lucky': *Mr Noon*, pp. 124, 123

60 'You are quite unaware of your husband': Michael Squires and Lynn K. Talbot, *Living at the Edge: A Biography of D. H. Lawrence and Frieda von Richthofen* (University of Wisconsin Press, 2002), p. 53

61 'You are the most wonderful woman in all England': *'Not I, But the Wind ... '*, p. 4

62 'She is ripping': *Letters*, 17 April 1912

63 'the catastrophic naivety': introduction to *The Selected Letters of D. H. Lawrence,* p. xxi

64 'I hated that death': *'Not I, But the Wind ... '*, p. 47

65 'I am married to an earthquake': *Living at the Edge*, p. 53

66 'I thought Ernest was Lancelot': *The Memoirs and Correspondence*, p. 85

67 'The misery I saw depicted': *A Personal Record*, p. 213

68 'suddenly': *'Not I, But the Wind ... '*, p. 5

69 'tongue-tied ... really free': *A Personal Record*, p. 216

70 'I hardly think I could have been': *'Not I, But the Wind ... '*, p. 3

71 'hatred' ... 'instinctively sorry': Frieda Lawrence, 'And the Fullness Thereof ...', in *The Memoirs and Correspondence*, pp. 470, 55

72 'The Lord can't have been such a bad psychologist': *The Memoirs and Correspondence*, p. 83

73 'chose' him: 'The Otto Gross–Frieda Weekley Correspondence', transcribed, translated and annotated by John Turner with Cornelia Rumpf-Worthen and Ruth Jenkins, *The D. H. Lawrence Review*, vol. 22, no. 2 (Summer 1990), p. 160

74 'My Beloved': 'Otto Gross–Frieda Weekley', p. 165

75 'the nearest approach': Ernest Jones, *Free Associations: Memories of a Psychoanalyst* (Basic Books, 1959), pp. 173–4

76 'The psychology of the unconscious': Gottfried M. Heuer, *Freud's 'Outstanding' Colleague/Jung's 'Twin Brother': The Suppressed Psychoanalytic and Political Significance of Otto Gross* (Routledge, 2017), p. 64

77 'giant shadow of Freud': 'Otto Gross–Frieda Weekley', p. 190

78 'far, far more brilliant than Freud': *Mr Noon*, p. 127

79 'in unison of pure love', *Mr Noon*, p. 141

80 'I cannot understand it': 'Otto Gross–Frieda Weekley', p. 166

81 'You won't find 3 people': 'Otto Gross–Frieda Weekley', p. 197

82 'have the right to gamble': 'Otto Gross–Frieda Weekley', p. 192

83 'almost destroyed': Martin Green, *The Von Richthofen Sisters: The Triumphant and the Tragic Modes of Love* (Basic Books, 1974), p. 53

84 'He was a marvellous lover': *Mr Noon*, pp. 126–7

85 'He lived for his vision': *The Memoirs and Correspondence*, p. 101

86 'reminiscent of the mood': *Freud's 'Outstanding' Colleague*, p. 173

87 'was almost as difficult': *Freud's 'Outstanding' Colleague*, p. 190

88 'like Gross and Frick': Martin Green, *Mountain of Truth: The Counterculture Begins: Ascona, 1900–1920* (University Press of New England, 1986), p. 34

89 'I could stand on my head for joy': *Letters*, 15 June 1912

90 'the vast patch work of Europe … so partial': *Mr Noon*, p. 107

91 'You will know by now': *Letters*, 7 May 1912

92 'thrown out of our paradisial state': *'Not I, But the Wind …'*, p. 40

93 'The children are miserable': *Letters*, 3 July 1912

94 'If my mother had lived': *'Not I, But the Wind …'*, p. 56

95 'Whatever the children may miss now': *Letters*, 14 December 1912

96 'word for word true': *Triumph to Exile*, p. 41

97 'It's I who've given you your self-respect': D. H. Lawrence, *The Fight for Barbara: A Comedy in Four Acts*, in *The Complete Plays of D. H. Lawrence*, p. 280

98 'I know it's a good thing': *Letters*, 9 June 1912

99 'curse the blasted, jelly-boned swines': *Letters*, 3 July 1912

100 'So many Christs': D. H. Lawrence, 'Christs in the Tyrol', in *Twilight in Italy and Other Essays*, ed. Paul Eggert (Cambridge University Press, 2002), p. 46

101 'I do not live any longer': *Mr Noon*, p. 252

102 'a man who was not a gentleman': *Living at the Edge*, p. 66

103 'an anarchist': David Garnett, *Great Friends: Portraits of Seventeen Writers* (Macmillan, 1979), p. 78

104 'a vast precipice': *Mr Noon*, p. 262

105 'a steady sort of force': *Triumph to Exile*, p. 40

106 a 'pure Italian': *Mr Noon*, p. 332

107 'dantesque sunrise': *'Not I, But the Wind ... '*, p. 70

108 'Well, I don't love her, mother': *Sons and Lovers*, p. 214

109 'I wish you could laugh at me just for one minute': *Sons and Lovers*, p. 189

110 'It's one of the creepiest episodes': introduction to *The Selected Letters of D. H. Lawrence*, p. xxiv

111 'The deer feed sometimes': *Letters*, 23 April 1913

112 'beastly, tight, Sunday feeling': *Letters*, 13 May 1913

113 'could not bear to look at it ... something else': *Twilight in Italy and Other Essays*, p. 209

114 'Love withers': *Shelley on Love: An Anthology*, ed. Richard Holmes (University of California Press, 1980), pp. 45–6

115 'in the Shelley direction': *Mr Noon*, p. 193

116 'an hours walk': *Letters*, 14 October 1913

117 'No words can tell you': letter to Mary Gisborne, R. Glynn Grylls, *Mary Shelley: A Biography* (Haskell House, 1969),pp. l, 164

118 'One gets by rail from Genoa': *Letters*, 30 September 1913

119 'hated me for being miserable': *Triumph to Exile*, p. 113

120 'I wish I could break my chains': *Shelley: The Pursuit*, p. 728

121 'made the yellow flames glisten': Edward Trelawny, *Recollections of the Last Days of Shelley and Byron* (Carroll & Graf, 2000), p. 137

122 'a bird with broad wings': *Letters*, 18 November 1913

123 'It seems to me': *Letters*, 2 December 1913

124 'the gush, the throb': Walt Whitman, *Leaves of Grass*, ed. David S. Reynolds (Oxford University Press, 2005), p. 85

125 'The fault about Whitman': *Letters*, 22 December 1913

126 'Whitman did not take a person': *Letters*, 22 December 1913

127 'look in my novel for the old stable ego': *Letters*, 5 June 1914

128 'poetical Character': *Complete Poems and Selected Letters of John Keats*, Introduction by Edward Hirsch (Modern Library of New York, 2001), p. 500

129 'the mind in creation': Percy Bysshe Shelley, 'A Defence of Poetry', *Selected Prose Works of Shelley*, with a foreword by Henry S. Salt (Watts & Co., 1915), p. 111

130 'diamond and coal': *Letters*, 5 June 1914

131 ''mid snow and ice': *Letters*, 18 June 1914

132 'Heaven, how happy we all were': *Triumph to Exile*, p. 143

133 'They discussed him before he came in': Hilda Doolittle [H.D.]., *Bid Me to Live: A Madrigal* (Virago, 1980), p. 137

134 'it was the spear': *Letters*, 30 January 1913

135 'long, slow, pernicious cold': *Letters*, 7 January 1915

136 'very sick and corpse-cold': *Letters*, 30 January 1915

137 'too timid and sensitive': *D. H. Lawrence's Nightmare*, p. 113

138 'the only one who seemed': *Bid Me to Live*, p. 65

139 'Let me tell you what happened': *Letters of Katherine Mansfield*, vol. 1, pp. 263–4

140 'one atom of sympathy for Frieda': *Letters of Katherine Mansfield*, vol. 1, p. 268

141 'Don't talk to me of Shelley. No, no': Aldous Huxley, *Point Counter Point* (Vintage, 2004), pp. 157–8

142 'Why should Shelley say of the skylark': 'Study of Thomas Hardy', p. 71

143 'It seems when we hear a skylark': D. H. Lawrence, 'The Poetry of the Present', in *The Bad Side of Books*, p. 77

144 'Whitman's is the best poetry': 'The Poetry of the Present', p. 80

145 'a soft valley': *Letters*, 29 May 1916

146 'really terrifying': *D. H. Lawrence's Nightmare*, p. 231

147 to take two couples: *A Personal Record*, p. 103

148 'So the two men entwined': D. H. Lawrence, *Women in Love* (Martin Secker, 1928), p. 283

149 'for the poet to yield himself': Merle Rubin, ' "Not I, But the Wind that Blows through Me": Shelleyan Aspects of Lawrence's Poetry', *Texas Studies in Literature and Language* (Spring 1981), p. 110

150 'through the tree fiercer and fiercer': *Sons and Lovers*, p. 61

151 'Man is an instrument': 'A Defence of Poetry', p. 76

152 'My God': *Women in Love*, p. 412

153 'What had she to do with parents': *Women in Love*, p. 482

154 'Murder': D. H. Lawrence, 'Edgar Allan Poe', in *Studies in Classic American Literature*, ed. Ezra Greenspan, Lindeth Vasey and John Worthen (Cambridge University Press, 2003), p. 239

155 'This playing at killing': *Women in Love*, p. 50

156 'tight round the neck': *Women in Love*, p. 199

157 'long, grave, downward-looking': *Women in Love*, p. 309

158 'She could not go on with her writing ... You hear?': *Women in Love*, p. 109

159 'I snatched up that iron paperweight': Fyodor Dostoevsky, *The Brothers Karamazov*, trans. Constance Garnett (William Heinemann, 1951), p. 666

160 'powerful, underworld men': *Women in Love*, p. 121

161 'darkness': *Women in Love*, pp. 409–10

162 'the navel of the world': *Women in Love*, p. 432

163 'so beautifully soft ... naked to heaven': *Women in Love*, pp. 498–504

164 'a pure balance of two single beings': *Women in Love*, p. 158

165 'a woman I don't see': *Women in Love*, p. 152

166 'of a world empty of people': *Women in Love*, pp. 131–2

167 'The acquaintance ... vigorous movement': 'Prologue to *Women in Love*', *Phoenix II*, pp. 92–106

168 'the achieved perfections': *Women in Love*, p. 478

169 'forward in life knowledge': D. H. Lawrence, 'Whitman', in *Studies in Classic American Literature*, p. 405

170 'a great hail storm ... characters': *D. H. Lawrence's Nightmare*, pp. 271, 262

171 'There was no story so absurd': *Conversations of Lord Byron*, p. 11

172 'about the sun': *Kangaroo*, p. 236

173 'freely of the end of the world': *Letters*, 5 May 1917

174 'One stormy night': *Triumph to Exile*, p. 404

175 'Lawrence has sent me his *awful* book': D. H. Lawrence, *The First Women in Love*, ed. John Worthen and Lindeth Vasey (Cambridge University Press, 1998), p. xlvi

176 'My word': *The Letters of Virginia Woolf*, vol. 5: *1932–1935*, ed. Nigel Nicolson (Chatto & Windus, 1979), p. 121

177 'And poor vindictive old Ottoline': *D. H. Lawrence's Nightmare*, p. 273

178 'so many single pieces': D. H. Lawrence, *Look! We Have Come Through!: A Cycle of Love Poems* (The Ark Press, 1958), p. 19

179 'After much struggling': *Look! We Have Come Through!*, p. 19

180 'destructive electricity': *Letters*, 23 August 1917

181 'was definitely not attractive': *Musical Chairs*, p. 138

182 'It surprises me': introduction to *Studies in Classic American Literature*, p. xxix

183 'thrilling blood-and-thunder': *Letters*, 30 August 1917

184 'There is a stranger on the face of the earth': D. H. Lawrence, 'The Spirit of Place' (first version), in *Studies in Classic American Literature*, p. 168

185 'All the best part of knowledge': *Psychoanalysis and the Unconscious*, p. 15

186 'in many ways a bore': *Letters*, 7 August 1917

187 'down the great magnetic wind': 'The Spirit of Place' (first version), p. 171

188 'it is necessary': D. H. Lawrence, 'Nathaniel Hawthorne', in *Studies in Classic American Literature*, p. 241

189 'magnetic propulsion': *Psychoanalysis and the Unconscious*, p. 24

190 'a sort of electric power': *Women in Love*, p. 67

191 'a lodestone': D. H. Lawrence, 'Edgar Allan Poe', in *Studies in Classic American Literature*, p. 231

192 'a virtuous Frankenstein monster': D. H. Lawrence, 'Benjamin Franklin', in *Studies in Classic American Literature*, p. 185

193 'conceive of themselves': D. H. Lawrence, 'Henry St. John de Crèvecoeur', in *Studies in Classic American Literature*, p. 191

194 'dark, primitive, weapon-like': 'Henry St. John de Crèvecoeur', p. 199

195 'does not pit himself against the sea': D. H. Lawrence, 'Herman Melville', in *Studies in Classic American Literature*, p. 334

196 'stick his head': *Letters*, 30 August 1916

197 'burrowed underground': D. H. Lawrence, 'Whitman' (1921–2), in *Studies in Classic American Literature*, p. 405

198 'like the song': 'Whitman' (1921–2), p. 417

199 'untranslatable otherness': 'The Spirit of Place' (first version), p. 168

200 'magical country': *Musical Chairs*, p. 122

201 'a country that makes a man psychic': *Kangaroo*, p. 226

202 'I cannot even conceive': *Letters*, 12 October 1917

203 'perfectly still, and pale': Richard Aldington, *D. H. Lawrence: Portrait of a Genius, But …* (William Heinemann, 1950), p. 199

204 'the people are not people': *Letters*, 17 October 1917

INFERNO: PART THREE

1 'In his eyes he saw the farm': *Kangaroo*, p. 258

2 'revulsed': *Bid Me to Live*, p. 109 ('I could not explain my revulsion to your writing, nor why it bored me')

3 'in your interminable novels': *Bid Me to Live*, p. 164

4 'flaming letters': *Bid Me to Live*, p. 138

5 'You said I was a living spirit': *Bid Me to Live*, p. 183

6 'feared and wondered over': *Kangaroo*, p. 248

7 'concentric, geometric': *Bid Me to Live*, p. 72

8 'great, over-sexed officer': *Bid Me to Live*, p. 47

9 'It's not that picture': *The Oxford Encyclopedia of American Literature*, vol. 3, ed. Jay Perini (Oxford University Press, 2004), p. 184

10 'One seems to be': *Triumph to Exile*, p. 412

11 'a perfect triangle': *Bid Me to Live*, p. 78

12 'I'm sick of the Ott': *Bid Me to Live*, p. 139

13 'Lawrence does not really care for women': *Magic Mirror, Compassionate Friendship, Thorn Thicket: A Tribute to Erich Heydt*, ed. Nephie J. Christodoulides (ELS Editions, 2015), p. 114

14 'all fixed up between them': *Bid Me to Live*, p. 78

15  'A waterlily': 'The Poetry of the Present', p. 78

16  'some sort of guide or master': Hilda Doolittle [H.D.], *Tribute to Freud: Writing on the Wall, Advent* (Carcanet, 1985), p. 141

17  'break the clutch': Hilda Doolittle [H.D.], *Collected Poems*, ed. Louis L. Martz (New Directions, 1983), p. xix

18  'this damn war': *Bid Me to Live*, pp. 83–4

19  'physical phenomenon': Janice S. Robinson, *H.D.: The Life and Work of an American Poet* (Houghton Mifflin, 1982), p. 10

20  'the laconic speech of the Imagistes': *The Life and Work of an American Poet*, p. 63

21  'You jeered at my making abstractions': *Bid Me to Live*, p. 164

22  'Of course, behind both': *The Life and Work of an American Poet*, p. 94

23  'Look': *Letters*, 6 November 1917

24  'unproud, subservient, cringing': *Letters*, 7 November 1917

25  'succession of musical notes', D. H. Lawrence, *Aaron's Rod* (Penguin, 1996), p. 39

26  'secret malady': *Aaron's Rod*, p. 22

27  'a fresh, stoutish … pince-nez and dark clothes': *Aaron's Rod*, pp. 27–30

28  'Each might have been born': *Aaron's Rod*, p. 106

29  'was conditioned, like herself': *Bid Me to Live*, p. 155

30  'Dis of the under-world': *Bid Me to Live*, p. 141

31  'I don't know why you and I': *Letters*, 12 March 1918

32  'This notebook is a replica': *Bid Me to Live*, p. 190

33  'it was not England … out of the world': *Bid Me to Live*, p. 145

34  'Perhaps you would say': *Bid Me to Live*, p. 176

35  'ghostly presences': *Tribute to Freud*, p. 173

36  'We don't want to be kicked out … so unapproachable?': *Bid Me to Live*, p. 193

37  'Somewhere, somehow': *Bid Me to Live*, p. 148

38  'they cannot stop you': *Bid Me to Live*, p. 165

39  'a very visible': *Bid Me to Live*, p. 158

40  'I have not seen Hilda for some time': *Letters*, 18 June 1918

41  'on a sort of ledge': *Letters*, 3 June 1918

42  'the passion of fighting': D. H. Lawrence, *Movements in European History*, ed. Philip Crumpton (Cambridge University Press, 1989), p. 117

43  'Every man has two selves': *Movements in European History*, p. 258

44  'an indescribable tone': *Kangaroo*, p. 253

45  'ill and unhappy': *Triumph to Exile*, p. 481

46  'I hope never to see you again': *Tribute to Freud*, p. 134

47  'Poor Hilda': *Letters*, 16 December 1918

48 'The wind is getting-up': *Letters*, 29 November 1918
49 'A putrid disease': *Letters*, 28 February 1919
50 'hail lashed down': *Kangaroo*, p. 256
51 'not to care': Richard Aldington, *Life for Life's Sake: A Book of Reminiscences* (Cassell, 1968), pp. 233–4
52 'a grey, dreary grey coffin': *Kangaroo*, p. 258

PURGATORY: PART ONE

1 'It was spacious': *Aaron's Rod*, p. 132
2 'a sincere half-mocking argument': *Triumph to Exile*, p. 536
3 'a very good book': Norman Douglas, *Looking Back* (Harcourt, Brace, 1933), p. 350
4 'The South!': *Letters*, 18 November 1919
5 'the past is so much stronger': *Letters*, 1 June 1920
6 'strange to me': D. H. Lawrence, Introduction to *Memoir of Maurice Magnus*, in *Memoirs of the Foreign Legion by M.M., with an Introduction by D. H. Lawrence* (Alfred A. Knopf, 1925), p. 7
7 'a mass of *café au lait*': D. H. Lawrence, 'David', in *Sketches of Etruscan Places and Other Italian Essays*, ed. Simonetta de Filippis (Cambridge University Press, 1992), p. 185
8 'has never … left me in the lurch': *Memoir*, p. 7
9 'wicked red face': *Memoir*, p. 8
10 'inspired provincial': *Looking Back*, p. 286
11 'I don't like it': *Looking Back*, p. 287
12 'a touch of down-on-his-luck': *Memoir*, p. 8
13 'buttoned up in their overcoats … introduce you to Magnus': *Memoir*, p. 8
14 'best piece single of writing, *as writing*': *Letters*, 26 January 1922
15 'just literal truth': *Letters*, 26 January 1922
16 'deeply disturbed': *'Not I, But the Wind …'*, p. 99
17 'a grrrreat littttterary period': Peter Wilson, *A Preface to Ezra Pound* (Routledge, 1997), p. 44
18 'the world broke in two': Milton Meltzer, *Willa Cather: A Biography* (Twenty-First Century Books, 2008), p. 112
19 'Lawrence's one attempt at biography': *Triumph to Exile*, p. 706
20 'just the kind of man': *Memoir*, p. 8
21 'an actor-manager' : *Memoir*, p. 8
22 'eyed me in that shrewd and rather impertinent way': *Memoir*, pp. 8–9
23 'all the shortcuts': *Memoir*, p. 9

24 'didn't care': *Memoir*, p. 9

25 'in a castle': *Aaron's Rod*, p. 210

26 'strange, vast, terrifying reality': *Movements in European History*, p. 7

27 'some impression … predict them': *Movements in European History*, pp. 8–9

28 'offered to man visions': *Movements in European History*, p. 165

29 'man was alive': *Movements in European History*, p. 166

30 'When Lorenzo was dying': *Movements in European History*, p. 154

31 'strange change … burned': *Movements in European History*, p. 154

32 'like a hot coal quenched': 'David', p. 186

33 'Why here you are': *Memoir*, p. 9

34 'queer smell … just wondered': *Memoir*, pp. 10–15

35 'Look here … half whimsically about the food': *Memoir*, pp. 11–12

36 'little pontiff': *Memoir*, p. 13

37 'heaven knows what … world of men': *Memoir*, pp. 13–35

38 'just the common … new bird to me': *Memoir*, p. 13

39 'You aren't going … good, good food': *Memoir*, pp. 15–16

40 'as grotesquely and alarmingly': H. M. L. Tomlinson, *Norman Douglas* (Chatto & Windus, 1931), p. 6

41 'no one had a keener sense': Cecil Gray, *Peter Warlock: A Memoir of Philip Heseltine* (Jonathan Cape, 1934), p. 121

42 'a natural copy-cat': David Garnett, 'A Reminiscence', Introduction to D. H. Lawrence, *Love among the Haystacks & Other Pieces* (Martin Secker, 1933), p. xv

43 'demoniacal possessions': John Worthen, 'Drama and Mimicry in D. H. Lawrence', in *Lawrence and Comedy*, ed. Paul Eggert and John Worthen (Cambridge University Press, 1996), p. 25

44 'He would work his congregation up': *'Not I, But the Wind …'*, pp. 43–4

45 'preferred the humorously satirical': Nancy Cunard, *Grand Man: Memories of Norman Douglas* (Secker & Warburg, 1954), p. 247

46 'On one side sat a tall, flashy …': Max Beerbohm, 'Enoch Soames', in *Seven Men*, ed. John Updike (New York Review Books Classics, 2000), p. 23

47 'Poor D. H. Lawrence': Joseph Epstein, *Charm: The Elusive Enchantment* (Rowman & Littlefield, 2018), p. 135

48 'He mimicked himself ruthlessly and continuously': 'A Reminiscence', p. xv

49 ' "Oh," said Magnus, "why that's the very time to spend money" ': *Memoir*, pp. 13–14

50 'the ordinary high-handed obstinate husband': D. H. Lawrence, 'Autobiograpical Fragment', in *Late Essays and Articles*, p. 51

51 'mostly … in one or other': *Memoir*, p. 14

52 'we find pages and pages of drivel': *Looking Back*, p. 345

53 'Isn't that all rather *Cinquecento*': *Grand Man*, p. 62

54 'malicious pederast': Vladimir Nabokov, *Letters to Vera*, ed. and trans. Olga Voronina and Brian Boyd (Vintage, 2014), p. 78

55 'Florence is taboo for me': Mark Holloway, *Norman Douglas: A Biography* (Secker & Warburg, 1976), p. 355

56 'ultimately boring': *Letters*, 23 May 1917

57 'extremely nice people': *Letters*, 24 November 1919

58 'world without time': Stanley Weintraub, *Reggie: A Portrait of Reginald Turner* (G. Braziller, 1965), p. 189

59 'Burn your boats!': *Looking Back*, p. 24

60 'How lovely your hair is': *Memoir*, p. 17

61 'Why should I go second?… Do come': *Memoir*, pp. 17–18

62 'So the little outsider was gone': *Memoir*, p. 17

63 'thrilled at the fireworks of wit': *'Not I, But the Wind …'*, p. 98

64 'What did *you* do in the Great War': Norman Douglas, *Alone* (R. M. McBride, 1922), p. 15

65 'I myself never considered Plato very wrong': *Letters*, 19 April 1915

66 'I have D. H. Lawrence … remote': *Reggie*, p. 193

67 'Morning in Florence …': 'David', pp. 185–6

68 'a line of Lawrence': *Reggie*, p. 191

69 'and I was charged with the odious task': *Looking Back*, p. 345

70 'Gradually the officer had become aware': D. H. Lawrence, 'The Prussian Officer', in *The Prussian Officer* (Penguin, 1968), p. 9

71 'straight in front of him': 'The Prussian Officer', p. 29

72 'bluey like fire': 'The Prussian Officer', pp. 9–10

73 'enviable flair, an enviable freshness': *Looking Back*, p. 351

74 'It has always seemed to me possible': *Norman Douglas: A Biography*, p. 337

75 'flit along': *Alone*, p. 111

76 'a low cliff, along whose summit': D. H. Lawrence, 'Vin Ordinaire', in *Selected Stories*, ed. Sue Wilson (Penguin, 2007), pp. 139–45

77 'At the Renaissance, mankind, and Florence perfectly': D. H. Lawrence, 'Looking Down on the City', in *Sketches of Etruscan Places and Other Italian Essays*, pp. 193–4

78 'The town lies below and very near': 'Looking Down on the City', p. 194

79 'amphitheatre of hills': 'Looking Down on the City', pp. 194–5

80 'far-off sadness': 'Looking Down on the City', pp. 194–5

81 'the pain which overcomes a man': 'Looking Down on the City', p. 195.

82 'first primal consciousness': 'Looking Down on the City', p. 196

83 'lovely, suave, fluid, *creative* electricity': *Psychoanalysis and the Unconscious*, p. 22

84 'the moonlight standing up': *Sons and Lovers*, pp. 23–4

85 'It happened before he was born': *A Personal Record*, p. 138

86 'hewing at a piece of rock': *Sons and Lovers*, pp. 30–2

87 'Oh, you never know what he's at': *Memoir*, p. 14

88 'her arms, her wrists, her hands': *Women in Love*, pp. 173–4

89 'backwards and forwards': *The Rainbow*, pp. 180–1

90 'I met him in Capri years and years ago': *Memoir*, p. 14

91 'I know it because I had fixed to leave': Norman Douglas, *D. H. Lawrence and Maurice Magnus: A Plea for Better Manners*, in *Memoir of Maurice Magnus*, ed. Keith Cushman (Black Swallow Press, 1987), pp. 109–10

92 'And now ... you must': *A Plea for Better Manners*, p. 110

93 'Here's your shirt': *A Plea for Better Manners*, p. 113

94 'Don't want anyone to know where I am ... under book cases': Norman Douglas Collection, Beinecke Rare Book and Manuscript Library, Yale University

95 'Cassino – Cassino – Cassino!': Maurice Magnus, 'Holy Week at Monte Cassino', *Land and Water*, 29 April 1920, p. 15

96 'He was in pensive mood ... such convulsions': *Alone*, pp. 134–5

97 'refinements': *A Plea for Better Manners*, p. 114

98 'such tremulously tender accents': *A Plea for Better Manners*, p. 114

99 'the cruel illusion of importance *manqué*': *Memoir*, p. 85

100 'so hollow': *Movements in European History*, p. 253

101 'royal nerves': *Memoir*, p. 86

102 'littérateur!': *Memoir*, p. 78

103 'to all my fellow sufferers': Louise E. Wright, *Maurice Magnus: A Biography* (Cambridge Scholars Publishing, 2007), pp. 9–10

104 'carefully ... told me': Edward Gordon Craig, *Index to the Story of my Days: Some Memoirs of Edward Gordon Craig, 1872–1907* (Hulton Press, 1957), p. 276

105 'A concert or a lecture to arrange?... he could have done it': *Index to the Story of my Days*, pp. 277–81

106 'He was not dishonest ... weak at the knees': *Index to the Story of my Days*, p. 281

107 'a saint, an artist, a gentleman, all in one': Maurice Magnus, 'Memoirs of Golden Russia', Norman Douglas Collection

108 'persistent, subtle jealousy': letter to Douglas Goldring, Norman Douglas Collection

109 'I was glad to lose sight of him': *Index to the Story of my Days*, p. 282

110 'seemed to have played him': *Maurice Magnus: A Biography*, p. 114

111 'the pale crouching Duomo … dull': *'Not I, But the Wind …'*, p. 98

112 'Few places in the West': Herbert Bloch, *Monte Cassino in the Middle Ages*, vol. 1 (Edizioni di Storia e Letteratura, 1986), p. 4

113 'crouching there above, world-famous': *Memoir*, p. 18

114 'riseth in height the space of three miles': *Life of St Benedict by Gregory the Great*, trans. Terrence G. Kardong (Liturgical Press, 2009), p. 20

115 'beyond the world into the pre-world': D. H. Lawrence, *The Lost Girl* (Martin Secker, 1920), p. 345

116 'It's a bit staggeringly primitive': *Letters*, 16 December 1919

117 'everything must be cooked … terrific beauty of the place': *Letters*, 16 December 1919

118 'It seems there are places which resist us': *The Lost Girl*, p. 343

119 'turned into a wandering Jew': *Triumph to Exile*, p. 546

120 'about 4 miles by 2 miles': *Letters*, 9 January 1920

121 'one of the most wonderful': *Letters*, 9 January 1920

122 'strange pieces of grey flannel underwear': *Triumph to Exile*, p. 568

123 'All the island life goes on beneath us': *Letters*, 4 January 1920

124 'watched him go down red into the sea': *A Composite Biography*, vol. 2, p. 21

125 'this island at one's feet, the dark sea all round': *Letters*, 12 January 1920

126 'the dim, sheer rocky coast': *Letters*, 25 January 1920

127 'lots of other people': *Letters*, 9 January 1920

128 'one feels generations of actors': *Letters*, 4 January 1920

129 'imperfect': Jeffrey Meyers, 'D. H. Lawrence and Homosexuality', in *D. H. Lawrence: Novelist, Poet, Prophet*, ed. Stephen Spender (Weidenfeld & Nicolson, 1973), p. 139

130 'Any chance for me?': Maurice Magnus to Norman Douglas, 18 July 1920, Norman Douglas Collection

131 'The Lord of the Isles': *Letters*, 12 September 1921

132 'I believe that hate': Compton Mackenzie, *The West Wind of Love* (Chatto & Windus, 1949), p. 320

133 'Man went off the track': *The West Wind of Love*, pp. 251–2

134 'where all the souls that never die': D. H. Lawrence, 'The Man Who Loved Islands', in *Love among the Haystacks and Other Stories* (Penguin, 1960), p. 99

135 'island idea': *Letters*, 5 February 1915

136 'I don't know what my next step will be': Maurice Magnus to Norman Douglas, Norman Douglas Collection

137 'I loathe you': *Letters*, 6 February 1920
138 'on ne meurt pas': *Letters*, 10 December 1918
139 'a wistful tone': *Memoir*, p. 18
140 'charity-boy of literature': *Letters*, 13 February 1920
141 'I felt … I owed': *Memoir*, p. 18
142 'Your cheque has saved my life': *Memoir*, p. 18
143 'a perfect selling novel': *Letters*, 27 December 1919
144 'I can't stay here all my life': *The Lost Girl*, p. 35
145 'How many infernos': *The Lost Girl*, p. 40

PURGATORY: PART TWO

1 'I always remember': *Memoir*, p. 19
2 'always loved': *Memoir*, p. 20
3 'Perhaps if I had missed it': *Memoir*, p 21
4 'a dirty little cart': 'Holy Week at Monte Cassino', p. 14
5 'We twisted up and up the wild hillside': *Memoir*, p. 21
6 'rather like a woman who': *Memoir*, pp. 21–2
7 'very short of money … one's college mates': *Memoir*, pp. 21–3
8 'charming and elegant': *Memoir*, p. 23
9 'Isn't it wonderful!': *Memoir*, p. 23
10 'I always wonder what the secrets can be … refectory': *Memoir*, pp. 24–5
11 lay brother 'with a bulging forehead … cornflowers': *Memoir*, pp. 25–6
12 'He showed me a wonderful photograph': *Memoir*, p. 27
13 'the farm cluster … child of the present': *Memoir*, p. 28
14 'so strange': *Memoir*, p. 28
15 'Roads … straight as judgment': *Memoir*, p. 30
16 'nobly animal, nobly spiritual … soul and body': John Ruskin, *Modern Painters*, vol. 5 (J. Wiley & Son, 1866), p. 321
17 'I could not bear it': *Memoir*, p. 30
18 'And what was the abyss, then?': *Memoir*, pp. 31–2
19 'rather raggedly typed out': *Memoir*, p. 31
20 'I was informed that a private soldier': *Memoirs of the Foreign Legion by M.M.*, pp. 219–21, p. 278
21 'in the red trousers and blue coat': *Memoir*, p. 77
22 'murderer': *Memoirs of the Foreign Legion*, p. 129
23 'John Smith': *Memoirs of the Foreign Legion*, p. 130
24 'it was a German regiment': *Memoirs of the Foreign Legion*, p. 130
25 'In addition to the filth': *Memoirs of the Foreign Legion*, p. 261
26 'No one is going to believe': *Memoirs of the Foreign Legion*, pp. 198–9

27 'Well, dearie, where is your protector today?': Maurice Magnus, *Dregs: Experiences of an American in the Foreign Legion*, in *Memoir of Maurice Magnus*, ed. Keith Cushman, p. 141

28 'I've given chapter and verse': *A Plea for Better Manners*, p. 115

29 'less vague and diffuse': Maurice Magnus to Norman Douglas. 'Lawrence, who had read it when he visited me, considered it good and told me to rewrite the five last chapters and finish it, since it was so nearly finished … and he would get me a publisher.' Norman Douglas Collection

30 'to being a scoundrel, thief, forger': *Memoir*, p. 78

31 'crying – crying, crying': *Memoir*, p. 32

32 'there speaks the first consciousness': *Psychoanalysis and the Unconscious*, p. 20

33 'gnarled bough': *Memoir*, p. 32

34 'The monks keep … turns to nothing': *Memoir*, p. 33

35 'They talk about love … the railway': *Memoir*, pp. 34–7

36 'I feel one comes unstuck from England': *Letters*, 19 March 1920

37 'I think one's got to go through': *Memoir*, p. 37

38 'He seemed to understand … never left him for long': *Memoir*, p. 38

39 'nothing is so hateful as the self one has left': D. H. Lawrence, 'A Modern Lover', in *The Woman Who Rode Away and Other Stories* (Penguin, 1950), p. 230

40 'wide old paved path': *Memoir*, p. 39

41 'felt that again': *Memoir*, p. 40

42 'We thought the old times': *Movements in European History*, p. 260

43 'gossipy, villa-stricken': *Triumph to Exile*, p. 556

44 'a good on-the-brink' feel: *Letters*, 25 March 1920

45 'ledged so awfully above the dawn': D. H. Lawrence, *Sea and Sardinia*, in *D. H. Lawrence and Italy: Sketches from Etruscan Places, Sea and Sardinia, Twilight in Italy*, ed. Simonetta de Filippis et al. (Penguin, 2007), p. 8

46 'witch-like': *Sea and Sardinia*, p. 10

47 'Here one feels': *Letters*, 31 March 1920

48 that bloomed for only a day: *Letters*, 2 March 1921

49 'a splendour like trumpets': *Memoir*, p. 42

50 'want to do a satire': *Letters*, 6 February 1920

51 'been in the musical-hall line': *The Lost Girl*, p. 97

52 'small felt hats … too impossible': *The Lost Girl*, pp. 99–111

53 'must have a good hotel': *The Lost Girl*, p. 137

54 so 'bad' it 'ought not to be allowed … on the prowl': *A Composite Biography*, vol. 2, p. 52

55 'He gave the slight': *The Lost Girl*, p. 198

56 'Can you *believe*': *The Lost Girl*, p. 158

57 'splendid gestures': *Sea and Sardinia*, p. 115

58 'coming out on the top … lost utterly': *The Lost Girl*, pp. 332–42

59 'live in this part of the world at all': *The Lost Girl*, p. 326

60 'not one memorable *word*': *A Composite Biography*, vol. 2, p. 52

61 'A terrible thing has happened … feeling kind': *Memoir*, pp. 42–7

62 'Whatever do you pick up': *Memoir*, p. 46

63 'Is it my duty to look after this man': '*Not I, But the Wind …*', p. 99

64 'But Magnus, there isn't a room for you in the house': *Memoir*, p. 46

65 without 'meaning or purpose': '*Not I, But the Wind …*', p. 99

66 'She, the bitch': Maurice Magnus to Norman Douglas, 9 May 1920, Norman Douglas Collection,

67 'there's an end to me at the monastery… humble': *Memoir*, pp. 50–1

68 'Lawrence heard my tale': Maurice Magnus to Norman Douglas, 9 May 1920, Norman Douglas collection

69 'It was final': *Memoir*, p. 53

70 'What good to me … were these few pounds?… She looked like nails': Maurice Magnus to Norman Douglas, 9 May 1920, Norman Douglas Collection

71 'my hotel bill ate up every cent I got': Maurice Magnus to Norman Douglas, 9 May 1920, Norman Douglas Collection

72 'Ah, I breathed free now he had gone': *Memoir*, p. 61

73 'Dear Lawrence': *Memoir*, p. 62

74 'Well, here was a blow!': *Memoir*, pp. 62–3

75 'like the grandest gentleman': *Memoir*, p. 65

76 'Yes, he passed all right': *Memoir*, p. 67

77 'bone-dry', 'bath-brick': *Memoir*, p. 69

78 'on the glittering mud': Richard Holmes, *Coleridge: Darker Reflections* (HarperCollins, 1998), p. 45

79 'I believe I should deserve the reproach': Maurice Magnus, 22 October 1920, Lawrence Manuscripts Collection, University of Nottingham Library

80 'What the hell will you do in Morocco': Norman Douglas to Maurice Magnus, 29 October 1920, Norman Douglas Collection

81 'shut up in that beastly island': *Memoir*, p. 70

82 'seized him, stood him': *Movements in European History*, p. 263

83 'shrill, penetrating, unforgettable voices': *A Composite Biography*, vol. 1, p. 497

84 'It's no good … And so to bed': *Triumph to Exile,* pp. 601–3

85 'spinning of sky winds': 'The Poetry of the Present', p. 79

86 'no rhythm which returns': 'The Poetry of the Present', p. 80

87 'in ourselves spontaneous': 'The Poetry of the Present', p. 81

88 'The world seemed to stand still for me': *Memoir*, p. 76

89 'a huge farce wrapped up in mystery': *Memoir*, p. 72

90 'I leave it to you': *Memoir*, p. 74

91 'I heard ... the other day': *Letters*, 16 November 1920

92 'I haven't any energy left': Maurice Magnus to Norman Douglas, 2 October 1920, Norman Douglas Collection

93 'Don't worry about Lawrence writing nasty': Maurice Magnus to Norman Douglas, 28 October 1920, Norman Douglas Collection

94 'very handsome, beautiful rather ... flowing together': D. H. Lawrence, 'Il Duro', in *Twilight in Italy and Other Essays*, p. 175

95 'Comes over one an absolute necessity to move': *Sea and Sardinia*, p. 7

96 'But why in the name of heaven': *Sea and Sardinia*, p. 48

97 'a naked town rising steep ... the Inferno': *Sea and Sardinia*, pp. 53–61

98 'The question is, shall we go on?': *Sea and Sardinia*, p. 61

99 'On we rush': *Sea and Sardinia*, p. 90

100 'Life was not ... only a process': *Sea and Sardinia*, p. 117

101 'One realises, with horror': *Sea and Sardinia*, p. 63

102 'Why, there is the monastery': *Sea and Sardinia*, p. 172

103 'Italy has given me back': *Sea and Sardinia*, p. 117

104 'Superficially there is something alike in them': *New Statesman*, 5 May 1923

105 'in his low sonorous voice': *A Composite Biography*, vol. 2, pp. 58–9

106 'A new place': *Aaron's Rod*, p. 103

107 'had fallen into country house parties ... out of the window': *Aaron's Rod*, pp. 134, 142, 149

108 'astonishment ... grievance to him': *Looking Back*, p. 286

109 'hovering ... jumbled, entangled hills': *Aaron's Rod*, pp. 148–57

110 'the long slim neck of the Palazzo Vecchio': *Aaron's Rod*, p. 211

111 'looked and looked': *Aaron's Rod*, p. 212

112 'And he never passed through': *Aaron's Rod*, p. 212

113 'a gleam almost of happiness ... unspeakably thankful': *Aaron's Rod*, pp. 227–64

114 'the last of my serious English novels': *Triumph to Exile*, p. 673

115 'The man's spirit has gone out of the world': *Aaron's Rod*, p. 101

116 'wicked whimsicality ... presence': *Aaron's Rod*, p. 218

117 'They've got the start of us': *Aaron's Rod*, p. 244

118 'caught the façade': *Aaron's Rod*, p. 232

119 'Little Mee': *Aaron's Rod*, p. 217

120 'being by oneself': *Aaron's Rod*, p. 166

121 'a black rod of power': *Aaron's Rod*, p. 258

122 'Flowers with good roots': *Aaron's Rod*, p. 232

123 'water-lilies twisted round my hat': *Letters*, 30 January 1915

124 'He was staying in a poorish hotel': Rebecca West, *Ending in Earnest: A Literary Log* (Doubleday, 1931), pp. 266–8

125 'five hundred pages of': *The Rainbow and Women in Love – A Case Book*, ed. Colin C. Clarke (Aurora Publishers, 1969), p. 68

126 'Why will men have theories about women?': E. M. Forster, *A Room with a View* (Penguin, 2006), p. 218

127 'his second self': *Aaron's Rod*, p. 286

## PURGATORY: PART THREE

1 'admirable and tranquil': Ernst Robert Curtius, *English Literature and the Latin Middle Ages*, trans. Willard R. Trask (Princeton University Press, 1953), p. 357

2 'I could ... by giving half my money': *Memoir*, p. 76

3 'no authority': Louise Wright, 'Disputed Dregs: D. H. Lawrence and the Publication of Maurice Magnus's Memoirs of the Foreign Legion', *Journal of D. H. Lawrence Studies* (1996), p. 58

4 'a dead dog': *Letters*, 10 November 1921

5 'lovely monuments of our European past': 'Foreword to *Studies in Classic American Literature*' (1920), in *Studies in Classic American Literature*, p. 384

6 it 'was the dark country': Van Wyck Brooks, 'The American Scene: General Thoughts on Henry James and America', *The Dial*, vol. 75 (July 1923)

7 'the flower of art blooms': Henry James, *Hawthorne* (Macmillan, 1887), p. 3

8 'whole tree of life': *Letters*, 26 October 1915

9 'display the role of the imagination': William Wasserstrom, *The Time of the Dial* (Syracuse University Press, 1963), p. 2

10 'two stories (or somethings)': Nicholas Joost and Alvin Sullivan, *D. H. Lawrence and The Dial* (Southern Illinois University Press, 1970), p. 9

11 'Nowadays I depend almost entirely': *Letters*, 10 November 1921

12 'real American book': epilogue to the American edition of *Fantasia of the Unconscious* (Thomas Seltzer, 1922)

13 'It is exactly two years': *Memoir*, p. 76

14 'stone-cold to this pink-faced ... lower classes': these remarks about Magnus's homosexuality were edited out of Lawrence's introduction to

the *Memoirs of the Foreign Legion by M.M.* (1924) and can be found in *Memoir of Maurice Magnus*, ed. Keith Cushman, pp. 93–4

15  'Let him die and be thrice dead': edited out of the 1924 introduction and found in *Memoir of Maurice Magnus*, ed. Cushman, p. 95.

16  'littérateur': *Memoir*, p. 78

17  'expurgated': *A Plea for Better Manners*, p. 115

18  'I like him for that … consciousness': *Memoir*, pp. 80–1

19  'Apparently the shades of Magnus': *Letters*, 20 December 1921

20  'Damn the Foreign Legion': Norman Douglas to D. H. Lawrence, 26 December 1921, D. H. Lawrence archive, University of Nottingham

21  'Lawrence's memoir … is sure to be full of bias': Norman Douglas to Grant Richards, 6 February 1922, Harry Ransom Humanities Research Center, The University of Texas at Austin

22  'All this is awkward': *A Plea for Better Manners*, p. 120

23  'the novelist's touch in biography': *A Plea for Better Manners*, p. 118

24  'He never borrowed a hundred': *A Plea for Better Manners*, p. 117

25  'what Lawrence wrote': Richard Aldington, introduction to D. H. Lawrence, *Apocalypse* (Penguin, 1974), p. xiii

26  270 satire of him in *Aaron's Rod*: Richard Aldington, *Pinorman: Personal Recollections of Norman Douglas, Pino Orioli and Charles Prentice* (William Heinemann, 1954), p. 185

27  'spiteful observations': *A Plea for Better Manners*, p. 125

28  'men cannot live': Norman Douglas, *South Wind* (Secker & Warburg, 1947), p. 153

29  'I like to taste my friends': *A Plea for Better Manners*, p. 108

30  'Let us examine this Siren-loving monster': Norman Douglas, *Siren Land* (Martin Secker, 1929), p. 71

31  'The news of his arrival': *Norman Douglas*, p. 314

32  'Rather a mess in here': *A Plea for Better Manners*, p. 113

33  'admirable': *A Plea for Better Manners*, p. 111

34  'bad breeding … age of eunuchs': *A Plea for Better Manners*, p. 125

35  'transition state is that of a girl': *Norman Douglas*, p. 334

36  'Lawrence is all wrong about my room': *Norman Douglas*, p. 334

37  'a masterpiece of unconscious': *A Plea for Better Manners*, p. 108

38  'Every place has its genius': Norman Douglas, *Old Calabria* (Martin Secker, 1920), p. 1

39  'reader of a good travel-book': Norman Douglas, *Experiments: A Miscellany* (Chapman & Hall, 1925), p. 13

40  'It is time that I said a word': *Memoir of Maurice Magnus*, ed. Cushman, pp. 135–7

41  'I induced Lawrence to': *Looking Back*, pp. 288–9

PARADISE: PART ONE

1 'November of the year 1916': this fragment of an untitled novel was first published in *The Princess and Other Stories*, ed. Keith Sagar (Penguin, 1972) under the name 'The Wilful Woman'. The edition used here is *St Mawr and Other Stories*, ed. Brian Finney (Cambridge University Press, 1987), pp. 199–203

2 'He had picked up a snake': 'The Wilful Woman', p. 199

3 'The time is different there': D. H. Lawrence, 'A Little Moonshine with Lemon', in *Mornings in Mexico and Other Essays*, ed. Virginia Crosswhite Hyde (Cambridge University Press, 2009), p. 97

4 'I had always regarded': *'Not I, But the Wind …'*, p. 136

5 *Intimate Memories*: Mabel Dodge Luhan wrote twenty volumes of autobiography, four of which were published in her lifetime. These four volumes, which together compose the series she called *Intimate Memories*, are *Background* (1933), *European Experiences* (1935), *Movers and Shakers* (1936) and *Edge of Taos Desert: An Escape to Reality* (1937)

6 'wanted to write an American novel': *Lorenzo in Taos*, p. 52

7 'a big, white crow': *Letters*, 5 December 1922

8 'she adored to change people': Edward Lueders, *Carl Van Vechten* (Twayne, 1965), p. 29

9 'changed me forever': D. H. Lawrence, 'New Mexico', in *Mornings in Mexico and Other Essays*, p. 176

10 'what I went through in my friendship': *Lorenzo in Taos*, preface and p. 3

11 'like a papyrus … not quite heard music': *Lorenzo in Taos*, pp. 4–5

12 'to get a little farm somewhere': *Letters*, 8 November 1921

13 'a few leaves': *Lorenzo in Taos*, p. 5

14 'Why hurry with the hurrying world?': Charles F. Lummis, *The Land of Poco Tiempo* (Charles Scribner's, 1893), p. 3

15 'smelt the Indian scent': *Lorenzo in Taos*, pp. 5–7

16 'strange, sinister spirit': *Sea and Sardinia*, p. 55

17 'understand things for me … laughing, aloof, genius of Taos': *Lorenzo in Taos*, pp. 3, 12

18 'The womb in me': *Lorenzo in Taos*, p. 37

19 'I foresaw': *Lorenzo in Taos*, p. 8

20 'I wonder which will give out first': *Lorenzo in Taos*, p. 255

21 'I also believe in Indians': *Lorenzo in Taos*, pp. 12–13

22 'We were coming *straight* to you': *Lorenzo in Taos*, p. 15

23 'I couldn't simply face America': *Letters*, 4 March 1922

24 'we will go with *you* to Taos': *Lorenzo in Taos*, p. 16

25 'It is vile of us to put off Taos': *Lorenzo in Taos*, p. 16

26  'You want to send [A. A.] Brill to hell': *Letters*, 28 January 1922

27  'He whom I was trying to draw to Taos': *Lorenzo in Taos*, p. 14

28  'I shall have to go to America at length': *Letters*, 27 January 1922

29  'Quite why Lawrence suddenly changed his mind': David Ellis, *D. H. Lawrence: Dying Game: 1922–1930*, vol. 3 of *The Cambridge Biography of D. H. Lawrence* (Cambridge University Press, 1997), p. 10

30  'Lawrence rewrote Koteliansky's translation': Nicholas Joost and Alvin Sullivan, *D. H. Lawrence and The Dial* (Southern Illinois University Press, 1970), p. 51

31  'gloomy and sultry depths of the inferno': D. H. Lawrence (trans.), ' "The Gentleman from San Francisco", by Ivan Bunin', in *Phoenix II*, pp. 198–212

32  'take a look': *Lorenzo in Taos*, p. 16

33  'most reasonably afraid': Catherine Carswell, *The Savage Pilgrimage: A Narrative of D. H. Lawrence* (Chatto & Windus, 1932), p. 168

34  'would have been the death of me': *Letters*, 4 March 1922

35  'AMERICA … knees lose their brassy strength': *Letters*, 17 August 1921

36  'Poor Magnus': *Letters*, 10 February 1922

37  'I did such a "Memoir" of Maurice Magnus': *Letters*, 12 February 1922

38  'Oh painted carts': *Sea and Sardinia*, p. 24

39  'Slowly came the evening': *Letters*, 7 March 1922

40  '*so* comfortable': *Letters*, 28 February 1922

41  'I feel … like a sea-bird must feel': *Letters*, 8 March 1922

42  'Time passes like a sleep': *Letters*, 7 March 1922

43  'long, slow lift': *Sea and Sardinia*, p. 30

44  'I wished in my soul the voyage might last forever': *Sea and Sardinia*, p. 30

45  'I do wonder how we shall feel when we get off': *Letters*, 7 March 1922

46  'I love trying things': *Letters*, 15 May 1922

47  'the thick, choky feel of tropical forest': *Letters*, 10 April 1922

48  'once asked me if I had heard': *Portrait of a Genius, But …*, p. 248

49  'rat-hole temples': *Letters*, 30 April 1922

50  'on the cinema': *Letters*, 3 April 1922

51  'hat tight on his head': *A Composite Biography*, vol. 2, p. 129

52  'They secretly hate him' … 'I find all dark people': *Letters*, 30 March 1922, 10 April 1922

53  'a little apology to Psychoanalysis': *Psychoanalysis and the Unconscious and Fantasia of the Unconscious*, p. 57

54  'I still am not quite sure where I am': *Letters*, 25 March 1922

55  'his piercing blue eyes': John Worthen, *D. H. Lawrence: The Life of an Outsider* (Penguin, 2005), p. 263

56  'the East doesn't get me at all … I come across': *Letters*, 10 April 1922

57  'in the heat': *Letters*, 3 April 1922

58 'The magnetism is all negative': *Letters*, 16 April 1922

59 'had never felt so sick in my life': *Letters*, 15 May 1922

60 'Even at night you sweat': *Letters*, 24 March 1922

61 'One sweats and sweats': *Letters*, 17 April 1922

62 'the feeling that there is a lid down': *Letters*, 16 April 1922

63 'It isn't so much the heat': *Letters*, 30 April 1922

64 'moment begins to heave': 'The Man Who Loved Islands', p. 99

65 'one feel that our day is only a day': D. H. Lawrence, 'Herman Melville's *Moby Dick*', in *Studies in Classic American Literature*, p. 138

66 'No more of my tirades': *Letters*, 30 April 1922

67 'Three months penalty for having forsworn Europe': *Kangaroo*, p. 20

68 'It is strange and fascinating': *Letters*, 30 April 1922

69 'high and blue and new': *Letters*, 15 May 1922

70 'the most democratic place I have *ever* been in': *Letters*, 13 June 1922

71 'little man': *A Composite Biography*, vol. 2, p. 138

72 'so I feel quite at home': *A Composite Biography*, vol. 2, p. 149

73 'haphazard and new': *Kangaroo*, p. 27

74 'an Australian humorism': *A Composite Biography*, vol. 2, p. 158

75 'The business of the novel': D. H. Lawrence, 'Morality and the Novel', in *Phoenix II*, p. 527

76 'a thought adventure': *Kangaroo*, p. 279

77 'gramophone of a novel': *Kangaroo*, p. 280

78 'only just what I felt': introduction to *Kangaroo*, p. lv

79 'Him! A lord and master!': *Kangaroo*, pp. 192–5

80 'you lonely phoenix': *Kangaroo*, p. 299

81 'Volcanic Evidence': *Kangaroo*, pp. 155–6

82 'more lava fire': *Kangaroo*, p. 262

83 'He had known such different deep fears': *Kangaroo*, p. 212

84 'fern-dark indifference': *Kangaroo*, p. 183

85 'Australianism in this book': introduction to *Kangaroo*, p. lv

86 'willed him to come': *Lorenzo in Taos*, p. 35

87 'Lawrence! … this is the best': David H. Usner, *Indian Work: Language and Livelihood in Native American History* (Harvard University Press, 2009), p. 121

88 'the Great American Mystery … opiate sun': *The Land of Poco Tiempo*, pp. 3–5

89 'in its lovely, lonely … mythology': *The Land of Poco Tiempo*, pp. 7–8

90 '*Ay!* … nineteen hundred years ago': *The Land of Poco Tiempo*, pp. 99–100

91 'Very interesting': *Letters*, 18 July 1922

92 'I became': *Lorenzo in Taos*, p. 35

93 'cold, snobbish': the description was discarded from the first typescript of *Kangaroo*. See *Kangaroo*, textual apparatus, Note 358.7, pp. 476–7

94 'Ricordi': *Letters*, 20 May 1922

95 'If you are thinking of coming here, don't': *Letters*, 22 August 1922

96 'the glamour of strangeness': T. E. Lawrence, *Seven Pillars of Wisdom* (Dover Publications, 2018), p. 9

97 'to me a brown skin is the only beautiful one': *A Personal Record*, p. 111

98 'These are supposed to be the earthly paradises': *Letters*, 31 August 1922

99 'Crowd of cinema people': *Letters*, 31 August 1922

100 'jeer at him': *Lorenzo in Taos*, p. 47

101 'soft puffy yellow fire': *St Mawr*, in *St Mawr and Other Stories*, ed. Brian Finney (Cambridge University Press, 1987), p. 134

102 'long, slow flash of lightning': *Lorenzo in Taos*, p. 44

103 'Something stood still in my soul': 'New Mexico', p. 175

104 'Never … is light more pure': 'New Mexico', pp. 176–7

105 'a sort of never-stop Hades': *Letters*, 6 September 1922

106 'live in the rapid and kaleidoscopic': D. H. Lawrence, 'Indians and Entertainment', in *Mornings in Mexico and Other Essays*, p. 60

107 'it would mean dollars!': *Lorenzo in Taos*, p. 107

108 'And was not Ursula's way': *Women in Love*, p. 326

109 'forced, false … distraught': *Lorenzo in Taos*, p. 36

110 'an agony … limited': *Lorenzo in Taos*, pp. 36–7

111 '"Oh, you and your hates"': *Lorenzo in Taos*, p. 39

112 'wrecking gang': Sharyn Rohlfsen Udall, *Spud Johnson and Laughing Horse* (Sunstone Press, 2008), p. 98

113 'It's your fault, Frieda!': Witter Bynner, *Journey with Genius: Recollections and Reflections Concerning the D. H. Lawrences* (The John Day Company, 1951), p. 2

114 'flee each harbor': *Journey with Genius*, p. 4

115 'The night had been the Lawrences' first': *Journey with Genius*, pp. 7–8

116 'headquarters for the future': Mabel Luhan to John Collier, 21 November 1922, quoted in Lois Palken Rudnick, *Mabel Dodge Luhan: New Woman, New Worlds* (University of New Mexico Press, 1984), p. 179

117 'not supposed to exist': *Mabel Dodge Luhan & Company: American Moderns and the West*, ed. Lois P. Rudnick (University of New Mexico Press, 2016), p. 123

118 'think with their heads': Carl Jung, *Memories, Dreams, Reflections* (Vintage, 1989), p. 249

119 'swinging carelessly': Mabel Dodge Luhan, *Winter in Taos* (Sunstone Books, 1934), p. 164

120 'one of those nasty little temples in India': *Lorenzo in Taos*, p. 45

121  'silent and seemingly unaware': *Lorenzo in Taos*, p. 49

122  'like looking from the top of a hill': *Letters*, 22 September 1922

123  'one of the monasteries of Europe': D. H. Lawrence, 'Taos', in *Mornings in Mexico and Other Essays*, p. 125

124  'Tony didn't want to take Lawrence': *Lorenzo in Taos*, pp. 47–8

125  'She was good company … something in myself, too': *Lorenzo in Taos*, pp. 48–9

126  'was like travelling with the landscape': Willa Cather, *Death Comes for the Archbishop* (University of Nebraska Press, 1999), p. 245

127  'Secret': *The Suppressed Memoirs of Mabel Dodge Luhan: Sex, Syphilis, and Psychoanalysis in the Making of Modern American Culture*, ed. Lois Palken Rudnick (University of New Mexico Press, 2012), p. 142

128  'What are you doing?… went down it': *Suppressed Memoirs*, p. 143

129  'filled with a secret': *Memories, Dreams, Reflections*, p. 249

130  'take *my* experience, *my* material': *Lorenzo in Taos*, p. 70

131  'a small, blond Southerner': *New Woman, New Worlds*, p. 173

132  'really likes Indians': *Winter in Taos*, pp. 215–20

133  'recognition of Indian civil rights': *New Woman, New Worlds*, p. 177

134  'I arrive in New Mexico at a moment of crisis': D. H. Lawrence, 'Certain Americans and an Englishman', in *Mornings in Mexico and Other Essays*, p. 105

135  'it does not seem to me very good': *Lorenzo in Taos*, p. 54

136  'energy, time, and money': *New Woman, New Worlds*, pp. 179–80

137  'We want *interest* and *appreciation*': *New Woman, New Worlds*, p. 180

138  'there is no bridge…': 'Indians and Entertainment', p. 61

139  'was much less vivid to him than the Inferno': *Movements in European History*, p. 163

140  'Supposing one fell on to the moon': 'Indians and an Englishman', in *Mornings in Mexico and Other Essays*, p. 112

141  'What holds the stars firm': *Lorenzo in Taos*, p. 171

142  'This narrative about Tony': *Edge of Taos Desert*, in *Intimate Memories: The Autobiography of Mabel Dodge Luhan*, ed. Lois Palken Rudnick (University of New Mexico Press, 1999), p. 237

143  'the points of Indian tents': 'Indians and an Englishman', p. 114

144  'old Spanish, Red Indian': 'New Mexico', p. 176

145  'their strong-weak, strong-weak pulse … feels final': 'Indians and an Englishman', p. 117

146  'up to the nose … in the air': 'Indians and an Englishman', pp. 117–20

147  'flat shapes, exactly like men': *St Mawr*, p. 131

148  'Internally, there is nothing': *Letters*, 15 August 1923

149  'was annoyed that Frieda … across the world': *Lorenzo in Taos*, p. 52

150 'averted his eyes ... with anyone else before': *Lorenzo in Taos*, p. 60

151 'were sinking down': *Lorenzo in Taos*, p. 251

152 'a secret life': *Suppressed Memoirs*, p. 16

153 'a Leyden jar': *Lorenzo in Taos*, p. 64

154 'I hardly knew whose baby': *Suppressed Memoirs*, p. 68

155 'YOU, lecturing ME': Patricia R. Everett, *Corresponding Lives: Mabel Dodge Luhan, A. A. Brill, and the Psychoanalytic Adventure in America* (Karnac, 2016), p. 135

156 'driving his awkward body': *Suppressed Memoirs*, pp. 69–71

157 'It was ... as though I had never known Karl': *Suppressed Memoirs*, p. 80

158 'Fly, my dear, fly': Emily Hahn, *Mabel: A Biography of Mabel Dodge Luhan* (Houghton Mifflin, 1977), p. 149

159 'For the first time in my life': *Mabel*, p. 100

160 'You are indeed the only one': *Corresponding Lives*, p. 37

161 'My heart was pounding with impatience': *Intimate Memories*, p. 189

162 'awakening at the different': *Lorenzo in Taos*, p. 63

163 'a complete, stark approximation': *Lorenzo in Taos*, pp. 60–2

164 'Frieda thinks we ought to continue': *Lorenzo in Taos*, p. 63

165 'seduce' Lawrence's 'spirit': *Lorenzo in Taos*, p. 69

166 'stamped around, sweeping noisily': *Lorenzo in Taos*, p. 64

167 'The meeting with Maurice': *Lorenzo in Taos*, p. 65

168 'put on to impress tourists ... dead battery': *Mabel*, p. 148

169 'You've got to remember': *Lorenzo in Taos*, p. 66

170 'Am doing a M. Sterne novel': *Letters*, 6 October 1922

171 'There is a kind of vitality': *Lorenzo in Taos*, p. 79

172 'America ... makes me feel': Letters, 14 August 1923

## PARADISE: PART TWO

1 'He bent a firm, gentle look': *Intimate Memoirs*, p. 245

2 'everlasting loneliness': *Suppressed Memoirs*, p. 129

3 'protested strongly': *Lorenzo in Taos*, p. 251

4 'a memory rushed back ... destructive': *Suppressed Memoirs*, pp. 157–8

5 'For the first time': *Suppressed Memoirs*, p. 161

6 'That damn bitch of Dr Sherman's': *Suppressed Memoirs*, p. 198

7 'I could never overcome': *Suppressed Memoirs*, p. 131

8 'some strong solution': *Intimate Memories*, p. 301

9 'ghastly secret things': *Suppressed Memoirs*, p. 131

10 'often wished one of those old men': *Suppressed Memoirs*, p. 138

11 'I have a very bad Oedipus complex': *Corresponding Lives*, p. 51

12 'family secret': *Suppressed Memoirs*, p. 26

13 'My father': *Suppressed Memoirs*, p. 30

14 'had to have': *Suppressed Memoirs*, p. 52

15 'If you ever so much': *Suppressed Memoirs*, p. 105 and endnote p. 211

16 'We have injured one another': *Suppressed Memoirs*, p. 128

17 Consumption shaped New Mexico: see Nancy Owen Lewis, *Chasing the Cure in New Mexico: Tuberculosis and the Quest for Health* (University of New Mexico Press, 2016)

18 'Mabel marched in and packed her up': *Mabel*, p. 190

19 And Frieda asked Mabel: *Lorenzo in Taos*, p. 105

20 'to the very worst climates': *Lorenzo in Taos*, p. 129

21 'It was like the end of the world': *Kangaroo*, p. 349

22 'a dynamo': Carl Van Vechten, *Peter Whiffle* (Alfred A. Knopf, 1922), p. 163

23 'You don't *know* your floor': *Lorenzo in Taos*, p. 73

24 'half-distressed and half-amused': *Lorenzo in Taos*, pp. 73–4

25 'our fingers touched in the soap-suds': *Lorenzo in Taos*, p. 71

26 'A woman is a woman': *Lorenzo in Taos*, p. 74

27 'the first reaction on me of America itself': *Letters*, 28 November 1922

28 'nightmares': *Studies in Classic American Literature*, p. lii

29 'The Perfectibility Of Man': 'Benjamin Franklin', p. 20

30 'Americanising': *Letters*, 11 November 1922

31 'sharper, quicker': *Letters*, 19 November 1922

32 'I AM HE... CHUFFFF!': 'Whitman' (1921–2), in *Studies in Classic American Literature*, pp. 421–2

33 'You may think them too violent now': *Letters*, 28 November 1922

34 'Paolo and Francesca': *Letters*, 14 November 1922

35 'put down exactly': Ezra Pound, 'Patria Mia: V', *New Age*, vol. 11, no. 23 (3 October 1912), pp. 539–40

36 'a sort of double meaning': 'The Spirit of Place' (final version), in *Studies in Classic American Literature*, pp. 14–15

37 'nice-as-pie': D. H. Lawrence, 'Nathaniel Hawthorne and *The Scarlet Letter*', in *Studies in Classic American Literature*, p. 81

38 'Never trust the artist': 'The Spirit of Place' (final version), p. 14

39 'It is love that causes': D. H. Lawrence, 'Edgar Allan Poe', p. 69

40 'He died wanting more love': 'Edgar Allan Poe', p. 80

41 'from her head': Knut Merrild, *A Poet and Two Painters: A Memoir of D. H. Lawrence* (Routledge, 1938), p. 36

42 'not physically attractive to women ... – like that!': *Lorenzo in Taos*, pp. 90–1

43 'was hopelessly empty': *A Poet and Two Painters*, p. 99

44 'We have to go on, on, on': 'Herman Melville's *Moby Dick*', p. 146

45 'The greatest seer': 'Herman Melville', p. 288

46 'The greatest seer and poet of the sea for me': 'Herman Melville's *Typee* and *Omoo*', in *Studies in Classic American Literature*, p. 122

47 'This is thy body': 'Herman Melville's *Typee* and *Omoo*', p. 125

48 'At first you are put off by the style': 'Herman Melville's *Typee* and *Omoo*', p. 133

49 'hunted, hunted': 'Herman Melville's *Moby Dick*', p. 146

50 'white as lard': *Lorenzo in Taos*, p. 183

51 'found Paradise': Raymond Weaver, *Herman Melville: Mariner and Mystic* (G. H. Doran, 1921), p. 250

52 'the inmost leaf ... a crabbed and darkly': *Mariner and Mystic*, pp. 323–4

53 'volcanic in energy': *Mariner and Mystic*, p. 28

54 'was so *much* greater than the man': 'Herman Melville's *Typee* and *Omoo*', p. 134

55 'hated the world': 'Herman Melville's *Typee* and *Omoo*', p. 126

56 'But I should not have been happy': 'Herman Melville's *Typee* and *Omoo*', p. 126

57 'No more Typees': 'Herman Melville's *Typee* and *Omoo*', p. 131

58 'Poor Melville!': 'Herman Melville's *Typee* and *Omoo*', p. 128

59 'pin ourselves ... That is life': 'Herman Melville's *Typee* and *Omoo*', pp. 128–9

60 'a snake and poison and a sick man': *Lorenzo in Taos*, p. 113

61 'will had been defeated': *Lorenzo in Taos*, p. 113

62 'She wants to bully me': *A Poet and Two Painters*, p. 30

63 'To quote Lawrence': *A Poet and Two Painters*, p. 89

64 'enjoying the deep forceful': *A Poet and Two Painters*, pp. 99–100

65 'When I think of it now': *A Poet and Two Painters*, pp. 101–2

66 'going off the stage': *A Poet and Two Painters*, p. 143

67 'So there you are': *A Poet and Two Painters*, p. 173,

68 'the most disinterested': *A Poet and Two Painters*, p. xvii

69 'underdeveloped, athletically speaking': *A Poet and Two Painters*, p. 208

70 'hermaphrodite': *A Poet and Two Painters*, p. 208

71 'a rotten, false, self-conscious': *Lorenzo in Taos*, p. 134

72 'I wish now to break the connection': *Letters*, 3 February 1923

73 'Mountsier didn't believe': *Letters*, 7 February 1923

74 'Feel as if old moorings': *Letters*, 2 February 1923

75 'I don't feel angry': *Lorenzo in Taos*, p. 112

76 'Lawrence was theatre': *Journey with Genius*, p. 63

77 'bony, pinched, pigeon-breasted': *A Poet and Two Painters*, p. 206

78 'a lake-city, like Mexico': *Aaron's Rod*, p. 288

79 'strain on the nerves': D. H. Lawrence, 'Au Revoir, USA', in *Mornings in Mexico and Other Essays*, p. 131

80 'some written "history"': *Lorenzo in Taos*, p. 253

81 'grovelled': *Journey with Genius*, p. 46

82 'gruesome': *Letters*, 28 March 1923

83 'same old dragon's blood': 'Au Revoir, USA', p. 132

84 'vibrations in the ether': 'The Spirit of Place' (first version), p. 173

85 'I hear Mabel married Tony': *Lorenzo in Taos*, p. 114

86 'I would never venture seriously to judge': *Lorenzo in Taos*, p. 273

87 ' "Really!" Mr. May seemed smitten': *The Lost Girl*, p. 250

88 'Your world must have come tumbling … In my *head*': *Letters*, 30 May 1923

89 'The Indians will save': *New Woman, New Worlds*, p. 183

90 'Did I feel a twinge': D. H. Lawrence, 'Surgery for the Novel – or a Bomb', in *Phoenix I*, p. 520

91 'I should never be able to write': *Letters*, 21 April 1921

92 'full dazzling gold … life *withheld*': D. H. Lawrence, *The Plumed Serpent*, ed. L. D. Clark (Cambridge University Press, 1987), p. 87

93 'Chapala paradise': *Letters*, 1 May 1923

94 'began to slant downward': *Journey with Genius*, p. 31

95 'With the tongue of a singing serpent': *Journey with Genius*, p. 135

96 'catch the spirit': D. H. Lawrence, 'America, Listen to Your Own', *New Republic*, 15 December 1920, p. 69

97 'real novel of America': *Letters*, 15 June 1923

98 'establish a system': D. H. Lawrence, *Quetzalcoatl*, ed. N. H. Reeve (Cambridge University Press, 2011), p. 218

99 'skipping, butting': *Quetzalcoatl*, pp. 319, 320, 324

100 'No … my new novel has nothing': *Letters*, 19 August 1923

101 'red': *Quetzalcoatl*, p. 312

102 'When I feel sick I want to go back': *Letters*, 3 May 1923

103 'He can go to blazes': *Dying Game*, p. 124

104 'It drove me crazy': F. A. Lea, *The Life of John Middleton Murry* (Oxford University Press, 1960), pp. 177–8

105 '*Fantasia* was more than a book': John Middleton Murry, *Reminiscences of D. H. Lawrence* (Henry Holt, 1933), p. 163

106 'I would prepare the place for him': John Middleton Murry, *Son of Woman: The Story of D. H. Lawrence* (Jonathan Cape, 1931), p. 328

107 'I should like to stay a night': *Letters*, 20 August 1923

108 'sixty years ago': *Letters*, 24 August 1923

109 'knew it out of the air … saw your mother': *Lorenzo in Taos*, p. 117

110 'Peccavi, peccavi': *Letters*, 19 November 1923

111 'may even yet be the rounding': *Lorenzo in Taos*, p. 119

112 'I submitted my will to him': *Lorenzo in Taos*, p. 134

113 'take your submission': *Lorenzo in Taos*, p. 120

114 'Don't trouble about the Indians': *Lorenzo in Taos*, p. 120

115 'to keep an invisible thread': *Lorenzo in Taos*, p. 122

116 'the whole strange episode': *Reminiscences of D. H. Lawrence*, p. 165

117 'the death-grey coast ... Not a man left: D. H. Lawrence, 'On Coming Home', in *Phoenix II*, pp. 250–6

118 'chumminess': *Savage Pilgrimage*, p. 192

119 'I can't bear it ... attack everything': *Son of Woman*, p. 331

120 'As if that weren't what I want': *Dying Game*, p. 145

121 'dull, heavy, mortified half-light': D. H. Lawrence, 'Dear Old Horse: A London Letter', no. 10, *Laughing Horse* (May 1924), pp. 3–6

122 'deaf, forty, very nice': *Lorenzo in Taos*, p. 130

123 'intelligent, witty and brilliant': Sean Hignett, *Brett: From Bloomsbury to New Mexico* (Franklin Watts, 1983), p. 29

124 'If it were not for my painting': *Brett*, p. 32

125 'On or about December 1910': Virginia Woolf, *Mr Bennett and Mrs Brown* (The Hogarth Press, 1924), p. 4

126 'was not quick enough': *Brett*, pp. 30–1. The section of *My Long and Beautiful Journey* relating to Brett's time with Lawrence in New Mexico was published in the *South Dakota Review*, June 1967, pp. 11–71. The manuscript is otherwise in private hands

127 'ambidextrous ... found out': *Brett*, p. 32

128 'I love you so much': *Brett*, p. 82

129 'a mild attack of malaria': *Savage Pilgrimage*, p. 200

130 'gloom – yellow air': *Letters*, 17 December 1923

131 'I don't belong over here': *Lorenzo in Taos*, p. 128

132 The host arrived late: Dorothy Brett, *Lawrence and Brett: A Friendship* (Lippincott, 1933), p. 21

133 "You'll see I'm quite up to this": *Savage Pilgrimage*, p. 206

134 'I am not a man': *Lawrence and Brett*, p. 21

135 'murderous dislike': *Savage Pilgrimage*, p. 208

136 'Did the search, the adventure': *Savage Pilgrimage*, p. 210

137 'I like you, Lawrence': *Savage Pilgrimage*, pp. 211

138 'Lawrence is a great man': *Savage Pilgrimage*, p. 209

139 'suddenly you put your arm': *Son of Woman*, p. 388

140 'I love you Lorenzo': *Reminiscences of D. H. Lawrence*, p. 175

141 'I *have* betrayed you': *Savage Pilgrimage*, p. 212

142  'an affair between men … detached': *Savage Pilgrimage*, p. 212

143  'I made a fool of myself': *Savage Pilgrimage*, p. 213

144  'in a moment of vision': *Reminiscences of D. H. Lawrence*, p. 171

145  'started attacking you': *Lawrence and Brett*, p. 32

146  'an outpouring stream': *Lorenzo in Taos*, p. 131

147  'One's got to put a new ripple': *Lorenzo in Taos*, p. 135

148  'The great god Pan is dead!': Plutarch, *Moralia*, vol. v, trans. F. C. Babbitt (Loeb Classical Library, 1936), p. 402

149  'no seriousness': *Lorenzo in Taos*, p. 135

150  'We'll laugh last': *Lorenzo in Taos*, p. 128

151  'the ever-ready amused jeer': *Lawrence and Brett*, p. 30

152  'pleasant devil's voice': *Journey with Genius*, p. 4

153  'thin man with a red beard … lightning': D. H. Lawrence, 'The Last Laugh', in *The Woman Who Rode Away and Other Stories* (Penguin, 1950), pp. 131–47

154  'a man who sees Pan by daylight': D. H. Lawrence, 'Pan in America', in *Mornings in Mexico and Other Essays*, p. 160

155  'The return of Lawrence is great news': *Brett*, p. 135

156  'Thirty years ago in literary circles': W. Somerset Maugham, *Cakes and Ale; Or, the Skeleton in the Cupboard* (Doubleday, 1930), pp. 331–2

157  'Dear Old Horse': 'Dear Old Horse: A London Letter', pp. 3–6

### PARADISE: PART THREE

1  'his mischievous naughty-boy mood': Brett, 'Autobiography: My Long and Beautiful Journey', *South Dakota Review*, vol. 5, no. 2 (Summer 1967), p. 12

2  'You ahead, I behind': *Lawrence and Brett*, p. 47

3  'breathless and shaking': *Lorenzo in Taos*, p. 165

4  'grotesque': *Lorenzo in Taos*, p. 166

5  'square, sturdy build': *Lawrence and Brett*, p. 49

6  'pervasive' as the 'air': *Lorenzo in Taos*, p. 166

7  'our second effort': *Lorenzo in Taos*, p. 167

8  'I am not the same as I was!': *Lorenzo in Taos*, p. 168

9  'I cannot describe to you': *Lorenzo in Taos*, pp. 172–3

10  "Here's Eve – the bitch": *Lorenzo in Taos*, p. 175

11  'cold and distrustful': *Lorenzo in Taos*, p. 192

12  'shadow-pictures': 'Indians and Entertainment', p. 62

13  'Pale, dry, baked earth': D. H. Lawrence, 'The Dance of the Sprouting Corn', in *Mornings in Mexico and Other Essays*, pp. 71–5

14  'Hah!' snorts Frieda: *Lorenzo in Taos*, p. 178

15 'that represented me taking Tony to Buffalo': *Lorenzo in Taos*, p. 190

16 'We have a hilarious evening': *Lawrence and Brett*, p. 125

17 'It's quite big enough, really': *Lawrence and Brett*, p. 70

18 'only the doctors know': *Suppressed Memoirs*, p. 167

19 'I have been learning the Truth!': *Lorenzo in Taos*, p. 230

20 'you want to *kill* me': *Lorenzo in Taos*, p. 206

21 'the roof of the world': D. H. Lawrence, 'The Woman Who Rode Away', in *The Woman Who Rode Away and Other Stories* (Penguin, 1950), pp. 57, 62, 80

22 'Do you like it?': *Lorenzo in Taos*, p. 238

23 'revealed the irresistible delight': *Intimate Memories*, p. 310

24 'where Lorenzo thought he finished me up': *Lorenzo in Taos*, p. 238

25 'monstrous ... technicolor': Kate Millett, *Sexual Politics* (Ballantine Books, 1978), pp. 405–11

26 'too *damn* mean': *Corresponding Lives*, p. 95

27 'Well ... I had the essence of him in my hands': *Lorenzo in Taos*, p. 243

28 '*wants* you *dead* ... lion's den': *Lorenzo in Taos*, pp. 240–1

29 '£50,000': *Lorenzo in Taos*, p. 250

30 'had had her own way ... eternal fire': *St Mawr*, in *St Mawr and Other Stories*, ed. Brian Finney (Cambridge University Press, 1987), pp. 19–139

31 'the forty-foot dynamos': Henry Adams, *The Education of Henry Adams* (The Modern Library, 1931), p. 380

32 'the greatest force the Western world': *The Education of Henry Adams*, p. 388

33 'touch of bronchial trouble!': *Laurence and Brett*, p. 141

34 'destroying himself': *Lorenzo in Taos*, p. 255

35 'thrice alone': *Lorenzo in Taos*, p. 266

36 'exchange spirits with them': D. H. Lawrence, 'The Hopi Snake Dance', in *Mornings in Mexico and Other Essays*, pp. 84, 91

37 'One wonders what one went for': D. H. Lawrence, 'Just Back from the Snake Dance – Tired Out', in *Mornings in Mexico and Other Essays*, p. 185

38 'not for the Horse to laugh at': *Lorenzo in Taos*, p. 268

39 'ragged ghost': 'The Hopi Snake Dance', pp. 84–5

40 'heavily built, rather short': 'The Hopi Snake Dance', pp. 88–92

41 'the gruesome convulsion of a decapitated frog': Aby Warburg, 'Kreuzinger Lecture', first published in translation as 'A Lecture on the Serpent Ritual' in the *Journal of the Warburg Institute*, vol. 2 (1938), pp. 277–92

42 'I don't care for that kind of thing ... little mad': D. H. Lawrence, 'The Princess', in *St Mawr and Other Stories*, ed. Finney, pp. 190–5

43 'the graveyard of humanity': D. H. Lawrence, 'Climbing Down from Pisgah', in *Phoenix I*, p. 740

44 'with all that is human': *Suppressed Memoirs*, p. 28

45 'Both you and Brill feel': *Lorenzo in Taos*, p. 276

46 'If I can once get started': *Corresponding Lives*, p. 92

47 'Perhaps we shall look': *Lorenzo in Taos*, p. 278

48 'dangerous': *Lorenzo in Taos*, p. 278

49 'frail failure': *Lorenzo in Taos*, p. 270

50 'The little town of Oaxaca is lonely': *Letters*, 15 November 1924

51 'You marry me': *Plumed Serpent*, p. 444

52 'How else, she said to herself': *Plumed Serpent*, p. 422

53 'I hear that Mabel thinks': *Journey with Genius*, p. 338

54 'simply transposed': *Lorenzo in Taos*, p. 114

55 a 'great cat': *Plumed Serpent*, p. 438

56 'I managed to finish my Mexican novel': *Letters*, 6 April 1925

57 'tail-end of influenza': *Letters*, 4 February 1925

58 'grippe' with 'a typhoid inside': *Letters*, 6 April 1925

59 'like a maniac the whole night': *'Not I, But the Wind ...'*, p. 151

60 'callow youth': Carl Van Vechten, *The Splendid Drunken Twenties: Selections from the Daybooks, 1922–30* (University of Illinois Press, 2003), p. 100

61 'glad' to put to 'some creative use': *Corresponding Lives*, p. 190

62 Critics of Mabel have assumed: see Christopher Lasche, *The New Radicalism in America, 1889–1963* (Penguin, 1997), p. 33: Mabel 'cared so little about art in general that when she was presented with the manuscript of *Sons and Lovers* ... she gave the manuscript to Dr Brill'. And David Ellis, *Dying Game*, p. 183: 'Some time later she gave the *Sons and Lovers* manuscript to Brill in payment for his help in treating a friend, so little did she appreciate having her urge to give transformed into a *quid pro quo*'

63 'disloyalty and treachery': *Corresponding Lives*, p. 133

64 'wrote incessantly': 'Autobiography: My Long and Beautiful Journey', p. 41

65 'serpents coiling and uncoiling': *Corresponding Lives*, p. 94

66 'to ignore each other's inward lives': *Intimate Memories*, p. 24

67 'would raise her eyes': *Intimate Memories*, p. 8

68 'ecstatic' night: *Intimate Memories*, p. 11

69 'I was thrilled to find': Mabel Dodge Luhan, 'My Attitude in the Writing of Autobiography', published in an abridged version in *The New York World-Telegram*, 19 April 1933, p. 2

70 'auriculas and saxifrage': *Sons and Lovers*, p. 8

71 'how far': *Suppressed Memoirs*, p. 118

72 'fox-red ... back its flame': D. H. Lawrence, *David*, in *Complete Plays*, pp. III–54

73 'Let's go to New Mexico': Aldous Huxley, preface to *A Poet and Two Painters*

74 'I want God, I want poetry': Aldous Huxley, *Brave New World* (Harper Perennial, 2007), p. 231

75 'Probably, it's going to be ... come to my attention': *Corresponding Lives*, p. 94

76 'the most serious "confession" ': *Corresponding Lives*, p. 95

77 'so that there would be nothing': *Lorenzo in Taos*, p. 394

78 'Remember, other people': *Lorenzo in Taos*, p. 296

79 'the greatest experience': 'New Mexico', p. 176

80 'very little about diseases': D. H. Lawrence, 'Introduction to These Paintings', in *Phoenix I*, pp. 554–5

81 'I feel so strongly': *Lorenzo in Taos*, p. 348

82 yield 'entirely': *Lorenzo in Taos*, p. 351

83 'always double': *Lorenzo in Taos*, p. 170

84 'Like a bird': *'Not I, But the Wind ...'*, p. 296

85 'extraordinary and potent woman': D. H. Lawrence, 'None of That', in *The Woman Who Rode Away and Other Stories* (Penguin, 1950), pp. 210–23

86 'somehow he could not give': *Lorenzo in Taos*, p. 253

87 'He was an artist first of all': Aldous Huxley, preface to *The Letters of D. H. Lawrence*, ed. Aldous Huxley (Viking, 1932), p. xv

88 'So glad to get your exciting letter': *Norman Douglas*, p. 414

89 'the ashes of Lawrence': *Frieda Lawrence and her Circle: Letters from, to and about Frieda Lawrence*, ed. Harry T. Moore and Dale B. Montague (Macmillan, 1981), p. 72

# Bibliography

## MANUSCRIPTS AND ARCHIVES

Berg Collection, New York Public Library

Harry Ransom Humanities Research Center, University of Texas at Austin

Lawrence Manuscripts Collection, University of Nottingham Library

Mabel Dodge Luhan Papers, Beinecke Rare Book and Manuscript Library, Yale University

Maurice Magnus Papers, Beinecke Rare Book and Manuscript Library, Yale University

National Archives of Malta

National Archives, Washington DC

Norman Douglas Collection, Beinecke Rare Book and Manuscript Library, Yale University (including Maurice Magnus, 'Memoirs of Golden Russia', 1920)

## BOOKS AND ARTICLES

Abel, Richard, *Americanizing the Movies and "Movie-Mad Audiences", 1910–1914* (University of California Press, 2006)

Acton, Harold, *Nancy Mitford: A Memoir* (Gibson Square Books/Hamish Hamilton, 1975)

Adams, Henry, *The Education of Henry Adams* (The Modern Library, 1931)

Adelman, Gary, *Reclaiming D. H. Lawrence: Contemporary Writers Speak Out* (Bucknell University Press, 2002)

Aldington, Richard, *D. H. Lawrence: An Indiscretion* (University of Washington Press, 1927)

Aldington, Richard, *D. H. Lawrence: Portrait of a Genius, But …* (William Heinemann, 1950)

Aldington, Richard, *Life for Life's Sake: A Book of Reminiscences* (Cassell, 1968)

Aldington, Richard, *Pinorman: Personal Recollections of Norman Douglas, Pino Orioli and Charles Prentice* (William Heinemann, 1954)

*Aldous Huxley: Bloom's Modern Critical Views*, ed. Harold Bloom (Infobase, 2010)

Alighieri, Dante, *The Divine Comedy: Inferno, Purgatorio, Paradiso*, trans. Allen Mandelbaum (Everyman, 1995)

Alighieri, Dante, *La Vita Nuova*, trans. Mark Musa (World's Classics, 1992)

Arnold, Armin, *D. H. Lawrence and America* (The Linden Press, 1958)

Arnold, Armin, *The Symbolic Meaning: The Uncollected Versions of Studies in Classic American Literature* (Centaur Press, 1962)

Atkin, Jonathan, *A War of Individuals: Bloomsbury Attitudes to the Great War* (Manchester University Press, 2002)

*The Bad Side of Books: Selected Essays of D. H. Lawrence*, ed. Geoff Dyer (New York Review Books Classic, 2019)

Beerbohm, Max, *Seven Men, and Two Others* (Penguin, 1954)

Blake, William, *The Marriage of Heaven and Hell* (Dover Publications, 2000)

Bloch, Herbert, *Monte Cassino in the Middle Ages*, vol. 1 (Edizioni di Storia e Letteratura, 1986)

Booth, Howard J., ' "To Desire, to Belong": Homosexual Identity in the Lives and Writing of Compton Mackenzie, Norman Douglas and D. H. Lawrence', PhD thesis, University of Kent at Canterbury, 1997

Brailsford, H. A., *Shelley, Godwin and their Circle* (Createspace, 2014)

Brett, Dorothy, 'Autobiography: My Long and Beautiful Journey', *South Dakota Review*, vol. 5, no. 2 (Summer 1967), pp. 11–71

Brett, Dorothy, *Lawrence and Brett: A Friendship* (Lippincott, 1933)

Brewster, Earl, *D. H. Lawrence: Reminiscences and Correspondence* (Martin Secker, 1934)

Brooks, Van Wyck, 'The American Scene: General Thoughts on Henry James and America', *The Dial*, vol. 75 (July 1923), pp. 29–42

Burke, Flannery, *From Greenwich Village to Taos: Primitivism and Place at Mabel Dodge Luhan's* (University Press of Kansas, 2008)

Bynner, Witter, *Journey with Genius: Recollections and Reflections Concerning the D. H. Lawrences* (The John Day Company, 1951)

Byrne, Janet, *A Genius for Living: A Biography of Frieda Lawrence* (Bloomsbury, 1996)

Byron, Lord, *Selected Letters and Journals*, ed. Leslie Marchand (Belknap Press, 1982)

Carswell, Catherine, *Open the Door* (Virago, 1986)

Carswell, Catherine, *The Savage Pilgrimage: A Narrative of D. H. Lawrence* (Chatto & Windus, 1932)

Cather, Willa, *Death Comes for the Archbishop* (University of Nebraska Press, 1999)

Chambers, Jessie [E.T.], *D. H. Lawrence: A Personal Record* (Frank Cass, 1935)

Clark, L. D., *The Minoan Distance: The Symbolism of Travel in D. H. Lawrence* (University of Arizona Press, 1980)

'The Collected Letters of Jessie Chambers', ed. George J. Zytaruk, *The D. H. Lawrence Review*, vol. 12, no. 1/2 (Spring and Summer 1979)

*Complete Poems and Selected Letters of John Keats*, introduction by Edward Hirsch (Modern Library of New York, 2001)

Corke, Helen, *D. H. Lawrence as I Saw Him* (Sisson & Parker, 1960)

Corke, Helen, *D. H. Lawrence: The Croydon Years* (University of Texas Press, 1965)

Corke, Helen, *D. H. Lawrence's Princess: A Memory of Jessie Chambers* (Norwood Editions, 1976)

Corke, Helen, *In Our Infancy: An Autobiography* (Cambridge University Press, 2008)

Corke, Helen, *Neutral Ground: A Chronicle* (A. Barker, 1933)

Cowley, Malcolm, *Exile's Return* (Penguin, 1994)

Craig, Edward Gordon, *Index to the Story of my Days: Some Memoirs of Edward Gordon Craig, 1872–1907* (Hulton Press, 1957)

Cunard, Nancy, *Grand Man: Memories of Norman Douglas* (Secker & Warburg, 1954)

Curtius, Ernst Robert, *English Literature and the Latin Middle Ages*, trans. Willard R. Trask (Princeton University Press, 1953)

*Dante: The Critical Heritage*, ed. Michael Caesar (Routledge, 1989)

Darnton, Robert, *Mesmerism and the End of the Enlightenment in France* (Harvard University Press, 1968)

Delany, Paul, *D. H. Lawrence's Nightmare: The Writer and his Circle in the Years of the Great War* (Basic Books, 1978)

Delavaney, Emile, *D. H. Lawrence: The Man and his Work: The Formative Years, 1885–1915* (Southern Illinois University Press, 1972)

*D. H. Lawrence: A Composite Biography*, ed. Edward Nehls (3 vols, University of Wisconsin Press, 1957–9)

*D. H. Lawrence and Comedy*, ed. Paul Eggert and John Worthen (Cambridge University Press, 1996)

*D. H. Lawrence: Novelist, Poet, Prophet*, ed. Stephen Spender (Weidenfeld & Nicolson, 1973)

Doolittle, Hilda [H.D.], *Bid Me to Live: A Madrigal* (Virago, 1980)

Doolittle, Hilda [H.D.], *Collected Poems, 1912–1944*, ed. Louis L. Martz (New Directions Publishing, 1982)

Doolittle, Hilda [H.D.], *Tribute to Freud: Writing on the Wall, Advent* (Carcanet, 1985)

Dostoevsky, Fydor, *The Brothers Karamazov*, trans. Constance Garnett (William Heinemann, 1951)

Douglas, Norman, *Alone* (R. M. McBride, 1922)

Douglas, Norman, *D. H. Lawrence and Maurice Magnus: A Plea for Better Manners*, in *Memoir of Maurice Magnus*, ed. Keith Cushman (Black Swallow Press, 1987)

Douglas, Norman, *Experiments: A Miscellany* (Chapman & Hall, 1925)

Douglas, Norman, *Late Harvest* (L. Drummond, 1947)

Douglas, Norman, *Looking Back: An Autobiographical Excursion* (Harcourt, Brace, 1933)

Douglas, Norman, *Old Calabria* (Martin Secker, 1920)

Douglas, Norman, *Siren Land* (Martin Secker, 1929)

Douglas, Norman, *South Wind* (Secker & Warburg, 1947)

Duncan, Isadora, *My Life* (Star Books, 1927)

Dyer, Geoff, *Out of Sheer Rage: In the Shadow of D. H. Lawrence* (Little, Brown, 1997)

Eliot, T. S., *The Complete Prose of T. S. Eliot: The Critical Edition: Literature, Politics, Belief, 1927–1929*, ed. Frances Dickey, Jennifer Formichelli and Ronald Schuchard (Johns Hopkins University Press, 2009)

Eliot, T. S., *To Criticize the Critic and Other Writings* (Farrar, Straus & Giroux, 1965)

Ellis, David, *Death and the Author: How D. H. Lawrence Died, and was Remembered* (Oxford University Press, 2008)

Ellis, David, 'D. H. Lawrence and Tuberculosis', in *Writing the Lives of Writers*, ed. Warwick Gould and Thomas F. Staley (Macmillan, 1998), pp. 204–11

Ellis, David, *D. H. Lawrence: Dying Game: 1922–1930*, vol. 3 of *The Cambridge Biography of D. H. Lawrence* (Cambridge University Press, 1997)

Ellis, David, *Love and Sex in D. H. Lawrence* (Clemson University Press, 2015)

Ellmann, Richard, *James Joyce* (Oxford University Press, 1959)

Everett, Patricia R., *Corresponding Lives: Mabel Dodge Luhan, A. A. Brill, and the Psychoanalytic Adventure in America* (Karnac, 2016)

Fay, Eliot, *Lorenzo in Search of the Sun: D. H. Lawrence in Italy, Mexico and the American Southwest* (Vision Press, 1955)

Ford, Ford Madox, *Mightier than the Sword: Memories and Criticisms* (Allen & Unwin, 1938)

Ford, Ford Madox, *Return to Yesterday* (Horace Liveright, 1932)

Ford, George H., 'Shelley or Schiller? A Note on D. H. Lawrence at Work', *Texas Studies in Literature and Language*, vol. 4, no. 2 (Summer 1962), pp. 154–6

Forster, E. M., *A Room with a View* (Penguin, 2006)

Forster, E. M., *Howard's End* (Penguin, 2000)

Forster, E. M., *Maurice* (Penguin, 2005)

Foster, Joseph, *D. H. Lawrence in Taos* (University of New Mexico Press, 1972)

Fraser, Keath, 'Norman Douglas and D. H. Lawrence: A Sideshow in Modern Memoirs', *D. H. Lawrence Review*, vol. 9 (1976), pp. 283–95

*Frederick Delius and Peter Warlock: A Friendship Revealed*, ed. Barry Smith (Oxford University Press, 2000)

*Frieda Lawrence and her Circle: Letters from, to and about Frieda Lawrence*, ed. Harry T. Moore and Dale B. Montague (Macmillan, 1981)

*Frieda Lawrence: The Memoirs and Correspondence*, ed. E. W. Tedlock (Alfred A. Knopf, 1964)

Furbank, P. N., *E. M. Forster: A Life* (Oxford University Press, 1979)

Fussell, Paul, *Abroad: British Literary Travelling between the Wars* (Oxford University Press, 1980)

Fussell, Paul, *The Great War and Modern Memory* (Oxford University Press, 2000)

Galea, Joseph, 'Maurice Magnus: His Stay in Malta', *Sundial* (Malta), (April 1943), pp. 229–32

Ganz, Earl, *The Taos Truth Game* (University of New Mexico Press, 2006)

Garnett, David, 'Frieda and Lawrence', in *D. H Lawrence: Novelist, Poet, Prophet*, ed. Stephen Spender (Weidenfeld & Nicolson, 1973), pp. 37–42

Garnett, David, *The Golden Echo* (Chatto & Windus, 1954)

Garnett, David, *Great Friends: Portraits of Seventeen Writers* (Macmillan, 1979)

Garnett, David, 'A Reminiscence', introduction to D. H. Lawrence, *Love among the Haystacks & Other Pieces* (Martin Secker, 1933)

Gay, Peter, *Weimar Culture* (Harper, 1968)

Gisborne, Mary and R. Glynn Grylis, *Mary Shelley: A Biography* (Haskell House, 1969)

Goldring, Douglas, *The Nineteen Twenties: A General Survey and Some Personal Memories* (Nicholson & Watson, 1945)

Goldstein, Bill, *The World Broke in Two* (Bloomsbury, 2017)

Gray, Cecil, *Musical Chairs; Or, Between Two Stools* (The Hogarth Press, 1948)

Gray, Cecil, *Peter Warlock: A Memoir of Philip Heseltine* (Jonathan Cape, 1934)

Green, Martin, *Mountain of Truth: The Counterculture Begins: Ascona, 1900–1920* (University Press of New England, 1986)

Green, Martin, *The Von Richthofen Sisters: The Triumphant and the Tragic Modes of Love* (Basic Books, 1974)

Griffiths, Eric and Matthew Reynolds, *Dante in English* (Penguin, 2005)

Hahn, Emily, *Mabel: A Biography of Mabel Dodge Luhan* (Houghton Mifflin, 1977)

Harrison, Andrew, *The Life of D. H. Lawrence: A Critical Biography* (John Wiley, 2016)

Heilbrun, Carolyn, *The Garnett Family* (Macmillan, 1961)

Heuer, Gottfried M., *Freud's 'Outstanding' Colleague/Jung's 'Twin Brother': The Suppressed Psychoanalytic and Political Significance of Otto Gross* (Routledge, 2017)

Hignett, Sean, *Brett: From Bloomsbury to New Mexico* (Franklin Watts, 1983)

Holbrook, May, 'Some Memories of D. H. Lawrence', in Jessie Chambers [E.T.], *D. H. Lawrence: A Personal Record* (Frank Cass, 1935), pp. 227–42

Holloway, Mark, *Norman Douglas: A Biography* (Secker & Warburg, 1976)

Holmes, Richard, *Coleridge: Darker Reflections* (HarperCollins, 1998)

Holmes, Richard, *Shelley: The Pursuit* (HarperCollins, 1974)

Holroyd, Michael, *Lytton Strachey: A Critical Biography*, vol. 2 (Holt, Rinehart & Winston, 1968)

Holroyd, Michael, *A Strange Eventful History: The Dramatic Lives of Ellen Terry, Henry Irving, and their Remarkable Families* (Vintage, 2009)

Hunt, Leigh, *The Selected Writings of Leigh Hunt*, vols 3 and 5, ed. Robert Morrison and Michael Eberle-Sinatra (Pickering & Chatto, 2003)

Hunt, Leigh, *Stories from the Italian Poets, with Lives of the Writers* (Baudry's European Library, 1846)

Hunt, Leigh, *The Story of Rimini: A Poem* (John Murray, 1816)

Huxley, Aldous, *Brave New World* (Harper Perennial, 2007)

Huxley, Aldous, *Point Counter Point* (Vintage, 2004)

Huxley, Aldous et al., *A Conversation on D. H. Lawrence* (UCLA Library, 1974)

Jackson, Rosie, *Frieda Lawrence, Including Not I, But the Wind* (HarperCollins, 1994)

James, Henry, *Hawthorne* (Macmillan, 1887)

Jones, Ernest, *Free Associations: Memories of a Psychoanalyst* (Basic Books, 1959)

Joost, Nicholas and Alvin Sullivan, *D. H. Lawrence and The Dial* (Southern Illinois University Press, 1970)

*Journal of Katherine Mansfield*, ed. John Middleton Murry (Persephone Books, 2006)

Jung, Carl, *Memories, Dreams, Reflections* (Vintage, 1989)

Kafka, Franz, *Letters to Friends, Family and Editors* (Shocken Books, 1977)

Kaplan, Sydney Janet, *Circulating Genius: John Middleton Murry, Katherine Mansfield and D. H. Lawrence* (Edinburgh University Press, 2010)

Kinkead-Weekes, Mark, *D. H. Lawrence: Triumph to Exile, 1912–1922*, vol. 2 of *The Cambridge Biography of D. H. Lawrence* (Cambridge University Press, 1996)

Lasche, Christopher, *The New Radicalism in America, 1889–1963* (Penguin, 1997)

Lawrence, Ada and G. Stuart Gelder, *Young Lorenzo: Early Life of D. H. Lawrence* (Martin Secker, 1932)

Lawrence, D. H., *Aaron's Rod* (Penguin, 1996)

Lawrence, D. H., 'America, Listen to your Own', *New Republic*, 15 December 1920

Lawrence, D. H., *Amores* (B. W. Huebsch, 1916)

Lawrence, D. H., *Apocalypse* (Penguin, 1974)

Lawrence, D. H., 'Au Revoir, USA', in *Mornings in Mexico and Other Essays*, ed. Virginia Crosswhite Hyde (Cambridge University Press, 2009), pp. 129–34

Lawrence, D. H., 'Autobiographical Fragment', in *Late Essays and Articles*, ed. James T. Boulton (Cambridge University Press, 2004)

Lawrence, D. H., 'The Bad Side of Books: Introduction to *A Bibliography of the Writings of D. H. Lawrence* by Edward D. McDonald', in *The Bad Side of Books*, ed. Geoff Dyer (New York Review Books, 2019), pp. 207–11

Lawrence, D. H., 'Benjamin Franklin', in *Studies in Classic American Literature*, ed. Ezra Greenspan, Lindeth Vasey and John Worthen

(Cambridge University Press, 2003), first version pp. 20–31, final version pp. 180–90

Lawrence, D. H., *Birds, Beasts and Flowers* (Cresset Press, 1930)

Lawrence, D. H., 'Certain Americans and an Englishman', in *Mornings in Mexico and Other Essays*, ed. Virginia Crosswhite Hyde (Cambridge University Press, 2009), pp. 103–11

Lawrence, D. H., 'Christs in the Tyrol', in *Twilight in Italy and Other Essays*, ed. Paul Eggert (Cambridge University Press, 2002), pp. 43–50

Lawrence, D. H., 'Climbing Down Pisgah', in *Reflections on the Death of a Porcupine and Other Essays*, ed. Michael Herbert (Cambridge University Press, 1988), pp. 223–30

Lawrence, D. H., *A Collier's Friday Night*, in *The Complete Plays of D. H. Lawrence* (William Heinemann, 1965), pp. 469–531

Lawrence, D. H., *Complete Poems*, ed. Vivian de Sola Pinto and Warren F. Roberts (Penguin, 1994)

Lawrence, D. H., 'The Dance of the Sprouting Corn', in *Mornings in Mexico and Other Essays*, ed. Virginia Crosswhite Hyde (Cambridge University Press, 2009), pp. 69–76

Lawrence, D. H., *The Daughter-in-Law*, in *The Complete Plays of D. H. Lawrence* (William Heinemann, 1965), pp. 203–69

Lawrence, D. H. 'David', in *Sketches of Etruscan Places and Other Italian Essays*, ed. Simonetta de Filippis (Cambridge University Press, 1992), pp. 183–90

Lawrence, D. H., *David*, in *The Complete Plays of D. H. Lawrence* (William Heinemann, 1965), pp. 63–155

Lawrence, D. H., 'Dear Old Horse: A London Letter', no. 10, *Laughing Horse* (May 1924), pp. 3–6

Lawrence, D. H., 'Edgar Allan Poe', in *Studies in Classic American Literature*, ed. Ezra Greenspan, Lindeth Vasey and John Worthen (Cambridge University Press, 2003), first version pp. 66–80, final version pp. 229–40

Lawrence, D. H., *Fantasia of the Unconscious* (Thomas Seltzer, 1922)

Lawrence, D. H., *The Fight for Barbara*, in *The Complete Plays of D. H. Lawrence* (William Heinemann, 1965), pp. 269–321

Lawrence, D. H., *The First Lady Chatterley* (Penguin, 1994)

Lawrence, D. H., *The First Women in Love*, ed. John Worthen and Lindeth Vasey (Cambridge University Press, 1998)

Lawrence, D. H., *The Fox*, in *The Complete Short Novels*, ed. Keith Sagar (Penguin, 1982), pp. 135–205

Lawrence, D. H. (trans.), ' "The Gentleman from San Francisco", by Ivan Bunin', in *Phoenix II: Uncollected, Unpublished, and Other Prose Works*, ed. Warren Roberts and Harry T. Moore (Viking, 1959), pp. 198–212

Lawrence, D. H., 'Henry St John de Crèvecoeur', in *Studies in Classic American Literature*, ed. Ezra Greenspan, Lindeth Vasey and John Worthen (Cambridge University Press, 2003), first version pp. 32–41, final version pp. 191–203

Lawrence, D. H., 'Herman Melville', in *Studies in Classic American Literature*, ed. Ezra Greenspan, Lindeth Vasey and John Worthen (Cambridge University Press, 2003), pp. 288–304

Lawrence, D. H., 'Herman Melville's Moby Dick', in *Studies in Classic American Literature*, ed. Ezra Greenspan, Lindeth Vasey and John Worthen (Cambridge University Press, 2003), pp. 133–47

Lawrence, D. H., 'Herman Melville's Typee and Omoo', in *Studies in Classic American Literature*, ed. Ezra Greenspan, Lindeth Vasey and John Worthen (Cambridge University Press, 2003), pp. 122–32

Lawrence, D. H., 'The Hopi Snake Dance', in *Mornings in Mexico and Other Essays*, ed. Virginia Crosswhite Hyde (Cambridge University Press, 2009), pp. 77–94

Lawrence, D. H., 'Hymns in a Man's Life', in *Late Essays and Articles*, ed. James T. Boulton (Cambridge University Press, 2004), pp. 128–34

Lawrence, D. H., 'Il Duro', in *Twilight in Italy and Other Essays*, ed. Paul Eggert (Cambridge University Press, 2002), pp. 173–8

Lawrence, D. H., 'Indians and an Englishman', in *Mornings in Mexico and Other Essays*, ed. Virginia Crosswhite Hyde (Cambridge University Press, 2009), pp. 111–22

Lawrence, D. H., 'Indians and Entertainment', in *Mornings in Mexico and Other Essays*, ed. Virginia Crosswhite Hyde (Cambridge University Press, 2009), pp. 57–68

Lawrence, D. H., *Introductions and Reviews*, ed. N. H. Reeve and John Worthen (Cambridge University Press, 2005)

Lawrence, D. H., 'Introduction to Pictures', in *Late Essays and Articles*, ed. James T. Boulton (Cambridge University Press, 2004), pp. 166–74

Lawrence, D. H., 'Introduction to These Paintings', in *Phoenix: The Posthumous Papers of D. H. Lawrence*, ed. Edward McDonald (Viking, 1964), pp. 551–87

Lawrence, D. H., 'Just Back from the Snake Dance – Tired Out', in *Mornings in Mexico and Other Essays*, ed. Virginia Crosswhite Hyde (Cambridge University Press, 2009), pp. 183–8

Lawrence, D. H., *Kangaroo*, ed. Bruce Steele (Cambridge University Press, 1994)

Lawrence, D. H., 'The Last Laugh', in *The Woman Who Rode Away and Other Stories* (Penguin, 1950), pp. 131–47

Lawrence, D. H., 'A Little Moonshine with Lemon', in *Mornings in Mexico and Other Essays*, ed. Virginia Crosswhite Hyde (Cambridge University Press, 2009), pp. 95–101

Lawrence, D. H., *Look! We Have Come Through!: A Cycle of Love Poems* (The Ark Press, 1958)

Lawrence, D. H., 'Looking Down on the City', in *Sketches of Etruscan Places and Other Italian Essays*, ed. Simonetta de Filippis (Cambridge University Press, 1992), pp. 191–6

Lawrence, D. H., *The Lost Girl* (Martin Secker, 1920)

Lawrence, D. H., *Love among the Haystacks and Other Stories*, ed. John Worthen (Cambridge University Press, 1987)

Lawrence, D. H., 'The Man Who Loved Islands', in *Love among the Haystacks and Other Stories* (Penguin, 1960), pp. 97–125

Lawrence, D. H., *Memoir of Maurice Magnus*, ed. Keith Cushman (Black Sparrow Press, 1987)

Lawrence, D. H., 'A Modern Lover', in *The Woman Who Rode Away and Other Stories* (Penguin, 1950), pp. 225–48

Lawrence, D. H., 'Morality and the Novel', in *A Selection from Phoenix*, ed. A. A. H. Inglis (Penguin, 1979), pp. 527–33

Lawrence, D. H., *Mornings in Mexico and Other Essays*, ed. Virginia Crosswhite Hyde (Cambridge University Press, 2009)

Lawrence, D. H., *Movements in European History*, ed. Philip Crumpton (Cambridge University Press, 1989)

Lawrence, D. H., *Mr Noon*, ed. Lindeth Vasey (Cambridge University Press, 1987)

Lawrence, D. H., 'Myself Revealed', in *Late Essays and Articles*, ed. James T. Boulton (Cambridge University Press, 2004), pp. 175–81

Lawrence, D. H., 'Nathaniel Hawthorne and *The Scarlet Letter*', in *Studies in Classic American Literature*, ed. Ezra Greenspan, Lindeth Vasey and John Worthen (Cambridge University Press, 2003), pp. 81–95

Lawrence, D. H., 'New Mexico', in *Mornings in Mexico and Other Essays*, ed. Virginia Crosswhite Hyde (Cambridge University Press, 2009), pp. 173–80

Lawrence, D. H., 'None of That!', in *The Woman Who Rode Away and Other Stories* (Penguin, 1950), pp. 203–14

Lawrence, D. H., 'Nottingham and the Mining Countryside', in *Phoenix: The Posthumous Papers of D. H. Lawrence* (Viking, 1964), pp. 135–6

Lawrence, D. H., 'The Novel', in *The Bad Side of Books*, ed. Geoff Dyer (New York Review Books, 2019), pp. 237–51

Lawrence, D. H., 'Odour of Chrysanthemums', in *Selected Stories*, ed. Sue Wilson (Penguin, 2007), pp. 74–95

Lawrence, D. H., 'On Being a Man', in *Reflections on the Death of a Porcupine and Other Essays*, ed. Michael Herbert (Cambridge University Press, 1988), pp. 211–23

Lawrence, D. H., 'On Coming Home', in *Phoenix II: Uncollected, Unpublished, and Other Prose Works by D. H. Lawrence*, ed. Warren Roberts and Harry T. Moore (Viking, 1959), pp. 250–7

Lawrence, D. H., 'Pan in America', in *Mornings in Mexico and Other Essays*, ed. Virginia Crosswhite Hyde (Cambridge University Press, 2009), pp. 153–65

Lawrence, D. H., *Pansies* (Martin Secker, 1929)

Lawrence, D. H., *Paul Morel*, ed. Helen Baron (Cambridge University Press, 2003)

Lawrence, D. H., *Phoenix: The Posthumous Papers of D. H. Lawrence*, ed. Edward McDonald (Viking, 1964)

Lawrence, D. H., *Phoenix II: Uncollected, Unpublished, and Other Prose Works*, ed. Warren Roberts and Harry T. Moore (Viking, 1959)

Lawrence, D. H., *The Plumed Serpent*, ed. L. D. Clark (Cambridge University Press, 1987)

Lawrence, D. H., 'The Poetry of the Present', in *The Bad Side of Books*, ed. Geoff Dyer (New York Review Books, 2019), pp. 77–82

Lawrence, D. H., 'The Princess', in *St Mawr and Other Stories*, ed. Brian Finney (Cambridge University Press, 1983), pp. 157–97

Lawrence, D. H., 'The Prussian Officer', in *The Prussian Officer* (Penguin, 1968), pp. 7–30

Lawrence, D. H., *Psychoanalysis and the Unconscious and Fantasia of the Unconscious* (Dover Publications, 2005)

Lawrence, D. H., *Quetzalcoatl*, ed. N. H. Reeve (Cambridge University Press, 2011)

Lawrence, D. H., *The Rainbow* (William Heinemann, 1961)

Lawrence, D. H., 'Return to Bestwood', in *Late Essays and Articles*, ed. James T. Boulton (Cambridge University Press, 2004), pp. 13–24

Lawrence, D. H., *St Mawr*, in *St Mawr and Other Stories*, ed. Brian Finney (Cambridge University Press, 1983), pp. 19–157

Lawrence, D. H., *Sea and Sardinia*, in *D. H. Lawrence and Italy: Sketches from Etruscan Places, Sea and Sardinia, Twilight in Italy*, ed. Simonetta de Filippis et al. (Penguin, 2007), pp. 137–326

Lawrence, D. H., *Sketches of Etruscan Places and Other Italian Essays*, ed. Simonetta de Filippis (Cambridge University Press, 1992)

Lawrence, D. H., *Sons and Lovers* (Duckworth, 1913)

Lawrence, D. H., 'The Spirit of Place', in *Studies in Classic American Literature*, ed. Ezra Greenspan, Lindeth Vasey and John Worthen (Cambridge University Press, 2003), final version pp. 13–20, first version pp. 167–79

Lawrence, D. H., *Studies in Classic American Literature*, ed. Ezra Greenspan, Lindeth Vasey and John Worthen (Cambridge University Press, 2003)

Lawrence, D. H., 'Study of Thomas Hardy', in *Study of Thomas Hardy and Other Essays*, ed. Bruce Steele (Cambridge University Press, 1985), pp. 3–133

Lawrence, D. H., 'Surgery for the Novel – or a Bomb', in *A Selection from Phoenix*, ed. A. A. H. Inglis (Penguin 1979), pp. 189–93

Lawrence, D. H., 'Taos', in *Mornings in Mexico and Other Essays*, ed. Virginia Crosswhite Hyde (Cambridge University Press, 2009), pp. 123–8

Lawrence, D. H., *The Trespasser* (Duckworth, 1912)

Lawrence, D. H., *Twilight in Italy and Other Essays*, ed. Paul Eggert (Cambridge University Press, 2002)

Lawrence, D. H., 'Vin Ordinaire', in *Selected Stories*, ed. Sue Wilson (Penguin, 2007), pp. 122–40

Lawrence, D. H., *The White Peacock* (Penguin, 1981)

Lawrence, D. H., 'Why the Novel Matters', in *The Bad Side of Books*, ed. Geoff Dyer (New York Review Books, 2019), pp. 252–9

Lawrence, D. H., 'The Wilful Woman', in *St Mawr and Other Stories*, ed. Brian Finney (Cambridge University Press, 1983), pp. 197–205

Lawrence, D. H., 'The Woman Who Rode Away', in *The Woman Who Rode Away and Other Stories* (Penguin, 1950), pp. 45-82

Lawrence, D. H., *The Woman Who Rode Away, St Mawr, The Princess*, ed. Brian Finney et al. (Penguin, 2006)

Lawrence, D. H., *Women in Love* (Martin Secker, 1928)

Lawrence, Frieda, 'And the Fullness Thereof …', in *Frieda Lawrence: The Memoirs and Correspondence*, ed. E. W. Tedlock (Alfred A. Knopf, 1964), pp. 3–128

Lawrence, Frieda, *"Not I, But the Wind …"* (Viking, 1934)

Lawrence, T. E., *Seven Pillars of Wisdom* (Dover Publications, 2018)

Lea, F. A., *The Life of John Middleton Murry* (Oxford University Press, 1960)

*The Letters of Aldous Huxley*, ed. Grover Cleveland Smith (Chatto & Windus, 1969)

*The Letters of D. H. Lawrence*, ed. Aldous Huxley (Viking, 1932)

*The Letters of D. H. Lawrence*, ed. James Boulton et al. (8 vols, Cambridge University Press, 1979–93)

*The Letters of John Keats*, vol. 2: *1819–1821*, ed. Hyder Edward Rollins (Cambridge University Press, 1958)

*The Letters of Katherine Mansfield*, ed. Vincent O'Sullivan and Margaret Scott (2 vols, Clarendon Press, 1984–7)

*The Letters of Virginia Woolf*, vol. 5: *1932–1935*, ed. Nigel Nicolson (Chatto & Windus, 1979)

Lewis, C. S., 'Shelley, Dryden and Mr Eliot', in *Selected Literary Essays*, ed. Walter Hooper (Cambridge University Press, 1969), pp. 187–209

Lewis, Nancy Owen, *Chasing the Cure in New Mexico: Tuberculosis and the Quest for Health* (University of New Mexico Press, 2016)

Lucie-Smith, Edward, 'The Poetry of D. H. Lawrence – With a Glance at Shelley', in *D. H. Lawrence: Novelist, Poet, Prophet*, ed. Stephen Spender (Weidenfeld & Nicolson, 1973), pp. 224–34

Lueders, Edward, *Carl Van Vechten* (Twayne, 1965)

Luhan, Mabel Dodge, *Intimate Memories: The Autobiography of Mabel Dodge Luhan*, ed. Lois Palken Rudnick (University of New Mexico Press, 1999)

Luhan, Mabel Dodge, *Lorenzo in Taos* (Alfred A. Knopf, 1935)

Luhan, Mabel Dodge, 'My Attitude in the Writing of Autobiography', *New York World-Telegram*, 19 April 1933, p. 2

Luhan, Mabel Dodge, *Winter in Taos* (Sunstone Books, 1934)

Lummis, Charles F., *The Land of Poco Tiempo* (Charles Scribner's, 1893)

*Mabel Dodge Luhan & Company: American Moderns and the West*, ed. Lois Palken Rudnick and MaLin Wilson-Powell (University of New Mexico Press, 2016)

Maddox, Brenda, *D. H. Lawrence: The Story of a Marriage* (W. W. Norton, 1996)

*Magic Mirror, Compassionate Friendship, Thorn Thicket: A Tribute to Erich Heydt*, ed. Nephie J. Christodoulides (ELS Editions, 2015)

Maugham, W. Somerset, *Cakes and Ale; Or, the Skeleton in the Cupboard* (Doubleday, 1930)

Mann, Thomas, *The Magic Mountain* (Vintage 1999)

Mansfield, Katherine, *The Collected Stories* (Penguin, 2007)

Magnus, Maurice, 'Holy Week at Monte Cassino', *Land and Water*, 29 April 1920, pp. 14–16

Magnus, Maurice, *Memoirs of the Foreign Legion by M.M., with an Introduction by D. H. Lawrence* (Alfred A. Knopf, 1925)

Mandelstam, Osip, *Conversation about Dante*, trans. Clarence Brown and Robert Hughes (Notting Hill Editions, 2011)

Medwin, Thomas, *Conversations of Lord Byron* (Princeton University Press, 1966)

Meltzer, Milton, *Willa Cather: A Biography* (Twenty-First Century Books, 2008)

*A Mere Interlude: Some Literary Visitors in Lyonnesse*, ed. Melissa Hardie (The Patten Press, 1992)

Merrild, Knut, *A Poet and Two Painters: A Memoir of D. H. Lawrence* (Routledge, 1938)

Meyers, Jeffrey, *D. H. Lawrence: A Biography* (Cooper Square Press, 2002)

Meyers, Jeffrey, *D. H. Lawrence and the Experience of Italy* (University of Pennsylvania Press, 1982)

Meyers, Jeffrey, 'D. H. Lawrence and Homosexuality', in *D. H. Lawrence: Novelist, Poet, Prophet*, ed. Stephen Spender (Weidenfeld & Nicolson, 1973), pp. 135–59

Meyers, Jeffrey, *Homosexuality and Literature, 1890–1930* (Athlone Press, 1977)

Millett, Kate, *Sexual Politics* (Ballantine Books, 1978)

Mills, Howard, ' "My Best Single Piece of Writing": "Introduction to *Memoirs of the Foreign Legion* by M.M." ', in David Ellis and Howard Mills, *D. H. Lawrence's Non-Fiction: Art, Thought and Genre* (Cambridge University Press, 1988), pp. 120–46

Monk, Ray, *Bertrand Russell: The Spirit of Solitude, 1872–1921* (The Free Press, 1996)

Moore, Harry T., 'D. H. Lawrence and the Flicks', *Literature/Film Quarterly*, no. 1 (Winter 1973), pp. 3–11

Murry, John Middleton, *Between Two Worlds* (Jonathan Cape, 1935)

Murry, John Middleton, *D. H. Lawrence: Two Essays* (The Minority Press, 1930)

Murry, John Middleton, *Fyodor Dostoevsky: A Critical Study* (Martin Secker, 1916)

Murry, John Middleton, *Reminiscences of D. H. Lawrence* (Henry Holt, 1933)

Murry, John Middleton, *Son of Woman: The Story of D. H. Lawrence* (Jonathan Cape, 1931)

Nabokov, Vladimir, *Letters to Vera*, ed. and trans. Olga Voronina and Brian Boyd (Vintage, 2014)

Nehls, Edward, 'D. H. Lawrence: The Spirit of Place', in *The Achievement of D. H. Lawrence*, ed. Frederick J. Hoffman and Harry T. Moore (University of Oklahoma Press, 1953), pp. 268–90

Neville, G. H., *A Memoir of D. H. Lawrence: The Betrayal*, ed. Carl Baron (Cambridge University Press, 1981)

Orwell, George, *The Road to Wigan Pier* (Penguin, 2001)

'The Otto Gross–Frieda Weekley Correspondence', transcribed, translated and annotated by John Turner with Cornelia Rumpf-Worthen and Ruth Jenkins, *The D. H. Lawrence Review*, vol. 22, no. 2 (Summer 1990), pp. 137–227

*The Oxford Encyclopedia of American Literature*, vol. 3, ed. Jay Perini (Oxford University Press, 2004)

Owen, Wilfred, *Complete Poems* (Blackthorn Press, 2013)

Parks, Adam, *Modernism and the Theatre of Censorship* (Oxford University Press, 1996)

Plutarch, *Moralia*, vol. v, trans. F. C. Babbitt (Loeb Classical Library, 1936)

Pound, Ezra, *Money Pamphlets by £* (Peter Russell, 1950)

*The Rainbow and Women in Love – A Case Book*, ed. Colin C. Clarke (Aurora Publishers, 1969)

Robinson, Janice S., *H.D.: The Life and Work of an American Poet* (Houghton Mifflin, 1982)

Rubin, Merle, ' "Not I, But the Wind that Blows through Me": Shelleyan Aspects of Lawrence's Poetry', *Texas Studies in Literature and Language* (Spring 1981), pp. 102–22

Rudnick, Lois Palken, *Mabel Dodge Luhan: New Woman, New Worlds* (University of New Mexico Press, 1984)

Ruskin, John, *Modern Painters*, vol. 5 (J. Wiley & Son, 1866)

*The Selected Letters of Bertrand Russell: The Public Years, 1914–1970*, ed. Nicholas Griffin (Routledge, 2001)

*The Selected Letters of D. H. Lawrence*, ed. Diana Trilling (Farrar, Straus & Cudahy, 1958)

*Selected Letters of E. M. Forster*, vol. 1: *1879–1920*, ed. Mary Lago and P. N. Furbank (Collins, 1983)

Seymour, Miranda, *Mary Shelley* (Simon & Schuster, 2018)

Seymour, Miranda, *Noble Endeavours: The Life of Two Countries, England and Germany, in Many Stories* (Simon & Schuster, 2013)

Seymour, Miranda, *Ottoline Morrell: Life on a Grand Scale* (Farrar, Straus & Giroux, 1993)

Shelley, Percy Bysshe, *Prometheus Unbound and Other Poems* (Humphrey Milford, 1931)

Shelley, Percy Bysshe, 'A Defence of Poetry', in *Selected Prose Works of Shelley*, with a foreword by Henry S. Salt (Watts & Co., 1915)

*Shelley on Love: An Anthology*, ed. Richard Holmes (University of California Press, 1980)

Skinner, M. L., *The Fifth Sparrow: An Autobiography* (Sydney University Press, 1972)

Smith, Barry, *Peter Warlock: The Life of Philip Heseltine* (Oxford University Press, 1994)

Smith, Helen, *The Uncommon Reader: A Life of Edward Garnett* (Jonathan Cape, 2017)

Smith, J. T., *Nollekens and his Times* (Richard Bentley & Son, 1895)

Squires, Michael and Lynn K. Talbot, *Living at the Edge: A Biography of D. H. Lawrence and Frieda von Richthofen* (University of Wisconsin Press, 2002)

*The Suppressed Memoirs of Mabel Dodge Luhan: Sex, Syphilis, and Psychoanalysis in the Making of Modern American Culture*, ed. Lois Palken Rudnick (University of New Mexico Press, 2012)

Thompson, Francis, *Shelley* (Burns & Oates, 1914)

Thomson, Ian, *Dante's Divine Comedy: A Journey without End* (Head of Zeus, 2018)

Thorne, Guy, *When It Was Dark: The Story of a Great Conspiracy* (Createspace, 2013)

Tindall, William York, *D. H. Lawrence and Susan his Cow* (Columbia University Press, 1939)

Tomalin, Claire, *Katherine Mansfield: A Secret Life* (Penguin, 2012)

Tomlinson, H. M. L., *Norman Douglas* (Chatto & Windus, 1931)

Trelawny, Edward, *Recollections of the Last Days of Shelley and Byron* (Carroll & Graf, 2000)

Udall, Sharyn Rohlfsen, *Spud Johnson and Laughing Horse* (Sunstone Press, 2008)

Usner, David H., *Indian Work: Language and Livelihood in Native American History* (Harvard University Press, 2009)

Van Vechten, Carl, *Peter Whiffle* (Alfred A. Knopf, 1922)

Van Vechten, Carl, *The Splendid Drunken Twenties: Selections from the Daybooks, 1922–30* (University of Illinois Press, 2003)

Wade, Francesca, *Square Haunting* (Faber & Faber, 2020)

Warburg, Aby, 'A Lecture on the Serpent Ritual', *Journal of the Warburg Institute*, vol. 2 (1938), pp. 277–92

Washington, Peter, *Madame Blavatsky's Baboon: Theosophy and the Emergence of the Western Guru* (Secker & Warburg, 1993)

Wasserstrom, William, *The Time of the Dial* (Syracuse University Press, 1963)

Weaver, Raymond, *Herman Melville: Mariner and Mystic* (G. H. Doran, 1921)

Weekley, Ernest, *The Romance of Words* (John Murray, 1913)

Weintraub, Stanley, *Reggie: A Portrait of Reginald Turner* (G. Braziller, 1965)

West, Rebecca, *Ending in Earnest: A Literary Log* (Doubleday, 1931)

Whitman, Walt, *Leaves of Grass*, ed. Malcolm Cowley (Penguin, 1959; first edition 1855)

Wilson, A. N., *Dante in Love: A Biography* (Farrar, Straus & Giroux, 2011)

Wilson, Peter, *A Preface to Ezra Pound* (Routledge, 1997)

Woolf, Virginia, *Mr Bennett and Mrs Brown* (The Hogarth Press, 1924)

Worthen, John, *D. H. Lawrence: The Early Years: 1885–1912*, vol. 1 of *The Cambridge Biography of D. H. Lawrence* (Cambridge University Press, 1992)

Worthen, John, *D. H. Lawrence: The Life of an Outsider* (Penguin, 2005)

Worthen, John, 'Drama and Mimicry in D. H. Lawrence', in *Lawrence and Comedy*, ed. Paul Eggert and John Worthen (Cambridge University Press, 1996), pp. 19–31

Worthen, John, '"Over Some Frontiers" at Monte Cassino: Lawrence and Maurice Magnus', in *Windows to the Sun: D. H. Lawrence's 'Thought Adventures'*, ed. Earl Ingersoll and Virginia Crosswhite Hyde (Fairleigh Dickenson University Press, 2009), pp. 50–68

Wright, Louise E., 'Disputed Dregs: D. H. Lawrence and the Publication of Maurice Magnus's Memoirs of the Foreign Legion', *Journal of D. H. Lawrence Studies* (1995–6), pp. 57–73

Wright, Louise E., *Maurice Magnus: A Biography* (Cambridge Scholars Publishing, 2007)

# Index

# Image credits

220  La Phot 1-10, University of Nottingham, Manuscripts and Special Collections

260  La L 11/1, University of Nottingham, Manuscripts and Special Collections

274  La Phot 1-30, University of Nottingham, Manuscripts and Special Collections

277  Alamy Stock Photo

303  Charles Lummis/Library of Congress/Getty Images

308  Collection Center for Creative Photography, The University of Arizona © The Ansel Adams Publishing Rights Trust

309  Bettmann/Getty

312  Mabel Dodge Luhan Papers. Yale Collection of American Literature, Beinecke Rare Book and Manuscript Library © The Ansel Adams Publishing Rights Trust

314  Bildagentur-online/Getty Images

357  La Wb 1-24, University of Nottingham, Manuscripts and Special Collections

380  La Wb 3, University of Nottingham, Manuscripts and Special Collections

381  La Wb 1-8, University of Nottingham, Manuscripts and Special Collections

384  Mabel Dodge Luhan Papers. Yale Collection of American Literature, Beinecke Rare Book and Manuscript Library

391  Collections and Center for Southwest Research, University of New Mexico Library

396  Warburg Institute, London

411  Collections and Center for Southwest Research, University of New Mexico Library

412  Albuquerque Museum, gift of the Albuquerque Museum Foundation from the Lucia v.B Batten Estate, PC2015.26.126.1

# Acknowledgements

The scholarship of John Worthen, David Ellis and Mark Kinkead-Weekes, authors of the monumental three-volume Cambridge University Press biography of Lawrence, has been invaluable; so too was the help of the staff at the New York Public Library's Berg Collection, the Lawrence Manuscripts Collection at Nottingham University, the National Archives in Malta, the Beinecke Rare Book and Manuscript Library at Yale University, and the Mabel Dodge Luhan House in Taos.

I am also grateful to Kate Bland, Lucia Boldrini, Kevin Cannon, Miranda Carter, Claudia Fitzherbert, Roy Foster, Ruth Guilding, Suzanne Hobson, Ken Kwami, Grainne Lamphee, Kate Miller, Constantine Phipps, Ray Ryan, Sarah Harrison Smith, Stacy Schiff, Al Storey, Inigo Thomas, Molly Van Amerongen, Janet Whitaker, Martin Wilson, A.N. Wilson, Clair Wills, Philomena Wills, Gaby Wood, Michael Wood, Andrew Wordsworth and Ada Wordsworth. Without the generous support of the New York Public Library's Dorothy and Lewis B. Cullman Centre for Scholars and Writers, this book would have taken a great deal longer to complete; thank you to Lauren Goldenberg, Paul Delaverdac and Salvatore Scibona, and to my fellow Cullman scholars, Vona Groarke, Corey Robin, Amanda Vaill, Mary Dearborn, francine harris, Marisa Silver, Jennifer Croft, Brooke Holmes, Faith Hillis, Martha Hodes, David Bell, Kirman Uribe and Karan Mahajan.

I am especially indebted to Paul Keegan, Bernard Richards, and Ophelia Field for their invaluable readings of the book in its first draft, and to James Lever, whose brilliance emboldened the narrative. Thank you also to my agent, Sarah Chalfant, to Michael Fishwick, Alexandra Pringle and Lauren Whybrow at Bloomsbury, and to Ileene Smith, Mitzi Angel and Jonathan Galassi at FSG. Peter James is a copyeditor without compare.

The two figures who bookended this project each died before it was completed: Evelyn Buchan (1955–2018) passed on the anecdote about Lawrence's ashes which inspired *Burning Man*, and the late friendship of James Atlas (1949–2019) kept the fires blazing. Thank you, both.

# A Note on the Type

The text of this book is set Adobe Garamond. It is one of several versions of Garamond based on the designs of Claude Garamond. It is thought that Garamond based his font on Bembo, cut in 1495 by Francesco Griffo in collaboration with the Italian printer Aldus Manutius. Garamond types were first used in books printed in Paris around 1532. Many of the present-day versions of this type are based on the Typi Academiae of Jean Jannon cut in Sedan in 1615.

Claude Garamond was born in Paris in 1480. He learned how to cut type from his father and by the age of fifteen he was able to fashion steel punches the size of a pica with great precision. At the age of sixty he was commissioned by King Francis I to design a Greek alphabet, and for this he was given the honourable title of royal type founder. He died in 1561.

# How to Survive the Titanic or The Sinking of J. Bruce Ismay

When the Titanic the iceberg on 14 April 1912 and a thousand men prepared to die, J. Bruce Ismay, the ship's owner and inheritor of the White Star fortune, jumped into a lifeboat with the women and children and rowed away to safety. The first victim of a press hate campaign, his reputation never recovered and while other survivors were piecing together their accounts, Ismay never spoke of his beloved ship again.

With the help of that great narrator of the sea, Joseph Conrad, Frances Wilson explores the reasons behind Ismay's jump, his desperate need to make sense of the horror of it all, and to find a way of living with lost honour.

'A gripping study – part reportage, part biography, part literary criticism – of the more intimate ramifications of a disaster which still haunts the public imagination' *Sunday Telegraph*

'Beautifully written and beautifully constructed' *Sunday Times*

'Wonderfully rich and multi-layered … Every sentence crackles with intelligence' *Mail on Sunday*

**Order your copy:**

By phone: +44 (0) 1256 302 699
By email: direct@macmillan.co.uk
Delivery is usually 3–5 working days.
Free postage and packaging for orders over £20.
Online: www.bloomsbury.com/bookshop
Prices and availability subject to change without notice.
bloomsbury.com/uk/author/frances-wilson